Latinas in the United States

Latinas in the United States

A Historical Encyclopedia

VOLUME 1

Introduction
Abarca through Guzmán

Edited by
Vicki L. Ruiz
and Virginia Sánchez Korrol

INDIANA UNIVERSITY PRESS
Bloomington and Indianapolis

Publication of this book is made possible in part with the assistance of a Challenge Grant from the National Endowment for the Humanities, a federal agency that supports research, education, and public programming in the humanities. Any views, findings, conclusions, or recommendations expressed in this publication do not necessarily reflect those of the National Endowment for the Humanities.

This book is a publication of

Indiana University Press
601 North Morton Street
Bloomington, IN 47404-3797 USA

http://iupress.indiana.edu

Telephone orders 800-842-6796
Fax orders 812-855-7931
Orders by e-mail iuporder@indiana.edu

The paper used in this publication meets the minimum requirements of American National Standard for Information Sciences—Permanence of Paper for Printed Library Materials, ANSI Z39.48–1984.

Manufactured in the United States of America

Library of Congress Cataloging-in-Publication Data

Latinas in the United States : a historical encyclopedia / edited by Vicki L. Ruíz and Virginia Sánchez Korrol.
p. cm.
Includes bibliographical references and index.
ISBN 0-253-34680-0 (set : alk. paper)—ISBN 0-253-34681-9 (vol. 1 : alk. paper)—ISBN 0-253-34683-5 (vol. 2 : alk. paper)—ISBN 0-253-34684-3 (vol. 3 : alk. paper) 1. Hispanic American women—Biography—Encyclopedias. I. Ruíz, Vicki. II. Sánchez Korrol, Virginia.
E184.S75L35 2006
920.72089'68073—dc22 2005034986

1 2 3 4 5 11 10 09 08 07 06

In honor of the women in whose footprints we follow, and for the women
who build community today and tomorrow.

En homenaje a las mujeres cuyos pasos seguimos, y para todas aquéllas
que construyen la comunidad de hoy y del mañana.

Contents

Contents

Preface

Latina history is a mosaic across time, region, gender, and borders. At the heart of this encyclopedia is a commitment to reclaim the lives of Latinas within their own historical moments and to recover their stories—frequently hidden, forgotten, or ignored. Since the founding of St. Augustine in 1565, Spanish-speaking women have left their imprints on U.S. soil. They appeared on the historical landscape before the establishment of English and French settlements. Many Latinas have Native American roots, while some trace their heritage to the rich contributions of the peoples of West Africa, brought to these shores as enslaved women. Still others descended from Spain and diverse European countries and, in time, combined their particular experiences with different communities of people in the Americas in the process of *mestizaje,* the blending of Spanish, African, and indigenous peoples. This pivotal point is important for understanding the cultural and biological syncretism that, in turn, gave form to Latinos in the United States in both the past and the present. As poet Aurora Levins Morales has aptly surmised: "I am new. History made me. My first language was spanglish. I was born at the crossroads and I am whole."[1]

Nomenclature for Latinas in and of itself reveals much about the diversity of Spanish-speaking peoples in the United States, past and present. There has never existed a single signifier of self-identification from Tejanos and Californios of the nineteenth century to Latinos and Hispanics today. In this encyclopedia Latina is an umbrella term that refers to all women of Latin American birth or heritage, including women from North, Central, and South America and the Spanish-speaking Caribbean. Mexicana and Mexicano refer to those born in Mexico, and Mexican American indicates U.S. birth. Chicana and Chicano reflect a political consciousness that emerged out of the Chicano student movement, often a generational marker for those who came of age during the 1960s and 1970s. Nuyorican refers to Puerto Ricans born on the mainland, not just in New York, while Puertorriqueña and Puertorriqueño include islanders and Nuyoricans alike. Boricua signifies endearment, empowerment, and unity for all Puerto Ricans. For some, regional identification becomes synonymous with nationality—Tejanos in Texas and Hispanos in New Mexico and Colorado. Others situate themselves in terms of racial location, preferring perhaps an Iberian connection (Hispanic) or emphasizing indigenous (mestizo/a) or African (Afro-Latino/a) roots. Cultural/national identification remains strong—Salvadorans, Dominicans, Brazilians, and Cubans, to name just a few. Divergent cultural locations mark the heterogeneity within Latino communities, a heterogeneity that occurs even within families. As Salt Lake City housing activist María Garcíaz reflected, "My mother is Spanish; one brother is Mexican; my sister Mexican-American; I am Chicana. Three brothers are Hispanic and the youngest is Latino."[2]

Within these pages the historical and literary narratives marking the U.S. Latina experience come to life. From *mestizo* settlements, pioneer life, and diasporic communities, *Latinas in the United States* documents women's contributions as settlers, healers, ranchers, and landowners, as community organizers and educators, and as writers, artists, and performers. Their experiences during and after Euro-American colonizing and conquests of the Southwest are also explored, in addition to the early-nineteenth-century migration of Puerto Ricans and Cubans. For the twentieth century, issues of immigration, literature, cultural traditions, labor, gender roles, community organizations, and politics are addressed, as well as individual biographical profiles of women who have left their marks on history, such as Puerto Rican feminist Luisa Capetillo, conservative New Mexican politician Concha Ortiz y Pino de Kleven, and Guatemalan labor and civil rights activist Luisa Moreno. This encyclopedia focuses on how Latinas have shaped their own lives, cultures, and communities through mutual assistance and collective action and how our understanding of pivotal events, such as the U.S.-Mexican War, the Great Depression, and World War II, becomes transformed when they are viewed through women's eyes.

Written to engage general and scholarly readers, this encyclopedia, the first to focus specifically on Latina history, consists of almost 600 entries (700,000 words) and nearly 300 photographs. The introduction features five comprehensive regional and historical overviews of Latina history in the Southwest, the Northeast, the Midwest, the Southeast, and the Pacific Northwest. Several themes interlace the diverse components within this compendium of new knowledge. First, the encyclopedia is essentially a working-class history of Latinas whose experiences and actions during three centuries helped build this nation. Second, it also represents an intellectual history of women who witnessed, defied, negotiated, and chronicled the forces that shaped Spanish American colonization and the present contours of this nation. Education, religion, activism, and labor and community have loomed large in the lives of Latinas, past and present. Representing cutting-edge scholarship, *Latinas in the United States* documents the divergences and convergences in the U.S. experiences of Mexican American, Puerto Rican, Cuban, Dominican, Central American, and South American women in a manner not possible before this publication. The coeditors are indebted to the cadre of talented authors who wrote entries for the encyclopedia, many of whom are among the most distinguished scholars in the fields of history, cultural studies, social science, and Latino studies. Their insights, hard work, and *corazón* shaped this collective, landmark enterprise.

This project began in the spring of 1998. The coeditors, widely recognized as leaders in the field of Latina history, embarked on this project as an intellectual conversation that moved the discussion from a one-group, one-coast perspective (whether Chicanas in California or Boricuas in New York) to an exploration of panethnic comparative perspectives that examined common legacies, divergent paths, and intersections of community activism and cultural production. The coeditors solicited nominations from five associate editors, specialists in various aspects of Latina studies, and an advisory board of well-known scholars. The majority of the profiles were generated through these recommendations, and the editors and board members played crucial roles in identifying subjects, photographs, and potential authors.

In 2000 publicity about the project spread across the nation based on a Knight-Ridder column, a *New York Times* feature article, a lead story in the *Miami Herald,* and subsequent exposure on television and other media sources, including the newspapers *Hoy* and *El Diario/La Prensa,* which, in turn, brought additional biographical profiles to our attention. The coeditors might never have known about Amelia Maldonado, a pioneer bilingual elementary teacher in Tucson, Arizona, who began her forty-year career in 1919, except for the correspondence of her nephew, Francis Brady. Perhaps, too, Verneda Rodríguez McLean, a pilot during World War II, would have gone unnoticed if museum director Bruce Ashcroft had not approached Vicki Ruiz after her lecture at the University of Texas, Austin. The entry on Madre María Dominga Guzmán, founder of a religious order and in the process of canonization, came to us in similar fashion. Even within the final week of putting the finishing touches on the manuscript, additional nominations kept arriving. To honor those who shared their stories and to provide examples of representative women, the coeditors have endeavored to include as many of these nominees as possible.

During the past three decades Latina educators from university professors to precollegiate teachers have contributed to the fluorescence of Latina history and Latina studies as recognized academic disciplines. They are acknowledged in these volumes through their scholarship. The advice of the associate editors and advisory board members provided critical guidance in selecting not only individuals, but also events and organizations with an emphasis on historical significance. The criteria for inclusion in *Latinas in the United States* favored older public women who had made a difference in their respective communities or on the national stage. A handful of young women representative of political activism and the arts are included, in addition to a few women like Sor Juana Inés de la Cruz and Felisa Rincón de Gautier whose influence transcended national boundaries. Although many present-day women are profiled, the coeditors sought to avoid a "who's who" approach. For this reason film legends like Carmen Miranda or Rita Moreno merited individual biographies, while their current counterparts may be included only in larger thematic entries. Contemporary representatives of women in the public eye were selected from a variety of fields—business, labor, literature, religion, social work, education, law, politics, entertainment, and the arts, to name a few. Encouraging comparative insights as well as discrete cultural narratives, the coeditors, as authors of numerous entries and editors of many more, have emphasized, whenever possible, a sense of real people—their dreams, routines, personalities, values, and contributions. From settlers to *curanderas* and from flappers to feminists, Latinas have indeed made history.

Contrary to popular media images that portray Latinos as recent immigrants, their legacies actually stretch back hundreds of years to the founding of St. Augustine in 1565. Indeed, this Spanish outpost was not just the realm of conquistadores and missionaries but also of women colonists and their families. St. Augustine was one of three military units in the primary line of defense established by the Spanish Crown throughout the Caribbean. Living under constant danger of British invasion, colonists in this neglected frontier settlement faced enormous obstacles. As *mulattos*, *negroes*, *indios*, *mestizos*, and *criollos*, they resisted and reinforced the injustices of life within a rigid class, color, and labor system that privileged Spaniards. Critical to the settlement's survival, St. Augustine women participated in every aspect of colonial life. Their lives were conditioned by race, class, and marital status. Indian and black women were concentrated at the bottom rungs of the social scale, often enslaved or indentured laborers in the house and the fields. However, free blacks, recent immigrants, and nonelites could also own property. By 1763 St. Augustine included some Catalan immigrants, Christianized Indians, and free blacks who added to the colony's already diverse and shifting demographic profile. Juana Ana María Paniagua, for example, was a *mujer mercenaria* (prostitute) who owned slaves and property. Most women were not, in fact, landowners, but more than a quarter of all landowners in the colony were single women, probably widows.[3] The story of St. Augustine, one that reveals the dynamic syncretism and fissures marking colonial society, provides an example of the histories tucked within this text. The five-part introduction, divided by region, provides the historical context for the encyclopedia as a whole and for the individual entries.

In the words of Chicana artist Irma Barbosa, "Stories are the spirit threads passed on from generation to generation."[4] Latina history has often been a private one, narratives told at the kitchen table. We hope that this encyclopedia inspires a new generation of historical research, including recording family memoirs and writing scholarly monographs. Many histories remain to be discovered and interpreted, especially of women with Central American, South American, Cuban, and Dominican roots. The preponderance of Mexican and Puerto Rican profiles reflects the current state of the field. As coeditors, we have also privileged the lives of women grassroots community organizers whose contributions have not had a wider hearing outside their respective towns or neighborhoods. Often underestimated in community politics and at city hall, these women demonstrate determination, resourcefulness, and tenacity. A Salvadoran immigrant and restaurant owner, Mirna Burciaga, successfully challenged discriminatory policies of a local southern California school district and in a recent interview related why she refused to be ignored. "I have an accent . . . when I talk . . . But that doesn't mean I have an accent . . . when I think."[5]

Burciaga is a naturalized U.S. citizen whose community engagement may be a bellwether for Latina politics in the twenty-first century. According to recent census figures, Latinos represent almost 50 percent of the foreign born in the United States (15 million out of 31 million total). In 2002 the Latino population could be categorized as follows: 67 percent Mexican, 14 percent Central and South American, 8 percent Puerto Rican, 4 percent Cuban, and 6 percent other groups (e.g., Dominicans). Moreover, 40 percent of all U.S. Latinos are foreign born.[6] This layering of generations and of diverse cultural groups, ranging from Hispanos in New Mexico whose roots extend back four centuries to recently arrived Dominican immigrants in New York City, speaks to an array of Latino/Latina experiences, past, present, and future. *Latinas in the United States: A Historical Encyclopedia* documents, chronicles, and traces the ways in which Latinas make meaning in their own lives and in the lives of others. *¡Pa'lante!*

Notes

1. Aurora Levins Morales and Rosario Morales, *Getting Home Alive* (Ithaca, NY: Firebrand Books, 1986), 50.
2. Vicki L. Ruiz, "Garcíaz, María," in this volume.
3. Susan L. Pickman and Dorcas R. Gilmore, "Women in St. Augustine," in "Spanish Borderlands" in this volume.
4. Chicana artist Irma Lerma Barbosa, quoted in María Ochoa, *Creative Collectives: Chicana Painters Working in Community* (Albuquerque: University of New Mexico Press, 2003), 68.
5. Jessica Garrison, 2001. "Orange County District to Overhaul English Instruction," *Los Angeles Times*, November 2, B1.
6. Social Science Data Analysis Network, "Nativity and Citizenship, 1990–2000." www.censusscope.org (accessed June 22, 2005); U.S. Bureau of the Census, June 2003. *The Hispanic Population in the United States: March 2002* (Washington DC: Government Printing Office) 1.

Acknowledgments

This project began in 1998, and through it all our managing editor, Carlos A. Cruz, has been the creative and organizational touchstone that sustained our efforts during the past eight years. In addition to managing all of our files, budgets, and contracts, he was responsible for the digital photography and reproductions and designed all of our e-mail and print postcards and publicity. As our biggest fan and toughest taskmaster, Cruz was a tireless office manager, photo researcher, resident artist, and enduring friend. *Latinas in the United States* would simply not exist without his efforts.

Substantial financial support was provided by the National Endowment for the Humanities and the Ford Foundation. We thank Helen Aguera, our program officer at NEH, and Janice Petrovich at the Ford Foundation. Cathy McKee, formerly of Motorola, provided a small seed grant at the beginning of the project. We have deeply appreciated the institutional funding we received, particularly during the last few months when our budget was bare. For Vicki L. Ruiz, the Arizona State University Office of the Provost allocated significant support monies, and she thanks Provost Milton Glick and Vice President for Research Jonathan Fink. At the University of California, Irvine, research funding provided by the Office of the Executive Vice-Chancellor, the School of Social Sciences, and the School of Humanities proved invaluable, and we acknowledge Michael R. Gottfredson, Executive Vice-Chancellor, Barbara Dosher, Dean of Social Sciences, and Karen Lawrence, Dean of Humanities. The Center for Latinos in a Global Society, directed by Leo Chávez, offered summer travel money and graduate research assistance during the project's last year.

For Virginia Sánchez Korrol, María E. Pérez y González and the faculty and staff of the Department of Puerto Rican and Latino Studies at Brooklyn College provided unwavering support, space, supplies, funds, and student assistants Jeannette Reyes and Bethsaida George. President Christoph M. Kimmich and Provost Roberta S. Matthews of Brooklyn College, as well as the former president, Vernon Lattin, provided funding for the project, and Nicholas Irons, Peggy Bergamasco, and the staff of Information and Technology Services gave us equipment and technical support. Christina Sferruzzo in the Office of Research and Program Development both was supportive and provided oversight of the project funds.

We both acknowledge day-to-day assistance of the staff members. Vicki Ruiz thanks Vera Galaviz of the Department of Chicana and Chicano Studies at Arizona State and Stella Ginez of the Program in Chicano/Latino Studies and Judy Morgan of the History Department at UC Irvine. Virginia Sánchez Korrol owes a debt of gratitude to Mildred Nieves Rivera and Raquel Fernández, Department of Puerto Rican and Latino Studies, Brooklyn College.

We relied on the wise counsel of the associate editors—Lillian Castillo-Speed, Bárbara Cruz, María Cristina García, Cynthia Orozco, and Nélida Pérez—whose hard work, prescient insights, and *corazón* contributed to the shaping of these volumes. We also thank our distinguished advisory board—Edna Acosta-Belén, Frances Aparicio, Albert Camarillo, María Raquel Casas, Daisy Cocco de Felippis, Deena González, Camille Guerin-Gonzales, Ramón Gutiérrez, Gabriel Haslip-Viera, Nancy Hewitt, Olga Jiménez de Wagenheim, Yolanda Chávez Leyva, Félix Matos Rodríguez, Lara Medina, Cecilia Menjívar, María Montoya, Milga Morales Nadal, Lorena Oropeza, Cynthia Orozco, María Pérez y González, Yolanda Prieto, Naomi Quiñonez, Raquel Rubio-Goldsmith, Elizabeth Salas, and Carmen Teresa Whalen. We also thank Margaret Stroebel and Susan Ware, who took time from their own reference works to assist us in the early stages of this project. We particularly appreciate those advisory editors who took the time to craft one or more entries for the encyclopedia.

Most of all, we owe a tremendous debt of gratitude to the more than 230 authors who made the encyclopedia possible. We are humbled by the overwhelming response we received from our contributors. The late Norma Williams deserves special mention, and we deeply regret that she did not live to see her contribution on the Latino family in print. Vicki L. Ruiz acknowledges with great gratitude the essays penned by her current and former graduate students: Carole Autori, Margie Brown-Coronel, Enrique Buelna, Yolanda Calderón-Wallace, Eve Carr, Phillip Castruita, Marisela Chávez, Julie Cohen, Marcelle Maese Cohen, Virginia Espino, Lilia Fernández, Matt García, Antonia García-Orozco, Margaret Jacobs, Irene Mata, Laura Muñoz, Marian Perales, Naomi Quiñonez, Annette Reed, Jean Reynolds, Alicia Rodríquez-Estrada, Maythee Rojas, Steven Rosales, Ana Rosas, Arlene Sánchez Walsh, Soledad Vidal, and Mary Ann Villarreal. Our Brooklyn College writers include Dorian Chandler, Georgina García, Luis Gordillo, Rachel Greene, Jorivette Quintana, and Jeannette Reyes. Mil gracias.

We are indebted to Christine Marin, head of the Chicano Research Collection at Arizona State University, for her assistance with photographs over the years and to Alicia, Dora, and Eugene Quesada for allowing us to reproduce the photo of their mother and best friend in "Comadres," the book cover image for *Latinas in the United States*. Maggie Rivas-Rodríguez also deserves special mention for allowing us to reproduce several narrative profiles and photographs from the University of Texas at Austin's U.S. Latinos and Latinas in World War II Oral History Project. We extend our deep appreciation to María Estorino and Esperanza de Varona of the Otto G. Richter Library, University of Miami, for their assistance with photos and research, and to Nélida Pérez and Pedro Juan Hernández of the Centro de Estudios Puertorriqueños Library and Archives, Hunter College, for their constant support and access to innumerable resources.

We also appreciate the dedication and generosity of the staff at the following repositories: Arizona Historical Society Library, Tucson; Autry National Center (especially Carolyn Brucken); Bancroft Library, University of California, Berkeley; California State Archives; Center for American History, the University of Texas, Austin; Center for Southwestern Research, University of New Mexico; City of Greeley (CO) Archives; Colección Puertorriqueña, Universidad de Puerto Rico, Rio Piedras; Colorado Historical Society; Corona (CA) Public Library Heritage Room; Fototeca del INAH, Pachuco, Hildalgo, Mexico (especially Susana Ramírez Vizcaya); Galerie Lelong, New York City; The Library of Congress; Los Angeles Public Library; Museum of New Mexico; New York Public Library; Patricia Correia Gallery, Santa Monica (CA); Rio Grande Historical Collection, New Mexico State University; Southwest Collection, Texas Tech University; Special Collections, Stanford University; Special Collections, Texas A&M, Corpus Christi; Tampa Bay History; Texas Labor Archives, University of Texas, Arlington; University of North Carolina, Chapel Hill Libraries; University of South Florida Library; University of Texas Institute of Texan Cultures, San Antonio (especially Patrick Lemelle); Vallejo Naval and Historical Museum; Walter P. Reuther Library, Wayne State University; and Western History Department, Denver Public Library.

Throughout the life of the project we were fortunate to receive enthusiastic media coverage that resulted in bringing potential subjects to our attention. For these efforts we extend our thanks to dozens of journalists, among them Lou Gonzales of the *Colorado Springs Gazette,* Barbara Crossette of the *New York Times,* Ana Veciana of the *Miami Herald,* and Albor Ruiz and Juan González of the *New York Daily News. El Diario/La Prensa, Hoy, Latina Magazine, Latina Style,* and *Hispanic Outlook* wrote about the project, and Univision Network and Lifetime TV brought it to the attention of the viewing public. Julie Frank of Latino Expo in New York was among the first to provide a venue for disseminating information about the Latina encyclopedia. We thank her and also Anita Vélez-Mitchell, Tania León, Angie Cabrera, and the late Antonia Pantoja, who unhesitatingly shared their life stories at the Latina encyclopedia's Latino Expo roundtable discussion. We are also grateful to journalists Betsy Wade and Kay Mills and to Rita Henley Jensen and the staff of Women's e-news for their encouragement, support, and recognition of our project.

Kudos goes to Robert Sloan of Indiana University Press for his faith, enthusiasm, and professionalism and to his entire staff for all of their efforts. It has been a long road and we thank you for standing by the project. We also acknowledge Lewis Parker of Westchester Book Services for his encouragement, efficiency, and patience. Our copy editor, Charles Eberline, deserves special mention for his superlative editorial skills, thoughtful queries, and meticulous attention to detail.

In some ways it seems bittersweet to end our eight-year collaboration. We started the project as friends and have concluded it as sisters. We have shared our lives in good times and in bad—through the death of a parent, the travails of major surgery, and the survival of cancer. We thank our families, especially our spouses Victor Becerra and Chuck Korrol, for their patience, good humor, and unflagging encouragement. Again, thanks to Carlos Cruz, who today remains the one person who knows where everything is.

Latinas
in the
United States

Introduction: A Historical and Regional Overview of Latinas in the United States

LATINAS IN THE SOUTHWEST

Since 1540 and the arrival of the Coronado expedition, Spanish-speaking women have migrated north decades, even centuries, before their Euro-American counterparts ventured west. They participated in the founding of Santa Fe in 1610, San Antonio in 1718, and Los Angeles in 1781, all part of the Spanish borderlands. The Spanish colonial government, in its efforts to secure its territorial claims, offered a number of inducements to those willing to undertake such an arduous and frequently perilous journey. Subsidies given to a band of settlers headed for Texas included not only food and livestock but also petticoats and silk stockings. Few women ventured to Mexico's far northern frontier alone as widows or orphans; most arrived as the wives or daughters of soldiers, farmers, and artisans.

The colonists themselves were typically *mestizos* (Spanish/Indian) or *mulattoes* (Spanish/African). Indeed, more than half the founding families of Los Angeles were of African descent. Those settlers who garnered economic and social power, as well as their children, would often position themselves as "Spanish," putting into practice the truism "money buys color" common throughout colonial Latin America. These successful individuals not only found economic opportunity on the frontier but also reimagined their racial identities. Women such as María Feliciana Arballo and Victoria Reid illuminate this privileging of a fictive Spanish past.

In the early years the concern was less about status than survival as settlements, especially in Texas, New Mexico, and Arizona, teetered on the brink of extinction through starvation or combative relationships with native peoples. However, the missions, pueblos (towns), and presidios (forts) took hold, and over the course of three centuries, Spanish/Mexican women raised families on the frontier and worked alongside their fathers and husbands herding cattle and tending crops.

Women also participated in the day-to-day operation of area missions. Whether heralded as centers of godliness and civilization or condemned as concentration camps, the missions, particularly in California, played instrumental roles in the economic development of an area and in the acculturation and decimation of indigenous peoples. In an environment of social indoctrination, acculturation, and servitude, missions relied on Indian labor to feed the growing colony and produce essential goods for trade. While the Francis-

"Comadres" Teresa Grijalva de Orozco and Francisca Ocampo Quesada, 1912. Courtesy of the Ocampo Family Collection, Chicano Research Collection, Department of Archives and Manuscripts, Arizona State University, Tempe.

cans were certainly zealous and energetic, they did not act alone. To support their endeavors, mission friars recruited women such as Apolinaria Lorenzana and Eulalia Pérez into their service as housekeepers, midwives, cooks, healers, teachers, seamstresses, and business managers.

The close proximity between Indian and Spanish/Mexican women engendered little pretense of a shared sisterhood. Indentured servitude was prevalent on the colonial frontier and persisted well into the nineteenth century. Indians and, to a lesser extent, people of African heritage were pressed into bondage. For instance, in 1735 Anttonía Lusgardia Ernandes, a *mulatta*, sued her former master for custody of their son. The man admitted paternity, but claimed that his former servant had relinquished the child to his wife since his wife had christened the child. The court, however, granted Ernandes custody. In other cases this pattern continued with tragic results. As noted by historian Miroslava Chávez-García, the murder of the Indian servant known only as Ysabel at the hands of her mistress Guadalupe Trujillo in 1843 offers but one example of the violence inflicted by one group of women on another. Race and class hierarchies significantly shaped everyday life on Mexico's far northern frontier.

Spanish/Mexican settlement has been shrouded by myth. Walt Disney's *Zorro,* for example, epitomized the notion of romantic California controlled by fun-loving, swashbuckling rancheros. Because only 3 percent of California's Spanish/Mexican population could be considered rancheros in 1850, most women did not preside over large estates, but helped manage small family farms. In addition to traditional female tasks, Mexican women were accomplished *vaqueras* or cowgirls. Spanish-speaking women, like their Euro-American counterparts, encountered a duality in frontier expectations. Although they were placed on a pedestal as delicate ladies, women were responsible for an array of strenuous chores. One can imagine a young woman being serenaded in the evening and then awaking at dawn to slop the hogs.

Married women on the Spanish borderlands had certain legal advantages not afforded their Euro-American peers. Under English common law, women, when they married, became *feme covert* (or dead in the eyes of the legal system) and thus could not own property separate from their husbands. Conversely, Spanish/Mexican women retained control of their land after marriage and held one-half interest in the community property they shared with their spouses. Rancho Rodeo de las Aguas, which María Rita Valdez operated well into the 1880s, is now better known as Beverly Hills. Rodeo Drive takes its name from Rancho Rodeo. Other women, such as Juana Briones, Victoria

"Cowgirls/vaqueras," circa early 1900s. Courtesy of Ocampo Family Collection, Chicano Research Collection, Department of Archives and Manuscripts, Arizona State University, Tempe.

Reid, Gretrudis Barceló, and María Calvillo, proved successful entrepreneurs and property holders, even defending their interests in court when necessary.

Life for Mexican settlers changed dramatically in 1848 (1836 for Tejanos given the Alamo and the Texas revolt) with the conclusion of U.S.–Mexican War, the discovery of gold in California, and the Treaty of Guadalupe Hidalgo. Mexicans on the U.S. side of the border became second-class citizens, divested of their property, political power, and cultural entitlements. Their world turned upside down. This period of conquest and migration was marked by pejorative stereotypes and widespread violence. In Euro-American journals, novels, and travelogues Spanish-speaking women were frequently portrayed as flashy, morally loose vixens.

At times these images had dire results. On July 5, 1851, a Mexican woman swung from the gallows, the only woman lynched during the California gold rush. Josefa Loraiza (also known as Juanita of Downieville) was tried, convicted, and hung the same day she had killed a popular Euro-American miner and prizefighter, a man who the day before had assaulted her. Nine days later a San Francisco newspaper editorialized, "Now we venture to say that had this woman been an American instead of a Mexican . . . had she been of the Anglo-Saxon race, instead of being hung for the deed, she would have been lauded for it."

For elite families, holding on to their ranchos assumed primary importance, and according to some historians, they believed that they had a greater chance of retaining their land if they acquired a Euro-American son-in-law. Intermarriage, however, was no insurance policy. In 1849 María Amparo Ruiz married Captain Henry S. Burton, and five years later the couple purchased Rancho Jamul, a sprawling property that covered much of present-day San Diego. When Henry Burton died in 1869, the ownership of the ranch came into question. After several years of litigation, the court awarded his widow only 8,925 acres. Squatters challenged even this amount, and she continued to lose acreage in the years ahead. Chronicling her experiences, Ruiz de Burton, considered the first Mexican American novelist, penned *The Squatter and the Don* (1885), a fictionalized account of the decline of the Californio ranching class.

Segregated from the Euro-American population, Mexican Americans in the barrios of the Southwest were relegated to lower-tier jobs, such as farm labor, domestic work, and food processing. Nineteenth-century Spanish-language newspapers reveal ample information on the social mores and expectations within these tightly knit communities. Newspaper editors upheld the double standard, and at times women wrote letters to protest. When one Tucson editor used biblical authority to bolster traditional views, one woman wrote that given that "the Bible itself was written by men and since 'all men were liars,' it could not be trusted." The Catholic Church couched its opposition to public schools in New Mexico and Arizona solely on moral terms, and one New Mexico priest in 1877 argued that women's suffrage imperiled both the family and the future of humanity.

Some women did transgress the bounds of convention. Gertrudis Barceló ran a successful gambling hall and saloon in Santa Fe, a business that became a popular landmark. Loreta Janeta Velázquez, an elite woman from Cuba, fought for the Confederacy disguised as a man, Lt. Harry Buford. Perceived as a heretic by the Catholic Church but as a saint by her followers, Teresa Urrea was a powerful *curandera* who for a time conducted public faith healings.

Despite conventions that relegated women to hearth and home, women worked for wages, most commonly because of economic necessity. Whether in cities or on farms, family members pooled their earnings to put food on the table. Some women worked at home taking in laundry, boarders, and sewing. Others worked in agricultural fields, in restaurants and hotels, and in canneries and laundries. Some sold food on the streets, while others operated small cafés or served their neighbors as *curanderas* and midwives.

In 1900 over 100,000 people of Mexican birth or heritage lived in the Southwest, but by 1930 this figure increased ten-fold as over one million Mexicans, pushed out by revolution and lured by prospective jobs came to the United States. They settled into existing barrios and forged new communities in the Southwest and the Midwest. Like their foremothers, women usually journeyed north as wives and daughters. Many, however, crossed the border alone or as single mothers. As in the past, women's wage earning proved essential to family survival. Urban daughters (less frequently mothers) worked in canneries and garment plants, as well as in the service industry. Entire families labored in the fields and received their wages in a single check made out to the head of the household. Peeling chiles by hand all day long at a cannery or picking berries for a penny per basket did not make for warm memories. Supporting her family at thirteen, Erminia Ruiz remembered the long hours at the doughnut shop and being hidden in the flour bins because of her age when health inspectors arrived.

Exploitation in pay and in working conditions prompted attempts at unionization. Through mutual-aid societies and progressive trade unions, Mexican women proved tenacious activists. In 1933 alone thirty-seven major agricultural strikes occurred in Cali-

Mother and infant, 1949. Courtesy of Lee (Russell) Photograph Collection, The Center for American History, The University of Texas at Austin, Neg. no. 13918-EF12.

fornia, twenty-four led by the Cannery and Agricultural Workers Industrial Union. The Los Angeles garment workers' strike (1933), the San Antonio pecan shellers' strike (1938), and the California Sanitary Canning Company strike (1939) provide examples of urban activism in the Southwest. Southern California cannery activists, such as Carmen Bernal Escobar, negotiated significant wage increases and benefits as members of the United Cannery, Agricultural, Packing, and Allied Workers of America (UCAPAWA/FTA).

Like the daughters of European immigrants, young Mexican women experienced the lure of U.S. popular culture. Considerable conflict emerged between daughters and parents because teenagers wanted to dress and perhaps behave like their Euro-American peers at work or like the heroines they encountered in movies and magazines. Evading traditional chaperonage became a major pastime for youth. Stories of ditching the *dueña* (chaperone) resonate in the memories of Latinas who came of age between the two world wars.

An employee of La Malinche Tortilla Factory, Corpus Christi, Texas, 1949. Courtesy of Lee (Russell) Photograph Collection, The Center for American History, The University of Texas, Austin, Neg. no. II DF-6.

While youth experienced the lure of Hollywood, a considerable number faced the specter of deportation. From 1931 to 1934 more than one-third of the Mexican people in the United States (more than 500,000) were either deported (summarily taken off the streets and transported across the border) or repatriated (leaving on their own, frequently under the threat of deportation), even though most were native U.S. citizens. Discrimination and segregation in housing, employment, schools, and public recreation further served to remind youth of their second-tier citizenship. A resident of the San Joaquin Valley of California put it this way: "I remember . . . signs all over that read 'no Mexicans allowed.' "

Operating small neighborhood businesses, the Mexican American middle class at times made common cause with their working-class customers, but in other instances they desired social distance. Members of the League of United Latin American Citizens (LULAC) did both simultaneously. Envisioning themselves as patriotic "white" Americans pursuing their rights (the other white group), LULACers restricted membership to English-speaking U.S. citizens. Taking a page from the early NAACP, LULAC stressed the leadership of an "educated elite" who would lift their less fortunate neighbors by their bootstraps. From LULAC's inception women participated in numerous grassroots service projects and quickly assumed leadership positions in

An elegant flapper, Luisa Espinel, a popular entertainer and great-aunt of singer Linda Ronstadt. Courtesy of the Arizona Historical Society, Tucson.

both local chapters and national posts. LULAC stalwarts such as feminist Alicia Dickerson Montemayor and folklorist Jovita González engaged in voluntarist politics and educational reform that sought to meet community needs. An important civil rights organization, LULAC used the courts to protest discrimination and played a vital role in *Méndez v. Westminster,* a landmark school desegregation case.

Taking a more working-class community action approach, El Congreso de Pueblos de Habla Española (the Spanish-Speaking People's Congress) was the first national Latino civil rights assembly, held in 1939. Luisa Moreno, an immigrant from Guatemala, and Josefina Fierro, a native of Mexicali, were the driving forces behind el Congreso, Moreno in organizing the first conference and Fierro in terms of the day-to-day activities of the southern California chapters. Welcoming all Latinos regardless of cultural background or citizenship and drawing delegates mostly from labor unions, mutual-aid societies, and other grassroots groups, el Congreso called for an end to segregation in public facilities, housing, education, and employment and endorsed the rights of immigrants to live and work in the United States without fear of deportation. Although el Congreso was short lived, it demonstrated the potential for building regional and national coalitions.

After World War II Mexican women were involved in a gamut of political organizations, such as LULAC and the Community Service Organization (CSO). While militant labor unions faltered during the cold war era, the classic film *Salt of the Earth* recorded the real-life story of the Mexican mining families who staged a successful strike in New Mexico. With an emphasis on local issues and voter registration, CSO brought together two dynamic organizers who would change trade union history, César Chávez and Dolores Huerta, cofounders of the United Farm Workers (UFW) during the early 1960s. Huerta, the principal negotiator and lobbyist, relied on extended kin and women friends to care for her eleven children during her absences. The idea of a "union family" undergirded UFW organizing campaigns that significantly improved the living conditions and wages of migrant farmworkers.

As part of global student movements of the 1960s,

Symbolizing a bicultural heritage, María Soto Audelo at a Fourth of July celebration, 1917. Courtesy of the Arizona Historical Society, Tucson.

Mexican American youth joined together to address continuing problems of discrimination, particularly in education and politics. Embracing the mantle of cultural nationalism, they transformed the pejorative term "Chicano" into a symbol of pride. "Chicano/a" represents a commitment to social justice and social change. A graduate student at UCLA, Magdalena Mora, not only wrote about trade union struggles, but participated in them as well. An activist since high school, she died of a brain tumor at the age of twenty-nine. The informal credo of the Chicano student movement was to return to one's community after one's college education. Mora never left.

Many Chicanas chafed at the sexism they experienced in the movement, but they avoided mainstream Euro-American feminist groups, which they perceived as condescending and indifferent. In forming their own agenda, Chicanas looked to the histories of their mothers and grandmothers and to role models of the past, such as Sor Juana Inés de la Cruz, Sara Estela Ramírez, Emma Tenayuca, and Luisa Moreno. Women, including Martha Cotera, Adelaida Del Castillo, and Ana Nieto Gómez, began to articulate a Chicana feminist vision that was predicated on the politics of the community, not the politics of the individual. No armchair activists, they provided leadership on a number of fronts, including welfare rights, immigrant services and advocacy, sterilization suits, community organizations, La Raza Unida Party, antiwar protests, and campus activism. Chicana lesbians, however, found themselves isolated in movement activities. As Cherríe Moraga revealed, "My lesbianism is the avenue through which I have learned the most about silence and oppression." Surprisingly, it was not until 1992 that the lesbian caucus of the National Association of Chicano and Chicana Studies was established. In their published works and community activities, Latina lesbian writers like Gloria Anzaldula and Moraga have strived to build interracial, transnational networks among women of color.

In the Southwest, where the majority of Mexican Americans live, a layering of generations has taken place from seventh-generation New Mexicans to recent immigrants. This layering has provided a vibrant cultural dynamic represented by artists Amalia Mesa-Bains, Judith Baca, and Carmen Lomas Garza and poets Sandra Cisneros, Pat Mora, and Demetria Martínez (to name a few). Substantial numbers of Latinos who are not of Mexican ancestry or birth have contributed to a new layering of communities and cultural orientations.

Since the 1980s more than 500,000 Salvadorans have immigrated to the United States and represent more than 40 percent of Central American arrivals, followed by Guatemalans and Nicaraguans, with smaller numbers from Costa Rica, Honduras, Panama, and Belize. Approximately 50 percent of Central Americans settle in California. Food can serve as a cultural barometer. In Los Angeles, for example, *pupusas* can be found as readily as tacos, and one of the premiere Cuban bakeries, Porto's, can be found in the southern California community of Glendale. Indeed, more than 60,000 Cubans reside in the Golden State. While tensions certainly exist among working class immigrant Latinos, service workers have come together as union stalwarts, as exemplified by Local 11 of the Hotel and Restaurant Workers' Union in Los Angeles, led by former Chicana student activist María Elena Durazo. Individuals have also made a difference, for example, Mirna Burciaga, a Costa Mesa mother and small-business owner who took on the local school district and won. Born in El Salvador, Burciaga noted how officials underestimated her intelligence and tenacity.

Erminia Ruiz at age nineteen. Courtesy of Vicki L. Ruiz.

A number of Latinas have capitalized on educational and entrepreneurial opportunities. Linda Alvarado of Colorado not only owns a major construction company but also is part owner of a major-league baseball franchise, the Colorado Rockies. A former farmworker, Amelia Ceja is the first woman president of a world-class winery, Ceja Vineyards in Napa, California. A rocket scientist once employed by NASA, France Córdova is the chancellor of the University of California, Riverside. As businesswomen, philanthropists, physicians, attorneys, and educators (to name a few), Latina professionals demonstrate the importance of education and educational access for individual dreams and community well-being. Indeed, the quest for educational equity has been an integral part of the history of civil rights among Latinos in the United States.

Latinos can be found throughout the Southwest. Five southwestern states have the largest proportion of people of Latin American birth and heritage relative to the overall population. New Mexico is first, with Latinos constituting 42 percent of the state's population, followed by California (32 percent), Texas (32 percent), Arizona (25 percent), and Nevada (20 percent). In 2000 Latinos could be found in every state of the union from Alabama to Wyoming. The Latino population has also become more diverse, with Dominicans in Dallas and Puerto Ricans in Phoenix. Latinas in the Southwest have a history rooted in a Mexican American past, but their future will reflect in some measure a political and cultural coalescence on *latinidad*.

SOURCES: Chávez-García, Miroslava. 2002. "Guadalupe Trujillo: Race, Culture, and Justice in Mexican Los Angeles." In *The Human Tradition in California,* eds. Clark Davis and David Igler. Wilmington, DE: Scholarly Resources; "Latinos in the United States," Winter, 1996. *OAH Magazine of History*; Ruiz, Vicki L. 1998. *From out of the Shadows: Mexican Women in Twentieth-Century America*. New York: Oxford University Press; and Virginia Sánchez-Korrol, eds. 2005. *Latina Legacies: Identity, Biography, and Community*. New York: Oxford University Press; Social Science Data Analysis Network. "Nativity and Citizenship, 1990–2000." www.censusscope.org (accessed May 23, 2005); U.S. Bureau of the Census, June 2003. *The Hispanic Population in the United States: March 2002*. Washington D.C.: Government Printing Office.

Vicki L. Ruiz

LATINAS IN THE NORTHEAST

In all probability the first families from the Hispanic Caribbean settled in New York, Boston, Hartford, and Philadelphia during the early nineteenth century. Records indicate that a small but energetic trade between the islands and key urban centers in the Northeast attracted merchant families involved in commerce. By the 1830s trade expanded sufficiently to warrant the establishment of a Cuban–Puerto Rican Benevolent Merchants' Association. In the federal census of 1845 some 508 individuals from Mexico and South America were found in New York City. A sizable Cuban community, including members of the Quesada, Arango, and Mantilla families, lived on 110th Street facing Central Park. Among the handful of Puerto Rican families in Connecticut was that of merchant José de Rivera, a wealthy sugar and wine trader who lived in Bridgeport from 1844 to 1855. De Rivera and his wife, son, and three daughters occupied an elegant residence on Stratford Avenue.

From the mid- to the late nineteenth century, immigration from the Hispanic Caribbean, Mexico, and South America increased. Political exiles and those who left on their own to escape tyranny and exploitation in the countries of origin were among the first to sow the seeds of identifiable Spanish-speaking com-

Carmen Cornejo Gallegos standing in the back row, third from the left. "Los Tomboys," Orange County softball champions of 1947. Courtesy of Lori Gallegos-Hupka.

munities in the Northeast. Others who came were artisans, labor leaders, professionals, or working-class individuals who were disillusioned with homeland conditions and sought a better way of life. Trade increased bringing a steady stream of merchants and well-to-do visitors to the North. Women were particularly attracted to the freedom enjoyed in large cities like New York in comparison with stricter gender expectations back home. "What a pleasure it is to see women here driving their own carriages, often alone, sometimes with a girl friend or young daughter," exclaimed the Cuban Aurelia Castillo de González on one such trip.

Among the earliest immigrants were students like the three daughters of Dr. Juan Fermín Figueroa and Angela Socarrás Varona, who graduated from pharmacy school in New York and returned to Havana to open the city's first female-owned pharmacy. María Dolores de Figueroa became Cuba's first licensed woman pharmacist. Rita Danau lived and studied in New York for years before returning to Cuba to open a school for fencing, cycling, and riding. Julia Martínez studied at Notre Dame in Baltimore and earned a doctorate from the University of Havana. Pilar Barbosa de Rosario was the first woman to teach at the University of Puerto Rico after receiving a master's degree and a doctorate from Clark University. Her contemporary, Amelia Agostini de del Río, also earned academic credentials from U.S. institutions. By the early 1900s American schools organized special programs for Spanish-speaking teachers such as the New York State Normal School at New Paltz, which invited thirty Cuban teachers every year. Similarly, Harvard University hosted some 1,300 Cuban teachers for instruction in the summer of 1900. Finally, among the handful of Dominican intellectuals who studied in the United States during this early period was the notable Camila Henríquez Ureña. The youngest daughter of an illustrious intellectual family, Henríquez Ureña received a master's degree from the University of Minnesota in 1919.

In concert with the rebellions for Antillean independence from 1868 to 1898, expatriate communities in the Northeast swelled with staunch supporters of liberation, political activists, skilled and unskilled workers, and professionals. The life of Puerto Rican patriot Lola Rodríguez de Tió offers a wonderful example of women's roles in these struggles, as does that of the Cuban Emilia Casanova de Villaverde. Noted for writing the Puerto Rican revolutionary anthem, Rodríguez de Tió lived much of her life in exile because of her political convictions. Her writings, poetry, readings, and fiery discourses on political reforms electrified audiences in New York at the height of the conflicts. Casanova de Villaverde wrote extensively in support of independence and sold her jewelry and home furnishings to finance the war efforts. Her guidance was instrumental in founding Las Hijas de Cuba, located on New York's Washington Square. Like Rodríguez de Tió and Casanova de Villaverde, numerous women in exile formed political clubs and organizations that raised funds, held bazaars, hosted dances and theatrical events, featured speakers and recitals, commemorated cultural and historical events, and proselytized about Antillean liberation.

Contingents of workers also made up early communities, many of whom were connected to either political or labor movements. Cigar workers were particularly identified with socialism and prioritized the plight of the working class. The practice of *la lectura,* reading aloud to cigar workers in Spanish-owned factories, honed class consciousness, raised awareness about workers' struggles, and promoted solidarity. Luisa Capetillo was perhaps the only female ever to read in the New York cigar factories. Known for her feminist writings, Capetillo, who belonged to the leadership of the Puerto Rican union Federación Libre de Trabajadores (Free Federation of Labor), wholeheartedly supported women's equality, free love, and human emancipation. During her residence in New York Capetillo ran a vegetarian restaurant and a boardinghouse on Twenty-second Street and Eighth Avenue where she raged against tyranny and gender injustice

Elisa Santiago Baeza, New York, circa 1927. Courtesy of Virginia Sánchez Korrol.

Butcher's shop at 111th Street and Park Avenue, New York. Courtesy of the Justo A. Martí Photograph Collection. Centro Archives, Centro de Estudios Puertorriqueños, Hunter College, CUNY.

and espoused strongly held views on revolution, classless societies, and anarchy. Indeed, boardinghouses, bodegas, dressmaking shops, and cigar factories were among the earliest entrepreneurial ventures in which Latinas were involved. One Cuban woman, Gertrudes Heredia de Serra, even ran the Midwife Clinic of Havana in New York City.

American citizenship, imposed on the people of Puerto Rico by an act of Congress in 1917, altered the migrant flow from the islands. Although Spaniards, Dominicans, and other Latin Americans continued to come to New York for study or business, Puerto Ricans, as citizens, came to predominate among the Spanish-speaking population throughout the Northeast, particularly because it was easier for citizens to enter the country than for noncitizens. The migrant flow followed two streams. Either they came voluntarily in search of better economic prospects not available to them in Puerto Rico, or they were actively recruited by American companies to work in the fields or factories. Whatever the reason, the dynamics of migration were intricately tied to the economic cycles of U.S. markets, ease of transportation, and job availability. In 1920 the 130 women recruited to work by the American Manufacturing Company joined dozens of Puerto Ricans already living in Brooklyn, site of the earliest enclave in the city. The company provided shelter and their basic needs, deducting a percentage of their salary for the initial steamship transportation and company-sponsored events.

By the early 1920s women immigrated to the United States for a myriad of reasons; they followed husbands or parents in the migration, or they came alone. Dominican writer Virginia de Peña de Bordas came to live and study in the United States by herself. Antonia Denis, an activist and community organizer in Brooklyn, arrived in New York in 1919 on board the *Caracas*. By the 1920s she was deeply involved in borough politics, was active in the Betances Democratic Club, and was the founder of the Hijas de Borinquen. Denis was known to provide room and board for needy compatriots in her Columbia Street house. In his memoir Joaquín Colón lauded Denis for accommodating nearly forty migrants during a crisis in 1920. Victoria Hernández was an entrepreneur who ran a record store and gave piano lessons in the back of the store. The sister of noted composer Rafael Hernández, Victoria became one of the most prominent women in the Latin music business. Elisa Santiago Baeza explained her reasons for coming to New York in 1930. "We were eleven, six females and five males," remarked Santiago Baeza, who stayed for thirty years and raised a family. "We were poor and as the oldest female, I was like a second mother. The burden of caring for the younger children was always on me."

Women were homemakers and worked in restaurants, the garment industry, and factories or as domestics and housekeepers. They contributed to both the formal and informal economic sectors and altered their lifestyles and gender roles in the process. Women took in boarders, helped expand fledgling communities through ritual kinship, provided child care for working mothers, sold their home cooking, did piecework in the home, and tended to growing families. In times of need women organized rent parties, helped reestablish evicted families, shared apartments with other families, and opened their homes to newly arrived migrants. In this spirit women helped extend communal

Rally for community rights, Chelsea, Massachusetts. Courtesy of Aura Sánchez Garfunkel.

bonds at a point when nuclear families predominated over extended-family compositions, and they made lifelong friendships and support networks in an otherwise hostile environment. By the 1930s Latinas like the noted Guatemalan labor leader Luisa Moreno were vigorously engaged in union organizing, were active in community groups and in the public schools that educated their children, and projected their views in a wide array of journalistic enterprises that flourished during the period. *Revista de Artes y Letras,* published in New York from 1933 until 1945, printed the work of major literary figures like Julia de Burgos and Gabriela Mistral. It published articles on family and child welfare, religion, society, the arts, and education. Founded and edited by Josefina Silva de Cintrón, this journal specifically targeted a sophisticated female readership but was not above confronting city officials on critical educational issues affecting the Puerto Rican community.

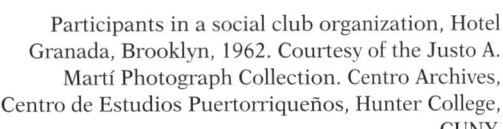

But for the most part, Latinas in the Northeast concentrated among the working class, and the 1930s and 1940s found them employed in factories, in garment-related occupations that relied heavily on the work of Puerto Rican women, as translators in civil service, as postal employees, in military service, and in other industries essential to the World War II war efforts. Nineteen-year-old Gloria Huertas, a native of Caguas, arrived in New Haven, Connecticut, with four children and no skills but soon found a job that allowed her to support her family. Community activist Antonia Pantoja arrived in New York in 1944 and worked in a series of factory jobs, all of which paid double what her salary had been as a rural teacher in Puerto Rico. Before she became the first woman mayor in the Western Hemisphere (she served as mayor of San Juan, Puerto Rico, from 1946 to 1968), Felisa Rincón de Gautier worked in New York factories, as did the city's first bilingual teacher, Ana Peñaranda, recruited to teach English to the growing numbers of Spanish-speaking children in the South Bronx's Public School 25. Most Latinas did not have the luxury to choose between working outside the home and being full-time homemakers. In the words of Connecticut community builder Genoveva Rodríguez, "What made me get up in the morning; it wasn't because I wanted to. It was because I was poor. And I wanted a better life . . . for my kids. And they wouldn't have a better life unless they went to school."

After World War II Puerto Rican barrios multiplied throughout the Northeast, in great measure because of the industrialization policies of the government of Puerto Rico. Migrant populations increased dramatically, and during the 1950s and 1960s an additional 20,000 seasonal contract farm laborers added to the migrant numbers. Seasonal workers, recruited to plant and harvest agricultural production, often remained in the regions of their contractual obligations, sent for their families, and gave rise to sizable communities in

Participants in a social club organization, Hotel Granada, Brooklyn, 1962. Courtesy of the Justo A. Martí Photograph Collection. Centro Archives, Centro de Estudios Puertorriqueños, Hunter College, CUNY.

Cubans in New York supporting the resistance against Batista's government, 1958. Courtesy of the Justo A. Martí Photograph Collection. Centro Archives, Centro de Estudios Puertorriqueños, Hunter College, CUNY.

places like Dover, New Jersey, Hartford and Bridgeport, Connecticut, Lorain, Ohio, and Chicago, Illinois. Until the 1970s, 80 percent of the migrant flow continued to come into New York City; 860,552 Puerto Ricans resided in New York, but 1.5 million appeared in the national census of 1990, with sizable populations in Chicago, Philadelphia, Newark, Hartford, and Jersey City. Moreover, the 1960s witnessed immigration legislation that eliminated preferences in the quota system based on national origins. Legal reforms encouraged Western Hemisphere emigration and family reunification and opened the door to an unprecedented immigration from the Caribbean, Mexico, and Central and South America. Economic uncertainty and political unrest were the most powerful factors in this immigration. The result was the emergence of a highly diverse, multilayered, ethnoracial Latino community that combined recent arrivals with longtime residents, citizens with aliens, and Spanish speakers with second-, third-, or fourth-generation English-dominant hyphenated Americans.

For Puerto Rican, Dominican, Cuban, and other Latina women, community issues, such as bilingual education, access to higher education, health, environment, employment, and adequate living conditions, reigned supreme. Communities mobilized, formed organizations for advancement, created the conditions for an emergent leadership, and combated racism and discrimination. Organizations like ASPIRA, the Puerto Rican Family Institute, the Puerto Rican Association for Community Affairs (PRACA), and the Puerto Rican Forum in New York spawned counterparts throughout the Northeast with different names but the same intentions. Indeed, many of the groups that originated throughout the civil rights period had national and international connections and continue to the present.

Women were front and center in many of these ventures. In New York, Pantoja worked alongside a dedicated group of social workers and educators that included high-profile figures like Josephine Nieves, Alice Cardona, Yolanda Sánchez, and María Canino to create ASPIRA, PRACA, and the Puerto Rican Forum. These organizations defined, structured, advocated, and provided for the urgent sociopolitical and economic survival of growing communities, often neglected by mainstream power brokers. Some belonged to the pioneer generation, like Patricia Rodríguez, a labor activist in Brooklyn, or Mamá Léo (Leoncia Rosado Rousseau), a Christian pastor who established a successful drug-abuse program in the South Bronx, but others were more recent arrivals. In Hartford María Clemencia Sánchez laid the foundations for the first Puerto Rican Day Parade, a celebratory feat that reinforced cultural nationalism but was also steeped in local politics. Described as a "one-woman social-service operation," Sánchez ran a candy store for a living where she held voter registration drives. She became the first Puerto Rican woman elected to the Hartford School Board in 1973 and the first Latina to serve in the state legislature. In Boston's South End Jovita Fontañez helped establish Inquilinos Boricuas en Acción (IBA), an organization that blocked the city from destroying a Puerto Rican community under urban renewal. Rallying to the cry "We shall not be moved from parcel 19," IBA led the way in creating a model development project, Villa Victoria. In New Jersey María DeCastro Blake, a passionate and determined woman, fought to open the doors of Rutgers University to Latino(a) students.

In spite of continuous struggles to provide basic necessities, achieve, and hold on to gains against mainstream backlash, Latina activist efforts were intended

Latinos in New York asking for support of the Dominican Revolution against Trujillo's government. Courtesy of the Justo A. Martí Photograph Collection. Centro Archives, Centro de Estudios Puertorriqueños, Hunter College, CUNY.

to yield long-range benefits, not self-aggrandizement. Edna Negrón succeeded María Clemencia Sánchez as the state representative for her district following Sánchez's untimely death. Negrón, Connecticut director of the Governor's Office of Puerto Rico, settled in Hartford in the 1960s and served as the city's coordinator for bilingual-bicultural education programs. Pantoja placed the directorship of ASPIRA, her most cherished organization, in the hands of Yolanda Sánchez and proceeded to blaze new trails in Puerto Rican and Latino community and educational advancement. María E. Sánchez, a leader in developing bilingual education in New York City, went on to direct the Department of Puerto Rican Studies at Brooklyn College, as did María Canino in the Department of Puerto Rican Studies at Livingston College of Rutgers University, New Brunswick, New Jersey.

Certainly women's political and union activism and intellectual and academic endeavors eroded the notion that Latinas were passive and uninterested in bettering their situations or in education. On the contrary, their contributions signaled another vibrant strand in the American mosaic. Claiming strong ties to cultural citizenship, Latina struggles in the Northeast ranged from securing bilingual education programs to admission into universities; from developing academic departments, programs, and research institutes on Puerto Rican, Latino, Dominican, or Hispanic American studies to incorporating Latino history and culture into the public school curriculum; and from marginalization on the job market to sitting at the negotiating table. By the 1980s and 1990s Latinas appeared to reap some of the fruits of this labor by assuming the reins of leadership in the public and private sectors.

Latina activists in bilingual education in the 1960s and 1970s like Carmen Pérez-Hogan, María Ramírez, and Hilda Hidalgo occupied decision-making positions at the state and national levels in the 1990s. Hidalgo served as assistant commissioner of education for the state of New Jersey, but before that she struggled with a cadre of committed individuals like Carmen Asencio in Trenton and Gloria del Toro in Newark to provide educational and social services for Puerto Ricans and Latinos. Bronx-bred Sonia Sotomayor, an assistant district attorney in New York, became U.S. district court judge for the Southern District of New York in 1992. The first Puerto Rican woman to serve in a U.S. federal court, Sotomayor earned her law degree from Yale University, where she edited the *Yale Law Journal.* Judge Carmen Beauchamp Ciparick, an associate judge of the New York State Court of Appeals in 1994, served as a staff attorney with the Legal Aid Society in New York City from 1967 to 1969. In medicine two Latinas from the Northeast stand out for their monumental service. Antonia Novello, the commissioner of health for the state of New York (and the first Latina

Community mobilization, Centro Latino de Chelsea, Massachusetts. Courtesy of Aura Sánchez Garfunkel.

surgeon general) advocated for quality health care and led the first national Latino initiative to identify and strategically address disease prevention. Helen Rodríguez-Trias directed the Department of Pediatrics at Lincoln Hospital in the Bronx, highlighting community-based involvement in health issues, AIDS among women, and sterilization. Isaura Santiago and Dolores Fernández each became president of Hostos College in the City University of New York system. Elsa Gómez was president of Kean College in New Jersey, and Marta Casals Istomin, cofounder of the internationally recognized Pablo Casals Festival in Puerto Rico, heads Manhattan's School of Music. Each of the women cited represents countless others who have enormously contributed to the legacy of Latinas in the Northeast.

In the twenty-first century a dramatic increase in the numbers of Mexican and Central American immigrants

Antonia Denis supporting Celia Acosta Vice's candidacy for the New York State Assembly. Courtesy of the Justo A. Martí Photograph Collection. Centro Archives, Centro de Estudios Puertorriqueños, Hunter College, CUNY.

in northeastern states has emerged that signifies how each incoming group finds its own way to connect to a historical legacy. Catering to the growing numbers of day laborers in Long Island, a group scorned for altering traditional work patterns in suburbs like Farmingville, Latinas have formed a door-to-door business. As *cocineras* (cooks), they provide homemade meals to men living away from wives and mothers. According to the *New York Times*, "These women make dinner, over-hear secrets, console those who cannot find work and quickly get used to grown men calling them *madre*." Hired to provide staples, cook, and clean house for legal or illegal communities of migrant workers, the women accommodate several homes a week. They cook the appropriate regional dishes required by each home, sometimes bring their children with them while they work, and serve as intermediaries with the surrounding societies when needed. Resilient and adapting to changing times, Latinas meet their own financial obligations, often earning more than they would at fast-food restaurants. Moreover, they serve as integral links in the preservation of community and heritage, carrying forth a legacy forged in the distant past.

The effects of migration, daily life in diaspora, identity, biculturalism, bilingualism, race, class, and gender become subjects for analysis in a variety of venues. During the 1980s and 1990s Latina writers like Nicholasa Mohr (*Nilda*), Julia Alvarez (*How the García Girls Lost Their Accents*), Esmeralda Santiago (*When I Was Puerto Rican* and *Almost a Woman*), and Judith Ortiz Cofer (*Silent Dancing*) explored these issues in semiautobiographical novels. In searching for their own answers, they gave voice to millions who experience the duality of "living on the hyphen." Aurora Levins Morales expanded the paradigm by introducing intergenerational and cross-cultural perspectives that spoke to yet another reality—the coalescence of something new on U.S. soil, neither Latin American nor U.S. American but a synthesis of both. Simply stated, Levins Morales declares in her poem *Child of the Americas*, "I am new. History made me. My first language was Spanglish. I was born at the crossroads and I am whole." In this spirit Latina history in the Northeast shares common ground.

SOURCES: Acosta-Belén, Edna, Margarita Benítez, José E. Cruz, Yvonne González-Rodríguez, Clara E. Rodríguez, Carlos E. Santiago, Azara Santiago-Rivera, and Barbara Sjostrom. 2000. *"Adíos Borinquen querida": The Puerto Rican Diaspora, Its History and Contributions.* Albany, NY: Center for Latino, Latin American, and Caribbean Studies, SUNY; Glasser, Ruth. 1997. *"Aquí me quedo": Puerto Ricans in Connecticut.* Middletown: Connecticut Humanities Council; Pérez, Louis A. 1999. *On Becoming Cuban: Identity, Nationality, and Culture.* New York: Harper Collins; Sánchez Korrol, Virginia. 1994. 2nd ed. *From Colonia to Community: The History of Puerto Ricans in New York.* Berkeley: University of California Press; Ruiz, Vicki L., and Virginia Sánchez Korrol, eds. 2005. *Latina Legacies: Identity, Biography, and Community.* New York: Oxford University Press.

Virginia Sánchez Korrol

LATINAS IN THE MIDWEST

Latina migrants began arriving in the Midwest in significant numbers during the early twentieth century as part of larger Latino migrant flows. The Mexican community was the largest Latina/o population in the region throughout the twentieth century, followed by Puerto Ricans, Cubans, and Central and South Americans. Latina/o communities have historically emerged in both urban and rural areas, and the group represents a diverse range of countries of origin, as well as class backgrounds. Many of the earliest residents, however, were working-class migrants in search of economic security.

The pre–World War II era saw largely Mexican immigrants, with smaller numbers of Central and South American and Caribbean immigrants. The first Latina/o immigrants to Chicago, for example, were workers contracted by the railroads in 1916. In that year 206 Mexicans were working on the railroads; by 1926, 5,255 Mexican men worked on the rail lines. Some wives, children, and other female relatives and single women also traveled to the Midwest. Women, however, made up a relatively small proportion of these communities. For example, of 17,000 Mexicans living in Chicago in 1927, only 1,650 were women and 3,350 were children. In the Indiana Harbor colony during this time, women numbered 500 and children 1,000 in a total population of 4,500 Mexican immigrants. Similarly, in Gary, Indiana, the population of 2,500 Mexicans included only 200 women and 350 children.

In urban areas like Chicago, Latina/o immigrants, predominantly males, were drawn by work in railroads, steel mills, and meatpacking houses. The railroads also drew workers to cities like Milwaukee and Kansas City, while cities like Gary and Indiana Harbor employed workers in steel mills. Detroit drew workers to the auto and other related industries. Overall, midwestern cities provided the opportunity for higher industrial wages compared with agricultural labor in the Southwest.

Many Latina immigrants worked outside the home, as well, in order to contribute to household economies. By the 1930s, according to Zaragosa Vargas, women constituted more than one-third of the Mexican immigrant workforce. Though women rarely found employment in heavy industrial work, some Mexicanas found jobs processing meats and sausages in the packinghouses or worked in candy, mattress, and paper factories. Smaller numbers found jobs as salesclerks or in office work. Although some men objected to women's employment outside the home because it disrupted the traditional gendered division of labor, for many families it was an economic necessity. Women also did work that blurred public/private boundaries, including taking in boarders, running restaurants that catered to single migrant men, or taking in piecework. Few Latinas during this period worked in domestic service.

In addition to paid labor, Latina immigrants also did the important work of sustaining social networks and kinship ties, performing productive labor in the home, and caring for other workers. Women, for example, often led collection efforts for fellow immigrants who were ill or had passed away. They organized cultural celebrations such as national independence days and other pageants.

Latinas and their families faced difficult conditions in midwestern cities because Mexican migrants often lived in the most overcrowded and poorest housing available. Railroad companies often relegated Mexican workers to boxcar camps. Here women had the especially difficult work of making suitable homes for their families in the direst of conditions, usually without heating, plumbing, modern cooking facilities, or adequate shelter from the elements. Mexican women struggled to maintain households and feed and care for their families in the most inhospitable conditions. Moreover, social service agencies and settlement houses neglected Mexican communities in comparison with European immigrants. Some agencies, however, did provide assistance to Latina/o immigrants, targeting Mexican women, for example, in their Americanization efforts.

Mexican women also migrated to rural areas throughout the region, where they and their families worked as agricultural laborers. Agricultural recruiters often sought entire families for fieldwork because this would ensure more hands in the fields. The first Mexican workers in Minnesota arrived in 1907, while the first workers in Ohio and Wisconsin (Milwaukee) arrived in 1917. By 1927 the Mexican population in the Midwest numbered 63,700. In summer months, when families headed north as migrant farmworkers, their numbers rose to as many as 80,000. Women, alongside male relatives and children, worked in the beet fields of Minnesota and Michigan, in the onion fields of Ohio, and on other crops throughout the region. Latina/o

Elena Rico and partner at one of the Chicago Fiesta Guild events. Courtesy of Elena Rico.

The Gómez family immigrated to Kansas City, Missouri, in 1917 from Jalisco, Mexico. The eighteen children pooled their resources from their jobs in the meatpacking houses and beer factories to support the family. Courtesy of Lara Medina.

immigrants also found themselves in rural or small-town communities in places like Nebraska, Kansas, and Iowa.

Not all Latinas during this time period, however, came from working-class backgrounds. A small number of professional Latin American migrants also made their homes in urban areas in the region. Argentinian, Colombian, Costa Rican, Cuban, Honduran, Mexican, and Panamanian consuls had offices in cities like Chicago, while Latin American doctors, lawyers, and other professionals relocated their families to midwestern cities where their services were in demand among the growing migrant population. The wives of these professional men often filled the roles of socialites, cultural ambassadors, and community leaders. They sometimes hosted or made appearances at social functions such as national independence celebrations where they represented their countries of origin to international government officials and the broader American society. Latin American students who studied in the Midwest also contributed to the migrant population. Latina young women from wealthy families who graduated from high school or college in the region were sometimes noted in local Spanish-language newspapers.

In Chicago Spanish-language newspapers of the 1920s and 1930s recognized the presence of Latina immigrant readers and printed columns that catered specifically to women. Advice columns addressed topics like beauty and homemaking. They advised readers on disciplining children and the cultural and moral education of Latin American children growing up in the United States. Women also found recipes and housekeeping tips in the pages of Spanish newspapers. In addition, numerous advertisements announced products like beauty creams and cosmetics designed to appeal to Latina migrant women. In the growing consumer culture of the United States, Latinas too were potential consumers. Latinas also used the newspapers for their own entrepreneurial interests—to advertise their boardinghouses or restaurants to fellow migrants. Such advertisements sometimes included a photograph of the proprietress of the business as a way to personalize the establishment and evoke a sense of "home" for potential migrant male customers.

After the Great Depression the Latina/o population in the Midwest declined dramatically. Deportation and repatriation campaigns depleted the Mexican migrant communities in urban and rural areas alike. By 1936, for example, only 1,200 Mexicans remained in Detroit, a city that had had 15,000 immigrants only seven years earlier and was the second-largest urban settlement of Mexicans in the Midwest. Mexican communities dwindled throughout the region and did not reemerge until after World War II. The postwar era, however, also saw a rise in the migration of Puerto Rican women, men, and children.

The years after World War II witnessed a renewed flow of Latina/o migrants. In particular, Puerto Ricans became an attractive source of labor for some American companies. Women and men were recruited for agricultural labor, picking crops as Mexican immigrants had done in earlier decades. Industrial employers, however, also began seeking out Puerto Rican labor. Puerto Rican women and men found work in factories in eastern and midwestern cities, but Puerto Rican women found employment in domestic work as well.

In 1946 more than 300 Puerto Rican women migrated to Chicago as part of an experimental domestic-

Two generations in 1939: a Mexican mother, Hermelinda Gómez Ornelas, with her Mexican American daughter, Ofelia "Rosemary" Ornelas. Courtesy of Lara Medina.

labor recruitment program. Because the women were hired as live-in domestics, they lived dispersed throughout the city in employers' homes rather than in concentrated ethnic communities. The recruitment program also included several dozen Puerto Rican men hired to work at the Chicago Hardware Foundry Company, which housed the men in a boxcar community on the company's premises. Within three months many workers began complaining about work conditions; some women worked as many as fifteen hours a day, others had poor living arrangements, and others complained of unfair wages. The women, who met one another at social gatherings sponsored by the local YWCA, gained the support of Puerto Rican students at the University of Chicago, including the famous Puerto Rican anthropologist Elena Padilla and Munita Muñoz Lee, the daughter of the then president of the Puerto Rican Senate (and soon to be governor of the island territory), Luis Muñoz Marín. Other sympathetic observers became involved as well, including a Puerto Rican social worker vacationing in Chicago at the time, Carmen Isales. After interviewing thirty women and researching local prevailing wages, Isales made the case that the women were discriminated against by a racially based wage differential: while employers paid white women as much as $35 or $40 per week for domestic work, Puerto Rican women earned only $15 per week. Eventually many of the recruited domestic workers quit their jobs and left the city. The episode, however, marked an important moment of Latina women in the Midwest advocating for one another and demanding equitable treatment as workers.

Small numbers of Latinas/os also continued migrating to the Midwest as university students. Puerto Rican and other Latina/o students attended universities throughout the region. Puerto Rican scholar Elena Padilla, for example, completed her master's thesis in anthropology at the University of Chicago in 1947. Though little was known about Latina/o immigrant populations in the Midwest during this time, Padilla's thesis compared Puerto Rican migration in Chicago and New York City. Her work made a significant contribution to the scholarship on Latinas/os in the Midwest.

Other Puerto Rican women also began migrating to the city after World War II. Those who did not live with their employers made their homes among Mexican immigrants (based on language affinities) or among African Americans (based on racial affinities). Many Puerto Rican women who migrated to the Midwest during this time had previous work experience in Puerto Rico, largely in the needle trades or in agricultural work. According to Gina Pérez, Puerto Rican women and men migrated as part of household units seeking a strategy for economic survival. Puerto Rican women's work both within and outside the home together represented women's survival strategies as members of families and extended communities.

Puerto Rican and Mexican women continued to arrive in the Midwest during the 1950s, particularly in urban areas, as part of larger migrant movements. As in the 1920s, women found employment in agricultural work, in meatpacking and other factories, and, increasingly, in domestic labor. Mexican and Puerto Rican communities grew dramatically during this decade. These new (im)migrants, however, continued to be marginalized by the city and were relegated to the poorest neighborhoods, the worst housing, and the lowest-skilled jobs. Moreover, because of the rapid deindustrialization of American cities like Milwaukee, Chicago, Detroit, and Cleveland, the Puerto Rican community experienced growing unemployment and underemployment and increasingly turned to public assistance for economic survival. Thus, while many Puerto Rican migrants initially came to the Midwest because of the promise of economic opportunities, the loss of industrial jobs made the times much more difficult for many. According to Gina Pérez, in Chicago by the 1960s, Puerto Ricans became stigmatized as culturally dysfunctional, an underclass, and largely dependent on welfare. Such characterizations of the Puerto Rican community rested largely on specifically gendered ideologies: like the denigrating views of African American women, these views described poor Puerto Rican women in very negative terms. Puerto Rican and other Latina women made efforts to better their socioeconomic conditions, however, by organizing around issues of welfare rights, education, and employment discrimination.

By 1965, when the Immigration and Naturalization Act reformed American immigration quotas, Mexican and Puerto Rican migrants to cities like Chicago and Detroit were increasingly accompanied by Cuban and Central and South American immigrants. Again, while Latin American men often immigrated alone as an economic strategy to provide for their families back home, women also immigrated as part of household units. Increasingly in the 1970s and 1980s, however, women also began immigrating alone, as men had done earlier, also seeking to provide economically for their families back home.

Cuban immigrants began arriving in larger numbers after the Cuban Revolution of 1959. The earliest waves of immigrants included mostly professionals and elites. By the 1980s the Cuban immigrant population included more working-class and less educated immigrants as well. Central and South Americans also included middle- and upper-class professionals, but particularly for Central Americans, migrants included large numbers of political refugees who were fleeing civil wars and political unrest in war-torn homelands. Mexican immigrants continued arriving, many of whom were fleeing Mexico's economic devastation during the late 1970s and early 1980s. Latina women from many of these sending countries played crucial roles in maintaining transnational ties and social networks between home and the U.S. mainland.

By the 1970s Latinas in the Midwest, especially the second and third generations, became increasingly politicized and more vocal about demanding services and rights for their communities. Women became the backbone of community organizing and grassroots activism and led various struggles for equitable housing, education, employment, and welfare rights. Maria Cerda, a Puerto Rican woman, became the first Hispanic to serve on the Chicago Board of Education in 1969. She advocated assiduously for bilingual education and a school curriculum that valued Latina/o children's cultural backgrounds. Six years later Cerda became the first executive director of the Latino Institute, a research and advocacy agency that provided technical assistance and support for local Latina/o community-based organizations. In 1973 Mexican and Puerto Rican women in Chicago founded Mujeres Latinas en Acción, a social service and advocacy agency that serves Spanish-speaking women. Mexican mothers in Chicago during the 1970s also led the struggle against inequitable, segregated, and inferior education for their children in overcrowded Mexican neighborhood schools. As small numbers of women began gaining access to higher education and professions, Latinas also became more visible as artists, educators and businesswomen and in other professional roles during the 1970s and 1980s. By the end of the twentieth century Latinas began flexing some political power as well, running for city, county, and state political seats and gaining political appointments in municipal government.

Still, Latinas in the Midwest struggle with gender and racial discrimination in education, housing, and employment. Recent immigrants, in particular, experience high rates of poverty, low wages, inequitable education, and inadequate housing. But U.S.-born Latinas also experience high rates of unemployment, poverty, and lack of educational resources. Latinas in the region have faced particular challenges over the decades. Being in a geographic region that is often overlooked by the East Coast–West Coast emphasis on Latinas/os, Latinas have had to work hard to make their communities visible on the national level. They have also encountered significant diversity within the Latina/o community in the region. Today Latina immigrants continue to arrive from countries throughout Latin America—Colombia, Guatemala, Chile, Peru, Cuba, Mexico, Nicaragua, and El Salvador. They also find, however, long-standing communities of women who trace their roots in the region back to the early twentieth century.

SOURCES: Fernández, Lilia. 2005. "Latina/o Migration and Community Formation in Postwar Chicago: Mexicans, Puerto Ricans, Gender, and Politics, 1945–1975." Ph.D. diss., University of California, San Diego; García, Juan R. 1996. *Mexicans in the Midwest, 1900–1932*. Tucson: University of Arizona Press; Padilla, Elena. 1947. "Puerto Rican Immigrants in New York and Chicago: A Study in Comparative Assimilation." Ph.D. diss., University of Chicago; Pérez, Gina M. 2004. *The Near Northwest Side Story: Migration, Displacement, and Puerto Rican Families*. Berkeley: University of California Press; Vargas, Zaragosa. 1993. *Proletarians of the North: A History of Mexican Industrial Workers in Detroit and the Midwest, 1917–1933*. Berkeley: University of California Press.

Lilia Fernández

LATINAS IN THE SOUTHEAST

When one thinks of traditional areas of settlement for Latinos, one thinks primarily of the Southwest and the Northeast of the United States. However, the first Spanish settlement in what is now the United States was in St. Augustine, Florida, in 1565. It was not until decades later that settlements were founded in New Mexico, Texas, and other areas of the Southwest. Since the sixteenth century Florida has been an important destination for many people who trace their ancestry to Spanish-speaking nations.

The Latino group most associated with the southeastern states is the Cubans. More than 1.3 million Cubans live in the United States today, and more than 60 percent of them live in southern Florida alone. Cuban migration to the United States can be divided into two distinct periods: the nineteenth-century migration prompted in part by the various wars of independence against Spain, and the post-1959 migration provoked by the Cuban Revolution. Cubans have migrated to the United States at other times, responding to a variety of political and economic crises in their country, but the largest migrations occurred during these two periods.

Thousands of Cubans migrated as a result of the Cuban wars of independence (1868–1878 and 1895–1898). Those who migrated to the United States settled in different cities around the country. Some settled in the Northeast, in places such as New York, Philadelphia, and Boston. The majority, however, settled in the southeastern United States, in cities like Key West, Tampa, Jacksonville, and New Orleans. Various Cuban cigar manufacturers relocated to Florida during this period, and Key West and Tampa emerged as the major cigar-manufacturing centers in the United States because of the Cuban factories that relocated to that area. These factories attracted thousands of Cuban workers who, faced with unemployment in Cuba in the midst of war, chose to leave for the United States and took their wives and children with them.

As a result of the relocation, many women were forced to work outside the home to supplement their family's income. They worked as seamstresses, laundresses, servants, cooks, midwives, peddlers, grocers, and boardinghouse keepers. By the 1870s Cuban women in Florida had a higher labor participation rate than women on the island. More women worked in the cigar industry than in any other trade, especially in Key West, where they constituted 9 percent of the industry's workforce. While men performed the highly skilled tasks of cutting, filling, rolling, classing, and selecting, women worked at semiskilled tasks, especially as *despalilladoras,* or tobacco strippers. Over time, however, more and more women gained access to the skilled occupations traditionally held by men. By 1890 women constituted up to one-quarter of all hand rollers in some factories in Tampa, working alongside the men. There was at least one case of a woman *lectora,* a reader in the cigar factory, occupying the most prestigious position on the factory floor.

Whether they settled in Florida or New York, most Cubans perceived themselves as exiles and planned to return to their homeland once it became an economically stable, independent nation. While they struggled to survive in the United States, they assisted in the liberation efforts. Throughout the Ten Years' War (1868–1878) Cubans raised money for the rebel forces. Women established organizations to assist the independence movement, among them the Hijas del Pueblo in New Orleans and the Junta Patriótica de Damas de Nueva York, which raised money to buy supplies for the rebel forces, and they rallied public support for the Cuban cause. Women also played a key role in José Martí's Partido Revolucionario Cubano (PRC). Of the 200 clubs that constituted part of the PRC, 25 percent were women's clubs. By 1898 Key West had the most *clubes femeninos,* with eighteen chapters, and Tampa had fifteen clubs. Total membership in the *clubes femeninos* in the United States and abroad reached nearly 1,500 by the end of 1898. Some of the *clubes* were named for female heroes of the revolution such as Mariana Grajales and Mercedes Varona. Often the names the women chose for their clubs reflected the role they perceived for themselves in the liberation effort, such as Protectoras de la Pátria (Protectors of the Nation), Obreras de la Independencia (Forgers of Independence), and Protectoras del Ejército (Protectors of the Army). The *clubes femeninos* organized dances, picnics, raffles, auctions, banquets, rallies, and parades through which they promoted the idea of independence and raised money to supply and feed the rebel army.

Apart from their active fund-raising and propaganda work, the women assisted the revolution in more subtle ways. As their men left to fight in Cuba, the responsibility of supporting their families fell on women's shoulders. Women successfully raised families, worked outside the home, and contributed to the political cause. They often neglected their own personal comfort in order to contribute more money to the PRC. Throughout the war, as more and more Cubans sought refuge in their communities, the women also took in the homeless, collected clothes, and set up soup kitchens. They took in widows, orphans, wounded soldiers, and other victims of the war. They kept medical supplies and even weapons and ammunition, and they opened their homes to the rebel leaders who made periodic visits to the exile communities to rally support.

After the Treaty of Paris that ended the Cuban-Spanish-American war of 1895–1898, a radical relocation to Cuba did not take place. Over the years Cubans had established ties to the United States in spite of their nationalism. Although they may have been torn by their desires to return home, they realized that they could fare better economically if they remained in the

United States. Many of those who repatriated following the war returned to Florida within a few years because of the political and economic instability on the island. They were joined by hundreds of new immigrants who chose to seek economic opportunities in the United States while Cuba rebuilt itself.

After independence the Cuban exile communities now channeled their energies into improving their domestic environment and especially their working conditions. The Cubans had a long tradition of militant trade unionism, but instead of joining U.S. labor organizations such as the Knights of Labor or the International Cigarmakers Union, they created their own labor unions such as the Union de Trabajadores and la Resistencia that addressed not only immediate concerns such as wages and benefits, but long-term issues such as class struggle. During the late nineteenth and early twentieth centuries Cuban cigar workers in Florida, especially in Tampa, went on strike on several occasions. Female cigar makers struck alongside the men for higher wages, better benefits, and union recognition. The women of the community assisted the protesters in countless ways. They set up soup kitchens, or *cocinas económicas,* to feed the striking cigar workers and their families, and they collected clothes, food, and medicine for them. When the strikers were evicted from their houses because of their inability to pay rent, women took families into their homes.

Less is known about Cuban women's lives after the 1920s because this period has received comparatively limited scholarly attention. Migration to the United States continued in the decades after Cuban independence because of high unemployment and a work climate hostile to organized labor. Records show that from 1921 to 1930, 16,000 Cubans immigrated to the United States. However, immigration decreased because of the Great Depression of the 1930s, as it did for most other immigrant groups. From 1931 to 1940 only 9,000 Cubans immigrated to the United States. A return migration to Cuba also characterized this period. Cigar workers were particularly likely to return. By the early 1930s the cigar industry in the United States had fallen on hard times, and many cigar makers either returned to Cuba or looked for factory jobs up north. Black and mixed-race Cubans were the most likely to move north during the first decades of the twentieth century because of segregation and heightened racial tension and discrimination in the South.

The political violence in Cuba during the 1940s and 1950s also compelled Cubans to emigrate, many as political exiles. From 1941 to 1950 some 26,000 Cubans immigrated to the United States. During the following decade 79,000 individuals immigrated. Cuban expatriates maintained contact with the homeland in multiple ways. They sent remittances to their relatives and kept Cuban traditions and the memory of their homeland alive through various cultural activities associated with religious or patriotic celebrations. Cubans published Spanish-language newspapers with news of the homeland, wrote books, and composed music that evoked their ties to both Cuba and the United States. Until 1959 Cubans on the island and on the mainland were able to travel back and forth, exchanging stimulating ideas and maintaining a sense of nationhood. They imported Cuban products and exported some of their own. Many emigrated to the United States with the hope of returning to their homeland one day; others never looked back. Like their nineteenth-century forebears, they played an active role in the politics of their homeland by raising money or campaigning for political candidates running for office back home. But the longer the Cubans stayed in the United States, the stronger the ties they developed to the country that gave them refuge.

By far the largest Cuban migration to the United States occurred as a result of the Cuban Revolution in 1959. Ironically, the revolutionary movement that produced the greatest reform also distanced the greatest number of people by its radicalism. More than one-tenth of Cuba's present-day population chose or was forced to emigrate after 1959; nearly 1 million settled in the United States and in the Commonwealth of Puerto Rico. Due to the visible and active U.S. presence on the island before the revolution, as well as a long historical connection between the two, it was logical that Cubans turned to the American nation in this time of need.

The postrevolutionary migration occurred in four distinct waves: 1959–1962, 1965–1973, 1980, and 1994 to the present. It also followed a socioeconomic progression. The first to leave were the upper and middle classes, followed closely by the working classes. The U.S. government granted the Cubans of the first two waves refugee status and welcomed them with a comprehensive assistance program, the Cuban Refugee Program (CRP). By 1973 CPR had dispensed more than $957 million in relief through job training, education programs, loans, medical care, surplus food distribution, and emergency relief checks, as well as a resettlement program. Subsequent arrivals did not receive the same levels of government assistance, but they did encounter a fairly open-door policy. Most Cubans who found the means to leave the island were accepted into the United States, even if they entered the country illegally.

Cuban women often found their first jobs more readily than men because they were willing to work for lower wages. These jobs, for the most part, were unskilled or semiskilled labor that did not require fluency in English or contact with the general public. Women found jobs as factory operatives, seamstresses, domestics and nannies, janitors, cooks, dishwashers, waitresses, sales personnel, and agricultural workers and in other low-level service occupations. The garment industry and textile manufacturing were important employers. By the mid-1980s more than 25,000 Cuban women worked in the garment industry and had become the backbone of that industry.

Because thousands of Cuban women were seeking employment, the Cuban Refugee Center in Miami created vocational training programs specifically for them. In 1964 a program titled "Training for Independence," or Aprenda y Supérese, was established by the center to help single women and heads of households become self-supporting. In two-month sessions women received intensive English instruction and training in a number of marketable skills: hand sewing, sewing-machine work, clerical office work, nursing assistance, housekeeping, and even silk-screen art work. Afterward the government assisted the women in finding employment, often resettling them to other parts of the country. Aprenda y Supérese trained more than 3,000 Cuban women and was so successful that it became a model for the amended Aid to Families with Dependent Children (AFDC) program during the Johnson administration in 1968.

Women also encountered opportunities in the teaching profession, where they contributed to the accommodation of thousands of refugee children into the Dade County school system. In 1961 Dade County, Florida, established a Cuban Teacher Training Program to prepare former and aspiring teachers for positions in southern Florida's rapidly growing school system. The Cuban "teacher assistants," the majority of whom were women, spent up to eight hours per day in a classroom, assisting in curriculum planning, teaching, and supervision and acting as interpreters for the refugee children. At night they took English-language and education courses to prepare for their certification exams. Once certified, the teachers headed their own classrooms in Dade County schools or were relocated to school systems around the country.

As each year decreased their chances of returning to Cuba, women began to work toward improving the quality of their lives in the United States. Many returned to school either to revalidate their professional credentials or to train for a more marketable career, accommodating language courses and college curricula into their busy schedules. To assist each other in these efforts, women helped found and maintain professional organizations that served as clearinghouses of information on job and educational opportunities. These professional associations had a largely male membership. However, in some associations, such as the Colegio Nacional de Bibliotecarios en el Exilio for librarians and the Colegio Nacional de Farmaceuticos en el Exilio for pharmacists, women constituted at least half the membership. For those women who did not have professional training, informal networks emerged to inform each other of job and educational opportunities.

Exile taught women to be resourceful and to work together within their families, neighborhoods, and communities. As their spheres of responsibility expanded, they found new and innovative ways of balancing work at home and in the workplace. Out of their common need they created networks of female relatives, friends, and neighbors to exchange services: they took care of each other's children and took turns doing the grocery shopping; they served as interpreters for one another; and in some cases they shared the expenses of major appliances that they traded from

Members of the Colegio Nacional de Bibliotecarias en el Exilio. Sitting from left to right: Evidia Blanco, Dolores Rovira, Ana Rosa Núñez, and Rosa Abella; standing from left to right: Elena Peraza, Carmen Martínez, María de los Angeles Menéndez, Sara Sánchez, and Lesbia Varona. Courtesy of the Cuban Heritage Collection, Otto G. Richter Library, University of Miami.

house to house. These networks of family and friends were crucial to women who worked outside the home. Although women expanded their roles to include wage earning, their spouses did not expand their roles to include housework. Elderly women, in particular, played a crucial role in this network. In three-generation households the elderly supplied an additional income from either outside employment or public assistance, which, in turn, helped assist their families financially. More important, they played a pivotal role in child rearing and home maintenance, allowing their daughters, granddaughters, and neighbors to go out and find work.

Some entrepreneurial women created lucrative businesses that catered to the needs of women who entered the workplace. They established housekeeping and delivery services, laundries and dry cleaners, home ateliers and dress shops, beauty parlors, day-care centers, driving schools, and even subscription home-delivery food services. Cubans discovered that any business that made life easier for women who worked outside the home had a good chance of succeeding.

The shift in roles and responsibilities has had a tremendous impact on Cubans' economic "success" as a group. As early as 1980 Cuban American median family income was almost equal to that of the total U.S. population. This was an important accomplishment for a community of predominantly first-generation immigrants. Women's high participation in the labor force helped raise the median family income. Without their contributions, these statistics would have been much different. While women's new roles brought them independence and power, it also strained marriages because many men felt threatened by these nontraditional relationships. By 1980 census figures showed that Cuban women had the highest divorce rates in the United States: 9.3 percent of Cuban women aged fifteen years and above identified themselves as divorced in the 1980 census, as compared with 7.3 of the total U.S. population.

While women's participation in the labor force had a notable impact on the economic success of both their families and the larger community, their participation in the political activities of the community was less obvious. During the 1960s exile politics was concerned more with Cuba than with the United States, and hundreds of political organizations emerged in Miami, Union City, New York, Los Angeles, and Chicago to lead the counterrevolution. Since politics was generally regarded as too hostile or violent an arena for women, for the most part, they were excluded from these organizations. The vast majority of women were also too preoccupied with domestic and economic responsibilities to be full-time advocates of *la causa cubana*. Tradition cast them in a supportive role. They could always be counted on to do the thankless and tedious work of sewing or painting banners, preparing food for protesters at demonstrations, writing letters and making phone calls, and marching in demonstrations. The handful of political organizations that emerged exclusively for women, among them the Union de Mujeres, the Cruzada Femenina Cubana, and the Movimiento Femenino Anticomunista de Cuba, functioned as auxiliaries, providing moral and financial support to different men's organizations by participating in their rallies and fund-raisers, organizing public relations campaigns and membership drives, and even sponsoring memorial services for the men who died for *la causa*. These organizations, however, offered no real political alternatives.

The one political issue that drew a significant participation from women was human rights. Numerous coalitions emerged dedicated to calling world attention to the plight of political prisoners in Cuba. Perhaps the most notable of these groups was the nonprofit organization Of Human Rights, founded in 1961 by Elena Mederos González to monitor human rights abuses in Cuba. Other groups that have emerged include the Committee to Denounce Cruelties to Cuban Political Prisoners, the Centro de Derechos Humanos del Movimiento Demócrata Cristiano, and El Movimiento Mujeres pro Derechos Humanos. Women played a crucial role in this political campaign, since it was their fathers, husbands, sons, and sisters who were imprisoned in Cuba. They wrote letters and sent petitions to Amnesty International, Americas Watch, the International Red Cross, and the PEN clubs, and they met with presidents, congressmen, and foreign dignitaries. They organized fund-raising banquets to raise money for their publicity campaign, arranged special memorial services to pray for the prisoners, and helped erect monuments honoring the prisoners in parks and public areas to keep them in the community's consciousness. It took years, however, to see the fruits of their work. It was not until the late 1970s and early 1980s that the Castro government finally began to release thousands of political prisoners.

Younger women who came of age in the United States and studied at U.S. colleges and universities tended to have greater opportunities for political expression than their mothers. Influenced by the civil rights movement, the feminist movement, and the student activism of the 1960s and early 1970s, they joined various student political groups and staged protests and demonstrations on college campuses. Some of these younger women, influenced by the radicalized milieu of the 1960s, came to adopt a more tolerant view of the revolution and began to work for the normalization of relations between both countries. Many

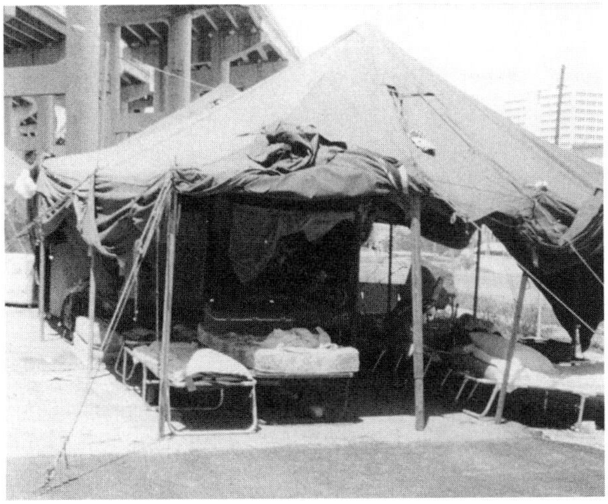

Refugee camp in Miami during the massive Cuban immigration known as the Mariel Boatlift, 1980. Courtesy of the Cuban Heritage Collection, Otto G. Richter Library, University of Miami.

young women also played key editorial roles in political journals of the 1970s such as *Areíto, Nueva Generación, Joven Cuba, Krisis,* and *¡Cuba Va!* that analyzed *la problemática cubana* and the plight of Cubans in the United States.

Since the 1980s a number of women have begun to distinguish themselves in local politics, serving in city and county governments. Ironically, because women were excluded from exile politics, they carved a niche for themselves in ethnic politics, that is, domestic policy making. Working with other racial and ethnic groups, they addressed issues of importance to the community as a whole, such as crime, racism, education, taxes, utilities, and urban development. As representatives of the Cuban community at the local level, they also addressed issues of specific importance to their fellow émigrés. In 1989 one Miami politician, Ileana Ros-Lehtinen, was elected to occupy the House seat long held by the late congressman Democrat Claude Pepper.

Cuban women were perhaps most influential in cultural matters, specifically, preserving *cubanidad,* or those customs, values, and traditions that they associated with being Cuban. Preserving *cubanidad* became a cultural mission in the exile community: an attempt to preserve those values they regarded as important for the distant day when repatriation became possible. Over time, however, as the exiles resigned themselves to a lengthy, if not permanent, stay in the United States, preserving *cubanidad* became important to establish the cultural boundaries that would allow Cubans to survive as a distinct community. Women reinforced *cubanidad* at both the family and community levels. As parents, they were traditionally responsible for instilling cultural values in their children and grandchildren and making sure that they learned to speak Spanish, as well as appreciate their cultural heritage. With this goal in mind, they established afterschool programs in churches, schools, and community centers that taught children the basics of Cuban history, geography, and culture for a few hours each day. On the community level, women created cultural organizations that sponsored various activities for the general public: lectures and seminars, literary contests, scholarship programs, variety shows, and festivals and parades. Through these activities they encouraged study and pride in *la tradición nacional.*

In their mission to preserve *cubanidad,* women also published newspapers and magazines and wrote essays, articles, and editorials for the Cuban exile press. A small few even had their own radio and television shows. Through these media they educated the public on a variety of cultural and historical topics. They entertained the public with stories and interviews and offered practical advice about life in exile. Initially, women did not hold as visible a representation in journalism, radio, and television as they did in cultural organizations, since men dominated the communications media. Of a sample of 665 periodicals at the Cuban Exile Archives of the University of Miami, published by Cuban exiles during the period 1959–1988, roughly 10 percent were published, edited, or directed by women. The percentage of female contributors varied, however, depending on the type of publication. Political newspapers employed few or no women, while the so-called women's magazines usually had a predominantly female staff. During the 1990s, however, the number of women in journalism and the communications media increased. At the *Miami Herald* and other city newspapers in the southeastern United States, Cuban women and other Latinas served as writers and editors. One Cuban woman, Liz Balmaseda, won a Pulitzer Prize for her work at the *Miami Herald*. Women served as reporters and anchors at local television stations, as well as national networks such as the Spanish-language Univisión and Telemundo. Among the women who have distinguished themselves in this medium are Cristina Saralegui, María Elvira Salazar, and Teresa Rodríguez. Cuban women from Miami also made names for themselves in the English-language mainstream and cable networks, for example, Daisy Fuentes and Maty Montfort.

As their spheres of influence expanded, women also demanded more of their organizations. The Cuban Women's Club (CWC), for example, founded in 1969 as a social club for middle-class women, diversified its activities to retain the participation of its wage-earning members. Modeled after the elite Liceo Cubano in Havana, the Cuban Women's Club sponsored luncheons, conferences, art exhibitions, and literary contests. Members were also involved in local charities and fund-raising activities, just as women of their social class were expected to be back in Cuba. By the mid-1970s, however, members demanded that the club do more than just organize social and charitable events. They wanted their club to address issues pertinent to their careers and their new roles in U.S. society. By the late 1970s, conferences addressed such issues as bilingual education, voting and political representation, salaries, and the workplace. The CWC ceased to be an exclusively Cuban social club and counted more than 300 members of various nationalities and professional and educational backgrounds by 1980.

Several business and professional organizations also emerged in southern Florida during the 1970s and 1980s, reflecting women's permanent shift into the workplace. Groups such as the Comité de Mujeres Latinas, the Latin Business and Professional Women's Club (LBPWC), and the Coalition of Hispanic American Women (CHAW) were created by younger women, graduates of U.S. colleges and universities, who regarded themselves as Cuban Americans. Whether at the local or national level, CHAW and the LBPWC addressed the problems all women in the U.S. workforce faced: unequal pay, inadequate child care, discrimination, and sexual harassment. Their workshops taught women strategies to achieve equal access to education, social services, and the judicial system. However, they also discussed issues relevant to the larger Latino community such as bilingual education, immigration reform, affirmative action, and domestic violence. Both organizations sponsored a scholarship program to help needy students attend college.

The exile experience, thus forced women to expand their participation in labor, the economy, politics, and the overall life of the community. To deal with the problems and challenges of life in a new country, they created social, familial, and professional networks. Women reconciled the past with the present and promoted an appreciation of the Cuban cultural heritage while contributing to their families' adaptation into the mainstream. They helped create a strong and stable ethnic community with ties to two countries and two cultures.

The Cuban population of southern Florida is the best known of the Latino/a populations of the southeastern United States, but it is not the only group to have settled in this state and region. Even in Miami and Dade County, long considered a Cuban stronghold, that group no longer constitutes the numerical majority. A recent influx from Central and South America, particularly from Nicaragua and Colombia, means that Cuban-accented Spanish is not the only form of the language heard on the streets of southern Florida. Puerto Ricans, Salvadorans, Dominicans, Mexicans, and others have also migrated to southern Florida and have established transnational economic and political connections that contribute to the city's reputation as the "gateway to the Americas." While Miami/Dade County was the most popular destination of Latinos, migration to other parts of the state also increased. By 1999 the Latino population in Florida stood at 2,334,403.

Elsewhere around the southeastern United States, Latinos have settled in towns and cities not traditionally associated with their populations. Some of them are recent immigrants, legal or illegal; others are contracted laborers who arrive with temporary visas; and still others are internal migrants who migrate from other areas of the country in search of better economic opportunities. The Latino/a population of Georgia is one of the fastest growing in the nation, doubling in size in just one decade. According to estimates from the U.S. Census Bureau, in 1999 there were 239,566 Latinos in Georgia, compared with 108,933 in 1990. Statistics for the Latino populations in 1999 in other southeastern states and their percentage increase since 1990 include the following: Alabama, 45,349 (84.1 percent); Louisiana, 119,496 (28.4 percent); Mississippi, 23,975 (49.9 percent); North Carolina, 175,707 (128.9 percent); and South Carolina, 54,299 (78 percent). Apart from a few studies of agricultural and oil workers in the region, non-Cuban Latinos of the Southeast remain one of the most understudied populations.

SOURCES: Estrade, Paul. 1987. "Los clubes femeninos en el Partido Revolucionario Cubano (1892–1898)." *Anuario del Centro de Estudios Martianos* 10:175–201; García, María Cristina. 1994. "Cuban Women in the United States." In *Handbook of Hispanic Cultures in the United States: Sociology*, ed. Felix Padilla, 203–217. Houston: Arte Público Press; Pérez, Lisandro. 1986. "Immigrant Economic Adjustment and Family Organization: The Cuban Success Story." *International Migration Review* 20 (Spring): 4–21; Pérez, Louis A. 1978. "Cubans in Tampa: From Exiles to Immigrants, 1892–1901." *Florida Historical Quarterly* 57 (October): 129–140; Prieto, Yolanda. 1984. "Reinterpreting an Immigration Success Story: Cuban Women, Work, and Change in a New Jersey Community." Ph.D. diss., Rutgers University.

María Cristina García

LATINAS IN THE PACIFIC NORTHWEST

A historical overview of Latinas in the Pacific northwestern states of Washington, Oregon, and Idaho reveals that according to the 2000 census, the Latino population of this region constituted about 7.8 percent of the total population. More than 75 percent of the Latino population in these states is of Mexican origin. The historiography of Latinas in this area remains almost nonexistent. Scholarly writing about Latinas appears here and there in brief mentions by scholars focusing on twentieth-century farmworkers, immigration, labor, and the family. Themes of importance for Latinas include the immigrant experience, farmworker women's issues, education, cultural preservation, political involvement, and the isolation of living in the Pacific Northwest.

Spanish exploration of the Pacific coast regions of Washington and Oregon began in the 1790s with the appearance of sailing ships and a few settlements. Latinas came into the Pacific Northwest as members of families and groups such as the wives and daughters of miners, vaqueros, mule packers, soldiers, and settlers. The most striking aspect of the Latina experience from the 1790s until the beginning of the twentieth century was the fact that women, along with their families, did not tend to become permanent residents in the Pacific Northwest. Most returned to the U.S. Southwest or headed into Canada and Alaska.

When the Spanish sent out forty-three ships of exploration in the late 1700s, indigenous women were often among the first to make contact with them. The rosters of the Spanish expeditions are scarce, but it seems that the crews were all men, with no women family members aboard. According to several scholars, the relationship between the Spanish sailors/settlers and indigenous women was not respectful or cordial. Native women faced abuse, rape, and enslavement by the Spaniards. In 1792 the Spanish established a two-year garrison of soldiers on Vancouver Island and another outpost at Neah Bay on Washington's Olympic Peninsula. The Spanish settlements consisted of about eighty mixed-race Spanish colonials, Peruvian Indians, and no female inhabitants. Some Spanish soldiers deserted and took up residence with local peoples such as the Mowachaht, one of the Nuu-chah-nulth (formerly Nootka) tribes of the area. Children born to these unions were reared in the mother's indigenous culture. By 1795 the last garrison contingent of twenty soldiers left Nootka.

The turmoil of the Mexican-American War (1846–1848) and its aftermath drew Mexican families to the Pacific Northwest from their homes in California or New Mexico. The most famous woman visitor to Oregon was María Josefa Tafoya, the wife of pioneer Oregonian Ewing Young. Young died in Oregon in 1843, far from his home in Taos, New Mexico. Tafoya and her son traveled to Oregon in 1855 to successfully claim Young's estate of $4,994.64. In her petition Tafoya detailed her dire poverty and her dependence upon the day labor of her son, as well as charity and assistance from her relatives.

Rosario Romero from Sonora, Mexico, settled in Yakima, Washington, during the 1860s. Although she is credited with starting the region's sheep-herding industry, she, like many others, did not remain in Washington as a permanent resident. Laurita Galina was another settler from Sonora. Born in 1830, she married and migrated with her husband to Oregon in 1862. By the 1870s Laurita had three children and lived in Josephine County, Oregon. Carmelita Colón, also born in Mexico, settled in Walla Walla, Washington, with her husband in the 1860s. Together they ran a mule-pack train from Walla Walla to Idaho. When their business failed, they stayed in the area to run a Mexican restaurant. Their descendants lived in Walla Walla until the 1950s.

The twentieth century witnessed a significant increase in the number of Latina migrants and immigrants to the Pacific Northwest, people who stayed on as permanent residents. Since the 1920s Yakima County, Washington, has ranked among the ten most productive agricultural counties in the United States and thus has required large numbers of workers (predominantly Mexican) from the April asparagus harvest to apple picking in October. The level of hardship and segregation earned Yakima County the unflattering nickname "Little Mississippi of the Northwest." Mexican American migrants came from New Mexico, Texas, and Wyoming, while immigrants arrived from Mexico. In recent times they have been joined by immigrants from Central and South America.

Juanita Ramírez migrated to Pocatello, Idaho, in 1916, and by the 1920s immigrant families lived in Nyssa, Oregon. Between 1915 and 1917 some of the early Latino migrants to Portland, Oregon, hailed from New Mexico. Born in Texas, Francisca García became part of the migrant labor stream that traveled from Texas to Ohio to pick sugar beets and tomatoes, then on to Wyoming for sugar beets, then on to Washington for asparagus, before moving further south to Oregon for hops and berries and then a final stop to pick cotton in California. Finally García and her family settled in Woodburn in Oregon's Willamette Valley. Catalina Trujillo remembered her family's journey from Mexico to Oregon via the railroads. Her father worked for the railroad, and the family's home was a railroad car, part of a boxcar barrio that had been set aside as housing for the workers.

Migration from the United States and immigration from Mexico and South America to the Pacific Northwest began to increase dramatically during the 1940s. Families that moved during this period represent the nucleus of the Latino communities that currently thrive in the Northwest. Born in La Junta, Colorado, in 1924,

Victoria Archuleta Sierra moved permanently to Pocatello, Idaho, in 1942. Sierra attended Idaho State University, became an electrician's helper and a railroad worker, and in 1945 joined the Women's Air Corps (WAC). She trained as a hospital aide and a medic in her eighteen months of military service. In a letter to her daughter, Antonia, Irene Castañeda detailed the family's move to Washington from Texas during the 1940s. Castañeda criticized the labor contractor for lying to the family that conditions in Toppenish were good and fair. The family experienced horrendous hardship, arriving in "bitterly cold weather" after traveling on a flatbed truck. The Castañedas discovered that their housing was "some old shacks, all full of knotholes in Brownstown—about twenty miles outside of Toppenish." Irene Castañeda recalled working in the hops fields in which women were paid 75 cents per hour while men received 85 cents per hour. Braceros (Mexican guest workers from 1942 to 1964) were also recruited to work in the Pacific Northwest. While the braceros in the Pacific Northwest were all men, women nonetheless wrote letters, trying to remain in contact with their departed husbands and sons.

By the 1950s the character of the settled Latino communities became evident in the celebration of cultural and religious events. *El Día de las madres* became an important annual event in Mexican communities. In Toppenish, Washington, on September 15–16, 1952, Margarita Rodríguez was crowned "Queen Liberty" in celebration of Mexican Independence Day. In summer migrant worker families abounded and at times held *tardeadas* (afternoon) and evening dances. Women such as Beatriz Escalante, the daughter of a migrant worker family in Sunnyside, Elaine Romero, the daughter of a family that operated a tiny Mexican restaurant in West Seattle, and María Dena, whose family had left field labor behind for other jobs, retained selected elements of Mexican border culture that fused the values of family, community, and small-town traditions with hard work. As part of this cultural preservation, Herminia Méndez began Spanish radio programming in the Yakima Valley in 1951. According to historian Erasmo Gamboa, in the hop fields when mechanization took place, "a division of labor by gender occurred with women and sometimes children going on the belt lines removing leaves and doing other 'light jobs' that required more dexterity, while males specialized in areas of the kiln where the hops were 'cooked' or dried. Naturally, a differentiated wage system for women and men also developed."

Eva Castellañoz, a *curandera* (healer) in Guanajuato, Mexico, in 1938 migrated with her husband Teodoro to the Snake River Valley in eastern Oregon. In addition to rearing nine children, she has worked as a migrant laborer, teacher, county activist, and traditionalist artist. For her creation of *coronas* (traditional wax and paper crowns used for weddings and quinceañeras), she received a National Heritage Award in 1988.

The arrival of Latinas from many different countries in South America occurred during the 1960s. The first groups that came from South America were called "the new Hispanics" and migrated to the Northwest for better jobs or a peaceful sociopolitical climate. Aida Pelaez Edenholm arrived in Washington during the 1960s, joining about a dozen Bolivian-born immigrants. She worked as a Pan American Airlines hostess and married a Seattle resident. Later during the 1960s a trickle of refugees from repressive regimes made their way into the Pacific Northwest. They remain most concentrated in the state of Washington. These "new Hispanic" Latinos in Washington grew from 1,371 in 1960 to 6,073 by 1980. Berta González fled Chile with her husband and two daughters during the Chilean military coup that ousted the popularly elected president Salvador Allende. The family settled in Seattle in 1977.

With the number of farm labor jobs decreasing year by year because of the decline in prices for the crops, unreliable water supplies, and farm land prices, increasing numbers of Latinos are migrating from small towns of the Pacific Northwest to urban areas. Most have not settled in defined barrios but remain scattered throughout city neighborhoods. One remedy for this scattered population has involved establishing settlement houses or community centers. In Seattle el Centro de la Raza established the Frances Martínez Community Service Center in 1983 as a tribute to the tireless activism of Martínez and her valiant struggle against leukemia. A former farmworker, she worked until the end of her life helping Latinos find jobs, housing, and counseling. Through el Centro de la Raza she organized emergency food programs and classes and secured legal advice for recent arrivals in Seattle.

Activism often became a family affair. Two women, Ninfa Tanguma and her daughter Yolanda Alaníz, provided leadership for Latinas in their transition from rural to urban areas. In 1970 Tanguma took her turn at picket duty in a hop-ranch strike in Yakima. Latinas were at the forefront of the strike and seemed "more willing to sacrifice than many men when it comes to supporting the union." Her daughter Yolanda joined the picket line at the age of six. Her sister recalled that Yolanda would study after working in the fields in order to educate herself out of farm labor. She attended the University of Washington in the early 1970s and recalled having to fight the "machismo" of El

Movimiento Estudiantil Chicano de Aztlán (MEChA). She wrote a pamphlet titled "In Defense of Adultery" because the male leaders of MEChA slanderously accused their Chicana comrades of being sexually promiscuous. Her struggles with sexist and nationalist men and her experience helping organize a campus union of low paid service workers led her to become a socialist feminist. In 1993 she ran unsuccessfully for the Seattle City Council as a socialist. She was by far the most important leader for the group Radical Women until the late 1990s, when she left the Pacific Northwest to become an activist in California.

The 1980s witnessed the first Latinas to win public office. Two Latinas currently serve in the Washington state legislature. In 1988 State Senator Margarita López Prentice, a Democrat representing the Eleventh District, was the first Latina elected to public office. Before going into politics, she worked as a registered nurse for thirty years. Health care and worker protection have long been of major concern for López Prentice. In 1989 she sponsored a bill that would require doctors to report pesticide poisoning cases to the state Department of Social and Health Services. Phyllis Gutiérrez-Kenney represents the Forty-sixth Legislative District in Seattle. Born into a farmworker family, she was one of eight children. Her father organized the first beet workers' union in the state of Montana. In Washington the family picked potatoes by hand. At the age of five, her job was to shake the vines free of potatoes so the older children could pick them up and put them in heavy sacks that they dragged behind them. Allergic to pesticides, she could not work in the hop fields. Gutiérrez-Kenny remembered picking asparagus for "seventy-five cents an hour and no bathrooms in the field." A mother of ten children, she stayed in the fields until the ninth month of her first pregnancy. Her own family would "pick grapes, prunes and other fruit in the Tri-Cities on weekends for extra money."

Her first stint at organizing began when she cofounded the Migrant Daycare Centers of Washington. She also cofounded the Educational Institute for Rural Families in Pasco. Two tragedies motivated her to focus on farmworker issues, one involving the death of a friend when she fell off a plank and into an irrigation ditch, the other death of a brother who died of pneumonia caused by the poor housing. Gutiérrez-Kenney recalled that "the snow would come in through the cracks and the windows would break and we'd have to cover them with blankets." Today she is the owner of her own retail business (Felipa's) and devotes much of her time to working for many professional and volunteer efforts toward quality education and social and economic equity for women and people of color. She has been a consistent spokesperson for the rights of farmworkers, especially in relation to education and housing. In 1998 she ran unsuccessfully for the position of secretary of state in Washington.

Latinas who have served as commissioners in Oregon's Hispanic Commission include María de Jesús García, Consuelo Lightner, Liliana Olverding, Nancy Padilla, Wendy Veliz, and Annabelle Jaramillo. The first Latina to be appointed to King County Superior Court in Seattle was Carmen Otero, and the second Latina appointed to the bench was Judge Debora Juárez.

Although some professional and entrepreneurial gains are evident, women in the Pacific Northwest share many of the same concerns that Latinas face in other parts of the United States. Education statistics in 2000 indicate about 51 percent of Latinos had completed at least a high-school diploma, compared with 83 percent of European Americans in the Pacific Northwest. In employment, about 36 percent of Latinas in Washington and Oregon were employed in the white-collar occupations of service and administrative support, while less than 8 percent of Latinas labored as farmworkers.

Latinas continue to form groups that seek to better their situation in the Pacific Northwest. Hortensia Villanueva formed a mothers' club in December of 1994. The wife of a union leader in eastern Washington, Villanueva used space at the Farm Workers' Clinic to organize the mothers of children who came down with contagious viral infections. Other groups include the long-standing Mujeres Unidas de Idaho in Boise, formed in 1989 to sponsor an annual conference and work as a network support system for Idaho's Latinas. Latinas have been leaders in groups such as the United Farm Workers of America, the Mexican American Women's National Association (MANA), Mujeres de Oregon, and the Oregon, Washington, and Idaho Commissions on Hispanic Affairs. Currently Rosalinda Guillen serves as Washington's regional director of the United Farm Workers, and Mona Mendoza is the cofounder of Hands off Washington, a gay/lesbian rights organization.

Entrepreneur Celia D. Mariscal and her family group own Juanita's Fine Foods in Hood River, Oregon, which grosses about $4 million per year. Her mother had wanted to own her own business and passed on this desire to her thirteen children, who decided to start a business when they were adults. In starting their tortilla factory in 1969, Mariscal recalled, "At night we made our tortillas—about 30 boxes. Since I was the only one who didn't work during the day I would take the tortillas out to the stores to try and sell them." She further emphasized that Mexican women can be successful and reflected that "in our company my brothers

Las Cuatas Diego, 1980. Painting in oil on canvas by and courtesy of Cecilia Concepción Alvarez.

respect my decisions because I am the oldest. They don't treat me with any less value because I'm a woman."

Latinas in the Pacific Northwest continue to be divided by cultural group, although the majority are of Mexican birth or heritage and have some connection to the rural areas and farm labor. Young rural Latinas, often reared in modest circumstances, feel torn between embracing traditional cultural values and wanting to further their education. In urban areas campus women's organizations, including Latina sororities, seek to address the lack of substantial women's networks and role models. Insitutions like Centro de la Raza also promote a sense of community. In 1989 a group of Latinas in Seattle formed the Hispanic Women's Network (HWN) to promote the personal, professional, and educational growth of its members.

Artist Cecilia Concepción Alvarez arrived in Washington State in 1975 and has developed a national reputation for her paintings. Her art reflects her experiences as a Chicana/Cubana, and through it she expresses her own vision of beauty and strength. In her opinion, people, art, and society have an obligation to advance humanity and find solutions to problems that threaten human coexistence and survival. Latinas living in the Pacific Northwest reflect in a variety of ways Alvarez's thoughts about combining selected cultural traditions with environmental concerns for today and the future.

SOURCES: Gamboa, Erasmo, ed. 1992. *Voces hispanas: Hispanic Voices of Idaho*. Boise: Idaho Commission on Hispanic Affairs; Gamboa, Erasmo, and Carolyn M. Buan. 1995. *Nostros: The Hispanic People of Oregon: Essays and Recollections*. Portland: Oregon Council for the Humanities; Valle, Isabel. 1994. *Fields of Toil: A Migrant Family's Journey*. Pullman: Washington State University Press; Villarreal, Luz E., and Sandra B. Fancher García. 1995. "A Cultural Profile and Status of Chicanas in the Northwest." In *The Chicano Experience in the Northwest,* ed. Carlos S. Maldonado and Gilberto García. Dubuque, IA: Kendall/Hunt Publishing Company.

Elizabeth Salas

A

ABARCA, APOLONIA "POLLY" MUÑOZ (1920–)

In June 1941 twenty-year-old Apolonia "Polly" Muñoz left her home in Mission, Texas, for Corpus Christi to pursue an education in nursing. Since the age of fifteen she had known that she wanted a career as a public servant. Abarca found her calling when she helped a nurse take handicapped children to a hospital in Galveston for treatment. Volunteering her time to help those in need became a way of life for her. While she was still a student, Abarca spent time volunteering at the Department of Immigration and working at the local dry-goods store on Saturdays—a task her father disapproved of. To Antonio Muñoz, the father of ten children, education was the primary goal.

When Apolonia Muñoz Abarca arrived at Fred Roberts Nursing School in Corpus Christi, she realized that she was the only Hispanic in the class. Although she had grown up in segregated schools in Mission, now she faced a whole new dilemma. Her roommate was frightened of her. In her hometown in Virginia, the young lady had been told that "Mexicans would kill you," Abarca recalled. Fortunately the fear was quickly dispersed, and the two became close friends. "We [Hispanics] always had to work a little bit harder to prove ourselves," she said.

During her first year at nursing school Abarca's older brother Antonio Muñoz was sent to Europe as a gunner in the air force. The next year her fiancé joined the army and was sent to Germany. Money was becoming scarce in the Muñoz family, and Abarca began to think that joining the Cadet Corps as a nurse was her only option. She wrote to her brother and her fiancé, whom she later married after the war, telling them of her plans, but both of them begged her to stay at home. Her brother sent money to pay for the remainder of nursing school, and she graduated in 1944 as a registered nurse. Abarca worked at Memorial Hospital in Corpus Christi, where she set up new operating and emergency rooms and soon became the supervisor of the outpatient clinic. In 1946 she joined the U.S. Public Health Service hospital in Corpus Christi and also began volunteering as a Red Cross nurse in the settlement house. There she taught home nursing in Spanish and English, again as a volunteer. For fifteen years she worked as a nurse at the City-County Health Department.

Apolonia Abarca (back, second from left) was a member of the 1944 nursing class at Fred Roberts Hospital, Corpus Christi, Texas. Courtesy of the U.S. Latino and Latina World War II Oral History Project, University of Texas, Austin.

In 1964 Abarca helped win the first federal grant in the United States for family planning—a milestone for health care. She said that she supported providing birth control after working as a public health nurse for so many years. Poor young women were constantly asking her how not to get pregnant too soon. Families lived in poverty. Children were neglected and undernourished. "At that time the word birth control was a no-no," commented Abarca. "I was daring, I guess." In 1965 Abarca was hired as the executive director of the area Planned Parenthood center and remained there until the services were turned over to the local health department. Abarca later worked as the director of nursing at the state-operated Corpus Christi school for mentally retarded children. She retired in 1974. Her husband, Antonio Abarca, died in 1984. Now in her eighties, Abarca still lives in Corpus Christi.

See also World War II

SOURCE: Stevens, Darcie. 2001. "War Granted Nurse Opportunity of Her Dreams." *Narratives: Stories of U.S. Latinos and Latinas and World War II* (U.S. Latino and Latina WWII Oral History Project, University of Texas at Austin) 3, no. 1 (Fall).

Darcie Stevens

ACOSTA, LUCY (1926–)

Born in 1926 in Miami, Arizona, Lucy Acosta was six years old when her family moved to El Paso, Texas. In the midst of the Great Depression Miami's copper mines, which had employed many of her family members, shut down, and many families, including Acosta's, were forced to seek employment elsewhere. Acosta's father was killed in one of these old copper mines when she was only three years old. Although her mother remarried a few years after they arrived in El Paso, Acosta remembers that it was pension payments her family received following her father's death that enabled them to survive the depression years. These payments meant that she could attend school full-time, unlike many of her friends and neighbors who had to work instead. Also, unlike many of her male peers, Acosta was free of the requirements of military service that withdrew most Mexican American boys in her high school. With a great love for her studies, Acosta excelled in school, graduating from Bowie High School in the top ten of her class. After high school she attended International Business College in El Paso, from which she graduated in 1945, and went on to hold several clerical and accounting jobs into the 1970s. Acosta married Alejandro Acosta in 1948 and gave birth to two children, Alex and Danny.

Acosta joined the League of United Latin American Citizens (LULAC) in 1957 and helped organize LULAC's Ladies Council No. 335, which was officially chartered in 1958. Although a Ladies Council in El Paso already existed (formed in 1934), Acosta and a few others felt that its dwindling membership signaled the need for a new council that might better represent the interests of a younger Mexican American generation. Beginning with "thirty some-odd" women, Ladies Council No. 335 grew to average between 50 and 100 members. Coinciding with the council's birth was the campaign of El Paso's first Mexican American mayor, Raymond Telles. Thus one of the council's first political actions involved raising funds to pay the poll taxes of Mexican Americans to ensure their right to vote in the mayoral election. Although LULAC's official policy prohibited the organization from endorsing specific candidates, it nonetheless offered essential support to the Telles campaign through its registration drives. Acosta recalls spending Saturdays fundraising in front of the local Sears, J. C. Penney's, numerous other stores, local churches, and the county courthouse. She remembers that a large part of their work required going door-to-door to register voters from south El Paso. Speaking of her involvement in LULAC's 1957 registration drive, Acosta recalls:

> I was still not very much in the political scene. I was there because Raymond Telles inspired all these people. . . . Let me tell you that people that had never, ever, ever voted—Mexican people I'm talking about—or ever, ever, taken . . . well, they couldn't vote because they never had a poll tax, would go out and buy a poll tax. Raymond Telles was a *mexicano,* and wouldn't it be wonderful if we would have the first Mexican-American mayor, the city of El Paso.

The registration drives were an enormous success. LULAC's efforts and Telles's election drew on the growing resolve of Mexican Americans across the nation. In particular, veterans returning home from World War II sought to challenge the discrimination they faced in the draft and the continuing discrimination they faced when they applied for jobs upon their return home.

Raymond Telles's election was a turning point for Acosta as well. Involvement in the campaign marked her entry into political activism and touched off what was to become a long and illustrious career with LULAC. She held numerous positions with her local chapter, as well as in the national administration of LULAC. In addition, she was appointed to various committees in Telles's administration. After his term she continued to hold appointments under Mayor Judson Williams and subsequent mayors. In 1972 she became the first woman in the history of El Paso to be appointed civil service commissioner.

The LULAC Ladies Council No. 335 continued to play an important role in registration drives. In 1960 it worked to organize Mexican American voters who backed John F. Kennedy for president. Raymond Telles left El Paso during his second term as mayor to work in the Kennedy administration. In 1970 he launched an unsuccessful bid for Congress. Acosta remained a close friend and supporter of Telles during the election in which Mexican Americans and Democrats were deeply divided. Of the election, she remembers that "a lot of people were just very hurt that he left, he took off and left us, you know. Like if we were his little chickens and he took off and he left us."

In addition to her continued involvement with LULAC, Acosta's public service included membership in the PTA, St. Joseph's Catholic Parish, and United Way and seats on the board of directors for multiple city and county agencies. Throughout her career she received numerous honors for her commitment to political activism and to the city of El Paso in particular. In 1963 and again in 1973 she was selected Outstanding LULAC National Woman of the Year and Outstanding LULAC Woman for the State of Texas and for the City of El Paso District No. 4.

See also League of United Latin American Citizens (LULAC)

SOURCES: Acosta, Lucy. 1957–1979. Collection. LULAC Archives, Nettie Lee Benson Latin American Collection, Rare Books and Manuscripts, University of Texas at Austin; ———. 1982. Interview by Mario T. García, October 28; García, Mario T. 1989. *Mexican Americans*. New Haven, CT: Yale University Press.

Julie Cohen

ACOSTA VICE, CELIA M. (1919–1993)

Hailed as a mixture of Mother Teresa, Felisa Rincón de Gautier (the first female mayor of San Juan), and Eleanor Roosevelt, Celia Acosta was a pioneer of the Puerto Rican community in New York City. She was born on June 20, 1919, in Guayanilla, a small municipality on Puerto Rico's southern coast. A committed public servant, Acosta founded the fifty-member Council of Brooklyn Organizations and was a member of the New York City School Decentralization Committee and of the advisory board of the Brooklyn branch of the Urban League. She became the first Puerto Rican female real-estate broker in Brooklyn and the first female grand marshal of the now National Puerto Rican Day Parade. Acosta was an established businesswoman who used her contacts and influences to advance the cause of social and economic equality, as well as the artistic heritage of the Puerto Rican people, both in New York City and on the island.

Her earliest years were spent in Puerto Rico. Acosta's father, Ramón, was a man of varied talents, having mastered the shoemakers' art while tending to a number of real-estate holdings and selling hardware and trinkets. Her mother, Flora, and her father decided to migrate to New York City in 1926, following the patterns of other migrants who came to U.S. shores not solely for economic reasons, but to seek educational advancement and to reunite with family members who had preceded them. The family settled in the Navy Yard area of Brooklyn among many Italian immigrants who themselves were recent arrivals and struggling to learn the English language. A precocious, slightly built, thin child, Acosta excelled in her acquisition of English and often served as a tutor to new arrivals from Puerto Rico. She has recounted how, given her appearance and the widespread fear of tuberculosis, school authorities would place her in special classes for children thought to be carrying this disease. When she was twelve, Acosta's family returned to Puerto Rico, nostalgic for the warmth and energizing climate of the island. During that one year Acosta found herself struggling to catch up in Spanish with island-raised classmates. This factor, coupled with her mother's desire to once more reunite the family, motivated their return to New York.

As a young Puerto Rican teenager, Acosta confronted many prejudices. However, she also met individuals who influenced the course her life would take. At thirteen she was encouraged by her mother's employer, a Mr. Kaufman, not to leave school for factory work. Although she did not accept this form of employment initially, Acosta's desire to provide for herself and her household led her to work in factories and offices throughout her young adult life. Acosta had wanted to graduate from Girls' Commercial High School but was discouraged by a school administrator who suggested that a girl reared near the dockyards came from the "other side of the tracks." Acosta persisted and eventually was enrolled.

This type of searing experience motivated her to ensure that others would not have to face the same discrimination. After completing her secondary education in night school, she set out to acquire the many skills she would need to advance her community. In the late 1930s she worked in a variety of jobs, including import-export, making artificial flowers, and the graveyard shift in a defense plant. A loan from her uncle allowed her to buy into a neighborhood business in Williamsburg, Brooklyn, that soon became an information and resource network for those most in need of social services.

Acosta's many interests led her to study literature, sociology, and business at Brooklyn College and Pace University on a non-credit basis. From 1942 to 1948 she developed additional skills as an accountant and translator while also serving the community as an interpreter and an informal curator of Puerto Rican artistic and cultural history. Her civic involvement covered many fronts, including active leadership in the local Democratic regular and independent political clubs. In 1954 she helped found the Fernando Sierra Vardeci Independent Democratic Club in Brooklyn. She successfully set out to unite the many disparate Puerto Rican/Hispanic organizations in Brooklyn by forming a powerful federation known as the Council of Brooklyn Organizations that was able to influence New York City's political hierarchy. In the absence of any government funding, Acosta asserted that she was obliged to pay "la renta y la luz del Concilio" (the rent and light bills of the council). She also stated that from these offices in Williamsburg, Boricua College, the first Puerto Rican institution of higher education in the United States, emerged. While she was immersed in the issues and problems affecting the Puerto Rican community, including voting rights and the struggle for bilingual services for a predominantly Spanish-speaking migrant community, she allied herself with the African American struggle for civil rights and made it her own. This commitment was realized through her work with the Urban League, the National Association for the Advancement of Colored People (NAACP), and the Lafayette Boys' Club.

Her leadership in the community was recognized in 1960 when she was named the first female grand marshal of New York City's Puerto Rican Day Parade. She described this position as significant because, in her own words, "el desfile no era solamente para fiestar, era ademas una fuerza política" (the parade was not just festive but a political force as well). Subsequently she was named to the Commission on Human Rights and served actively on the Williamsburg-Greenpoint local school board. In this capacity she was able to utilize her mediation and conflict-resolution skills to bring together white ethnics and communities of color. Amid all the political involvement Acosta Vice found time, in 1961 to organize the first Three Kings Day Parade in Brooklyn, distributing free toys during the Christmas season to families who could not afford them. She was approached to run as coleader of the Brooklyn Democratic Party representing the Puerto Rican community, a position she did not relish, given its largely ceremonial status. In addition, in 1964 Acosta Vice was asked to head a major government-sponsored social service agency, the Eleanor Roosevelt Job Orientation in Neighborhoods Center (JOIN), to help troubled youth. Her proven leadership and ability to mobilize the community led her to become the director of information and community relations for the Community Corporation of Williamsburg in 1968.

Celia M. Acosta Vice, Democratic candidate for the New York State Assembly. Courtesy of the Justo A. Martí Photograph Collection. Centro Archives, Centro de Estudios Puertorriqueños, Hunter College, CUNY.

A lifelong supporter of the Puerto Rican arts, she maintained an extensive book collection, considered the foundation for New York's Museo del Barrio. In the 1970s she founded the first library and bookstore on Puerto Rico in New York City, the Puerto Rican Heritage Bookstore, and made frequent trips to the island to purchase art and handicrafts. By 1979 Acosta returned to her homeland. Continuing her unstinting support of Puerto Rican arts and culture, she established the Kiosko Cultural in Plaza de las Americas, Puerto Rico's most prominent commercial center.

Celia Acosta Vice died following a bout with cancer on January 30, 1993. Her service was attended not only by her three daughters, but also by the former director of the renowned Institute of Puerto Rican Culture, Dr. Ricardo Alegria. She leaves a long legacy of unflinching engagement as a female pioneer in the economic, political, social, and cultural affairs of the Puerto Rican community in New York City and in Puerto Rico. In the tradition of the "servant leader," Acosta Vice selflessly sought to empower disenfranchised constituencies and provided a vision for the pursuit of social equity and justice.

SOURCES: Acosta Vice, Celia. 1973. Interview, Long Island Historical Society Oral History Project (PROH #002), Centro de Estudios Puertorriqueños, Hunter College, CUNY, August 7; Board of Education of the City of New York. 1965. *Call Them Heroes.* Morristown, NY: Silver Burdett Co.; Ferrer, Mila. 1993. "P.R. Cultural Leader in NY Interred in Old San Juan." *San Juan Star,* February 2; *Puerto Ricans in NY: Voice of the Migration.* New York, NY: Centro de Estudios Puertorriqueños; 1988. Celia Acosta Vice Interview, June 6; *San Juan Star.* 1993. "Celia Acosta Rodriquez," February 2. Centro Archives, Centro de Estudíos Puertorriqueños, Hunter College, CUNY.

Milga Morales

AGING

The research on aging gives limited attention to racial/ethnic groups. It was not until the 1960s that studies of older African Americans emerged, and attention to Latinas/Latinos in general began to appear during the 1970s. Most of the literature focused on Chicanas/Chicanos, the largest proportion of Latinas/Latinos in the United States. Nevertheless, within this population social scientists paid little attention to the elderly, partly because of misconceptions and stereotypes about their place within the family and the broader society. Social science literature tended to paint a rather romanticized picture of the extended Latino or Hispanic family, which was believed to support the aged and protect them from a "hostile" world. As a result, the problems of older individuals, unlike their counterparts in other racial/ethnic groups, were minimized by the "supportive qualities" of the Latino family. While such ideas continue to the present, this position has attracted critical attention in recent years.

Until the 1980s the available research on Latinos generally ignored critical gender analyses or differences. With respect to gender, differences among Latinos are similar to those of other elderly groups. For example, women generally live longer and outnumber men. Older Latino men marry or remarry more often than men in other racial/ethnic minority groups. Sanchez-Ayendez (1986), who studied "the interplay between values and behavior in family and community of a group of older, low income Puerto Rican women in Boston," describes how women create and utilize familial and community networks in a supportive, productive nature. Bastida (1984) explored age- and gender-linked norms among Mexican, Puerto Rican, and Cuban women and found that core cultural elements of the collective identity system exist among all three populations. In other words, women's lives are shaped by sex-appropriate behavior and the pursuit of realism regarding age and aging. A comprehensive work on older Latinas, edited by Marta Sotomayor (1995), helps understand current research and its implications for policy development. Particular attention and advice are available for program administrators, psychologists and counselors, doctors, nurses, and service providers.

Espin's (1992) work on contemporary sexuality and the Hispanic woman suggests that "the honor of Latin families is strongly tied to the sexual purity of women. And the concept of honor and dignity is one of the essential distinctive marks of Hispanic culture." Hispanic or Latina sexuality, as culturally defined, is linked to assumed lifelong roles in both the family and community. In many instances women's roles may render them both powerful and powerless. For example, middle-aged and elderly Hispanic women retain important roles in their families, even after their sons and daughters are married. Grandmothers remain present and highly vocal in family affairs and have more status and power than their white American counterparts, who may suffer depression due to "empty-nest syndrome." Espin is one of the few writers who critically examine the relationship between sexuality, gender, and woman's roles in old age.

In general, research and writings on older Mexican women remain scarce. Aging among Mexican women appears as a uniform process because research has failed to address the lives of older Chicanas in a critical manner. In studies on aged Chicanas the plight of older women is masked by notions of familism. As defined in the literature, that concept embraces familial cultural values of unity and expected mutual aid, respect for the aged, and a positive gender hierarchy considered specific to Chicano families but found among other Latinos as well.

Studies guided by the concept of familism describe characteristics of strength and vitality among older Chicanas, who nonetheless defer to their husbands and male relatives. Generally, older women are viewed from a traditional perspective in which gender differences are neither challenged nor questioned. More specifically, the role of the Chicana grandmother is portrayed as that of the nurturing elderly child-care provider, facilitator of religious and cultural values (cultural teacher), and the main individual in the extended family. Alignments between women, both within the family and outside it, often constitute the core of family networks.

Scholars claim that older women perform a variety of tasks for their families. Nonetheless, familism as an empirical phenomenon, a manifestation of expected mutual aid and support, is changing, although certain elements of it, particularly family unity, still remain. The multigenerational household and extended family do not operate as the literature would have people believe, in part because older women are establishing modified networks with other older Chicanas, not necessarily within their own family. While they still value family unity, it may stem not from familism or culture but rather from gender and age dynamics.

The value placed on motherhood by most Latinas continues with the transition to grandmotherhood. Current research suggests that older Chicanas find grandmotherhood "confining" and "limiting" and seek ways to avoid meeting the expectations associated with the status. Many women expressed joy and pride on becoming grandmothers, but they were less willing to take on child care.

Gender, also a major component of Chicano familism, continues to manifest itself throughout the life cycle. Familism serves to explain and understand women as wives, mothers, and grandmothers. Older women in general struggle with past traditions in the midst of contemporary realities that create contradictions and challenges in advanced age. Although they are socialized with conventional ideas about old age (harmony, status, respect, and solace), the reality of their present lives is poverty, family structural changes, differential life expectancies, and longevity. Older women confront traditions that reinforce a gender hierarchy. Chicano and Latino cultural norms expect older women, whether they are biological or surrogate grandmothers, to conform to the role of caregivers, and they are generally discouraged from seeking male companionship. They are steered instead toward the role of *abuelas* (grandmothers) and an old age spent as caregivers. Older Chicanas are dealing with conflicting cultural traditions and structural constraints through community organizations, senior-citizen centers, the Catholic Church, and their own families. Within these contexts women actively define or construct varied meanings of aged womanhood.

Among Chicanas attempts to define and resolve issues of womanhood lead to challenging cultural expectations at the risk of being disrespected. Capitalizing on respect is critical because it facilitates the process of self-definition. The family presents a means of support, love, and respect, but stresses conformity and ultimately control. In moving toward alternative definitions of womanhood among older Chicanas, the concept of *abuela* or grandmother merits attention. The term *abuela* connotes a romanticized image of a matriarch that only serves to disempower women within their families and in the community. It is interesting to note that when older Chicanas are discussed in the literature, they are almost always referred to as grandmothers. Thus the terms *grandmother* and *older woman* are synonymous.

The element of powerlessness lies in the potential exploitation of older Chicanas as convenient caregivers or baby-sitters. While grandmothering is a difficult task, of greater concern are limited views of older women simply as caregivers. The process of establishing oneself as a cultural teacher differs for widowed and married women and involves retaining and capitalizing on the respect granted to older women who conform to the caregiver role. The widowed grandmother respects the memory of her past marriage, remains widowed, and conforms to the nurturer role. Since convention discourages older women from seeking male friendship, this proscription ultimately controls their sexuality. While older Chicanas do have a sense of sexuality, cultural expectations, ageism, and patriarchy define and subsequently influence the expression of sexuality. A widowed grandmother who challenges this expectation risks being judged a "bad" woman, or *una mujer sin vergüenza*. The dichotomy of the "good" versus "bad" woman serves to ensure that widowed grandmothers will commit themselves to cultural expectations of caregiving. If they do not concede, they risk losing the respect needed to establish themselves as cultural teachers.

The social construction of womanhood for older Chicanas involves reconceptualizing the traditional expectation of caregiving and the role of cultural teacher. Along with other Latinas, Chicana grandmothers are altering such traditional roles and will provide child care out of necessity but not for convenience's sake. This, in turn, grants them independence and leverage in defining their relationship to the family. Under these conditions child-care services are viewed as important to the family, and grandmothers attempt to construct the caregiver role as familial support rather than a form of control. Nonetheless, their womanhood, with respect to grandmothering, continues to be defined within a traditional context.

The process of socially constructing elderly womanhood also involves utilizing the symbolic respect for the aged. Younger generations are expected to acknowledge the presence of their elders, not render them invisible. They are taught to respect the aged for their wisdom, knowledge, and survival into old age. Older women's quest for self-definition often depends on their relationship to their children, and requiring respect for the aged places Chicanas in an advantageous situation. It enables them to maintain contact with their children, grandchildren, and, for some, great-grandchildren. Such contact, whether through visits, social gatherings, or caregiving services, allows older women to establish themselves as cultural teachers and subsequently to redefine their womanhood while maintaining positive familial relationships.

As cultural teachers, women socialize grandchildren and/or great-grandchildren with certain cultural values and traditions, particularly their behavior toward older people and the maintenance of the Spanish language. The preservation of traditional music, food, and, for some, religion is equally as important. Older women are thus placed in a position where they can leave a legacy of cultural rather than monetary value.

SOURCES: Bastida, E. 1984. "Age and Gender Linked Norms among Older Hispanic Women." In *The Hispanic Older Woman,* ed. Roberto Anson. Washingtion, DC: National Hispanic Council on Aging; Espin, O. M. 1992. "Cultural and Historical Influences on Sexuality in Hispanic/Latin Women: Implications for Psychotherapy." In *Race, Class, and Gender: An Anthology,* ed. M. L. Andersen and P. H. Collins. Belmont, CA: Wadsworth; Facio, E. 1996. *Understanding Older Chicanas: Sociological and Policy Perspectives.* Thousand Oaks, CA: Sage

Publications; Sánchez-Ayendez, M. 1986. "Puerto Rican Elderly Women: Shared Meanings and Informal Support Networks." In *All American Women: Lines That Divide, Ties That Bind,* ed. J. B. Cole. New York: Free Press; Sotomayor, M., ed. 1995. *In Triple Jeopardy: Aged Hispanic Women: Insights and Experiences.* Washington, DC: National Hispanic Council on Aging.

Elisa Linda Facio

AGOSTINI DEL RÍO, AMELIA (1896–1996)

Born in Yauco, Puerto Rico, in 1896, scholar Amelia Agostini del Río grew up a diligent student and avid reader. After completing high school she received a scholarship to study at the University of Puerto Rico's Normal School, from which she graduated in 1917. She was part of a select group of women students being trained mostly as teachers, but her exposure to academic life at Puerto Rico's main center of learning resulted in many friendships with prominent male and female writers and intellectuals of this period. After graduating from the university she worked as a high-school teacher. In 1918 she left the island to further her education at Vassar College. She also studied at the Centro de Investigaciones Históricas and received a doctoral degree from the University of Madrid. Afterward she continued teaching in Santurce's high school for several years, but was also involved in writing, directing, and performing in some theatrical productions.

In 1926 she married the well-known Spanish literary critic Angel del Río, who had been her professor at the University of Puerto Rico. They moved to New York, where her husband taught at New York University and later at the Hispanic Institute of Columbia University. Angel del Río and other intellectuals from Spain were living in exile in New York and Puerto Rico during the years before and after the Spanish civil war and the fascist Francisco Franco dictatorship. These Spanish exiles played a key role in the founding not only of Columbia's Hispanic Institute, but also of a prestigious Department of Hispanic Studies at the University of Puerto Rico.

Agostini's broad intellectual formation and close contact with Spanish and Latin American literary circles is reflected in many of her writings. She lived for forty years in New York, where she was involved in teaching and other scholarly pursuits, including creative writing. She was a professor of Spanish language and literature and chair of the Spanish Department at Barnard College for many years. Along with her husband, she taught at Middlebury College's Spanish immersion summer program. The couple also coedited the widely used textbook *Antología general de la literatura española* (General Anthology of Spanish Literature) (1960). From her experiences in the New York Latino community, she wrote a book of narrative portrayals, *Puertorriqueños en Nueva York* (1970).

After four decades of living in New York, Agostini returned to Puerto Rico in the late 1960s, a few years after the death of her husband. On the island she continued her teaching and writing activities and became a frequent cultural columnist for the Puerto Rican newspaper *El Imparcial*. Her articles from this period are collected in the book *Rosa de los vientos* (Rose of the Winds) (1980). Most of these articles relate personal anecdotes involving distinguished figures of Puerto Rico's literary world and that of other Spanish-speaking countries. These writings represent a mixture of cultural commentary, autobiographical account, and literary criticism, but most of all, they are a clear testimony of how numerous intellectual friendships shaped and enriched Agostini's life.

An earlier book, *Viñetas de Puerto Rico* (Puerto Rican Vignettes) (1965), is an intimate recollection of the author's years growing up in the small town of Yauco, Puerto Rico, and provides some human-interest stories about a few of the town's most picturesque characters. Her connections to the homeland are also reflected in her poetry collection *Canto a San Juan de Puerto Rico y otros poemas* (Song to San Juan de Puerto Rico and Other Poems) (1974). She also authored several books of children's stories and songs.

For her many literary and cultural contributions, Agostini was honored in 1973 by the Puerto Rico Chapter of the American Women's Union. She was also elected president of the Sociedad de Autores Puertorriqueños (Society of Puerto Rican Authors).

See also Education

SOURCES: Agostini del Río, Amelia. 1980. *Rosa de los vientos.* San Juan: Instituto de Cultura Puertorriqueña; Rivera de Alvarez, Josefina. 1974. *Diccionario de literatura puertorriqueña.* Vol. 2, tomo 1. San Juan: Instituto de Cultura Puertorriqueña.

Edna Acosta-Belén

ALATORRE, SOLEDAD "CHOLE" (1927–)

Soledad "Chole" Alatorre was born in 1927 in San Luis Potosi, Mexico. She came from an upper-middle-class background in Mexico. Her father was an officer in the Railroad Workers Union. At the age of twenty-seven Alatorre immigrated to the United States with her husband and sister. She settled in the San Fernando Valley of greater Los Angeles and began a career working as a bathing-suit model for a clothing-manufacturing company in downtown Los Angeles. Through her work

Alatorre began to establish relationships with the workers in the garment industry. In the manufacturing plant Alatorre became known for her personal contact with workers and eventually took on the role of an intermediary between the union rank and file and garment-industry manufacturers. This launched a career of labor organizing in the greater Los Angeles region. Alatorre became affiliated with unions such as the Teamsters, the United Auto Workers, the Maritime Union, and the United Farm Workers.

A strong labor activist, Alatorre became a prominent leader in the Chicano civil rights movement. In 1968, along with Bert Corona, whom she met through labor organizing, Alatorre founded el Centro de Acción Social Autónomo Hermandad General de Trabajadores, also known as CASA. CASA became a leading organization advocating for immigrant worker rights and provided a host of services for immigrant workers, including legal assistance, social policy advocacy, and education. Alatorre was a vital force in the operation of CASA. She was responsible for administrative duties and maintained a behind-the-scenes approach to her activism. Close friends say that this was one of Alatorre's strengths. She firmly believed in the collective spirit of activism and organizing and refrained from any sort of self-promotion.

To this day, Alatorre remains politically active. She maintains a prominent role but a behind-the-scenes profile in the Chicano/Latino communities of southern California. She has protested the resurrection of the Ku Klux Klan and vigilante action in San Diego and has worked toward ensuring representation of the Latino community in local political campaigns and elections in Los Angeles. Like many individuals in the movements for labor and civil rights, Alatorre championed community efforts and continuously identified herself as a member of the movement, rather than as an individual leader.

See also Centro de Acción Social Autónomo (CASA)

SOURCES: García, Mario T. 1994. *Memories of Chicano History: The Life and Narrative of Bert Corona*. Berkeley: University of California Press; Gutiérrez, David G. 1995. *Walls and Mirrors: Mexican Americans, Mexican Immigrants, and the Politics of Ethnicity.* Berkeley: University of California Press; Ruiz, Vicki L. 1998. *From out of the Shadows: Mexican Women in Twentieth-Century America.* New York: Oxford University Press.

Margie Brown-Coronel

ALBELO, CARMEN (1925–)

When Carmen Albelo sailed from San Juan, Puerto Rico, to the United States in 1939, she envisioned a land of opportunity and freedom, not war, discrimination, and loneliness. "When I came here I thought I was going to have a better life, but it wasn't like that," Albelo recalled. Born on October 1, 1925, in Sábana Grande, Puerto Rico, Albelo was introduced to an independent lifestyle at an early age. When she was only eight years old, young Albelo's mother divorced her husband and left Albelo and her siblings with relatives so she could try to make a better life for them in America. "It wasn't very easy when she left us," Albelo said, but her mother had no choice. Albelo stayed in Puerto Rico with her brother, two sisters, and grandparents. One by one, the children moved to the United States to rejoin their mother. Carmen Albelo was first.

"My mother sent me clothes for that day—shoes, clothes and ten dollars," Albelo said. She sailed to the United States by herself, wearing clothes ten times too big for her. "My aunt sent a letter to my mother saying I was [a size] 16; that was the size she wore. I was about 80 pounds," Albelo said.

At fourteen years of age, draped in layers of clothing, sunburned from the boat ride, and ill from motion sickness, she arrived in the United States almost unrecognizable to her mother, but with hope for the beginnings of a prosperous future. Two years later she was engaged to Higinio Albelo, a boy from the apartment building where she lived. "I had a dream with him," Albelo recalls. "I saw him dressed like a soldier, and he had a bag on his back. That's the way I saw him the first time." Although her mother disapproved of her getting married at such a young age, problems at home with her new stepfather pushed Albelo toward the altar. "He didn't want us," Albelo said of her stepfather. "So I told my mother, 'I'm going to get married.' . . . I didn't want my mother, because of me, having problems."

On November 19, 1941, Carmen and Higinio Albelo exchanged vows, promising to cherish and love each other, in good times and in bad. One of their cherished moments was the birth of Higinio Jr., whom they called Gene, on January 14, 1943, in Metropolitan Hospital in New York. Albelo spent three days in labor, without medication and without her mother or husband at her side. Higinio Albelo had been called to serve his country and was visiting his parents in Puerto Rico before going to fight with the navy in World War II. He did not see his son until a year later. The birth of her baby boy, however, made the time away from her husband easier for Albelo. "That was a joy because he was something that belonged to me, not to my family, not to anybody, me and my husband. And for years, I didn't have any joy, until I had my son," Albelo said.

With Higinio Albelo away at war, Carmen Albelo had a difficult time working, taking care of her son, and dealing with missing her husband all at once. While working as a seamstress sewing uniforms for members of the military, Albelo found that the nanny she

Carmen I. Albelo and her son, Gene Albelo, in California, 1948. Courtesy of the U.S. Latino and Latina World War II Oral History Project, University of Texas, Austin.

had hired to care for her son was leaving him alone for hours at a time. Albelo had to quit her job and stay home. She recalls writing to her husband in tears, asking what they were going to do, and feeling helpless because the checks she received from the navy were not enough. "I was alone in New York, and my mother was two hours away," Albelo said. "The problem was, I was very, very lonely."

Higinio Albelo began staying in while the other navy men had free time, ironing uniforms to make extra money to send home to his wife and baby boy. The extra money helped ease some of the family's financial woes, but they were still apart. "I remember one Christmas I was so alone. I was crying, I said, 'Oh my God, it's so awful to be alone on Christmas.' And I said, 'Well, I have my baby boy. That's good enough for me,' " Albelo said.

That same Christmas Albelo was surprised by someone at the door. Thinking someone might be trying to break in, she was shocked to see her husband walk in. "That was so nice, because my baby was happy, I was happy, and he was happy," Albelo said. When Higinio Albelo finally returned for good after serving for three years in the war, the couple's daughter, Carmen Albelo, was born, and the family was complete. The children inherited their mother's sense of independence and hard work; Higinio became the first in his family to graduate from college, from Columbia University, and Carmen got her associate's degree and fulfilled a lifelong dream to teach elementary school. Albelo said she had achieved all she set out for when she sailed to the United States in 1939. "I had bad days, but I had good days, too. So I can't complain that much."

See also World War II

SOURCES: Albelo, Carmen. 2002. Interview by Helen Aguirre Ferre, Miami Vet Center, September 14; Mendoza, Sylvia. 2003. "New Baby Helped Woman Endure Lonely War Years." *Narratives: Stories of U.S. Latinos and Latinas and World War II* (U.S. Latino and Latina WWII Oral History Project, University of Texas at Austin) 4, no. 1 (Spring).

Sylvia Mendoza

ALFAU GALVÁN DE SOLALINDE, JESUSA (1890–1943)

Novelist, painter, and educator Jesusa Alfau Galván was the daughter of Antonio Abad Alfau Baralt and Eugenia Galván Velázquez. She spent much of her life in the shadows of her illustrious grandfather, the Dominican Manuel de Jesús Galván, author of *Enriquillo,* one of the better-known and best-regarded *indianista* (idealized-Indian-themed) novels in the Spanish Caribbean and Latin America. Alfau's husband was the distinguished *hispanista* (Hispanic studies professor) Antonio G. Solalinde. She spent many years living in her native Spain and in the Dominican Republic, land of her ancestors. She received her formal education in Spain and later worked with her husband in research on philology and education. Jesusa Alfau Galván authored at the age of eighteen the novel *Los débiles,* published four years later in 1912 in Spain.

Alfau Galván de Solalinde lived in the United States on and off beginning in 1916. In the United States she was a regular contributor to the weekly *Las Novedades,* edited between 1916 and 1918 by her father. Her essays published in *Las Novedades* are meant to interpret for many in the Latino communities, within and outside the United States, customs and values of North American culture, much as José Martí and Pachín Marín, among many, had done before her. Among the titles of articles published in *Las Novedades* are "Sábado" (Saturday), "Thanksgiving," and "Visiones del Norte" (Visions of the North).

For several decades most Dominican literary histories have indicated that *Los débiles* had been translated into English in the United States. There is a 1930 edition of *Los débiles* that was published by Prentice-Hall, with a prologue and notes by Professor J. Horace Nunemaker of the Department of Foreign Languages at the State College of Washington. This edition was prepared for use as a textbook in intermediate to advanced Spanish-language courses. The brief prologue is the only section written in English. There is also a vocabulary in the back and a series of exercises. A copy of this second edition of *Los débiles* was found by

Daisy Cocco De Filippis on the shelves of the Queens College library, one of the colleges of the City University of New York. Cocco De Filippis edited the novel and published it in a slim volume titled *Como los crisantemos lila, obra escogida de Jesusa Alfau Galván de Solalinde,* with eight of the articles written by Galván de Solalinde for *Las Novedades.*

Jesusa Alfau Galván de Solalinde began writing her thesis "Nomenclatura de los tejidos españoles del siglo XIII" in English for the master of arts degree at the University of Wisconsin, but she died in Mexico in 1943 before completing the project. Her thesis was translated into Spanish by her nephew Antonio Gobernado de García and published in 1969 by the Real Academia de la Lengua Española. Her life and work are early precursors of what became the diasporic Dominican/Hispanic family in the twentieth century.

SOURCES: Alfau Galván, Jesusa. 1912. *Los débiles.* Madrid: Imprenta Artística José Blas; ———. 1930. *Los débiles.* Prologue and annotations by J. Horace Nunemaker. New York: Prentice-Hall; ———. 2000. *Como los crisantemos lila, obra escogida.* Selection and prologue by Daisy Cocco De Filippis. Colección Tertuliando, no. 5. New York: Ediciones Alcance.

Daisy Cocco De Filippis

ALLENDE, ISABEL (1942–)

Noted writer Isabel Allende was born in Lima, Peru, where her father Tomás Allende served as a diplomat. She is a second cousin of socialist Chilean president Salvador Allende Gossens (1908–1973). After her father abandoned the family, her mother, Francisca Llona, was left with three children. She moved back to her parents' house in Santiago de Chile in 1945 and later married Ramón Huidobro, also a diplomat. He was appointed to Bolivia and Beirut, where Allende attended private schools. In 1958 the writer returned to Chile and met her first husband, Miguel Frías. They married in 1962 and had two children, Paula and Nicolás.

In 1970 Salvador Allende was elected president of Chile, but three years later, on September 11, there was a coup d'état led by Pinochet Ugarte and supported by both Chilean aristocrats and the U.S. government. Salvador Allende was assassinated, and Isabel Allende was forced to leave the country in 1975.

From 1967 to 1974 Isabel Allende worked as a bilingual secretary at the United Nations Food and Agriculture Organization (FAO) in Chile. She also wrote for *Paula* magazine and was in charge of the humorous column "Los impertinentes." From 1973 to 1974 she contributed to the children's magazine *Mampato* and published two stories for children: "The Grandmother Panchita" and "Lauchas y lauchones." In addition, between 1970 and 1975 she worked for television channels 13 and 7 in Santiago.

In 1975 Allende and her family were exiled to Venezuela, where they lived for thirteen years. In Caracas she contributed to the newspaper *El Nacional* and from 1979 to 1982 worked as an administrator for Marroco College, a secondary school in the Venezuelan capital. In 1978 Allende and her husband separated for two months. They eventually divorced in 1987.

In 1981, when her grandfather was about to die, Allende began to write him a letter that later became the manuscript for *The House of the Spirits.* The novel, published a year later, brought her international attention. She published nine more books in the next twenty years: *Of Love and Shadows, Eva Luna, Stories of Eva Luna, The Infinite Plan, Paula, Aphrodite, Daughter of Fortune, Portrait in Sepia,* and *City of Beasts.*

In 1988 she married Willie Gordon; since then, they have both lived in San Rafael, California. Today the Chilean novelist is dedicated to writing, lecturing, and giving conferences. After fifteen years of exile Allende returned to Chile to receive the Gabriela Mistral Award. A year later her daughter, Paula, suffered a porphyria attack and went into a coma. She died in 1992, and in her memory Allende began to write *Paula.*

Gregory D. Lagos-Montoya has stated, "Although Allende's literary awards as well as her honorary degrees are numerous, some literary critics have alleged that her works are imitations of Nobel laureate Gabriel García Márquez's masterpiece *Cien años de soledad* (*One Hundred Years of Solitude,* 1967)." Even though one can see a similarity in elements of the so-called magic realism, it is undeniable that Allende is a prolific author who has developed her own style and who has managed to succeed as a best-selling novelist.

See also Literature

SOURCES: Correas Zapata, Celia. 1998. *Isabel Allende, vida y espíritus.* España: Plaza y Janés; Isabel Allende online. http://www.isabelallende.com/ (accessed October 4, 2004); Tompkins, Cynthia Margarita, and David William Foster, eds. 2001. *Notable Twentieth-Century Latin American Women.* Westport, CT: Greenwood Press.

Maria E. Villamil

ALONZO, VENTURA (1904–2000)

Ventura Alonzo was born in Matamoros, Mexico, on December 30, 1904. She was the fifth of eight children born to José Martínez and Maria de Pilár Cuevas Escamilla. When she was five, she and her family fled the Mexican Revolution to live in Brownsville, Texas. Shortly thereafter they continued their migration to

Ventura Alonzo was known as the Queen of the Accordion. Mural by Teodoro Estrada, 1996. Photograph by David Carrera Jr. Courtesy of Mary Ann Villarreal.

Kingsville, Texas. Her love for music began when her older brother ordered a piano from New York City. She recalls that she was only twelve years old when a piano teacher came from Mexico and gave several children, including her sister, piano lessons. Alonzo, however, just wanted to play and did not want lessons. She recounted, "Entonces vino el profesor y me examinó en el piano. . . . El dijo 'Esta muchachita no es de nota, es de aquí de la cabeza.' " (Then the professor came and gave me an examination on the piano. . . . He said [to my parents], "This little girl does not go by note, but it's here in her head.") Her father passed away in Kingsville, and the onset of the depression forced Alonzo, her mother, and her siblings to move to Houston to find employment.

Alonzo gave birth to eight children, three sons with her first husband and five children with her second husband, Francisco Alonzo. In the mid-1930s she and Francisco started their orchestra, Alonzo y sus Rancheros, which was composed of family members, including Alonzo as the singer and accordion player. Before starting on the circuit, the group performed for free at the Immaculate Heart of Mary Catholic Church's annual bazaar in Houston. She was a hit wherever they performed, traveling from Fort Worth to Kingsville. One story goes that "during one set, Alonzo's arm got tired from holding the accordion and she put it down, stepping up to the microphone to sing publicly for the first time. She was a hit." The orchestra performed live on the radio to increase its popularity and also to introduce music it had recorded. She eventually earned the title "Queen of the Accordion" or "la Reina del Acordéon." Her talents did not end with her playing or singing abilities. She wrote several songs that the group recorded, including "Magnolia Park." They performed throughout Houston's Magnolia Park until they opened La Terraza in 1956, a ballroom located at 1515 McCarty Drive. At the ballroom Alonzo had multiple duties, from performing to collecting the cover charge at the door. She knew the importance of keeping her audience happy, playing the songs they requested, and keeping the regulars returning week after week.

Ventura and Francisco Alonzo retired from the nightclub business and from performing as an orchestra in 1969. In retirement she dedicated her time to playing the piano for senior citizens of the Denver Harbor community every Friday at the Centro Alegre. A mural dedicated to Alonzo was painted by local art teacher Teodoro Estrada in 1996 and is located on the side of a Houston Firestone store at 6901 Harrisburg Blvd.

SOURCES: Alonzo, Ventura. 1999. Oral history interview by Mary Ann Villarreal, May; Peña, Manuel. 1999. *The Mexican American Orquesta: Music, Culture, and Dialectic of Conflict.* Austin: University of Texas Press; Rust, Carol. 1996. "Ventura Alonzo Honored in Magnolia Mural/Queen of the Accordian." *Houston Chronicle,* August 14, 1; Vargas, Deborah Rose Ramos. 2003. "Las tracaleras: Texas-Mexican Women, Music, and Place." Ph.D. diss., University of California, Santa Cruz; Villarreal, Mary Ann. 2003. "*Cantantes y Cantineras*: Mexican American Communities and the Mapping of Public Space." Ph.D. diss., Arizona State University.

Mary Ann Villarreal

ALTARS

The tradition of altar making or "the arrangement of objects with symbolic meaning" has its roots for Latinas among the ancient indigenous cultures of Mexico and Latin America. In Mexico the Toltecs maintained small shrines or altars to deities in the privacy of domestic space. The Mexica carried on the tradition in their dwellings with small alcoves designed for an effigy of a deity and a container for burnt offerings. Among the Maya, Toltec, and Mexica, large stones with flat surfaces suitable for the burning of oblations served as public altars.

During the colonial period elite Spanish and criollo families constructed home chapels with elaborate altars dedicated to Catholic icons. Indigenous peoples continued the practice of domestic altar making. Despite efforts by church officials to curtail the importance of home altars for native peoples, these sites of spiritual vitality persisted, but with Christian symbols included. For mestizo populations, the complexity of *nepantla* (a Nahua term meaning "in the middle") began to be visualized in religious iconography. In time, mestizo home altars revealed the emerging syncretic nature of Mexican Catholicism with its distinct symbol system incorporating indigenous and Christian elements in one object, for example, the crucified body of Jesus surrounded by the moon and sun, or a crucifix made of cornhusks. These images connect the Christian deity to the sacred cosmic forces and the sacred food of Mesoamerican indigenous religions.

The curtailment of church authority during the Reform era and the Juárez presidency in the mid-1800s, along with the decline in the number of priests and churches, increased the importance of domestic shrines where families could continue their prayers and rituals. The *rezadora* or female prayer leader took on a central role in the maintenance and transmission of the faith among family members. In rural communities the virtual absence of clergy made the spiritual healing abilities of *curanderas* or specialized healers extremely significant. The last decade of the nineteenth century witnessed a reinstatement of church vitality in Mexico with a new cadre of priests trained in ideas of social action. Church buildings and church attendance increased, yet the home altar remained a central site for the practice of personal and familial devotions.

With the annexation of one-half of Mexico by the United States in 1848, Mexican Catholics became members of the U.S. Roman Catholic Church. Overt discrimination, European-born clergy, and unequal monetary and staff allocations to new Mexican American dioceses often created a distance between Mexican Americans and the institutional church. Once again, the home altar maintained its importance in the preservation of the faith among Mexican families. During the mid-twentieth century, as part of efforts to universalize Catholic worship, Mexican American Catholics often succumbed to the pressure to drop domestic altar making. Numerous families, however, continued the tradition that celebrates spirituality beyond the boundaries of institutionalized religion and often signifies a Latina feminist spirituality.

For Latina Protestants, the construction of home altars with symbols other than a cross and the Bible are rare, because Protestant Christianity traditionally prohibits the display of icons or the practice of praying through material objects. Rather, *el altar familiar,* the family altar, takes the form of time and space set aside for Bible study and prayer. Latinas practicing Santería or Lucumí construct altars regularly as part of their ritual practice of making oblations to deities and the ancestors.

Depending on the *oricha* or sacred spirit being honored, a *santera*'s altar will contain food and drink offerings, richly colored fabrics designating the *oricha,* elaborately decorated ceramic pots holding the *ashé* or

Catholic women took great pride and comfort in their home altars. Courtesy of Lee (Russell) Photograph Collection, The Center for American History, The University of Texas at Austin, Neg. no. CN06311.

spiritual power of the *oricha,* ritual instruments to call forth ancestors and spirits, and images of the *oricha,* at times a statue of a Christian saint that conceals the identity of the *oricha*.

Chicana artists such as Amalia Mesa-Bains, Ofelia Esparza, and Enedina Casarez Vásquez have influenced significantly the reclamation of altar making as a central expression of spirituality by contemporary Chicanas and Latinas. For Latinas who have left organized religion and for those who remain, altars provide the space for women to create and express what for them has ultimate meaning. For women, the act of altar making reinforces their claim to name the sacred. Through the arrangement of symbols, photographs, candles, and icons, all imbued with meaning, altars connect the spiritual world with the physical world, the living with the dead, goddesses/gods or the spirit world with humans, and the altar maker with the viewer. Altars become sites of historical memory, of creativity and imagination. They communicate family histories and personal and political identities through the images and symbols displayed. Altars can take a variety of forms, from more abstract to traditional expressions and from personal and private creations to public and communal works of art. They represent fluid expressions of ever-changing personal and social locations. Chicanas and Latinas inherit a rich legacy of women creating sacred spaces for spiritual and psychic nourishment.

See also Religion

SOURCES: Cortez, Constance, ed. 1999. *Imágenes e historias/Images and Histories: Chicana Altar-Inspired Art.* Medford, MA: Tufts University Gallery; McMann, Jean. 1998. *Altars and Icons: Sacred Spaces in Everyday Life.* San Francisco: Chronicle Books; Romero Cash, María. 1998. *Living Shrines: Home Altars of New Mexico.* Santa Fe: Museum of New Mexico Press; Salvo, Dana. 1997. *Home Altars of Mexico.* Albuquerque: University of New Mexico Press; Turner, Kay. 1999. *Beautiful Necessity: The Art and Meaning of Women's Altars.* New York: Thames and Hudson.

Lara Medina

ALVAREZ, AIDA (1949–)

Aida Alvarez, the first Hispanic woman and first Puerto Rican to head the federal Small Business Administration, was born in Aguadilla, the oldest of the six daughters and sons of Héctor and Aurelia Alvarez. The family moved to New York when Alvarez was not yet a year old, and when she was of school age she helped at her mother's businesses—a luncheonette first, later a restaurant—between classes. That experience, she later said, gave her an understanding of the needs of small-business owners.

The first person in her immediate family to obtain a college education, Alvarez graduated from Harvard College with a degree in English literature in 1971 and then spent two years as a high-school Spanish teacher before starting a successful career as a newspaper and television journalist and anchor. With a series of articles for the *New York Post,* "Latins in New York," she won a Front Page Award for Journalistic Excellence, and her television reporting from El Salvador during that country's civil war won an Emmy nomination in 1982. Although she considered the possibility of continuing as a war correspondent, after her experience in Central America Alvarez decided that she wanted a role that allowed her to work for social change. "In the media, you have to be objective. But as I matured, I had some strong beliefs, and I really wanted to be an advocate," she told an interviewer.

Leaving what was considered an enviable position in the prime television news market of New York City, in 1984 Alvarez became vice president for public affairs and special projects for the city's Health and Hospitals Corporation, a post she occupied until the following year. After that brief initial experience in government Alvarez worked in the investment banking industry for more than a decade, specializing in public finance at Bear Stearns and Company and at the First Boston Corporation. During that period she met her husband, Dr. Raymond Baxter. They have two daughters.

In private industry Alvarez served on several governmental panels, among them New York City's Charter Revision Commission, which was in charge of rewriting the city's charter. She developed a reputation for directness, an illustration of which was seen in her statements to the press after the commission's final vote in 1989. As one of the few dissenters from the commission's recommendations, Alvarez declared that the process had been a missed opportunity and called the final draft "a patchwork of political accommodations rather than a progressive vision."

Alvarez was also engaged in national Democratic politics, participating in Al Gore's presidential campaign and working in the development of a Hispanic agenda for the 1988 election. She was co-chair of the women's committee for Bill Clinton's campaign in 1992, and after Clinton's victory she served on his economic transition team. Alvarez returned to government in 1993 when Clinton nominated her as director of the Office of Federal Housing Enterprise Oversight, a new government entity created to regulate the nation's two largest housing finance agencies.

In December 1996 President Clinton nominated Aida Alvarez to head the Small Business Administration (SBA). She was sworn in on March 7, 1997, and remained in the post throughout the full second term of the Clinton presidency. Those were years of high tension between the Republican-led Congress and the Democratic executive branch, and the SBA's managerial practices under Alvarez's direction were reviewed by Congress on several occasions. Although Alvarez's background in finance was an asset, her lack of professional small-business experience was pointed out by critics when she was nominated, and when she took office, there were questions about the future of the agency, which had been frequently targeted for budgetary reductions.

It was therefore considered a credit to Alvarez that during the four years of her tenure, the amount of loans and guarantees given by the SBA increased significantly. The agency also developed programs to address the needs of special constituencies, from rural businesses to independent filmmakers, and began initiatives to increase small businesses' participation in international trade.

Under Alvarez's direction the SBA reached an agreement with the big three U.S. automakers to increase their contracts with minority-owned small businesses. Alvarez also developed partnerships with ethnic business organizations and offered new bilingual services. Her vigorous advocacy for women- and minority-owned small businesses, which led to a dramatic increase in loans to both sectors, was one of her most strongly noticed accomplishments as an administrator.

SOURCES: Birnbaum, Jeffrey H. 2001. "Aida's Exit Interview: She Made the SBA Bigger and Better Than Ever, but Does the Outgoing Boss Have Any Regrets?" *FSB (Fortune Small Business),* March 1; Nixon, Brian. 1994. "Inventing Government: A Profile of Aida Alvarez." *Savings and Community Banker,* April.

Maria Vega

ALVAREZ, CECILIA CONCEPCIÓN (1950–)

Dynamic self-taught artist Cecilia Alvarez is a Cuban Mexican American born to Jorge Guillermo Alvarez and Cecilia Alejandra Diego de Alvarez in National City, California. She was raised on the San Diego–Tijuana border and eventually attended San Diego State University, where she pursued a degree in sociology. At the age of twenty-three, however, Alvarez quit school in order to help support her family. Eventually Alvarez moved to Canada, where the spatial distance from her community provided her the environment to begin to think freely. According to Alvarez, this experience allowed her to see racism in a different light and to grow as an individual.

Alvarez's work as an artist is centered on family in a symbolic sense that discusses issues in both her life and the world. Her use of female images transcends the literal meaning of gender to portray the aspects of life that are considered inferior or less important in an industrial consumer society. Female perspectives on the symbolic things people give up to survive, such as culture and earth, are those aspects that are unfortunately given female attributes. Examining the female form in Alvarez's work demonstrates that she is essentially redefining femininity. In the piece *La Malinche Tenia Sus Rasones* Alvarez portrays La Malinche, Hernán, Cortés's indigenous concubine, as a remorseful heroine. Another factor in the imagery used reflects aspects of Alvarez's upbringing in the San Diego area, where the proximity to Mexico and the influxes of migration constantly create political unrest and cultural shifts. Alvarez explains that growing up in the San Diego–Tijuana area, she quickly learned that people tend to disregard family and culture, and that when these are sacrificed, they become commodified. In this way her work is a visual discourse on reality and the changes of humanity within a collective society. As an artist, Alvarez attempts to redefine beauty, power, and importance from the context of cultural values: "Without dreams of beauty, of power—there is no reason to live."

La Tierra Santa, Las Cuatas Diego, and *El Eterno Danzón del Sueño de la Unidad* exemplify Alzarez's use of culture, often depicted as family figures or indigenous figures, and the Earth, represented by flowers or animals. The use of family figures and the Earth is an important aspect in her art because they embody her ideas on the preservation of culture and community. Beyond the aesthetic qualities of her art, Alvarez's artistic strength lies in her ability to incorporate the observer into a dialogue of current social issues within the context of culture. *Si Te Puede Pasar a Ti, EL SIDA* is perhaps the best example of this capacity. This installation piece utilizes the image of the skeleton to demonstrate the inevitable, yet her use of the woman with the condom illustrates the power that people hold to avoid destruction through sexually transmitted diseases, such as AIDS. Through the process of immersing the observer into a discussion on power and social issues, Alvarez invites introspection about personal biases, hate, and prejudice.

Alvarez aims to help youth understand the complex world that they live in so that they may grow to be healthy individuals. She feels that her upbringing in the San Diego area and her subsequent residence in Washington State have allowed her to become a freethinker. Alvarez also believes that to achieve dynamic changes in the community, people must educate themselves.

La Tierra Santa, 1986. Painting in oil on canvas by and courtesy of Cecilia Concepción Alvarez.

Among her achievements, she lists being blessed with the opportunity to articulate through her art what is important to her community locally, nationally, and internationally. Her work has been featured in many books and several international art shows.

See also Artists

SOURCES: Alvarez, Cecilia Concepción. 2002. Oral history interview by Marylou Gómez, May 24; Beardsley, John, and Jane Livingston. 1987. *Hispanic Art in the United States.* New York: Abbeville Press; Griswold del Castillo, Richard, Teresa McKenna, and Yvonne Yarbro-Bejarano, eds. 1991. *Chicano Art: Resistance and Affirmation, 1965–1985.* Los Angeles: Wight Art Gallery, University of California, Los Angeles; Quirate, Jacinto. *Mexican American Artists.* Austin: University of Texas Press.

Marylou Gómez

ALVAREZ, DELIA (1941–)

An outspoken critic of U.S. military intervention in Southeast Asia, Delia Alvarez is also the sister of Everett Alvarez Jr., who was held as a prisoner of war during the Vietnam conflict for eight and one-half years. Delia Alvarez's antiwar activism reflected both her increasing involvement in the Chicano movement during the late 1960s and her steadfast conviction that ending the war was the fastest way to bring her brother home.

When they were growing up in the California town of Salinas, the two Alvarez siblings, of whom Delia was the younger by three years, were extremely close. When Delia Alvarez found out that her brother, a U.S. Navy pilot, had been shot down in August 1964 during the Gulf of Tonkin incident, she immediately wished that she, as a woman, could join the military to help rescue him. At the time, like many Americans, she accepted the necessity of U.S. involvement in Vietnam to stop the spread of Communism. Her brother's capture, however, prompted her to read everything she could about Vietnam's colonial past and American intervention. She concluded that the conflict was essentially a civil war in which the U.S. military had no legitimate role to play. For a member of a military family in the mid-1960s, however, the notion of expressing such doubts publicly was inconceivable. Her reluctance faded as the years passed and her brother remained a prisoner.

Furthering her opposition to the war was Delia Alvarez's participation in the Chicano movement. When she was working in San Jose to promote Mexican American college recruitment and retention, she noticed that Chicanos were particularly vulnerable to the draft because they were not receiving college deferments. Similarly, when she pressed for better health care and improved local housing, she resented the federal government's cuts in funding for domestic social programs while it was spending billions on the war overseas. As she explained years later, "I would have come out against [the war] if [my brother] hadn't been a POW," but "there's no doubt in my mind that I became so involved because I had an emotional involvement to end the war."

Determined to do everything in her power to hasten her brother's release, Delia Alvarez became a featured speaker at national antiwar rallies. She also traveled repeatedly to Washington, D.C., to demand that the Nixon administration stop the war. In 1970 she cofounded a group of antiwar POW families. As a member of that group, Delia Alvarez also met with Indo-Chinese women twice in the early 1970s, in Vancouver and Paris. All along, she realized that she was risking her brother's disapproval. In fact, while he was still a captive in North Vietnam, Everett Alvarez Jr. was dismayed to learn of his sister's antiwar activism. Like many POWs, he viewed such protest as tantamount to siding with the enemy. But after Everett Alvarez's release in 1973, familial bonds ultimately proved more powerful than the siblings' political differences. Delia Alvarez retired as the director of public health for Santa Clara County in 1993 and now lives in San Francisco.

SOURCE: Oropeza, Lorena. 2005. *Raza Sí!, Guerra No!: Chicano Protest and Patriotism during the Viet Nam War Era.* Berkeley: University of California Press.

Lorena Oropeza

ALVAREZ, JULIA (1950–)

The first Dominican American novelist to bring Dominican culture to the attention of an English-speaking readership, Julia Alvarez was born in 1950 in New York City but was raised in the Dominican Republic in an extended upper-class Dominican family that exerted a powerful influence on Alvarez and her sisters, who grew up on her mother's family property surrounded by aunts, cousins, and maids. Despite these early experiences on the Caribbean island, the enormous impact of U.S. culture on those of her class has led Alvarez to assert, "Mine was an American childhood."

Politics intruded on her idyllic youth, however, and compelled her and her family to experience life in the United States firsthand. Because of his opposition to the regime of the Dominican dictator Rafael Leónidas Trujillo, Alvarez's father, a medical doctor, was forced to flee the country to the United States with his wife and daughters in 1960. The homesickness and alienation Alvarez experienced as an immigrant and her struggle to find a place for herself in a new environment are the foundation of much of her writing, particularly her first novel, *How the García Girls Lost Their Accents* (1991), a work described as a Dominican female bildungsroman that garnered the author critical praise as an evocative storyteller. Alvarez has also published several award-winning collections of poetry, including *Homecoming* (1984) and *The Other Side: El otro lado* (1996). A graduate of Middlebury College in Vermont and Syracuse University (M.F.A., 1975), Alvarez became an English professor at Middlebury in 1988. The author and her husband divide their time between their home in Vermont and their farm in the mountains of the Dominican Republic.

While *García Girls* parallels autobiographical elements of Alvarez's own experiences, her second work of fiction, *In the Time of the Butterflies* (1994), delves more specifically into the history of her homeland as it follows the story of the Mirabal sisters, three of whom were murdered for their political resistance to the brutal Trujillo regime. In 1997 Alvarez returned to characters in *García Girls* in her novel *Yo!,* which continues themes found in her first novel related to the complexity of the bilingual-bicultural experience of Latina women in U.S. culture. "Sometimes I hear Spanish in English (and of course, vice versa). That's why I describe myself as a Dominican American writer. That's not just a term. I'm mapping a country that's not on a map. . . . It's a world formed of contradictions, clashes, cominglings—the gringa and the Dominican, and it is precisely that tension and richness that interests me."

Julia Alvarez is a writer whose work is in demand in the popular media. Her thoughtful yet lively essays can be found in a range of publications, from *Latina* magazine to the Sunday magazine section of the *New York Times*. Her work *Something to Declare* (1998) is a collection of essays that trace the diverse lessons she has learned on the way to becoming a writer. In keeping with her interest in illuminating the lives of remarkable Dominican women, Alvarez has published *In the Name of Salomé* (2000). The story concerns the famous nineteenth-century national poet of the Dominican Republic, Salome Ureña, who, among other accomplishments, established the country's first free school for females, and her daughter, Camila Henríquez Ureña, who retired from her position as a professor at Vassar College in 1960 to join the Cuban Revolution. While Julia Alvarez's class origins may distinguish her experiences from those of the typical Dominican immigrant to the United States, she nevertheless was the first writer to provide a voice in English for that community and, in particular, for the concerns of Dominican women.

See also Literature

SOURCES: Castelluci Cox, Karen. 2001. "A Particular Blessing: Storytelling as Healing in the Novels of Julia Alvarez." In *Healing Cultures: Art and Religion as Curative Practices in the Caribbean and Its Diaspora,* ed. Margarite Fernández Olmos and Lizabeth Paravisini-Gebert. New York: Palgrave–St. Martin's Press; *Notable Hispanic American Women Book II.* 1998. Detroit: Gale Research; Rosario-Sievert, Heather. 2000. "The Dominican-American Bildungsroman: Julia Alvarez's *How the García Girls Lost Their Accents.*" In *U.S. Latino Literature: A Critical Guide for Students and Teachers,* eds. Harold Augenbraum and Margarite Fernández Olmos. Westport, CT: Greenwood Press.

Margarite Fernández Olmos

ALVAREZ, LINDA (19??–)

Almost three decades in journalism and frequent involvement in charitable causes have made reporter Linda Alvarez one of the most recognized Latino television presences in Los Angeles. Born Hermelinda Alvarez, she was one of the four children of Ray Alvarez, a gas-station owner of Mexican origin, and Margarita Larios, a Californian of Mexican and Chilean descent who worked as an administrative assistant at the University of California, Los Angeles.

When the couple separated, the children—three sisters and a brother—fell upon difficult times. As Alvarez once told an interviewer, "We depended on each other growing up. I wouldn't have been able to graduate from college if I hadn't had scholarships and people who cared about me." Linda Alvarez's education and early career were oriented toward the learning and teaching of languages. She attended Catholic schools and Venice High School, and in 1963 she graduated from UCLA with an English degree. After an additional year earning her teaching credentials, Alvarez taught English and Spanish for two years at Venice High School.

In her spare time she also taught Spanish to Peace Corps volunteers, an experience that eventually inspired her to relocate to Venezuela, where she taught at the Universidad de Carabobo and started an English-language school. After she returned to the United States, she taught at schools in New York and Connecticut and at the United Nations Secretariat. For one summer she also worked at the Universidad Autónoma de México in Mexico City. Upon returning from Mexico, she became director of an adult basic education program for the federal Department of Health, Education, and Welfare in Chicago. Noticing her excellent pronunciation of both Spanish and English, an acquaintance encouraged her to record bilingual public announcements for television station WTTW. That marked the beginning of a career in the media for Alvarez. In 1973 she was hired by station WMAQ, initially as a weather forecaster. After a short time she was offered a regular news reporting job and, after a year, became cohost of *Chicago Camera,* a ninety-minute program that was transmitted live from various locations in the city.

In 1977 Alvarez moved from Chicago to Los Angeles. For a brief period she was one of the hosts of KNBC's *Saturday Show* before relocating again to Phoenix, Arizona. There, at station KPNX, Alvarez was anchor of three daily newscasts and was the reporter and producer of the station's documentary unit. It was in Phoenix that she met her husband, cameraman Bill Timmer.

In August 1985 Alvarez returned to Los Angeles' KNBC as weekend anchor. A year later, at the same station, Alvarez became the first Latina to anchor a major weekday newscast in the Los Angeles area. After eight years at KNBC, in 1993 Alvarez joined station KCBS, where she has worked as anchor and news reporter.

Among the events Alvarez has covered during her career are the 1985 earthquake in the Mexican capital, the California earthquakes of 1987 and 1989, Pope John Paul II's 1987 visit to Los Angeles, and the 1988 Summer Olympics in Seoul. At various journalism conferences Alvarez has spoken about the need for strong ethical standards in the profession and for better representation of women and minorities in the media. "There is a race to get advertisers and audiences," she said at a meeting of the National Association of Hispanic Journalists. "Crime and sex stories get audiences. The media overlook the community issues that affect Latinos."

Alvarez has also spoken frequently in favor of youth service and educational programs. Active in many not-for-profit organizations, she has been a frequent participant in fund-raising events and has been a board member of the YMCA of Metropolitan Los Angeles, Big Sisters of Los Angeles, and the National Conference of Christians and Jews, among other charities. Alvarez has won eight Emmy awards and honors from many media organizations.

See also Journalism and Print Media

SOURCES: Alexander, Katina. 1988. "Linda Alvarez Wears Her Heritage Proudly—Even without Makeup." *Orange County Register,* December 2; Guensburg, Carol. 1999. "Taming the Beast." *American Journalism Review,* July.

María Vega

ALVAREZ V. LEMON GROVE SCHOOL DISTRICT (1931)

Although limited in scope and local in nature, the California court case *Alvarez v. Lemon Grove School District* was one of the earliest challenges to school segregation in the United States. A small farming community east of San Diego, Lemon Grove seemed an unlikely place for litigation because European American and Mexican American children attended the same elementary school in 1930. Such integrated education seemed exceptional for the time period, because segregated "Mexican" schools were the norm in southern California. This situation, however, soon changed.

On January 5, 1931, when the children returned to school after the holidays, the school superintendent, Jerome Greene, met the Mexican youngsters at the door and instructed them to walk over to their "new school" constructed across the tracks in the barrio. The "new" two-room facility resembled a barn hastily built and hastily furnished with secondhand equipment, supplies, and books. The students returned to their homes, and their parents took action. Forming el Comité de Vecinos de Lemon Grove (the Lemon Grove

Neighbors Committee), they voted to boycott the segregated school and to seek legal redress. Except for one household, every family kept the children home. With the assistance of the Mexican consul, Enrique Ferreira, the Comité hired an attorney on behalf of the eighty-five children affected and filed suit.

Using the Americanization banner, board members justified their actions on the grounds that a separate facility was necessary to meet the needs of non-English-speaking children. They argued that the Mexican students were behind in their studies and that the new school would offer them remedial instruction. To counter this argument, students "took the stand to prove their knowledge of English." Twelve-year-old Roberto Alvarez testified as the lead plaintiff in the case. An honor student, Alvarez contradicted the school board's claims of alleged learning difficulties among local Mexican youth.

In *Alvarez v. Lemon Grove School District* (1931) Judge Claude Chambers ordered the "immediate reinstatement" of the Mexican children to their old grammar school. Chambers, however, in this landmark case made a fairly narrow ruling; he argued that Mexicans were "white" and therefore not subject to segregation. Alvarez graduated from high school, joined the navy during World War II, and later became a multimillionaire as the owner of an international produce-distribution firm. His son Roberto Alvarez Jr., an anthropologist who teaches in the Department of Ethnic Studies at the University of California, San Diego, wrote about his family's involvement in the case and worked closely with filmmaker Paul Espinosa to bring the story to life in the PBS docudrama *The Lemon Grove Incident*. Making history runs in the family, because Luis Alvarez, the son of Roberto Alvarez Jr., is a historian at the University of Houston.

During a reign of deportations and repatriations during the Great Depression, Mexican immigrants had mustered the courage to protest segregation in education and they had won. These immigrant parents, moreover, had sought the assistance of the Mexican consul in their effort to provide equal opportunities for their children born in the United States. Equally important, according to anthropologist Roberto Alvarez Jr., the case may represent "the first successful court action in favor of school desegregation in the United States." Certainly it was an early victory.

See also Education; Mexican Schools

SOURCES: Alvarez, Roberto, Jr. 1987. *Familia: Migration and Adaptation in Baja and Alta California, 1800–1975*. Berkeley: University of California Press; Balderrama, Francisco. 1982. *In Defense of La Raza: The Los Angeles Mexican Consulate, and the Mexican Community, 1929–1936*. Tucson: University of Arizona Press; Espinosa, Paul (producer). 1984. *The Lemon Grove Incident*. Videocassette documentary; Ruiz, Vicki L. 2004. "Tapestries of Resistance: Episodes of School Segregation and Desegregation in the U.S. West." In Peter Lau, ed. *From Grassroots to the Supreme Court: Exploration of Brown. v. Board of Education and American Democracy*. Durham, NC: Duke University Press.

Vicki L. Ruiz

AMERICANIZATION PROGRAMS

Between 1910 and 1930 more than 1 million Mexicanos migrated northward to the United States. Escaping widespread poverty and the violence and chaos of the Mexican Revolution, they represented the first modern wave of Mexican immigration. In response, from Los Angeles, California, to Gary, Indiana, state- and religious-sponsored Americanization programs swung into action. Imbued with the ideology of "the melting pot," teachers, social workers, and religious missionaries envisioned themselves as the standard-bearers of salvation and civilization as they targeted their messages and activities toward women and children. Like their counterparts several decades earlier who had lived in east coast and midwestern settlement houses working among recent immigrants from southern and eastern Europe, these reformers emphasized classes in hygiene, civics, cooking, language, and vocational education (e.g., sewing and carpentry). Whether seated at a desk in a public school or on a sofa at a Protestant or Catholic neighborhood house, Mexican women received similar messages of assimilation.

Examples of Americanization efforts spanned the Southwest and Midwest from secular settlements in Watts, Pasadena, and Riverside to Hull-House in Chicago and Catholic neighborhood centers, such as Friendly House in Phoenix. Protestants also operated an array of settlements, health clinics, and schools. During this time, for example, the Methodist Church sponsored one hospital, four boarding schools, and sixteen settlements and community centers, all serving a predominantly Mexican clientele.

In addition to these social services, the advocates of Americanization held out unrealistic notions of the American dream and romantic constructions of life in the United States. Just as Madison Avenue advertisers exhorted consumers to buy particular products to find romance, happiness, and financial security, many Americanization workers made similar promises of behaviors that would provide the key for immigrant success if they were embraced. In the words of one missionary at the Rose Gregory Houchen Settlement in El Paso, Texas, "Sanitary conditions have been improving—more children go to school—more parents are be-

Celia M. Acosta Vice and Ivan Vice with their daughters at a Brooklyn celebration, 1960. Courtesy of Centro Archives, Centro de Estudios Puertorriqueños, Hunter College, CUNY.

coming citizens, more are leaving Catholicism—more are entering business and public life—and more and more they taking on the customs and standards of the Anglo people."

This statement ignores economic segmentation and racial-ethnic segregation. Focusing on El Paso, historian Mario García (1980) demonstrated that the curricula in Mexican schools, which emphasized vocational education, served to funnel Mexican youth into the factories and building trades. In the abstract, education raised expectations, but in practice, it trained them for low-status, low-paying jobs. Settlement workers seemed to ignore that racial-ethnic identity involved not only a matter of personal choice and heritage but also an ascribed status imposed by external sources. Indeed, Houchen Settlement operated an employment bureau for neighborhood women that placed them as domestic workers in "Christian" homes. At the Eighth Street School in Tempe, Arizona, the segregated "Mexican" elementary school, girls were taught not only reading, writing, and arithmetic, but also cooking, bed making, sewing, and other domestic chores. This emphasis on domesticity (lessons that one could argue young girls learned at home) prepared the children for future work in the service sector as maids and housekeepers.

There are a few exceptions worth noting in terms of promoting individual mobility. The Hull-House Kilns,

Patriotic parade in Spanish Harlem. Courtesy of the Justo A. Martí Photograph Collection. Centro Archives, Centro de Estudios Puertorriqueños, Hunter College, CUNY.

Dance recital. Courtesy of Houchen Community Center, El Paso, Texas.

for example, represented a cottage industry that emphasized self-help, artistic innovation, and sales, and as a result, several immigrant artisans became well-known artists in their own right. A Methodist all-girls boarding school, the Frances De Pauw School in Los Angeles, educated approximately 1,800 young Mexican women from 1900 to 1946. According to one source, "Among [the school's] graduates are secretaries, bookkeepers, clerks, office receptionists, nurses, teachers, waitresses, workers in cosmetic laboratories, church workers, and Christian homemakers." While preparing its charges for the workaday world, the school never lost sight of women's domestic duties. "Every De Pauw girl is graded as carefully in housework as she is in her studies."

Americanization workers were not always praised for their activities. Reverend Robert McLean, who worked among Mexicans in Los Angeles, referred to his congregation as "chili con carne" bound to give Uncle Sam a bad case of "heartburn." While one can certainly cringe at the ethnocentrism that permeated settlement work, one should also acknowledge its contributions in terms of providing medical and childcare services. For example, the hospital and clinic associated with El Paso's Houchen Settlement were important community institutions for more than half a century.

Americanization programs in the Southwest, most of which were sporadic and poorly financed, had little impact. For example, Mexican women in El Paso derived substantive services in the form of health care and education from Houchen Settlement; however, they refused to embrace the romantic idealizations of American life or to attempt to make themselves over into white Anglo-Saxon Protestants. Latinas have sought to claim a place for themselves and their families in the United States without abandoning their cultural affinities.

The idea that Latino cultures inherently "lack" certain ingredients for success was a widely held premise among advocates of Americanization, people who did not recognize the very real economic impediments for mobility. This culturally deficient model continues to haunt Latinos today from the novels of Oscar Lewis to the attitudes of some contemporary social workers and educators. For example, one university outreach program is based on the assumption that Latino parents need to be instructed by undergraduate volunteers on the proper ways to read and play with their preschool children. The legacies of Progressive-era Americanization projects remain in the twenty-first century.

See also Education

SOURCES: Ganz, Cheryl R., and Margaret Strobel, eds. 2004. *Shaping Clay, Shaping Lives: Mexicans, Reformers, and Pottery at Chicago's Hull House, 1920–1940.* Urbana: University of Illinois Press; García, Mario T. 1980. *Desert Immigrants: The Mexicans of El Paso, 1880–1920.* New Haven, CT: Yale University Press; Ruiz, Vicki L. 1998. *From out of the Shadows: Mexican Women in Twentieth-Century America.* New York: Oxford University Press; Sánchez, George J. 1993. *Becoming Mexican American: Ethnicity, Culture, and Identity in Chicano Los Angeles, 1900–1945.* New York: Oxford University Press; Yohn, Susan. 1995. *A Contest of Faiths: Missionary Women and Pluralism in the American Southwest.* Ithaca, NY: Cornell University Press.

Vicki L. Ruiz

ANTONETTY, EVELINA LÓPEZ (1922–1984)

Educator and community activist Evelina López Antonetty is a woman of legendary status known to some as the "mother of the Puerto Rican Community" and to others as the "hell lady of the Bronx." Nobody was neutral about Antonetty. On a gray September day in 1933, Evelina López arrived alone in New York City aboard the boat *El Ponce*. She was ten years old and disembarked lamenting the loss of her long hair that had been cut before her voyage. The earliest impression of the drabness of her new surroundings remained in her memories forever. She had come to stay with her mother's sister, Vicenta, who lived in El Barrio, or

Spanish Harlem. Back in Ponce her mother Eva saved for boat fare to New York, but it was not until 1935 that she and her two younger daughters, Lillian and Elba, joined Evelina, thus beginning their new life as a migrant family in New York. Eva López worked long hours in the laundry room of the Hotel New Yorker to provide for her daughters and keep them in school.

As a young girl in East Harlem, Evelina López became the spokesperson for her neighbors, often helping them resolve problems with landlords and city agencies. Her sisters described López as courageous and quick to notice injustices. At the age of sixteen she and her sister Lillian joined the Young Communist League. She attended public schools and graduated from Wadleigh High School in Central Harlem. The depression and lack of money prevented her from going on to college.

From 1946 to 1956 Antonetty worked as a job developer and organizer for District 65, a militant union that organized small shops. She not only was instrumental in bringing more than 4,000 Spanish-speaking workers into the union, but also organized the Spanish Affairs Committee within the union. Mentored by community activists like Jesús Colón and Bernardo Vega, Antonetty developed into a formidable activist and community leader.

In 1965, frustrated by the lack of response on the part of the public school system to the needs of Puerto Ricans and other minorities, Antonetty joined forces with other parents to create United Bronx Parents (UBP), a grassroots organization dedicated to community development in the South Bronx area with special emphasis on educational reform. Under Antonetty's dynamic leadership UBP flourished, broadening its mission, adding new projects and constituencies that extended well beyond its Bronx headquarters, and providing technical assistance in parent training to diverse groups in New York and other cities. In 1970 UBP began to expand its program activities to other arenas, establishing a bilingual-bicultural day-care center, an adult education program, a youth leadership program, and a citywide summer lunch program. Antonetty was the executive director of UBP until her death in 1984.

Evelina López Antonetty at a rally. Courtesy of the Justo A. Martí Photograph Collection. Centro Archives, Centro de Estudios Puertorriqueños, Hunter College, CUNY.

Antonetty was greatly admired for her organizing skills and her understanding of political issues. She mobilized parents throughout the city for quality education, organized sit-ins against library closings, and was instrumental in the struggle for school decentralization and community control of schools. She was a forceful, persuasive, pioneering leader who was widely respected for her ability to bring people together. She is fondly remembered by many younger activists as an influential mentor and as a model for Puerto Rican leadership in New York.

Antonetty never earned a college degree, although she attended classes at Brooklyn, Hunter, City, and Manhattan Colleges. In 1970 she received an honorary doctorate of humane letters from Manhattan College and ever after was respectfully called Dr. Evelina Antonetty. She taught a course, the Puerto Rican Child in New York City Schools, in the Black and Puerto Rican Studies Department at Hunter College. Her affiliations and awards are numerous.

In 1990, six years after her death, a tribute celebrating her legacy was held in City College. The program focused on her efforts at coalition building and the social transformation of communities of color. In 2001 a play was produced titled *Evelina's Heart/El corazón de Evelina* that tells the story of her life accomplishments and reaffirms her important place in Puerto Rican community history. In memory of her achievements, the library and archives of the Centro de Estudios Puertorriqueños at Hunter College carry her name.

See also Education

SOURCES: Antonetty, Evelina López. 1997, 2001. Oral history interviews by Lillian López. Centro Archives, Centro de Estudios Puertorriqueños, Hunter College, CUNY; Maldonado, Adál Alberto. 1984. *Portraits of the Puerto Rican Experience.* Eds. Louis Reyes Rivera and Julio Rodríguez. New York: IPRUS Institute; Mohr, Nicholasa. 1993. *All for the Better.* Austin, TX: Steck-Vaughn; Rodríguez, Sandra, and Gloria Zelaya. 2001. *Evelina's Heart.* Multimedia play; United Bronx Parents, Inc. 1966–1989. Records. Centro Archives, Centro de Estudios Puertorriqueños, Hunter College, CUNY.

Nélida Pérez

ANTONIO MACEO BRIGADE (1977–)

After the revolution that took place in Cuba in 1959, both the United States and Cuba barred Cuban exiles from returning to visit their homeland. All that changed in 1977, when President Jimmy Carter lifted the ban on travel to Cuba, and the Cuban government invited a group of young Cuban professionals for a return visit. The group's members called themselves the Antonio Maceo Brigade (Brigada Antonio Maceo, BAM) after a black Cuban military strategist of the nineteenth century known for his fierce military fighting against Spain in defense of his homeland. The trip home marked a major turning point in the relationship of the Cuban government to its diaspora of exiles and immigrants. It also marked the first time that Cubans residing in the United States openly dared to break ranks with the more vocal and organized anti-Castro leadership in the Cuban exile community.

The Antonio Maceo Brigade was made up of fifty-five women and men—young professionals and students from the United States, Puerto Rico, Spain, and Mexico. They were united around a common theme: support for the normalization of relations between the United States and Cuba, lifting of the U.S. trade embargo against Cuba, and the cessation of hostile acts of aggression against Cuba by the U.S. government or members of the Cuban exile community. The brigade only accepted as members those individuals who had left Cuba as youngsters through parental decision, and who had not participated in acts of organized violence against the Cuban government. The latter conditions not only responded to restrictions set by the Cuban government itself as security measures, but also reflected the youthful idealism of the members of the BAM themselves. For the most part, the first BAM members, or *brigadistas,* had been activists against the Vietnam War, participants in progressive movements in the Puerto Rican and Chicano communities in the United States, or members of *Jóven Cuba,* a magazine for Cuban Americans.

But the driving force behind the first Antonio Maceo Brigade was really the members of *Aréito,* a magazine founded in 1974 by young Cuban intellectuals who had consistently advocated a rapprochement with Cuba. Cuba's Instituto Cubano de Amistad con los Pueblos extended the historic 1977 travel invitation to the members of *Aréito* magazine. Two women, in particular, were the principal movers and shakers behind *Aréito* and the organization of the first brigade: Lourdes Casal, Ph.D., and Marifeli Pérez-Stable, Ph.D. Casal, a black woman of considerable literary talent, is considered one of the most accomplished Cuban exile intellectuals of the period. She died only a few years after that historic trip. Pérez-Stable is a respected political science professor who now openly favors a U.S.-style democracy in Cuba.

The Antonio Maceo Brigade was organized in January 1978 upon the return of the *brigadistas* to the United States. Since then, hundreds of young Cubans who had spent most of their lives outside their homeland have returned to Cuba under its auspices in search of family and roots. For them, that return has been as emotionally charged as it was for the first *brigadistas.* The echo of the experience is summarized in what one of the first BAM members told the *New York Times* upon his return home: "The country is the people and the family we still have there. While we were there with our families, we were true Cubans, revolution or not, and there was an instant rapport."

In Cuba the first Antonio Maceo Brigade not only visited family and friends, but also met with top-ranking government officials, including Cuban president Fidel Castro. That first visit by Cuban exiles to their abandoned homeland opened the way for the Cuban government to relax its antagonism toward the exile community and led Castro to call for a dialogue between Cuba and Cubans living abroad. It resulted in agreements to release political prisoners and find ways of reuniting separated families and in new regulations to allow Cubans abroad to visit relatives in Cuba. In December 1978 three members of the first Antonio Maceo Brigade opened Marazul Tours, the first U.S.-based travel agency to arrange routine trips to Cuba, and another BAM member opened a similar agency in Puerto Rico.

But the attempt to establish a bridge to the homeland angered the anti-Castro leadership in the Cuban exile community. There were numerous sharp media attacks and even violence. In April 1979 Carlos Muñiz Varela was assassinated in Puerto Rico, and in November of the same year the Cuban terrorist organization Omega 7 took credit for the assassination of *dialoguero* Eulalio Negrín in West New York, New Jersey.

The Antonio Maceo Brigade continues to exist today, falling far to the left of the political spectrum of most groups in the Cuban American community. Although many former *brigadistas* publicly hold a more moderate and often critical political stance toward their country of origin, on one issue agreement is certain: After that first visit to Cuba by the Antonio Maceo Brigade in 1977, the lives of Cubans living on the island and their counterparts abroad were never the same again. Because of the Antonio Maceo Brigade, the divide between Cuba and its exile community was forever broken.

SOURCES: *Aréito.* 1978. Special edition entirely dedicated to the Antonio Maceo Brigade. 4 (Spring); Grupo Aréito. 1978. *Contra viento y marea.* Havana, Cuba: Casa de las Americas; Pérez-Stable, Marifeli. 1978. "Young Cuban Exiles Visit Homeland." *Guardian* (New York), March 8, 24; Smothers, Ronald. 1978. "Cuban Exiles Visiting Home Find Identity." *New York Times,* February 14, 37.

Dagmaris Cabezas

ANZALDÚA, GLORIA (1942–2004)

Descended from seven generations of ranchers in a small southern Texas ranching settlement known as Jesús María, Gloria Anzaldúa was born in 1942. The oldest child in a family of four, as an infant she developed a rare illness that caused her to have a menstrual period at the age of three months. According to Anzaldúa, "I started bleeding in my diaper and went into puberty when I was six." The resultant physical imbalances caused her to stop growing physically at the age of twelve. Acutely aware of her difference at an early age, Anzaldúa believes that "I was born a queer." This perception had both physical and political ramifications for the rest of her life.

Anzaldúa recalls that at about the age of eight "my coming to voice had to do with feeling oppressed because of race. I noticed very early on the difference between how the white kids were treated and how I was treated." Anzaldúa attended segregated schools until high school. She received her elementary education in a one-room schoolhouse where one teacher taught all the grades in Spanish.

Anzaldúa's thirst for knowledge and her budding intellectual efforts served as a double-edged sword. Although her schoolmates recognized her as "a brain," her teachers treated her intelligence as a novelty. Anzaldúa was aware early on of the racism that cast her as an exception to the rule for Mexicanas. Her intelligence also drew criticism from family members who considered her love for reading and writing to be unusual. Constantly ridiculed for her efforts, she nonetheless continued her studies. Anzaldúa recollects an image of herself as an "eighty pound kid who carried around the complete works of Aristotle." She always felt herself to be a philosopher trying to make sense of life.

By the time she was twelve, Anzaldúa's family moved to Hargill, Texas, and two years later her father died. In order to survive, she and her family labored as migrant workers. During this period Anzaldúa came to understand the social disparities and injustices of migrant life. The shock of her father's death worsened Anzaldúa's physical condition. The severity of her menstrual pain caused her to disassociate herself from her body and enter a fantasy world. "I would go into my imagination; I would go into the world of the book." Reading and writing allowed Anzaldúa to both confront and escape her realities. Anzaldúa found that she wrote most about what bothered her—"injustice against women." During this time she developed a consciousness about a family double standard that flagrantly privileged males. "I knew that in my culture the males were favored and I could see it in my own family." Although Anzaldúa esteemed her single mother's strength and hard work to keep the family together, she rebelled against her mother's attempt to impose strict and limiting rules of tradition on her daughters. Anzaldúa believes that Chicanas are influenced by many sectors that socialize girls into silence. The larger social message "calls for us to keep our mouths shut." Disrupting silence and asserting voice are issues that breathe through many of Anzaldúa's writings.

Anzaldúa continued to work in the southern Texas fields throughout high school and college while pursuing a B.A. degree from Pan American University. After graduating in 1969, she enrolled in an M.A. program in English education at the University of Texas, Austin, where she received her degree in 1972. Upon completion of her degree Anzaldúa was selected to teach migrant children in a Texas state education program. She then moved to Indiana and worked as the director of the Migrant Bilingual Program. In 1974 she began writing poetry. One of her first essays, "Growing Up Chicana," was written during this period.

In 1974 Anzaldúa entered a doctoral program at the University of Texas, Austin. However, she soon became disgusted with the narrow limitations of a department that did not recognize Chicana literature as a field. She left in 1977. This experience strengthened her resolve to devote herself to creative expression, and soon she was on the road to San Francisco, where she embraced a life of writing and in the process became one of the foremost Chicana writers in the nation.

Anzaldúa's work has inscribed an indelible mark on the American literary and political landscape. A Chicana lesbian, feminist, writer, theorist, and activist, Anzaldúa coedited *This Bridge Called My Back: Writings by Radical Women of Color* with colleague Cherríe Moraga. It became a groundbreaking book on feminism among women of color. Published in 1981, *Bridge* remains a cornerstone in explicating the unique social, cultural, and political foundations of Chicana feminism.

Speaking of her intense motivations for writing the book, Anzaldúa states, "For me the being different, the class thing, the being a little Chicanita, the gender thing, the race thing, the family, my father's death, just seeing what death and pain are like were motivations for me to write." San Francisco also ignited Anzaldúa's social consciousness, and she became active in a number of causes, including the United Farm Workers union. She also continued to work with migrant children. However, her involvement in the Feminist Writers Guild and the Women's Writers' Union brought her face-to-face with the racism and sexism in white, mainstream feminist organizations that further motivated her to edit *This Bridge Called My Back.*

Despite the positive popular recognition Anzaldúa

gained for her work, she continued to struggle with her family's negative reactions to controversial themes such as lesbianism, sexuality, and family relationships. Her family perceived such public disclosures of her personal life as a kind of cultural betrayal. "I was betraying the culture by exposing all these things." Anzaldúa remains philosophical about this contradiction and encourages Chicana writers to overcome such pressures and to challenge assumed roles.

Another important work published by Anzaldúa is *Borderlands /La frontera: The New Mestiza*. *Borderlands* constructs an important framework for negotiating a complex legacy of colonization and offers a new paradigm for transcendence in a form Anzaldúa refers to as "Mestiza Consciousness." It continues to be a primer for Chicana/o feminists, scholars, writers, and activists. Anzaldúa wrote *Borderlands* while living in Santa Cruz. She moved there in 1985 to complete a Ph.D. in the History of Consciousness Program at the University of California, Santa Cruz. Although she was an invited distinguished visiting professor in Women's studies, the program did not accept her because "they felt I was too established. . . . I didn't know enough theory and was too far behind and wouldn't be able to catch up. The final blow was the fact that I was a creative writer and they already had too many creative writers." Although she did not enter the program, Anzaldúa continued her goals and in 1990 published a sequel to *Bridge* titled *Making Face, Making Soul/Haciendo caras.*

Through her writing Anzaldúa hoped to give younger Chicanas a sense of continuity to the Chicana feminist and queer experience by telling them her stories. For her, "this is how I continue the Chicano struggle. I can use my writing as a feminist, as a queer and as a Chicana to question, to identify, and to open up minds."

Anzaldúa's most recent contribution to the field of feminist studies is *This Bridge Called Home: Radical Visions for Transformation,* coedited with Ana Louise Keating and released in 2002. According to Vanessa Bush, "this feminist anthology acknowledges the enormous contribution to feminist literature of the first *Bridge* and explores continuing challenges for feminist thought." On May 15, 2004, Gloria Evangelina Anzaldúa lost her struggle with diabetes and passed away at her Santa Cruz home.

See also Feminism; Literature

SOURCES: Anzaldúa, Gloria E. 1987. *Borderlands/La frontera: The New Mestiza.* San Francisco: Spillsters/Aunt Lute; ———, ed. 1990. *Making Face, Making Soul/Haciendo caras: Creative and Criticial Perspectives by Feminists of Color.* San Francisco: Aunt Lute; ———. 1994. Interview by Naomi H. Quiñonez, Santa Cruz, CA; *Dictionary of Literary Biography.* 1992. Vol. 122, *Chicano Writers, Second Series.* Detroit: Gale Research; Monaega, Cherríe, and Gloria Anzaldúa, eds. 1981. *This Bridge Called My Back: Writings by Radical Women of Color.* Watertown, MA: Persephone Press.

Naomi H. Quiñonez

APODACA, FELICITAS (1912–1997)

Community activist Felicitas Córdova Apodaca was born on March 6, 1912, in a small town outside of Guanajuato, Mexico. Her mother, Irene Santos Córdova, customarily left El Paso, Texas, for Mexico to deliver her babies surrounded by female relatives. Although her husband, Ignacio Córdova, did not approve, Irene traveled in the midst of the Mexican Revolution to deliver Felicitas, and it was six months before the infant was brought to El Paso.

Apodaca's father worked at the smelter outside of El Paso, and the family lived in company homes. Nevertheless, the industrious Ignacio began to buy property on Raynor and Central in El Paso, Texas, where the family eventually moved. Some of Apodaca's earliest remembrances are of this moving day. She believed that her family was rather grand using a horse-drawn wagon to carry their belongings and the small children, while her mother rode in a fringed black surrey. Apodaca recalled, as well, the large mounds of grease left over from the smelting of the ore.

It was perhaps an incident with the Migra (the INS Border Patrol) that influenced the girl to become fluent in English. One day while the women in the home were in the kitchen making Mexican sausage, La Migra invaded the house and took all the occupants away. Upon hearing the noise, the five-year-old Apodaca hid in the corral. Afterward she entered the kitchen and saw the pots boiling and her grandmother rocking in her chair. When Ignacio came home, he became angry, took the immigration papers to the detention center, and got the family released.

Ignacio encouraged his daughter, a perceptive child, to get a college education, promising that he would be there to play mariachis when she graduated. Apodaca never saw that day because her father died when she was in the eighth grade. Reading was her passion, and she often negotiated household chores in exchange for reading time. More acculturated than her siblings, Apodaca spoke both Spanish and English. She was proud of her Mexican heritage, relished the display of both the Mexican and American flags, and soon became the family's interpreter.

During the depression she attended El Paso High School, but dropped out one semester short of graduation. To help her widowed mother, Apodaca went to work. In 1937 she married Juan Apodaca. For thirteen years she was a traditional wife and mother. She man-

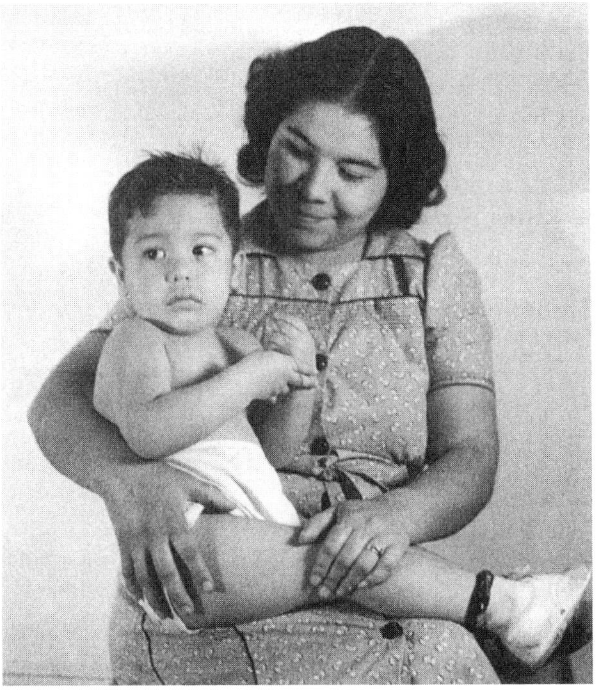

Felicitas Apodaca, circa 1940. Publicity photograph for El Paso Planned Parenthood. Courtesy of Linda Apodaca.

aged household finances and joined Planned Parenthood, becoming a poster mom with her son Juan. A resourceful woman, Apodaca earned extra money selling hosiery and clothes. She worked as a maid at the Campo Grande Motel on Alameda and, in time, was hired as a seasonal sales employee at the Popular, a leading area department store.

Apodaca experienced many changes in her life, moving from Texas to California as a middle-aged woman. Her work as an activist became her third career. She retired from Bonds Stores in 1973 and embarked on a new chapter in work and activism. Apodaca joined the Community Service Organization (CSO), a long-standing grass roots civil rights confederation in California, as a community development specialist. At the age of sixty-two, she began her work with the CSO chapter based in El Monte, a predominantly Mexican community near Los Angeles.

From her first day at the El Monte office, Apodaca fell into the rhythm of community work, organizing, activism, and peer counseling. To organize the El Monte chapter, Apodaca needed people, and so she recruited longtime customers from Bond into the CSO. She also recruited parents of students involved in the Young Adult Leadership Program sponsored by the CSO. Apodaca taught new members how to run meetings and elections themselves. With chapter members, Apodaca organized fund-raisers, youth activities, the annual Navidad en el Barrio (Christmas in the Neighborhood) pageant, and a food pantry for low-income residents. At the biweekly food pantry food was brought in from the main distribution center in Los Angeles and put into baskets. Apodaca coordinated these activities with the help of chapter members and also did the paperwork to verify the distribution of food. To her recollection, no one was ever turned away from the pantry.

Apodaca acquainted new members with the CSO's food co-op, buyers' club, death-benefit society, and credit union and also helped distribute groceries to members. Mexican immigrant families were introduced to banking by way of the CSO credit union. People who lived on minimum wages were able to save for cars and then purchase them through the credit union. Many of the people Apodaca worked with were undocumented immigrants for whom she provided consumer and paralegal information and family counseling. With advice from the CSO legal team, she helped families with financial planning, property investments, IRAs, mutual funds, and writing wills. She counseled women in abusive relationships by providing referrals to women's centers in the San Gabriel Valley. In addition, Apodaca helped families avoid foreclosures and maneuver through the maze of the immigration system.

This work gave her additional experience in advocacy, helping clients with unscrupulous lawyers who had been paid by the undocumented immigrants, but who had not provided the contracted legal services. Through these programs Apodaca often empowered her clients so they could advocate for themselves.

When Apodaca finally retired at the age of seventy-nine, she had not missed a day of work since 1950. Nor did she completely retire even then. Apodaca took classes at California State University, Los Angeles, and worked on a master's degree in sociology. Until the final days of her life, Apodaca was active in her community and with her family. She died on December 26, 1997.

Felicitas Córdova Apodaca was a feminist long before the National Association for Chicano Studies dedicated its 1984 conference to the issue of Chicana feminism. She empowered her children, nieces, and nephews to build a better life for themselves and their families. She empowered the disadvantaged and underrepresented to become part of the American fabric. Though she never became a U.S. citizen, she believed in the United States and its political processes. Above all, she had a deep commitment to education.

See also Community Service Organization (CSO)

SOURCES: Apodaca, M. Linda. 1999. "There Is Nothing as Gentle as Strength and Nothing as Strong as Gentleness: The

Life and Times of Felicitas Córdova Apodaca, 1912–1997." *Frontiers: A Journal of Women Studies*, 20:1 (Spring): 45–58; Rooke, Luisa. 1992. "Lessons—Old and New: 80 Year Old Still Learning, Shares Anti-drug Message." *San Gabriel Tribune*, July 21, D1.

Linda Apodaca

APRENDA Y SUPERESE (1965–1973)

During the second wave of post-Castro Cuban immigration to the United States (1965–1973), the federal government experimented with various programs to help Cuban refugees adapt to the U.S. labor market. Aprenda y Superese, also known as "Training for Independence," was one such program. Unlike the majority of job-training programs, which targeted male workers, Aprenda y Superese targeted Cuban women, particularly those who had signed up to receive assistance from the Cuban Refugee Program.

Because of the Castro government's restrictions, which prevented men of military age from emigrating, as well as political prisoners or those holding skills vital to the revolution, this second wave of Cuban immigration had a disproportionate number of women and elderly. Many Cuban women suddenly found themselves alone in the United States, or the sole support of their parents and children. Since three-quarters of Cuban women did not work outside the home prior to the Castro revolution, few had skills, job experience, or English fluency that they could successfully use in the U.S. labor market. The women who took part in Aprenda y Superese received intensive training in any of a number of skills, including hand and machine sewing, clerical work, nursing assistance, silk-screen art work, and domestic service. Day care was provided, as well as a monthly stipend to cover transportation costs to the training site. Upon completion of the course, the women agreed to resettle outside of Miami if jobs in the city were unavailable.

Aprenda y Superese was regarded as one of the most successful programs under the umbrella of the federally funded Cuban Refugee Program. It served as a model for the amended Aid to Families with Dependent Children (AFDC) program in 1968. Together with the other CRP programs, Aprenda y Superese was phased out by 1973.

SOURCES: García, María Cristina. 1996. *Havana USA: Cuban Exiles and Cuban Americans in South Florida, 1959–1994*. Berkeley: University of California Press; U.S. Cuban Refugee Program. 1968. *Training for Independence: A New Approach to the Problems of Dependency*. Washington, DC: Social and Rehabilitation Service.

María Cristina García

ARAGÓN, JESUSITA (19??–)

After learning the skill of midwifery from watching her grandmother, Hispanic New Mexican *partera* (midwife) Jesusita Aragón delivered more than 12,000 infants in her life. Aragón's clients were women who worked in ranching and subsistence farming and lived under extremely difficult conditions in the northern New Mexican frontier. Working and living on shared land marked by extended-family networks, patriarchal rulings, *patrones,* and folk Catholicism, Aragón delivered her first baby when she was fourteen. Unable to finish school, Aragón took over her grandmother's practice as a local *partera* and willingly devoted her life to the service of the community whose members sought her out to bless, heal, advise, and cure them day and night. Through Aragón's life one can learn about folk medicinal practices and the various ways in which *parteras'* skills and knowledge met the critical health and emotional needs of the Spanish-speaking community in New Mexico during the early and mid-twentieth century.

Stressing the importance of maintaining a balance between the natural and the supernatural, Aragón believed that her ability to cure others was a direct blessing from God that required her to be available to heal, treat, and pray over patients and their families at any time. Her methodology as a *partera,* which was supported by the larger *curandera* (healing) community, held diseases to be the result of natural imbalances, bewitchments, or punishments for sins. However, these could be effectively treated with knowledgeable use of herbal teas, cleansings, massages, and prayers to local saints.

Historian Fran Leeper Buss referred to Aragón as the last of the traditional Hispanic midwives in New Mexico, who learned the skills of midwifery and healing by riding along on horseback with her grandmother and helping her deliver the villages' babies. Aside from assisting her grandmother, Aragón also became an expert field worker, laboring in the fields with her father, who raised her like a boy and taught her how to protect herself from snakes, to work with wood, and to shoot weapons. Early in her childhood Aragón assumed the place of the oldest son in her family. Forced to leave school after completing the eighth grade, she helped her father herd sheep and goats in the seasonal rhythms of farm life. Growing up in the village of Trujillo, working in the fields, herding, planting, driving wool to the market, and assisting with deliveries, Aragón recalled a happy childhood with big fiestas, dancing, local fairs, sewing special gowns, and sharing good food.

Aragón's mother died at the age of thirty-four when Aragón was only ten. Raised by her grandparents and her father, she helped the family survive until she was sent away following two pregnancies outside of marriage. Ashamed and ostracized, she attempted to run away, but had nowhere to go, so she returned to the family home, where she was closely watched. When Aragón was able to afford it, she moved out of the family home with her three little children. She built her own home and decided to farm and work as a midwife. In order to support her family, Aragón cleaned houses, washed, and ironed in Trujillo until she moved with her three children to Las Vegas, New Mexico in 1952 so they could attend high school.

Recalling her experiences as a midwife, Aragón remembered riding long distances on horseback, wagons, or cars to help deliver babies. She confessed that sometimes her job had dangerous aspects, especially when she was following a strange man to his home, trusting that his wife was about to give birth. Aragón would always pray on her way to deliveries and remembered to bring along a clean white apron and to keep her nails trimmed. Aragón kept a meticulously clean delivery room in the back of her home. She made sure that her hands were soft and smooth and she tried to comfort stressed pregnant women by making them laugh and trying to distract them.

Aragón remembered that many mothers pinched, scratched, and yelled at her, often blaming her for their condition. Still, Aragón understood their anxieties and remained calm, especially when mothers tried to deliver breech babies. She was a skillful and experienced midwife, but when Anglo medical practices were introduced through nursing campaigns to educate and license *parteras,* she opted to refer difficult deliveries to the local hospitals to ensure a mother's safest delivery environment.

Aragón helped deliver babies and later in her career obtained a practicing license and joined a midwife club. She baptized babies, helped with adoptions, cared for children and mothers when they were sick, and suffered the painful and difficult experiences of losing mothers and babies in difficult deliveries. In these times of profound sadness, grandmothers were left with the grief of losing a child and the challenge of raising grandbabies at a late age. Because she understood her job as a *partera* as a blessing from God, she only charged fifty dollars for deliveries, and in difficult financial situations she delivered babies for free. Aragón also treated young women who were victims of rape, cured kids with *empacho* (food poisoning), and healed ulcers and illnesses through expert use of alcohol, *azafrán,* snake weed, *romerillo,* teas, and chamomile. To supplement her income, Aragón took in boarders who were outpatients from a local mental hospital. With the rise of birth control and the spread of institutional medicine, fewer mothers needed her help. Still, she remained in the area to take care of people, her family, and her ranch.

See also Medicine

SOURCES: Buss, Fran Leeper. 1980. *La Partera: Story of a Midwife.* Ann Arbor: University of Michigan Press; Comunicación e Información de la mujer. Ruiz, Miriam. 2002. "Las parteras: un trabajo historicamente despreciado." June 22. www.cimacnotlocas.com (accessed October 4, 2004); el-mundo.es (online newspaper based in Spain). 2002. "Vuelven las parteras." www.el-mundo.es (accessed October 4, 2004).

Soledad Vidal

ARBALLO, MARÍA FELICIANA (1762–?)

Known as the "Merry Widow" of California history, María Feliciana Arballo journeyed to California as part of Captain Juan Bautista de Anza's 1775–1776 colonizing expedition. Of Spanish birth and thus at the pinnacle of colonial society, this resident of Sinaloa was a rebellious teen who defied her parents by marrying a common mestizo soldier named Juan Gutiérrez. The couple had two daughters and had hoped to travel with Anza in search of a new life. Regrettably, her husband died before the expedition, but rather than remain behind, as Father Font suggested, Arballo convinced Captain de Anza that she and her daughters could complete the journey. With one daughter riding in front and the other in back, the three traveled by horseback all the way to California.

According to Antonia I. Castañeda, Arballo paid for her assertiveness and determination. Father Font rebuked her on several occasions throughout the journey; the most notable incident occurred on December 17, 1775, when the colonists staged a fandango (dance) celebrating the successful crossing of the treacherous Colorado River. Font grew increasingly angry and incensed with the colonists for their inappropriate celebration and suggested prayer rather than music and dance. Noting that she had had a bit too much to drink, he wrote about "a very bold widow [who] sang some verses that were not at all nice, applauded and cheered by the crowd." Although reprimanded and physically beaten for her actions, Arballo and her two daughters survived the journey and became permanent settlers in California.

While atypical in her willful independence, Arballo was representative of Spanish-speaking women's experiences in Spanish borderlands frontier society and particularly of the women who journeyed north to California. Statistically, Arballo deviated just slightly from the other women because twenty-nine of the thirty-four women on the Anza expedition were wives of soldiers. Their average age was twenty-eight; they had married in their mid-teens. At the time of the expedition they had been married an average of twelve years and had given birth to an average of four children. Most of the women were in the middle of their childbearing years, and eight of the thirty-four women were or became pregnant during the journey, but five had miscarriages, and one woman, Manuela Ygnacia Pineuleas, died in childbirth. No extended families joined the expedition, and as a result, wives were highly self-reliant, and older children were pressed into needed labor for household tasks.

While she statistically shared many common points with the other women, Arballo's actions reveal a strong, assertive, and headstrong woman who faced frontier hardships and changes of fortune with resolve and determination. As a widow, she was, ironically, in both the strongest and weakest social position a woman could occupy in Spanish/Mexican society. The fact that she constantly ignored Father Font's attempt to restrict and admonish her actions indicates a woman who made her own decisions.

The hardships of the journey failed to lessen Arballo's bold nature. On January 4, 1776, the expedition reached the San Gabriel Mission and rested before finishing the last leg of its journey to Monterey, California, but when it began the journey north, the expedition was missing Arballo and her daughters. She caused "a minor sensation" by remaining at the San Gabriel Mission and quickly marrying Juan Francisco López, a soldier, on April 7, 1776. She survived her second husband and on March 10, 1800, three months after López's death, married her third husband, Mariano Tenorio, at the fairly advanced age for the time of forty-eight. Arballo's life reveals that opportunities and good fortune were available to women on the far northern frontier, and some women made the best of them depending on their means and abilities, that is, if they were bold enough. She also leaves a lasting political legacy, because she became the grandmother of two California governors, Andrés and Pío Pico.

See also Spanish Borderlands

SOURCES: Bouvier, Virginia Marie. *Women and the Conquest of California, 1542–1840.* Tucson: University of Arizona Press; Castañeda, Antonia I. 1990. "Presidarias y Pobladoras: Spanish-Mexican Women in Frontier Monterey, Alta California, 1770–1821." Ph.D. diss., Stanford University; Taggert, Frederick J. 1913. *The Anza Expedition of 1775–1776, Diary of Pedro Font.* Berkeley: University of California Press.

María Raquel Casas

ARGUELLO, MARÍA DE LA CONCEPCIÓN (SISTER MARÍA DOMINICA) (1791–1857)

The life of María de la Concepción Arguello spans a period of sixty-seven years during which her native California evolved from Spanish colonial rule to Mexican rule to U.S. conquest in 1848. She was born in 1791 at the presidio in San Francisco, where her father, Don José Arguello, served as commandante. Commandante Arguello and his wife, María Ignacia Moraga, like many other military families during this period, represented and protected the Spanish Crown's interest in Alta California. They responded to the Spanish Crown's Reglamento Laws of the 1770s that promoted colonization in Alta California by establishing presidios and missions in the empire's far northern territories in an effort to discourage Russian, British, or French expansion. Arguello's life, as a member of a military family, reveals the varied roles of Spanish-speaking women in Alta California. In addition to the traditional roles of wife and mother, women in this frontier society assumed other responsibilities that were essential to mission and presidio self-sufficiency.

Arguello is best remembered as the "Juliet of California" as a result of her ill-fated romance with Count Nickolai Rezanov. In 1806 Count Rezanov, chamberlain to Czar Alexander I, sailed into San Francisco Bay, desperately seeking supplies for his starving Russian colony in Sitka, Alaska. Despite the Spanish Crown's ban on trade with Russia, Commandante Arguello allowed the Russians entrance in order to repair their vessel, as well as to obtain needed supplies. During the count's stay at the presidio, he was immediately taken with the commandante's beautiful daughter. The fifteen-year-old Concepción Arguello reciprocated his feelings, and anxious to secure a trading relationship with this Spanish outpost, the forty-two-year-old Rezanov asked for her hand in marriage. Although the count's proposal met with great disapproval from her parents and local priests, Rezanov's journal states, "her resoluteness finally overcame them all." It took a very strong and daring young woman to stand up to all the authority figures in her life.

Because the pope, the king of Spain, and Alexander I all would have to grant permission for the marriage, the two planned a ceremony to take place within two years upon Rezanov's return from Russia with the necessary dispensations. Because of a fatal accident in Siberia, he never returned to California. Concepción Arguello heard rumors of Rezanov's death two years after his departure.

The story of the young Spanish beauty falling in love with a Russian count has inspired literary figures such as Bret Harte, Gertrude Atherton, and Alberta Denis to pen highly romantic interpretations of the affair. While Denis implores, "Let us keep our romance," Hubert Bancroft pragmatically states that although he does not want to spoil a good story, the "celebrated courtship had a very solid superstructure of ambition and diplomacy." The strong-willed Arguello, however,

Artist rendition of María de la Concepción Arguello. Photograph by Jan Café. Courtesy of the Interfaith Center at the Presidio in San Francisco.

was not a pathetic and fragile young woman, nor out of sorrow did she don the nun's habit "in spirit" after her fiancé failed to return.

To focus on only one incident in her life negates her years of social service to the poor in both California and Mexico. In reality, she did not have the luxury of dwelling on her misfortune, because her father's reassignment to a post in Loreto caused great financial hardship. A robust and confident Arguello accompanied them to Loreto, becoming her parents' caretakers until their deaths in Guadalajara fourteen years later. As one of the few literate women in the area, she shared her knowledge with others. She certainly did not conform to Brigida Briones's observation that women of Alta California "were born and educated here; here they lived and died; in complete ignorance of the world outside." On the contrary, Arguello traveled up and down the coast of the Californias ministering to the poor as a secular nun.

Upon her return to California in the 1830s, she offered her assistance to the missions and the newly created diocese. From 1846 to 1850 she represented the Catholic presence in the region until a new bishop could be appointed. Although she was in her sixties, Arguello eagerly petitioned for admittance to the first convent in California in 1851. A year later she became Sister María Dominica, California's first native-born nun. She assisted in the establishment of the order's new headquarters and school in Benicia, where she remained until her death in 1857. Forty years of lifelong service to her family, community, and church and her role as an educator in early California certainly eclipse the romantic image as the "Juliet of California."

See also Spanish Borderlands

SOURCES: Arguello, María Dominica, Sr. Correspondence. Dominican Convent Archives, San Rafael, CA; Bancroft, Hubert Howe. 1886. *History of California*. Vol. 11. San Francisco: History Company; Castañeda, Antonia. 1988. "Comparative Frontiers: The Migration of Women to Alta California and New Zealand." In *Western Women: Their Land, Their Lives,* ed. Lillian Schlissel, Vicki L. Ruiz, and Janice Monk. Albuquerque: University of New Mexico Press; ———. 1990. "Presidarias y Pobladoras: Spanish-Mexican Women in Frontier Monterey, Alta California, 1770–1821." Ph.D. diss., Stanford University.

Yolanda Calderón-Wallace

ARÍAS, ANNA MARÍA (1960–2001)

Anna María Arías was the founder of *Latina Style* magazine, the premiere national magazine for professional Hispanic women. Born and raised in San Bernardino, California, Arías came from a politically active family. Her father, Jesse, was the first Latino city council member in San Bernardino, and her mother was elected to the same seat in 1995.

From early childhood Arías was outgoing and dynamic. In high school she was a cheerleader and student body officer. After a trip to Hawaii as a teenager, Arías was deeply drawn to the state and decided to enroll at Hawaii Pacific University. After obtaining her B.A. degree in communications, she won a fellowship in 1988 from the Congressional Hispanic Caucus Institute (CHCI) that brought her to a position at CNN's Washington, D.C., office.

Opinionated and energetic, Arías was well suited for the city's competitive, political atmosphere. Soon after she arrived, she met numerous influential members of the Latino community. Always drawn to stories of accomplished women, Arías developed a passion for Latina advocacy. She believed very strongly in promoting the position of Latinas through economic empowerment and through greater representation of professional Latinas in the national media.

Anna María Arías. Courtesy of *Latina Style* magazine.

From the moment she arrived in Washington, Arías enjoyed a varied and accomplished communications career. She worked as a radio news anchor, newswriter, and media and campaign organizer for presidential and local candidates at the Democratic National Committee. She was also a member of CNN's *Crossfire* program.

Arías earned a respected reputation for her work in the Hispanic media and served for five years as managing editor of *Hispanic* magazine. Her editorial direction and keen insight into the issues affecting the Hispanic community were instrumental in making the publication one of the most respected media vehicles in the Hispanic market. However, she was struck by the exclusion of Latinas from the general market media and even from the Hispanic media. Her experience inspired Arías to produce a publication that would address that inequality by promoting a positive and accurate image of Latinas. With only her family's support and a small inheritance from her father, Arías took on the arduous task of publishing a start-up magazine. Working intensely from her small apartment with just one computer, she began designing the magazine that would become her life's mission.

In October 1994 Arías launched *Latina Style* magazine. In her seven years at the helm of the publication, Arías was able to establish a relationship with Latina readers that remains unsurpassed. To this day the magazine is the only national publication that is 100 percent Latina owned. *Latina Style* is the first national magazine that covers issues pertinent to the contemporary, professional, Hispanic working woman from a Latina point of view. Today, with a national circulation of 150,000 and a readership of more than 600,000, *Latina Style* reaches the Latina professional, business owner, and college student with all the information she needs to succeed in her endeavors. Through special programs like the *Latina Style* Business Series and the *Latina Style* Special Report of the top fifty companies for Latinas, the magazine maintains an active relationship between its readers, political leaders, and the corporate world.

During her years at *Latina Style* Arías bravely fought a seven-year battle with aplastic anemia. However, she refused to let her illness affect her joy in life or her desire for success. Her determination paid off both in the growth of her magazine and in public recognition of her work. She received many accolades, including the Washington Hispanic Chamber of Commerce's 1999 Entrepreneur of the Year. She counted among her many admirers members of Congress, community leaders, corporate executives, and former Second Lady of the United States Tipper Gore. After her death Congresswoman Nydia Velázquez remarked about Anna María Arías: "She was an amazing woman, a loyal colleague, and a first-rate editor. . . . *Latina Style,* a smart, witty, colorful magazine, is a real reflection of Anna María and what she represented. She was a real inspiration for Hispanic women everywhere."

In many ways Arías lives on through her magazine, her outreach programs, and the scholarships named in her honor. These include the GM–Anna María Arías Communications Scholarship, the CHCI Anna María Arías Trailblazer Scholarship, the MANA (a National Latina Organization)/State Farm Insurance Companies Scholarship, and the Anna María Arías Memorial Business Fund Awards. In the words of Congressman Silvestre Reyes, "The same hope, excitement and joy shared by Anna María will shine bright as others follow in her footsteps to ensure that the Hispanic community and Latinas specifically, are properly represented in all spheres of society."

SOURCE: Anna María Arías Memorial Foundation. www.annamariaarias.com (accessed September 10, 2004).

Julia Young

ARIZONA ORPHAN ABDUCTION (1904–1906)

The dramatic story of the Arizona orphan abduction in 1904 began in New York City. There, in the late nineteenth century, child welfare advocates developed a system of "rescuing" the city's so-called orphans by shipping them west on orphan trains. Most of the children shipped out were not orphans but children of poor single mothers who could not manage to support their offspring and had no welfare programs to help them. The so-called rescuers were motivated not only by sympathy for the children but also by their desire to combat disorder and violations of what they considered proper family values among the poor, to rid the city of undesirables, and to avoid spending tax money on aid to the poor. Most of these orphans were Catholics, while the leading child savers were Protestants who placed the waifs in Protestant homes. To the Catholics, this policy seemed a form of genocide. In response, the Irish Sisters of Charity opened the New York Foundling Hospital, which proceeded to run its own orphan trains, placing children in Catholic homes in the West.

In 1904 a priest from two small towns, Clifton and Morenci, Arizona, rounded up parishioners to volunteer to take forty orphans aged two to six. A group of Irish Catholic children was shipped out on September 25, accompanied by three sisters, three nurses, and one male logistics agent. When they arrived, the priest gave the children over one by one to their assigned foster mothers.

But the New York Catholics did not understand who the Arizona Catholics were. The Clifton and Morenci Catholics were, of course, all Mexicans. The twin towns Clifton and Morenci had arisen around copper mines and smelters, and their combined population of 4,500 to 5,000 was at least 65 percent Mexican.

The nuns thought that they were placing poor Catholic children with poor Catholic parents, but the Clifton and Morenci Anglos saw "white" children being given to Mexicans. They organized an "indignation" meeting and threatened the Foundling Hospital's staff with tarring and feathering and even lynching. The Anglo women began to convince each other that placing the white children with Mexicans was a form of child abuse from which the children needed "rescue," and they mobilized Anglo men to form a posse. This group of twenty-five went to the Mexican homes and kidnapped the children at gunpoint. The men delivered the children to the Anglo women, who kept some for themselves and distributed others among the Anglos, and all refused to give them back to the Foundling Hospital.

The nuns, meanwhile, had capitulated to the Anglos' racist complaints. They agreed to take all the children back to New York and re-place them with suitable "white" Catholics, but now the Anglos would not give up the children. Their defense consisted of vile allegations about the housekeeping standards and morals of the Mexicans, a defense that simultaneously reflected and constructed an ideology of Mexican inferiority. The Foundling Hospital brought suit, and the case made its way through three layers of courts, ending at the U.S. Supreme Court in 1906. All the courts ruled in favor of the vigilantes and allowed them to keep the children. The legal logic included several abstruse points, but the central finding rested on the best-interests-of-the-child doctrine and was accompanied by an explicit statement about the unfitness of Mexicans as parents to "white" children. The vigilante families kept the children forever.

The case illustrated some of the peculiarities of racial formations in the United States. The U.S. government had officially categorized Mexicans as "white." This logic stemmed partly from the Treaty of Guadalupe Hidalgo, which had conferred U.S. citizenship on residents of the territory taken from Mexico. Since the law at that time allowed only whites and blacks to become naturalized citizens, the fact that Mexicans were citizens seemed to make them white. To Arizona Anglos by the turn of the century, Mexicans were not "white" and were rapidly being segregated. In contrast, the Irish orphans were by no means entirely white in New York—they were said to be "of the Irish race."

The most resonant aspect of this case was the Anglos' sincere conviction that Mexicans could only be inferior parents, not qualified to raise "white" children, and that the whites had a responsibility to "protect" the children. This perspective has led throughout the world to abduction of the children of subordinated peoples by dominant peoples—a practice used against Aborigines in Australia, American Indians in the United States, Irish in the United Kingdom, Sephardic Jews in Israel, antidictatorship activists in Argentina, and, in a well-known individual case, the Cuban boy Elián González in Miami.

SOURCES: Gordon, Linda. 1999. *The Great Arizona Orphan Abduction.* Cambridge, MA: Harvard University Press; Heyman, Josiah McC. 1991. *Life and Labor on the Border: Working People of Northeastern Sonora, Mexico, 1886–1986.* Tucson: University of Arizona Press; Rubio-Goldsmith, Raquel. 1994. "Seasons, Seeds, and Souls: Mexican Women Gardening in the American Mesilla, 1900–1940." In *Women of the Mexican Countryside, 1850–1990,* ed. Heather Fowler-Salamini and Mary Kay Vaughan, 140–156. Tucson: University of Arizona Press; Ruiz, Vicki. 1998. *From out of the Shadows: Mexican Women in Twentieth-Century America.* New York: Oxford University Press.

Linda Gordon

ARMIÑO, FRANCA DE (C. 1900–19??)

The available details about Franca de Armiño's life are still very sketchy. She worked as a tobacco stripper (*despalilladora*) in Puerto Rico and was one of the most active feminists in the island's socialist labor movement during the 1910s and 1920s. This was a period of intense labor unrest on the island when Puerto Rican women workers joined men in the socialist Federación Libre de Trabajadores (Free Federation of Labor) and participated in many of its sponsored strikes, demonstrations, and organizing activities. Both men and women workers were combating the low wages and exploitative working conditions in the sugar, tobacco, and needle industries mostly controlled by U.S. absentee corporations and Creole proprietors.

In 1919 the Primer Congreso de Mujeres Trabajadoras (First Congress of Women Workers) was held in Puerto Rico to define an agenda focused on the needs of women workers. Franca de Armiño was a delegate to the congress representing women workers from the town of Cataño. One of the congress's results was the founding, a year later, of the Asociación Feminista Popular (Popular Feminist Association) aimed at securing equal rights for women, including the right to vote. Franca de Armiño was elected president of this working-class suffragist association. As a result of the efforts of both working- and middle-class suffragist organizations, Puerto Rican women were first allowed to vote in 1929 when suffrage was granted to literate women. It would take six more years before the passage of an amendment to allow universal women's suffrage.

During her years of labor activism in Puerto Rico, Armiño published a few articles in *Justicia* (Justice), the workers' leading newspaper. Her article "A la mujer obrera" (To the Woman Worker) argues for the need for women workers to come together, assert their rights as citizens, and demand social justice. In her own words: "La Organización se impone. Sin Organización no hay salvación" (Organizing is the rule. Without organizing there is no salvation).

Armiño migrated to New York during the years of the Great Depression, but little has been discovered about her activities in the U.S. metropolis, except for the self-publication of her play *Los hipócritas: Comedia dramática social* (The Hypocrites: A Social Drama) in 1937. According to its introduction, *Los hipócritas* is a drama dedicated to "the oppressed and all those who work for ideas for social renovation." Thus this work is a continuation of the author's earlier ideological stances and labor activism. The play focuses on the clashes between the poor and the wealthy and ends with a call for a socialist workers' revolution. The action begins with the Great Depression of 1929 that shattered the lives of most workers worldwide, and takes place in a Spanish setting shortly before the outbreak of the civil war between Republicans and fascists. It was also during this period that a large number of Spanish exiles began to come to New York, and this perhaps explains the chosen thematic focus of Armiño's play. In the inside cover of *Los hipócritas* it is mentioned that the author was working on three other works—a book of poems, a collection of essays, and another play—but so far these works have not been found.

See also Journalism and Print Media; Theater

SOURCES: Armiño, Franca de. 1937. *Los hipócritas: Comedia dramática social.* New York: Modernistic Editorial; Kanellos, Nicolás. 1993. *The Hispanic-American Almanac.* Detroit: Gale.

Edna Acosta-Belén

AROCHO, JUANITA (1910–1998)

A pioneering presence in the Puerto Rican community of East (Spanish) Harlem, Juanita Arocho was a dedicated organizer and *independentista* who worked for the rights and freedoms of Puerto Ricans both on the island and in her adopted home of New York. An active political figure, she was in addition an integral member of the Orden de la Estrella de Oriente, a local Puerto Rican Masonic order that figured prominently in both her personal and political activities.

Born in Lares, Puerto Rico, in 1910, Arocho migrated to the United States in 1933 on the USS *San Jacinto,* joining the many other Puerto Ricans who took advantage of increased steamship travel between New York and the island to seek better opportunities abroad. Settling with her mother on 112th Street and Seventh Avenue, Arocho quickly became active in community and independence politics. Taking impetus from her work on the women's right-to-vote campaign in Puerto Rico and the inspirational political work of Pedro Albizu Campos, Arocho was involved in the founding of Casa Borinquen, la Asociación Cívica Lareña, and the Comité de Manhattan del Partido Independentista Puertorriqueño, of which she was president. She also worked as a political assistant to Congressman Vito Marcantonio, who represented East Harlem, during three of his campaigns, starting in 1936. In addition, Arocho was an active journalist and wrote weekly columns for a number of Spanish-language newspapers. These columns included commentaries on the state of women in the Puerto Rican community, editorials, and discussions of community events.

In the course of her political and community work Arocho became acquainted with such figures as the poet Julia de Burgos, political leaders Pedro Albizu Campos and Gilberto Concepción de Gracia, political prisoner and nationalist Lolita Lebrón, and political activists Erasmo and Emilí Vando. Of particular note was her relationship with Albizu Campos, who looked to her to heighten the awareness of women's issues in the independence movement.

Juanita Arocho (sitting in the middle) and other members of the Orden de la Estrella de Oriente. Courtesy of the Justo A. Martí Photograph Collection. Centro Archives, Centro de Estudios Puertorriqueños, Hunter College, CUNY.

In 1948 Arocho married Homero Rosado. He was also active in independence and nationalist circles, and the couple supported each other's efforts toward the empowerment of Puerto Ricans in New York and on the island. In 1959 they moved to Brooklyn, where they resided for the rest of their lives. Arocho remained with her husband until his death in 1994.

Juanita Arocho died on August 22, 1998, in Brooklyn, New York. A seminal presence in the *pionero* community of East Harlem and the general Puerto Rican community of New York, she left a legacy exemplified by her extensive community work and support for the independence of Puerto Rico. A collection of Arocho's memorabilia is held at the Library and Archives of the Center for Puerto Rican Studies at Hunter College, City University of New York. It provides but a hint of the extent of her activism and is supplemented by interviews that are part of the Centro Oral History Project.

SOURCE: Arocho, Juanita. 1940–1994. Papers. Centro Archives, Centro de Estudios Puertorriqueños, Hunter College, CUNY.

Mario Ramírez and Pedro Juan Hernández

ARROYO, CARMEN E. (1933–)

Carmen Arroyo is the first and only Puerto Rican woman elected to the New York State Assembly and also the first Puerto Rican woman elected to any state assembly in the United States. She represents the Eighty-fourth Assembly District, which includes the South Bronx, Mott Haven, Melrose, and part of Highbridge. Describing Arroyo, the *Village Voice* calls her "a mixture of political pragmatism and deep sense of moral responsibility." She was born in Corozal, Puerto Rico, in 1936, where she lived a life of struggle and raised seven children, often as a single parent. She arrived in New York in 1964 intending to find her husband, who had come to the city and stayed several years before. Instead, she found a man no longer interested in maintaining a relationship. In her own words, "When I found him, he was drinking, had a negative attitude. . . . And I said no. I don't need this." Rather than return to the island, Arroyo found a job at a bookbinding factory in the Bronx, saved enough money to send for her mother and children, and established a new life in New York City.

When Arroyo's mother and oldest daughter returned to Puerto Rico, Arroyo found herself unable to care for the children and work at the same time. Unable to find day-care services, she quit her job and applied for public assistance, a situation that continued for nine months until her youngest child was in school. An involved, outspoken figure in her children's education, Arroyo soon became adept at managing the systems of welfare and the politics of the New York City schools. She became an advocate for others in both arenas and in the process laid the foundations for a career in politics. The welfare experience was humiliating for Arroyo. She recalls, "But it was training for me. I went to school; I learned English and I got involved in the community." She organized a welfare mothers' organization, the South Bronx Action Group, that succeeded in attracting funding for subsidized housing and helped prepare women on welfare for employment. In addition, Arroyo became involved in Democratic Party politics and helped launch the careers of local politicians. Among the many politicians endorsed by Arroyo was the young Herman Badillo, who went on to become the first Puerto Rican congressman in the U.S. House of Representatives. "In those days," Badillo remembers, "it was mostly women who filled the volunteer pools; men just liked making the speeches." For Arroyo, the political system became an important venue for community advancement.

Throughout the 1970s Arroyo continued to work in party politics and to expand her own opportunities.

She graduated from Hostos Community College with an associate's degree in 1978; two years later, at forty-four years of age, Arroyo earned the baccalaureate degree from the College of New Rochelle. Arroyo became the executive director of the South Bronx Community Corporation, a nonprofit social service organization, and chairperson of School Board 7. In both positions Arroyo's contribution was tempered by her own experiences as a struggling welfare mother and a commitment to bettering the life of those around her. She established senior citizens' food programs, promoted health issues, worked in drug rehabilitation, and continued to work closely with the district's assemblymen.

From 1978 until 1993 Arroyo served as district leader of the then Seventy-fourth Assembly District. She sat on the Lincoln Hospital Advisory Board for seventeen years. In 1973 Governor Nelson Rockefeller appointed Arroyo to the New York State Medicaid Council.

In 1994 Arroyo ran in a special election called by Governor Mario Cuomo to replace the district's assemblyman. Arroyo won the election with 50 percent of the vote and the support of the Bronx Democratic Party establishment. In 1998 she won reelection with 98 percent of the vote. She serves on the following committees: Alcoholism and Drug Abuse, Children and Families, Education, and Aging. Arroyo's political positions have not always found favor within the party. A pro-choice advocate, Arroyo also considers herself a Catholic. She is among the most respected political leaders in the state. Her determination to advocate for others remains her primary focus.

SOURCE: New York State Assembly. 2005. Official Biography of Assemblywoman Carmen E. Arroyo, 84th Assembly District, New York. http://assembly.state.ny.us/mem/?ad=084&sh=bio (accessed June 15, 2005).

Virginia Sánchez Korrol

ARROYO, MARTINA (1937–)

Gifted soprano and distinguished professor of music at Indiana University Martina Arroyo was born in Harlem in 1936 during the Great Depression. Her father, Demetrio Arroyo, who hailed from Puerto Rico and was a mechanical engineer employed by the Brooklyn Navy Yard, provided a stable home environment for his family. Martina's mother, Lucille Washington, came from Charleston, South Carolina. Lucille taught Martina to play the piano and encouraged her passion for performing. With few black or Puerto Rican role models in the world of classical performance, Arroyo's zeal was greatly driven by film musicals popular in the 1940s and 1950s. "I had a lot of dreams when I was a kid, and my mother humored them," explained Arroyo in a *New York Times Magazine* interview. Nonetheless, her mother also instilled the idea that Arroyo should have a career to fall back on in case the stage was unattainable. An exceptionally bright student, Arroyo graduated from the prestigious Hunter High School and majored in romance languages and literature at Hunter College. Following her mother's sound advice, Arroyo prepared herself for a teaching career.

In college Arroyo joined a graduate-level opera workshop and impressed the director, Joseph Turnau, with her abilities. He subsequently arranged a meeting with Marinka Gurewich, a noted voice teacher who accepted Arroyo as a student. Turnau, Gurewich, and Thea Dispeker, Arroyo's concert manager, remained with her from those first encounters and throughout her career. But in those early college years opera was not a serious option for Arroyo, and the dearth of black women opera singers failed to offer an optimistic picture of singing as a profession. It was not until 1952 that the Puerto Rican soprano Graciela Rivera debuted at the Metropolitan Opera House in *Lucia di Lammermoor,* and it was not until 1955 that Marian Anderson also sang there. Licensed to teach high-school literature, Arroyo accepted a position in the Bronx but continued to train with Gurewich. An effort to devote more time to her music led to another position with the New York City Welfare Department as a case worker. Arroyo immersed herself in the process of helping others.

Her big break came in 1958 when she sang an aria from *Aida* in the Metropolitan Opera's Auditions of the Air competition. Awarded $1,000 and a scholarship, Arroyo embarked on the study of German, English diction, drama, and fencing. The following year she debuted at Carnegie Hall in *Assassinio nella cattedrale* and received critical acclaim from the press. Resigning from her position with the Welfare Department, Arroyo officially entered the world of classical performance with an overseas tour of European opera houses singing minor roles. Arroyo earned a reputation for dependability and for tackling difficult roles. In Italy she met and married violist Emilio Poggioni and joined the Zürich Opera Company. Soon thereafter, according to a *New York Times Magazine* interview, a visit to her family in Harlem opened a whole new chapter in her career.

As the story goes, she received a call from Rudolf Bing, general manager of the Metropolitan Opera, which she immediately assumed was a hoax. He invited her to substitute for the suddenly ill soprano Birgit Nilsson as the lead in *Aida.* Clearing up the embarrassing situation, Arroyo debuted at the Met on February 4, 1965. The audience's standing ovation at the final curtain was extraordinary and convinced Bing to offer her a contract with the company. Arroyo's career soared. Rave reviews and recording contracts accompanied her interpretations of the works of the masters. At London's Covent Garden she appeared as Valentine in *Les Huguenots* and was the first Puerto Rican/African American artist to portray Elsa in *Lohengrin.* A series of triumphs throughout the years brought fame on both sides of the Atlantic, and Arroyo also became a celebrated personality in popular culture through numerous appearances on national television. Marking his 1,000th performance with the New York Philharmonic, Leonard Bernstein specifically invited Arroyo, one of his favorite singers, to perform with him in concert.

Married for a second time to financier Michel Maurel, Arroyo maintains residences in New York City, where she keeps in touch with the old family neighborhood from time to time, and in the Caribbean. Remembering her own experiences as a child in Harlem, she is acutely aware of the importance of role models in all professions and devotes time to Hunter College, where she sits on the board of trustees, and the Carnegie Hall board. Nowhere is this sentiment more pronounced than in an interview with *Opera News,* in which Arroyo posits the importance of extending a helping hand to young generations of opera hopefuls.

SOURCES: Cole, Thomas. 1968. "Martina, You Watch What You Say, Hear?" *New York Times,* April 28, sec. 1, p. 21; Levy, Alan. 1972. "Life at the Opera with Madame 'Butterball.' " *New York Times Magazine,* May 14, 20, 26–31, 38; Story, Roslyn M. 1991. "Positively Martina." *Opera News,* September, 26–28.

Virginia Sánchez Korrol

ARTISTS

Latina visual artists offer a wide range of expression representative of the cultures from which they derive their inspiration. As a result, it is as problematic to define what constitutes a Latina aesthetic as it is to circumscribe the parameters of what it means to be a Latina in the United States. Their aesthetic products describe the many ways in which women of Latin American descent interpret and reinvent the quotidian elements of their lives. Because the traditions that form the basis of Latina artistic expression are so varied, many artists enjoy success in a variety of art forms. They excel as printmakers, easel and wall painters, sculptors, photographers, textile artists, and crafters of *papel picado* (intricate paper cut-outs), as well as creators of assemblage, digital, conceptual, and installation art. As a result, there are many cultural influences woven into the tapestry of Latina visual artistry.

In spirit and articulation, Latina artistic production is rooted in the many ethnic heritages found in the Americas. Some artists speak directly to the role of *mestizaje* in the development of Latina/o identity. One such work, *Un nuevo mestizaje: The New Mix* (1987–2001), an oil-on-canvas and oil-on-wood series by Chicana artist Margaret García, is comprised of sixteen canvases. García's painting borrows from caste-system typographies created in the Americas during the eighteenth and nineteenth centuries. Illustrations depicting different visages were labeled and positioned in a social hierarchy that valued the lightest complexion. In opposition to this racial phenotypic hierarchy, García's paintings present an intensely humane visual accounting of the ethnic complexity that shapes contemporary Latina/o identity.

Numerous inspirational elements are blended in varying amounts within Latina visual art. The outcome is complex, rich, and deeply rooted in the cultural elements—indigenous, African, and Spanish; modern, traditional, handmade, mass produced, emotive, and intellectual—that form a multifaceted foundation. Exemplary utilization of a nontraditional genre that repositions traditional iconography is seen in the work of multimedia Chicana artist Alma López. Her *Lupe y Sirena* (1999–2000) digital print series juxtaposes two popular images in Mexican culture: the Virgen de Guadalupe and the mermaid, or *la sirena,* from the bingo game, *la lotería.* One print in the series situates the figures in an alluring environment and, in doing so, evokes an erotic atmosphere. López says of this print, "In *Lupe & Sirena in Love* (2000) they embrace, surrounded by angels with the Los Angeles cityscape and the U.S./Mexico border as their landscape. Guadalupe and Sirena stand on a half moon held by a Viceroy butterfly instead of the traditional angel."

Another example of a traditional form redefined through its juxtaposition within a contemporary medium is the *Totem* series created by Cuban artist María Martínez-Cañas. This series derives its inspiration from the indigenous totem pole, whose function is to narrate the story of a clan, family, or community. Yet Martínez-Cañas's work is not the usual carved wooden form; instead, she creates a series of collaged fragments, including personal photographs and reproductions of ancient manuscripts and cartographic illustrations, duplicated as contact prints on photographic paper. Her silver print *Totem Negro XVI* (1992) recollects her search for an ethnic identity.

For many Latinas, artistic expression often emerges from concerns about human welfare and social justice. The vernacular aspects of life inspire artists to tell the stories of ordinary people in the course of everyday life: factory workers and farmworkers, domestics in the home, teachers in the classroom, and cultural workers in public venues. The resulting artistic representations depict women and men clothed not in military uniform, but in the uniform of service work. The heads of their subjects are crowned not with feathers, but with sweat, and the hands of their subjects are raised not in the rage of battle, but in the task of daily labor. These highly accessible images belie complex social and political significance.

Juana Alicia's mural *Las lechugeras* (1983), Yolanda López's digital print *El trabajo de las mujeres no termina nunca: Homenaje a Dolores Huerta* (1995), and the mural masterpiece *Latinoamerica* (1974) created by Las Mujeres Muralistas, a Chicana/Latina group, all draw inspiration from the role that Latinas play in the labor force. Using a less polemical but no less potent approach, the work of Carmen Lomas Garza captures the fantastical delight and mystery found in everyday domestic life. She calls upon childhood memories for her inspiration. Such a moment is seen in her gouache-on-paper *Tamalada* (1987), in which she details the multigenerational, multifaceted work that takes place when families gather together for the making of tamales. For historical scale, particularly in documenting Latinas/os' contributions in Los Angeles, the work of Chicana muralist Judith Francesca Baca is unparalleled. Although disparate in presentation, all of these artists' works are evidence that it is possible to relay the historical development of the Latina/o communities without relying on a reductive heroic saga that forecloses the contributions of numerous individuals.

Many Latina artists locate themselves as agents of social change operating within various liberation movements. These identities are rooted in the social activism of the 1960s and 1970s when such expression assumed a scope of mass mobilizations. This period serves as an activist antecedent for popular political expression among Latinas/os in the United States today. Latina artists who came of age during this time responded to the social and cultural potency of the time in their artistic expressions. Inspirational social justice issues for Latina artists included the farmworker struggles, civil rights, student protests, antiwar demonstrations, and land-grant concerns. Two works on paper that capture different expressions from the period are *Libertad* (1976), a lithograph by Ester Hernández that recasts the Statue of Liberty as an Amerindian stele being carved by a Chicana who foregrounds a contemporary skyline, and Linda Lucero's *Lolita Lebrón* (1978), a silk-screen print that foreshadows the U.S. Latina/o activism of the 1980s and 1990s that occurred in response to U.S. military intervention in Latin American countries such as Jamaica, Cuba, El Salvador, Nicaragua, Chile, Peru, and Colombia.

Because of the civil unrest that results from such intervention, Latin American artists have frequently sought asylum in the United States from their native lands. Such artists include Salvadoreña Martivón Galindo, whose monoprints *Mujer Maya devorada por los perros* (1998) and *Fuga del mito* (1998) are influenced by the social conditions that exist in her homeland of El Salvador. Chicana artist Yreina Cervántez expresses the solidarity between Chicanas/os and the people of Central America in the title and imagery of her silk-screen print *El pueblo Chicano con el pueblo centroamericano* (1986). In Cervántez's work recurrent images of Rigoberta Menchú, Augusto Sandino, and Che Guevara border an urban landscape through which Chicanas/os traverse. Their means of travel is the ubiquitous automobile, whose bumper sticker displays an anti-intervention message.

Although struggles exist around the sexual politics of the various liberation movements, Latina artists receive encouragement for their involvement as creative contributors to the movements. The holistic meld of their artistic talent and social consciousness results in artwork that functions as a form of critical reflection. Some Latina artists emerged from predominantly male organizations with painting styles so strong that their work is readily identifiable. Such Chicana artists include Irma Lerma Barbosa, Lorraine García, and Celia Rodríguez from the Royal Chicano Air Force (RCAF), Judith Hernández from Los Four, and Patssi Váldez from ASCO, a cutting edge East Los Angeles art collective.

The autobiographical paintings of Mexican artist Frida Kahlo established the representational foundation for some of the late-twentieth- and early-twenty-first-century artistic production by Latinas in the United States. Artists influenced by Kahlo's work recognize her dual aesthetic commitment to political action and cultural allegiance. The simultaneity of Kahlo's representations depicts the celebrations and challenges of being Latina. Artists such as Chicanas Barbara Carrasco, Diane Gamboa, and Xochitl Nevel Guerreo, as well as Costariqueña Marta Chávez and Chilena Paula Pía Martínez, have produced profoundly emotive and thoughtful autobiographical works. In Carrasco's silk screen *Self-Portrait* (1984), she illustrates herself as a runner breaking the finish-line tape in a race against time. Instead of breaking a sweat, the paintbrush she holds aloft like a victory torch splashes color against a calendar whose days are being rolled out of existence by a giant paint roller. Her image reminds us that there is little leisure time for Latina artists. As Ester Hernández quips "All of my work is done with a child in one hand, a brush in the other."

Photography is another medium used for autoreflective narratives. Chicana photographers Laura Aguilar, Christina Fernández, Delilah Montoya, and Kathy Var-

Looking at the Primitive. By and courtesy of Delilah Montoya.

gas demonstrate the breadth of form, style, and worldview possible in this singular genre. Aguilar's provocative self-portraiture, such as that found in *Three Eagles Flying* (1990), *In Sandy's Room* (1990), and *Don't Tell Her Art Can't Hurt* (1993), draws upon her identity as a Chicana lesbian artist. Aguilar's intimate work contrasts with Fernández's stylized figurative approach exemplified by her series *María's Great Expedition* (1995), whose sociohistorical presentation provides the backdrop to her visual narrative. Montoya presents her abstracted figurative prints as installation art, as in the case of *Shooting the Tourist* (1995), an antidocumentarian work. Vargas, best known for her compelling use of multiple exposure and text, as in the series *My Alamo* (1995), brings to her art a Tex-Mex influence that derives from living on the border. Parallel in spirit is the *Arbol de la vida* (1977) series of the now-deceased interdisciplinary Cuban artist Ana Mendieta, who produced as a sculptor, as well as a conceptual and performance artist. Mendieta's performance piece, which she documented as a series of photographic prints, placed her nude body, covered in mud, against a mammoth tree trunk. Mendieta both emerges from and is engulfed by the power of the tree as she demonstrates the essential connection between nature and human life.

Latina artistic production is embedded within the overarching social and cultural structures and pressures that result from mainstream racism and misogyny. Paramount for success as a working artist is identifying and affiliating with mentors. In their quest to develop as mature artists, Latinas are challenged by the persistent lack of mentors who understand artistry culled from traditions other than mainstream culture and shaped by the unique vision that springs from being a woman of Latin American descent. Novelist Ana Castillo dramatically illustrates how some Latinas are unable to overcome the paucity of support and the social pressure placed on them for their gender-role transgressions when she says: "Many women who showed great creative promise did not continue. Some were forced to stop. Some went mad. Others died." In an effort to sustain their artistic impulses and find rigorous critical commentary, some Latina artists form collective organizations. One such group of middle- to elder-aged Chicanas based in Sacramento, California, Co-Madres Artistas, has worked together since 1992. Their success as a collective is due in large measure to the strength of presentation derived from their cooperative art-making processes and the commercial success of their paintings. As one member of the group says, "Solo, we are not that important. But, as Co-Madres we are giants. We belong as a whole to the community."

Latinas also form alliances with feminists, most notably with other women of color, as a means of gaining

Sewa Virgen. By and courtesy of Consuelo J. Underwood.

support and inspiration; these collaborations frequently result in hybridized expressions that reflect the cultural traditions of contributing artist members. The mural *Maestrapeace* (1994) was painted by the multicultural, multiracial group of the same name and is described as the "largest mural in the San Francisco–Oakland Bay Area." The group counts among its seven members Chicana artists Juana Alicia and Irene Pérez.

Artistic embellishment of everyday goods also provides for an outpouring of expression that celebrates life and self. Quilts, serapes, rebozos, *arpilleras, comida, altares,* and *monitos* are but some examples of the material culture that is incorporated into Latina artistic expression. This particular formulation of visual art provides the means for their largely Latina/o audiences to contextualize and reflect on the daily realities of their lives. Consuelo Jiménez Underwood, a textile artist, combines elements of quilt making with *colcha* embroidery and graphite illustrative work in the piece *Virgen de los Caminos* (1994) and creates a powerful work of art that conveys the dangerous act of crossing the physical and psychological borders separating the United States and Mexico. Textile art also serves as a form of historical memory and sustainable development for those who elect to work cooperatively within a traditional framework in the application of contemporary design. Tierra Wools, a northern New Mexico–based weaving collective of Hispanas founded in 1992, is unique for its growth as an arts and cultural group that enjoys success as an economic development venture providing college credits and employment for its member weavers.

Hybrid formulations of contemporary form and traditional iconography are also apparent in the works of installation and conceptual artists. The art of Amalia Mesa-Bains elicits praise for her use of abstract concepts embedded and presented within readily accessible formulations. Cuban artist Coco Fusco presents her installation and performance pieces as satirical challenges to mainstream notions of Latina identity. Working on a more intimate scale, Chicanas Celia Alvarez Muñoz, Santa Barraza, and Patricia Rodríguez and Puertorriqueña Marina Gutiérrez create works that hearken to the ex-voto or *retablo* traditions. Their allegorical, multimedia boxes depict the miraculous occasions found in the secular sphere rather than the usual telling of the religious moment.

Among the emergent generation there are those Latina artists whose works resist traditional boundaries of expression and sources of inspiration. These artists pull from animation and cartoon or anime (futuristic Japanese animation) for their inspiration and frequently rely on contemporary processes of creation such as *gicleé* (a high-resolution digital print process). One such Chicana artist, Camille Rose García, is described as deploying "personally edgy contemporary iconography and language" as she "explores themes of invasion and replication" in intriguingly titled paintings such as *Cherry Girls vs Contaminatron, Creepcake Annihilation Plan,* and *Parasite Eradication Squad.*

Ana Mendieta, Silueta, Mexico, 1971. Courtesy of the *Estate of Ana Mendieta Collection*. Galerie Lelong, New York.

It is important to restate that Latina visual artists are prolific and multidimensional and reframe their forms of expression as their artistic trajectories shift in interest. No one artist or group of artists can stand as the essential representatives of Latina aesthetic expression. The approaches and articulations of Latina artists share only the coincidence and richness of complexity born from a hemisphere of influence. What this artistry might be said to hold in common is that the works cause their audiences to marvel at the vibrancy of each piece.

SOURCES: Arnoldo, García, and Elizabeth Martínez, eds. 1993. "A Salute to Latinas in the Arts." *Crossroads Magazine: Contemporary Political Analysis and Left Dialogue,* May; Goldman, Shifra. 1994. "Mujeres de California: Latin American Women Artists." In *Dimensions of the Americas: Art and Social Change in Latin America and the United States.* Chicago: University of Chicago Press; Guzmán, Juana. 1987. *Latina Art: Showcase '87/ Arte de Latinas: Muestra '87.* Chicago: Mexican Fine Arts Museum; Ochoa, María. 2003. *Creative Collectives: Chicana Painters Working in Community.* Albuquerque: University of New Mexico Press; Smithsonian Institute Latino Art

Archives. http://artarchives.si.edu/guides/latino (accessed January 8, 2003).

María Ochoa

ASOCIACIÓN NACIONAL MÉXICO-AMERICANA (ANMA) (1949–1954)

As the cold war and McCarthyism intensified their grip on the domestic life of the United States in the late 1940s and 1950s, Mexican Americans organized to challenge what many regarded as their status as second-class citizens. One such group, the Asociación Nacional México-Americana (ANMA), was formed in 1949 as a progressive and leftist civil rights group with a significant multiethnic coalition base. The association promoted immigrant rights, cultural and social rights, political representation, and opposition to the Korean War. By 1950 ANMA boasted a membership of more than 4,000, with thirty or more locals throughout the Midwest and Southwest. Mexican American women gained prominence within the association as leaders, intellectuals, and organizers. In the struggle for first-class citizenship, these women challenged racial, class, gender, and sexual barriers that circumscribed their daily lives.

ANMA women brought significant experience in progressive and radical political activism. Some had long advocated the development of a national organization for the defense of the Mexican American community. Few exemplified this more than Francisca Flores. Born in 1913 and reared in San Diego's poorest barrios, Flores was profoundly influenced by the political climate within the barrios following the Mexican Revolution. She moved to Los Angeles during the 1940s, a time of heightened anti-Mexican sentiment. In 1943 twelve Mexican American youth were unjustly convicted of murder in what was called "The Sleepy Lagoon Case." Francisca Flores joined a grassroots defense committee, composed of such prominent activists as Josefina Fierro and prominent author Carey McWilliams. This committee generated visibility for the defendants' plight and raised money for their appeal. In 1944 the 2nd District Court of Appeals overturned their convictions. The case and the defense committee would be memorialized in the popular 1979 play *Zoot Suit*. Francisca Flores emerged as a local civil rights leader during her work with the Sleepy Lagoon Defense Committee. She became a mentor to young Mexican American activists who looked to her for intellectual guidance and inspiration. Ralph Cuarón, an organizer with the furniture workers and ANMA's first national youth director, remembered that Flores introduced him to the political milieu of the Left in Los Angeles.

Flores supported grassroots democratic projects and organizations that educated the Mexican American electorate and working class. She was a board member of the statewide California Legislative Conference and worked as an instructor for the California Labor School. In 1949 she taught a course on the problems of Mexican American people and methods for organizing this community. At ANMA's founding national convention in October 1950, she and Alfredo Montoya, the national president, coauthored a pamphlet, *Towards the Unity of the Mexican People in the United States,* that outlined the group's long history of struggle and resistance. Despite her poor health stemming from tuberculosis at a very young age, she remained active and a key figure influencing the course of Mexican American intellectual development, leadership, and political activism.

Isabel Gonzáles and Virginia X. Ruiz also gained prominent positions on ANMA's national executive board. A longtime activist in Denver, Colorado, Gonzáles operated an agency that provided social services to the Mexican American and immigrant communities. Described as a firebrand, she frequently spoke and wrote critically of the nation's racist policies that forced Mexican Americans into the margins of society. A regular outlet to the public was a local publication out of Denver called the *Letter;* she was on its editorial advisory board. In 1949 Gonzáles was elected first vice president of ANMA's executive body. In the same year Virginia X. Ruiz became secretary general of the national executive board. Highly visible and active, Ruiz addressed issues of civil rights, immigration policies, and the plight of immigrant workers. She spoke for the repeal of the 1940 Smith Act, the first peacetime sedition act in American history; the 1950 Internal Security Act; and the 1952 Immigration and Nationality Act.

Others involved in ANMA's formative phase included Celia Luna Rodríguez and her sister, Julia Luna Mount. Both supported unionizing efforts and civil rights. Active in regional and state conventions, the sisters spearheaded the organization of the Eastside chapter and held offices in the organization. Julia was secretary-treasurer to the southern California regional office; María Galloway was vice president; and Celia became vice president of the national office.

ANMA represented a new spirit that was moving Mexican American communities to resist oppressive conditions nationwide. It reached out to other communities of color, such as African Americans, to form progressive coalitions. Unfortunately, ANMA's activities raised the ire of anti-Communist and conservative groups that readily labeled the association as subversive and anti-American. By 1954 ANMA could no longer withstand the continued harassment of the Immigration and Naturalization Service, local police, and federal and state investigative committees charged with ferreting out Communist organizations. The association fell into disarray and never recovered.

SOURCES: Acuña, Rodolfo. 2004. *Occupied America: A History of Chicanos.* 5th ed. New York: Longman; García, Mario T. 1989. *Mexican Americans: Leadership, Ideology, and Identity, 1930–1960.* New Haven, CT: Yale University Press; Ruiz, Vicki L. 1987. *Cannery Women, Cannery Lives: Mexican Women, Unionization, and the California Food Processing Industry, 1930–1950.* Albuquerque: University of New Mexico Press; Vargas, Zaragosa, ed. 1999. *Major Problems in Mexican American History.* Boston: Houghton Mifflin.

Enrique M. Buelna

ASPIRA (1961–)

ASPIRA was founded as a nonprofit community organization in 1961 by the Puerto Rican educator and activist Dr. Antonia Pantoja and other community leaders. The name ASPIRA is derived from the Spanish verb that means "to aspire." The group's stated goal was and continues to be the socioeconomic development of the Puerto Rican community in the United States through the education of its youth. According to Pantoja, a staunch supporter of education, "ASPIRA's program is based on the absolute belief that there is only one certain avenue remaining for the Puerto Rican to lift himself out of the grip of poverty—education." ASPIRA's primary objectives are high-school retention, college placement, and college retention. It operates a wide range of programs and services for Puerto Rican and other Latino young people and their families, including educational counseling, academic tutoring, and information about financial assistance. ASPIRA also sponsors parent workshops.

An important aspect of its mission was to foster cultural awareness and pride in Puerto Rican identity through social activities and Puerto Rican history and culture classes. The organization continues to do that but has broadened its focus in recent years to include other Latino communities. Funded originally by private foundations and corporations, ASPIRA has subsequently been supported by government money, as well as continued foundation and corporate support. ASPIRA first operated in Manhattan but later expanded to four borough offices throughout New York City. In 1968 it became ASPIRA of America and established centers in New Jersey, Pennsylvania, Chicago, and San Juan, Puerto Rico. Throughout the years ASPIRA has served many thousands of Puerto Rican and Latino students and has sought to influence public education policy through its efforts as a pressure and interest group. A prime example of this was its successful 1972 class-action legal suit brought in partnership with the Puerto Rican Legal Defense and Education Fund against the Board of Education of New York City for failing to educate the city's limited-English-speaking children. The result was the ASPIRA Consent Decree that established bilingual education in the city's public school system.

ASPIRA recognizes that its achievements can only be acknowledged within the context of progress against unequal access to adequate schools, decent housing, good jobs, and better business and career opportunities. Several generations of *aspirantes* or ASPIRA alumni, now found in leadership positions in local, state, and national government, the health professions, universities, schools, and law and corporate offices, attest to the organization's success.

See also Education

SOURCES: ASPIRA of New York. 1974. Annual Report; Santiago Santiago, Isaura. 1981. *ASPIRA v. Board of Education*

ASPIRA founder Antonia Pantoja (seated in the middle with a black vest) with organizers and *aspirantes*. Courtesy of Centro Archives, Centro de Estudios Puertorriqueños, Hunter College, CUNY.

of the City of New York: A History and Policy Analysis. Ann Arbor, MI: University Microfilms International.

Carlos Sanabria

ASPIRA V. NEW YORK CITY BOARD OF EDUCATION (1972–1974)

On September 20, 1972, ASPIRA, a Puerto Rican community educational organization, employing attorneys from the Puerto Rican Legal Defense and Education Fund, filed suit against the Board of Education of the City of New York. This class-action suit alleged that as a result of their ethnicity and language, 182,000 Puerto Rican children of little or no English-language ability in the New York City public schools were being discriminated against and denied an equal educational opportunity because they were unable to understand their teachers or read their textbooks. The plaintiffs argued that the city's school system had failed to provide adequate educational programs to meet these student's special pedagogical and cultural requirements. ASPIRA petitioned the court to order the board of education to initiate bilingual education programs as the only way to satisfactorily meet the needs of non-English-speaking Puerto Rican children in the public schools.

As a result of the suit, an agreement known as the ASPIRA Consent Decree was signed by both parties on August 29, 1974. This decree provided that the New York City Board of Education would establish and implement a bilingual education program and that it would identify students whose limited English-language proficiency precluded them from completely availing themselves of the education being offered. Instructors and support personnel would be provided to all children entitled to the program. Moreover, the consent decree promoted minimum educational standards to be met by all districts in the school system and stipulated that a maximum effort be made to obtain the needed financial resources and the number of teachers required to implement a bilingual program by September 1975.

The policies on special educational programs that resulted from *ASPIRA v. Board of Education* augmented national rulings and laws, among them *Lau v. Nichols* and the Civil Rights Act of 1964, on the rights of language-minority children. Federal policy now mandated federal aid to hundreds of school districts throughout the nation to provide language-minority students with equal opportunities for full participation in the educational process.

See also Bilingual Education

SOURCES: Santiago Santiago, Isaura. 1978. *A Community's Struggle for Equal Educational Opportunity: ASPIRA v. Board of Education*. Princeton, NJ: Educational Testing Service, Office for Minority Education; ———. 1981. *ASPIRA v. Board of Education of the City of New York: A History and Policy Analysis*. Ann Arbor, MI: University Microfilms International.

Carlos Sanabria

AVILA, MARÍA ELENA (1953–)

Born on April 18, 1953, in a small village in Guanajuato, Mexico, María Elena Avila has become one of the most successful Latino entrepreneurs in Orange County, California. She and her brothers, the children of Salvador and Margarita Avila, own and operate the popular Avila's El Ranchito restaurants, with ten locations in southern California. A former bracero, her father brought the family to the United States when María Elena was only five years old. With the help of relatives, the Avilas put down roots in Huntington Park, California, and there in 1966 her parents, borrowing pots and pans, started their first restaurant. Her mother was the cook, her father, the janitor, and her grandfather, the dishwasher. After school and on weekends, María Elena and her siblings (three brothers and one sister) went to work at the family restaurant. Her parents taught the children the importance of family unity, faith, hard work, and cultural pride. In María Elena's words, "I know first hand what it means to be an immigrant."

In 1974 María Elena Avila started her first restaurant. Although she was only twenty-one years old and a single mother, she was determined to succeed in business despite her father's misgivings. "After I got divorced, my dad said, 'Honey, you're a woman. You don't belong in the restaurant business. You can't run the restaurant on your own. We'll take care of you and your daughter.' But I said, 'I've got a daughter to support and I'm going to make it.' So I rolled up my sleeves and I was determined." She continued, "I saw my mom as a partner in the business; I had her as a role model." Avila owns Avila's El Ranchito in Costa Mesa and the family catering business. As the keeper of her mother's cherished recipes, she oversees the quality control at all of the restaurants. In addition, she has tinkered with a few of the dishes over the years in order to create more heart-healthy versions that remain true to authentic flavors.

María Elena Avila is one of the area's most recognized Latina civic leaders. For example, she has served as a founding member of the Orange County Hispanic Education Endowment Fund and the Latino Leadership Council. A devout Pentecostal, Avila credits her success as a businesswoman, philanthropist, and mother to her Christian faith. She is justifiably proud of her daughter Elizabeth, who is now an attorney. A tireless fund-raiser for college scholarships, Avila has partici-

María Elena Avila, a successful Latina entrepreneur, with her daughter Elizabeth. Courtesy of María Elena Avila.

pated on a number of local university boards. Since 2001, she has been the *madrina* of the University of California at Irvine's Community Outreach Partnership Center, which engages faculty, staff, and students in applied research, service learning, and outreach activities that foster community development through initiatives that promote collaboration, inspire civic engagement, and advance the cultural, social, and economic welfare of neighborhoods, focusing on Orange County. Reflecting on her family's business philosophy, María Elena Avila stated, "They're not just restaurants. . . . They are an extension of our family."

See also Entrepreneurs

SOURCES: Avila, María Elena. 2004. Interview by Vicki L. Ruiz, August 23; Newspaper clippings on María Elena Avila (private collection of María Elena Avila); Tertrault, Sharon. 2003. "Orange County Families: The Avilas." *Orange Coast,* March, 152–156.

Vicki L. Ruiz

AVILA, MODESTA (1867–1891?)

Modesta Avila was born into a ranching family in 1867. Her kin lived on a small plot of land in southern California's San Juan Capistrano that they owned until about 1888 and continued to occupy and cultivate after having sold it. This land and the region's cultural and gender politics thrust Avila into the center of a dramatic tragedy of great personal and symbolic import.

In 1889, when Avila was in her early twenties, some of the region's Anglo residents wanted to secede from the larger Los Angeles County and create Orange County. Rapidly populating the area, migrants of all origins joined Mexicans who had been there for generations. More often than not, the newcomers did everything possible to acquire (or appropriate) Mexican-owned land. Among those who looked voraciously at the region were the owners of the railroad companies who sought to spread their tracks into the south.

Modesta Avila and the Santa Fe Railroad almost literally collided shortly before Orange County was created. The railroad, increasingly the most powerful economic interest in southern California, expanded over people's property without permission or recompense, and in Avila's case the Santa Fe did just that: their tracks ran through her former property, and she had no say in the matter. Nonetheless, like many others violated in this way by the powerful railroads, Avila objected strenuously. Sometime in June 1889 she challenged the railroad through a gesture that would come back to haunt her a few months later. She laid a railroad tie or a wooden post across the tracks that passed through her property. It is said that she attached a paper to the post on which she had written, "This land belongs to me!" Shortly thereafter she informed a railroad agent, and he removed the tie before a train passed.

Four months later the newly elected sheriff of the recently created Orange County, together with the newly elected district attorney, had Modesta Avila arrested and charged her with obstructing a railroad track. She was tried before a jury twice; the first trial ended in a hung jury, and the second with her conviction on November 1, 1889. (It is interesting to note that between the first and second trials, people had learned that Avila was pregnant, a socially unacceptable condition for a young single woman in nineteenth-century San Juan Capistrano.) Avila was sentenced to three years in the California State Penitentiary at San Quentin, where she joined a handful of other women imprisoned there.

There is every reason to believe that the sequence of legal events that occurred four months after Avila's symbolic protest was connected to the fact that Orange County's criminal justice apparatus had yet to accomplish a successful prosecution. Its first felony trial had culminated earlier with an acquittal, and county leaders were anxious to show the state leaders that they could make a strong stand against crime. Avila thus became the vehicle for polishing Orange County's law-and-order image. It did not hurt the prosecution's cause that Avila was portrayed in the press of the time as a loose woman, nor that she was one of many Mexicans who had once owned land.

Her lawyer, George Hayford, represented her during her two trials at no cost to her and continued to help

Modesta Avila when she was incarcerated in San Quentin. Courtesy of California State Archives.

her while she was at San Quentin. He petitioned unsuccessfully for a writ of habeas corpus in February 1890 and subsequently petitioned two governors, again unsuccessfully, for a pardon. Hayford argued that Avila's conviction was more a reflection of the community's moralistic disapproval of her unwed pregnancy than of the strength of the criminal case against her. He also maintained that Orange County's political leaders needed a conviction on the books in order to measure up to the larger and more established Los Angeles County from which they had seceded. Finally, he accused Avila's father of having misled her as to her rights as a property owner, implying that the father had received some benefit by allowing the railroad to build tracks on the land.

In any event, Avila remained in San Quentin, and prison records show that she was discharged on March 3, 1892, eight months before the end of her three-year sentence. Other sources, however, allege that she died in prison. Indeed, her obituary appeared in the *Santa Ana Standard* on September 26, 1891.

Modesta Avila led a short life, one that might have gone unnoticed but for her short burst of celebrity, the stark symbolism of her spontaneous protest against the violation of her rights, and the brutal punishment she received for it. While the details of her death are not chronicled, and even the details of her daily life are unknown, the image of that young and fearless female David challenging the railroad Goliath is appealing and dramatic. Her actions ensure her a place beside thousands and thousands of nameless Chicanas and other Latinas who have stood up to demand their rights.

SOURCE: Haas, Lisbeth. 1995. *Conquests and Historical Identities in California, 1769–1936*. Berkeley: University of California Press.

Victoria Ortiz

AZTLÁN

Scholars generally believe that the word Aztlán derives from *Aztatlan,* a Nahuatl-language contraction of two words: *aztatl,* which means heron, and *tlan,* which means close together. According to the oldest Mexica sources, which became known and transcribed after the 1521 Spanish conquest, Aztlán was described as a place in Mexico's north, populated by many white herons, with seven caves, and surrounded by water. Those who interpret the details of Aztlán literally place it variously in Lake Chapala in the Mexican state of Jalisco, in Puget Sound near Seattle, Washington, in New Mexico, and on the island of Mezcaltitlán in Nayarit, Mexico.

Even to the Aztecs themselves, Aztlán was already a place deeply shrouded in mythology and little concrete reality by the fifteenth century. Sometime between 1440 and 1469, for example, Moctezuma Ilhuicamina, the Mexica ruler, is said to have summoned his priests, hoping to learn what was known of their place of origin. According to Fray Diego Durán, who recounted this story in 1581, the royal historian Cuauhcóatl appeared before Moctezuma Ilhuicamina to explain:

> Our forebears dwelt in that blissful, happy place called Aztlán, which means "Whiteness." In that place there is a great hill in the midst of the waters, and it is called Colhuacan because its summit is twisted; this is the Twisted Hill. On its slopes were caves or grottos where our fathers and grandfathers lived for many years. There they lived in leisure, when they were called Mexitin and Azteca. There they had at their disposal great flocks of ducks of different kinds, herons, water fowl, and cranes. . . . Our ancestors went about in canoes and made floating gardens upon which they sowed maize, chili, tomatoes, amaranth, beans and all kinds of seeds which we now eat and which were brought here from there. However, after they came to the mainland and abandoned that delightful place, everything turned against them. The weeds began to bite, the stones became sharp, the fields were filled with thistles and spines. They encountered brambles and thorns that were difficult to pass through. There was

> no place to sit, there was no place to rest; everything became filled with vipers, snakes, poisonous little animals, jaguars and wildcats and other ferocious beasts. And this is what our ancestors forsook. I have found it painted in our ancient books. And this, O powerful king, is the answer I can give you to what you ask of me. (Durán 1964, 134)

While a few other historical sources from the colonial period offer more details on Aztlán, most are highly suspect because they are thoroughly saturated with Spanish influences and tell more about Mexica acculturation under colonial rule than about any authentic pre-Columbian past.

In 1885 William G. Ritch, then secretary of the Territory of New Mexico and the recently elected president of the New Mexico Bureau of Immigration, issued a promotional book on the resources of New Mexico titled *Aztlán: The History, Resources and Attractions of New Mexico,* which was meant to attract Anglo immigrants to the territory. Published in more than 100,000 copies, the book asserted that archaeologists generally agreed that Aztlán was "near the portion of New Mexico and Arizona bounded by the 35th and 37th parallel of latitude." The bulk of *Aztlán* was devoted to a glorious description of all the resources and opportunities that awaited American immigrants, promising investment returns as high as 80 percent. "Rich mines are found in almost every direction . . . our mountains contain illimitable treasures, in the shape of lead, iron, copper, silver, mica and gold, and in the near future this beautiful country is destined to be known as the true El Dorado."

The fantasy of Aztlán that William G. Ritch cultivated was one in which Anglos would become so numerically dominant that they would subordinate the Mexican and Indian residents of the territory, and that New Mexico would become a state. Ritch promised Anglo immigrants a place "on the *top of the ladder,*" but if they were "not prepared to take their place *at the top,* it would have been better if they stayed away." Through Anglo industry, individualism, and republican spirit New Mexico would be brought into the "last" epoch of history, to be ushered in by the "advent of the ever restless and irresistible American, to whom has been reserved the gigantic task of developing the illimitable resources of this most wonderful country, and by whom, eventually, the entire universe will be enriched in a most material manner."

Aztlán was a particularly poignant example of how a myth was selectively appropriated, reinterpreted, and selectively transformed to serve concrete political gain far from central Mexico. In 1885 William G. Ritch wanted to attract immigrants to New Mexico so that Anglos would outnumber Hispanos to create an Anglo-dominated state. Indeed, Ritch accomplished his goal in 1912.

For Chicanos and Chicanas, Aztlán is both a very specific geographic concept, which encompasses the southwestern states of the United States, and a very general sentiment, a national sense of belonging to an oppressed racial group that yearns for the return of their homeland known as Aztlán. This specific place and general sentiment came to consciousness among Chicanos in 1967 because of the writings of a San Diego, California, poet known simply as Alurista. In 1967 Alurista picked up a copy of *Life* magazine that contained an article on the discovery of the main altar of the Aztecs' high temple in Mexico City when the underground metro was being constructed in preparation for the 1968 Olympics. The article reported that the Aztecs had come from Aztlán, which was generally believed to exist somewhere in northern Mexico, perhaps even in the U.S. Southwest. Alurista was so intrigued by what he learned that he began to wax lyrically in his poems about Aztlán as the stolen homeland of Chicanos that he and others hoped would soon be returned, if necessary as the result of a national revolution.

Embracing cultural nationalism, Chicano students sought to reclaim a glorious Aztec past. Courtesy of the Denver Public Library, Western History Department.

Alurista's role in placing the concept of Aztlán into circulation was certainly catalytic, but it was not until March 1969, at the National Chicano Youth Liberation Conference in Denver, Colorado, organized by Rodolfo "Corky" Gonzales, that Aztlán took concrete form in the ideology of the Chicano radical students gathered there. With more than 1,500 persons in attendance, representing more than 100 different student groups from all over the United States, the participants declared their quest for nationhood and announced that Aztlán was the stolen homeland they wished restored. Articulating their demands in a conference manifesto, which they called *El plan espiritual de Aztlán* (The Spiritual Plan of Aztlán), they proclaimed:

> We, the Chicano inhabitants and civilizers of the northern land of Aztlán, from whence came our forefathers, reclaiming the land of their birth and consecrating the determination of our people of the sun, declare that the call of our blood is our power, our responsibility, and our inevitable destiny.
>
> We are free and sovereign to determine those tasks which are justly called for by our house, our land, the sweat of our brows and by our hearts. Aztlán belongs to those who plant the seeds, water the fields, and gather the crops, and not to the foreign Europeans. We do not recognize capricious frontiers on the Bronze Continent.
>
> Brotherhood unites us and love for our brothers makes us a people whose time has come and who struggle against foreigner "Gabacho," who exploits our riches and destroys our culture. With our heart in our hands and our hands in the soil, We Declare the Independence of our Mestizo Nation. We are a Bronze People with a Bronze Culture. Before the world, before all of North America, before all our brothers in the Bronze Continent, We are a Nation, We are a Union of free pueblos, We are Aztlán. (Valdez and Steiner 1972, 402–403)

Within a month of the Chicano Youth Liberation Conference in Denver, the Chicano Coordinating Council on Higher Education (CCHE), a network of faculty, students, and staff in California institutions of higher education, organized another conference, this one on the campus of the University of California, Santa Barbara, in April 1969. The goal of the group was to improve Mexican American access to higher education through the elaboration of curricula and appropriate support services. Armed with *El plan espiritual de Aztlán,* brought by some of the student activists from Denver, the students at the conference made their first order of business the adoption of a militant identity and name that would unite many different student organizations into a national force. Many students were determined that whatever name was chosen, it had to include Chicano and Aztlán. After much debate they chose to call themselves el Movimiento Estudiantil Chicano de Aztlán (the Chicano Student Movement of Aztlán), referred to by the acronym MEChA, which literally means matchstick. Through MEChA students orchestrated and coordinated their curricular and pedagogical demands at various colleges and universities across the land. If by the early 1970s many Chicano studies programs looked similar in shape, content, and outreach activities, it was because students had been successful in imposing the plan, or some part of it, on their campus.

Aztlán inflamed the imagination of Chicanos and Chicanas in 1967 and 1968 precisely because of the racism, segregation, poverty, police brutality, and lack of educational access they faced in American society. They imagined a land of plenty, of justice and racial equality, an autonomous nation governed by self-determination, and those sentiments seemed possible in a mythic place called Aztlán. In the decade that followed, a number of literary and artistic works used Aztlán as a potent symbol of Chicano identity. In 1969 at UCLA the scholarly journal *Aztlán* published its first issue, introduced by Alurista's "Poem in Lieu of Preface." In 1974 Miguel Méndez's novel *Peregrinos de Aztlán* described a U.S. Southwest in which Chicanos were an oppressed and occupied population. Rodolfo Anaya's novel *Heart of Aztlán* followed in 1976, in which the reverse journey from Mexico City/Tenochtitlán to Aztlán was imagined as a return to an original state of might and splendor. These are the lineages of the concept of Aztlán as it has been used over the ages.

See also Chicano Movement

SOURCES: Alurista. 1971. *El ombligo de Aztlán*. San Diego: San Diego State College, Centro de Estudios Chicanos Publications; Anaya, Rudolfo. 1976. *Heart of Aztlán*. Berkeley: Justa Publications; Anaya, Rudolfo, and Francisco Lomelí, eds. 1989. *Aztlán: Essays on the Chicano Homeland*. Albuquerque: Academia/el Norte Publications; Bruce-Nova, Juan. 1980. "Alurista." In *Chicano Authors: Inquiry by Interviews*. Austin: University of Texas Press; Durán, Diego. 1964. *The Aztecs: the History of the Indies of New Spain*. Trans. Dories Heyden and Fernando Horcasitas. New York: Orion Press; Gutiérrez, Ramón A. 1989. "Aztlán, Montezuma, and New Mexico: The Political Uses of American Indian Mythology." In *Aztlán: Essays on the Chicano Homeland,* eds. Rudolfo Anaya and Francisco Lomelí. Albuquerque: Academia/El Norte Publications; Méndez, Miguel. 1979. *Peregrinos de Aztlán*. Berkeley: Justa Publications; Muñoz, Carlos. *Youth, Identity, Power: The Chicano Movement*. New York: Verso; Ritch, William G. 1885. *Aztlán: The History, Resources and Attractions of New Mexico*. Boston: D. Lothrop and Co.; Valdez, Luis, and Stan Steiner, eds. 1972. "El Plan Espiritual de Aztlán." *Aztlán: An Anthology of Mexican American Literature*. New York: Alfred A. Knopf.

Ramón A. Gutiérrez

B

BABÍN, MARÍA TERESA (1910–1989)

Dedicated to a life of learning, teaching, and the dissemination of Hispanic culture, María Teresa Babín had been encouraged as a young girl by her mother to pursue a life in literature and higher education. Born in Ponce, Puerto Rico, Babín went on to study at the University of Puerto Rico in Río Piedras, where she received a master's degree in Hispanic studies in 1939. There her interest in the work of the famous Spanish author Federico García Lorca took root and was the topic of her master's thesis, which was later published as *Federico García Lorca y su obra* (1939). From 1932 to 1940 Babín taught Spanish and French in high schools in Puerto Rico and the United States, and in 1940 she became an associate professor of Spanish at the University of Puerto Rico.

In the mid-1940s Babín moved to the United States and taught as an instructor at Hunter College in New York. She began to write what would be considered one of her major literary contributions, *Introducción a la cultura hispánica* (1949), which was used as a textbook on several college and university campuses. Babín's passion for Lorca's writing became the topic of her doctoral dissertation from Columbia University in 1951, as well as that of several books, among them *El mundo poético de Federico García Lorca* (1954), *García Lorca: Vida y obra* (1955), and *La prosa mágica de García Lorca* (1962). At Columbia Babín met her first husband, Estevan Vicente, a Spanish artist.

Her scholarly interests were not limited to Lorca; Puerto Rican themes also became a focus of her prolific intellectual output. *Panorama de la cultura puertorriqueña* is an overview of the island's cultural development before the date of the work's publication in 1958, and Babín's literary creativity is expressed in her *Fantasía Boricua: Estampas de mi tierra* (1956). This work combines nostalgic remembrances of the island with Puerto Rican customs, folk traditions, and diverse cultural and historical data. In 1962 Babín compiled an anthology of the respected but controversial nineteenth-century poet Francisco Gonzalo (Pachín) Marín, whose poetry championed the cause of Puerto Rican independence. Her own affinity for poetry was revealed in her collection of poems, *Las voces de tu voz,* published in 1962. In the 1960s Babín met her second husband, José Nieto, also a college professor.

Babín's professional career in higher education transpired on a number of campuses. In the 1950s she became an assistant professor of Spanish at New York University; in the late 1960s she joined the faculty of Lehman College of the City University of New York, where she founded and headed the Department of Puerto Rican Studies, in addition to holding a faculty position at the City University of New York Graduate School.

Recognized for her literary accomplishments, as well as her promotion of Puerto Rican culture, with numerous awards and honors from her native Puerto Rico, Babín received the Instituto de Literatura Puertorriqueña literary prize in 1954, the Ateneo Puertorriqueño literary prize in 1955, the Unión Mujeres Americanas prize in 1962, and the Prize of the Year in literature from the Instituto Puertorriqueño in 1970. The Puerto Rican author Cesáreo Rosa-Nieves has expressed his admiration of María Teresa Babín, citing her "passionate attachment" to the culture of her country and her work as an educator on the island and in the United States.

See also Literature

SOURCES: *Diccionario de literatura puertorriqueña*. 1974. Vol. 1. San Juan: Instituto de Cultura Puertorriqueña; *Notable Hispanic American Women*. 1993. Detroit: Gale Research.

Margarite Fernández Olmos

BACA, JUDITH FRANCESCA (1946–)

Judith Baca's influence on the development of public art in Los Angeles is such that any discussion of contemporary wall art in the United States must reference Baca's many murals found throughout the city. Baca is a native of Los Angeles. Her early childhood was influenced by her grandmother, mother, and two aunts. When she was six, her family moved to a suburb north of Los Angeles. Baca keenly felt the loss of her grandmother, who remained in the city. She also experienced a cultural uprooting that resulted from her family's departure from the neighborly atmosphere of the barrio. Artistic expression became Baca's source of affirmation and consolation. Her early interest and talent in art developed as she matured into a young adult. Baca earned a baccalaureate degree in 1969 and an M.A. in fine art from California State University, Northridge, in 1979.

Murals painted at Hollenbeck Park (1970) and Venice Pavilion (1974) were among Baca's first encounters with the power and promise of collaborative mural work. After the completion of her undergraduate studies, she taught art in a high school and was also a member of the local parks and recreation staff. While she was coordinating a community art program, Citywide Mural Project, she invited gang members from rival neighborhoods to successfully work together on mural projects. Baca is credited with coordinating the first mural in Los Angeles to be painted by a racially mixed group of artists. These germinal experiences provided Baca with a vision for utilizing mural painting as a means of bridging cultural difference and articulating commonality among people of diverse backgrounds. Central to Baca's approach is her emphasis on collective practice that brings artists, community members, civic leaders, and young people together in creative partnership. Billed as the "longest mural in the world," *The Great Wall of Los Angeles* (1974–1984) was created by more than 400 people, mostly youths, working with Baca. The resulting heritage mural is notable for its illustration of the quotidian elements of peoples' lives. A decade in the making, the mural is more than 130 feet high and more than 2,400 feet in length; restorative work on it was begun in 2002.

In 1976 Baca founded the Social and Public Art Resource Center (SPARC). A cross-cultural art service center, SPARC serves as an institutional home to muralists and interested art historians, educators, and collectors from around the world. The organization exists as Baca's enduring contribution to public discourse regarding wall art, its artists, and the relationship of community to public artwork. Its programs and services reach beyond the boundaries of Los Angeles and touch the lives of people around the world. Baca coordinated *The World Wall: A Vision of the Future without Fear* (1987–1994), which consists of fourteen panels, seven of them painted in Los Angeles and the remaining seven by artists in countries that served as sponsors of this traveling mural. *The World Wall* was first exhibited in Finland in 1990; it later traveled to Moscow, where it was on display in Gorky Park.

Baca works in the traditional mural genre of painting, as well as in digital art format. *La memoria de nuestra tierra* (2000) was commissioned for the Denver Airport. Digitally produced on aluminum tile, this mural tells the stories of indigenous, Mexicana/o, and Anglo residents of the area. It required two years of historical research conducted by Baca while on fellowship at Harvard University. The City of Durango, Colorado, commissioned Baca to create *reCollections* (2002), a digital mural whose figurative narrative relates the stories of local residents living in this small rural town.

In addition to her work as a muralist and art administrator, Baca serves as a faculty member affiliated with the César Chávez Center for Chicana/o Studies at the University of California, Los Angeles. She previously taught at California State University, Monterey Bay, and at the University of California, Irvine.

The Liberty Hill Foundation honored Baca in 2000 for her leadership and artistic contributions with the Creative Vision Award. She received the National Hispanic Heritage Award from the Hispanic Heritage Awards Foundation in 2001.

See also Artists

SOURCES: Barnett, Alan. 1984. *Community Murals: The People's Art.* New York: Art Alliance Press; Cockcroft, Eva, and Holly Barnet-Sánchez, eds. 1990. *Signs from the Heart: California Chicano Murals.* Albuquerque: University of New Mexico Press; Cockcroft, Eva, John Weber, and James Cockcroft. 1998. *Toward a People's Art: The Contemporary Mural Movement.* Albuquerque: University of New Mexico Press; Social and Public Art Resource Center. www.sparemurals.org (accessed June 19, 2005).

María Ochoa

BACA BARRAGÁN, POLLY (1941–)

Among the earliest Chicanas to hold public office, Polly Baca was born in 1941 on a small farm in Weld County, between Greeley and La Salle, Colorado. Reared in a family that valued education for women, Polly and her two sisters were encouraged to aspire to higher education. "My mother always talked about the importance of education. We would never know, when we got married, if our husbands would die or leave us." Despite hardships and discrimination against Mexican Americans, Baca attended Colorado State University on a state scholarship and in 1963 earned a baccalaureate degree in political science. In 1992 she earned a master of arts in public administration. She was named honorary doctor of humane letters by the University of Northern Colorado at Greeley and received an honorary doctor of law from Wartburg College in Waverly, Iowa. Baca married civil rights activist Miguel Francisco Barragán and has two adult children. Her areas of interest are leadership/management styles and women, how Hispanics dealt with the "old guard" in established institutions, and investigating different leadership/management styles of Hispanic men and women.

Baca was a member of the Colorado state legislature for twelve years. Elected to the Colorado House of Representatives in 1974 and to the Colorado Senate in 1978, Polly Baca became the first minority woman to serve in a leadership capacity in any state senate in the United States. In 1977 Baca chaired the House Democratic Caucus. From 1981 until 1989 she was vice-chairman in the Democratic National Committee (DNC), and in 1992 and again in 1996 she cochaired the Colorado campaign for the Clinton/Gore ticket. In 1994 President Bill Clinton named Polly Baca his special assistant to the Office of Consumer Affairs. As the chief consumer advisor for the president, Baca served as chair of the Consumer Affairs Council and chaired the delegation to the Organization of Economic Development's Committee on Consumer Policy.

Before joining the Clinton administration, Baca was the executive director of the Colorado Hispanic Institute, a nonprofit agency whose goal is to promote multicultural leadership. Her primary responsibility was as director of Visiones. A statewide leadership development program, Visiones assisted community leaders from different ethnic and racial groups in becoming more conversant with each other's needs and contributions.

Polly Baca has received numerous recognitions, among them induction into the national Hispanic Hall of Fame. She can be found in *Who's Who in American Politics* and in *Who's Who in the West*. In 1993 she received the Martin Luther King Jr. Humanitarian Award and was recognized as an outstanding humanitarian by the Denver branch of the NAACP. She also earned the 1994 Leadership Award from the Hispanic Chamber of Commerce. Baca was inducted into the Colorado Women's Hall of Fame and in 2002 was appointed executive director of the Latin American Research and Service Agency (LARASA), a prominent Colorado nonprofit organization whose educational, health, and community programs reach 500,000 area Latinos yearly.

From 1995 to 1998, Baca served as regional administrator of the General Services Administration (GSA), Rocky Mountain Region VIII. With a staff of 474 employees, she oversaw a six-state region that supported 48,000 government employees for forty-three federal agencies and had a budget of $246 million. Currently, Polly Baca is chief officer of Sierra Baca Services, a consultant firm that specializes in motivational presentations, multicultural leadership development, and diversity training. In 2004, she was appointed to the Diversity Action Council for Burger King.

In an interview given for the *9News Profile*, "Chief Executive Office of Sierra Baca Services, Polly Baca," she referred to several community problems that she saw as still unresolved, among which were teaching people to appreciate and trust the diversity of others, the lack of quality education for all children, and universal health care. She listed the need for safe neighborhoods and streets and affordable housing.

Baca believes that hard work and her faith have brought her to her current position in life. "I've been so lucky." she stated in an interview. "I met John Kennedy and Bobby Kennedy and worked for Lyndon Johnson. My young, single life was an incredible opportunity and I loved it. My second life was as a mother. We will see how my third life goes."

See also Politics, Electoral

SOURCES: Bonilla-Santiago, Gloria. 1992. "Polly Baca, Pioneer for Hispanic Women in Politics." In *Breaking Ground and Barriers: Hispanic Women Developing Effective Leadership*. San Diego: Main Publications; InSites (Colorado non-profit organization). "Polly Baca." http://www.insites.org/board/baca.html (accessed June 19, 2005); RockyMtNews.com (online version of *Rocky Mountain News*). Olvera, Javier Erik. 2004. "Shifting spectrum: Anglos no longer majority in Denver, census indicates." September 30. http://www.rockymouintainnews.com/drmn/census/article/0,1299,DRMN_429_3219406,00.html (accessed June 19, 2005).

Linda C. Delgado

BAEZ, JOAN CHANDOS (1941–)

Joan Chandos Baez was born on January 9, 1941, in Staten Island, New York, the middle daughter of Joan Bridge and Albert Baez. She is named after her mother, who is of Scottish descent, and her father, who is Mexican. Baez inherited not only her parents' multiethnic heritage, but also their nonviolent Quaker religious beliefs, which eventually sparked her interests in acquiring peace and justice for society. Despite growing up in a peaceful and tolerant family environment, Joan Baez was confronted with the harsh realities of racism and discrimination at an early age. In junior high school Baez's multiethnic roots and her dark complexion were cause for ridicule among her peers. Those early and impressionable years were filled with isolation and displacement for Baez.

In an attempt to gain popularity and recognition and escape her loneliness, coupled with rejection, Baez took up singing. She developed her voice and soon became known as an entertainer around school. Baez made her first stage appearance in a school talent show. The very people who initially ignored and discriminated against her began to praise Baez's singing and artistic talents.

In June 1958 Baez graduated from Palo Alto High School in Palo Alto, California. After graduation she

Folk singer and civil rights activist Joan Baez. Courtesy of Joan Baez. Photograph by Dana Tynan.

and her family moved from California to Boston, Massachusetts, where she enrolled in Boston University. In college her focus was diverted from her studies, and her music became top priority. During the 1950s folk music was reemerging, and the public's interest in this genre of music was at an all-time high. Baez displayed her talent as a folk musical artist on a small scale in local coffeehouses. Initially, Baez sang duets with her roommate, but her decision to become a solo artist proved successful as she gained a large following of fans.

In 1959, while Baez was singing in a Chicago nightclub, Bob Gibson, a popular folksinger of the time, discovered her. Gibson invited Baez to perform with him at the first annual Newport Folk/Jazz Festival in California. Baez's performance and her unique voice captivated a crowd of 13,000. With this singular performance Joan Baez became an instant star, and several record companies fought to get her on their labels. Ultimately Baez signed her first record contract with Vanguard, a small independent label.

In 1960 Joan Baez's self-titled album was released. Within the album Baez embraced her heritage by integrating both her Scottish and Mexican musical roots. As she toured for three years alongside legendary entertainer Bob Dylan, her political activism began to develop. Baez grew more aware of the injustices plaguing society, and with her newfound fame she felt an obligation and had the advantage to make positive changes. In 1963 Baez stood beside civil rights pioneer Martin Luther King Jr. at the March on Washington. She led a crowd of more than 300,000 in singing the black spiritual "We Shall Overcome." Baez performed at a concert for Lyndon Johnson, where she petitioned the president to pull U.S. troops out of Vietnam. In protest of the Vietnam War, Baez refused to pay federal income tax. She believed that the money acquired from this federal tax was going directly to support the U.S. Defense Department and its war efforts.

In 1965 Joan Baez created the Institute for the Study of Nonviolence in Palo Alto, California. Today it is known as the Resource Center for Nonviolence. Despite her many supporters, Baez had an equal number of opponents. Her antiwar beliefs drew anger from conservative groups such as the U.S. military and the Daughters of the American Revolution (DAR). In 1967 Baez's strong opposition to the Vietnam War ultimately landed her in jail, where she served a ninety-day sentence.

On March 26, 1968, Joan Baez married David Harris, a former leader in the draft resistance movement. In the summer of 1969 she experienced one of the highlights of her musical career when she performed at Woodstock, New York. After only three years of marriage and the birth of their son, Gabriel, Joan and David Harris divorced in 1971. The following year Baez had her biggest commercial hit with the song "The Night They Drove Old Dixie Down."

Joan Baez served on the national advisory board of Amnesty International, a worldwide organization that advocates for the release of people imprisoned for their religious or political beliefs. She not only served on the board, but also helped create the group's California branch, Amnesty, West Coast. In 1979 she founded another organization, Humanitas International, which promotes human rights, disarmament, and nonviolence through seminars and other educational opportunities.

By the 1980s, Baez's popularity began to decline. Nevertheless, in 1985, in a familiar fashion, she used her music and a concert forum, Live Aid, to rejuvenate her career and awaken people's awareness of injustice and oppression around the world. During the 1990s, she served as a mentor for several emerging women singers and composers and on her 1995 album *Ring Them Bells,* some of the guest performers included the Indigo Girls and Tejana sensation Tish Hinojosa. In 2003, Universal Music released a special boxed set of her music from the 1970s. Joan Baez's living legacy is based upon the premise of staying true to one's self and on the principal of nonviolence and freedom. Her talents, words, songs, and activism, coupled with her compassion for humanity and equality, have served as an example and have proven to be powerful instruments throughout her career.

SOURCES: Chabran, Richard, and Rafael Chabran, eds. 1996. *The Latino Encyclopedia*. Pasadena: Salem Press; Joan C. Baez/Diamonds and Rust Productions; Levy, Arthur. 2003. "Official Biography of Joan Baez." www.joanbaez.com (accessed June 19, 2005); Meir, Matt S. 1988. *Mexican American Biographies: A Historical Dictionary, 1836–1987*. Wesport, CT: Greenwood Press; Perry, Joellen. 2002. "Music & America." *U.S. News and World Report,* July 8/July 15; Tardiff, Joseph C., and L. Mpho Mabunda, eds. 1996. *Dictionary of Hispanic Biography*. New York: Gale Research; Unterburger, Amy L. 1995. *Who's Who among Hispanic Americans, 1994–95*. New York: Gale Group.

Dorian Chandler and Jeannette Reyes

BARCELÓ, MARÍA GERTRUDIS ("LA TULES") (1800–1852)

First and foremost, María Gertrudis Barceló, familiarly known as "La Tules," was an astute New Mexican businesswoman. The red-haired, bejeweled, and cigarillo-smoking La Tules was also a dexterous monte card dealer who combined her intelligence, conviviality, and card skills to become the wealthiest citizen of Santa Fe. She earned her fortune as the proprietor of a thriving gambling hall and saloon that served as the social center for Santa Fe's Spanish Mexican citizenry, Euro-Americans, foreign merchants, and traders who passed through town. After the U.S. war with Mexico (1846–1848) her establishment became a haven for the newly posted American officers from whom she took pleasure and gambling profits while introducing them to Santa Fe's distinctive Spanish-based culture and customs.

Hispanic Santa Fe was an amalgam of Spanish tradition, frontier spirit, and Native American influence that allowed women a considerable degree of independence. Single and married women enjoyed the right to own personal property, retain their maiden name after marriage, have their own money, sue in court, obtain a legal separation, and will their property to their daughters if they chose to do so. When corsets, bustles, and floor-length hoopskirts were considered proper attire in the East, and female ankles risqué, Hispanic women could dress for an active outdoor life in off-the-shoulder low-cut blouses with short sleeves and midcalf-length full skirts. Women, as well as men, took pleasure in dancing, drinking, and gambling, as often as not, as customers of La Tules's saloon. Some women presumed themselves to be on an equal footing with men and shared a single sexual standard. La Tules (meaning "reed" in Spanish and used as an affectionate diminutive referring to her size) was a unique and colorful woman in a vibrant town that allowed her entrepreneurial talent to flourish.

However much she was appreciated by the majority of her community, La Tules was the target of slander aimed at her by Euro-Americans and a handful of resentful local women who begrudged her popularity and power. She dealt with the latter by taking them to the alcalde court and winning apologies. The Euro-

La Tules (Gertrudis Barceló) dealing monte in her Santa Fe gambling house. Courtesy of the Library of Congress, American Women: A Gateway to Library of Congress Resources for the Study of Women's History and Culture in the United States (Digital ID: ppmsca 02901).

American traders and travel writers of the day presented a different problem. They created a legend around La Tules that enveloped her in Santa Fe intrigue that reverberated as far as the Atlantic seaboard. Misunderstanding the cultural milieu that was Santa Fe in the 1830s and 1840s, these traders and writers unfairly judged the redheaded saloon keeper who dealt cards, served whiskey, and raked in gambling profits as a woman of loose morals and scandalous escapades.

Rumor and innuendo continually swirled about her because of the mystery that surrounded her early years, when she may have operated a brothel in Tome, and her choice of business in Santa Fe, along with her self-possessed ease in male company. Some believe that everything was exaggerated in proportion to her being a woman. Although married to Manuel Sisneros in 1823, she maintained a close friendship with New Mexico's governor Manuel Armijo, with whom she may have shared a more private relationship. Adultery, while not totally unheard of in Santa Fe, was nonetheless against the law. Whatever La Tules's relationship with Governor Armijo may have been, she remained his trusted friend and political confidante. As one of the few literate women in town, La Tules was in a position to know and understand the political ramifications of what was told to her, and the governor may have appreciated this wealthy woman's counsel.

Amassing a fortune in business, María Gertrudis Barceló bought properties and entertained lavishly. However, she was always conscious of her obligation to the less fortunate. She frequently made charitable gifts to the Catholic Church and to her own and other needy families and adopted a number of children. Her civic-minded foresight prompted her to contribute more than her share of taxes in the form of a "forced loan" to keep the government functioning during periodic budget shortages. She created goodwill among her Euro-American customers, too, by ingeniously lending money to the U.S. Army to pay its troops in 1846, thereby assuring their continued patronage. La Tules was held in high esteem by her community, and even those who disdained this remarkable character acknowledged the admiration showered on her by the "best society."

In 1852 La Tules died, leaving behind a legend and a legacy. Her industriousness and resourcefulness defied Euro-American stereotypes of "lazy and degenerate" Spanish Mexican women. La Tules smoothed the path for the first Americans to be accepted in Santa Fe by encouraging the use of her saloon as an economic and social center that brought the two worlds together. La Tules herself was the drawing card because her opinions were sought by merchants, army officers, and politicians on a range of subjects affecting the well-being of the community. Astute businesswoman that she was, she used her notoriety to attract visitors who brought much-needed currency into Santa Fe's beleaguered economy. She was an unusually clever woman who assisted the peaceful transition of the inevitable American takeover of Hispanic New Mexico.

See also Spanish Borderlands

SOURCES: González, Deena J. 1993. "La Tules of Image and Reality." In *Building with Our Hands: New Directions in Chicana Studies,* ed. Adela de la Torre and Beatríz M. Pesquera, 75–108. Berkeley: University of California Press; Lecompte, Janet. 1981. "The Independent Women of Hispanic New Mexico, 1821–1846." *Western Historical Quarterly.* Vol. 22 (January): 17–35; ———. 1989. "When Santa Fe Was a Mexican Town: 1821 to 1846." In *Santa Fe: History of an Ancient City,* ed. David Grant Noble, 79–95. Santa Fe: School of American Research Press.

Carole Autori

BARNARD, JUANA JOSEFINA CAVASOS (1822–1906)

During her lifetime Juana Josefina Cavasos Barnard's experiences ranged from Indian captive to African American slave owner in Texas. Born in Mexico to María Josefina Cavasos, she was reportedly of Spanish, Italian, and Canary Island descent. Her grandfather was Narciso Cavasos, a large landowner in southern Texas.

In 1900 she related her life in an oral testimony to her granddaughter, Verdie Barnard Alison, titled "My Life with the Indians." According to her narrative, in 1840 a group of Comanches raided southern Texas and took the eighteen-year-old Cavasos captive. She testified that they held her for about a month. When her captors visited the Tehuacana Creek Trading House just south of present-day Waco, they sold her to George Barnard for $300 in horses and merchandise. She married his brother, Charles Barnard of Connecticut, who reportedly was on good terms with various Indian nations.

Juana Josefina Cavasos Barnard worked with her husband and brother-in-law operating the trading post known as the Comanche Peak Trading House for fifteen to twenty years in an area considered remote for white settlers. The post served as a church, as a jail, and later as a courthouse. Business was brisk until the U.S. government removed the Comanches to the Fort Belknap reservation in Oklahoma. She did not romanticize her captivity in her later years, but did remember the Indians as friendly traders.

Cavasos Barnard and her husband owned African American slaves; she reported owning "plenty." The slaves built a limestone mill in 1859, the first building in the present-day town of Glen Rose near Waco. The family estate was valued at $100,000, but they sold the mill in 1870 for $65,000. The family fortune declined steadily after this period.

In her oral narrative Cavasos Barnard saw herself as a mother, grandmother, gardener, pioneer settler, slave owner, trader with Indians, and wife. She related, "I am the mother of fourteen children. Ten dead and four living. . . . I have twenty-five grandchildren and thirteen great grandchildren. . . . I raise a big garden every year. . . . We were the first settlers in Hood County. For months and months I never saw a white woman. We had plenty of Negro slaves. We kept our trading house for the Indians for fifteen or twenty years." Juana Josefina Cavasos Barnard had fourteen children, but only six reached adulthood. She and her husband also raised Ambrosio Hernández, a Mexican boy ransomed from Indians. Contemporary writer Pearl Andrus wrote a fictional account of Barnard's life titled *Juana, a Spanish Girl in Central Texas* in 1982.

Josefina Juana Cavasos Barnard developed a reputation as a gifted healer, no doubt learning about the medicinal qualities of local herbs from the Indians with whom she traded. Intersecting Mexican, Indian, African American, and European American worlds, her life reflected on a daily basis the heterogeneity of the Mexican North, and certainly her position as a slaveholder was unusual for a Tejana. She died of a stroke in 1906.

See also Spanish Borderlands

SOURCES: Elliot, Raymond, and Mildred Padon. 1979. *Of a People and a Creek*. Cleburn, TX: Bennett Printing; Nunn, W. C. 1975. *Somervell: Story of a Texas County*. Fort Worth: Texas Christian University Press; Orozco, Cynthia E. 1996. "Juana Josefina Cavasos Barnard." *New Handbook of Texas,* 2: 2:385. Austin: Texas State Historical Association.

Cynthia E. Orozco

BARRAZA, SANTA CONTRERAS (1951–)

Santa Contreras Barraza, daughter of Frances and Joaquín Barraza, was born in Kingsville, Texas, among the desert cacti, javelinas, and vast landholdings of the King and Kenedy Ranches where members of the Barraza family earned their living. In this harsh southern Texas environment Barraza's artistic sojourn, marked by resistance, self-empowerment, self-definition, and survival began. Barraza grew up in a traditional Catholic home and participated in church activities such as las San Juanitas, catechism classes, and the Catholic Youth Organization. Her knowledge of Catholic images, especially the Virgin, and the dusty, coarse landscape of southern Texas eventually found an important place in her artwork. Today many of these images are recycled and incorporated in her paintings.

As a child Barraza did not have opportunities to develop her art, but her parents wanted her to have every chance. In 1969 she enrolled at Texas A&I University (now Texas A&M University, Kingsville), the same institution her mother had attended in the mid-1940s, to pursue a career in science and math. However, she enrolled in a printmaking class and took courses in art history, pre-Columbian, and Mexican art. Overwhelmed by the subject matter, Barraza changed her major to pursue a bachelor's degree in fine arts.

The late 1960s and 1970s reverberated with the voices of the Chicano movement, the women's movement, and the peace protests against the Vietnam War across many university campuses in the Southwest, including Texas A&I. While the voices of the activists that fueled these movements informed Barraza, it was the Chicano movement, particularly the Mexican American Youth Organization (MAYO), formed by Carlos Guerra, that made the greatest impression on Barraza. Artists such as César Martínez, Carmen Lomas Garza, and Amado M. Peña, among others, became major figures in Chicano activist organizations. The impact of these experiences and contacts with Chicano social reformers eventually informed Barraza's philosophy of life and art. It was a pivotal moment in her life.

With the support of Chicano artists like César Martínez, she began to exhibit her work in alternative spaces for Chicano art. By the mid-1970s Barraza was invited to join Los Quemados (The Burned Out Ones), an association of Chicano visual artists based in Austin and San Antonio with progressive political views and objectives. Santa Barraza was one of three women who formed the group. Later Barraza left the group and founded a Chicana/Latina visual arts organization, Mujeres Artistas del Suroeste (MAS). Their mission was to support Chicana and Latina visual artists. In 1979 MAS organized one of its most ambitious programs in the Austin area, the Conferencia Plástica Chicana. The conference, a forum for scholars and visual artists of Mexican descent, was recognized as a historic step. It was the first platform where Mexican American visual artists engaged in cultural exchanges with other artists of Mexican American and Mexican national descent.

In 1980 Barraza was accepted into the graduate program in studio art at the University of Texas at Austin. The program, entrenched in the Western classical tradition, was for a Chicana cultural artist like Barraza a disappointing experience, but cultural bias could not prevent this woman of sturdy character from graduating two years later with a master of fine arts. In 1985 Barraza left Texas and moved to Pittsburgh, Pennsylvania, to accept a teaching position at La

Roche College. It was a difficult period for Barraza, who was raising a child as a single parent and establishing an artistic career. By this time she began to incorporate printmaking with drawing and painting in her artworks. In 1986 Barraza received a fellowship to study printmaking at the Robert Blackburn Printmaking Workshop in New York City. She became a member of the advisory board of the INTAR Latin American Gallery and soon thereafter joined the faculty of the School of Visual Arts at Pennsylvania State University. These associations led to numerous exhibitions in major U.S. and European cities, including New York, Chicago, Mexico City, and Rome. Grants from Pennsylvania State University's Arts and Humanistic Studies and the Reader's Digest–Lila Wallace fund took Barraza to Mexico to continue research on Mexican images, especially the Virgin of Guadalupe, and indigenous and folklore formats of the codex and *retablo* tradition (small paintings on sheets of tin presented to a holy personage to commemorate a favor received or a miracle performed). From 1993 to 1996 Barraza was associate professor at the Art Institute of Chicago in the Painting and Drawing Division, and after a long absence from Kingsville and South Texas, she returned to her homeland. In Barraza's words, "Twenty-five years ago, I left my birthplace seeking knowledge to enrich myself as a person and as an artist. Ironically I discovered that the information I sought always had been at my disposal, in my own family, home and town."

In 1996 she was commissioned to paint a dramatic mural at the Biosciences Building of the University of Texas at San Antonio. The mural, forty-three feet in diameter, combined ancient Aztec symbols, Mayan concepts, pictographs from the Texas Pecos region, and contemporary scientific images. Since 1998 she has chaired the art department at Texas A&M University, Kingsville.

Throughout her career Barraza has sought a vision and a voice in her myriad of drawings, paintings, and mixed-media creations. The surfaces she utilizes in her compositions include canvas, handmade and standard paper, and aluminum, tin, and galvanized steel. Her painting and drawing media incorporate oils, acrylics, enamel paint, pastels, ink, crayon, and mixed media. She also utilizes printmaking techniques such as lithography, silk screen, and collagraphy (a printing technique using found objects affixed to a template, inked and rubbed on a surface). The result is vivid and colorful paintings that express her identity as a Mexican American with deep roots in the heartland of the Texas-Mexican border. Many of her paintings broaden the *retablo* tradition to include contemporary visions of ordinary or historical figures as central characters in the visual story. Additionally, she has introduced collaged surfaces with photographic and xerographic reproductions and paintings modeled after the pre-Columbian codices. Some of her works have also included silver *milagros* (charms of small body parts placed in a church in search of a physical cure). In her latest works Barraza features frontal figures against flat, bright-colored landscapes such as *La Diosa de Maiz con la Llorona,* the weeping woman who is a ghostly apparition of a female wanderer crying for her lost children. Her most recent installation work, in collaboration with disenfranchised and undocumented women, depicts *Adelitas* and *Cihuateteos*.

Today Barraza's résumé reflects three decades of dedication and hard work. Among her achievements are numerous individual and collective exhibitions in galleries and museums across the United States and Mexico, commissions, awards, and publications. In addition to her countless credits, in 2001, Texas A&M University Press published *Santa Barraza, Artist of the Borderlands,* the first scholarly work on the life and work of a Chicana artist. The book received the 2001 Southwest Book Award. As chair of the art department at the Texas A&M, Kingsville, campus, Barraza has initiated many programs in her department through collaboration with regional museums and internship programs. Additionally, Barraza has played an important role in instituting a faculty and student exchange program with the faculty of the Visual Arts Department of the Autonomous University of Nuevo León in Mexico. In Oaxaca Barraza developed and established the Art Institute of Texas A&M summer program for students to study at the Art Institute of Benito Juárez.

See also Artists

SOURCES: Block, Gay, Annette Carlozzi, and Laurel Jones. 1986. *50 Texas Artists*. San Francisco: Chronicle Books; Chicago, Judy, and Edward Lucie-Smith. 1999. *Women and Art: Contested Territory*. New York: Watson-Guptill Publications; Henkes, Robert. 1999. *Latin American Women Artists of the United States: The Works of 33 Twentieth-Century Women*. Jefferson, NC: McFarland. Herrera-Sobek, María, ed. 2001. *Santa Barraza: Artist of the Borderlands*. College Station: Texas A&M Press.

María de Jesús González

BARRERA, PLÁCIDA PEÑA (1926–)

Born on July 13, 1926, to Reynaldo and Josefa (Ramírez) Peña in Guerra, Texas, forty miles northwest of Roma, Plácida Peña was the oldest of three children. She vividly remembers her childhood days in the dry heat of Guerra, also known as El Colorado Ranch, where she helped her father plant corn, pumpkins, and watermelons. During the depression the economics of the country and the availability of goods were sharply different than today. Coffee cost ten cents per pound; the average working wage was twenty-five cents an hour; a stamp cost three cents; and an average meal consisted of beans, rice, and a little meat.

"It was a really strange life back then, especially during the Depression," Barrera said. "It was a hard life, but we never did without." Food assistance sent to the county commissioner provided some people in Guerra with apples and flour, but the politics underlying the welfarelike assistance did little to help the community. "The county commissioner would hold back relief goods because it wasn't profitable for the stores in town," Barrera recalled. "We really didn't get too much help from anyone or anything."

As a teenager, she stayed with her mother's youngest sister, "Tia Cata," in Mission during the week so she could attend school. One Sunday, as Tia Cata was driving her the 100 miles from the family's ranch back into Mission, they heard the news about the attack on Pearl Harbor. She remembers arriving at the school auditorium on December 8 to hear President Franklin Roosevelt declare war on Japan.

Upon graduation in 1945, Peña Barrera enrolled in Texas A&I University at Kingsville with aspirations of becoming a nurse or teacher. Although she thought that it would be easy, attending college was harder than she expected, and she withdrew three weeks later. "I cried because I wanted to go to school, but financially we couldn't afford it," she recalled. Her father was suffering from multiple sclerosis. "I panicked," she said.

Plácida Peña Barrera. Courtesy of the U.S. Latino and Latina World War II Oral History Project, University of Texas, Austin.

In 1948 Peña Barrera met her husband-to-be while visiting her aunt in Mission. "It was funny because I knew him while in school in Mission, Texas, when I was 14 years old," said Barrera, adding that they were neighbors, "but he was too quiet." He seldom talked to her when they were young. Drafted on March 31, 1944, Raymundo Barrera pursued her, courting her with letters while he was stationed in Delaware as a soldier with the U.S. Air Force. "He proposed to me by mail, our courtship was by mail and he even sent the rings by mail," Barrera said.

Following their marriage on June 4, 1950, Raymundo and Plácida Barrera began a military life of constant moves. Equipped with a $1,400 Buick convertible and, eventually, six children, the Barrera family became world travelers, moving from sweltering climates to bitter winters. In 1950 Peña Barrera traveled by car with her husband to Cleveland, Ohio, where he received his transfer orders. During this time Peña Barrera was trained as a nurse at the Cleveland Lutheran Hospital and earned 65 cents per hour. Months later the couple moved to Rome, New York, and then to Presque Isle, Maine.

"Maine was very primitive," she said. "We had no gas . . . and were without a refrigerator." They used charcoal stoves, she said, "and because it was so cold, we had an icebox on an outside window ledge where we would keep our milk, but then it would freeze and expand, and there was milk everywhere." Before they moved back to Mission for two months, their first child, Nora Myrna Barrera, was born on June 24, 1951.

In 1952 the Barreras were transferred to Fort Ethan Allen, Vermont, where Raymundo Jr. was born on January 26, 1953. Sgt. Barrera went to Korea in 1954, and Peña Barrera, who was expecting, moved back to Mission, where Cynthia Yvonne was born on April 5, 1954.

Upon returning from Korea, Sgt. Raymundo Barrera was assigned to Wichita, Kansas, and again Peña Barrera joined him. There Sandra Yvette was born on May 14, 1956. Soon after her birth, the Barreras received new orders, this time to Tachikawa Air Force Base in Tokyo, Japan. The Barreras traveled for nineteen days in a ship across the Pacific Ocean from Seattle, Washington. The ship traveled through the Yellow Sea to Inchon, Korea, to drop off some soldiers and pick up others who were to be returned to the United States. The Barreras lived in Tokyo for three years. Sgt. Barrera was the sergeant of communications and supply.

Peña Barrera said that the Japanese viewed most Americans as likable and loved the American children; however, there were demonstrations against the war and the ships in Tokyo Bay. "Sometimes I felt as if they didn't want us there," Peña Barrera said. "We were interfering with their lives."

Carlos Humberto and Judith Margot rounded out the Barrera family, both born at the air force hospital in Tokyo, in 1957 and 1959. After Judith's birth, the Barrera family moved back to Texas—a thirty-six-hour flight with six children—and Sgt. Barrera was assigned to Laredo Air Force Base. But in 1963 Raymundo Barrera was reassigned to Korea, and later that year his family flew overseas to be with him. The following year he was reassigned to Japan, and again the family followed. They stayed there until July 1968.

The family was sent to Forbes Air Force Base in Topeka, Kansas, on September 30, 1969. Sgt. Barrera retired as a technical sergeant and relocated to Laredo, where he and his wife pursued additional education.

In 1971 Peña Barrera began taking courses at Laredo Junior College and received her degree in 1978 from Texas A&I University at Laredo, with a major in political science and Spanish, at age fifty-two. Her husband received a bachelor of science degree in political science and law enforcement. Both taught in the United Independent School District in Laredo. He retired from teaching in 1990, and she retired a decade later. Throughout all the struggles and travels during the war, Peña Barrera said that she is very pleased with her life and experiences. "I am very happy with the way my life has turned around. I feel that I have accomplished a lot," she said.

See also World War II

SOURCES: Barrera, Plácida Peña. 2002. Interview by Virgilio Roel, Laredo Vet Center, September 28; Burgess, Emily. 2003. "Texas Girl Traveled World as Air Force Wife." *Narratives: Stories of U.S. Latinos and Latinas and World War II* (U.S. Latino and Latina WWII Oral History Project, University of Texas at Austin) 4, no. 1 (Spring): 18

Emily Burgess

BELPRÉ, PURA (1899–1982)

A pioneer in shaping the early New York Puerto Rican community, Pura Belpré was born in 1899 in Cidra, Puerto Rico. Her father was a building contractor who moved the family frequently, and she attended school in various towns throughout the island. In 1919 she graduated from Central High School in Santurce and enrolled in the University of Puerto Rico, intending to become a teacher. Her studies were interrupted in 1920 when she accompanied her family to the wedding of her sister Elisa in New York City. New York turned out to be her home for the rest of her life. At the start she worked briefly in the needle trades industry. In 1921 she accepted a position as Hispanic assistant at the 135th Street branch of the New York Public Library (NYPL). She began working with adults, but soon discovered a preference for working with children. This was the beginning of her legendary career as a children's librarian, storyteller, folklorist, and writer.

"I grew up in a home of storytellers listening to stories which had been handed down by word of mouth for generations," recalled Belpré. A story her grandmother told her as a child about the courtship and marriage of a mouse named Pérez and a cockroach named Martina was the first Puerto Rican folktale to be shared with New York children at a story-hour session in the public library. The story became her "golden key," said Belpré in an interview. It opened up a special place for her inside the library and established her reputation as a gifted storyteller. The publication of *Perez and Martina: A Porto Rican Folk Tale* in 1932 was the first of her many successes as an author. Some years later, in 1946, she compiled and published *The Tiger and the Rabbit and Other Tales,* the first collection of Puerto Rican folktales in English published in the United States. Subsequently, she became a well-published writer, editor, and translator of children's stories. Although she collected children's tales from many countries, her primary concern always remained the preservation and dissemination of Puerto Rican folklore.

As a librarian, Belpré was a pioneer in advocating for services to Spanish-speaking communities and instituted bilingual story hours. She implemented programs based on traditional Puerto Rican holidays such as Three Kings Day and insisted that the libraries buy Spanish-language books. Belpré was also an active participant in the life of the Puerto Rican community and attended the meetings of organizations such as the Porto Rican Brotherhood of America and La Liga Puertorriqueña e Hispana. She helped these kinds of groups organize activities and obtain library space for gatherings.

In 1943 Belpré married African American composer Clarence Cameron White and a year later resigned her position at the library to go on tour with him and to devote herself to writing. Throughout their lives together the couple maintained their residence in Harlem. Upon White's death in 1960 Belpré returned to the NYPL as the Spanish children's specialist. She had principal responsibility for branches serving a predominantly Latino population and traveled all over the city, delighting children, as well as adults, with her stories.

Despite her full schedule during this period, she published *Juan Bobo and the Queen's Necklace: A Puerto Rican Folk Tale* in 1962. This story introduced one of

Pura Belpré tells a story to children. Courtesy of the Pura Belpré Papers, Centro Archives, Centro de Estudios Puertorriqueños, Hunter College, CUNY.

the best-known characters in Puerto Rican folklore to the American public. In 1966 a long-overdue Spanish translation of *Perez and Martina* was also published.

Although she retired in 1968, Belpré was persuaded to return to work with the South Bronx Library Project, a community outreach program to promote library use among Latinos and other minorities. Belpré was an accomplished puppet maker and puppeteer, a skill she had developed over the years. For the project she designed a mobile puppet theater and gave performances throughout the Bronx based on all of her favorite folktales.

Between 1968 and 1978 Belpré published five more books and translated numerous stories. One of these books was *Once in Puerto Rico* (1973), which drew on Puerto Rico's early history, including stories about the Taínos and the Spanish conquest.

Her interviews and personal papers give testimony to her great love of children and of storytelling. In describing her experiences with children in the library, she used words like "magical," "priceless," "rich," and "beautiful." These very words also describe the extraordinary effect her stories had on people. She died in 1982, leaving a rich literary and public service legacy.

See also Literature

SOURCES: Belpré, Pura. 1976. Oral history interview by Lillian López. Centro Archives, Centro de Estudios Puertorriqueños, Hunter College, CUNY; Belpré, Pura. 1896–1985. Papers. Centro Archives, Centro de Estudios Puertorriqueños, Hunter College, CUNY; Hernández Delgado, Julio. 1992. "Pura Teresa Belpré, Storyteller and Pioneer Librarian." *Library Quarterly* 62, no. 4 (October): 425–440; Mapp, Edward. 1974. *Puerto Rican Perspectives*. Metuchen, NJ: Scarecrow Press.

Nélida Pérez

BENCOMO, JULIETA SAUCEDO (1923–)

As a fourteen-year-old, Julieta Saucedo Bencomo convinced her mother that she could drive. The high-school freshman promptly crashed her oldest brother's car into a fire hydrant, and her older sister wound up with a broken nose. That same daring spirit—tempered by experience—later led her to challenge Arizona's education system. Bencomo was the fourth of five children born in El Paso, Texas, to Guadalupe García Saucedo and José Silvano Saucedo, immigrants from Durango, Mexico. Her father was a locksmith. Her mother had been a business teacher and a college graduate, a rare occurrence for a Mexican woman in the early 1900s. Julieta embraced her mother's love of learning and became valedictorian of El Paso High School's class of 1941. Because of the outbreak of World War II she decided to decline a college scholarship in order to work in the family's locksmith shop. In her words, she met "the love of my life," Joseph D. Bencomo, in 1941. They married in 1944. After work-related moves to Arizona, Ohio, and New Jersey, the couple and their growing family moved to Phoenix permanently in 1959.

Julieta Bencomo blossomed. From advocating for special education instruction for Arizona's incarcerated youth to helping pass state legislation to fund programs for the gifted and talented, Bencomo frequently testified before state and local officials, demanding that children's needs be met. Making sure that resources for non-English-speaking students were provided led her to become a volunteer tutor. "I champion vulnerable people," she said with pride. Her own eight children provided opportunities for taking a stand. When her youngest children were not being challenged academically in the local school district, she transferred them to another district. She then ran for the school board, intent on making changes, and won. In 1979, after serving as the first Latina president of the Phoenix Elementary School District Board of Trustees, she was appointed to the Arizona State Board of Education by Governor Bruce Babbitt. She became the first Latina to serve on the board and later was its vice president.

Julieta Saucedo Bencomo at her seventy-eighth birthday celebration. Photograph by Armando Bencomo. Courtesy of the Bencomo family.

While education was her focus, her activities often extended beyond the classroom. Bencomo's community activism included fighting for the rights of older Americans and immigrants, promoting the arts, and serving on urban planning committees. When the Arizona state legislature refused to recognize the birthday of the late Reverend Martin Luther King Jr. as a national holiday, she marched in support of the holiday. She was also involved in the protests against an anti-bilingual education initiative. Other activities have included distributing condoms as a Planned Parenthood volunteer. She has also counseled Spanish-speaking parents for Parents Anonymous. One of her proudest moments was when a former elementary student she had tutored appeared at her home with an invitation to her college graduation. The young woman told her, "I became a teacher because of you." Her own children have excelled, with one Harvard, two Stanford, and two Northwestern University graduates. The other three have attended Arizona colleges.

Bencomo's accomplishments as a mother who was determined to make a difference have been widely recognized. In 1985 Arizona State University named her one of the state's 100 most influential people and awarded her a Medallion of Merit for Leadership in Public Education. In 1990 the local NBC station named her one of the "12 Who Care," for which she received the Hon Kachina Award. She also received the Jefferson Award Medallion presented by Luke's Men and the American Institute of Public Service. One profile of her work succinctly stated: "Without a doubt, she has been a leading force in education and civil rights for the minority communities. . . . When there was nowhere left to turn, Julieta was always there."

SOURCES: *Arizona Republic*. 1977. "School Board's Chief Refuses to Step Down." March 16; *Phoenix Gazette*. 1979. "Senate Panel Oks Bencomo Nomination." March 15; Rose-Clapp, Margery. 1985. "High Profile: Improved Education from Hispanic Tops Advocate's Priority List." *Arizona Republic*, May 23; Shanahan, Deborah. 1982. "Two Members Oppose Enlarging Board of Education." *Arizona Republic*, August 24.

Julia Bencomo Lobaco

BERNAL, MARTHA (1931–2001)

Noted psychologist Martha Bernal was born to Alicia and Enrique de Bernal on April 13, 1931, in San Antonio, Texas. Originally from Mexico, Bernal's parents came to Texas as young adults and raised their daughter in El Paso, where she received most of her schooling. In 1962 Martha Bernal graduated from Indiana

University and became the first Latina to receive a Ph.D. in clinical psychology in the United States.

During a span of four decades Bernal made significant inroads in the profession, broadening the paradigm to include an emphasis on women clinicians, diversity in the faculty and scholarship, and ethnic identity, particularly as it pertained to treatment modalities and the university curriculum. Bernal's colleague Dr. Melba J. T. Vásquez remarks, "She contributed to an increase in the use of empirically validated interventions in child treatment . . . through both her scholarship and professional activities, she helped to advance a multicultural psychology—one that recognizes the importance of diversity in training, recruitment, and research."

In bringing about changes in the field of psychology, Bernal focused on creating academic opportunities for Latinos/as and other people of color by finding ways to increase access to university education and developing strategies for retention. Congruent with major shifts in higher education, increases in minority student populations, and curricula revisions throughout the United States, Bernal repeatedly called attention to the invisibility of scholars of color in her profession and the lack of diversity in treatment modalities. As part of her ongoing research, Bernal statistically documented poor minority representation in university departments of psychology across the nation. Moreover, she supported the inclusion of coursework on the experiences of people of color in the graduate and undergraduate curriculum. Such changes, she believed, should also extend to the institutions and organizations that further structured the profession. Equally important was the need to acknowledge the importance of the contributions, past and present, of ethnic minorities.

Awarded numerous National Research Service Awards while on the faculty at the University of Denver and later at Arizona State University, Bernal pushed for developing methods and opportunities to educate clinical psychologists about the culture, issues, and needs of ethnic minorities. The dimensions and characteristics of ethnic identity, particularly among Mexican American children, became an important area of research for Bernal, and she created the first courses on ethnic identity in the field.

An active participant in the American Psychological Association, Bernal helped draft the bylaws for the Board of Ethnic Minority Affairs. She served on its committee on training and education and on the Steering Committee Task Force that was charged with creating the National Latino/a Psychological Association. Bernal sat on the American Psychological Association's Commission on Ethnic Minority Recruitment, Retention, and Training and on the Board for the Advancement of Psychology in the Public Interest and was also an active member of Gay, Lesbian, and Bisexual Affairs.

Bernal was an important, inspirational role model and mentor to young Latinas in the profession. Her accomplishments garnered recognition and praise from many sectors. She received the Distinguished Life Achievement Award from the Society for the Psychological Study of Ethnic Minority Issues, the Hispanic Research Center Lifetime Award from Arizona State University, the Carolyn Attneave Award, and the American Psychological Association's Distinguished Contribution to Psychology in the Public Interest Award.

By 2001, however, Bernal's involvement in public and professional activities was on the wane due to continued bouts with various types of cancer. On September 28, 2001, Bernal succumbed to the disease in Arizona. Her students, colleagues, and friends remember her as a formidable pioneer in the field, an inspiration for an entire generation of psychologists of color. An obituary published in *American Psychologist* (2002) describes Bernal as passionate about her ideas, outspoken against injustice, an advocate of high standards in scholarship and professionalism, and compassionate for fellow human beings.

SOURCES: Bernal, Martha E., and George P. Knight, eds. 1993. *Ethnic Identity: Formation and Transmission among Hispanics and Other Minorities.* Albany: State University of New York Press; Vásquez, Melba. 2003. "The Life and Death of a Multicultural Feminist Pioneer: Martha Bernal (1931–2001)." *Feminist Psychologist* (Newsletter of the Society for the Psychology of Women, Division 35 of the American Psychological Association) 30, no. 1 (Winter); Vásquez, Melba. 2002. "Martha E. Bernal (1931–2001)." *American Psychologist* 57: 880–888.

Virginia Sánchez Korrol

BERNASCONI, SOCORRO HERNÁNDEZ (1941–)

Socorro Hernández Bernasconi was born in 1941 to Ruperto and Ramona V. Hernández on the outskirts of Guadalupe, Arizona, a community established in 1910 as trust land for local Yaqui Indians. The family moved to Guadalupe after fire destroyed their home. In this tiny town, bordered on all sides by Tempe and Phoenix, Mexican Americans and Yaquis lived and intermarried, and most worked in the surrounding fields. Growing up in a strongly Catholic family, Socorro decided as a teenager to become a nun. She saved enough money to join the Precious Blood Convent in San Luis Rey, California, at the age of sixteen and later transferred to the motherhouse in Ohio. There, in 1967, she trained to become a nun and pursued a teaching degree at the University of Dayton, becoming the first Guadalupe resident to earn a bachelor's degree in elementary education. After graduation she hoped to return to Guadalupe and serve its residents.

Instead, the order sent her to various locations to teach, and eventually to Phoenix. After deep consideration Socorro chose not to renew her vows to ensure that she would remain in Guadalupe. In 1969 she began working for the Tempe School District No. 3, which oversaw Guadalupe's Veda B. Frank Elementary School. Socorro supported the emerging Arizona United Farm Worker union movement and worked for the AFL-CIO in its labor organizing efforts. She received an opportunity to attend Texas Tech University to train as a counselor and earned her master's in education counseling in 1970. Later that year she married Santino Bernasconi, a member of the Guadalupe Organization, a citizens group. In 1970 Socorro Bernasconi became a counselor at the Frank School. There she noticed a disproportionately large number of Spanish- and Yaqui-speaking students attending "special-needs" classes for the mentally handicapped.

Concerned about the placement of Mexican American and Yaqui students of normal intelligence in special-needs classes through English-only testing methods, she conferred with local parents, the district, and the U.S. Office of Civil Rights. She discovered that parents were not notified of their children's placement, and that students were not routinely retested to determine if they needed to stay in the classes, which restricted their educational advancement. In 1971 the Guadalupe Organization filed a lawsuit against Tempe District No. 3 and the Arizona State Board of Education, alleging discrimination based on ethnicity, race, and language. The court case revealed that Yaquis and Mexican Americans composed only one-fifth of the district's student population, but more than two-thirds of special education classes. The U.S. district court ruled in favor of the Guadalupe Organization in 1972, mandating that the school district institute a new set of regulations regarding special education testing. The following year the district transferred Bernasconi to a nearby school and changed her position from counselor to teacher. She entered into another legal battle with the district, and in 1977 the U.S. Ninth Circuit Court of Appeals ruled that this transfer had violated Bernasconi's rights.

Bernasconi went on to other important work. She raised eight children, and in the 1980s she helped found an alternative school, I'tom Escuela, which provided a trilingual education for local children. In 1987 Bernasconi became director of Guadalupe's Refugio de Colores, the first women's domestic violence shelter to offer bilingual services and traditional cultural practices in the Phoenix area. After the death of her nineteen-year-old son, Sergio, she organized a community group in 1995 called Guadalupe Libre de Alcohol, Armas, y Drogas (GLAAD), initiating a program that encouraged teenagers to exchange their guns for rewards. GLAAD gave the guns to local welders who fashioned art and tools out of them, including candleholders for the altar of the Guadalupe church. In addition, Bernasconi started a college scholarship fund for local youths.

In 1996 she won the Petra Foundation Award and was honored in 1999 as a Peacemaker at the National Conference on Peacemaking and Conflict Resolution. In 2002 she received the Arizona State University Martin Luther King Jr. Servant Leadership Award. A fierce advocate for women, children, and her community of Guadalupe, she holds the honor of being the first resident to receive a college degree and the first Latina counselor in the Tempe School District.

See also Education

SOURCES: Hernández, Leticia. 1987. "Hernández Family." Manuscript, CHSM-326, Chicano Research Collection, Arizona State University Libraries, Tempe. December 1; Marín, Christine. 1992. "From the Cesspool to Equality: The Tempe Elementary School District No. 3 and Guadalupe." Manuscript, E-244, Chicano Research Collection, Arizona State University Libraries, Tempe; Shattuck, Jessica. 1998. "Hellraiser: Socorro Hernández Bernasconi." *Mother Jones,* July–August.

Jean Reynolds

BETANCES JAEGER, CLOTILDE (1890–197?)

Writer Clotilde Betances Jaeger was born in San Sebastián, Puerto Rico, in 1890 and was the grandniece of the island's most prominent nineteenth-century independence leader, Ramón Emeterio Betances. Most of what is known about Clotilde Betances Jaeger's literary pursuits is related to her still-scattered contributions to newspapers and journals in Puerto Rico and New York. Some of these include the island's *Puerto Rico Ilustrado* (Puerto Rico Illustrated), *La Democracia* (Democracy), *Alma Latina* (Latin Soul), and *El Mundo* (The World) and New York's *Grafico* (Illustrated) (1927–1931), *Revista de Artes y Letras* (Journal of Arts and Letters) (1933–1945), and *Pueblos Hispanos* (Hispanic Peoples) (1943–1944).

Betances Jaeger went to elementary and secondary school in Puerto Rico, but left the island in 1912 to complete an undergraduate degree in natural sciences at Cornell University. After she graduated in 1916, she taught in Puerto Rico's public schools for a few years. She moved to New York in 1923 and remained in the United States for the rest of her life. For many years she was a teacher at the Beth Jacob Teachers' Seminary of America in New York. She also continued her graduate education, earning a master's degree from Butler University in Indiana and completing additional studies at the Sorbonne and the University of Salamanca. She was married to a North American of German descent.

For several decades Betances Jaeger continued to write on a variety of topics, including socialism, women's issues, music, religion, and the historical significance of the Lares insurrection and the separatist movement. She wrote for periodical publications in Puerto Rico, New York, and other Latin American countries. She was a member of the Asociación de Escritores y Periodistas Puertorriqueños (Association of Puerrto Rican Writers and Journalists). According to literary critic and historian Josefina Rivera de Alvarez, Betances Jaeger left several unpublished works, including a biographical profile of her famous granduncle, a novel, and a couple of plays.

SOURCES: Reyes Bermúdez, José. 1937. "Puertorriqueños Ilustres: Clotilde Betances." *Puerto Rico Ilustrado,* no. 1522 (May 20). Rivera de Alvarez, Josefina. 1974. *Diccionario de literatura puertorriqueña.* Vol. 2, tomo 1. 203–205. San Juan: Instituto de Cultura Puertorriqueña.

Edna Acosta-Belén

BETANZOS, AMALIA V. (1928–   )

A native New Yorker, Amalia Betanzos was born and raised in the South Bronx of Puerto Rican parents. A graduate of New York University, Betanzos became a vital force in the New York Puerto Rican community through her efforts to advance women's and working-class concerns. In particular, Betanzos concentrated on education as a transformative outlet, and her initiatives brought her to the attention of city and state elected officials.

Amalia Betanzos has extensive administrative experience in the public and private sectors. She was appointed to numerous government positions in New York City under mayors John Lindsay, Abraham Beame, and Edward Koch. An outstanding administrator, Betanzos has served as chairperson of the New York Commission on the Status of Women and as a member of the Temporary New York State Commission on Constitutional Revision, the Citizens' Commission on AIDS, the New York City Board of Education, the Mayor's Advisory Committee on Police Management and Personnel Policy, the Commission on Integrity in Government, and the New York City Housing Authority. She has chaired the Rent Guidelines Board and was commissioner of the Youth Services Agency, commissioner of relocation and management services in the Housing Development Administration, and executive secretary to John Lindsay in charge of programs for the poor, physically handicapped, and mentally challenged.

Before joining city government, Amalia Betanzos was executive director of the Puerto Rican Community Development Project and president of the National Association for Puerto Rican Civil Rights. She now serves as chairperson of the National Puerto Rican Coalition. Since 1978 Amalia Betanzos has been president and chief executive officer of the Wildcat Service Corporation. This organization was established in 1972 as a nonprofit education, training, and employment program. The corporation works with chronically unemployed individuals such as ex-offenders, public assistance recipients, former alcohol and drug abusers, high-school dropouts, and people with limited English-language skills in order to successfully bring them into the labor force.

The Wildcat Service Corporation also sponsors the John V. Lindsay Wildcat Academy, an alternative high school founded in 1992 and funded by the New York City Board of Education, as well as private corporations such as the Soros Foundation. Perhaps Betanzos's most important achievement, the Wildcat Academy has been touted among the most successful alternative schools, a model for charter schools and similar initiatives throughout Latin America. The school, which began with only 100 students, had by 2001 served more than 4,000 individuals. The objectives, according to Betanzos, are to help students realize their potential, expose them to the arts and humanities, and then facilitate future employment.

SOURCE: Unterburger, Amy L., ed. 1995. *Who's Who among Hispanic Americans, 1994–95.* Detroit: Gale Research.

Carlos Sanabria

BILINGUAL EDUCATION

Contrary to popular opinion, bilingual-bicultural education has existed in the United States since the eighteenth century, reflecting the nation's diversity from its very beginnings. Bilingual education was practiced among the Dutch and German communities of the colonial era and was used as an accepted instructional methodology for some religious group education in American society. Ohio was the first state to officially adopt a bilingual education law. Responding to parental requests, in 1839 the state authorized classroom instruction in German and English. In 1847 the state of Louisiana provided for French and English instruction, and the territory of New Mexico followed suit for Spanish and English instruction in 1850. Until the mid-nineteenth century public and private educational institutions in northern Mexico, what is today the American Southwest, primarily taught in Spanish. By the century's end bilingual education laws were enacted in a dozen states; however, other states unofficially provided bilingual instruction in languages such as Norwegian, Italian, Polish, Czech, and Cherokee.

During World War I the political climate in the United States discouraged pluralism, multiculturalism, and instruction in any language other than English. Viewed as a loyalty issue in American society, non-English speakers, especially German Americans, were ostracized, and states embarked upon Americanization programs in the schools and other institutions that left no room for "foreign" cultures. English-only instruction dominated pedagogical practice, and bilingual schools throughout the nation drastically declined. By the 1930s children with limited English-language skills were fully expected to leave the home culture and language at the schoolroom door. In the classroom they only received total English immersion instruction. For more than thirty years limited English proficiency (LEP) students experienced low academic achievements and increased dropout rates. Some did well in the sink-or-swim learning environment, but many did not.

By the 1950s Latino youngsters constituted the largest population of LEP students. Alarming rates of poor academic achievement became a rallying cry in Latino communities throughout the country during the civil rights era. Confronted with ethnocentrism and discrimination, Latino communities organized for equal educational opportunity, bilingual education, and English as a second language. In 1963 the first bilingual two-way program for grades one through twelve was established in the Coral Way School in Dade County, Florida, in response to the needs of the children of Cuban refugees in the district. Directed by Pauline Rojas, the school served as a model for the rest of the nation and became the focus of extensive pedagogical research.

Throughout the 1960s and 1970s communities increasingly mobilized to argue for bilingual and bicultural education as a civil right. Coupled with an unprecedented rise in immigration, community activism resulted in the passage of the Bilingual Education Act (Public Law 90-247) on January 2, 1968. This federal regulation provided for bilingual education in the public schools and secured funds for program development, teacher and staff training, evaluation standards and procedures, curricular initiatives, and other resources. Priority was given to those states with the largest concentrations of LEP students, among which were New York, Massachusetts, New Jersey, Florida, Illinois, California, and Texas.

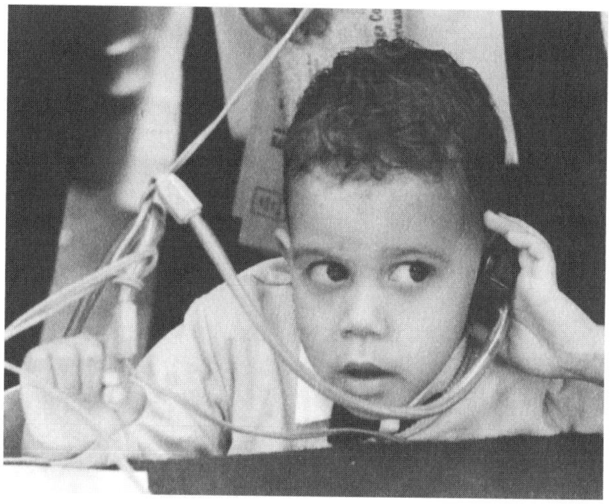

A child listens to a message in a bilingual program, 1968. Courtesy of Virginia Sánchez Korrol.

Puerto Rican Discovery Day, food-tasting party, November 1969. Courtesy of Virginia Sánchez Korrol.

In 1974 two court cases on bilingual education attracted national attention. In *Lau v. Nichols* the Supreme Court ruled that 1,800 Chinese students in San Francisco were denied their rights under Title VI of the Civil Rights Act of 1964 because the federally aided public school district did not provide for their language needs. In New York City, then the largest urban public school system in the country, ASPIRA of New York, the Puerto Rican Legal Defense and Education Fund (PRLDEF), and a class of children plaintiffs brought a suit against the New York City Board of Education on the grounds that thousands of students of Spanish-speaking background were denied their civil rights. City schools had failed to provide an education that met their language needs. The result was the ASPIRA Consent Degree, which mandated that the city offer a broad-based instructional program for children with limited English proficiency. The Bilingual Education Act was also revised in 1974 to create a National Advisory Council on Bilingual Education charged with articulating a national policy on bilingual education.

A meeting of parents and teachers, 1968. Courtesy of Virginia Sánchez Korrol.

The actual implementation of bilingual programs was left in the hands of the states. Although the overall goal in educating LEP students remained the mastery of the English language and content in academic areas, different methods of instruction emerged. Immersion required teachers to use simple language in teaching academic subjects, allowing the students to absorb the English language while learning. Transitional bilingual programs offered instruction in the students' language over the course of several grades but gradually shifted into total English-language instruction. Developmental or maintenance programs prioritized the students' skills in the native language as they became proficient in English as a second language.

In the 1990s bilingual and multicultural education became controversial. Opposition arose among Anglo and Latino parents who wanted faster results. Bilingual education was deemed too costly or ineffective by organizations like English First and U.S. English, which led the political movement to mandate English as the official language of the United States. Several states, including California and Arizona, repealed bilingual education laws. But supporters of bilingual education, as well as foreign-language programs, cited multiple academic benefits. They believed that proficiency in more than one language is well worth the effort, particularly in light of increased globalization, foreign commerce, advanced technologies, and national intellectual advancement.

See also Education

SOURCES: Acosta-Belén, Edna, Margarita Benítez, José E. Cruz, Yvonne González-Rodríguez, Clara E. Rodríguez, Carlos E. Santiago, Azara Santiago-Rivera, and Barbara Sjostrom. 2000. *"Adíos Borinquen querida": The Puerto Rican Diaspora, Its History and Contributions*. Albany, NY: Center for Latino, Latin American, and Caribbean Studies, SUNY; Cockcroft, James. 1995. *Latinos in the Struggle for Equal Education*. New York: Franklin Watts; Nieto, Sonia. 2000. *Affirming Diversity: The Sociopolitical Context of Multicultural Education*. 3rd ed. New York: Longman.

Virginia Sánchez Korrol

BLACK LEGEND

In 1914 Spanish intellectual Julián Juderías coined the phrase "Black Legend" to describe the prevalent belief among European intellectuals that the Spanish were not only a backward people but also lecherous, deceitful, and cruel. Juderías traced this defamatory tradition of Spanish cruelty to the writings of Bartolomé de Las Casas, whose defense of the Indians subsequently provided damning examples and criticisms of Spanish colonial rule and fueled anti-Spanish propaganda, beginning in the sixteenth century. Spain's far-reaching and successful colonization in North Africa and the New World engendered tremendous antagonisms from its European enemies, particularly among emerging Protestant countries. There are two distinctive phases in defining the significance of the Black Legend: first, the historical events surrounding the writings of Bartolomé de Las Casas; second, why Spain's foreign rivals continuously engaged in and promoted anti-Spanish propaganda based on Las Casas's writings.

In the sixteenth century the Spanish Crown faced a two-pronged religious battle within its wars of expansion. The Spanish Crown spearheaded the spread of

Catholic hegemony in the New World while simultaneously battling the Protestant Reformation in Europe through the establishment of the Holy Office of the Inquisition, which sought to maintain religious orthodoxy in both the Old and New Worlds. Initial Spanish Christianizing efforts met with uneven success that prompted imperial officials to reform their Christianizing and judicial administration in the New World. Central to these reforms were establishing the legal rights of native Indians and their effective conversion to Catholicism. The most antagonistic opponents of these reforms were the conquistadores who resurrected the almost extinct *encomienda* system. Effectively used against the Moors in the reconquest of Spain, the *encomienda* system rewarded Spanish warriors with grants of labor in newly conquered territories. In New Spain labor tribute led to wealth. Therefore, extracting labor was often brutal, excessive, and dehumanizing.

Formerly a soldier in the Aztec Conquest, Bartolomé de Las Casas became a Dominican friar after an intense religious experience. He eventually became the bishop of Chiapas and the most vociferous champion of Indian rights. In a celebrated debate against Juan Ginés de Sepúlveda, who argued that the doctrine of natural slavery legitimized Spain's Indian wars and the *encomienda* system, Las Casas argued that all humans were naturally free and rational beings with rights to self-determination; therefore, the *encomienda* system relegated Indians to the status of hereditary serfs, a condition with potentially disastrous results to Indian and royal interests. In 1552–1553 Las Casas published in Seville nine treatises severely critical of the Spanish conquest in America, one of which was his *Brevisima relación de la destrucción de las Indias* (A Brief Account of the Destruction of the Indies). The *Brevisima Relación* described in horrifying detail examples of murder, rape, torture, and shameless abuse by the Spanish overlords. Las Casas's persistent criticisms encouraged the abolition of the *encomienda* system, and the Reform Laws of 1572 effectively ended the conquest era.

Las Casas's *Brevisima Relación* found a wider audience among Spain's enemies after 1552; the first foreign translation (Dutch) appeared in 1578, followed by French (1579), English (1583), and German (1599) versions. The Black Legend was born in these foreign translations. Envy of Spain's New World riches and the desire to carve out their own empires at Spain's expense assured the blackening of Spain's international reputation. Pointing to Spanish wrongdoings justified the righteousness and aggressive actions of European rivals such as the English, French, Italians, and Dutch in the New World. As early as the fourteenth century Italians published unfavorable opinions of Spaniards, and after Spain invaded the Dutch Low Countries, the Dutch became their most strident critics. In one of the most circulated editions, the Dutchman Theodore de Bry added horrific sketches depicting Spanish torture and violence against defenseless Indians. De Bry's images of Spaniards dashing out the brains of Indian infants and feeding their bodies to dogs and of Indians being simultaneously hung and burned were quickly and uncritically accepted by the English. After the defeat of the Spanish Armada in 1588 international rivalry between these two countries increased. England's rise as the staunchest defender of Protestantism brought forth a surge of fanatical Protestant writers who advanced the development of a national consciousness that made Englishmen distinctive. As the staunchest of enemies, fanatical English Protestants promoted the Black Legend in North America to remind other Europeans of the innate defectiveness of the Spanish and all their institutions.

See also Spanish Borderlands

SOURCES: Hilgarth, J. N. 2000. *The Mirror of Spain, 1500–1700: The Formation of a Myth*. Ann Arbor: University of Michigan Press; Keen, Benjamin. 1998. *Essays in the Intellectual History of Colonial Latin America*. Boulder, CD: Westview Press; Maltby, William S. 1971. *The Black Legend in England: The Development of Anti-Spanish Sentiment, 1556–1660*. Durham, NC: Duke University Press.

María Raquel Casas

BLAKE, MARÍA DECASTRO (1911–2001)

María DeCastro Blake, Puerto Rican community activist and pioneer, was the second oldest of six children born into an impoverished family on the island of Vieques, Puerto Rico, in 1911. Her father, Francisco DeCastro, a fisherman and a native of Cabo Rojo, Puerto Rico, abandoned the family while she was still young. Her mother, Clotilde Smaine, supported the family as a cook. A literate woman with a passion for romantic novels, Smaine instilled a love of learning in her children. Blake graduated from high school and completed a secretarial course before her mother died. Her mother's death in 1932 left Blake in the difficult role of having to support her younger siblings during the Great Depression.

After more than a year of failed job searches, she placed her siblings with various relatives and migrated to New York City. A family she had known in Vieques welcomed her into their tiny apartment on Ridge Street and for several years let her sleep on a cot in the living room. The women in that family also helped her find work in a garment factory, because she did not yet speak English. Without any other skills besides her secretarial training, Blake was hired as a "dress finisher." Her tasks were to inspect the garments and to trim any loose threads. The job paid ten dollars a week.

From this sum she contributed two dollars a week for her board, covered her daily expenses, and purchased clothing and books. She also saved in order to bring one of her sisters to New York. On evenings and Saturdays she took courses to improve her English.

Four years after her arrival in New York, Blake had saved enough to pay for her sister Nilda's passage and to rent a one-bedroom apartment on Sixteenth Street and Eighth Avenue. Nilda found work in a factory, and together they saved for the fares for the remaining sisters in Puerto Rico, Genoveva and Margarita.

Blake continued to take courses in stenography, English, and typing in preparation for a secretarial job. She also enrolled in the extension division of Columbia University and the New School. In time she was hired for her bilingual skills by some of the import-export companies on Wall Street that did business with Latin America. At Columbia she met Thomas Blake, an insurance underwriter and part-time fencing instructor. A college graduate, "Tom was," according to María Blake, a "frustrated white-collar worker" who "preferred carpentry to office work," but not wishing to "disappoint his immigrant parents, who had sacrificed to give him an education," he never pursued that line of work. María Blake, on the other hand, was happy with her secretarial work. By the time she married Thomas Blake in 1942, her salary had increased to fifty dollars a week. After marriage she continued to work for nearly a year, until their first child, Clotilde, was born.

Civic leader María DeCastro Blake. Photograph by Máximo Blake. Courtesy of the Blake family.

The need for additional space for their daughter, and Thomas's frustrations at work, led the couple to move from Manhattan to Jersey City, New Jersey, in 1943, where Thomas opened a stationery store. The business failed after five years. With two additional children, the couple decided to purchase a home in East Orange, a suburb close to Newark, New Jersey, so that Thomas could return to the insurance business.

Thomas died shortly thereafter, leaving María to support and care for the three children. She took a part-time job as a Berlitz instructor and rented the upper floor of her house to a young couple. By the late 1950s the children were in middle school and quite active in sports. Blake in turn began to do volunteer work at St. Patrick's Church in Newark. Mostly she taught English to the Puerto Rican families that had begun to settle in the city along Plane Street, now known as University Avenue. She taught the children in the afternoons and adults in the evenings.

In 1960 she returned to full-time work, taking a secretarial job at the Alumni Department of Rutgers University at Newark. Still interested in helping the Puerto Rican community, she mobilized the Alumni Office to partner with St. Patrick's in its campaign to send Newark's poor children to camp. She was particularly interested in this project because the children who were selected were also given medical exams and free sneakers. As a staff member of Rutgers University, she began to promote the idea of enrolling Hispanic students at the Newark campus for the first time. In the early days she had to convince the parents as well. In all cases she helped the students fill out the application forms and apply for financial aid. In many instances she provided the needed aid whenever the financial aid funds were late or fell short. Many of those who went on to become professionals are proud to say that without María Blake's help they could not have done it. By the time the first seven Hispanics graduated from Rutgers, Newark, Blake had become a very instrumental ally, known affectionately among them as "the Dean." Rutgers took notice of her efforts and promoted her to the position of assistant dean of admissions five years after she was first hired. With a secretary of her own, a small budget, and a large office, Blake recruited hundreds of Hispanic students for Rutgers, Newark. Never one to limit her role, she sought scholarship funds and internships for her students from corporations and government agencies. She served the university and the larger community for twenty-four years. Hundreds attended her retirement party in 1984 and eagerly paid homage to the woman who had helped them obtain the college education she was unable to secure for herself.

Part of Blake's activism led to the creation of several institutions, such as ASPIRA of New Jersey, the Association for the Professional Education of Puerto Ricans, the Puerto Rican Congress, and the Black and Puerto Rican Convention. For her many efforts she was recognized as Woman of the Year by the Hispanic Women's Task Force of New Jersey (1991) and by the 208th New Jersey Legislature (1998), which placed her name alongside those of Clara Barton, Millicent Fenwick, and other notable New Jersey women.

Many of her former students continued to visit her at the small apartment she rented in New York after she left Rutgers and New Jersey. She moved, she said, "to speed her commute to the New York Public Library and to the Museum of Natural History," the two places where she volunteered her services every week for the next seventeen years. She stopped only when her legs could no longer carry her. But until her death, July 22, 2001, one day short of her ninetieth birthday, she remained a concerned citizen and an eager student.

SOURCES: Blake, Brian. 2001. Draft of "Maria's Obit." July 24; Blake, María DeCastro. 1997. Oral interview by Olga Jiménez de Wagenheim, April 8; Hidalgo, Hilda, and Elia Hidalgo-Christensen. 1979. "Two Women: A Story of Success." In *The Puerto Rican Woman,* ed. Edna Acosta-Belén. New York: Praeger.

Olga Jiménez de Wagenheim

BORRERO PIERRA, JUANA (1877–1896)

Cuban poet Juana Borrero, like many women artists, has only recently been "rediscovered" by literary and art critics and has yet to receive the attention that many feel she deserves as one of the continent's first modernists. Indeed, even the basic biographical information published on Juana Borrero is contradictory.

She was born in Puentes Grandes, Cuba, on May 18, 1877, one of three daughters of an aristocratic Creole family. Her love for literature and the arts began at a very early age, perhaps encouraged by her father, Don Esteban Borrerro y Echevarría, a physician and poet who hosted numerous gatherings at the family home that were attended by the leading artists and intellectuals of Cuban society. Among the visitors to her home was the poet Julian de Casal, who became her literary mentor and great friend, and who dedicated several of his poems to her. Borrero wrote her first poem at the age of four and published her first work at the age of thirteen in the literary magazine *La Habana Elegante,* one of the leading periodicals of this period.

In 1895 Cuban rebels, led by José Martí, initiated another war of independence against the Spanish Crown. As a rebel combatant during the Ten Years' War (1868–1878), Don Esteban came under the suspicion of colonial authorities. The Borrero family fled to the United States to avoid certain imprisonment and perhaps death. They settled in the cigar-making community of Key West, Florida, which, along with Tampa and New Orleans, had one of the largest Cuban exile communities of the nineteenth century.

After their departure the ancestral home was destroyed by Spanish authorities, who burned the family's vast collection of books, paintings, and manuscripts, an act that forever scarred Borrero, exacerbated her frail health, and perhaps contributed to her early death. In Key West she met and became engaged to the Cuban poet Carlos Pío Uhrbach, who returned to Cuba to fight in the war of independence and died on the Cuban battlefields.

Borrero produced five volumes of poetry. Her best-known work is *Rimas* (1895), a collection of poems that earned her international acclaim. Among her literary admirers were José Martí and Rubén Darío. The collection includes the poem "Los proscriptos," which

Poet Juana Borrero. Courtesy of the Cuban Heritage Collection, Otto G. Richter Library, University of Miami.

was written shortly after her arrival in Key West and describes her last night in Cuba. Because many of her poems describe the pain and loneliness of exile, she has become a favorite of a new generation of Cuban exiles—those who arrived after the Castro revolution of 1959. Like Casal and Pío Uhrbach, she was a central figure in the modernist movement known as Kábala—the only female modernist in Cuba. The Kábala also included such writers as Eulogio Horta, Raúl Cay, José Francisco Piedra, and Vicente Tejera. She was a prolific letter writer. Her letters are compiled in the two-volume *Epistolario*.

Juana Borrero died of typhoid fever at the age of eighteen on March 9, 1896. She was buried in Key West in a tomb belonging to friends of her family. The grave site remained unidentified until 1972, when it was rediscovered following a lengthy study by the Cuban Society of Archeology and Ethnology in Exile. The remains were exhumed and transferred to her own tomb, with a gravestone that reads "Glory of Cuba."

See also Literature

SOURCES: Borrero, Juana, 1966. *Juana Borrero: Epistolario.* Havana: Instituto de Literatura y Linguística, Academia de Ciencias de Cuba; Hauser, Rex. 1990. "Juana Borrero: The Poetics of Despair." *Letras Femeninas* 16 (Spring–Fall): 113–120; Nuñez, Ana Rosa. 1975. "Juana Borrero: Portrait of a Poetess." Trans. Graciella Cruz Taura. *Carrell: Journal of the Friends of the University of Miami Library* 16:1–24; Vertical Files, Cuban Heritage Collection, Otto G. Richter Library, University of Miami; Rivero, Eliana. 1990. "Pasión de Juana Borrero y la critica." *Revista Iberoamericana* 56 (July–December): 829–839.

María Cristina García

BOYAR, MONICA (1920–)

Dominican entertainer Monica Boyar was born in Santiago de los Caballeros in the Dominican Republic. Her birth name was Argentina Mercedes María González Morel Valerio Ureña. Her parents, Pablo Duarte and Juanita, moved to the United States when she was six years old for political reasons. She grew up in New York City, where she attended Manhattanville Junior High School and Textile High School.

At the age of twelve Boyar performed in a choral group at the Metropolitan Opera House singing soprano, which she disliked, and she developed an allergy to tenors as well; in later years she became a contralto. Her love of the theater developed in her early school years. She appeared in many plays and won the yearly dramatic award for her portrayal of Miriam in Maxwell Anderson's *Winterset*.

After her mother's death her father was taken ill. To bring money into the house, and with her father's permission, she auditioned at the famous club La Conga in New York City. She was hired instantly to replace Diosa Costello, the star of the show, who was hospitalized. Borrowing the graduation prom dresses of two friends and lowering the necklines, she opened for a four-week engagement. This was the beginning of her long and successful professional singing career. Her songs were orchestrated by Desi Arnaz, who led the band at La Conga.

Boyar was the first to sing commercial calypso in the supper clubs of New York City. She recalls, "Harry Belafonte and I both sang calypso well, but neither of us was authentic. We just helped to make calypso popular by watering down the lyrics so they could be understood."

Boyar is proud of the heritage of West Indian folk music and has lectured on the varied rhythms and musical origins of the Caribbean. She sang in seven languages and four dialects. The songs in her large repertoire of music ranged from the earthy chants of the sugarcane workers to the gentle whisper of a lullaby. She sang the blues and dramatized their anguish, along with songs about the love of a woman for her man. Her singing had the fire of the Latin she is, as well as the American sense of humor that she grew up with. She set a record of forty-two weeks singing at Le Ruban Bleu supper club and six months at the Vien-

Dominican singer and actress Monica Boyar. Photograph by James Kreigsmann, New York. Courtesy of Monica Boyar.

nese Lantern, both in Manhattan, with yearly return engagements. Her appearances in New York included performing at the Waldorf-Astoria, the Blue Angel, Café Society Downtown, and the Château Madrid.

In a review written by Lee Mortimer of the *New York Daily Mirror,* Boyar is described as "tall, olive-complexioned and slim. Her hair is forty inches long. Her eyes are light brown when in good spirits, almost black when annoyed. Her mouth, sensuous and pouting, is quick to express an opinion. Her hands are as much a part of her songs as the very lyric and music she is feeling. She is an exciting performer to watch as you experience her constantly changing moods." He once dubbed her the "Satin Latin," and the appellation has stuck with her throughout her life. The international press praised her style and individuality.

During World War II she performed in many benefit shows in the War Bond Drive headed by President Franklin Delano Roosevelt. She worked with the coordinator of Inter-American affairs, broadcasting Dominican folk music, and recorded for the Library of Music of the World for its files in Washington, D.C. She entertained in hospital units for the USO Camp Shows and introduced the first postwar V-E song, called "Hail, Hail, There's No More Heil." While appearing at the Blackamoor supper club in Miami Beach, Florida, she sang requests from the audience on one condition: that they deposit $10 in a March of Dimes cash box she passed around on behalf of the National Foundation for Infantile Paralysis, the disease that plagued President Roosevelt. She is also proud of having received her U.S. citizenship papers in 1947.

Boyar was involved with her second husband, Federico Horacio Hénríquez, in the first unsuccessful attempt to overthrow the brutal dictator Rafael Leónidas Trujillo Molina. Hénríquez, who had enlisted in the U.S. Navy so he could remain in the United States, was killed during the revolution in 1949. He was the nephew of Horacio Vázquez, who was president of the Dominican Republic until he was deposed by Boyar's godfather, Rafael Estrella Ureña. Estrella Ureña was the provisional president until he was ousted by Trujillo. In 1960 Boyar became the secretary to Captain Enríque Jiménez Moya, who led a second unsuccessful attempt to topple Trujillo. In 1961 Trujillo was assassinated.

Years later Boyar married the American film star Leslie Nielsen. Their honeymoon was abruptly interrupted when she was invited to return to New York City to open as the solo act at the new Château Madrid nightclub.

Boyar has been an international singing star who has also appeared as an actress on Broadway. She originated the role of Rosa González in the Broadway production of the Tennessee Williams play *Summer and Smoke,* which opened at the Music Box Theatre on October 6, 1948. She also costarred as Don Ameche's "lovely and vibrant native Hawaiian wife, Emmaloa," in the Broadway musical *13 Daughters,* which played at the Fifty-fourth Street Theatre.

Her résumé is filled with international singing engagements, including many exclusive hotels, supper clubs, cabarets, boîtes, and *salones de gala* throughout the world. Honored by being asked to sing a command performance for His Highness Prince Bernhard of the Netherlands, Boyar also sang at a benefit performance for Prince Rainier of Monaco and a special concert for Aristotle Onassis. She was invited, as well, to appear for a request performance at the Dominican Embassy in Washington, D.C., in celebration of her country's 101st Independence Day.

Monica Boyar is not just a singer/actress. She is a major personality and the epitomé of a chanteuse. She introduced the merengue, the native dance of the Dominican Republic, to the United States at the 1939 New York World's Fair after teaching it to Arthur Murray, the dance maven. Xavier Cugat told her, "The merengue will never catch on. It's too similar to the samba." Boyar proved him wrong.

An ardent baseball fan and aficionada of the bullring, Boyar defends both sports with equal vehemence, as she does with everything she believes in. She is also an accomplished painter, working mostly with watercolors. Boyar is now retired and lives in Las Vegas, Nevada.

SOURCES: Blum, Daniel, ed. (*Theatre World 1952–1953.*) Greenberg; Hirschfield, Al. 1961. *American Theatre as Seen by Hirschfeld.* New York: G. Braziller; Nathan, George Jean, ed. *Theatre Book of the Year, 1948–1949.* New York: Alfred Knopf; *Theatre World, 1960–1961.* Philadelphia: Chilton Co.; *Who's Who in Theatre, 1948–1949.* New York: Pitman.

Ben Tatar

BOZAK, CARMEN CONTRERAS (1919–)

Carmen Contreras was born on New Year's Eve, 1919, in Cayey, Puerto Rico, near San Juan, the oldest of three children. She attended elementary school in Puerto Rico, where her mother, Lila Baudilia Lugo Torres, worked as a seamstress and raised her children by herself. The family moved to New York City, and young Carmen attended Julia Richman High School. Upon graduating from high school she went to work for the National Youth Administration. Shortly afterward she took the civil service test and accepted a job as a payroll clerk in the War Department in Washington, D.C. Bozak found that the job at the War Department ignited her patriotism and excitement at the beginning of World War II and drove her to join the Women's Army Auxiliary Corps (WAAC). "Oh, I had to go," Bozak re-

Carmen Contreras Bozak in Rome with a carabiniere, 1944. Courtesy of the U.S. Latino and Latina World War II Oral History Project, University of Texas, Austin.

called. "I thought, 'It'll be a change. I'll get to travel.' I was so happy that I did join, that I got a good job."

As one of 195 members of the 149th WAAC, Bozak set sail from New York for Europe in January 1942. She remembers watching as her ship passed the Statue of Liberty and realizing that they were sailing off to battle. The women who made up the 149th were chosen for their ability to speak more than one language. Bozak felt special to be among them. "I was only out of basic training not two months, and I was going overseas already," she said. "I was so happy, even though I got seasick." She was stationed in Algiers, Algeria, for most of her time overseas. There she worked as a teletype operator, transmitting encoded messages to the battlefield.

Algiers was not far from battlefield action. Bozak recalled that during her eighteen months there, she witnessed four air raids and the dropping of a bomb near one of the residences. She and one of her friends seldom sought cover like the rest of the women in her unit. They liked to go up on the roof of the hotel where they worked nights to watch the artillery fire. "We were never afraid," Bozak said. "Some girls were scared, but I never was."

After her time in Algiers Bozak spent a short time in Italy before returning to the United States. She was discharged as a technician fourth grade and earned several medals, including the European-African–Middle Eastern Campaign Medal, two Battle Stars, a World War II Victory Medal, an American Campaign Medal, a WAAC Service Medal, and the Good Conduct Medal.

After she came home, an eye infection she had contracted in Algiers flared up, and she was sent to Valley Forge General Hospital in Pennsylvania in July 1945, which turned out to be a fortunate twist of events. During a trip back to the hospital from Washington, she met her future husband, Theodore J. Bozak, who was also a patient at the hospital. After dating for less than five months, the two married. "That was my lucky day (the day he was transferred to Valley Forge)," Carmen Bozak said. "That was the day I met my husband."

The couple was married for forty-six years until his death in 1991. They had two sons, Brian and Robert, and a daughter, Carmen. Bozak maintained that her Puerto Rican heritage never deterred her from accomplishing any of her goals and that she was never the victim of discrimination based on her culture or her gender. She did not teach her children to speak Spanish because her husband was of Polish descent and did not speak the language. In retrospect, Bozak said that she has some regrets about "not teaching the children the Spanish language."

It has been nearly sixty years since Bozak served in the U.S. Army in World War II, but her time in the war continues to be a part of her everyday life. In 1989 she started a chapter of WAC Vets in Fort Lauderdale, Florida, where she currently lives. She was the chapter's first president and also founded a chapter of the Society of Military Widows in 1998. She volunteers at the Oakland Park VA Outpatient Clinic, attends Veterans of Foreign Wars meetings, and travels to WAC reunions and conventions. Bozak is living a life whose course was determined by a simple decision to enlist in the army.

See also Military Service; World War II

SOURCES: Bozak, Carmen Contreras. 2002. Interview by Vivian Torre, Miami Vet Center, September 14; Kennon, Katie. 2003. "Choice to Enlist Changes Course of Woman's Life." *Narratives: Stories of U.S. Latinos and Latinas and World War II* (U.S. Latino and Latina WWII Oral History Project, University of Texas at Austin) 4, no. 1 (Spring): 55.

Katie Kennon

BRACERO PROGRAM (1942–1964)

On August 4, 1942, Mexico and the United States launched a contract labor program, commonly known as the Bracero Program. The United States originally proposed this program as a temporary measure to alleviate perceived World War II agricultural labor shortages. The Mexican government urged its men to lend *sus brazos* (their arms, hence the term *bracero*) in this effort to expose them and, upon their return, its citizenry to modern U.S. agricultural skills, values, and work habits. An estimated 4.6 million Mexican men between the ages of twenty and forty left their families and friends to temporarily maintain railroad lines and plant and harvest U.S. cotton, fruit, sugar-beet, and vegetable fields, previously worked by poor black, Latino, and white laborers who opted for better-paying jobs in war production.

Under the 1942 agreement and supplementary legislation in 1943, the U.S. Employment Service of the Department of Labor, its state branches, and the Immigration and Naturalization Service, in collaboration with Mexico's Dirección General del Servicio Consular, the Oficialia Mayor, and the Dirección de Asuntos de Trabajadores Agricolas Migratorios of the Secretaria de Relaciones Exteriores, all offices of participating state governments and municipal county presidents, recruited, transported, and supplied bracero candidates to U.S. agricultural employers. Soon thereafter centers located closer to or at the U.S.-Mexico border in Aguascalientes, Chihuahua, Hermosillo, Mexicali, Monterrey, Tampico, and Zacatecas were included. Depending on whether one uses Mexican or U.S. statistical sources, the yearly number of legally contracted braceros ranged from 49,000 to 80,000 in 1942–1946. The yearly estimates ranged between 116,000 and 141,000 from 1947 to 1954 and were approximately 333,000 in 1955–1964.

From 1942 to 1946 and less so from 1947 to 1964, at the insistence of the Mexican government, U.S. agricultural employers attempted to enforce protective clauses on behalf of braceros that were not then available to domestic U.S. laborers. For example, these clauses assured that upon signing a contract, 10 percent of the prevailing wage would be placed into a savings account and redeemed upon completion of the worker's contract. Both the administration of the program and contract compliance rested on the governments of Mexico and the United States. With the assistance of the United States, agricultural employers would pay for workers' transportation and subsistence costs. Discrimination against braceros, securing their labor for the purpose of displacing U.S. domestic workers, or depressing wages were prohibited. Nonetheless, the U.S. government and agricultural employers often violated these terms and failed to provide braceros with fair wages or the same social benefits available to U.S. domestic laborers. Furthermore, in 1947 Texas's overt violation of these terms resulted in the Mexican government's refusal to export legally contracted braceros into this state.

Approximately 2,600,000 braceros were separated from their wives and children, and by 1964 an estimated 1,375,000 of these men permanently separated from their families because they remained in the United States or journeyed to Mexico's urban centers instead of returning to their families and places of origin. Although these figures reflect high rates of bracero family separation, they cannot possibly approximate the exact number of bracero families that participated in this program. Not all participating braceros signed official contracts with agricultural employers or Mexican government agents. Therefore, the participation of hundreds of bracero families was not documented and is not reflected in these figures. It is uncertain approximately how many braceros reunited with their families in the United States or Mexico.

Overwhelmingly, bracero wives in Mexican rural villages and urban towns did not have a say in their husbands' participation and were abandoned, ostracized, and stigmatized. Adela Piñeda, a former bracero wife, remembers anxiously waiting at her door for her husband to return from work, only to find out two days later that he had left and joined the Bracero Program. Convinced that he would quickly send "letters stuffed with money," her family and friends failed to understand her shock and desperation. They did not sympathize or offer emotional or financial support, and letters "stuffed with money" never arrived. Consequently, and much to their horror, Adela sold her furniture and livestock and left with their child for Guadalajara, Jalisco.

Upon her arrival she opened a *fonda* (makeshift lunch counter) and introduced herself to her neighbors and customers as a single teenage girl of recently deceased parents caring for her newborn brother. It struck her as a plausible story; after all, she was only seventeen years old. Committed not only to make ends meet, but to prosper socially and financially, she desperately used whatever means were necessary to start anew.

Parents and relatives did offer emotional and financial support to some bracero wives, but not unconditionally. One example was the case of María Elena Jiménez, who endured her husband's desertion. She repaid his debts, commuting two hours to and from work as a laundress, seamstress, and restaurant hostess. Her parents and siblings repeatedly urged her to restore their and her reputation by moving in with them and relying on their limited financial support. Working eleven hours a day, six days a week, among women and men in the service sector shamed her family. Jiménez explained that rather than live at the "mercy of her mother, father, or anybody else's whim that she preferred working three times as hard to make ends meet."

However, there were women like Julia Méndez who relied on their parents' and other relatives' moral and financial support to cope with their husbands' negligence, so much so that these relatives took an active role in reprimanding their sons-in-law's behavior. In fact, angry letters like those written by Arturo Ortega, in which he condemned Angel Méndez for never bothering to "send so much as a few coins" to his daughter, were fairly common. He, like many other angry fathers and relatives, stressed in lengthy letters that like Angel, their estranged sons-in-law "never sent their daughters enough money to buy a loaf of bread, let alone a dress, and that they were not men but *desgraciados*."

Not all braceros abandoned their wives and families. Many marriages endured while partners lived for long periods apart. María Ruiz, Ester García, and Laura Camacho would hand over their husband's remittances to either their parents or mothers-in-law. They in turn would purchase shoes for their grandchildren, rebozos (shawls), *tejanas* (cowboy hats), *guaraches* (sandals), and *zarapes* (warm drapes) for themselves, and a large supply of maize and other grains, beans, bread, coffee, cheese, and milk for the entire family and save whatever was left. Nevertheless, bracero wives were not permitted to administer these funds or purchase so much as a dress or a new pair of shoes for themselves. These wives asserted that had they managed their husband's remittances themselves, this would have been interpreted by society as selfish and disrespectful and would have made them the talk of the town.

Bracero wives' experiences further confirm that their husbands' absence augmented the intensity of gender norms. They abided by their respective families' and peers' values or risked losing their support, reputation, and marriage's livelihood. Women's behavior was severely scrutinized, forcing many to assume subordinate or autonomous roles in the extreme to survive.

In sharp contrast, and in spite of strong opposition from the National Association for the Advancement of Colored People, the National Farm Labor Union, and the American Federation of Labor, U.S. agricultural employers were satisfied with the Bracero Program. Moreover, upon the program's expiration in 1947, they managed to secure a substitute. Again, U.S. and Mexican government officials proved sympathetic, and the result was a new set of arrangements that allowed U.S. agricultural employers themselves to recruit braceros. This was the general procedure under the agreements of March 1947, April 1947, February 1948, and August 1949. All of these agreements except that of 1948 also allowed employers to sign contracts with illegal Mexican workers already in the United States.

Employers regarded this postwar arrangement as more satisfactory than the wartime program. Mexico, however, complained about employer abuses and the drainage of vitally needed labor from the border area. In 1951 the Mexican government refused to renew the agreement unless the United States guaranteed compliance with employment contracts, penalized employers of illegal Mexican workers, and agreed to some system of interior recruitment. U.S. agricultural employers mobilized their forces and astutely secured the ratification of Public Law 78. This law authorized U.S. agricultural employers to recruit braceros, transport them to reception centers near the border, and assist them in negotiating contracts and guaranteed contract compliance. Illegal Mexican workers who had been in the United States five years or longer could also obtain a contract. However, there were a number of restrictions and protective clauses. Mexican workers could not be recruited or imported until the U.S. secretary of labor had certified that there was a need for them. The government would be reimbursed for transportation costs, and in accordance with the executive agreement of 1951 and its later extensions, agricultural employers had to pay braceros the prevailing wage, guarantee employment for at least 75 percent of the contract period, provide compensation for occupational injuries and diseases, and furnish adequate housing and transportation facilities.

Despite persistent criticism on the part of the aforementioned labor groups throughout the 1950s, Mexican Americans, and humanitarian reformers and the 1954 implementation of Operation Wetback, which resulted in the deportation of thousands of illegal Mexican workers, the program established under Public Law 78 remained substantially intact. Repeatedly, critics called for reform. They wanted to establish minimum wages, determine labor shortages in public hearings, and require that agricultural employers offer U.S. domestic laborers the same fringe benefits guaranteed to braceros. They failed, however, to achieve anything of the sort. On the contrary, only minor changes were made. In 1955, for example, an amendment required the Employment Service to consult with laborers, as well as employers, to determine agricultural labor shortages. The Interstate Commerce Commission was empowered to regulate the transportation of braceros and forced a raise in minimum wage rates under a stricter set of administrative rules. Nevertheless, braceros, and to a lesser extent U.S. domestic laborers, were still overwhelmingly discriminated against and were dealt poor working and living conditions and miserable wages.

On December 31, 1964, the Bracero Program came to an end. Agricultural labor shortages declined, and U.S. agricultural employers replaced braceros with machines and illegal Mexican workers without contract labor guarantees. Ultimately, this program was an agent for Mexican solidarity and turmoil, demonstrating that agricultural interests and gender conventions conditioned opportunities and responses and enabling people to participate and interact in very different ways. Most important, this program laid the foundation for what would become the second-largest wave of Mexican and Central American immigration to the United States.

See also Immigration of Latinas to the United States

SOURCES: Calavita, Kitty. 1992. *Inside the State: The Bracero Program, Immigration, and the INS*. New York: Routledge; Galarza, Ernesto. 1964. *Merchants of Labor: The Mexican Bracero Story*. Santa Barbara, CA: McNally and Loftin; Gamboa, Erasmo. 1990. *Mexican Labor and World War II: Braceros in the Pacific Northwest, 1942–1947*. Austin: University of Texas Press; García y Griego, Manuel. 1996. "The Importation of Mexican Contract Laborers to the United States, 1942–1964: Antecedents, Operation, and Legacy." In *Between Two Worlds: Mexican Immigrants in the United States*, ed. David G. Gutiérrez. Wilmington, DE: Scholarly Resources.

Ana E. Rosas

BRAGA, SONIA (1950–)

The life of Sonia Braga is one of transcendence. She was born in 1950 to a black-Portuguese father and white-Indian mother in one of Brazil's poorest states, Paraná. After her father's death in 1958 she worked to support her mother and six siblings. Braga's life influenced her advocacy on behalf of children's rights to education, food, and shelter.

Braga became a typist at fourteen; she also starred as a princess on a children's television show. By age eighteen Braga caused a scandal by appearing nude onstage in the Broadway show *Hair*. Her fame soared as she took lead roles on Brazilian soap operas and in various Brazilian films during the early 1970s, and in 1976 her starring role in *Dona Flor e seus dois maridos* gave her career an international character. Among her best-known films are *Moon over Parador* (1988) and *Angel Eyes* (2001), in which Braga portrays Jennifer López's battered mother. Throughout her career Braga has produced two films and appeared in more than twenty-five films and nineteen television series.

For many, Sonia Braga both personifies and reproduces an international perception of Brazilian women as sexy and erotic bombshells. Following Carmen Miranda, Braga reinforced an ideal for Brazilian femininity that became synonymous with her physical appearance. Whether appearing nude in *Hair,* in *Dona Flor e seus dois maridos,* or in *Playboy* (1984, 1987), Braga has used her sexuality to market herself as an actress. Despite this, Braga does not embody a simplified heterosexuality; she has never married and admits to having once fallen in love with another woman. Braga's career demonstrates that women's sexuality moves beyond the reductionism that often characterizes Carmen Miranda's public image. Braga uses sex to challenge women's vulnerability, the cult of virginity, gender roles, age stereotypes, and homophobia. In her first film, *O bandido da Luz Vermelha,* she plays a nineteen-year-old rape victim. In what is perhaps her most famous international role, in *Kiss of the Spider Woman* (1985), Braga is the subject of a gay man's (Molina's) fantasy. In Molina's imagination Braga is both conventional femme fatale and the force that allows him to transcend the confines of his imprisonment. In *Tieta of Agreste* (1996) a forty-six-year-old Braga plays a rich woman who has a sexual affair with her young nephew, who is headed for the priesthood. Finally, she plays the role of a lesbian in several episodes of the hit television series *Sex and the City.*

Braga's life and career also confronted political conflict. She knew activists jailed or killed during Brazil's military dictatorship. In her role in the 1988 film *The Milagro Beanfield War,* Braga plays an activist body-shop owner who rallies the town in defense of the bean field. In 1995 Braga was nominated for an Emmy and a Golden Globe award (best supporting actress) for her role in 1994's *The Burning Season,* a film about the infamous Amazon rain-forest preservation activist Chico Mendes. She was also nominated in 1986 for a Golden Globe award (best supporting actress) for *Kiss of the Spider Woman* and for another in 1989 for *Moon over Parador.*

See also Movie Stars

SOURCES: Braga, Sonia. 1993. Interview by Edney Silvestre, New York, on July 25. *Revista da TV, O Globo*. http://geocities.yahoo.com.br/novela_dancindays/entrevista_sonia.html (accessed October 11, 2003); Ferber, Lawrence. 2001. "Return of the Spider Woman: As the 1985 Classic Kiss of the Spider Woman Returns to Theaters, Sonia Braga Talks about Falling in Love with a Woman, Gay Men's Fantasies, and Her Secret *Sex and the City* Role." *Advocate* 841 (July 3): 42; Richman, Alan. 1988. "'Ugly' Teen Turned Temptress, Sonia Braga Clouds Male Minds but Brightens a Beanfield." *People Weekly* 29, no. 15 (April 18): 66–69.

Nicole Trujillo-Pagán

BRIONES, MARÍA JUANA (1802–1889)

Businesswoman and landowner María Juana Briones was a woman of vision who served as a role model for later generations. María Juana Briones y Tapia de Miranda was born in 1802 in Villa de Branciforte, or present-day Santa Cruz, California. Her father, Marcos Briones, originally from San Luis Potosi, Mexico, was a corporal in the military, and her mother, María Isadora Tapia de Briones, came from Culiacán, Sinaloa, Mexico.

María Juana Briones lived with her family at Polin Springs near the San Francisco Presidio. Her mother Isadora died when Briones was only ten years of age.

However, she was able to teach her daughter survival skills, how to sew, and about the power of the *yerbas* (herbs) before her death.

In 1820 Briones married Apolinario Miranda. They lived in Polin Springs until 1833, when he received a land claim, el Rancho de Ojo de Agua de Figueroa, near the presidio. Throughout the time Briones lived at this ranch, she helped mistreated young sailors, who sometimes were virtually enslaved by their captains. These young sailors escaped the horrendous conditions of the ships and took refuge in the Miranda home, where Briones sheltered and healed them.

About this time Miranda became abusive toward his wife, causing Briones to pack up her children and belongings and petition the authorities for her own land grant. In 1836 Briones received a grant called Yerba Buena, now known as Washington Square in San Francisco. Although the *militario* reprimanded Miranda five times because of his abusive behavior, in 1844 Briones sent a letter to Bishop Diego in Santa Barbara asking for a separation. The bishop then asked the alcalde (mayor) to protect her, and he did.

Briones supported her eight children in a number of ways, including raising cattle, selling and trading the hides and tallow, selling milk, growing and selling vegetables, and working as a seamstress. The single head of a large household, she also adopted an orphan girl named Cecilia Chohuilhuala.

Along with her various business ventures, Briones never stopped caring for people. She was known as a *curandera* (healer) and *partera* (midwife). Her first lessons in healing with herbs were from her mother. Later she continued to develop this expertise by studying with local Indian healers. Historian J. N. Bowman noted that the pioneers of the late 1830s, as well as travelers of the early 1840s, seldom failed to mention her. She was unafraid of disease. Ships arrived in port bringing in men who were suffering from smallpox and scurvy, and Briones took them in as readily as if all they had was the mildest fever. She was known to say, "I want no pay. If they get well, I am satisfied."

In 1844 Briones paid $300 for 4,438 acres of land in Mayfield, in what is now the Los Altos Hills and a small part of Palo Alto. She moved there in 1847 and continued her life as a rancher. In that same year Briones's husband Miranda died. The following year the United States annexed California. In 1851 the U.S. Land Commission came to California to verify land deeds. The Land Commission ruled that since Briones's husband had died, the land was no longer in use. Briones petitioned the commission, stating that she used the land to raise cattle, horses, and vegetables. After twelve years she won her case in the U.S. Supreme Court. Although she never learned to read or write, Briones chose trustworthy people to read and write for her. She was also very careful with her paperwork and precise in the drafting of her contracts.

Throughout the remainder of her life she continued her work as a healer, traveling from Santa Clara to Half Moon Bay, healing people, and helping women bring children into the world. In addition, Briones continued to take in people who were ill and gave them shelter.

In 1884 Briones finally bought a house in Mayfield so she could be close to her daughters. By this time arthritis made it difficult for her to be alone. Five years later, on December 3, 1889, Briones died. She lived long enough to see the railroad come into the area and change the way of traveling. She saw governments change twice in her lifetime. She witnessed the changes in San Francisco as the presidio grew from a wide-open space with few inhabitants to a very crowded city. She lived through the gold rush and the changes it caused in the land and the people. Despite a patriarchal system, Briones thrived as she did what she loved best—raising her children, managing the affairs of her ranch, healing the sick and the infirm, and buying and selling property.

María Juana Briones's contributions were viewed negatively by some who believe that she exploited the labor of the very people she saved from hardship, but others emphasize her humanitarian qualities within the historical context in which she lived. On October 5, 1997, María Juana Briones's contributions to early California were recognized when a monument was erected in her honor in San Francisco's Washington Square, not far from where her Yerba Buena house stood nearly 150 years earlier. Briones remains a strong role model who has set an example for women everywhere.

See also Spanish Borderlands

SOURCES: Bowman, Jacob N. 1957. "Juana Briones de Miranda." *Historical Society of Southern California Quarterly* 39:3 (September): 227–241; Gates, Mary J. 1895. *Contributions to Local History: Rancho Pastoria de los Borregas, Mountain View, California*. San Jose: Cottle and Murgotten Printers; Pitt, Leonard. 1970. *The Decline of the Californios*. Berkeley: University of California Press.

Olga Loya

BURCIAGA, MIRNA RAMOS (1960–)

Mirna Burciaga, an activist and entrepreneur, immigrated to the United States in 1980 as a direct result of death threats issued by citizens of El Salvador rebels in the midst of the civil war that had begun a year earlier. Like Burciaga, the citizens of El Salvador were caught between the government and the rebels and were often the innocent victims of both factions.

In the spring of 1980 Burciaga was riding in the back of a pickup truck when a government soldier wielding an automatic weapon strafed the rear of the truck with bullets because the driver misunderstood an order to pull over for document verification. One bullet ripped the heel of her hand and thumb from her palm, and another tore into her leg. After several months in the hospital she returned home, but it was no longer a safe refuge.

Terrorism in the form of murder, kidnapping, and violence was used by extremist groups in an effort to block the political process. Soldiers warned her that she was on a terrorist list and had only a few days of safety because a close relative was in the military and working for the government. Convinced that she was a target, she left El Salvador and crossed the border into Guatemala. This was the start of a four-month odyssey that ended in southern California and reunited her with her father and two younger sisters, who had left before the civil war erupted.

Burciaga, a third-year university student studying to become a pediatrician, borrowed money from her stepmother in the United States for living and traveling expenses while waiting for official papers to enter the country from Mexico. Hundreds of thousands of people left the carnage of war-torn El Salvador before the peace accords were signed in 1992 between the government and leftist guerrilla forces of the Farabundo Martí Para Liberacion Nacional (FMLN).

Burciaga arrived with few resources other than her intelligence, a strong work ethic, and a will to succeed. Whatever her expectations had been of her family, she was told that she would have to support herself and repay the loan. This was true for most people who emigrated from El Salvador because families and friends did not have the financial resources to help them. Within a week she started work as a live-in nanny/housekeeper in a household with five children. With the aid of a Spanish-English dictionary she was able to communicate with her employers after six months. Her small salary was turned over to her stepmother until she paid off the debt for her escape. After sharing the rent and food expenses, Burciaga saved enough to leave her job and look for more lucrative employment.

Studies reveal that Central American women now dominate in private domestic jobs, but their sheer numbers push wages down. Within a short period Burciaga circumvented this pattern by working for a number of clients and hiring an assistant. Cleaning private homes gave her more money and the time to return to school. While continuing to work, she received her associate's degree in fashion from a local community college, married Sal Burciaga, a man who had emigrated from Mexico in 1983, and gave birth to three children, Natalie, Sal, and Stephanie.

Salvadoran entrepreneur Mirna Burciaga. Courtesy of Mirna Burciaga.

Armed with her degree in fashion and her savings, she opened a clothing store, but success eluded her. Undaunted, she looked around for another opportunity. On the site of a failing Mexican restaurant she opened a Salvadoran restaurant. Without professional expertise, but with faith in her abilities and recipes from her native country, she introduced a new cuisine to the neighborhood. Ten years later, when her lease could not be renewed, she found a better location and opened a larger restaurant, El Chinaco, with great success.

Burciaga's striving and unrelenting hard work made her a successful businesswoman, and, as the mother of three school-age children, she was determined to use the same energy to create a better and safer educational environment for the children in her community. To accomplish this new goal, she sought out and worked with local politicians and community organizations devoted to children's welfare. She is on the board of the University of California at Irvine's Community Outreach Partnership Center, among many other organizations. Her unwavering commitment to her adopted country and her close association with the political process have led her to run for election to the Costa Mesa City Council in 2004. Though she was unsuccessful in her first bid for political office, she vows to run again and someday serve as the first Hispanic woman mayor of Costa Mesa.

SOURCES: Burciaga, Mirna Ramos. 2004. Interview by Carole Autori, October; Hamilton, Nora, and Norma Stoltz Chinchilla. 2001. *Seeking Community in a Global City: Guatemalans and Salvadorans in Los Angeles*. Philadelphia: Temple University Press; Hondagneu-Sotelo, Pierrette. 2001. *Doméstica: Immigrant Workers Cleaning and Caring in the Shadows of Affluence*. Berkeley: University of California Press; Menjívar, Cecilia. 2002. *Fragmented Ties: Salvadoran Immigrant Networks in America*. Berkeley: University of California Press.

Carole Autori

C

CABALLERO, DIANA (1947–)

Diana Caballero is an educator, community organizer, and activist. She has dedicated much of her life to developing civil rights and educational reform organizations. She was a member of the Young Lords Party (1970s), president of the National Congress for Puerto Rican Rights (1983–1987), and director of the Puerto Rican/Latino Education Roundtable (1984–1997).

Caballero was born and raised in the South Bronx area of New York and went to public schools. After receiving an associate's degree in secretarial studies from the Borough of Manhattan Community College (1967), she went on to complete a B.A. in elementary education at City College of the City University of New York (1970). In 1978 she graduated summa cum laude with a master's degree in elementary and bilingual education from Long Island University, and she obtained both an M.A. and an Ed.D. in educational administration and bilingual education from Teachers College of Columbia University in 1996. From Hofstra University she received a certificate of advanced study in educational administration.

In 1972 Caballero successfully coordinated the efforts of a coalition formed to pressure the Public Broadcasting Network, WNET, Channel 13, to produce and fund *Realidades,* the first bilingual television series transmitted in the United States. Later, as a member of the project team, she helped develop program philosophy and content. From 1972 to 1984 Caballero worked in different settings, but always as an advocate for bilingual education. She was, for example, an elementary-school teacher, and as a trainer and resource specialist, she presented workshops for teachers, administrators, and parents.

As the director of the Puerto Rican/Latino Education Roundtable based at the Centro de Estudios Puertorriqueños, Hunter College, she effectively advocated for educational reform and the needs of Latino students throughout the public school system. As a strong proponent of the right to a bilingual education, she served as coordinator of the Bilingual Education Task Force of the National Congress for Puerto Rican Rights

Educator Diana Caballero. Courtesy of the Luis O. Reyes Papers. Centro Archives, Centro de Estudios Puertorriqueños, Hunter College, CUNY.

and the New York Coalition for Bilingual Education. Caballero participated on numerous boards, committees, and commissions concerned with public education, such as the Manhattan Borough President's Task Force on Education and Decentralization, Chancellor Fernández's Multi-cultural Advisory Board, and the City-wide Community School Board Elections Committee. She also served on Education Commissioner Thomas Sobol's Task Force on Minorities: Equity and Excellence that published the controversial report "Curriculum of Inclusion," which was highly critical of the exclusionary school curriculum in effect throughout the system. Her activism went beyond educational advocacy, as is demonstrated by her work with the Committee against Fort Apache (1980–1981) (formed to counter media racism and oppose the film *Fort Apache: The Bronx*) and the Black and Latino Coalition against Police Brutality (1979–1980).

Caballero has been widely recognized for her educational advocacy, her organizational leadership, and her dedication to upholding the democratic and civil rights of Puerto Ricans and other Latinos. In 1990 she received an award from the Women for Racial and Economic Equality and in 1989 from the Parents Coalition for Education of New York City. She was also the recipient of the Charles Bannerman Memorial Fellowship Award in 1988.

Caballero is currently an assistant professor in the Bilingual Education Program of the Department of Childhood Education at the City College of New York. The Diana Caballero Papers at the Library and Archives of the Center for Puerto Rican Studies at Hunter College are important sources in the areas of bilingual education, language rights, and educational reform. They provide information about organizations such as the Committee against Fort Apache and the National Congress for Puerto Rican Rights and community activism in the 1980s.

See also Education; Young Lords

SOURCE: Caballero, Diana. 1967–1999. Papers. Centro Archives, Centro de Estudios Puertorriqueños, Hunter College, CUNY.

Ismael García, Nélida Pérez, and Pedro Juan Hernández

CABEZA DE BACA, FABIOLA (1894–1991)

Fabiola Cabeza de Baca, a Hispanic New Mexican writer also known as Fabiola C. de Baca Gilbert, was born on May 16, 1894, in La Liendre, New Mexico Territory, to Graciano and Indalecia C. de Baca. As a writer and folklorist, Cabeza de Baca touched the lives of many people throughout her long career. Some historians and folklorists consider her a "legendary" figure of New Mexico, while among Hispanic literary critics her writings are viewed as a precursor of Chicana literature.

C. de Baca, as she often identified herself, lived a life of privilege. Her wealthy and influential family included lawyers, writers, politicians, and a New Mexico governor. C. de Baca idealized this society in her books and identified with it throughout her life. She was inculcated by her paternal grandmother with the practice of noblesse oblige, the obligation of the rich to help those less fortunate. It profoundly affected her life and work.

C. de Baca lived in a highly stratified society steeped in interethnic racism. Many Hispanos felt genetically superior to Mexicans and Indians because of their light skin, blue eyes, and Iberian origins. Still, C. de Baca crossed class lines frequently; she socialized with elites, but taught in rural schools. For most of her life she worked with the poor and needy.

C. de Baca attended Loreto Academy, where Hispanic elites sent their daughters. Because of insubordination (she slapped a nun) she was expelled from kindergarten and enrolled at New Mexico Normal, where she earned a teaching credential in 1912.

During C. de Baca's childhood education among Hispanos was limited. School statistics show that while illiteracy fell from 79.0 percent in 1875 to 14.0 percent in 1920 throughout the state, more than 50 percent of Hispanos were not literate. Few women progressed beyond third grade. Appalled at the lack of education among the poor, C. de Baca applied to teach in a rural schoolhouse. Hired to teach for the Santa Rosa School District, she rode a pony to the schoolhouse. In bad weather she was forced to take the train. The mostly poor students from nearby ranches rode ponies to the one-room school that lacked drinking water and a privy. C. de Baca appealed to her father for funds to purchase the school supplies the cash-strapped district could not afford. She taught school for twelve years while attending college. Her efforts were rewarded when she became the first female in the C. de Baca clan to attain an advanced degree. She earned a baccalaureate in domestic science at what is today New Mexico Highlands University and a master's degree in pedagogy from New Mexico State University.

As the first Hispana hired by the New Mexico Agricultural Extension Service (NMAES), a New Deal government agency, C. de Baca worked with farm women. NMAES was an important component of the 1930s reform programs designed to "Americanize" (native Indian) women. For more than thirty years C. de Baca taught domestic skills and food preservation. She is often credited with reviving the Hispano *colcha* (quilting) tradition. During World War II she helped organize victory gardens and child-care centers for women working in war-related industries. The high-school 4-H clubs that she developed became a source of personal pride, especially when in 1940 her students won blue ribbons in dressmaking at the New Mexico State Fair.

In the 1940s C. de Baca rebelled against her conservative Catholic grandparents to marry Carlos Gilbert, a divorced man. There were no children from this union, and in time she and Gilbert divorced. Soon afterward, while she was driving on a country road, C. de Baca's car collided with a train, and she almost lost her life. She was hospitalized for more than a year, and her rehabilitation was hampered by a limited supply of antibiotics. Ultimately she lost her left leg to gangrene. Fitted with a prosthesis, she continued her work with NMAES.

As the family historian, C. de Baca knew well the history of most Hispanos in northern New Mexico's Staked Plains. She documented many historical events throughout the state. Her writing career began with her translations from English to Spanish of NMAES nutrition pamphlets. Her first recipe books, *Historic Cookery* (1939) and *The Good Life: New Mexico Traditions and Food* (1949), placed traditional Hispanic recipes within a cultural context. *We Fed Them Cactus* (1945) chronicles the history of Hispanos in northern New Mexico, her family among them. It was one of the first works to cite the important contributions of Hispano ranch women to the settlement of that state.

The Chicano movement of the 1970s led to the rediscovery of C. de Baca's writings. *We Fed Them Cactus* is today considered an important contribution to early Hispanic American literature. C. de Baca has been honored by numerous organizations, including her alma mater, New Mexico State University. Among her best-known publications are *Los alimentos y su preparación, Historic Cookery, The Good Life,* and *We Fed Them Cactus.*

See also Literature

SOURCE: Kanellos, Nicolás, ed. 2002. *Herencia: The Anthology of Hispanic Literature in the United States.* New York: Oxford University Press.

Merrihelen Ponce

CABRERA, ANGELINA "ANGIE" (1927–)

Angelina (Angie) Cabrera was born to Puerto Rican parents in Brooklyn Heights, New York, where she continues to live. Upon graduation from Girls' Commercial High School during World War II, Cabrera's ambition was to join the air force, but "nice" Puerto Rican girls were expected not to leave home until they were married nor to work far away from home. Instead, she became a secretary at Fort Hamilton Army Base in Brooklyn and unsuspectingly entered a lifelong career that would be filled with glamour, travel, excitement, politics, finance, and advocacy for minority and women's rights.

At Fort Hamilton she met and married a young navy man, and soon thereafter they moved to Pittsburgh, Pennsylvania, where he pursued an architectural degree at Carnegie Institute of Technology. From 1952 to 1954 Angie Cabrera worked for H. J. Heinz Company as its official Spanish translator. Assigned to the Foreign Sales Division, she became secretary to the director and also translated for H. J. Heinz Sr. because of his many holdings in Spain. Returning to New York, Cabrera attended Fordham University and completed a baccalaureate degree in political science. She was employed at the Office of the Commonwealth of Puerto Rico as executive secretary to the director of tourism, but graduated to confidential executive secretary to the governor of Puerto Rico, Luis Muñoz Marín. In this position Cabrera traveled extensively throughout Puerto Rico and accompanied the governor on his many trips to Washington, D.C. This was a heady time in Puerto Rican politics because the island was embarking on a massive economic reorganization, Operation Bootstrap. Cabrera's deep involvement in Puerto Rican affairs stems from this experience. "I learned to take risks even though I was afraid," remarks Cabrera. "That experience was responsible for the strong commitment I have to help my Puerto Ricans." That phase of her life also opened other doors for Cabrera, particularly connected with Democratic Party politics.

From 1965 until 1968 Cabrera was the New York secretary for Senator Robert F. Kennedy and special staff assistant on Hispanic affairs. At the forefront of the American political scene, Cabrera traveled extensively with the Kennedys and organized rallies, meetings, and personal matters. Cabrera became the liaison between the senator and the Latino community. On June 5, 1968, Robert F. Kennedy was assassinated, and Cabrera faced the most heartbreaking responsibility of her career when she was called upon to personally arrange for the closing of the senator's New York apartment and office. When Cabrera was sworn in as New York governor Hugh Carey's deputy director of the Women's Division in 1975, Ethel Kennedy's presence at the ceremony indicated the closeness that had developed between the two women.

After Kennedy's assassination Cabrera branched out into her own business. She founded Capital Formation (1969–1972), the first nonprofit pioneering organization of its kind. Devoted to assisting minority entrepreneurs in preparing business plans and loan packages, Capital Formation acted as an intermediary between the Small Business Administration and banking institutions. In 1972 Cabrera decided that it was time for a change, and she was offered the position of national director for public relations and community affairs at the National Puerto Rican Forum, a nonprofit organization designed to provide a variety of services to the Latino community throughout the city. At the forum she created a cultural center "to develop awareness of our fabulous artists, many of whom had never been properly exposed."

Cabrera's political contacts and understanding of government and community services provided her with the broad experience needed for appointments to a number of administrative positions. She was a member of the Manhattan Women's Political Caucus and a board member of ASPIRA, the Puerto Rican Family Institute, the National Association of Puerto Rican Women, and the National Association of Minority Busi-

Angelina Cabrera, president of Cabrera and Associates, a well-respected leader in Puerto Rican, minority, and women's causes. Courtesy of Angelina Cabrera.

ness Women. She was advisor to the First Women's Bank and the Citizens' Union. Cabrera served as a delegate to the Democratic National Convention in 1972 and was vice-chairperson of the State Democratic Committee and a member of the Compliance Review Commission created by the Democratic National Committee to oversee affirmative action in delegate selection for the 1976 Democratic National Convention. At that point Cabrera was working as assistant deputy director for the Women's Division for the Executive Chamber of the State of New York. For ten years Cabrera was in a position to represent women's and minority issues to state legislators, reaching out especially to African Americans, Latinos, and small-business entrepreneurs.

In May 1984 Cabrera became the business development specialist in the New York State Department of Economic Development's Division of Minority and Women's Business Development. Two years later Governor Mario M. Cuomo appointed her assistant deputy commissioner for that division. Cabrera held this position for eleven years. In 1998 Cabrera was appointed as a commissioner in the Equal Employment Practices Commission by Rudolph Giuliani, then mayor of the city of New York. She completed the previous commissioner's two remaining years and was reappointed.

Cabrera has been honored on countless occasions for her service and dedication to the city, the state, and the Latino community. However, her greatest reward has been the opportunity to "encourage all Hispanics, especially Hispanic women, to participate more fully in city, state, and national politics, so that our children can have a fair share of the benefits enjoyed by other American citizens."

See also Politics, Party

SOURCES: *Hispanic America*. 1995. "Angela Cabrera, Assistant Deputy Commissioner." Special edition. 1, no. 1 (May); Maldonado, Adál Alberto. 1984. "Angela Cabrera." In *Portraits of the Puerto Rican Experience,* ed. Louis Reyes Rivera and Julio Rodríguez. New York: IPRUS Institute.

Hector Carrasquillo and Virginia Sánchez Korrol

CABRERA, LYDIA (1899–1991)

Lydia Cabrera, one of Cuba's foremost Afro-Cuban culture writers of the twentieth century, was born in Havana on May 20, 1899, and died in Miami on September 19, 1991. She has become an indispensable source of study for scholars and individuals interested in the African presence in Cuba, especially its religious and linguistic aspects.

Born into an educated and socially prominent family of Havana—her father was Raimundo Cabrera, writer and editor of *Cuba y América,* one of the most important Cuban cultural journals of the early twentieth century—she had the opportunity of being immersed from childhood in the magic realism of Afro-Cuban reality through the "nanas" who took care of her and fed her with the folktales, religious stories, legends, and rhymes that filled her imagination with the sense of awe that would be evident in the years to come. Hers was a firsthand early life experience that left a unique imprint on her future work. Equally important was the influence of Fernando Ortiz, Cuba's most renowned scholar of Afro-Cuban culture.

The Paris of the 1920s and 1930s influenced Lydia Cabrera's cultural life decisively. The years during which she lived in that city—almost two decades, with brief trips to her homeland—awakened and strengthened in her the memories and feelings of her childhood and adolescence. It was the Paris of Josephine Baker, "La Revue Nègre," and "Le Bal Nègre" at the Théâtre de Champs Elysées; of the encounter of a city with jazz and the realization of Negritude as a transforming and powerful social and cultural force. It was in Paris, in 1936, that *Contes Nègres de Cuba,* her first collection of short stories, was published in a French translation.

After her return to Cuba in 1939, she published the original Spanish version titled *Cuentos negros,* which appeared in 1940. Another collection of short stories, *¿Por qué?,* followed in 1948. In 1954 *El monte,* a monumental work now in its eighth edition, appeared in print for the first time. The book, which, according to the author, studies "the religions, magic, superstitions and folklore of black 'criollos' and of the Cuban people," has become a classic in the genre. Between 1955 and 1958 three other books were published: *Refranes de negros viejos* (1955), *Anagó (vocabulario Lucumí)* (1957), and *La sociedad secreta Abakuá* (1958). In 1960, after the Cuban Revolution, she went into exile and never returned to Cuba.

Lydia Cabrera's work is impressive for its vastness and originality, and most of it has been published outside Cuba. After leaving the island she went to Spain, where she published *La laguna sagrada de San Joaquín* (1973) and another extraordinary work, *Anaforuana: Ritos y símbolos de iniciación en la sociedad secreta Abakuá* (1975). The latter included a substantial number of her own symbolic drawings.

Lydia Cabrera's passionate love for Cuban culture in general and Afro-Cuban culture in particular translated into a remarkable and extensive body of work, written and published in the United States during a twenty-year span. Significantly, this began when she was already in her seventies and ended near her death at ninety-two years of age. Perhaps the most productive period of her life, the years 1970–1988, demonstrated, once again, the sensitivity, astounding knowledge, intellectual rigor devoid of arrogance, and the human touch, so ingrained in both her scholarly and creative discourses, of a woman full of vitality and joy for life. Titles for this period include *Otán y Iyebiyé: Las piedras preciosas* (1970), *Ayapá: Cuentos de jicotea* (1971), *Yemayá y Ochún* (1974), *Francisco y Francisca* (1976), *Itinerarios del insomnio: Trinidad de Cuba* (1977), *La regla kimbisa del Santo Cristo del Buen Viaje* (1977), *Reglas de Congo: Palo Monte Mayombe* (1979), *Koeko Iyawó: Aprende novicia, pequeño tratado de regal lucumí* (1980), *Siete cartas de Gabriela Mistral a Lydia Cabrera* (1980), *Cuentos para niños, adultos y retrasados mentales* (1983), *Vocabulario Congo* (1984), *La medicina popular en Cuba* (1984), *Supersticiones y buenos consejos* (1987), and *La lengua sagrada de los ñáñigos* (1988). In 1993 Isabel Castellanos posthumously published Lydia Cabrera's *Consejos, pensamientos, y notas de Lydia E. Pinbán* and, in 1994, *Páginas sueltas.* A person of courage, full of intellectual vitality, with a deep sense of personal integrity and a compassionate view of life, ahead of her times in many ways, Lydia Cabrera stands as an exemplary woman who paved the way for others to walk along the path she discovered.

Specialist in Afro-Cuban culture Lydia Cabrera. Courtesy of the Cuban Heritage Collection, Otto G. Richter Library, University of Miami.

See also Literature

SOURCES: Castellanos, Isabel, and Josefina Inclán, eds. 1987. *En torno a Lydia Cabrera.* Miami: Ediciones Universal; Hiriart, Rosario. 1988. *Cartas a Lydia Cabrera: Correspondencia inédita de Gabriela Mistral y Teresa de la Parra.* Madrid: Ediciones Torremozas.

Reinaldo Sánchez

CALDERÓN, ROSE MARIE (1956–)

Born to New Mexican parents, Rose Marie Romero Calderón has combined her workplace responsibilities and family roles with community organizing. Alongside her husband, José Calderón, she helped develop a community-based organization and center in Greeley, Colorado, Al Frente de Lucha. Through this organization Calderón organized yearly community fundraisers, marches, and fiestas to commemorate Mexican holidays and to economically sustain the organization. Believing that gender transformations must begin in the home, Calderón instituted a division of labor in which the males in the family all took part in the domestic chores. In Monterey Park, California, she headed a parents' group in her children's day-care center that led to the establishment of various neighborhood groups. She connected her roles in the family

Rose Marie Calderón. Courtesy of José Z. Calderón.

with community activism by supporting political candidates for local, state, and national positions.

With her husband, Calderón organized various parent groups in the Alhambra School District to challenge the practice of tracking Latino students into vocational education classes and the lack of a multicultural educational focus in the curriculum. Working with parents from diverse backgrounds, she advocated for her sons, as well as pushing for changes that affected the entire school district. As part of the Multi-ethnic Task Force, she helped develop a list of ten proposals that included a policy for dealing with hate-motivated behavior. This policy required principals to create an environment that would allow all persons "to realize their full individual potential through understanding and appreciation of society's diversity of race, ethnic background, national origin, religious belief, sex, age, disability, or sexual orientation." As part of this policy, the school district institutionalized conflict-resolution classes and gave students the option of mediation as an alternative to expulsion.

Calderón also helped establish another parent advocacy group at the local Boys' and Girls' Club that brought Latino and Asian youth together around sports programs and issues of diversity. In recent years she served on the board of the House of Ruth, a domestic violence shelter in Claremont, California. She is also a staunch advocate for the rights of immigrant workers to obtain driver's licenses, good jobs, quality education, and adequate health care.

SOURCES: Calderón, José. 1995. "Multi-ethnic Coalition Building in a Diverse School District." *Critical Sociology* 21, no. 1: 101–111; Horton, John, and José Calderón. 1995. *Politics of Diversity*. Philadelphia: Temple University Press; Pardo, Mary. 1998. *Mexican American Women Activists: Identity and Resistance in Two Los Angeles Communities.* Philadelphia: Temple University Press.

José Z. Calderón

CALIFORNIA MISSIONS

In 1769 Junípero Serra, a Franciscan missionary, founded the first of twenty-one Catholic missions as part of Spain's effort to colonize California. Serra and his missionary colleagues had two goals. Most important, they intended to convert the Indians to the Roman Catholic faith. Second, they meant to inculcate Spanish ways, the Spanish language, and Spanish social mores in the Indian converts, whom the missionaries called neophytes. This task necessarily involved an effort to reconstruct the gender roles and relations of California Indians. Missionaries regarded their work as a divinely sanctioned effort to save Indian souls and improve Indian society. For Indians, the missionaries' demands were often confusing and sometimes cruel.

Indian and Spanish societies constructed gender roles according to long-standing customs and religious beliefs. Generalization about Indian ideas concerning gender is difficult because the social structures of native California were complex and varied. There were more than 100 languages spoken in California and dozens of distinctive tribal cultures. In general, California Indians were hunters and food collectors who exploited well-established territories. For the most part, men hunted and fished, while women collected wild plant foods. According to anthropologists, women probably provided more food for their communities than men. Oak trees were ubiquitous in California, and the acorn meal that women processed was a staple of the Indian diet. Spanish and Indian ideas about men's and women's economic roles overlapped at many points. In the Spanish system women were expected to prepare food and work at other domestic tasks such as sewing, much as Indian women were expected to cook and make baskets and clothing. However, missionaries expected men to till fields, which was more like women's work than anything that they had done before.

Men held most of the spiritual and leadership roles among Indians in pre-Spanish times, but in some societies there were female chiefs and shamans. In Spanish society religious and political authority was vested in the men. The mission system provided some appointive and elective positions for neophytes, such as alcalde (mayor), and these went to men. Within the missions there were few leadership roles available to women that the priests sanctioned. However, some neophyte women held considerable influence by virtue of their jobs within the mission. For example, priests named a woman to oversee the unmarried female barracks (*monjero*). She reported on the women inmates and locked them in at night to stymie illicit sexual liaisons or perhaps closed her eyes to certain transgressions. Priests' attempts to transform Indian sexual and marriage customs probably caused the most trouble. They taught that spousal intercourse was the only permissible sexual activity. All other sexual activity was execrable sin. In native society there were fewer constraints on sexuality, especially before marriage, when sexual experimentation usually occurred. Once married, however, spouses were expected to be loyal to their partners. Sexual misbehavior was a legitimate ground for divorce, which usually occurred if one of the parties desired it. Some Indian cultures permitted polygamy, but the practice of taking multiple wives was usually restricted to wealthy men and chiefs. Among Catholics marriage was a permanent arrangement ordained by God, and divorce was extremely difficult. There was no provision for polygamy in Catholic or Spanish society. These rules seemed unnecessarily strict to neophytes who were accustomed to serial monogamy.

Santa Barbara Mission, Santa Barbara, California. Courtesy of the Library of Congress, American Landscape and Architectural Design, 1850–1920 (Reproduction no. 117845).

The presence of *berdache,* males who dressed as women and performed female roles, among California Indians shocked and horrified Spanish priests and laymen alike. Evidently Indians regarded the *berdache* as a third gender with male and female characteristics, although researchers disagree on this matter. High-ranking Indian men often took a *berdache* as a second wife because it was believed that they could work harder than women. Priests, however, regarded *berdache* behavior as a sin against nature and punished them, and their male partners, wherever they were found. The *berdache* were common when the missionaries first arrived, but eventually became rare in the vicinity of Spanish settlements.

While marriages occurred between Spanish-Mexican men and Indian women, there were comparatively few of these formal unions in California. They evidently preferred to marry their own. Nevertheless, there were many informal unions between soldiers and Indian women. Some of these were based on mutual attraction, but missionaries frequently complained about soldiers raping Indian women. Sexual assaults were among the causes of Indian rebellion against Spanish authority. Prostitution seems not to have been practiced in California before 1769, but references to Indian prostitutes were common by the end of the eighteenth century.

Priests' concerns about illicit sex of all kinds led them to construct *monjeros* at the missions. Once they reached sexual maturity, unmarried female neophytes had to sleep in these locked rooms in order to prevent philandering. Sequestering young women failed to prevent illicit sex, but the close living quarters fostered the spread of communicable diseases. Some researchers think that these living conditions contributed to high death rates among women. Despite the efforts of priests to instruct neophytes in the normative sexual behavior of eighteenth-century Catholic Spaniards, many Indians continued sexual behavior that offended priests. Whether this was a form of rebellion or the continuation of age-old customs is an open question. One of the unintended results of Spanish settlement was the spread of sexually transmitted diseases, especially syphilis, to which Indians had not been previously exposed. This was especially true in the missions, where large numbers of Indians were concentrated in novel living conditions. Syphilis lowered the birthrate, raised the death rate, especially among women, and contributed to the overall decline of Indian population in the missions.

In sum, the missions affected Indian gender roles and relations in several ways. Men and women's roles were altered. The once numerous *berdache* were eliminated or driven underground. Indian sexual behavior came under surveillance. New diseases reduced the native population in general and were especially deadly among women, thus reducing the birthrate. Therefore, it must be said that the attempts to reconstruct gender roles in the mission had a disastrous effect on the neophytes. Nevertheless, substantial numbers of Indians survived the mission experience, and some of them are practicing Catholics today.

See also Spanish Borderlands

SOURCES: Castañeda, Antonia I. 1990. "Presidarias y Pobladoras: Spanish-Mexican Women in Frontier Monterey, Alta California, 1770–1821." Ph.D. diss., Stanford University; Castillo, Edward D. 1994. "Gender Status and Decline, Resistance, and Accommodation among Female Neophytes in the Missions of California: A San Gabriel Case Study." *American Indian Culture and Research Journal* 18, no. 1:67–94; Cook, Sherburne F. 1976. *The Conflict between the California Indian and White Civilization*. Berkeley: University of California Press; Hackel, Steven W. 1997. "The Staff of Leadership: Indian Authority in the Missions of Alta California." *William and Mary Quarterly* 54 (April): 347–376; Hurtado, Albert L. 1992. "Sexuality in California's Franciscan Missions: Cultural Perceptions and Sad Realities." *California History* 71 (Fall): 370–385; ———. 1999. *Intimate Frontiers: Sex, Gender, and Culture in Old California*. Albuquerque: University of New Mexico Press.

Albert L. Hurtado

CALIFORNIA SANITARY CANNING COMPANY STRIKE

On August 31, 1939, at the height of the peach season, 400 (out of 430) workers walked off their jobs at the California Sanitary Canning Company (Cal San), one of the largest food-processing firms in Los Angeles. The next day sixteen of the thirty who stayed behind joined their picketing co-workers outside the plant. Though their jobs were at stake and they pounded the pavement in record-breaking heat, the strikers (the majority were Mexican and Russian Jewish women) were demanding not only higher wages and better plant conditions but also the recognition of their union, Local 75 of the United Cannery, Agricultural, Packing, and Allied Workers of America (UCAPAWA). Their militancy marked the beginning of unparalleled labor activism among cannery workers in southern California.

This canning labor force included young daughters, newly married women, middle-aged wives, and widows. Occasionally three generations worked at a particular cannery—daughter, mother, and grandmother. They pooled their resources to put food on the table. Carmen Bernal Escobar recalled, "And to keep the family going . . . in order to bring in a little more money . . . my mother, my grandmother, my mother's brother, my sister and I all worked together at Cal San."

At Cal San women clustered into specific departments—washing, grading, cutting, canning, and packing—and were paid according to the production level. Women jockeyed for position near the chutes or gates where the produce was plentiful. Standing in the same spots month after month, women often developed friendships that crossed family and ethnic lines. Their day-to-day problems (slippery floors, peach fuzz, production speedups, tyrannical supervisors, and even sexual harassment) cemented feelings of solidarity. They even employed a special language when talking among themselves, often referring to an event in terms of when specific fruits or vegetables arrived for processing at the plant. For instance, the phrase "We met in spinach, fell in love in peaches, and married in tomatoes" indicated that the couple met in March, fell in love in August, and married in October.

In July 1939 Dorothy Ray Healey, a UCAPAWA organizer, began to distribute union leaflets outside the Cal San gates. Meetings were held in workers' homes so entire families could listen, and membership cards traveled from one kin or peer network to the next. Within three weeks 400 Cal San employees had joined. The cannery owners, the Shapiro brothers, refused to recognize the union, and a strike was called. In addition to the twenty-four-hour picket line around the plant, the workers set up boycotts and picketed local grocery stores that refused to take Cal San products off their shelves. After a two-and-one-half-month standoff the workers implemented an innovative strategy that brought management to the bargaining table—their children picketed the front lawns of the Shapiros' homes. Within days of the child pickets, who carried signs such as "I'm underfed because my Mama is underpaid," a settlement was reached.

Wages and conditions improved at Cal San as workers nurtured their local. In 1941 Luisa Moreno, a UCAPAWA vice president, arrived to organize other canneries in southern California. She enlisted the aid of Cal San workers in union drives at several area food-processing firms. The result was Local 3, the second-largest UCAPAWA affiliate in the nation. Moreno encouraged cross-plant alliances and women's leadership. In 1943, for example, Mexican women filled eight of the fifteen elected local positions. The local provided benefits that few industrial unions could match—free legal advice and a hospitalization plan. A fierce loyalty developed as the result of rank-and-file participation and leadership. Forty years after the strike Carmen Bernal

Women of the California Sanitary Canning Company, 1936. Courtesy of Carmen Bernal Escobar.

Escobar declared, "UCAPAWA was the greatest thing that ever happened to the workers at Cal San. It changed everything and everybody."

See also United Cannery, Agricultural, Packing, and Allied Workers of America (UCAPAWA/FTA)

SOURCES: Ruiz, Vicki L. 1987. *Cannery Women, Cannery Lives: Mexican Women, Unionization, and the California Food Processing Industry, 1930–1950.* Albuquerque: University of New Mexico Press; ———. 1998. *From out of the Shadows: Mexican Women in Twentieth-Century America.* New York: Oxford University Press.

Vicki L. Ruiz

CALLEJO, ADELFA BOTELLO (1923–)

Adelfa Callejo, attorney, civic leader, and activist, was born in Millett, Texas, on June 10, 1923, the eldest of four children of Felix Botello and Guadalupe Guerra. Her father migrated to Texas in 1911, but her mother was Texas born. Although her parents lacked in formal education, they encouraged and assisted her to gain an education. Callejo aspired to become a lawyer after seeing an uncle deported without the benefit of a hearing. Educated in the "Mexican" schools of southern Texas, Callejo graduated from high school in Cotulla, Texas. She moved to Dallas with her family and began the first of many years of night-school study at Southern Methodist University (SMU). Her education was postponed near the end of World War II when she moved to California to assist her brother, who had been wounded in the war.

In California she met William "Bill" F. Callejo, and they married in Dallas. Adelfa Callejo returned to night classes at SMU and earned her law degree in 1961. She was the only Hispanic and one of only three women in the class. Passing the bar exam, she became one of only two Hispanic lawyers in Dallas at that time. By 1966 Bill added a law degree to his degrees in architecture and engineering, and they formed the law partnership of Callejo and Callejo, with Adelfa specializing in personal injury, criminal, and family law. These specialties allowed her to concentrate on one of her goals, aiding the disadvantaged.

In addition to representing criminal defendants and those who had suffered catastrophic injuries, Adelfa Callejo also was active in the community. An advocate for minorities in the fields of education, housing, immigration, voting rights, and other social justice issues, she challenged at-large elections to the Dallas City Council, a violation of the Voting Rights Act, and was successful when the local federal district court agreed that the process diluted minority votes. In education she lobbied six Dallas district superintendents until a dropout-prevention program was implemented.

Among the many boards on which she served were the Dallas Housing Authority, Dallas Area Rapid Transit, Dallas County Mental Health and Mental Retardation, Mexican American Legal Defense and Educational Fund, and Dallas Fort Worth International Airport (where during her time on the board 72 percent of $75 million for concessions at the airport were awarded to women- and minority-owned businesses). She served as president of the Dallas County Criminal Bar Association and as regional president of the Hispanic National Bar Association, an organization she helped found.

Recognized for service to both the community and the legal profession, Callejo has received the 1998 Spirit of Excellence Award from the American Bar Association Commission on Opportunities for Minorities in the Profession, the Martin Luther King Justice Award (the first Hispanic ever to receive this award), a Lifetime Achievement Award from the Mexican American Bar Association of Texas, the 1996 Distinguished Alumni of the SMU Dedman School of Law, the Ohtli Reconocimiento award from the government of Mexico for her dedication and commitment to the rights of persons of Mexican origin, the 2002 Award for Excellence in Community Service for Volunteer Community Leadership, and the 2004 Dallas Bar Association's Fellows Award. Additionally, she was profiled during the American Bar Association's celebration of National Hispanic Heritage Month in 2001.

In 2004 it was announced that she and her husband were donating $1 million to create the Adelfa B. Callejo Leadership and Latino Studies Professorship at the SMU School of Law. This gift will create a leadership institute that includes coursework on ethics, governance, dispute resolution, and arbitration.

SOURCES: American Bar Association, Division of Public Education. 2001. "Raising the Bar: Pioneers in the Legal Profession: National Hispanic Heritage Month, Adelfa Botello Callejo." http://www.abanet.org/publiced/callejo.html (accessed July 21, 2005); Callejo, Adelfa B. 2004. Personal correspondence with Kinchen C. Pier III, April; Olivera, Mercedes. 2004. "Alum to SMU law school: Thanks a million." *Dallas Morning News,* April 16, 3B.

Kinchen C. Pier III

CALLIS DE FAGES, EULALIA FRANCESCA Y JOSEPHA (1758– ?)

Eulalia Callis was the first woman to petition for divorce in Spanish colonial California (1785), creating what was considered the scandal of the century in that region. She was born in Barcelona, Spain, on October 4, 1758, the daughter of Don Agustín Callis and Doña Rosa Casañas Masón. Doña Rosa and her children followed Don Agustín to New Spain around 1771, after he was commissioned captain of the Free Company of Catalonian Volunteers charged with stabilizing the northern provinces of New Spain. Among the troopers was fellow Catalonian Lieutenant Pedro Fages.

The Callis family was part of a prominent group of Catalans who lived in Mexico City. Eulalia enjoyed a privileged upbringing, receiving formal education and living in a sumptuous home amid many servants. Although Pedro Fages was almost twenty-nine years older than Eulalia, Don Agustín considered him a fitting suitor for his daughter. In 1780 Fages, now a lieutenant colonel in command of the Company of Catalonian Volunteers assigned to Sonora, married Callis in Mexico City. His position required frequent travel to places such as Guadalajara, Hermosillo, Santa Cruz, and Mexico City. Callis sometimes traveled with her husband but more often remained behind. Shortly after they married, while Callis was five months pregnant, the couple moved to Fages's new assigned post at Arizpe, in the frontier province of Sonora. One month after their arrival, in May 1781, Callis gave birth to a son, Pedro José Fernando Fages. Soon after the birth of their son Fages again left his wife to fight the Seri Indians and, later that year, to battle with the Yumas. This assignment kept the couple apart for almost two years and left Callis in isolated, solitary, and unimpressive surroundings.

When Fages was appointed governor of California in 1782, he attempted to persuade his wife to join him at Monterey, the capital of Alta California. Fearing further loneliness and isolation, Callis at first refused to go, but after much pleading by Fages, she reluctantly followed her husband to that northernmost frontier region of New Spain. The trip to Monterey was a very arduous one for Callis and her infant son. From her initial arrival at the Pacific coast, where she set sail across the Gulf of California, she encountered great difficulties. The ship from San Blas was very small, and thus her carriage and some of her luggage were left behind. Fages joined her at Mission Loreto in Baja California to escort her on the remaining trip north. The rugged journey would have been strenuous and fatiguing for any person, but even more so for a woman of the elite unaccustomed to the hardships of the frontier. During this trip Callis, now pregnant with her second child, suffered a miscarriage.

Her tenure as the governor's wife was largely an unhappy one. Although the colonists throughout Baja and Alta California enthusiastically welcomed Callis, she was not impressed by the condition of the settler communities. She appeared distressed at the nakedness of the Indians and gave them some of her own clothing. In addition, Callis continued to suffer from ill health. Callis was six months pregnant when she again traveled with her husband to the dedication of the church at Santa Clara Mission. She was, however, unable to complete the journey and stayed at Mission San Francisco until she gave birth in August 1784 to her daughter María del Carmen. Callis was forced to temporarily remain there to recuperate from a postpartum illness. Shortly after her return to Monterey, because of her continued frail health and nostalgia for Mexico City, Callis began to request that her husband allow her to return there. He adamantly refused. This reportedly caused significant conjugal discord, and some propose that it ultimately led to the infamous scandal.

In February 1785, after discovering her husband in a compromising position with an adolescent Yuma Indian girl, Callis accused her husband of adultery and petitioned for divorce, something unheard of in the region at that time. According to colonial honor codes, which held a woman honor-bound to submit to both her husband's and the church's will, Callis's accusation of adultery against her husband was deemed censurable, if not condemnable. Her role as the wife of the Spanish colonial governor was to uphold the honor status of her husband. She was severely berated by the mission authorities for making her accusations public. Callis refused to recant her charges, and as a result, the missionaries attempted to silence her. At the request of her husband the missionaries detained her and transferred her under military guard to Mission Carmelo, where she was to meditate on her actions, was subjected to harsh conditions, and was prohibited contact with family and friends under the threat of excommunication. Ultimately Callis, under continued pressure by the missionaries, reportedly retracted the charges and renewed marital life with her husband. During her tenure in California Callis was pregnant two more times. One child, Josefa Agustina Rosa, born in May 1786, died eight days later; the other, María Josefa, was born in May 1788. The Fages family eventually returned to Mexico City after the governor resigned his post in 1790. Little else is known about Callis after her departure from California and the death of her husband in 1794, which left her a widow at the age of thirty-six.

Some of the residents of Monterey spoke fondly of Callis's generosity and sympathy for the indigenous people of the region. Until recently historians, however, referred to Callis as a hysterical woman suffering from either premenstrual syndrome or postpartum depression, or as a fiery, tempestuous Catalan woman who was disgraceful, scandalous, and headstrong. Inevitably, Callis will be remembered as the First Lady who, attempting to free herself from the severity of the frontier and from a philandering husband, became one of the most infamous women of early Spanish colonial California.

See also Spanish Borderlands

SOURCES: Dakin, Susanna Bryant. 1963. *Rose, or Rose Thorn? Three Women of Spanish California*. Berkeley, CA: Friends of the Bancroft Library; Nuttall, Donald A. 1998. *The Señoras Gobernadoras of Spanish Alta California: A Comparative Study*. Santa Barbara: Santa Barbara Trust for Historic Preservation.

Bárbara O. Reyes

CALVILLO, ANA MARÍA DEL CARMEN (1765–1856)

Ana María del Carmen Calvillo, a successful rancher and entrepreneur, was born in San Antonio de Bexar in 1765. Her father, Ignacio Francisco Xavier Calvillo, married Antonia Arocha, daughter of prominent cattle raiser Francisco de Arocha and Juana Curbelo, originally settlers from the Canary Islands. They had four children, one of whom was Ana María del Carmen.

Ana María del Carmen Calvillo's marriage to Juan Lucas Gavino de la Trinidad Delgado, also descended from Canary Islanders, is recorded in census records in the Bexar Archives and in Frederick Chabot's genealogical studies. The marriage took place around 1781 (no record of it has been found) and produced two sons, Juan Bautista in 1783 and José Anacleto in 1784. Ecclesiastical proceedings record their baptisms and the younger son's death seven months after he was born. There is no known death date for the firstborn, but he is not listed in his mother's will. One may assume that the firstborn preceded her in death.

The census of 1795 listed María Calvillo (no age given) and Gavino Delgado (age thirty-six) as living in Villa de San Fernando and gave Delgado's occupation as rancher. In 1811, however, the couple was living on La Santa Cruz y Paso de la Mugeres [*sic*] Ranch that belonged to her father, Don Ignacio Calvillo, and that his daughter would eventually inherit. Gavino Delgado was a revolutionary involved in the political intrigue that surrounded San Antonio de Bexar in 1813.

María Calvillo inherited Rancho de las Cabras (Wilson County, Texas), formerly an outpost of Mission San Francisco de la Espada located in San Antonio de Bexar, from her father. He had successfully petitioned for land that had formerly been part of the extensive ranch lands owned by Mission Espada. Rancho de las Cabras adjoined his holdings situated on El Paso de las Mujeres on the San Antonio River. Unlike other women who relinquished control over their assets to their husbands, and who assumed control of spousal holdings only after his death, Calvillo left her husband for unknown reasons and established economic independence, single-handedly operating her ranching enterprise.

Calvillo added to her inheritance by petitioning for land within the mission compound where she had been living. She also expanded the ranches' operations by building a granary, a sugar mill, and an extensive irrigation system with the help of neighboring ranching families and families that lived on the ranch with her.

Widows enjoyed a degree of social acceptability and were granted full protection of the law; however, a woman who abandoned her husband was a different matter. Surely she was scorned by frontier society of the time. Yet Spanish law protected women from spousal abuse in general and liability in regard to debt, as well as giving them the right to sue and be sued. Petitions found in the Bexar Archives demonstrate that Calvillo knew her legal rights. She kept her maiden name and thus her individuality and maintained her property separate from that of her husband. A strong and determined woman, not unlike others shaped by harsh frontier conditions, Calvillo defended her inheritance in 1828. She asked the court to provide her with a legal survey of her holdings "because the deeds which she had to it by her deceased father together with the chest were taken from her by officials of the Spanish Government."

According to her grandnephew, Jacobo Cruz, she dressed like a man and could shoot and rope like one. On one occasion a surveyor spent long, tedious hours astride a horse, marking off and measuring her lands, and Calvillo went along, seeing to it that her interests were properly looked after. No one dared cross her. She endured the angry criticisms of her neighbors by paying tribute to rampaging Indians. She offered them beef in exchange for protection of her property.

According to unsubstantiated sources, raising cattle and sheep was not Calvillo's only source of income. One of her relatives carried on a flourishing trade in contraband between Texas and Louisiana. Since the ranch was situated on two main roads, it served as an excellent base for such operations, and Calvillo was rumored to be a very agreeable silent partner.

By 1833, however, she was again having troubles with the Indians. She filed a petition citing "deterioration of her landed property caused by the hostile wars of the enemy tribes." She also stated that she had given whatever aid she could to help wage war against them. By 1851 her legal representative appeared in court on her behalf. Calvillo was declared non compos mentis. She died on January 15, 1856, at the age of ninety-one.

According to local folklore, her ghost still roams the countryside around Rancho de las Cabras astride a great white horse, her raven hair flowing in the wind. One Texas writer used the same description but added the words "scandalizing the countryside."

Like other women of the frontier, Calvillo broke through societal confines to assert her personhood, expand her economic outlook, and, most important, open the doors to political and legal recognition enjoyed by women today. Evelyn Carrinton, in *Women in Early Texas,* portrayed Doña María Calvillo as a modern-day feminist: "Cherished by no one, ostracized by all women," she refused to accept the lot of the women of her era, which was "inexorable wifehood and motherhood."

See also Spanish Borderlands

SOURCES: Bexar Archives, 1781. "Inventory of Rancho de las Cabras, San Fernando de Bexar." October 10; ———, 1782. "Report on the Roundup Ordered by Governor Domingo Cabello." February 26; ———, 1806–1828. "Petition for Return of Property and Various Other Land Petitions and Request for Title Searches," Eugene C. Barker Center for American History, University of Texas, Austin; Carrinton, Evelyn. 1994. *Women in Early Texas.* Austin: Texas State Historical Society; Chabot, Frederick C. 1970. *With the Makers of San Antonio.* San Antonio: Artes Graficas; McMillan, Nora E. Rios. 1999. " 'Siendo mi derecho . . . ' The Hispanic Woman's Legal Identity in the Spanish Southwest," *South Texas Studies,* 102–142; San Fernando Church Marriage Records. 1811. Archdiocese of San Antonio.

Nora E. Rios McMillan

CANALES, LAURA (1954–2005)

Laura Canales was born in Kingsville, Texas, on August 19, 1954. The undisputed "reina de la onda Tejana/Queen of Tejano music" broke through the traditional male-dominated genre in the 1970s, making her singing debut with Los Unicos in 1973, a year after graduating from H. M. King High School in Kingsville, Texas. Canales briefly performed with the legendary El Conjunto Bernal from 1973 to 1975. She then became part of Snowball and Co., led by Ramiro de la Cruz, with whom she recorded her first hit, "Midnight Blue," in 1975 on the Fireball Records label. Canales's bands went through several structural changes, but her popularity and impact on the Tejano music market never faltered. In 1978 Canales and her band became Felicidad, and in 1981 the band disassembled into two groups. From there Canales moved on to form her next band, Laura Canales y Encanto. It was with this band that Canales released one of her most significant albums, *Si viví contigo,* in 1981. The title-track single to this album established Canales as the top female artist in Tejano music. The early 1980s represented a major shift for the Tejano music industry with the formal establishment of the Texas Talent Musicians Association and the Tejano Music Awards, and it was Canales who symbolically assured the larger public that Tejanas would not be left out. Over the years she has appeared on a wide range of television programs, such as *Siempre en Domingo, Mundo Latino,* and *The Johnny Canales Show.*

Canales was nominated for Tejano Music Awards in Female Vocalist of the Year and Female Entertainer of the Year categories from 1982 to 1990. Beginning in 1982, Canales won the Tejano Music Awards for Female Vocalist of the Year and Female Entertainer of the Year for four consecutive years, a record broken only by Selena in the 1990s. December 22, 1985, marked her last public performance with Encanto before taking several years of leave from the music industry. She remained involved in the music scene as a disc jockey for KYST in Houston in 1988. In 1989 Canales signed a five-year contract with Capital/FM Latin, with whom she recorded "No Regrets," a gesture of affirmation to those who doubted her decision to take a leave of absence. The early 1990s showed that Canales's presence within the Tejano music industry was as assertive as ever; she produced such hits as "Cuatro caminos," "Dile a tu esposa," and "Frente a frente." In 1994 Canales signed a contract with Fonovisa Records. By the end of the 1990s Canales was arguably the most significant female presence within the musical landscape of Tejano music since the post–World War II era, when Tejana duets and other solo artists created a significant space for women. No other Tejana singer since the 1970s can display a Tejano music career that has spanned nearly three decades. Although still releasing Tejano music CDs, Canales's priorities were also invested in the area of higher education. In 1997 she obtained her bachelor of arts degree in communication disorders from Texas A&M University in Kingsville. She pursued her master of arts degree in psychology from the same institution. In April 2005 Laura Canales died unexpectedly after gallbladder surgery.

SOURCES: Burr, Ramiro. 1999. *The Billboard Guide to Tejano and Regional Mexican Music*. New York: Billboard Books; "Laura Canales, 50, Star of Tejano Music, Is Dead." 2005. *New York Times,* April 20.

Deborah Vargas

CANALES, NOHELIA DE LOS ANGELES (1974–)

Born in Nicaragua and raised in Los Angeles since the age of five, Nohelia Canales is a nationally recognized activist who has fought for the rights of Latinas/os in California and throughout the United States. As a young immigrant in Los Angeles, Canales's own experiences of "living between two cultures" and facing discrimination in the school system drove her "to see what is just and unjust" and greatly influenced her perspective on racism, cultural rights, and women's rights in U.S. society.

In 1996 Canales completed her B.S. in biology and philosophy at Mount St. Mary College (MSMC) in Los Angeles. While attending Mount St. Mary College, Canales and two other students in the MSMC Leadership Program were selected to participate in the National Education for Women (NEW) Leadership Program, a national workshop held at the Center for American Women and Politics (CAWP) at Rutgers University. She describes this workshop as "one of the most amazing experiences" she had because she was given "an opportunity to feel connected, become politicized, and meet women revolutionaries" like Bella Abzug, Geraldine Ferraro, and Ruth Mandel. With a public policy grant from CAWP, Canales and her fellow classmates returned to Mount St. Mary College to co-found the first women's group on campus, WAKE-UP (Women Advocates for Knowledge and Empowerment, also called WAKE), an organization created to "bring women of color into feminism." A primary goal of WAKE was to "make feminism relevant to the lives of women of color" and to challenge the stereotype that "feminism is only for white women." She co-founded another student advocacy group, Latinas Unidas, a first-of-its-kind organization that was dedicated to addressing the intersection of gender, race, class, and sexuality in the lives of Latina students. Canales organized with members of WAKE and Latinas Unidas to bring Eleanor Smeal and Dolores Huerta to campus, worked with the United Farm Workers, volunteered in the campaign against Proposition 187, and created public forums to address complex issues such as abortion rights, women's autonomy, and sexuality.

In 1996 Canales deferred medical school at the Mayo Clinic in order to work with Freedom Summer/Fall '96, a Feminist Majority Foundation affirmative action and voter registration project. As a full-time intern and later as "the only woman of color" core staff member for Freedom Summer/Fall '96, Canales helped spread the word to Latino communities in East Los Angeles to vote against Proposition 209, legislation designed to dismantle hard-won affirmative action policies in California. As a result of her work educating Latino communities about Proposition 209, Canales was awarded a Gloria Steinem Award from the MS. Foundation in 1997, making her one of the youngest women ever to receive this honor. During the same year Canales was nationally recognized by *Ms. Magazine* in its twenty-fifth anniversary issue as one of the top twenty-one most accomplished, promising young feminists aged thirty and under.

Canales entered the master's program at the Mayo Clinic in 1997, where she focused on tumor biology with an emphasis on breast cancer research. She continues to integrate her feminist perspective into the "white, male-dominated field" of science and medicine and hopes to challenge dominant perceptions of women, ethnic minorities, and sexual minorities in medicine, including "the very structures of knowledge that shape medical professionals' views on medicine, bodies and women's health." Being the only Latina in her graduate program at the Mayo Clinic, Canales faced "a huge contrast" between her professional field and the Latino community in Los Angeles. She continues to "stay in touch" with her activist side, participates regularly in third-wave feminist conferences and workshops, and continues her educational work to bring awareness around issues of racism, sexism, homophobia, and heterosexism in the medical field. In 2005, she is working on her doctorate in Oral Biology and Medicine at the University of California, Los Angeles. She also serves as the program manager for the Anti-Violence Project of the Los Angeles Gay and Lesbian Center and sits on the advisory board of *Ms. Magazine*.

For Canales, the most rewarding thing about being an activist is "creating a community and being the impetus for change." She states, "Unless you put yourself out there it's never going to happen . . . that's how I see all of the great women who have put themselves out there for me." Canales integrates her beliefs into her passion for science, where she hopes to break down stereotypes about scientists as "objective and non-biased" and educate people about the revolutionary role of scientists in creating a more humane society.

SOURCE: *Ms. Magazine*. 1997. "Next Generation: 21 for the 21st." September/October.

Amy Lind

CANINO, MARÍA JOSEFA (1944–)

Dr. María Josefa Canino's academic work and public service range over a thirty-year career centered on community-based institution building, the development of professional education curricula, and advocating on behalf of the poor, the non-English-dominant, and the disenfranchised, as well as pioneering the establishment of an academic department, Puerto Rican and Latino Studies at Rutgers University, Livingston. A product of New York City, Canino was born in the heart of El Barrio on 106th Street and Fifth Avenue. The daughter of a *bodeguero,* Canino is a proud and outstanding representative of that fusion of the island and the urban experience.

Educated in the Northeast, Canino holds an Ed.D. (1981) in administration, planning, and social policy from Harvard University, an M.S. (1967) in social work with a specialization in community organization from Columbia University, and a B.A. (1964) in sociology from the City College of New York. She was appointed by New York mayor John Lindsay to the Board of Trustees of the City University of New York and subsequently served on Governor Mario Cuomo's Task Force on Poverty and Social Welfare. She was honored by her alma mater when she received the 125th Anniversary City College Alumni Medal. Throughout her career she has been affiliated with several committees and organizations, such as the Board of Directors of El Barrio Popular Education Project, the Puerto Rican Association for Community Affairs (PRACA), ASPIRA, the National Congress of Puerto Rican Rights, and the Board of Directors of the Field Foundation.

Her career has been characterized by her dedication and commitment to the point of personal sacrifice, as was evident in 1993 when she withdrew her candidacy to direct the prestigious Center for Puerto Rican Studies at Hunter College in order to break the deadlock in which the president and chancellor had placed the center because, despite demonstrations held by students and staff along Lexington Avenue in support of her nomination, they ignored the recommendation made by the research committee. It was, ironically, her support for the very creation of that research center, along with her stand on issues such as remedial education and the preservation of Hostos Community College while she was a CUNY trustee, that played a part in the political undertones surrounding that decision.

One of the most exciting periods of her career was a ten-year effort as a member of an educational team that pioneered in the design and implementation of competency-based curricula in social work and public administration, the experimental Master's in Social Work Program for Hispanics and the Graduate Bilingual Program in Public Administration. Canino has also served on the faculty of the University of Puerto Rico's Graduate School of Social Work during its implementation of a new curriculum geared to preparing a cadre of professionals in social service, policy, and administration.

At Rutgers University, Newark, Canino co-coordinated the public administration certificate in nonprofit management, an innovative graduate-level credential open to personnel from the nonprofit sector, as well as graduate students from all disciplines. She has served as acting chairperson of that department, directed its Executive MPA Program, and taught in the master's program. She is presently working on publishing the research results of a Nonprofit Sector Research Fund grant to study Latino advocacy and welfare reform in New Jersey, editing a book on higher-education policy in Cuba, Puerto Rico, and the Dominican Republic, and, with other founders, establishing a Hispanic Foster Care Family Recruitment agency in New Jersey.

Canino sits on various nongovernmental organization (NGO) boards. She is vice-chairperson of the Puerto Rican Legal Defense and Education Fund (PRLDEF), a founding board member of the New Jersey Policy Perspective (NJPP), and cofounder of the Children's Advocacy Resource Association of New Jersey (CARANJ). She most recently served on the Advisory Committee to the Newark Museum for its exhibit Puerto Rican Santos de Palo: Sculptures between Heaven and Earth. Canino's advice to young Latino/a students is simple and exemplifies her credo and entire career: "Have integrity, and by which I mean personal honesty about what they are confronting, what their role is in the community and what their contribution is to the collective welfare, while asking themselves questions about what they can do to advance that welfare."

See also Education

SOURCES: Canino, María Josefa. 2002. Oral history interview by Luis Gordillo, March 19; Cruz, Evidio de la. 1993. "Critican al presidente del Hunter College por vetar a educadora boricua." *El Diario/La Prensa* (New York), July 7, 3; Rutgers, the State University of New Jersey. "María Josefa Canino." http://www.rutgers-newark.rutgers.edu/pubadmin/phd/faculty/Canino.htm (accessed March 1, 2002).

Luis G. Gordillo

CANNERY AND AGRICULTURAL WORKERS INDUSTRIAL UNION (CAWIU) (1931–1934)

The Cannery and Agricultural Workers Industrial Union (CAWIU) was formed in 1931 as the agricultural arm of the Communist Party's (CP) national federation of unions, the Trade Union Unity League (TUUL). The TUUL entered California agricultural fields in 1930, joining strikes by Mexican agricultural workers in the Imperial Valley. Continuing this work, the CAWIU organized strikes during the contentious depression years of 1931 to 1935. Although it was briefly active in Arizona, the union organized primarily in California.

In 1933 a wave of strikes by some 47,575 workers hit California; twenty-five of these, involving 37,565 workers, were under the aegis of the CAWIU. This "general strike" in agriculture began in southern California with the El Monte berry strike, moved north into the San Joaquin Valley, crested in the October 1933 cotton strike, and then began again in the Imperial Valley in early 1934. By 1933 CAWIU leaders had studied agricultural wages and working conditions, developed a union strategy, and attempted to establish a regional confederation using as its base the camp committees, composed of farmworkers elected by their fellow workers. Yet the organization remained skeletal, and as one organizer said, "it was a union in name, a rally point, but as far as organization . . . it was actually nonexistent." CAWIU activist Caroline Decker pointed out that even without the union "there would have been strikes anyway. Strikes were breaking out all over. . . . Those strikes would have happened union or no union."

As strikes broke out, the CAWIU joined workers. The union began to take on a shape and identity as the strikes spread across the state. The CAWIU had a good reputation among agricultural workers, especially those who had worked with the CP in unemployed workers' councils or in various fights for civil rights. Yet the union was small. The few formal organizers received little or no salary, depended on sympathizers for food and donations, and traveled on freight cars or in dilapidated automobiles; they even hitchhiked. The 1933 cotton strike had only six CAWIU organizers covering the 200-mile-long San Joaquin Valley. Some, such as Pat Chambers, had worked with Mexican workers. Others had not, and few spoke Spanish.

The union sounded impressive in newspaper accounts and party minutes, and a red-baiting press, growers, and federal and state officials' denunciations of the Communist union magnified the organization's size. The CAWIU was important as a rallying cry, as an organization that could make demands and negotiate for workers, and as a structure around which the informal networks, families, crews, and groups could coalesce. Yet as organizer Pat Chambers recognized, "Although the directives in some superficial way could come from the outside, the actual organization had to come from the workers themselves." The CAWIU depended on Mexican Communists, leftists, fellow travelers, and workers experienced in labor fights who served as the conduits between the union and Mexican labor camps, families, and labor crews in the fields. These workers met with CAWIU organizers, strategized, and organized in their own communities. The union's base and much of the strategy and leadership came from the Mexican workers themselves.

Few workers, male or female, actually joined and paid dues, although they felt that they belonged to the union. Women seemed ignored by the union structure. Some women attended strike meetings. Younger bilingual women translated for union organizers. While some women were aware of the CAWIU, it is possible that the majority did not know the union by name. Yet focusing on union structure obscures the crucial role of women and women's networks. Groups of women set up soup kitchens, fed strikers, and organized child care. Mexican women hid CAWIU organizers in the Imperial Valley, transporting them house to house and successfully eluding police. They organized picket lines, and at least one Euro-American migrant worker learned from a Mexican striker how to shout "Huelga pizacadores." Women confronted growers, law enforcement, and vigilantes, fought both strikebreakers and deputy sheriffs, and were arrested in these conflicts.

California business and agriculture pressured officials to stop the CAWIU. In the wake of the San Francisco general strike of 1934, and under mounting pressure from business, police raided the CAWIU office in Sacramento and arrested union organizers. Fifteen were indicted on charges of violating the Criminal Syndicalism Act. The lengthy trial effectively removed the CAWIU from the fields. Eight of the union organizers were convicted and sent to jail. Yet the Communist Party itself administered the coup de grace to the union. In 1934 the party shifted to the popular-front strategy and abandoned separate unions to work within established labor organizations.

See also Labor Unions

SOURCES: Weber, Devra. 1989. "*'Raiz Fuerte'*: Oral History and Mexicana Farmworkers." *Oral History Review* 17, no. 2:47–62; ———. 1994. *Dark Sweat, White Gold: California Farm Workers, Cotton, and the New Deal*. Berkeley: University of California Press.

Devra A. Weber

CÁNTICO DE LA MUJER LATINA (1998–)

In 1998 pastoral musician Rubi Martínez Bernat received a call from Father Virgil Funk, president of the National Association of Pastoral Musicians. He said, "We are coming to Grand Rapids, can you do something Hispanic?" Martínez Bernat knew that the Latino population in Grand Rapids was growing. Thus she wanted to do something that showcased Latino culture. She received the application for the conference entry and considered what she wanted to do. She recalled, "I knew I wanted to do music, poetry, and readings by Latinas." She went to the choir she directed and talked to the members. She explained, "I told the women we would not be paid; it would just be for the glory of the performance." From this discussion Cántico de la Mujer Latina was born.

The founder of Cántico, Martínez Bernat came to pastoral music at the age of nineteen. Her parents, Nohemy González and Pedro Martínez, believed that piano lessons would keep Martínez Bernat from smoking, hanging out with the wrong crowd, or getting into trouble. Thus she took music lessons throughout her childhood.

Her pastoral career began in an unlikely way. After the birth of her first son Derrick, Martínez Bernat went to St. Francis Church in Ecorse, Michigan, to request baptism. During her meeting the priest explained to her that they needed a volunteer musician to play the organ for the morning masses. Martínez Bernat did not know how to play the organ, and she had just become a mother. The priest allowed her to use the church to practice, and a young couple from the church offered to take care of her son during her practice times. Later Martínez Bernat went to Sacred Heart Seminary in Detroit, where she studied organ, pastoral music, and theology. As Martínez Bernat explained, "Before I knew it, I went from being a volunteer to being a full-time employee."

Martínez Bernat eventually left St. Francis Church and went to St. Anne's shortly after her divorce. Martínez Bernat has questioned her role within the church. She stated, "I am a woman, Mexican, divorced, a single woman. . . . I am on the edge before I open my mouth. . . . How can I be a Church lady and divorced?" Martínez Bernat has received support from the pastor of St. Anne's, Father Robert Duggan, and the parish community. It was at St. Anne's that she founded Cántico de la Mujer Latina.

At its first performance in Grand Rapids, Cántico received the conference's highest evaluation. After the concert the choir members returned home. Martínez Bernat recalled, "We thought this would be a one-time opportunity." However, a short time later they received an invitation to perform at the Southwest Liturgical Conference in Albuquerque, New Mexico. Someone from Albuquerque had heard Cántico perform in Grand Rapids. The group learned new songs and new material and headed to Albuquerque. From its performance in Albuquerque, it was invited to Chicago. Since its appearance in Chicago, Cántico's success has continued to grow. In August 2002 it performed at the Basilica of Our Lady of Guadalupe in Mexico City.

Cántico is composed of eighteen women from diverse ethnic backgrounds. Their music blends literature and poetry by Latinas such as Gloria Anzaldúa and Esmeralda Santiago with Latina theology by Ada María Isasi-Díaz and liturgical music by Mary Frances Reza. The group also showcases the creativity of members, such as poetry by Martínez Bernat and music by Marcela Salas. Cántico teaches awareness about the role of Latinas in the church, celebrates the achievements and accomplishments of Latinas, and empowers women to be agents for change in the church and in society.

Cántico reflects the grassroots community activism in the church, and it challenges the hierarchical and patriarchal structures that exist in the church and society. Building on the theories of Anzaldúa, Martínez Bernat stated that the church, like society as a whole, views Latinos as "optional people." She elaborated, "Other people are making decisions for us and about us without even consulting us." Through their music and creative ministry Martínez Bernat and Cántico make the lives, history, experiences, and accomplishments of Latinas and Latinos central to the church and to society.

See also Religion

SOURCES: Anzaldúa, Gloria. 1987. *La frontera/Borderlands: The New Mestiza*. San Francisco: Aunt Lute Books; Isasi-Díaz, Ada María. 1996. *Mujerista Theology: A Theology for the Twenty-first Century*. Maryknoll, NY: Orbis Books.

Elaine Carey

CAPETILLO, LUISA (1876–1922)

Although Luisa Capetillo was recognized in her lifetime as an important labor and feminist pioneer in the Americas—one of her essays was included in a 1921 anthology of leading international feminist and radical figures, such as Clara Zetkin, Rosa Luxemburg, and Emma Goldman, among others—there has been little historical writing about her. Luisa Capetillo was born out of wedlock in the northern town of Arecibo, Puerto Rico, in 1876. Her mother, Margarita Perone, was a domestic of French ancestry, and her father was Luis Capetillo Echevarría, an unskilled worker born in Spain. Capetillo's mother made sure that her daughter received a solid education at home and encouraged her interest in literature. Capetillo became active in the Federación Libre de Trabajadores (FLT, Free Federation of Workers) from its inception in 1899. The FLT was Puerto Rico's most important labor organization during the first three decades of the twentieth century, and Capetillo figured as one of its more prominent leaders. At that time Capetillo worked in cigar factories in Arecibo. She was also a reader in these factories, paid by cigar workers themselves to read novels, philosophical and political essays, and other writings aloud as they prepared the cigars. This job was one of great prestige among turn-of-the-century cigar workers in the United States and the Caribbean.

In 1904 Capetillo started what became a lifelong endeavor: writing short pieces for labor newspapers and magazines. Throughout the decade she continued her activism and her writing on behalf of the FLT. Her first book, *Ensayos libertinos,* published in 1907, engaged socialist and anarchist discourses familiar to the Puerto Rican (and international) working class. In 1909 she founded a short-lived feminist working-class magazine called *La mujer* and moved to Puerto Rico's capital, San Juan. Unfortunately, researchers have not been able to find any remaining copies of this magazine.

Capetillo published a utopian novel, *La humanidad del futuro,* in 1910. The novel is organized around the anarchist concept of a general strike. In 1911 Capetillo published her most important and influential book, *Mi opinión sobre las libertades, derechos, y deberes de la mujer.* This book is considered the first feminist treatise in Puerto Rico and one of the very first in Latin America and the Caribbean. By 1911 Capetillo was a well-known figure both in Puerto Rico's labor movement and in literary and feminist circles.

In 1912 Capetillo began her work as an international labor intellectual and organizer. She moved to New York and worked closely with the Hispanic labor press. Her commitment to working-class issues led her in 1913 to collaborate with Cuban, Spanish, and African American cigar workers in Ybor City and Tampa. In 1915 she moved to Havana, Cuba. There she was arrested and subsequently acquitted for wearing trousers, considered at the time exclusively men's clothing, in public. Capetillo continued the practice of wearing men's trousers at public events after this incident. In 1916 Capetillo was deported for her work on behalf of syndical and anarchist organizations in Cuba.

Back in Puerto Rico, Capetillo published her fourth and final book, *Influencias de las ideas modernas.* Although the book was published in Puerto Rico in 1916, the project had been gestating since her days in Tampa. Between 1916 and 1919 Capetillo actively organized and participated in strikes and collaborated with working-class newspapers and magazines. She moved back to New York City in 1919–1920, where she ran a hostel, continued to serve as a reader in cigar factories, and kept writing for the local Spanish press. She returned to Puerto Rico and died of tuberculosis in 1922, at the age of forty-six, in San Juan.

A feminist, union organizer, journalist, and activist for social justice, Capetillo argued for nonconformism premised on a profound sense of natural harmony, gender, and social equality. She often questioned deeply held social, sexual, political, and economic assumptions of her time.

See also Cigar Workers; Feminism; *Tabaqueros'* Unions

SOURCES: Hewitt, Nancy. 2005. "Luisa Capetillo: Feminist of the Working Class." In *Latina Legacies: Identity, Biography, and Community,* ed. Vicki L. Ruiz and Virginia Sánchez Korrol, eds. New York: Oxford University Press; Quintero Rivera, Angel. 1976. *Workers' Struggle in Puerto Rico: A Documentary History.* New York: Monthly Review Press; Ramos, Julio, ed. 1992. *Amor y anarquía: Los escritos de Luisa Capetillo.* Río Piedras: Ediciones Huracán; Sánchez González, Lisa. 1996. "Luisa Capetillo: An Anarcho-Feminist Pionera in the Mainland Puerto Rican Narrative/Political Tradition." In *Recovering the U.S. Hispanic Literary Heritage,* ed. Erlinda González-Berry and Chuck Tatum, 2:148–167. Houston: Arte Público Press; Valle Ferrer, Norma. 1990. *Luisa Capetillo: Historia de una mujer proscrita.* Río Piedras: Editorial Cultural.

Félix V. Matos Rodríguez

CARBONELL, ANNA (1952–)

In July 2002 Anna Carbonell was named vice president of the National Broadcasting Corporation for Station Relations at NBC4 and Telemundo East Coast. Carbonell's responsibilities include philanthropic budgets, development of public service announcements, and maintaining the FCC public inspection files. She serves on the NBC Diversity Council and has been a key senior advisor on ethnic diversification issues at NBC. Her appointment was publicly hailed by industry insiders because of her outstanding work in the media.

She was born Anacandia Fermaints and came to New York City from Arecibo, Puerto Rico, in the early 1950s when she was a year old. Her parents, Francisco Fermaints, a merchant seaman, and Adela Sánchez, left the oppressive poverty of Puerto Rico and came looking for a better life. Adela had suffered from tuberculosis during her pregnancy with her daughter but felt that her health had improved and that with better medical care she would prosper in New York City. Shortly after their arrival their daughter Anacandia was hospitalized because she was found to have a tubercular growth in her knee.

Anacandia was taken to an upstate hospital, which made it almost impossible for her parents to visit often or for an extended amount of time. To be an infant hearing a strange language for the first two years of life without her parents became Anacandia's lot. Upon release she spoke only English and was taken to a home where only Spanish was spoken. These early traumatic experiences made communication a priority for this young child and helped shape her successful future in media.

"Be good to yourself, be proud of yourself" has been the trademark signoff for Anacandia, today known as Anna Carbonell. She is well known today to millions in the New York metropolitan area who have seen her for more than twenty-five years on public service television shows, at colleges, universities, and public events, and at the numerous boards and organizations where she serves.

Carbonell is a product of the public school system and attended New York University, where she majored in English. Initially Carbonell began to work with community organizations but soon became employed as supervisor of press relations for the International Paper Company. In 1981 she was offered the opportunity to work for the American Broadcasting Company in the press information office. In 1983 she launched the station's first major public affairs issues program geared to the interests and needs of the growing Hispanic community in the tristate area. For more than thirteen years she produced and hosted the program, *Tiempo,* which was broadcast every Sunday morning.

All socioeconomic issues that affected Hispanics were of interest to Carbonell. She became very active in all facets of New York life. In 1995 she joined the National Broadcasting Corporation as director of press and public affairs for WNBC-TV. She was a member of the board of directors of the Puerto Rican Legal Defense and Education Fund, the National Puerto Rican Coalition, the Association of Hispanic Arts, the New York Investment Fund, Marymount Manhattan College, YWCA of New York, the National Association of Puerto Rican Women, and numerous other organizations. A strong advocate for fairness in media, she directed the Northeast Region of the National Association of Hispanic Journalists and served on the editorial board of WABC-TV.

For her many efforts, Carbonell garnered critical recognition. She is the recipient of numerous awards. Because of her activism, Carbonell has been honored by the Hispanic Academy of Media Arts and Sciences, the U.S. Department of Health and Human Services, the National Conference of Puerto Rican Women, and numerous other organizations. She was named one of the 100 Most Influential Hispanics in the Nation by *Hispanic Business Magazine* in 1989 and was listed among 50 Influential Latinos by the *New York Daily News* in 1995. Carbonell resides in Staten Island, New York, is divorced, and has one daughter, Diana Carbonell, who is an attorney with a major brokerage firm in New York City.

See also Television

SOURCES: The New Tomorrow (online publication for Black and Hispanic Young Adults). "Anna Carbonell." http://www.tntomorrow.com/A&L_speakers_and_consultants_pg12.html (accessed June 21, 2005); wnbc.com (NBC Channel 4 New York City web site). "Anna Carbonell." http://www.wnbc.com/station/1169234/detail.html (accessed June 21, 2005).

Edward Mercado

CARDONA, ALICE (1930–)

Grassroots political activist and community organizer Alice Cardona was born and raised in New York City, one of nine children of Puerto Rican parents who came to New York in 1923. Her family was part of the pioneer generation of migrants who left the island before World War II. Cardona was reared in a large and loving family. "My childhood," she recalls, "was rich in love and friendship, if not always [in] material possessions. . . . we learned early to share what we had with those less fortunate." Sharing, collaboration, collective action, and group empowerment permeated Cardona's early years and were reflected in the organization and group efforts she engendered in later life. Above all, Cardona's dedication to the advancement of the disenfranchised, especially the Puerto Rican and Latino communities of the city, has served her as a steady guiding principle. This mission is most evident in Cardona's contributions to her brother Luis Antonio's efforts to research and write *The Coming of the Puerto Ricans.* Self-published in 1974 to fill the abysmal void on documentation of the U.S. Puerto Rican experience, this historical compilation ranks among the earliest resources on this group.

In the 1960s Cardona worked as a program coordinator for the United Bronx Parents, a group founded by community leader Evelina López Antonetty to advocate for minority rights and quality education. Cardona developed knowledge and expertise about the public schools, encouraged parental involvement, and worked with summer youth employment programs. All of this prepared Cardona for a position with ASPIRA in the 1970s. Founded in 1961 by the venerable Antonia Pantoja, ASPIRA promoted an educational agenda designed to develop youth leadership and provide access to a university education. One of a cadre of organizers who worked with Pantoja in several of her empowerment initiatives, Cardona became a counselor at ASPIRA and later directed its Parent Student Guidance program.

As was the case with many Puerto Rican and Latino leaders during the late 1960s and early 1970s, Cardona was an experience-based activist without the academic credentials that would later become requisite for employment once these organizations became institutionalized or received government funding. In 1973, however, at the age of forty-three, Cardona received a college degree from New York University. The university recognized Cardona's life experience and credited long-distance studies at Goddard College.

That life experience included a wealth of contributions. She was a charter member of the National Conference of Puerto Rican Women (NACOPRW), cofounder with Norma Stanton of the Hispanic Women's Center (HACER), a mediator, a policy maker, and an advocate for numerous community programs. In 1995, Cardona worked alongside Shirley Rodríguez Remeneski and others to create the group 100 Hispanic Women. Among its activities, the group is involved with voter registration and electoral participation.

Cardona was appointed program associate director of the New York State Division for Women in 1983. She promoted an impressive array of issues, from bilingual education to AIDS and domestic violence. She retired in 1995.

As an intrepid septuagenarian, Cardona has turned her attention to the trauma of being a first-time voter. "It hit me like thunder, right on top of my head," Cardona exclaimed to a *Newsday* journalist in 2000. "People are afraid to vote . . . when you go to vote, the first thing you see is a police officer in uniform." This revelation motivated Cardona to develop a new voter education pamphlet with the help of a Queens College professor. The table of contents includes a history of minority voting rights, filling out various voter forms and ballots, a synopsis of the party system and primary elections, and the rationale for stationing police officers at the polls.

After a lifetime of grassroots and organized activism, Cardona has received countless recognitions and awards. Not one to rest on past achievements, Alice Cardona remains committed to empowering marginalized communities for generations to come.

SOURCES: Cardona, Luis Antonio. 1974. *The Coming of the Puerto Ricans*. Bethesda, MD: Carreta Press; Duggan, Dennis. 2004. "A life that is far from random." *Newsday,* November 28, G2; Gudrais, Elizabeth. 2000. "Walking Tall into the Polling Booth." *Newsday*, July 7, G6; Maldonado, Adál Alberto. 1984. "Alice Cardona." In *Portraits of the Puerto Rican Experience*. New York: IPRUS Institute.

Virginia Sánchez Korrol

CARR, VIKKI (1940–)

Born Florencia Bisenta de Casillas Martínez Cardona to Carlos and Florence Cardona in El Paso, Texas, Vikki Carr was the oldest of eight children. Her family moved to Rosemead, California, when she was only an infant. At age eighteen, with the stage name "Carlita," she performed as a singer with a band in Palm Springs and in 1961 landed a contract with Liberty Records. Her first headliner shows were at the Coconut Grove in Los Angeles. Her fame began that same year with the hit song "He's a Rebel." It was soon followed by another hit single, "It Must Be Him," which was later featured in the movie *Moonstruck* (1987).

In the late 1960s she changed "Carlita" to Carr and added Vikki as her first name. Her father's initial disappointment with her name change reinforced Carr's commitment to her heritage and the desire to record in Spanish. Carr soon persuaded Columbia Records to record her first Spanish-language album in 1972. Although she remains one of the most successful and prolific Latina singers, the early days at Las Vegas hotels reflect harder times. In the public relations materials announcing her 1999 PBS special, *Vikki Carr: Memories, Memorias,* Carr recalled when she was starting her career in the 1960s and was performing in the lounge of the Sands Hotel in Las Vegas. Nat King Cole was headlining in the hotel's Copa Room, where Carr watched his act nearly every night before performing in her own lounge show. One night Cole brought a group of his friends to hear her sing. She was disappointed by their lack of interest. She recounts, "I was devastated. When I finished my set, I walked away feeling pretty low and suddenly, I felt a tap on my shoulder. I turned and there he was, Nat King Cole. He smiled and said, 'I'd like to apologize for my friends. Maybe you thought no one was listening, but I was, and you keep singing.' "

She has won three Grammy awards: in 1985 for Best Mexican-American Performance for *Simplemente mujer*; in 1992 for Best Latin Pop Album for *Cosas del amor,* which included a duet with Mexican artist Ana Gabriel; and in 1995 for Best Mexican-American Performance, Vocal or Instrumental, for *Recuerdo a Javier*

Solis. Carr has made many television appearances, including an appearance as a guest host for Johnny Carson on *The Tonight Show* and as guest star on *The Carol Burnett Show.* She has performed in theater and on the radio. In 1971 she founded the Vikki Carr Scholarship Foundation, which has distributed more than 200 scholarships. The scholarship encourages Mexican American youth to pursue a higher education. She has received numerous other awards, including Hispanic Woman of the Year in 1984 for her civic and humanitarian contributions. Her public service includes 1998 radio spots to educate the Hispanic community on how to deal with credit.

Over the years she has performed for the queen of England and for five U.S. presidents. Her 1999 PBS special *Vikki Carr: Memories, Memorias* celebrated Mexican and Latin American music in the United States in the 1940s and 1950s. Having divorced twice, Carr is currently married to San Antonio physician Dr. Pedro DeLeón.

SOURCES: Burr, Ramiro. 1999. *The Billboard Guide to Tejano and Regional Mexican Music.* New York: Billboard Books; *Hispanic Times.* 1998. "Avoiding Bankruptcy: Educating Latinos to Use Credit Wisely." 19, no. 3 (June 30): 46; Telgen, Diane, and Jim Kamp, eds. 1993. *Notable Hispanic American Women.* Detroit: Gale Research; *Vikki Carr: Memories, Memorias.* 2001. http://www.kcet.org/vikkicarr (accessed October 3, 2002).

Mary Ann Villarreal

CARRILLO DE FITCH, JOSEFA (1810–1893)

Born on November 27, 1810, María Antonia Natalia Elija Carrillo was affectionately called Josefa in honor of her godmother. She was the oldest of thirteen children born to María Carrillo López and Joaquín Victor Carrillo, captain of the San Diego Presidio. The Carrillos were an influential and socially well connected family with relatives through blood or marriage scattered throughout the various presidios and settlements in California, and by the 1820s they developed their rancho holdings and were raising livestock to supplement the family's limited military salary. Landholding was the surest means of aggrandizing social and economic status for the second generation of Californios. Josefa Carrillo was born into this ranchero elite.

Carrillo early life was rather typical of the ranchero class. She had little formal education but became adept at the female skills of sewing, cooking, cleaning, raising children, and ordering Indian servants; in short, she acquired the necessary skills for maintaining a rancho household. Two socioeconomic factors greatly affected nineteenth-century California. First, the aftermath of Mexican independence and its liberalizing social forces ushered in the secularizing of the California missions, thereby removing hundreds of thousands of cultivated acres from the power of the clergy. Second, the introduction and steady growth of a trade route that established the hide and tallow trade with New England merchants expanded the rancheros' economic power and social ascendancy.

Young Californianas were expected and pressured to marry early. Rather than marrying a fellow Californio, Carrillo fell in love with Henry Delano Fitch, an American merchant seaman, who formally presented a written marriage request to her parents in 1827. On April 15, 1829, the wedding ceremony was in progress, but was stopped by order of the governor, José María Echeandía. Carrillo believed "that the governor's persecution of herself and her husband was . . . prompted by the hatred which possessed his soul when he realized that she preferred a rival whom he detested." Echeandía actually detested Fitch's failure to become a naturalized citizen and his smuggling activities. Undaunted, the couple eloped, escaping in Fitch's ship, and they were married in Valparaiso, Chile. The elopement was the greatest social scandal of its time.

Business brought the Fitches and their newborn son Eduardo back to California in July 1830. According to Carrillo "All the resident ladies of the port came to visit her and within a few days her mother and sister came, they welcomed her and after so many greetings her mother told her that her father was very offended with her." Upset by this news, since "she preferred risking death rather than live in anger with the author of her days," she attempted reconciliation. Finding her father sitting next to a shotgun, Carrillo literally begged on her knees for forgiveness, and moved by this emotional display, Joaquín Carrillo reluctantly reconciled with his daughter.

While the Fitches reconciled with one male authority, they greatly displeased another, Governor Echeandía. The governor declared the couple's marriage illegal, imprisoned Fitch, and simultaneously placed Carrillo in *deposito,* the practice of separating eloped couples in order to ascertain whether the young woman had consented of her own volition. The ecclesiastical authorities investigated the governor's acts but simultaneously initiated an annulment trial in October 1830. Carrillo was removed from the state's control and placed under another house of *deposito* in San Gabriel, while Fitch was sent to the prison at Monterey. In December 1830 the ecclesiastical authorities found the marriage valid but not legitimate under canonical law. To show penance and put an end to the scandal, the recalcitrant couple was ordered to hold lit candles while attending a high mass at the San Gabriel Mission and was instructed to pray the third part of the Rosary of the Virgin Mary for thirty days. In time Henry and

Josefa Carrillo Fitch had eleven children and settled in northern California, where the couple purchased the Sotoyomi rancho. According to Carrillo, Henry Fitch had promised to make her happy "for the rest of her days" on the night they eloped. Later in her life she related that her husband kept that promise loyally and faithfully for the twenty years she lived at his side. She never remarried after Fitch's death in 1849 and died on January 26, 1893.

See also Spanish Borderlands

SOURCES: Sánchez, Rosaura. 1995. *Telling Identities: The Californio Testimonios.* Minneapolis: University of Minnesota Press; Weber, David J. 1992. *The Spanish Frontier in North America.* New Haven, CT: Yale University Press.

María Raquel Casas

CASAL, LOURDES (1938–1981)

Cuban writer and public intellectual Lourdes Emilia Irene de la Caridad Casal y Valdés was born in Havana. Her life was consumed by a passionate love of learning. Casal believed that the purpose of knowledge was to further human development. Thus she devoted her life to finding the answers that she ardently believed would bring progress and justice to society, and she did this with extraordinary honesty and integrity.

Born to professional, mulatto parents, Casal enjoyed the benefits of middle-class life. Her commitment to education was probably due to the influence of her parents. Her father, Pedro Casal, was a physician and dentist, and her mother, an elementary-school teacher. Like many other middle-class mulattoes, Casal struggled with the tensions between race and class in prerevolutionary Cuban society. There were always reminders of the "color line." In a short story Casal relates how a girlfriend did not invite her to her birthday party because (Casal) "was a pretentious mulatto girl who felt she was better than everybody else because her father was a doctor."

The Catholic University of Villanueva in Havana, from which Casal graduated with a degree in chemical engineering, was the stage for her first involvement in student activities. She edited student newspapers, participated in literary contests, and, as a practicing Catholic, became involved in organizations of religious women. It was obvious that Casal was moving away from the natural sciences and evolving into a multifaceted, Renaissance-like intellectual and activist. Later her commitment to Catholicism waned.

As happened with most Cubans, the Revolution of 1959 marked Casal's life in dramatic ways. As a university student at the time, Casal participated in revolutionary activities. With other Catholic students she became involved with the Directorio Estudiantil Revolucionario (Student Revolutionary Directorate), an important anti-Batista movement. But in the midst of intense ideological conflicts, and disappointed at what she saw as a betrayal of the original objectives of the Cuban Revolution, Casal became active in counterrevolutionary affairs in Cuba for a while and eventually left for exile. She came to New York in 1962, where she worked and studied, always with Cuba on her mind.

Her desire to understand human behavior had led Casal to take some psychology courses at the University of Havana shortly before leaving Cuba. In New York she enrolled at the New School for Social Research, where she completed a Ph.D. in social psychology. She taught at the City University of New York and later at Rutgers University in Newark, New Jersey. At the same time, she wrote prolifically, not only about social science research, but also about literature and politics. Among her early literary works are *El caso Padilla* (1971), about the Cuban dissident writer, and *Los fundadores: Alfonso y otros Cuentos* (1973), both published in Miami, Florida. She wrote many poems about the exile experience and about life in New York, a city that she also loved. Although she wrote in Spanish, many of her poems have been translated into English.

As a social scientist, Casal's research focused on the fate of U.S. minorities, especially African Americans and Latinos. In this society, where race categorizations are more rigid than they are in Cuba, Casal clearly became "black" rather than mulatto. Her position as a black woman awakened her interest in the study of race and ethnicity. In 1974 she published *The Cuban Minority in the United States* with Rafael Prohias, another Cuban-born scholar, a report that identified the needs of those Cubans in the United States who were not as "successful" as other Cuban exiles of the 1960s. She also studied black Cubans (only about 3 percent of the total Cuban immigration of the 1960s and 1970s) who concentrated between white Cuban and black neighborhoods in Miami. But a great deal of her energy was devoted to the study of Cuba. In 1969 she cofounded the Institute of Cuban Studies, a group of Cuban academics in the United States committed to scholarship and pluralism. She also contributed to the magazine *Nueva Generación,* a publication that called for measured analysis and new ideas about Cuban reality.

Casal's life took a decisive turn in 1973 when she was invited by the Cuban government to visit the island. This invitation was an uncommon occurrence at the time, since Cuba considered exiles betrayers for having left the country, especially those who had left voluntarily as adults. Casal accepted, and her journey to Cuba opened the door for future exile visits and perhaps was instrumental in the eventual Cuban government's policy change toward the Cuban community in the United States. The trip had a profound impact on Casal. Her intellectual attempts to understand the 1959 Cuban Revolution turned into an open, albeit critical, support for it. Upon returning to the United States, she accepted an invitation from a Cuban-born colleague and friend to edit and publish a new magazine, *Areíto*. They talked to various individuals, including many members of *Nueva Generación*, who agreed to add their names to a long list of supporters of this new project. But when the first issue of *Aréito* came out, many strongly criticized the content, which they saw as an unconditional support of the revolution, and they asked for their names to be removed. Casal's evolution had caused a rift among existing groups of Cuban Americans. At the same time, many other Cubans, especially among the young, became attracted to Lourdes Casal's ideas and joined her projects. She helped found the Antonio Maceo Brigade, a group of young, progressive Cuban Americans who had come to the United States at a very early age. In 1978 she participated in the Dialogue, a meeting between members of the Cuban government and a group of exiles that led to the release of political prisoners, family reunification, and travel agreements. At the academic level Casal immersed herself in the analysis of Cuban society and politics. She continued to be an important voice at the Institute of Cuban Studies, where she contributed sympathetic, yet rigorous assessments of the Cuban Revolution.

Casal's love of life was often frustrated by poor health. She was diabetic. Beginning in 1977, she had to receive dialysis treatment due to renal dysfunction. In December 1979, during one of her trips to Cuba, Casal was hospitalized. Her health continued to deteriorate, and she stayed in Cuba, where she died on February 1, 1981.

Casal served as a bridge between Cubans on the island and in the diaspora. She wanted to bring them together in a spirit of dialogue. Although she was a controversial figure in exile circles, Casal had the ability to express her positions firmly without disrespecting those who opposed her beliefs. Her untimely death represented a great loss for all Cubans who yearn to end years of hostility between Cuba and the United States.

Her last book, *Palabras juntan revolución,* received a posthumous award by Casa de las Américas in Cuba. This collection of poems reflects different facets of Casal's rich life. For example, "Siempre he vivido en Cuba" is a proud statement of loyalty to her native land. Another poem, "Para Ana Veldford," is a sorrowful reflection on the uprootedness of exile, the high cost of multiple identities: "I carry this marginality inside me, immune to all returns, too *habanera* to be New Yorker, too New Yorker to be—even to become again—anything else."

Lourdes Casal's honest quest influenced many who knew her. Her integrity gained her much respect, even among those who disagreed with her views. She is terribly missed.

SOURCES: Bryce-Laporte, Roy S. 1981. "Obituary to a Female Immigrant and Scholar, Lourdes Casal (1938–1981)." In *Female Immigrants to the United States: Caribbean, Latin American, and African Experiences*. Washington, DC: Smithsonian Institution; Cuesta, Leonel Antonio de la. 1982. *Perfil biografico, itinerario ideologico: Antología de Lourdes Casal.* Miami, FL: Instituto de Estudios Cubanos; Sunshine, Catherine, and Keith Warner, eds. 1998. "Poems of Exile: Lourdes Casal." In *Caribbean Connections: Moving North*. Washington, DC: Network of Educators on the Americas.

Yolanda Prieto

CASALS, ROSEMARY (1948–)

Rosemary Casals is known in the world of tennis as "Rosebud," but it is said in the world of sports that she was far from the picture of serenity suggested by that nickname. She was born in San Francisco on September 16, 1948, to Central American parents, immigrants from El Salvador. While she was still an infant, she and her sister Victoria were placed in the care of a great-aunt, María, and a great-uncle, Manuel Casals, who raised them as their own. Manuel Casals introduced Rosemary to tennis on the city's public courts. He served as Casals's only coach throughout her impressive career.

Casals enjoyed the competitiveness of the sport, but like other pioneers who achieve recognition for their accomplishments, she faced numerous challenges along the way. Tennis was considered a sport of the upper classes, played on country estates and at expensive country clubs. Casals's poor family background and Latino heritage immediately set her apart. She could not afford the pricey trappings of the sport: the expensive clothes, shoes and rackets, tournament fees, and transportation. In time Casals revolutionized the sport by wearing bright colors on the court, breaking a long tradition of wearing only white clothes during matches. This act of necessity became a signature style for her, and Casals, who often received standing ovations for her robust games, became known for her colorful tennis outfits.

Determined to be the best tennis player ever, at five feet, two inches, Casals faced another disadvantage in playing taller players. As a result, she developed an explosive playing style on the court, with incredible acrobatic strokes and stamina honed from constant competition in tournaments against older, more experienced players. In an interview for the International

Tennis Hall of Fame, Casals remarked, "I'm out there with [5-foot-11 Margaret 'The Arm'] Court with those arms and legs that stretch forever, and I had to make my shots count right away." Before her eighteenth birthday Casals was ranked as the top junior and women's player in northern California and eleventh in the country.

Professional women's tennis in the 1970s fought for equality on several fronts and paved the way for acceptance of women tennis players on a par with men. Casals emerged as a leading figure, along with Billie Jean King, in bringing about changes. Women players attempted to boycott tennis tournaments in 1970, citing the differences in the prize purses awarded men as opposed to women players. They demanded that equal prize monies be given to both men and women. The U.S. Lawn Tennis Association ignored their demands, and women players led by Casals and King established the Virginia Slims Invitational tournament. The slogan of Virginia Slims cigarettes, "You've come a long way, baby," could not have been more appropriate as Casals, King, and others marched into history. "Those early Slims days were an exciting time, and a little scary, too," recalls Casals. "We knew we had to break away, go on our own. . . . the USTA didn't like our rebel ways and threatened to suspend us Americans if we played. They did, and for a while we wondered if that was the end of tennis for us. Of course it wasn't."

Casals was inducted into the Tennis Hall of Fame in 1996. Her victories include the 1966 U.S. hard-court and indoor doubles tournaments with Billie Jean King and the doubles crown at Wimbledon and at the U.S. and South African championships in 1967, also with King. King and Casals remain the only doubles team to have won U.S. titles on grass, clay, indoor, and hard-surface courts. An incomparable team throughout the 1970s, the two women won fifty-six titles and were unbeatable. Casals also entered tournaments as a single contender in all the majors. During her career, she won 11 singles and 112 pro doubles titles. Five years later Casals underwent knee surgery and left competition. She started a business in California but continued to promote a women's classic tournament for seniors. At the age of forty-one, Casals and Martina Navratilova won the U.S. Open Seniors' women's doubles championship in 1988.

SOURCES: International Tennis Hall of Fame. 1996. "Rosie (Rosemary) Casals, 1996 Enshrinee." http://www.tennisfame.org/enshrinees/rosie_casals.html (accessed October 6, 2004); Kanellos, Nicolás, ed. 1998. "Rosemary Casals." In *The Hispanic American Almanac.* Detroit: Gale Research; Thomson Gale online. "Rosemary Casals." http://www.galegroup.com./free_resources/whm/bio/casals_r.htm (accessed September 10, 2004).

Virginia Sánchez Korrol

CASANOVA DE VILLAVERDE, EMILIA (1832?–1897)

Born in Cuba in 1832 or 1833, Emilia Casanova was the first Cuban woman to write political essays, address the Congress of the United States as the representative of Cuban women fighting for independence, and make an attempt to internationalize Cuba Libre by writing to both Victor Hugo and Giuseppe Garibaldi. At the age of twenty-two she became the wife of the noted Cuban novelist Cirilo Villaverde, the author of *Cecilia Valdés,* a nineteenth-century Cuban literary masterpiece dedicated to "all Cuban women." The second version of the novel was written in New York City during Villaverde's political exile and documented the complex universe of slavery in Cuba and the Ten Years' War in light of the American Civil War and Reconstruction.

Most of the information about Emilia Casanova de Villaverde comes from the text and context of her political addresses. A pamphlet published in New York in 1874 included a biography and selections from her political writings. In it Cirilo Villaverde describes his wife as an exemplary woman patriot. She was born to a rich slaveholding family of Cárdenas, and she did not have coquettish manners "which were natural in young girls," because from an early age she was consumed by "the fire of freedom." Young, beautiful, vivacious, and rich, Casanova "was adored by her parents, and idolized by her slaves." A member of the Creole elite, young Casanova distanced herself from her father's conservative views. At a banquet, in the presence of the Spanish authorities, she lifted her glass and courageously toasted "to the freedom of the world and to the independence of Cuba," making the cheerful reunion dissolve.

Her first trip to the United States in 1852, in the company of her father and two brothers, had a profound impact on her. There she could admire the monuments erected to the heroes of Cuban independence and find a solid confirmation of her republican principles. She thought to stay in New York to continue her education and polish her English, but a letter from her adored mother, who felt lonely and sad, made her decide to spend only three months in the city and return to Cuba. But the period she spent in New York was enough for her to come in contact with eminent members of the Cuban exile community, and she agreed to bring some important documents back to the island. Casanova avidly read these subversive documents and with the help of her two brothers circulated them in Cuba. She was still a girl when she helped one of her brothers, accused of conspiracy, flee to the United States.

In 1854 the entire family moved to Philadelphia. There the twenty-two-year-old Casanova met and married Cirilo Villaverde, who was twenty years older. When her family returned to Cuba, she moved with her husband to New York, sharing with him "the bitter bread of exile." She quickly integrated into the exile community, organized public meetings, and opened her home to the friends of the Cuban revolution. She witnessed the events of the Civil War, in which "she discovered the symptoms that later stirred the revolution in her country." When the Ten Years' War broke out in 1868, she welcomed it as the beginning of the end of slavery and the beginning of Cuban independence. To raise funds for the Cuban army, she founded the first political club of women, the Liga de las Hijas de Cuba. Informed that her father, a naturalized American citizen who held property in the United States, had been imprisoned in Havana, she immediately wrote to the U.S. secretary of state, Hamilton Fish, asking for the protection of the American government. The following day she traveled to Washington to meet members of Congress and managed to meet President Grant in the White House, who, apparently moved by her passionate attempts to free her father, promised that the Spaniards would not dare touch him. After her father was released, Casanova continued to build networks with eminent Americans and foreigners friendly to the cause of Cuba Libre.

In January 1869 she wrote to Giuseppe Garibaldi, who was then living on the island of Caprera, about the Cuban quest. She explained that "the beginning of our revolution means the freedom of our slaves, giving them arms and incorporating them in our patriotic ranks." She could not understand why European leaders kept silent about the Cuban cause. After a full year Garibaldi responded that he would always be on the side of the oppressed "whether the oppressors are kings or nations," and that he wished that beautiful Cuba would gain independence. Casanova had hoped for a more substantial commitment.

In 1871, as the representative of "Cuban mothers," Casanova went to Washington for the third time to petition the government to make all diplomatic efforts on behalf of the students of the medical school imprisoned by the Spanish authorities in Havana, and to bring them to the United States. In 1872 she returned to Washington representing the Liga de las Hijas de Cuba to petition Congress to recognize the state of belligerence against the Cuban insurgents. She explained the situation in Cuba as a "popular, political and social revolution" against a U.S.-supported Spanish colonial domination. She provided evidence that attempts made from the 1820s to the 1850s to abolish slavery in Cuba had faced opposition from the United States, as had efforts to liberate the island because that would have ended slavery as well. Casanova's powerful arguments failed to gain support. It was in the best economic interests of the United States to preserve a weak colonial power rather than a strong newly independent republic.

Portrait of Emilia Casanova de Villaverde, in Juan Casasus, *La emigración cubana y la independencia de la patria* (Havana, 1953). Courtesy of Alexandra Lorini.

Emilia Casanova de Villaverde remained in exile until her husband died in 1894. She transported his remains to Cuba as he had wished, but returned to New York City, where she died on March 4, 1897. She never abandoned the cause of Cuban independence.

See also Journalism and Print Media; Ten Years' War

SOURCES: *Apuntes biográficos de Emilia Casanova Villaverde.* 1874. "Escritos por un contemporaneo." New York; Pertierra Serra, Enrique. 2000. *Italianos por Cuba.* Havana: Editorial José Martí; Villaverde, Cirilo. 2002. *Cecilia Valdés.* Havana: Editorial Letras Cubanas.

Alessandra Lorini

CASITA MARIA, NEW YORK (1934–)

The oldest settlement house serving New York City's Latino community is Casita Maria, a Catholic but nonsectarian institution. Its hub location is at 928 Simpson Street in the borough of the Bronx, but it originated in Spanish Harlem in 1934 during Mayor Fiorello La Guardia's first term in office. Serving primarily Puerto Rican youth, Casita Maria was founded by two public school teachers, Elizabeth and Claire Sullivan, with the assistance of a Catholic nun, Sister Mary Imelda. The Puerto Rican community in East Harlem originated in the early 1920s and was culturally reflected in the area's thriving business sector, complete with movie houses, record stores, and markets often refurbished to meet Puerto Rican needs. Tenements in East Harlem (Spanish Harlem or El Barrio) sheltered Italians, Jews, African Americans, West Indians, and Puerto Ricans. In the 1930s and 1940s eastern Europeans and Italians began to move northward to the Bronx. As the black and Puerto Rican communities expanded in the densely populated region, property values declined, and unemployment and poverty increased. Rapidly El Barrio deteriorated into a city slum area, an environment particularly deleterious to the cultivation of potential leadership among the youth.

With few social service agencies available, limited open park spaces, and restrictions on the use of certain recreational facilities, the Sullivan sisters and Sister Mary Imelda encouraged the formation of clubs and youth activity programs. The Royals and their rival club, the Dukes, composed of teenage boys, who organized to play stickball and cards in the homes of club members but also posed problems of delinquency, were invited to join Casita Maria. The Sullivan sisters supplied funding to furnish the Royal Club in a vacant ground floor, attracting the interest of barrio residents and volunteers. Community volunteers, including the Sullivans, Royal Club members, and local leaders constituted an organizing committee. They met at the Catholic Church, La Milagrosa, to draw up plans for structuring, financing, and expanding Casita Maria. In 1934 the group established Casita Maria on the first floor of the building at 32 West 113th Street. This, in essence, became the first Puerto Rican community house in the city. It is noteworthy that the Dukes rarely participated in the venture, and eighteen of their twenty-three members had run-ins with the law, but the sports-conscious Royals, who supported the settlement house, completed school. Some received scholarships and became professionals. Among the members of girls' clubs and other gangs joining Casita Maria, many became leading citizens, including Judge John Carro, who was a member of a teen gang, the Zeniths.

The earliest Casita Maria programs targeted children during and after school, offering English-language instruction, games, and activities. Soon parents joined the organization, and classes in English for adults developed, taught by city teachers. Casita Maria rapidly outgrew its space and opened a second building on East 110th Street that was renovated to incorporate two adjacent houses. The City Housing Authority invited Casita Maria to sponsor a center at Carver Houses, a low-income development on East 102nd Street. In 1945 Casita Maria was able to buy another building at 61 East 107th Street, but was forced to sell it in the 1960s to the municipal government as the future site of the Madison Park Housing Project. After demolition of the 107th Street building Casita Maria moved to larger quarters in the South Bronx. By this time it had become one of the largest multiservice organizations of its kind. Assisted by funding from the city of New York, initiatives such as remedial reading classes, preschool Head Start programs, child care, day camps, summer camps, youth clubs, and job and leadership training became hallmarks of the organization.

Offering a wide range of services, Casita Maria continues to serve the Latino population of the South Bronx and East Harlem, and education remains its focal point. From its humble, self-funded origins in a

Casita Maria organized summer youth activities. Courtesy of Centro Archives, Centro de Estudios Puertorriqueños, Hunter College, CUNY.

Sister Carmelita, a reformer at Casita Maria, with a group of children at the Doctor White Settlement House in Brooklyn, 1920s. Photograph by C. Spero. Courtesy of Missionary Servants of the Most Blessed Trinity archives.

vacant ground-floor apartment to its headquarters in the South Bronx, Casita Maria developed into one of the city's premier institutions. With the Carver and Corsi Centers in East Harlem, the Mount Pleasant Senior Housing complex, social services, and educational and recreational programs, Casita Maria has earned its place in the history of New York Puerto Ricans and Latinos.

See also Americanization Programs

SOURCES: Casita Maria, United Neighborhood Houses. www.unhny.org/member/agency_detail.cfm?ID=5017 (accessed September 10, 2004); Ribes Tovar, Federico, ed. 1970. "Casita Maria" and "Some Outstanding Former Juvenile Members of Casita Maria." In *Enciclopedia puertorriqueña,* vol. 2. New York: Plus Ultra Educational Publishers.

Virginia Sánchez Korrol

CASTILLO, ANA (1953–)

Born on June 15, 1953, in Chicago, Ana Castillo ranks among the most prolific and versatile writers in Chicano literature. Although her Mexican American family was originally from the Southwest, Castillo has strong midwestern roots. She attended community college and received her undergraduate degree from Northwestern University. Castillo discovered her poetic talents during her college years and gave her first public poetry reading at the age of twenty. Her poetry reflected on the instances of racism and sexism that she and her family encountered. Through this outlet Castillo began to realize her voice not only as a poet, but as an emerging Chicana feminist.

After graduation from Northwestern Castillo moved to Sonoma County, California, and for one year taught courses in ethnic studies. She returned to Chicago and completed a master's degree in Latin American and Caribbean studies at the University of Chicago. She later earned a doctorate in American studies at the University of Bremen in Germany.

Castillo's first three publications were collections of poetry: *Otro canto, The Invitation,* and *Women Are Not Roses.* Her poetry ranges from the emotional explorations and meditations of modern poets to works with a distinctly Chicana activist overtone. Her "protest poetry" and unabashedly feminist insights garnered the attention of other Chicana artists and activists. Castillo became a prominent influence in the Chicana/o movement. *The Invitation,* a self-published chapbook, represents a bold critique of sexism within the Chicano movement. She elaborated on these themes in her later fiction and nonfiction essays. During the 1980s Castillo's poetry began to take on a much more musical tone as the result of her involvement with the Al-Andalus Flamenco Dance Company. The rhythm and meter of her work display distinctly aural qualities that are complemented by the chosen word.

One of her most celebrated publications is *The Mixquiahuala Letters* (1986). The novel tracks the lives of two women who travel to Mexico to discover their place in a world that has them divided between being American and being Mexican. It is narrated through letters written between these two women, providing an emotionally captivating and thought-provoking medium. The novel received much praise for its discussion of gender roles in both American and Mexican societies and the traps that such roles create for women. The book won the American Book Award from the Before Columbus Foundation.

Castillo's novel *So Far from God* gained even more critical acclaim. The novel incorporates folk mythology, political and social commentary, and issues of gender within Chicano society into a story that at heart helps provide a positive answer for the darkest questions. The novel won the Carl Sandburg Literary Award and further cemented Castillo's position as one of the important voices in Chicana literature.

Castillo's work includes journalism and editing. Along with Cherríe Moraga and Norma Alarcón, Castillo edited *The Sexuality of Latinas,* a collection of essays that explored issues of sexual liberation and repression in Latino culture. Castillo's most recognized nonfiction work is her collection of essays *Massacre of the Dreamers: Essays on Xicanisma*. For Castillo, *Xicanisma* is an ever-present consciousness of Chicana interdependence specifically rooted in Chicana culture and history. Although *Xicanisma* is a way to understand Chicanas in the world, it may also help others, both men and women, who are not necessarily of Mexican background. Its philosophy is yielding, never resistant to change, one based on wholeness, not dualism. For women, men are not their opposites, their opponents, their 'other.'" As feminist philosopher, poet, and novelist, Castillo continues to expand her own literary style by publishing children's books, newspaper articles, and nonfiction essays. A vibrant literary voice and guardian of Latina feminist traditions, Ana Castillo is currently Writer in Residence at DePaul University in Chicago.

See also Literature

SOURCES: Ana Castillo online. www.anacastillo.com (accessed October 6, 2004); Benson, Sonia G., ed. 2003. *The Hispanic American Almanac.* 3rd ed. Detroit: Thomson/Gale Publishing; Castillo, Ana. 1994. *Massacre of the Dreamers: Essays on Xicanisma.* Albuquerque: University of New Mexico Press; Palmismo, Joseph M., ed. 1998. *Notable Hispanic American Women, Book II.* Detroit: Gale Publishing.

Daniel Ruiz

CASTILLO, GUADALUPE (1942–)

Born and raised near the Mexican border in Tucson, Arizona, on March 23, 1942, Guadalupe Castillo has always maintained a strong affinity with immigrant rights, workers' issues, and history. Driven by the memories and oral histories of her venerable Tucsonense ancestors, Castillo became a historian in order to document and highlight Mexicano and Chicana/o contributions to the area's and nation's development. She was the first Chicana to obtain a master's degree in history from the University of Arizona, pursued doctoral studies, and received a Ford Foundation Fellowship for three years. Castillo became an early advocate of education, urging academia to recognize and institutionalize Chicana/o studies programs and was one of the first professors to develop Chicana/o studies courses. Guadalupe Castillo, along with Herminio Rios, pioneered in the field by publishing detailed bibliographic resources on Chicana/o history in *El Grito.*

Castillo's commitment to social justice is also evident in her pedagogical methods. As a professor at Pima Community College since the 1980s, she requires that students take an active role in community events and organization. Activists in southern Arizona often credit Castillo with playing a vital role in awakening, formulating, and encouraging their political activism.

Castillo is also recognized for her commitment to social justice issues. She played a pivotal role in launching the Chicano movement in Tucson. A founder of the Movimiento Estudiantil Chicano de Aztlán (MEChA) at the University of Arizona, she rallied to ensure Chicana/o representation in the political arena through her work in La Raza Unida Party. Ultimately these grassroots efforts resulted in a heightened political awareness in Tucson about Chicana/o issues and the movement. The struggle forced the city of Tucson to establish local community centers, like El Rio Neighborhood Center, designed to promote Chicana/o cultural, intellectual, and health needs.

In the 1980s Castillo focused on another pressing issue as a mounting number of Central American refugees arrived in the United States desperately in need of protection and legal information. Their dilemma motivated Castillo to devote herself to providing critical assistance. A member of the Manzo Area Council, a social service organization, Castillo and others organized asylum counseling and legal recourse work for El Salvadoran refugees. These actions set in motion the sanctuary movement, and Castillo personally assisted refugees by processing hundreds of asylum petitions to ensure shelter and safety in the United States. During this period Castillo founded La Mesilla Organizing Project, an advocacy group to educate and demand immigrant rights.

In the 1990s Castillo helped found and cochaired the Derechos Humanos Coalition, an advocacy organization designed to promote respect for human and civil rights in southern Arizona and along the U.S.-Mexican border. The organization emerged as the flagship agency of its kind in the region. It challenged the increasing militarization on the border and exposed human rights abuses by federal, state, and local law enforcement officials of migrants and U.S. citizens. A speaker on radio programs and at community and educational events, Castillo passionately argues that "ningún ser humano es ilegal" (no human being is illegal). As a result of her activism on immigrant rights and border issues, Castillo has received many awards, including the National Lawyers Guild Recognition Award in 1999. Other awards are the Dedication to Community Arts by Borderlands Theater, the Recognition Award for Best Teacher by Minority Affairs at Pima

Guadalupe Castillo at an immigrant rights conference in Tucson, Arizona, 2004. Photograph by and courtesy of Lydia R. Otero.

Community College, and the Presidential Teacher Award from the League of United Latin American Citizens (LULAC). In the fall of 2001 Castillo received the Outstanding Alumnus Award from the University of Arizona's Department of History for her "effective teaching and political activism."

SOURCES: Castillo, Guadalupe, and Margo Cowan. 2001. *"It is not our fault": The Case for Amending Present Nationality Law to Make All Members of the Tohono O'odham Nation United States Citizens, Now and Forever.* Sells, AZ: Tohono O'odham Nation, Executive Branch; Rios, Hermino C., and Lupe Castillo. 1970. "Toward a True Chicano Bibliography: Mexican-American Newspapers, 1848–1942." *El Grito* 3, no. 4 (Summer): 17–24.

Lydia R. Otero and Raquel Rubio-Goldsmith

CASTRO, ROSIE (1947–)

Longtime activist Rosie Castro has been an advocate for the rights of women and minorities both in and out of the political arena since her college days. An only child raised by her mother, Castro grew up on San Antonio's West Side after immigrating to the United States from Mexico. She went to Little Flower High School. When Castro first got involved in politics, her mother was alarmed. Reflecting on changing attitudes, Castro commented, "It's very different now, but at that period of time, it was a real shock that I would want to be involved because that was not a womanly thing to do." As a student at Our Lady of the Lake University, she studied to become a teacher and began her journey of political campaigning and activism. She founded a chapter of Young Democrats and later served as president at the county level and vice president at the state level of that group. Early on, Castro "came to really believe the only way to make significant change in this country is through the political process, to affect public policy. At that time public policy was so stacked against people of color."

In 1971 Castro, then twenty-three, ran for city council. She finished second out of four candidates running on the Committee for Barrio Betterment slate. "Of course, we didn't win," Castro says, but the organization was able to claim a victory: "We increased the number of *mexicanos* that started to run, and we brought out the issues." After the loss Castro vowed, "We'll be back." Castro once told reporter Elda Silva, "I think most of my life what I've tried to do is to look at where the deficits are that most minorities encounter and then try to do something about those deficits. Also what I've tried to do is to take the strengths inherent in our culture and use that as much as possible to forward a positive agenda." That agenda led to more than thirty years of volunteer teaching for migrant children, the establishment of a Latino collection of books at the San Antonio Central Library, and important work with the San Antonio Housing Authority.

Pregnancy and motherhood did not deter Rosie Castro from her commitment to politics. In fact, she went into labor while working on a Raza Unida campaign. On September 16, 1974, Castro gave birth to twins Julián and Joaquín, born one minute apart. Now the mother of two, she took the twins to a multitude of activities, including political rallies and meetings. Her sons graduated from Harvard Law School in 2000 and in 2001. Julián became San Antonio's youngest city council member with Joaquín's help as campaign manager. In November 2002 Joaquín won the District 125 Texas House seat with Castro as his campaign manager. Castro has reiterated in several interviews, "They are my legacy."

Castro remains active in the San Antonio community, addressing a variety of issues, including Hispanic voter turnout and Latinas in public policy at San Antonio College. Her history as an organizer in La Raza Unida Party and a veteran of the Chicano movement remains a part of her reputation as a leader and advocate for women and poor people.

SOURCES: Cardenás, José A. 1997. "Rosie Castro a success as civil rights pioneer and a mother." *San Antonio Express-News,* June 29, 6J; Gutiérrez-Mier, John. 1998. "Mexican Americans 'birth' commemorated at daylong discusión." *San Antonio Express-News,* February 2, 7A; San Antonio Community College. "Rosie Castro: Civil Rights Advocate, Member of La Raza Unida." http://www.accd.edu/pac/lrc/chicanaleaders/castro.htm (accessed July 21, 2005); Schiller, Dane. 2001. "Castro upholds family's involvement." *San Antonio Express-News,* May 20, 18A.

Mary Ann Villarreal

CASTRO, VICTORIA M. "VICKIE" (1945–)

Los Angeles educator and activist Victoria M. Castro was born and raised in the Boyle Heights area of Los Angeles. Her parents were a seamstress from El Paso and a furniture maker from Mexico. She attended area schools and eventually went to Roosevelt High School, where she describes herself as "a little above-average student" and very active in school. Because she grew up in a traditional family and was the only girl among four other siblings, Castro's parents held few educational expectations for her other than to finish high school. Yet her parents influenced her greatly and contributed to her emerging social and political awareness. "They were quietly leaders in their workforce," Castro recalls. In particular, her mother was part of the organizing of the downtown garment industry, and Castro remembers going on picket lines with her at a young age.

Castro's social awareness continued during her high-school years. As a senior, Castro experienced a moment of "awakening." When she inquired about an application to attend Mills College, a school counselor urged her to consider a local community college instead. "I was devastated [and] that's where my hostility [emerged]. . . . I started reflecting on my own education and I could just see where it lacked." Soon after, Castro was invited to attend a Mexican American youth leadership conference sponsored by the Los Angeles County Human Relations Commission. Students from all over the county participated, and Castro for the first time heard others talk about ethnic discrimination. It was at the youth conference that Castro made lasting connections with a group of students who went on to forge the Chicano student movement in Los Angeles.

After graduation Castro attended California State University, Los Angeles, where she remembers the shock of a predominantly Anglo campus, a stark contrast to her largely Latino high school. Here, increasingly active, Castro tapped into her growing network and helped organize the Young Citizens for Community Action (YCCA, later renamed Young Chicanos for Community Action), an organization committed to a variety of issues, including the improvement of the educational system.

In March 1968 Castro and the YCCA helped organize the East Los Angeles high-school walkouts, or "blowouts," which Castro describes as a "massive display of discontent with the education system." On March 1, 300 students walked out of Wilson High School, and by the end of the next week 15,000 high-school students had walked out of five Los Angeles schools. The students demanded attention to long-ignored problems afflicting their schools. Citing high dropout rates (described by some as "push out rates") and regular discrimination from faculty and administration, they called for immediate change and put forth a list of demands ranging from the inclusion of Mexican American history into the curriculum and the hiring of more Mexican American teachers to an end to the tracking system that channeled Chicano students into a vocational education curriculum and discouraged them from enrolling in college-bound classes. Of her role in the first day of the walkouts, Castro remembers, "I was being interviewed for a teaching assistant assignment, but my thing was to stall the principal. . . . I made [the appointment] . . . specifically for the time that the rest . . . were gonna go into the hallways and yell 'walkout.' . . . [The principal] . . . takes me into his office . . . [but] he starts to go in and out of his office . . . and I know exactly why! And then he finally just comes to tell me that he has an emergency and will have to reschedule, and then I just skipped out!" The blowouts mobilized many Chicano youths and brought widespread attention to the need for educational reform. Further, the events launched Castro's lifetime commitment to educational advocacy.

Castro remained active, particularly in United Mexican American Students (UMAS), while she pursued a bachelor's degree in math. After graduating from college in 1973, Castro worked in an array of educational posts that ranged from teaching math to administration. Active in the Association of Mexican-American Educators, she eventually served as the organization's state president and acquired invaluable experience and knowledge in the politics of California's educational system. She also pursued her own education, receiving teaching credentials from the University of California at Santa Cruz and a master's degree from Pepperdine University. In 1986 she assumed her first position as school principal at Belvedere Junior High School.

In 1993 Castro was elected to the Los Angeles Unified School District (LAUSD) Board. She served for eight years on the board, including one year as president. Castro describes her decision to run for office: "I had been the principal of Belvedere Junior High and I had just had a horrific year where I lost five kids to gang violence in one year. I think we took three or four shootings during the day, and I . . . just could not . . . get assistance. . . . I was under siege and losing kids, and I was being blamed more than being assisted. And so I was very angry. . . . I could not get assistance for my students in the sense of additional police, programs. . . . I sort of had to fend for myself. . . . So I ran for office!"

As a member of the LAUSD Board, Castro worked tirelessly to improve the Los Angeles school system.

Chicano movement student leader and, years later, school board member, Victoria Castro. Courtesy of Victoria Castro.

She faced frustrations, including a political firestorm over construction of new high school. The problems with the Belmont school site continued to obstruct the need for a high school in the area. In addition, she fought against the firing of Superintendent Ruben Zacarias by outside political and financial influences. Castro explains her disappointment "just seeing a political force of the city, and I mean the old white guard of the city . . . determine what our politics were, and not being in a position to fight it."

Yet despite the difficulties of the job, Castro accomplished a great deal for the Los Angeles district. In her first year she focused on school safety and also helped bring more college counselors to the schools. She cites as her greatest accomplishment work on a successful bond measure that provided desperately needed funds for school repair and construction. It was the first bond measure put to voters in seventeen years and did much to address the serious problem of overcrowding. In addition, she helped the district create a parent-community service organization that gave a powerful voice to the parents of Los Angeles.

After her eight years on the board of education, Castro returned to school administration in 2001 as the principal of Hollenbeck Junior High School in Los Angeles. When she is not focusing all her energies at school, Castro concentrates on her family, spending time with her daughter and two grandchildren. She reflects, "It's just a great place to be in life because I'm not building a career. . . . [I have a strong] knowledge level of how to work with the system . . . and I have no fears!" As an activist, an educator, and a community leader, Castro leaves a significant legacy for the city of Los Angeles. Her activism, dedication, and leadership continue to contribute to community empowerment and educational reform.

See also Chicano Movement; Education

SOURCES: Castro, Victoria M. 2003. Interview by Julie Cohen, September 22; Los Angeles Unified School District. "Los Angeles Unified School District Board Member: Victoria M. Castro." www.lausd.k12.ca.us/lausd/board/castro.html (accessed February 10, 2004); National Latino Communications Center, Galán Productions, Inc., and KCET, producers. 1996. "Taking Back the Schools." *CHICANO! History of the Mexican American Civil Rights Movement,* vol. 3. 57 min. Videocassette. Los Angeles; Rosales, F. Arturo. 1996. *Chicano! The History of the Mexican American Civil Rights Movement.* Houston: Arte Público Press; Ruiz, Vicki L. 1998. *From out of the Shadows: Mexican Women in Twentieth-Century America.* New York: Oxford University Press.

Julie Cohen

CEJA, AMELIA MORAN (1955–)

The life of Amelia Moran Ceja provides a unique example of attaining the American dream. When she was born to Felipe and Francisca Moran on June 13, 1955, in the village of Las Flores, Jalisco, Mexico, not even Amelia's devoted parents and family could have possibly envisioned her dynamic future. She spent her childhood years in Las Flores, a small agrarian village that consisted of a population of "no more than sixty people, had no electricity or running water," and was a place where one "rode donkeys to the river to wash clothes!" Amelia was primarily raised by her mother and grandparents, because her father worked in the United States. While her family had very little in material things, her life "was richer than most people" due to the unconditional love and nurturing she received from her mother and family members. This loving, accepting environment provided her with a strong sense of self-confidence and "can-do" attitude that has served her well throughout her life.

The Morans also instilled the importance and love of education in their daughter. Although her parents had not received an education, they understood that it was "the bridge" to bettering oneself in life. The Morans took great pride in knowing that despite their long separations, they were able to provide education for their daughters beyond the one-room village school that had only six grades. Thus Ceja was sent to the larger town of Teocaltiche in order to complete seventh and eighth grade, while her older sister attended the well-known Colegio La Paz, a private girls' preparatory boarding school in the city of Aguascalientes.

After years of making the journey to northern California by himself, Felipe Moran decided that it was time for his family to join him in the Napa Valley. The family arrived in September 1967, just in time for the fall harvest and the start of school. While Ceja was very eager to join her father in the lovely land of "el Norte," she found herself experiencing a great deal of culture shock when she started her school year at Robert Louis Stevenson Junior High in St. Helena. It was a difficult transition for her. Although she had always been a top student in Mexico, the teachers at this school placed her in special education classes, as they did all non-English speakers. Fortunately, a Spanish-speaking teacher quickly determined that Ceja did not belong in special education and placed her in an entry-level class until her English improved. Ceja also received her first taste of prejudice when classmates made fun of her accent and culture. While it hurt her deeply, it also made her determined to succeed. She drew on her sense of self-confidence and on her parents' encouragement for her to "just be very happy and proud to be who she was." At the end of junior high she received numerous achievement awards, had participated in various school sports, and was fluent in English.

Having arrived at harvest time, Ceja discovered the wonderful world of the vineyards and winemaking, and her father proudly showed her the vineyards where he had earned his livelihood. She eagerly joined him during weekends and observed all the tasks involved in maintaining a vineyard. She recalls "falling in love with the smell of the harvest" and began entertaining the possibility of working in the wine industry someday. "I just knew that someday, I'd be part of it."

Her newly acquired fascination with the vineyards was put aside in 1969 when she accepted her parents' offer to attend the same preparatory school from which her sister had graduated in Aguascalientes, Mexico. Not only did the next two years enable Ceja to reconnect with her Mexican culture and family, but she also discovered another passion—a love of cooking. She had the unique opportunity to learn and prepare the regional cuisines of Mexico. Returning to California to finish high school and pursue a degree in history and literature at the University of California at San Diego, she was well versed in the history, culture, and cuisine of Mexico. Studying in Mexico for two years was a life-changing event for her. "I was so proud of my heritage and I felt so empowered!"

Always close to her family and mindful of her first passion, the vineyards, she returned to the valley during college vacations and learned how to prune vines and other viticulture practices. It was during this period that she was able to get reacquainted with Pedro Ceja, whom she had known since junior high school. As they dated, they discovered that they shared the same dream of someday owning a vineyard. In 1980, two years after her college graduation, Amelia and Pedro Ceja were married after the harvest season.

In 1983, while residing in the Silicon Valley with their three preschool-age children, Amelia and Pedro Ceja, along with family members, purchased their first piece of vineyard property. The following years were difficult and required great sacrifice from all family members. When the senior Cejas lost their jobs, Amelia and Pedro promptly moved their family to a tiny, one-room studio on the property in order to contribute more to the mortgage. Although a "for sale" sign went up, fortunately no offer was received, and by 1986 the first vines were planted. Their first harvest was sold to the well-respected Domaine Chandon Winery. In turn, the Cejas were presented a great business opportunity when the winery assisted them in obtaining root stocks to plant on their property. In the coming years the family continued investing in land until they eventually owned 113 acres of prime Carneros vineyards.

As their vineyard operation prospered, in the late 1990s the Cejas explored the possibility of expanding their operation to include bottling their own wines on a commercial scale. They were well aware that one person was needed to take charge of this part of the business. The logical choice was Amelia, because she had been busy working for well-known wineries and educating herself in all aspects of the winery business since their first harvest. The family encouraged her, stating, "You're not afraid of anything!" During 1999 she immersed herself in writing a marketing plan, incorporating the vineyard, and overseeing the development of a website, along with a company logo and label. Her determination saw the "birth" of Ceja Vineyards, which bottled commercially for the first time in 2000. As the president of Ceja Vineyards, she became the first Mexican American woman to head a winery operation. With her typical hands-on approach, she handles a myriad of duties from marketing and sales to public relations and compliance issues. Despite her heavy schedule, she always welcomes the opportunity to promote Ceja wines. She demonstrates how well the wines and food complement each other by serving one of her many specialties with a matching Ceja selection to visiting distributors, retailers, and writers and at numerous benefits.

Amelia Ceja, president of Ceja Vineyards.
Courtesy of Amelia Ceja.

Fulfilling the roles of wife, mother, gourmet chef, and president of a winery with great finesse, Amelia Ceja is adamant about her belief in "giving back to the community." Her involvement spans a variety of both civic and professional organizations, as well as many charitable endeavors throughout the Napa Valley and beyond. She is especially proud of her work with outreach and mentoring programs that are aimed at youths and teens in her community. Having experienced discrimination firsthand, she has great empathy for youths who are facing their own struggles. She eagerly shares her family's story in order that it may inspire young Latinos to create and attain their own dreams.

Ceja is determined to dedicate the rest of her life to building Ceja Vineyards into a viable enterprise in order that the company can continue to serve future generations. Her goal is to change the perception of Mexicans in the wine industry, emphasizing that the wine industry could not exist without the hard labor and dedication of the vineyard workers. "I want people to realize that we don't work only in the vineyards or cellars; we're wine makers, we're growers, and we have college degrees."

See also Entrepreneurs

SOURCES: Farr, Louise. 2003. "Field of Dreams." *More,* October; Heeger, Jack. 2004. "Ceja Honorary Co-Chair of Three Tenors' Concert." *Napa Valley Register,* June 7; Macias, Robert. 2004. "The Worker's Wine." *Hispanic Business,* 25th anniversary issue, June; Shaw, David. 2003. "Braceros to Vintners in a Generation." *Los Angeles Times,* June 5.

Yolanda Calderón-Wallace

CENTRAL AMERICAN IMMIGRANT WOMEN

The presence of Central Americans in the United States began to attract notice since the 1980s. However, Central Americans have a long history of migration to the United States. Since 1900 Guatemalans, Salvadorans, Nicaraguans, Costa Ricans, Hondurans, and Panamanians have immigrated to many cities in the United States. Salvadoran and Nicaraguan coffee growers traveled back and forth for business motives and pleasure in the early 1900s. Arriving on commercial ships that transported bananas from Honduras to the United States, Hondurans became acquainted with opportunities in the United States. In spite of this enduring immigration, Central Americans remained relatively invisible, "passing" as, or often being mistaken for, Mexicans. They constituted a relatively small group, and many arrived at a time when immigration laws were far more relaxed.

This changed when the political and economic crisis that had been brewing for decades erupted in civil wars and armed confrontations in Central America in the late 1970s. A civil war from roughly 1979 to 1991 in El Salvador, an armed conflict in Guatemala that flared for more than thirty years, and another in Nicaragua that began in the mid-1970s, when Anastasio Somoza was in power, and continued for a decade after he was deposed in 1979 contributed to tripling and sometimes more than quintupling, as in the case of the Salvadorans, the number of these immigrants in the United States. These immigrants established vibrant communities and constitute one of the fastest-growing Latino groups in the United States. Salvadorans are the most numerous, accounting for 43 percent of all Central Americans in the United States; Guatemalans account for 20 percent, and Nicaraguans for 15 percent. Costa Ricans, Hondurans, Panamanians, and Belizeans make up the rest.

Central Americans come from dissimilar contexts and constitute sociocultural and economic groups different from one another. Moreover, they have received differential treatment from the U.S. government as well. The U.S. Latin American population includes well-educated and unskilled immigrants, political refugees, wealthy landowners, and peasants, as well as a variety of ethnic groups such as Garifuna (black Caribs) from Belize and Honduras and several Maya groups from Guatemala. They have settled in a number of U.S. destinations, such as metropolitan Los Angeles, Houston, San Francisco, Miami, New York and New Jersey, and Washington, D.C.

Women have figured prominently in Central American migration, sometimes as pioneers. For instance, women, mostly Salvadorans, initiated the Central American immigration to Washington, D.C. American diplomats working in El Salvador and other Central American regions in the 1960s brought their housekeepers back to the United States. In the United States these women petitioned for their relatives, who in turn brought other family members, thus initiating an enduring pattern of chain immigration. In the 1980s Central American immigration increased exponentially, quintupling the Salvadoran population and quadrupling the Guatemalan group. Women took part in this exodus in great numbers. Some moved to reunite with or accompany husbands, parents, or other relatives, but many came on their own. In fact, two-thirds of the Central American women made the decision to leave on their own, without the collaboration or assistance of male partners or fathers, and thus demonstrated an unusual degree of autonomy. These women sought a better future for themselves and their children and to avoid the consequences of political conflicts occurring in Central America during that period.

The 2000 Census revealed that as a whole, for Central American immigrants, there is almost an equal number of men and women (50.5 percent are men and 49.5 percent are women) with some striking differences by country. At one end, 56 percent of Belizeans and 59 percent of Panamanians are women, and at the other end 55 percent of Guatemalans are men. Salvadoran men and women maintain almost equal representation. Women head approximately one-fifth of Central American households; however, in the Panamanian case this proportion reaches one-third. Central American women's educational levels are varied. In general, men have higher levels of education than women. Panamanians and Costa Ricans are highly educated; one fourth of them have a high-school diploma, one third some college education, and slightly more than 10 percent have completed bachelor's degrees. In contrast, about 16 percent of Guatemalans and Salvadorans have a high-school diploma, approximately 15 percent have some college, and fewer than 4 percent have bachelor's degrees.

Central American immigrants and their descendants have settled everywhere in the United States, and with the exception of Panamanians, the overwhelming majority of Central Americans live in large metropolitan areas. California receives more than half, followed by Florida, Texas, New York, New Jersey, and the Washington, D.C., area, with increasing concentrations in other states, such as Arizona, North Carolina, Georgia, and Kansas. But Los Angeles remains the preferred destination for half of all Central Americans in the country, with more than half of Salvadorans and Guatemalans residing there. More than half of Nicaraguans call Miami their home, whereas New York is the most popular destination for Panamanians.

The bulk of the Central American immigrants arrived in a period of stiffer U.S. immigration laws, and for many, obtaining permanent residence or a legal permit becomes nearly impossible. The Immigration and Naturalization Service (INS) estimates that close to 60 percent of Salvadorans and Guatemalans and approximately 40 percent of Nicaraguans are in the United States without proper documentation. Indeed, Salvadorans and Guatemalans are described as especially vulnerable because of their undocumented and non-refugee status. Immigration law, theoretically gender neutral, affects men and women dissimilarly, and often the legal status of women is tied to reunification with a husband or family group. Considerably more Central American women than men remain in the United States without proper documentation.

Central American women work in clerical and administrative jobs, as well as in housekeeping, babysitting, and cleaning services. Although education acquired in the home country can make a difference in the kinds of jobs these women obtain, it is noteworthy that the legal status of many Central American women and men greatly determines their options in the labor force. Even women with higher educational levels, including college graduates, and substantial work experience are found in unskilled or limited-skills positions due to their undocumented status in the United States. For instance, a former mathematics and physics high-school teacher and a woman with a degree in psychology and philosophy from the National University in El Salvador worked, respectively, as a clerk and housekeeper in San Francisco. Neither could afford to look for a job more in line with their education—or to obtain necessary language instruction—because, as undocumented refugees, they did not have any other means of support. Thus many Central American women, sometimes despite semiprofessional or professional educational skills, care for the elderly and children and clean homes and offices in urban areas. Some Central American immigrants have opened businesses that cater mostly to compatriots and other Latino clientele, and there exists a growing proportion who are self-employed, many as street vendors.

The jobs that women perform tend to be available even during recessionary times. Such jobs tend to be unregulated and away from the public eye, which makes it easier for employers to hire these women under informal terms. For these reasons Central American women can often find jobs more easily than men, and in some cities, such as Los Angeles, Salvadorans, and other Central American women seem to have taken over the domestic work niche. For instance, Salvadoran women in Los Angeles are twelve times and Guatemalans are thirteen times more likely than the general population to work as private servants, cleaners, and child-care workers, whereas for Mexican women this factor is only 2.3. Salvadorans and Guatemalans are also five to six times more likely to work as maids. However, in spite of the relative ease with which these women find jobs in both the formal and informal economies, when men and women both work, men earn more than women do, and women experience less occupational mobility than their male counterparts.

Work outside the home has been said to promote changes in gender relations among immigrant women. Central American women provide an interesting case to test this notion, since the overwhelming majority had paid work experience before their migration. Among these women U.S. paid work has not been equated with changes in gender relations in the home.

Some Central American women have come to the United States single and have established families here; others have arrived alone but have left their families back home. Many women came undocumented, meaning that their journeys had to be undertaken by land, which would put accompanying children in much danger. However, some have brought their children, but because of the high crime rates and ubiquity of drugs in the neighborhoods where many of these immigrants live, have sent their children back to their countries to shield them from such dangers. Meanwhile their mothers labor in the United States to send them money for school supplies and for the necessities of life. Many Central American women suffer the painful consequences of these separations, but they have little choice. If the children remain back home, the women worry about their children's well-being, and if the children are with them in the United States, these mothers express concern about their neighborhoods and their schools and ultimately wonder about the ever more tenuous benefits of life in the United States.

In some cases women, as well as their male counterparts, have established new families in the United States, rearrangements that do not always work out smoothly. These new family arrangements, coupled with the increased economic contributions of these women, have had important repercussions for gender relations among this group, though not always in the expected direction. For instance, as some women acquire more status within their families as a result of their increased economic contributions, gender relations become more egalitarian; other times gender relations become more unbalanced in favor of men because the women do not want to upset delicate arrangements in the home that would threaten the men's position. In still other cases, most notably among indigenous Guatemalans who start out from relatively more egalitarian gender relations, no discernible change in gender relations occurs with women's increased economic participation as a result of migration.

The types of jobs that Central American women perform have been found to affect their social networks in important ways. Guatemalan indigenous women who worked as live-in domestics, for example, had reduced and weaker social networks than men. Women who work as domestics but do not live in their employers' homes were found to have wide-reaching networks in the community. In fact, precisely because women actively sought resources in specific community organizations, given their responsibilities to provide for employer family needs, their networks proved to be more comprehensive than those of men. Spending time in community organizations gave women opportunities to forge networks independent of those of men and to learn and share crucial information about their rights and other important issues, such as legal protection for women against domestic violence. Through their informal networks Guatemalan women procured a range of medical treatments for themselves and their families. Thus, in the process of caring for their families, Central American women forged strong ties that enabled them to deal with their lack of access to formal assistance and services.

One of the most important places for Central Americans to forge community ties and to obtain varied forms of assistance is the church. They attend Catholic or mainline Protestant services, as well as evangelical Pentecostal churches. Churches have instituted a range of services that help the immigrants with their settlement, such as legal counseling, job placement, food and clothing distributions, free clinics, and emotional and spiritual support. Additionally, they have created spaces that enable these immigrants to remain connected to their communities of origin. Thus, as was the case for early-twentieth-century immigrants, for current Central Americans, particularly Salvadorans and Guatemalans, organized religion, whether Catholic, mainline Protestant, or Pentecostal, plays a key role in their incorporation into U.S. society regardless of where they eventually settle.

SOURCES: Hondagneu-Sotelo, Pierrette. 2001. *Doméstica: Immigrant Workers Cleaning and Caring in the Shadows of Affluence.* Berkeley: University of California Press; Lopez, David E., Eric Popkin, and Edward Telles. 1996. "Central Americans: At the Bottom, Struggling to Get Ahead." In *Ethnic Los Angeles,* ed. Roger Waldinger and Mehdi Bozorgmehr, 279–304. New York: Russell Sage Foundation; Menjívar, Cecilia. 1995. "The Ties That Heal: Guatemalan Immigrant Women's Networks and Medical Treatment." *International Migration Review* 36:427–466; 1995. ———. 1999. "The Intersection of Work and Gender: Central American Immigrant Women and Employment in California." *American Behavioral Scientist* 42, no. 4:595–621; ———. 2000. *Fragmented Ties: Salvadoran Immigrant Networks in America.* Berkeley: University of California Press; Repak, Terry A. *Waiting on Washington: Central American Workers in the Nation's Capital.* Philadelphia: Temple University Press; Rodriguez, Nestor P., and Jacqueline Hagan. 1999. "Central Americans." In *The Minority Report: An Introduction to Racial, Ethnic, and Gender Relations,* ed. Anthony Gary Dworkin and Rosalind J. Dworkin, 3rd ed. Dallas, TX: Harcourt Brace Jovanovich.

Cecilia Menjívar

CENTRO DE ACCIÓN SOCIAL AUTÓNOMO (CASA) (1968–1978)

In 1968 the Centro de Acción Social Autónomo (Center for Autonomous Social Action) emerged as a mutual-aid and social service agency for Mexican immigrants in Los Angeles, California. By 1975 it had become the self-proclaimed vanguard of an ethnic Mexican class-based revolution. New membership infused the mutual-aid organization with a Marxist-Leninist ideology. Yet while women's issues often took a backseat to what were deemed the real issues of "the cause," women remained a central part of the leadership and life of the organization.

The Centro de Acción Social Autónomo (CASA) emerged out of the Hermandad Mexicana Nacional (National Mexican Brotherhood) founded in the Los Angeles area in 1968 by local politician and educator Bert Corona and labor organizers Soledad Alatorre, Francisco Amaro, María Cedillos, Juan Mariscal, and Rafael Zacarias. As an offshoot of an already established Hermandad in San Diego, the Los Angeles Hermandad provided mutual aid and social services to Mexican immigrants in the area. As the popularity of Hermandad grew, its founders established CASA to provide expanded services such as processing residency papers and teaching English classes. CASA centers were also established in cities such as San Jose, San Diego, and Greeley, Colorado. Given its immigrant focus, CASA also supported workers' struggles to improve their working conditions and wages and became involved with the National Alliance against Racism and Political Repression, an advocacy group for political prisoners. Through this involvement CASA came into contact with the Committee to Free Los Tres (CTFLT), an organization based in East Los Angeles, which struggled for the freedom of three young men (Los Tres) whom the CTFLT believed had been wrongfully imprisoned for trying to protect their neighborhood from drugs.

In its struggle for Los Tres' freedom, the CTFLT had merged Chicano cultural nationalism and Marxism to argue that the drug trade was a tool used by the capitalist system against working people, and therefore, Los Tres were political prisoners. In 1975, after their cause waned, the young, college-educated Chicano/a students and professionals saw a prime opportunity in CASA to continue an expanded struggle against capitalism because of CASA's base among Mexican working-class immigrants. The two organizations merged in 1975, and the infusion of CTFLT members changed CASA's political framework from one of traditional self-help and advocacy to one of a Marxist vanguard.

The men and women who became the leadership of the new CASA viewed their cause in Marxist-Leninist terms and struggled for the liberation of the Chicano/Mexicano working class in the United States and Mexico. The new leadership also restructured the organization according to the ideals of democratic centralism. *Sin Fronteras* (Without Borders), the title of the organization's newspaper, became the mantra for CASA's struggle and spoke to its vision of a transnational working class and its focus on immigration. In fighting for the equal rights of undocumented workers, CASA waged battles against federal and state legislation that the organization believed did not benefit immigrants, and helped organize workers in Los Angeles, Santa Barbara, and the San Francisco Bay Area. In doing so, it organized around both labor rights and human rights and especially targeted abuses by the Immigration and Naturalization Service (INS).

In addition to these activities, CASA participated in and organized conferences on various topics related to immigration and even on the "woman question," participated in marches and demonstrations against immigration policy, participated in coalitions against unfair immigration laws and against political imprisonment, and published *Sin Fronteras,* which had an average circulation of 3,200 per month in Los Angeles. An additional 2,000 to 3,000 copies of the newspaper were sold through the other CASA centers in San Diego, Santa Barbara, Oakland/San Jose, Seattle, Chicago, and Colorado. CASA had subscribers as far east as New York and as far south as Florida. *Sin Fronteras* also had an international audience in Cuba, Colombia, the Philippines, and Venezuela.

While CASA members focused on issues affecting the Chicano/Mexicano community, they also linked themselves to a larger world picture, positing themselves as another manifestation of the liberation struggles of third-world peoples. Thus they had ties to the Puerto Rican Socialist Party, the Communist Party of Cuba, the revolutionary forces in Angola, and student and labor groups in Mexico.

In 1978, because of dissatisfaction with leadership, financial difficulties, infighting, family obligations, and the stress of constant surveillance from the Federal Bureau of Investigation, CASA folded as an organization. Historian Ernesto Chávez argues that CASA's attempt to merge nationalism and Marxism-Leninism led to a fundamental contradiction in philosophy, which became the major cause of CASA's demise. CASA had espoused the most openly Marxist political rhetoric of the Chicano movement and, therefore had situated itself at the far left of the movement's ideological spectrum. Although members of CASA were influenced by the cultural nationalist thought of their contemporaries, they questioned the U.S.-specific nature of this ideology by imagining themselves as the representatives of a transnational Mexican working-class community. By doing so, CASA brought the plight of the immigrant to the forefront of the Chicano movement, as well as the class and racialized nature of inequality in the United States.

In CASA, though the tenets of Marxism-Leninism and the ideology of cultural nationalism implied the liberation of women, issues that addressed women both explicitly and implicitly were often subsumed under the "real" cause, which was class liberation. For example, a study guide, "The Woman Question," issued by CASA stated, "Women must awaken to the fact that the main fight is not with their men. Men are oppressed by the same evil, but not to such an extent. If women are not trained to take part in the revolution, they will become obstacles and hold the revolution back." In this framework women themselves became subsumed in CASA's organizational structure and took few leadership positions in CASA. Those women who did hold prominent positions found it difficult to wield power. Nevertheless, CASA did manage to have a significant female participation that in fact provided the backbone of the organization.

It is easy to dismiss CASA as yet another example of Chicano movement organizations that placed women in supportive rather than leadership roles. Yet the women members of CASA, including Isabel H. Ro-

Children of CASA line up to march. Historian Marisela Chávez, pictured in pigtails, stands in the second row. Courtesy of Department of Special Collections, Stanford University Libraries.

dríguez, Evelina Márquez, Patricia Vellanoweth, and Teresa Rentería, to name a few, dedicated their lives to this organization. To dismiss CASA as an organization is to dismiss the sacrifices and contributions that these women made to the Chicano movement as a whole. However, most of the women, as well as the men in CASA, presently work as professionals serving the needs of the working class and poor, as well as being involved in community and political issues. In essence, CASA was a training ground for future activism.

SOURCES: Centro de Acción Social Autónomo Papers. M0325, Department of Special Collections, Stanford University Libraries, Stanford, CA; Chávez, Ernesto. 2000. "Imagining the Mexican Immigrant Worker: (Inter)Nationalism, Identity, and Insurgency in the Chicano Movement in Los Angeles." *Aztlán* 25 (Spring): 109–135; Chávez, Marisela R. 2000. " 'We lived and breathed and worked the movement': The Contradictions and Rewards of Chicana/Mexicana Activism in el Centro de Acción Social Autónomo–Hermandad General de Trabajadores (CASA-HGT), Los Angeles, 1975–1978." In *Las obreras: Chicana Politics of Work and Family*, ed. Vicki L. Ruiz, 83–105. Los Angeles: UCLA Chicano Studies Research Center Publications; Gutiérrez, David G. 1984. "CASA in the Chicano Movement: Ideology and Organizational Politics in the Chicano Community, 1968–1978." Stanford Center for Chicano Research, Working Paper Series, no. 5.

Marisela R. Chávez

CENTRO HISPANO CATÓLICO (1959–)

In 1959 Roman Catholic bishop Coleman F. Carroll, of the recently created Diocese of Miami, opened the Centro Hispano Católico to assist the growing influx of refugees from Castro's Marxist revolution. Located in downtown Miami, near Little Havana, the Centro offered services such as housing and job referrals, English classes, preschool and educational programs for children, an outpatient and dental clinic, home visits to the elderly and infirm, food, toiletries, and used clothing. When the Belén Jesuit High School, one of Cuba's best private Catholic preparatory schools for young men, was forced to close in Havana, it reopened first at the Centro Hispano Católico. Eventually it relocated to Little Havana and later to a middle-class suburb in southwestern Miami. During the early 1960s the Centro was one of eight refugee centers in southern Florida specifically set up for humanitarian assistance. It assisted hundreds of people each day, most of them women who acted as representatives and intermediaries for their families.

Until the 1970s more than 90 percent of the Centro's caseload was Cuban refugees. Since then the Centro has expanded its mission to assist immigrants from various Latin American countries, including the more recent arrivals from Nicaragua, El Salvador, Colombia, and Mexico. Women have played a key role in operating the Centro since its inception. In the early 1960s most of the people who staffed the offices and directed the various programs were nuns and laywomen, many of them of Latin American origin who could easily converse with—and often relate to—their clients. Over time the clients became the staff: Cuban women who were once the beneficiaries of the Centro's generosity now donate their time and services to help others who find themselves in situations similar to theirs. A Ladies Auxiliary organization raises funds for the Centro's various programs. Forty years after its creation the Centro Hispano Católico continues to be one of the most influential social welfare agencies in southern Florida.

See also Religion

SOURCES: "Centro Hispano Católico." Vertical File, Cuban Heritage Collection, University of Miami; García, María Cristina. 1996. *Havana USA: Cuban Exiles and Cuban Americans in South Florida, 1959–1994*. Berkeley: University of California Press.

María Cristina García

CENTRO MATER (1968–)

Centro Mater was founded in 1968 in southern Florida's Little Havana to assist Cuban refugees and other immigrants. Over the years this nonprofit social welfare center has become a fixture in Miami's Spanish-language community, assisting low-income families—and especially women and children—from twenty different nations.

The Centro is run by a staff of more than 400 volunteers, the majority of whom are Latinas. It offers a variety of services to low-income mothers so they can work or study knowing that their children are cared for: a prekindergarten program, an after-school program for elementary-, middle-, and high-school students, and a summer camp program. In addition, the Centro offers medical and dental care and psychological counseling, as well as classes for parents on hygiene and nutrition.

Latinas in southern Florida play an instrumental role not only in staffing and running the Centro but in its funding: Centro Mater receives most of its operating budget from fund-raisers such as fashion shows and banquets that are organized by middle- and upper-class Latinas in southern Florida. The Centro has been honored with a number of awards since 1973. Among its distinctions include the "Point of Light" Excellence in Education Award and the National Hispanic Heritage Presidential Tribute.

SOURCE: "Centro Mater." Vertical Files, Cuban Heritage Collection, University of Miami.

María Cristina García

CEPEDA-LEONARDO, MARGARITA (1965–)

Margarita Cepeda-Leonardo, president of the Dominican American National Roundtable (2002–2003), was born in San Francisco de Macoris, Dominican Republic, on May 10, 1965. She is one of nine children born to María Trinidad Peña and Justo Ramón Cepeda. She came to the United States during her infancy. As a young woman she completed her education at Rhode Island Community College and Bryant College, where she studied management.

Cepeda-Leonardo's involvement in community service began at age sixteen after she won the Miss Hispana de Rhode Island contest. One of her early achievements included raising $3,000 to aid the victims of the eruption of the volcano Nevado del Ruiz in Colombia, where more than 100,000 natives perished. In 1987 she founded Quisqueya en Acción ("Quisqueya" is the indigenous name of the Dominican Republic), a community center that provides services for youth.

Completing her formal education, Cepeda-Leonardo received a fellowship for leadership training under the National Fellowship Network of New Generation Leadership Program. As a leader and community activist, she received state and local government appointments, such as positions on the Commission on State Hispanic Affairs Advisory Board, the Rhode Island National Community Service Commission, and the City of Providence Minority Business and Women Development Enterprise. She was the keynote speaker at the 1994 Women's Leadership Conference sponsored by Radcliffe College, Harvard University, and the John F. Kennedy Government Institute.

Since 1995 Cepeda-Leonardo has served as founding executive director of the Miami Beach Hispanic Community Center, the first Hispanic social service agency in the city, which offers a variety of programs and services. She has overseen the development of the center to its current funding status of more than $2 million. Through a number of activities she has worked for the political empowerment of the Hispanic community of Miami Beach. She has been involved in election campaigning to support the first Hispanic public officials in the history of Miami Beach. Her other activities include voter registration drives, community education, and personal advocacy.

The Dominican American National Roundtable is an advocacy organization that serves the interests of the Dominican community living in the United States and Puerto Rico. Margarita Cepeda-Leonardo's involvement with this national organization dates back to the time of its creation in 1997, when she served as president of the Dominican American National Foundation of South Florida, a civil rights and community empowerment organization concerned with low-income Dominican communities. During the early period of the organization's creation Cepeda-Leonardo participated in organizing and hosting the initial meeting in Miami of more than 200 Dominican American leaders who gathered from different parts of the country to discuss issues of common concern. Later, as president of the Dominican American National Roundtable, she encouraged Dominicans in the United States to become involved in the political process at all levels of government from local to national.

For her leadership efforts Cepeda-Leonardo has gained recognition and received numerous community service awards, including the Rhode Island Citizen Citation, the City National Youth Service Program Moccasin Award, and the Rhode Island State House of Representatives Citizen Citation for her contribution to promoting a positive image of youth and the Hispanic community. She received the Honorary Alumni Award from Rhode Island University for community services and the Leadership Award from the Rhode Island Chapter of the Boy Scouts of America.

Margarita Cepeda-Leonardo is married to Julio Enrique Leonardo and has two children, Julian Enrique and Celina. She holds the greatest admiration for her mother, María Trinidad Peña, whom she considers her source of inspiration because of her dignity, courage, and love.

SOURCE: Cepeda-Leonardo, Margarita. 2003. Oral history interview by José A. Díaz, October 17.

José A. Díaz

CERVANTES, LORNA DEE (1954–)

Lorna Dee Cervantes was born in San Francisco on August 6, 1954, and was raised in San Jose. Cervantes was five years old when her parents separated and she and her mother and brother went to live with her Chumash maternal grandmother in San Jose. Her grandmother exerted a profound influence on Cervantes's sense of power and language. "My grandmother was sold into slavery at the age of eleven after her family lost their land in the land grabs of the late nineteenth century." At the mercy of the California apprenticeship laws of the early 1900s, her grandmother, along with many other native people, was essentially forced into indentured servitude. Although her grandmother longed to learn to read and write, she lived as a servant to a white family until she married.

A creative family fueled Cervantes's poetic aspirations. Her brother possessed musical abilities, her grandmother made and created prize-winning costumes for the Santa Barbara fiestas, and her father was a talented visual artist. Although the family was rich in creativity, it struggled to make ends meet. Cervantes's mother and grandmother worked as domestics and also received public assistance. Life in a woman-centered household allowed Cervantes to appreciate independence. Both her mother and grandmother derived their sense of autonomy from Native American tradition. "I think there is an indigenous feminism from the natural social patterns of the California Native Americans. It is an independence passed on from mother to daughter."

Cervantes composed her first poem at the young age of eight. However, she was accused of plagiarism and was threatened with suspension after showing the poem to her second-grade schoolteacher. Stunned into silence, Cervantes never shared her work with a teacher again. Nonetheless, she continued to write and developed an ear for poetry from listening to audio recordings of famous writers. At the age of seventeen she recalls ceremoniously accepting her role and destiny as she secretly wrote in her journal, "I am a writer," forever committing herself to the joys and sacrifices of the craft. She shared her love of poetry with her brother, and they spontaneously collaborated; he played music while she "scribbled" poetry.

Cervantes was influenced by the idealism of the Chicano movement and became involved in social protest in high school, participating in the antiwar movement, the school feminist debate team, teach-ins, and the Chicano cultural movement. During this time she heard Chicano poet Corky Gonzales's reading of "I Am Joaquín" on a local radio program. She listened to feminist debates with Gloria Steinem, Betty Friedan, and Phyllis Schlafly and felt that "all the doors in my mind suddenly opened and everything was put into place. My experience living with my grandmother and mother . . . their experience, the sources of my mother's bitterness" all blended into a developing political consciousness. She understood more clearly the economic, class, and gender forces that affect women's lives.

While Cervantes was a student at San Jose City College in 1972, her Chicano theater group accepted an invitation to participate in a Latin American Theater Festival in Mexico City. On the trip she wrote feverishly and completed up to five poems a day. During the festival she recited poetry between acts, and her brother accompanied her. She translated what became one of her most celebrated poems, "Refugee Ship," into Spanish and recited it before a large and appreciative audience. In the audience were the editor of one of Mexico City's daily newspapers and also the head of *Revista Chicana-Riqueña,* Nicolás Kanellos. Both men praised her work and encouraged her to continue writing. Her presentation was featured in a Mexico City newspaper's Sunday supplement, where the entire text of "Refugee Ship" was first printed. The poem later appeared in her first book, *Emplumada,* published in 1981. She was one of the first Chicana poets of her generation to be published. Her voice affirmed ideas of social change.

Crossing the borders between language and silence, Cervantes connected readers to the complex and often contradictory circumstances of contemporary life. Cervantes combined a palette of memory, social commentary, storytelling, and prophecy to paint memorable images in rich poetic language.

One of Cervantes's literary projects that supported early Chicano writers in northern California was *Mango,* a home-pressed literary journal. In 1974 she used her savings to buy an offset printing press. After learning how to operate it, she began to publish chapbooks, and eventually the literary journal, *Mango,* was born. In 1978 she attended a retreat in Provincetown, Massachusetts, where she studied with accomplished writers. During this time she completed her poetry manuscript and submitted it to the University of Pittsburgh Press. In 1981 *Emplumada* was released. Cervantes describes her book as strongly influenced by cultural nationalism and an understanding of language and power. "There is always this relationship between language and power for me: Being unable to speak Spanish was always a big issue for me, a personal issue and an ideological issue, and an issue in my writing certainly." Nonetheless, *Emplumada* conveys an understanding of how "the intersection of all three multiple ironies as a woman, as an indigenous woman, and as a lower class welfare woman" define the complexities of the Chicana experience.

Shortly after the book's release *Emplumada* won the American Book Award. Cervantes's ascent as a major poet, however, was accompanied by tragedy. In 1982 her mother was brutally killed in San Jose. Cervantes was paralyzed by the trauma and stopped writing. Years of healing allowed Cervantes to earn a B.A. from California State University, San Jose. She entered the history of consciousness program at the University of California, Santa Cruz, where she engaged in writing a dissertation on the aesthetics of black music. Upon recovery Cervantes began the manuscript for *From the Cables of Genocide: Poems on Love and Hunger* (1991). The book gained wide recognition both nationally and internationally and won the Latino Literature Prize and the Paterson Poetry Prize.

Cervantes's political and cultural activism is critical to her literary aspirations. "I have always thought of myself as a cultural worker—this has been my way of working for and with Chicanos." As a cultural worker, Cervantes sees art as a social force. "Art is not some elitist thing, but is a part of everyday life and is a part of understanding the history and spiritual practices and just joy."

See also Literature.

SOURCES: Cervantes, Lorna Dee. 1981. *Emplumada*. Pittsburgh: University of Pittsburgh Press; Cervantes, Lorna Dee. 1991. *From the Cables of Genocide: Poems on Love and Hunger*. Houston: Arte Público Press; Cervantes, Lorna Dee. 1995. Oral history interview by Naomi H. Quiñonez; 1989. Lomelí, Francisco A. and Carl R. Shirley, eds. *Dictionary of Literary Biography. Vol. 82: Chicano writers, First Series.* Detroit: Gale Research.

Naomi H. Quiñonez

CHABRAM, ANGIE GONZÁLEZ (1926–)

Born on April 19, 1926 in El Paso, Texas, Angie González Chabram was part of the Mexican American generation that came of age during World War II. Her parents, Isabel and Cruz González, had journeyed to El Paso from Chihuahua, Mexico during the Mexican Revolution. Although they struggled financially, Isabel and Cruz had high hopes for their daughter's education and sent her to a Catholic grammar school. However, when Cruz broke his spine, Angie had to quit school. The day after she completed the eighth grade, she went to work at her first job—as a salesclerk at the White House, a department store in El Paso. As was the case for most Mexican American youths, in order to ensure the survival of the family, wage work took precedence over education. Working at the White House, particularly during the depression, was considered a very good job for a Mexican American of any age. In 1930, for example, according to the U.S. census, only 10 percent of Mexican women workers in the Southwest held clerical or sales positions. In contrast, 20 percent of these women worked in factories and another 19 percent as farmworkers.

During World War II Angie González secured employment as a messenger at Fort Bliss and at the base hospital. While enjoying a Sunday afternoon at the park with her girlfriends, she caught the eye of a young Puerto Rican serviceman. Her parents did not approve, but the couple wed on January 6, 1946, when she was only nineteen. Within ten years of their marriage, they had four children—Rafael, Yolanda, Richard, and Angie.

In the photo that accompanies this entry, Angie González Chabram is twenty years old and sports the hairdo that she fashioned as a teenager, armed with the help of an old-fashioned curling iron and a petroleum lamp.

Newlyweds Harry and Angie González Chabram. Courtesy of Angie Chabram-Dernersesian.

In 1960 Chabram reached a crossroads. With no education or technical skills, she had to work outside the home to support her four children because her husband left the family. Her parents urged her to come home to El Paso, but her oldest son Rafael, then a teenager, argued that educational opportunities were better in California than in Texas. Keeping all four children in parochial school, she scrubbed floors at a hospital, cooked for the nuns at the school, and cleaned private residences. She also made sure that though her children were third-generation Mexican American, they would speak fluent Spanish. Three of her children became significant Chicano studies scholars—Rafael Chabram, a professor at Whittier College, Richard Chabram, a University of California librarian who helped launch ChicanoNet, and Angie Chabram-Dernersesian, a dynamic literary critic and professor at the University of California, Davis. Angie González Chabram is one of two El Paso residents who became matriarchs of academic dynasties. Her compatriot Alma Araiza García also notes with pride the accomplishments of her sons Mario and Richard, well-known historians, and her daughter Alma, a distinguished Chicana feminist scholar.

Needing health insurance, Angie González Chabram went to work for the French Company, a garment firm that was a subcontractor for a number of high-end designers. She and her daughter Yolanda worked there for several decades. Now retired, she resides in Chino, California, with Yolanda and her son-in-law. When she recalled the difficulties of educating four children as a single parent, she explained, "God helped me a lot." She firmly believes that with faith and family anything is possible. Angie González Chabram hopes that young women, including those who are rearing their children alone with few resources, can pursue their dreams and lead happy, productive lives. Her motto is "You can do it."

SOURCE: Ruiz, Vicki L. 1998. *From out of the Shadows: Mexican Women in Twentieth-Century America.* New York: Oxford University Press.

Angie Chabram-Dernersesian

CHACÓN, SOLEDAD CHÁVEZ (1890–1936)

Politician Soledad Chávez Chacón, "Lala," was born in 1890 in Albuquerque, a decade after the railroad arrived. The railroad ushered in monumental changes for Hispanos. Albuquerque witnessed a population and building explosion that included schools of higher learning and a stream of new social and political ideas.

The daughter of Melitón Chávez, a bank clerk, and Francisca Baca, Chacón had a middle-class upbringing. She played the mandolin and the piano. After graduating with honors from Albuquerque High School in 1908, she earned an accounting degree from the Albuquerque Business College.

Fresh out of college in 1910, Chacón married Ireneo Eduardo Chacón, a furniture store manager in Albuquerque. Within two years she gave birth to Adelina and Santiago. Soledad Chacón and her husband held high expectations for their children. Adelina was one of the first Hispano graduates from the University of New Mexico, earning a bachelor's degree in education. Santiago earned a law degree and became a businessman.

In addition to her duties as a housewife, Chacón joined literary, civic, and service clubs: el Club Literario, el Club Latino, the Women's Club, and the Minerva Club. One day, when she was baking a cake in her home in Albuquerque, five Democrats came to ask her to run for statewide office. The year was 1922, and Democratic power brokers—including her cousin, future U.S. senator Dennis Chávez, and two future governors—wanted thirty-two-year-old Chacón on the ticket to help retake control of the state legislature. They wanted to take advantage of the passage in 1920 of the women's suffrage amendment. Democrats did not want to concede the women's vote to Republicans, who had two women candidates. Although Chacón was a political novice, she was nonetheless college educated, belonged to several women's civic and service organizations, and came from a prominent political family. After securing Chacón's consent, as well as the permission of her husband and father, Democrats nominated her for New Mexico secretary of state. In addition to Chacón, Democrats nominated Isabel Eckles for superintendent of public instruction. Every New Mexico Democratic candidate for state and federal office was elected that year.

The 1922 election was a pivotal moment in New Mexico history. The state was one of the most conservative in the American West in terms of granting women political power. From 1869, when Wyoming became the first state to allow women the right to vote, to 1920, almost every state in the West extended voting to women. New Mexico was one of the exceptions. In 1921 an amendment to the New Mexico Constitution was ratified that granted women the right to hold public office. New Mexican women moved swiftly into public service. From 1922 to 1934 seventeen women were elected to the New Mexico legislature.

Chacón's first decision as secretary of state was selecting an assistant. After a female cousin declined the position, Democratic leaders were in a quandary. Following much debate they strongly urged Ireneo, Chacón's husband, to take the job. He reluctantly accepted. In 1924 Lieutenant Governor José Baca died. Governor James Hinkle departed the state for two weeks to attend the Democratic National Convention, leaving Chacón as acting governor.

The *Albuquerque Morning Journal* noted, "Mrs. Chacon is the daughter of a line of governors reaching back into the days when New Mexico was under Mexican rule." On her first day in office she could do little but greet the throng of well-wishers who visited her. In a statement she honored the memory of the deceased lieutenant governor and thanked Governor Hinkle for his faith in her abilities. She understood the historic significance: "[I]t is my earnest desire to carry out the plans and wishes of our governor during his absence, in as fearless and conscientious a manner as has been his policy."

Chacón was reelected in 1924 when she defeated a Republican Hispano. She was invited to attend Franklin D. Roosevelt's 1933 inaugural as an Electoral College representative. She was elected to the state legislature the following year. Her assignments included chairing the Rules and Order of Business Committee. In 1936, at age forty-five, Chacón died of peritonitis after an operation. In her short lifetime Chacón distinguished herself by being the first *Hispana* to be elected to a New Mexico state office and the first woman (acting) governor in the United States.

See also Politics, Electoral

SOURCES: "Hand of Woman is Guiding N.M. Ship of State." 1924. *Albuquerque Morning Journal,* June 22; Chávez, Dan D. 1996. "Soledad Chávez Chacón: A New Mexico Politi-

New Mexico's Soledad Chávez Chacón, the first Hispanic woman to serve as an acting governor in the United States, circa 1925. *The New Mexico Blue Book*. Courtesy of the Secretary of State of New Mexico.

cal Pioneer, 1890–1936." Self-published pamphlet, Center for Southwest Research, University of New Mexico; Coan, Charles F. 1925. *A History of New Mexico*. Vol. 3. Chicago and New York: American Historical Society; Salas, Elizabeth. 1995. "Ethnicity, Gender, and Divorce: Issues in the 1922 Campaign by Adelina Otero-Warren for the U.S. House of Representatives." *New Mexico Historical Review* 70:4 (October): 367–382; Vigil, Maurilio E. 1996. "The Political Development of New Mexico's Hispanas," *Latino Studies Journal*. 7:2 (Spring): 3–28.

Benny Andrés Jr.

"CHARO" (MARÍA ROSARIO PILAR MARTÍNEZ MOLINA BAEZA) (1942–)

María Rosario Pilar Martínez Molina Baeza, known popularly as Charo or the "cuchi-cuchi" girl, was born in Spain on January 15, 1942. (Charo had a judge change her legal birth date to 1952.) She began playing guitar in school at the Catholic convent of the Sacred Heart when she was only nine years old. She eventually trained under Andrés Segovia, one of the fathers of modern classical guitar music, and became a classical guitarist. During the 1960s Charo met and soon married the "Rhumba King," Xavier Cugat, who brought her to the United States. Charo's mother and sister were also brought to live in the United States.

An accomplished musician, dancer, comedienne, actress, and singer, Charo is fluent in Spanish, English, French, Italian, and Japanese. Her professional achievements are impressive. Her album *Guitar Passion* (1994) remained on the Billboard Top 50 album charts for four months. *Billboard Magazine* named it the best Latin pop album by a female artist in 1995. In the following years Charo also released *Dance a Little Bit Closer* (1996) and *Gusto* (1997). She won the *Guitar Player* magazine's Readers Poll as Best Flamenco Guitarist two years in a row and received the Distinguished Career Award from Hispanic Exhibitor and Distributor. Charo also appeared in several movies, including *Tiger by the Tail* (1968), *Joys* (1976), *The Concorde: Airport '79* (1979), and *Moon over Parador* (1988), and was the voice of Mrs. Toad in *Thumbelina* (1994). She often performs on the nightclub circuit in Las Vegas and Atlantic City.

Despite Charo's professional accomplishments, she is perhaps best remembered by audiences in the United States for her earlier performances on television shows, including *Fantasy Island, The Love Boat, Hollywood Squares, The Carol Burnett Show, Cher, Chico and the Man, The Facts of Life, That '70s Show, The Sonny and Cher Show, The Ed Sullivan Show, The Tonight Show,* and two *Pee-Wee Herman Christmas Specials*. During the 1970s, in Charo's first appearances in the United States, she performed in big blond-hair wigs and tight and flamboyant clothes, squealing "cuchi-cuchi," while hip-shaking her voluptuous figure. In a *Rolling Stone* magazine interview, however, Charo claimed that "around the world I am known as a great musician. But, in America I am known as the cuchi-cuchi girl. That's okay because cuchi-cuchi has taken me all the way to the bank."

SOURCES: Club Josh. "Charo." www.clubjosh.com/charo (accessed June 22, 2005); Internet Movie Database. "Charo" (I). www.imdb.com/name/nm0004819 (accessed June 22, 2005); TV Tome. "Charo: Biographical Information." www.tvtome.com/tvtome/servlet/PersonalDetail/personid-6756 (accessed June 22, 2005); William Morris Agency. "Charo: Biography." www.wma.com/charo/bio/CHARO.pdf (accessed June 22, 2005).

Nicole Trujillo-Pagán

CHÁVEZ, DENISE (1948–)

Growing up in Las Cruces, New Mexico, Denise Chávez gathered experiences on *la frontera* that she would later craft into her plays, short stories, and novels of small-town life in southern New Mexico. Chávez came from a family of readers, artists, and educators who prized literature and learning, as well as service to family and community. Chávez's father, E. E. Chávez, grew up bilingual and bicultural in the barrio Chiva Town, the historical heart of Las Cruces. After obtaining a law degree at Georgetown University in the 1920s, "something that was unheard of for any Mexican-American," her father returned to practice law in Las Cruces. Chávez's mother, Delfina Rede Chávez, was a beloved schoolteacher in Las Cruces for forty-two years. Growing up in western Texas, "my mother's family were the first Latino graduates of Sol Ross University." One aunt was named Texas Mother of the Year, and another started a library in her grocery store.

As a child, Chávez began her love affair with literature. She spent much of her free time in the public library in Las Cruces. When her parents divorced when she was ten, "we'd spend the summers in West Texas with my aunt in El Polvo, a very remote town. Of course there was nothing to do there; there were about 20 people in the town. And so we read, everybody read." Chávez also began writing at age eight and kept a diary and wrote stories throughout her childhood.

After attending Madonna High School, a private all-girls Catholic school, Chávez earned her B.A. in drama from New Mexico State University in 1971 and her M.F.A. in drama from Trinity University in 1974. In 1984 she completed an M.A. in creative writing from the University of New Mexico.

Combining her interests in theater and literature, Chávez considers herself a "performance writer." Her one-woman play *Women in the State of Grace* was originally written as *Novenas narrativas* in 1988. It features Chávez in the role of nine different Chicanas, aged seven to seventy-eight. Chávez has also written two plays for young people, *The Flying Tortilla Man* (1990) and *The Woman Who Knew the Language of the Animals/La mujer que sabía el idioma de los Animales* (1993); numerous short stories, some of which are collected in *The Last of the Menu Girls* (1986); and two novels, *Face of an Angel* (1994) and *Loving Pedro Infante* (2001).

Chávez has also worked as an actress and educator in many different settings. While she was in northern New Mexico for seven years, Chávez took part in la Compañía de Teatro, a bilingual theater company based in Albuquerque, and Theatre-in-the-Red. She has taught at such varied institutions as the American School of Paris, the College of Santa Fe, Northern New Mexico Community College, the University of Houston, New Mexico State University, and the Radium Springs Center for Women, a medium-security prison.

Although Chávez ventured far from Las Cruces, she eventually moved back to her hometown. "I never thought of living any other place," Chávez declares. She still lives in the house in which she grew up. "This is where my roots are," Chávez asserts. "I personally love living on the border. I'm a frontera person." It is indeed the border and small-town life of southern New Mexico that provides the setting, characters, plots, and struggles for Chávez's writing. She observes, "I've always worked with border characters, border themes, people who are working their lives out on the border, linguistically, spiritually, and so on."

In her work Chávez concentrates on themes of identity, balance, and service. She explores "how people become authentic human beings while embracing and taking the best from culture and traditions and retaining their intrinsic roots." Chávez notes that her characters "are trying to find equilibrium, a state of grace, a state of balance." She also believes that "the theme of service is very important to me: what it means to serve and be served." Chávez ties this theme to her own experience. "It was just a given in our family," she observes. "We were servers and we were served by other people. I think it's a frontera thing, it's a trading of personal services for different things."

Like her characters, Chávez is an exemplar of the service ethic. She initiated the Border Book Festival in 1994, an annual weeklong event that brings world-renowned writers to Las Cruces to read from their work and to hold writing workshops for community members. The Border Book Festival also conducts a

New Mexico author Denise Chávez. Photograph by Marisol Garza. Courtesy of Mary Ann Villarreal and Marisol Garza.

year-round program, Emerging Voices, of writers-in-residence at local schools, domestic violence shelters, prisons, senior centers, and other community organizations.

For her writing, as well as her community service, Chávez has received numerous awards, including the American Book Award for *Face of an Angel* in 1995. Chávez has also been awarded the New Mexico Governor's Award in Literature (1995) and the Woman of Distinction Award in Education (1996), as well as many other state and local awards. In 2000 Chávez received a Lila Wallace–Reader's Digest Fellowship for her project La Frontera Divina/The Divine Frontier to gather oral histories with senior citizens in the historic Mesquite District in Las Cruces. Asserting that "all of my role models were within my family," Chávez found inspiration in the everyday life of her small town and developed a unique frontera voice. She continues to write and to serve her community in her own ongoing quest for a state of grace.

See also Literature; Theater

SOURCES: Chávez, Denise. 1986. *The Last of the Menu Girls*. Houston: Arte Público Press; ———. 1994. *Face of an Angel*. New York: Farrar, Straus and Giroux; ———. 2001. Interview by Margaret D. Jacobs, April 23; ———. 2001. *Loving Pedro Infante*. New York: Farrar, Straus and Giroux; Heard, Martha. 1988. "The Theatre of Denise Chávez: Interior Landscapes with 'sabor nuevo mexicano.'" *Americas Review: A Review of Hispanic Literature and Art of the USA* 16, no. 2 (Summer): 83–91; Mehaffy, Marilyn, and AnaLouise Keating. 2001. "'Carrying the Message': Denise Chávez on the Politics of Chicana Becoming." *Aztlán: A Journal of Chicano Studies* 26, no. 1 (Spring): 127–156; Richter, Francine K. Ramsey. 1999. "Romantic Women and la Lucha: Denise Chávez's Face of an Angel." *Great Plains Quarterly* 19, no. 4 (Fall): 277–289.

Margaret D. Jacobs

CHÁVEZ, HELEN (1928–)

Born in Brawley, California, near the Mexican border, the second of five children in a poor, rural Mexican immigrant family, Helen Fabela Chávez represents the unsung Latinas who combined domestic responsibilities with social activism. The Fabela family survived by working in the fields and orchards of southern California's fertile valleys before migrating to the central San Joaquin Valley near Delano during the Great Depression. Meager wages and inferior working conditions led to a life of substandard housing, inadequate sanitation, malnutrition, limited educational opportunities, and poverty. Helen Fabela began working around the age of seven. Lacking transportation, she walked with her family to the local ranches to pick cotton, grapes, peaches, strawberries, peas, and walnuts during the summer, on weekends, and after school. The death of her father caused her to drop out of school at the age of fifteen to help her mother support the family.

Courtship and marriage dramatically changed Helen Fabela's life. During World War II she met César Chávez at a local malt shop. Two years after his service in the navy the couple married in a civil ceremony in Reno, Nevada, followed by a church wedding in San Jose in 1948. She was just nineteen years old. During the next eleven years Chávez bore and reared eight children. As was the case with her parents, economic survival required every member of the household, including the children, to contribute to the family finances. Traveling with her husband's family, the Chávezes migrated up and down the state in search of work. Recognizing the bleak future that farm labor offered, Helen agreed with César's decision to take a position with the Community Service Organization (CSO), a civic-minded, self-help, Mexican American civil rights group that had sprung up in the barrios of the postwar urban Southwest. As a loyal wife, she moved her growing family to the small towns that dotted central California and then to Los Angeles to further her husband's organizing activities. To advance his career, she spent her evenings writing in longhand the daily reports he dictated to her, as well as addressing envelopes and postcards and helping prepare for chapter meetings.

Chávez supported her husband's resolve to leave his CSO position, the first real economic security the family had ever enjoyed, to found the National Farm Workers Association (the precursor to the United Farm Workers union). She chose this course of action not only out of commitment to her husband's aspirations, but also because of her own working-class experience in the fields and the memory of her mother as a struggling widow trying to raise her family. Without César's steady income, this choice held momentous consequences for her. In 1962, at the age of thirty-four, Helen Chávez reentered the agricultural work force. "I think the beginning of the Union was the roughest time we had," she later recalled. In an interview César conceded, "Helen did most of the worrying about money for food and clothing," freeing him to concentrate on the union.

In addition to caring for the children, running the household with a largely absent husband, and working in the fields and packing sheds, Helen Chávez found time to demonstrate her commitment to a better life for "campesinos." Her activism evolved in the context of her extended family. With her children and relatives she joined picket lines and marches. Taunts and threats came with the territory, and occasionally violence disrupted the normally peaceful protests. Chávez took her ideals to another level when she went to jail to publicize La Causa. A particularly notable event occurred in 1965 when she was arrested for shouting *huelga* (strike) with forty-four others at a demonstration against a local grower. The charges were later dismissed. Helen Chávez's example gave other wives and mothers the courage to join picket lines, marches, and boycotts.

But an emphasis on Helen Chávez's arrests and participation in public protests distorts an important aspect of her quiet legacy to the union. Her dedication for nearly thirty years to one of the UFW's earliest projects, the credit union, is an enduring, but less well known, contribution. Though initially reluctant because of her lack of education and experience, she began to work at the credit union full-time. Through her positions as secretary, bookkeeper, and finally treasurer-manager, she maintained an important service for union members who were traditionally denied credit at mainstream institutions. She grew to see the credit union as her own special charge, lobbying for its inclusion in union contracts. "Don't you come back without that!" she admonished her husband when the union entered preliminary negotiations with a grape grower. The credit union helped a generation of farmworkers raise themselves out of poverty and provided opportunities for their children to enter the Chicano middle class.

Comfortable with protesting in a group, Helen Chávez was by nature a shy and modest individual and resisted demands to make public speeches. Despite numerous requests from media and other organizations, she has preferred to stay in the background. Even after the unexpected death of her husband in 1993, she refrained from a more public presence, only venturing out to accept posthumous awards on behalf of her husband and to mark the annual celebrations of his birthday, now a state holiday in California.

Helen Chávez practiced a more traditional form of social activism, one that merged family, work, and union activism. Despite shunning a prominent profile, she made a vital, but often hidden, contribution to the founding of the United Farm Workers. Her quiet strength and unassuming temperament led many in the union family to regard her as the union's backbone. In the process of supporting the unionization of farmworkers, she has inspired many traditional Chicanas and Mexicanas of her generation, who suffered from lack of education and marginalization in the most impoverished sector of society, to raise their voices and join the most significant Mexican American protest movement in the second half of the twentieth century on behalf of agricultural workers and their families.

See also Labor Unions; United Farm Workers of America (UFW)

SOURCES: Levy, Jacques E. 1975. *Cesar Chavez: Autobiography of La Causa*. New York: W. W. Norton; Rose, Margaret. 1988. "Women in the United Farm Workers: A Study of Chicana and Mexicana Participation in a Labor Union, 1950 to 1980." Ph.D. diss., University of California, Los Angeles; ———. 1990. "Traditional and Nontraditional Patterns of Female Activism in the United Farm Workers of America, 1962–1980." *Frontiers* 11:26–32; Ruiz, Vicki L. 1998. *From out of the Shadows: Mexican Women in Twentieth-Century America*. New York: Oxford University Press.

Margaret Eleanor Rose

CHÁVEZ, LINDA (1947–)

Among the most outspoken voices in American politics and society, Linda Chávez is the product of a working-class family who made their living painting houses or working in department stores or restaurants. Exposure to working-class values during her early years influenced Chávez's conservative attitudes toward privilege and labor in her adult years. She was born on July 7, 1947, in Albuquerque, New Mexico, but by her tenth birthday her family moved to Denver, Colorado. There Chávez received much of her education. In 1970 she earned a baccalaureate degree from the University of Colorado. During the next two years Chávez completed graduate coursework in English literature at the University of California at Los Angeles. This background helped prepare Chávez for numerous positions she would hold in later years.

Although Chávez writes a nationally syndicated political column that appears in numerous papers throughout the country, she is best known for her book *Out of the Barrio: Towards a New Politics in Hispanic Assimilation* (1991). The book, described as a text that "should explode the stereotypes about Hispanics that have clouded the minds of patronizing liberals and xenophobic conservatives" by the *Denver Post,* is considered highly controversial. Chávez sets forth conventional views regarding the rate and degree of assimilation among Hispanics, opposition to affirmative action programs, and to bilingual education. According to Chávez, who is a member of the American Civil Rights Union and heads a center that researches issues of race, ethnicity, and assimilation, people of color can succeed without government programs or special privileges. This ideology was evident when, as a U.S. Commissioner on Civil Rights (1983–1985), Chávez reversed government policies supportive of diversity, gender issues, and minority civil rights, alienating liberals in the U.S. Congress and civil rights groups throughout the nation.

From 1977 until 1983 Chávez edited the award-winning *American Educator,* the journal of the American Federation of Teachers, then headed by Albert Shanker. She served as Shanker's assistant from 1982 to 1983 and was assistant director of the union's legal division. In the ensuing years she held a number of appointed positions. Among these, Chávez was staff director of the U.S. Commission on Civil Rights (1983–1985) and White House director of public liaison (1985), sat on the Administrative Conference of the United States (1984–1986), was chair of the National Commission on Migrant Education (1988–1992), and sat on the United Nations Human Rights Commission. The latter position required Chávez to serve on the Sub-commission on the Prevention of Discrimination and Protection of Minorities. Also a member of the Council on Foreign Relations, Chávez co-chaired the council's Committee on Diversity (1998–2000).

A failed attempt to become the Republican senator from the state of Maryland was a setback for Chávez in 1986. However, her influence on civil rights policy continued with her political analysis for the Fox News Channel, a syndicated column, and authorship of a second book, *An Unlikely Conservative: The Transformation of an Ex-Liberal* (2002). She became president of U.S. English, an organization dedicated to making English the official language of the United States, and served as an advisor to Ron K. Unz, the proponent of Proposition 227, a ballot initiative in California that essentially eradicated bilingual education legislation in that state.

In 2000 President-elect George W. Bush named Chávez his secretary of labor, but she was forced to withdraw before confirmation because of a controversial incident involving the hiring of an illegal immigrant woman to care for Chávez's children. She is currently the founder and president of the Center for Equal Opportunity, a nonprofit public policy research institute in Virginia. Chávez is married to Christopher Gersten, and the couple has three children.

SOURCES: ABC NEWS.com; "Profile: Linda Chavez." http://abcnews.com/sections/politics/DailyNews/Chavez_profile010201.html (accessed July 13, 2004); Chávez, Linda. 1991. *Out of the Barrio: Toward a New Politics of Hispanic Assimilation*. New York: Basic Books; Chávez, Linda. 2001. *An Unlikely Conservative: The Transformation of an Ex-Liberal, or, How I Became the Most Hated Hispanic in America*. New York: Basic Books; Kamen, Al. 2002. "Chavez Torching the Bridge." *Washington Post*. January 21, A 15. Linda Chávez home page. "Linda's Bio." http://www.lindachavez.org (accessed June 24, 2005).

Virginia Sánchez Korrol

CHÁVEZ RAVINE, LOS ANGELES

Today the site of Dodger Stadium near downtown Los Angeles, in 1950 Chávez Ravine was a bustling Mexican American barrio that included small numbers of Chinese Americans and one African American family. It is one of the best-known incidents of the use of eminent domain to destroy a racial-ethnic community, first in the name of public housing and later for private profit.

Named after Julian Chávez, a native of New Mexico who settled in Los Angeles during the 1830s, Chávez Ravine developed as a specific neighborhood with the influx of families who migrated to southern California during the Mexican Revolution. By 1950 two to three generations of Mexican Americans called the ravine home. Although most of the houses were poorly constructed and lacked adequate plumbing, and overcrowding was common, many families took great pride in their humble homes. Even Robert Alexander and Robert Neutra, the architects in charge of designing the new public housing units for the ravine, had to admit that the area was "charming" and that the residents themselves shared a strong sense of community. More than homes, Chávez Ravine had a grammar school, a Roman Catholic church, Santo Niño, and neighborhood merchants. As Henry Cruz later recalled to photographer Don Normark, "It wasn't . . . Beverly Hills, but we were happy people here in this neighborhood."

In August 1949 the Los Angeles City Council endorsed a public housing plan that would use $110 million of federal money to construct 10,000 new housing units in eleven sites around Los Angeles, including Chávez Ravine. On July 24, 1950, in a memorandum, residents were notified about the city's plans. "This letter is to inform you that public housing development will be built on this location for families of low income. . . . The house you are living in is included. . . . You will be visited by representatives of the Housing Authority who will . . . inspect your home in order to estimate its value. It will be several months at least before your property is purchased. . . . *Later you will have the first chance to move back into the new Elysian Heights development.*" Frank Wilkinson, manager of the City Housing Authority of Los Angeles (CHA), met with the residents of Chávez Ravine on several occasions to quell their concerns and to persuade them that a new and improved neighborhood was on the way in the form of twenty-four apartment buildings that would rise thirteen stories tall, along with 163 more modest two-story structures.

Public housing was not embraced by powerful interests in Los Angeles. The *Los Angeles Times*, home builders' associations, the Chamber of Commerce, and local real-estate boards began a concerted campaign to get the city out of the public housing business, calling it "creeping socialism." In December 1951 the city council responded to the pressure and by one vote rescinded the public housing contract with the City Housing Authority. The CHA went to court, and the California Supreme Court in 1952 ruled unanimously that the Los Angeles City Council could not cancel the contract. Council members decided to put the matter to the people in the form of a referendum, and the voters backed their decision to void the contract. California senators Richard Nixon and William Knowland then worked to pass federal legislation that would legitimate the council's action. The targets of rampant red-baiting by the press and conservative state politicians, Frank Wilkinson and other members of the CHA lost their jobs. With the election of Norris Poulson, the anti–public housing candidate for mayor, in 1953, any hope for public housing in Chávez Ravine was effectively dead.

What would happen to the families who had sold their homes under eminent domain, and what would happen to the land? Chávez Ravine was now desolate, a shell of a poor, but vibrant community with only a few families left who stubbornly refused eviction. In 1954 the U.S. Congress authorized the CHA to sell Chávez Ravine to the city for a $4-million loss and to void the public housing contract, but with the stipulation that the land could be used for public purposes only, not for private development. The Brooklyn Dodgers then became involved. After a series of controversial negotiations and much deal making the city council voted on October 7, 1957, to approve giving Chávez Ravine to Walter O'Malley in exchange for Wrigley Field, land O'Malley had recently purchased in South Los Angeles. The city also agreed to cover the costs of making the ravine suitable for the construction of the new stadium and to provide the necessary access roads.

Outraged, current and former neighbors of Chávez Ravine filed suit, arguing, "It has been held (by the U.S. Supreme Court) that the *power of eminent domain* may be exercised only for public purpose and not for a private purpose." Prominent civil rights activist Fred Ross (the mentor of César Chávez), labor organizer María Duran, and attorney Phil Silver worked with residents who formed the Committee to Save Chávez Ravine for the People. The committee gathered 85,000 signatures to put a referendum on the ballot that would allow voters to decide between baseball and housing. Proposition B went to the voters in December 1958, and by only a 2 percent margin they chose baseball. The next month the California Supreme Court rejected the claims brought by the residents and approved the actions of the city council. On May 8, 1959, the bulldozers arrived and more than thirty people were forcibly evicted from their homes. One newspaper described the scene: "Amid shouting and cursing the deputies arrived and carried one of the women bodily out the door. The others went but not quietly. . . . Ten minutes later, the roar of two giant bulldozers drowned out Mrs. Aréchigas's sobs as she sat on a curb and watched the machine reduce the frail dwelling to rubble." Los Angeles city councilman Ed Roybal declared, "The eviction is the kind of thing you might expect in Nazi Germany and the Spanish Inquisition." Aside from displacing 7,500 people, destroying some 900 homes, and costing taxpayers $5 million, the arrival of baseball to Los Angeles did not change things much.

However, the former residents of Chávez Ravine have not forgotten their past, a history that has now received a wider hearing. Judy Baca's famous mural *The Great Wall of Los Angeles* recorded the destruction of Chávez Ravine (with the Dodgers depicted as aliens from outer space). In 1949 photographer Don Normark, unaware of the brewing controversy, recorded the daily rhythms of the barrio; fifty years later he published these photos for the first time alongside commentary from the people who called it home in *Chávez Ravine, 1949: A Los Angeles Story*. In 2003 Culture Clash, the popular Latino comedy troupe, opened its play *Chávez Ravine* at the prestigious Mark Taper Forum in Los Angeles. At the time of the evictions one resident maintained a sense of hope. "Everyone in this area has suffered many losses, both personal and financial. . . . I shall not quit fighting for justice . . . for it may pave the way for [a] better and more glorious generation."

SOURCES: Acuña, Rodolfo. 1988. *Occupied America: A History of Chicanos*. 3rd ed. New York: Harper and Row; Avila, Erik. 2004. "Revisiting Chávez Ravine: Baseball, Urban Renewal, and the Gendered Civic Culture of Postwar Los Angeles." In *Velvet Barrios: Popular Culture and Chicana/o Sexualities*, ed. Alicia Gaspar de Alba and Tomás Ybarra Frausto, 125–139. London: Palgrave Macmillan; Becerra, Victor. 1982. "The Untold Story of Chávez Ravine." Paper, History Research Holdings, Chicano Studies Library, University of California, Los Angeles; Normark, Don. 1999. *Chávez Ravine, 1949: A Los Angeles Story*. San Francisco: Chronicle Books.

Victor Becerra

CHÁVEZ-THOMPSON, LINDA (1944–)

During World War II Linda Chávez-Thompson was one of eight second-generation Mexican American children born into a cotton sharecropping family in Lubbock, Texas. The family struggled to make ends meet, and the children were all needed to labor alongside their parents in the hot, dusty western Texas fields. For their backbreaking efforts, adults earned fifty cents an hour, and the children received thirty cents an hour. Because it was necessary for the children to help support the family, schooling became sporadic, dependent on the crops and economic and agricultural cycles. Like countless other migrant children, Chávez-Thompson was forced to leave school without graduating from high school because of financial difficulties. In 1963, at the age of twenty, Chávez-Thompson married and embarked on her first "adult" job, cleaning other people's houses.

Chávez-Thompson joined the Laborers' International Union in 1967 and became secretary for the Lubbock local. This position connected the young activist with the region's Latino membership because she was one of the few Spanish speakers in the union. The position also provided Chávez-Thompson with a broad education in the daily operation of the labor union, the issues, and the personal and work-related problems faced by the membership. Four years later Chávez-Thompson was employed at the American Federation of State, County, and Municipal Employees (AFSCME). In comparison with her previous employment, AFSCME carried a wider, more far-reaching range of opportunities and responsibilities. Chávez-Thompson rapidly became acquainted with labor legislation, negotiations, grievances, education programs, compensation issues, and politics.

In 1995 Chávez-Thompson's bid for elective office within the union proved successful. She became the first Latina executive vice president of the AFL-CIO, a position she holds today. Calling upon her own experiences as a leader, a woman of color, and a migrant laborer, Chávez-Thompson brings powerful perspectives to the union table. While she connects the labor movement to diverse Latino communities throughout the nation, Chávez-Thompson also calls for increasing the numbers of women in leadership positions. Since her high-profile election to the AFL-CIO Council, she has served on numerous boards and organizations. She sits on the board of governors of the United Way and is a vice-chairperson of the Democratic National Committee, a member of the executive committee of the Congressional Hispanic Caucus Institute, and a member of the board of trustees for the Labor Heritage Foundation. Most important, in projecting for future advances for workers, Chávez-Thompson brings to bear the voices and concerns of thousands of individuals previously marginalized.

See also Labor Unions; United Farm Workers of America

SOURCE: National Women's History Project. "Linda Chávez-Thompson: A Woman Pioneering the Future." www.nwhp.org/tlp/biographies/chavez-thompson/chavez-thompson-bio.html (accessed July 10, 2004).

Virginia Sánchez Korrol

CHICANA CAUCUS/NATIONAL WOMEN'S POLITICAL CAUCUS (1972–1973)

The Chicana Caucus evolved out of the 1971 organizing conference of the National Women's Political Caucus (NWPC) in Washington, D.C. The NWPC committed itself to increasing the number of women in all aspects of political life. After that meeting the Texas Women's Political Caucus (TWPC) was created. Each state held its own caucus meetings, so when the Texas Women's Political Caucus State Convention held its meeting in Mesquite, Texas, on March 11, 1972, Chicana activists from throughout Texas came to participate. Almost 100 Chicana activists, including Martha Cotera and Evey Chapa, formed the Chicana Caucus when it became clear that NWPC leaders ignored the voices of *raza* women. Although Chicanas gave their full energies to their role in the NWPC, many Chicanas felt caught between the Chicano movement and the feminist movement. They negotiated their position by addressing concerns in both arenas, forming caucuses in both feminist and Chicano organizations to address their specific needs. In an address to the 1972 TWPC, Martha Cotera stated, "We are Chicanas and women. We have nothing now because of these two factors. And we can go for 'broke.' We certainly can't do worse than we are doing now with the present system." Chicanas who joined the NWPC found that the larger caucus was forced to recognize and find solutions for Chicanas as a group. Chicana organizers believed that if the NWPC was to succeed, it must include the point of view of Chicanas, and that only Chicanas could speak to the problems of Chicanas or advocate for their solution. More important, Chicanas felt that their Anglo counterparts were unaware of the power Chicanas held in their homes, an advantage that many Anglo women still did not have. The TWPC had the opportunity to host its first NWPC convention in February 1973 in Houston. More than sixty Chicanas from seven states met during the NWPC convention to address problems specific to employment, education, welfare, and politics, and in the end they focused their attention on seven resolutions.

The Chicana Caucus presented two resolutions supporting the strike against the Farah Manufacturing Company and the lettuce boycotts sponsored by the United Farm Workers. A third resolution focused on the Education Act of 1973, garnering the NWPC's support to address the problems of Chicanas in education. A fourth resolution recognized the National Chicana Welfare Rights Organization as separate and autonomous from the National Welfare Rights Organization. This allowed Chicanas to deal with the cultural and economic differences facing Chicano families. The fifth resolution opposed the Talmadge Amendment, which would require every person on welfare to register and accept whatever job was offered without being provided day care or job training. The sixth resolution made it official that NWPC would acknowledge the Raza Unida Party in its literature. At that time the Raza

Unida Party had become the most supportive and viable option for Chicanas to run for office. A final resolution called for the creation of Chicana political caucuses, proposing "that in those states where Chicanos reside, Chicana Political Caucuses be established and maintained on equal basis with the other State caucuses." This resolution received the most opposition because those outside the Chicana Caucus did not understand why there was a need to form a separate official caucus. After much debate the NWPC finally approved the resolution.

SOURCES: Chapa, Evey. 1964. "Report from the National Women's Political Caucus." Martha Cotera Papers, Benson Latin American Collection, General Libraries, University of Texas at Austin; Cotera, Martha. 1972. "Feminism As We See It." Keynote address to the Texas Women's Political Caucus. Gloria Steinem Papers, Sophia Smith Collection, Smith College, Northampton, MA.

Mary Ann Villarreal

CHICANA RIGHTS PROJECT (1974–1983)

The Chicana Rights Project was a feminist civil rights and legal rights program that reflected the Chicana feminist movement of the 1970s. Under the auspices of the Mexican American Legal Defense and Educational Fund (MALDEF), this program sought to enhance Chicana self-sufficiency in employment, health, education, and housing. Founded in 1968, MALDEF continues to address the civil and legal rights of Latinos, using litigation for empowerment. In 1974 MALDEF's first Mexican American woman director, Vilma Martínez (a native of San Antonio, Texas), initiated the Chicana Rights Project by establishing offices in San Francisco and San Antonio. Patricia M. Vásquez headed the Texas effort, and Carmen A. Estrada took charge of the San Francisco office. Norma V. Cantú served as a staff attorney from 1979 to 1983.

The Chicana Rights Project included litigation, research, and community education. It monitored the impact of the Comprehensive Employment and Training Act (CETA), a federal program designed to assist low-income persons. In 1976 the project filed suit, *Hernández et al. v. Cockrell et al.,* against the city of San Antonio, alleging that the city did not include Mexican American women on equitable terms in its CETA programs. After the complaint the percentage of women and people of color in the San Antonio CETA programs rose from 20 percent to 50 percent.

The project also filed a class-action suit against the Texas Employment Commission to seek unemployment compensation benefits for pregnant women. Lawsuits challenging sterilization abuses and health service cutbacks were also filed in California and Texas. The Chicana Rights Project obtained compliance reviews and audits of San Antonio's largest banks so as to assure equal opportunities for women.

This pioneering Chicana feminist program initiated a pamphlet series on abortion, sterilization, mental health, immigrant rights, and employment. It also published information about immigration, employment rights, the 1980 census, and Texas women's legal rights. The pamphlets were printed in English and Spanish. These publications included *Profile of the Chicana: A Statistical Fact Sheet,* with census data; *Chicanas: Women's Health Issues,* on abortion and sterilization; *CETA: An Economic Tool for Women; Chicanas and Mental Health,* which addressed cultural sensitivity; *Hispanic Women: Immigration Issues*; *Hispanic/Women's Employment Rights*; *The 1980 Census: Impact on Hispanics and Women*; and *Texas Women's Legal Rights,* a handbook on federal and state laws. The Chicana Rights Project served as a resource for other Latina organizations, as well as state and federal agencies on the local, state, and national levels. Corporate sponsors included the following foundations: Ford, Rockefeller, Revlon, and Playboy. The project ended in 1983 because of a lack of funds.

Though short lived, the Chicana Rights Project was significant for its concrete contributions and made a difference in the lives of thousands of Mexican American women. Furthermore, it demonstrated the gendered nature of legal rights because most Chicano organizations focused only on race and Chicano male nationalism. The Chicana Rights Project represented Chicana feminism in action, and several contemporary Chicana civil rights leaders, such as Norma Cantú, began their careers with this project.

SOURCES: O'Connor, Karen, and Lee Epstein. 1985. "A Legal Voice for the Chicano Community: The Activities of the Mexican American Legal Defense and Educational Fund, 1968–82." In *The Mexican American Experience,* ed. Rodolfo O. de la Garza, Frank D. Bean, Charles Bonjean, Ricardo Romo, and Rodolfo Alvarez. Austin: University of Texas Press; Orozco, Cynthia E. 1996. "Chicana Rights Project." *In New Handbook of Texas* 3:69. Austin: Texas State Historical Association.

Cynthia E. Orozco

CHICANO MOVEMENT (1965–1980)

The Chicano movement, which flourished in the southwestern United States from roughly 1965 to 1980, was a coalition of organizations and individuals that sought to address the effects of racial discrimination, low socioeconomic status, and police violence on persons of Mexican ancestry. The movement arose in embryonic form out of churches, community organizations, labor unions, and mutual-aid societies during the 1950s. It gradually expanded from local and particular concerns to address the larger national issues of segregation, political disenfranchisement, and legal injustices. Inspired during the late 1950s by the rhetoric and tactics of decolonization movements around the globe and by the black civil rights movement, Mexican American activists increasingly drew attention to long-term structural inequalities produced by poor education, inadequate employment, residential segregation, and lack of access to good housing in their communities. By systematically focusing on these local concerns in many places they were able to forge a larger national movement. The campaign to improve the lives of ethnic Mexicans in the United States was often referred to as "La Causa" (the Cause); activists called themselves members of "La Raza" (the Race), implying a host of inequalities born of institutional racism.

What differentiated the Chicano movement from the activities of such groups as the League of United Latin American Citizens (LULAC), the American GI Forum, or the numerous mutual-aid societies that Mexicans had created to better their socioeconomic situation in the United States was the movement's radical political stance. Civil rights organizations during the 1940s and 1950s had sought slow, peaceful change through assimilation, through petitions for governmental beneficence, and through appeals to white liberal guilt. Chicanos, in a revolution sparked by rising expectations, demanded equality with white America, demanded an end to racism, asserted their right to cultural autonomy, particularly in education, and demanded self-determination as an independent nation. Eschewing the ethnic label their parents had embraced as "Mexican Americans" during the 1940s and 1950s, these young men called themselves Chicanos, announcing their oppositional identity and resistance to assimilation and Americanization.

Since much of the ethnic militancy that Chicanos articulated was profoundly influenced by black nationalism of the same period, it is important to recall one of the truly poignant insights in the autobiography of Malcolm X. Reciting the psychic violence that racism and discrimination had wreaked on African Americans, Malcolm X noted that the most profound had been the emasculation of black men. In the eyes of white America blacks were not deemed men. Thus whatever else the Black Power movement was, it was also about the cultural assertion of masculinity by radical men, most of them quite young.

Chicanos faced what was undoubtedly a rather similar experience—social emasculation and cultural negation—by seeking strength and inspiration in a heroic and militant Aztec past. The Aztec past they chose emphasized the virility of warriors and the brute exercise of force. Young Chicano men, a largely powerless group in American society, invested themselves with images of power, a symbolic inversion commonly found in the fantasies of powerless men worldwide and a gendered vision that rarely extends to women. Chicanos dreamed of reclaiming a lost homeland they called Aztlán, that mythical place of Aztec genesis, which they claimed consisted of the contemporary states of California, Arizona, New Mexico, Colorado, and Texas. Despite all the fuzziness of Aztlán as an actual spatial concept, meshed as it was in the deep recesses of Aztec mythology, the dream of an independent Aztlán sank deep roots in the imaginations of Chicano radicals, despite the fact that the nation had very imprecise geographic boundaries and previous claims to the territory that American Indians could justly assert.

Aztlán was an internal colony of the United States that required national liberation, the radicals maintained. Chicanos were an internally colonized population that was socially, culturally, and economically subordinated and territorially segregated by white Anglo-Saxon America. This colonization was most profoundly felt in the barrios (ghettos) and *colonias* (shantytowns) of the Southwest. If they were to be liberated, Chicanos had to identify with *la raza* (the race or people), collectively promoting the interests of *carnales* (brothers) with whom they shared a common language, culture, and religion stemming from the putative Aztec blood that ran through their veins.

The personal political identities young ethnic Mexican men living in the United States crafted as "Chicanos" clearly reflected their idealization of the Aztecs. The etymology of Chicano is the Nahuatl word *mexica*. In pre-Columbian times the Aztecs had been known in their own language as the *mexica,* whence the country's name, Mexico. The "x" in *mexicanos,* or Mexicans, is pronounced as "ch." Dropping the first syllable of *mexicanos* and replacing the "x" with a "ch" created the word *chicanos.* In Mexico the word *chicano* had long been a vulgar, derogatory, class-based term used to refer to persons of dubious character, to persons of lower-class origins, to tramps, and to guttersnipes. In the 1960s militants embraced this class-based term of insult and derision as an ethnic identity and transformed it into a badge of pride, thereby identifying with the downtrodden and weak of the world. For persons born into second- and third-generation Mexican immigrant households, Chicano identity, tied as it was etymologically to a heroic past of Aztec warriors, provided an alternative tradition of resistance to marginality and discrimination and proved a particularly expansive rhetorical arsenal for the construction of a usable national past.

Sociological studies show that young men called themselves Chicanos more often than young women, undoubtedly because of the vulgarity previously attached to the term's older connotations; proper Mexican American women did not use such language in public. Economic status and Chicano self-identification were inversely related; the higher one's socioeconomic status, the less likely one was to identify as Chicano. The term was also quite generationally deployed. First- and second-generation Mexican-origin immigrants rarely embraced the identity. Chicanos were most often third-generation assimilated Mexican American males of radical political tendencies, often below the age of twenty-five, who did not speak Spanish, knew little of Mexico's history, and had only the most marginal cultural memories of Mexico, its regions, and its peoples. Chicano identity was initially quite localized, popular primarily in California. But with time, and particularly after two nationwide student conferences on Chicano issues—the Chicano Youth Liberation Conference held in Denver in March 1969 and the Chicano Coordinating Council on Higher Education held in April 1969 at the University of California, Santa Barbara—Chicano as a political identity became more widely diffused and embraced, at least among young males. Chicano identity seems to have provided the political glue to unify what had previously been a host of quite local and distinct concerns. Having arrived as students of Mexican American, Latin American, and Hispanic origin at the Denver Chicano Youth Liberation Conference in 1969, by the meeting's end they proclaimed: "We, the Chicano inhabitants and civilizers of the northern land of Aztlán . . . We are a Nation. We are a Union of free pueblos, We are Aztlán" ("El Plan Espiritual de Aztlán" 1969). Elsewhere in the American Southwest the older ethnic Mexican populations had forged much more place-specific identities as Latin Americans, Spanish Americans, Hispanics, Hispanos, Mexicanos, and Mexican Americans. Indeed, to outsiders, particularly to sociologists and anthropologists, the only thing that seemed to unite all of these groups was that they were "Spanish speakers" whose linguistic deficiencies hampered their Americanization and upward mobility.

Many organizations and leaders, too numerous to discuss here, were to become the Chicano movement's major participants. Four charismatic men stand out. Each had a unique organizational style, personal political commitments, a local constituency, and a specific set of social concerns. They were to become the organizational muscle that gave the Chicano movement its specific forms.

César Chávez is perhaps best known for his peaceful, pacifist tactics inspired by Gandhi and often compared to those of Dr. Martin Luther King. Working with a largely rural constituency to improve the wage and work conditions of unskilled farm laborers in agribusiness, he was active mostly in California, later in Colorado, New Mexico, and Texas, and through a series of nationwide boycotts of agricultural products gained international visibility. The United Farm Workers of America, the labor union he began, still exists.

Reies López Tijerina, a charismatic Baptist minister, militated on behalf of Hispanos of northern New Mexico and southern Colorado who had seen their ancestral land grants known as *mercedes* fraudulently stolen by unscrupulous lawyers and legal chicanery. Seizing federal property, engaging in armed confrontation with local authorities, and pressing his claims before the United Nations as international treaty violations, Tijerina sought to regain land through his organization, the Alianza Federal de Mercedes.

José Angel Gutiérrez began his activities as a student in Crystal City, Texas, there seeking Mexican American participation in school curriculum and governance. Faced with resistance from local school board members, he successfully organized, taking over the school board and city council and finally seeking political change through the formation of a political party known as La Raza Unida Party, which developed chapters throughout the Southwest.

Rodolfo "Corky" Gonzales, a professional prizefighter in his youth, with a "can-do" spirit, sought to improve the living conditions of ethnic Mexicans in and around Denver. Through his militant organization called the Crusade for Justice he organized high-school and college students locally and then nationally around a number of issues—educational reform, police violence, protest against the war in Vietnam and FBI surveillance, and, most important, the need for the creation of an independent nation that would be known as Aztlán. He is responsible for forging disparate and regionally isolated student militants into a national force, having hosted in Denver the March 1969 Chicano Youth Liberation Conference, from which emerged the Plan Espiritual de Aztlán, a foundational agenda for the betterment of Chicanos.

The years 1965 to 1969 were heydays of Chicano activism, in the fields and streets, in courtrooms and classrooms, protesting racism, police violence, and limited access to educational opportunities, low wages, poor working conditions, and, eventually, the mounting number of Chicano deaths in Vietnam. Movement activists articulated most of these concerns largely in gendered terms, as problems faced primarily by men and their families. While the movement persistently advocated the self-actualization of all Chicanos, the term Chicanos really referred to men.

A burgeoning feminist movement had begun to grip the imaginations of the young women participants in the movement, and by 1969 it was being given symbolic lip service. At the 1969 Chicano Youth Liberation Conference organized by "Corky" Gonzales, for example, women met as a group to explore their common concerns. But when their discussions were reported to the conference as a whole, the facilitator declared, "It was the consensus of the group that the Chicana woman does not need to be liberated." Reflecting on her experiences at the Denver conference, Enriqueta Longeaux y Vásquez reported, "I felt this as quite a blow. . . . Then I understood why the statement had been made and I realized that going along with the feelings of the men at the convention was probably the best thing to do at that time." While some women at other conferences devoted to Chicana feminist issues during the early 1970s expressed a similar lack of interest over their liberation, more common was the growing realization that Chicanas were triply oppressed—by their race, their gender, and their class.

Within the Chicano student movement women were being denied leadership roles and were invited to perform in only the most traditional stereotypic roles—cleaning up, making coffee, executing the orders men gave, and servicing their needs. If women did manage to assume leadership positions, as some of them did, they were ridiculed as unfeminine, sexually perverse, and promiscuous and all too often were taunted as lesbians.

A 1970 incident at San Diego State University was particularly telling about the tenor of the times. There women had managed to assume leadership over the campus Chicano student group. When it was announced that "Corky" Gonzales was going to visit the campus, an intense debate ensued. "It was considered improper and embarrassing for a national leader to come on campus and see that the organization's leadership was female," recalled one of the campus leaders. "Consequently, the organization decided that only males would be the visible representatives for the occasion. The female chairperson willingly conceded."

By 1969 articles began appearing in the movement press highlighting the contradiction between racial and sexual oppression in the Chicano movement and drawing attention to the rampant sexism. "Machismo or revolution?" was an often articulated question. Chicano men initially regarded the feminist critique as an assault on their Mexican cultural past, on their power, and, by implication, on their virility. If Chicanos were going to triumph in their anticapitalist, anticolonial revolt, divisiveness could not be tolerated. Men responded to the assault by resorting to crass name-calling, labeling Chicana feminists as *malinchistas,* traitors who were influenced by ideas foreign to their community—namely, bourgeois feminist ideology. Be "Chicana Primero," the men exhorted, asking the women to take pride in their cultural heritage and to reject women's liberation. Chicanas responded rather uniformly that they did not want to dominate the movement. They only sought full equality and participation for all.

The increased mobilization of women in the Chicano movement shifted the political agenda to a broader set of issues. If the aim of the Chicano movement was to decolonize the mind, as the novelist Tomás Rivera once proposed, Chicanas were determined to decolonize the body. Male concerns over job discrimination, access to political power, entry into educational institutions, and community autonomy and self-determination increasingly appeared alongside female demands for birth control and against forced sterilization, for welfare rights, for prison rights for *pintas* (women prisoners), for protection against male violence, and, most important, for sexual pleasure both in marriage and outside it. "La Nueva Chicana," the new woman, was determined to see sexism as a form of oppression equal to racism.

Unlike Chicanos who took their sex/gender privileges for granted, Chicanas, as victims of those privileges, realized that an essential part of their identity as political subjects had to include an exploration of their sexuality. "Our sexuality has been hidden, subverted, distorted within the 'sacred' walls of the 'familia'—be it myth or reality—and within the even more privatized walls of the bedrooms. . . . In the journey to the love of female self and each other we are ultimately forced to confront father, brother, and god (and mother as his agent)," wrote Norma Alarcón, Ana Castillo, and Cherríe Moraga. Subjects that formerly had been taboo began to be openly discussed in the 1970s. Incest, sexual abuse, domestic violence, and lesbianism became frequent themes at conferences and in movement newspapers, which by necessity focused naturally on generational relations.

Assessing the impact of feminism on the Chicano movement, one can easily say that women's concerns highlighted the complexity of the ethnic Mexican population in the United States. It was a population that largely shared a similar class location as poor and working class. Yet it was a population deeply stratified by race and color, by gender and sexual preferences, by intractable generational divisions, by region and locale, and, most important, by differing political attitudes toward assimilation and Americanization. The failure of the Chicano movement was due not only to the limited political vision of its militant activists, but also to extensive government repression and large segments of the ethnic Mexican population who believed deeply in the possibilities of the American dream.

SOURCES: Acuña, Rodolfo. 1988. *Occupied America: A History of Chicanos.* 3rd ed. New York: Harper and Row; Barrera, Mario. 1988. *Beyond Aztlan: Ethnic Autonomy in Comparative Perspective.* New York: Praeger; "El Plan Espiritual de Aztlán." www.panam.edu/orgs/MEChA/aztlan.html (accessed July 21, 2005); Gonzales, Rodolfo "Corky." 2001. *Message to Aztlán.* Houston: Arte Público Press; 1969. Gutiérrez, José Angel. 1998. *The Making of a Chicano Militant: Lessons from Cristal.* Madison: University of Wisconsin Press; Gutiérrez, Ramón A. 1986. "Unraveling America's Hispanic Past: Internal Stratification and Class Boundaries." *Aztlán: A Journal of Chicano Studies* 17, no. 1 (Spring): 79–101; López Tijerina, Reies. 2000. *They Called Me "King Tiger": My Struggle for the Land and Our Rights.* Houston: Arte Público Press; Márquez, Benjamin. 1993. *LULAC: The Evolution of a Mexican American Political Organization.* Austin: University of Texas Press; Miller, Michael V. 1976. "Mexican Americans, Chicanos, and Others: Ethnic Self-Identification and Selected Social Attributes of Rural Texas Youth." *Rural Sociology* 41:234–247; Moraga, Cherríe. 1983. *Loving in the War Years: Lo que nunca pasó por sus labios.* Boston: South End Press; Moraga, Cherríe, and Gloria Anzaldúa, eds. 1983. *This Bridge Called My Back: Writings by Radical Women of Color.* New York: Kitchen Table Women of Color Press; Muñoz, Carlos. 1989. *Youth, Identity, Power: The Chicano Movement.* New York: Verso; Navarro, Armando. 1998. *The Cristal Experiment: A Chicano Struggle for Community Control.* Madison: University of Wisconsin Press; ———. 2000. *La Raza Unida Party: A Chicano Challenge to the U.S. Two-Party Dictatorship.* Philadelphia: Temple University Press; Rosales, F. Arturo. 2000. *Testimonio: A Documentary History of the Mexican American Struggle for Civil Rights.* Houston: Arte Público Press; Ruiz, Vicki L. 1998. *From out of the Shadows: Mexican Women in Twentieth-Century America.* New York: Oxford University Press; Trujillo, Carla. 1991. *Chicana Lesbians: The Girls Our Mothers Warned Us About.* Berkeley, CA: Third Woman Press; Vigil, Ernesto. 1999. *The Crusade for Justice: Chicano Militancy and the Government's War on Dissent.* Madison: University of Wisconsin Press.

Ramón A. Gutiérrez

CHICANOS POR LA CAUSA (CPLC) (1969–)

In the 1960s young Latinos and Latinas from minority and mainstream groups in the United States vigorously called on established leadership to honor the democratic ideals that were purportedly core values in the country. In the nation's history no other era embodies the rise of youthful self-conscious idealism. Such a heady mix was bound to inspire Mexican Americans in universities who in college-mall rap sessions or in campus hangouts excitedly discussed potential reforms to ameliorate the subordination of their people. Caught up in this historic moment, students at Arizona State University organized the Mexican American Student Organization (MASO) in 1968. The group mainly pressed the university to meet the educational needs of the Chicano community. In their very first confrontation, MASO members occupied the administration building and forced the university to sever a contract with a Phoenix linen service that discriminated against Chicano workers. After making this commitment to their community, students Alfredo Gutiérrez, Arturo "Frank" Rosales, Rosie López, and others quickly took the movement into the Phoenix barrios. In 1969 the students joined with community activists like Joe "Eddie" López, Manuel Domínguez, Terry Cruz, and farmworker organizer Gustavo Gutiérrez and incorporated Chicanos Por La Causa (CPLC), a strident civil rights and community development organization.

Arizona labor leader and board member of the Southwest Council of La Raza Maclovio Barraza steered the fledgling organization toward the Ford Foundation. CPLC acquired a small seed grant from the foundation and hired Juan Alvarez, a farmworker organizer, as director. The ambitious, idealistic group of young militants proceeded to transform the Phoenix Chicano community. The group's initial activities dealt with educational and political issues. For example, CPLC ran a slate for an inner-city school board election consisting of the Basque activist parish priest Frank Yoldi and other barrio residents. The CPLC slate lost, but the event provided the first electoral experience for many activists who today form the core of Chicano political leadership in Maricopa County, Arizona. Regarding education, CPLC organized walkouts at Phoenix Union High School to protest inadequate funding, the lack of relevant courses, and the failure of the school to deal with constant racial tension between Mexican American and black students. Alfredo Gutiérrez, cochairman of MASO, helped organize the walkouts and formed a local Brown Beret chapter.

In 1970 the Ford Foundation provided the group with full funding, and Ronnie López became director. Under his leadership the organization's militant edge gave way to a more accommodating approach in dealing with government officials and potential funders. CPLC's direction became more programmatic. By 1974, in the midst of an economic recession, Ford reduced funding, but within three years CPLC received $2 million in federal funds. The organization could now focus on economic development, job training, and housing issues in a more structured fashion. Tommy Espinoza succeeded López, who became a special assistant to the governor of Arizona in 1978. Until Espinoza's resignation in 1988, he guided CPLC into its contemporary profile. During his directorship the organization opened centers in Tucson and Yuma, Arizona.

Under the new director, Peter García, *Hispanic News* selected the organization as the second-top Hispanic nonprofit in the country because of its "22 years of dedicated service to their community." Today CPLC has thirty offices in twenty-three Arizona cities. The organization estimates that 45,000 people annually receive CPLC services through youth counseling programs, affordable housing, formation of positive cultural identity, senior citizen housing and recreation, rehabilitation, domestic violence prevention, and, true to its original goal, economic development. Few other organizations that came out of the Chicano movement have survived, let alone reached the mammoth proportions of CPLC.

See also Chicano Movement

SOURCES: Chávez, John R. 1998. *Eastside Landmark: A History of the East Los Angeles Community Union, 1968–1993.* Stanford, CA: Stanford University Press; Luckingham, Bradford. 1994. *Minorities in Phoenix: A Profile of Mexican American, Chinese American, and African American Communities, 1860–1992.* Tucson: University of Arizona Press; Luey, Beth, and Noel J. Stowe, eds. 1987. *Arizona at Seventy-five: The Next Twenty-five Years.* Tempe: Arizona State University Public History Program and the Arizona Historical Society; Navarro, Armando. 2000. *La Raza Unida Party: A Chicano Challenge to the U.S. Two-Party Dictatorship.* Philadelphia: Temple University Press; Rosales, F. Arturo. 1996. *Chicano! The History of the Mexican American Civil Rights Movement.* Houston: Arte Público Press.

F. Arturo Rosales

CIGAR WORKERS (1860s–1940s)

The thick sweet smell of tobacco permeated the lives of tens of thousands of women in the late-nineteenth- and early-twentieth-century United States. In small Pennsylvania towns, among Bohemian and German immigrants in New York City, Rochester, Detroit, and Chicago, amid the fields and factories of the Carolinas and Puerto Rico, and in the ethnic enclaves of Tampa and Key West, Florida, women stripped the wide green leaves from the stem, bunched or chopped tobacco in preparation for rolling, and placed brand-name bands around each cigar. Some gained highly skilled positions as cigar rollers, but women only came to dominate cigar production in the 1930s and 1940s when automation diminished the skill, pay, and prestige accorded cigar workers. Nonetheless, for many Cuban and Puerto Rican women in the United States, work in cigar factories offered better pay and working conditions than most sex-typed jobs and provided entrée to powerful *tabaqueros'* unions and to a wide range of other social and political movements.

Rolling tobacco leaves for smoking was an ancient art in the Americas and was taught to European invaders and settlers by native inhabitants. By the early nineteenth century women in Spain had become closely identified with the cigar trade. They were hired to work in the royal factory of Seville beginning in 1812; images of beautiful Hispanic women graced many cigar labels; and Bizet's opera *Carmen* fueled the imaginations of smokers, writers, and audiences. The mass production of cigars in the United States developed in the 1860s, 1870s, and 1880s as Bohemians, Germans, Cubans, and Puerto Ricans migrated in large numbers. In northern cities the factory production of cigars was almost entirely a male affair in this period, although home production in tenement districts used the skills of thousands of Bohemian and smaller numbers of Cuban and Puerto Rican women. In the South, however, especially in the "Cigar Cities" of Key West and Tampa, Florida, immigrant women played critical roles in both factory and home-based production from the establishment of the industry.

In southern Florida cigar production followed the model developed by Spanish officials and factory owners in nineteenth-century Cuba. Beginning in the early 1800s, men, including slaves, produced cigars in factories owned and managed by Spanish entrepreneurs. During the 1820s women and children, mainly residents of charity homes, were introduced into the labor force to cut costs, but men continued to dominate the industry. By the 1880s and 1890s Spanish, white Cuban, Creole, African and Afro-Cuban (slave and free), and Chinese immigrant men vied for the wide range of skilled and unskilled positions in the tobacco factories, while women, mainly African and Afro-Cuban, were relegated to the least prestigious job of stripping tobacco leaves from the stem. During these same decades Puerto Rican women were also entering male-dominated cigar factories, again working mainly as tobacco stemmers.

When the wars for independence erupted in Spain's Caribbean possessions in the late nineteenth century, they sparked a mass movement of Cuban cigar workers and factory owners to southern Florida and led to the development of the industry first in Key West and then in Tampa. The first wave of refugees fled to Key West during the Ten Years' War (1868–1878), after an unsuccessful attempt by Cuban insurgents to overthrow their colonial rulers. The independence movement and Key West's émigré community both included white and Afro-Cuban men and women drawn from across the class spectrum. Like Jewish immigrants fleeing persecution in eastern Europe, most Cubans came with families and the bare minimum of necessities. This ensured that many Cuban women—those who were older and married, as well as those who were young, single, or widowed—would be forced to find work. The newly built cigar factories offered immediate employment along with higher and steadier wages than domestic service or other jobs open to women immigrants. Because the Cuban émigrés were a highly politicized group, workers organized more effectively than did their native-born counterparts in the late-nineteenth-century South. Moreover, because of the economic boost the cigar industry brought to Key West, white civic leaders initially ignored the interracial and mixed-sex character of the cigar labor force and the militant unions it established.

By the mid-1880s, however, extensive labor organizing, a series of volatile strikes, and a fire that destroyed much of Key West's commercial district drove factory owners to search for a new home. In 1886 Don Vicente Martínez Ybor constructed the first factory on the eastern edge of Tampa, and the first 200 cigar workers and their families arrived that spring. Other owners quickly followed suit, and within two years Ybor City was home to a dozen factories, several churches and mission stations, two Spanish-language newspapers, coffee shops, bakeries, a brass band, Cuban restaurants, Chinese laundries, and hundreds of cigar workers.

The Cuban cigar workers brought their unions and mutual-aid societies, along with another tradition that had important implications for their education and political activism. The reader, *el lector,* had been introduced into cigar factories in Cuba and Puerto Rico in the mid-1800s. Because cigar making was a relatively quiet process—only the rustle of tobacco leaves and the click-click of the cutting blades disrupted the silence—readers were paid by the workers to provide entertainment and education. In the mornings they generally read stories from Spanish-language newspapers and political tracts that presented a range of socialist and anarcho-syndicalist perspectives. In the afternoon they read novels in serial form, often selecting those with socialist realist themes or working-class heroes. Although most readers were men, women stemmers in at least one Ybor City factory hired their own reader in the 1880s, and those who gained positions as bunchers and rollers would listen to *el lector* alongside male cigar makers.

By the early 1890s the education provided by *los lectores,* combined with renewed claims for independence in the Caribbean and the expansion of the cigar industry in the United States, increased women's participation in factory work and political organizing. The independence movement also brought a new flood of Cuban and Puerto Rican exiles to southern Florida and to New York City. The resurgence of the Cuban independence movement rested on the political vision of José Martí. A member of New York's exile community and active in the Partido Revolucionario Cubano (PRC), Martí argued that only a truly democratic movement, one that engaged the loyalties of whites and Afro-Cubans, workers and the middle class, could succeed in overthrowing Spanish tyranny. Many of the more affluent leaders of the PRC sought independence from Spain, but had little interest in a more thoroughgoing revolution in social relations. To gain leverage for his vision, Martí traveled to the Cigar Cities of southern Florida in 1892 to seek support from the workers there. White and Afro-Cuban women and men turned out by the thousands to hear Martí's speeches, applaud his vision, and honor his heroism. Young Cuban girls presented Martí with flowers and gifts from the assembled throng, and some, like ten-year-old Pennsylvania Herrera, made impassioned pleas for Cuban independence before large audiences of exiles.

In Ybor City two of Martí's most ardent supporters were Paulina Pedroso, a boardinghouse keeper, and her husband Ruperto, a cigar roller. Leaders of Afro-Cuban educational and mutual-aid organizations in

Tobacco stemmers, southern Florida, circa 1900. Courtesy of University of South Florida Library, Tampa.

Key West and Tampa, they helped assure Martí's success. So, too, did Carolina Rodríguez, a white Cuban who had served as a courier between separated insurgent forces during the Ten Years' War. Working in an Ybor City cigar factory in the 1890s, she joined Martí in his efforts to establish organizations in support of the revolution. Women's revolutionary clubs flourished among Cuban exiles during the next several years, and Ybor City and Key West were soon home to more than a dozen.

When the war against Spain recommenced in February 1895, Cuban women exiles played increasingly prominent roles. As factory workers, they, like the men, often contributed a day's pay per week to the independence struggle. As community activists, women cigar workers joined the wives of factory owners and professionals in establishing revolutionary clubs and hosting picnics, dances, bazaars, and other events to raise funds for the PRC and assist widows, orphans, and wounded soldiers. Martí recognized the critical importance of these donations by calling Ybor City "the civilian camp of the revolution." As the war against Spain widened to include Puerto Rico, exiles from that island settled in New York City. There they became part of a vibrant radical community that, like its counterparts in southern Florida, relied on the wages of cigar work to fuel its political agenda and social development.

The United States entered the war against Spain in the spring of 1898, and the status of Cuban and Puerto Rican immigrants changed dramatically after the American victory. The U.S. government controlled the postwar settlement. Cuba became a protectorate of the United States and Puerto Rico a colony within it. Cubans who remained in southern Florida after the war retained their status as immigrants. Puerto Ricans became American citizens, although clearly second-class citizens. Yet as long as cigars remained profitable and the industry dependent on Caribbean labor, Cuban and Puerto Rican workers could sustain their militant traditions despite the new political context.

As the industry expanded in Puerto Rico and southern Florida, women increased their significance in the cigar labor force and in the social activism it spawned. In 1899, for instance, only 60 women were listed as "operators," that is, workers, in tobacco factories in Puerto Rico. By 1910 the number rose to 3,204 and in 1920 to 8,473. In Tampa women's employment also grew with the industry. Beginning with a dozen or so factories operating in the 1880s, Ybor City counted 129 by 1900. The overall workforce numbered more than 5,000 by the turn of the century and reached more than 12,000 by 1920. Ancillary trades—box factories, bakeries, laundries, and coffeehouses—provided further employment. During this period the population of Ybor City included a growing number of Italians, who, along with Cuban and Spanish workers, were considered, and considered themselves, part of a larger Latin community. By 1910 women constituted some 20 percent of the Latin cigar labor force—1,800 of nearly 8,800 workers—and their numbers continued to grow during the next decade. Among Italians, married women were as likely to work for wages as single women; among Cubans, single women outnumbered married, but many women who left the factory in the 1910s and 1920s to raise families returned once their children were old enough to care for themselves. In addition, a significant number of women, especially Cuban women, stripped and bunched tobacco and rolled cigars in home-based shops known as *chinchales.*

In both Puerto Rico and southern Florida women were welcomed into the unions, a position at odds with the traditions established by the Cigar Makers' International Union and other U.S.-based labor organizations. Moreover, women's participation was important not only because it engaged them in shop-floor issues, but also because it encouraged their unions to consider society-wide debates over gender equity. La Federación Libre de los Trabajadores (FLT), the massive anarcho-syndicalist union in Puerto Rico, which included large numbers of women cigar workers among its members, advocated women's education, improved infant and maternal health care, and female suffrage. Indeed, in 1908 it became the first organization in Puerto Rico to demand women's enfranchisement. The FLT also provided opportunities for a few women to serve as organizers, building bridges with women cigar workers in the United States and Cuba. The most famous was Luisa Capetillo, who not only mobilized workers in Puerto Rico but also wrote articles for a variety of progressive Spanish-language publications, authored books and essays on workers' and women's rights, and carried the FLT's vision of social change to New York City, Ybor City, Key West, and Havana.

During her sojourn in southern Florida in 1913–1914, Capetillo must have felt right at home. She was hired as a reader by workers at an Ybor City factory, and a local printer published a volume of her essays. But more important than these personal triumphs was the culture she shared with the area's Latin workers. Embracing a mutualist ethos and anarcho-syndicalist principles of organization, Cuban and Italian workers in Ybor City, West Tampa, and Key West organized food and clothing cooperatives, established day nurseries, and supported mutual-aid societies. These societies built substantial clubhouses that included cafés, theaters, ballrooms, lecture halls, and libraries, and they also managed health care programs. For a small monthly fee, they provided medical care, including midwives, as well as death and burial benefits. Several operated cemeteries for their members; two opened hospitals. In all, these organizations provided critical support for women and their families during personal and community crises, including strikes.

Although first- and second-generation immigrants from across the class spectrum joined the mutual-aid societies, cigar workers formed a significant share of the membership. Whereas the unions brought together white Cuban, Afro-Cuban, and Italian working women and men on behalf of class issues, the mutual-aid societies brought together professionals, small shopkeepers, artisans, cigar workers, and housewives from the city's various ethnic and racial groups. Within the ethnic clubs women generally organized separate *comités de las damas* (women's committees) to raise funds, provide emergency relief, and improve medical facilities. The first was founded by members of la Unión Martí-Maceo, the Afro-Cuban club; women in el Centro Español, el Centro Asturiano, el Círculo Cubano, and l'Unione Italiana soon followed suit. Although men most often viewed the clubs as gathering places for food, drink, relaxation, and entertainment, women generally emphasized the material benefits they offered. Within their own committees, moreover, women honed leadership skills and gained increased authority. Cigar worker Dolores Patiño Río, who was active in el Centro Asturiano, recalled that in 1925 the women's committee wanted to hold a dance to aid hurricane victims in Cuba. The men opposed the decision, but the women "had it anyway, and it was a success."

By the middle of the depression the unions were shattered and large numbers of workers were unemployed. However, women cigar workers in southern Florida, Puerto Rico, and Cuba maintained their commitment to collective action. They were especially active in donating money, ambulances, and other forms of material support to aid the Republicans and their allies in the Spanish civil war. In Ybor City women workers also carried on earlier political traditions by raising money for the Scottsboro Boys Defense Fund, attending Highlander Folk School to learn organizing techniques, and protesting various forms of discrimination in the implementation of New Deal programs.

For many Cuban and Puerto Rican women, in their homelands and in the United States, cigar work provided steady employment, relatively decent wages, and an introduction to a range of political and social issues in the late nineteenth and early twentieth centuries. Active in unions, women cigar workers also contributed to the Puerto Rican and Cuban independence movements, the establishment of mutual-aid societies, and the maintenance of Caribbean cultural traditions. As the hand-rolled cigar industry declined in the 1930s and 1940s, it was primarily Cuban and Puerto Rican women who made the transition to machine work, thereby maintaining their economic role in the family and their political role in the larger community.

See also Labor Unions; *Tabaqueros'* Unions

SOURCES: Azize, Yamila. 1985. *La mujer en la lucha*. Río Piedras, Puerto Rico: Editorial Cultural; Hewitt, Nancy A. 2001. *Southern Discomfort: Women's Activism in Tampa, Florida, 1880s–1920s*. Urbana: University of Illinois Press; Patiño Río, Dolores. Interviews by Nancy A. Hewitt, September 4, 1985, and April 7, 1986, Special Collections, University of South Florida Library, Tampa, Florida; Stubbs, Jean. 1985. *Tobacco on the Periphery: A Case Study of Cuban Labour History, 1860–1958*. Cambridge Latin American Studies 51. Cambridge: Cambridge University Press; Valero-Lago, Ana. 1997. "'*No pasarán*!': The Spanish Civil War's Impact on Tampa's Latin Community, 1936–1939." *Tampa Bay History* 19 (Fall–Winter): 5–35.

Nancy A. Hewitt

CINEMA IMAGES, CONTEMPORARY

Latinas have worked in the film industry since the early days of Hollywood. The first Latina leading ladies of the silent screen included actresses like Beatríz Michelin and Myrtle González. Images of Latinas in the early years of filmmaking were blurred by movie and social codes. Because the Latino population was small and the majority of Mexican descent, films predominantly related stories focusing on them. Films with Mexican characters before the 1920s commonly had titles like *The Greaser's Gauntlet* (1908), *Tony the Greaser* (1911), *Broncho Billy and the Greaser* (1914), and *The Girl and the Greaser* (1915). Movies depicted Mexicans as nonwhite villains, and sexual or romantic relationships between Anglos and Mexicans were taboo.

In the 1920s Dolores Del Río and Lupe Vélez were the most significant Mexican actresses in Hollywood. Dolores Del Río portrayed European peasants in her early work; later she played sophisticated ingénues. The opposite occurred for Vélez, whose image evolved into the stereotypical Hollywood "Mexican Spitfire" and "Hot Tamale."

About this time Lupita Tovar's career took another route. While she did not obtain as great a reputation as did Del Rio and Vélez, she appeared in numerous Hollywood Spanish-language films. She was cast as the lead in the Spanish version of Rupert Julian's *The Cat Creeps* (1927). *La voluntad del muerto* did so well in Mexico that Universal cast her in the Spanish version of *Dracula*.

In the 1930s Hollywood bombarded both the U.S. and Latin American markets with Latin-themed films like *Down Argentine Way* (1940) and *Weekend in Havana* (1941). Probably the most famous Latina to come out of this period was the Brazilian Carmen Miranda. Another well-known Latin actress of the 1940s was María Montez, who hailed from the Dominican Republic. Then there was Rita Hayworth, who made the transformation from being an ethnically identifiable Latina to an American "sex goddess." Hayworth rarely acknowledged her ethnic roots, although she worked as her Spanish father's dancing partner in Aguascalientes and Tijuana.

The 1950s saw a few Latinas make it onto the screen, including Sarita Montiel and Linda Cristal, but the most memorable performance by a Latina of the 1950s was Katy Jurado's appearance in *High Noon* (1952), for which she won a Golden Globe. One of the most significant films involving Latinas was released in 1954. Based on actual events, *Salt of the Earth* detailed the zinc strike of 1950–1952 in Grant County, New Mexico. Playing the lead was Rosaura Revueltas, a Mexican actress. Miners' families lived in deplorable conditions that ultimately led to the strike. The miners were not successful until the women came to their aid. Not long after its release the film was labeled "communistic" in its message and banned.

Originally from Puerto Rico, Rita Moreno signaled the appearance of a new crop of actresses. Awarded the Oscar for Best Supporting Actress as Anita in *West Side Story* (1961), Moreno hoped for more serious roles. Instead, she did not work for seven years, rejecting conventional stereotypical roles. Awarded the Emmy, Tony, and Grammy for roles off the screen,

Rita Moreno received an Oscar for her role as Anita in *West Side Story.* Courtesy of the Offices of the Government of Puerto Rico in the United States. Centro Archives, Centro de Estudios Puertorriqueños, Hunter College, CUNY.

Moreno serves as an excellent example for aspiring Latinas in the film industry.

Besides Moreno, Raquel Welch, the daughter of a Bolivian engineer, has carved out an enduring acting career. Welch's breakthrough film was *One Million Years B.C.* (1966). Welch portrayed mostly vamps and vixens, but in 1974 she earned a Golden Globe Best Actress award for her role in *The Three Musketeers* (1973).

In the 1970s and 1980s there were standout performances by such actresses as Rachel Ticotín in *The Wanderer* (1979) and *Fort Apache, the Bronx* (1981), María Conchita Alonso in *Moscow on the Hudson* (1984), and Elizabeth Peña as the sultry maid in *Down and Out in Beverly Hills* (1986). Sonia Braga appeared in *Kiss of the Spider Woman* (1985), *The Milagro Beanfield War* (1988), and *Moon over Parador* (1988). Rosie Pérez debuted in Spike Lee's *Do the Right Thing* (1989) and was nominated for an Academy Award as Best Supporting Actress in *Fearless* (1993).

Latinas did better in the 1990s. While the movie industry still failed to reflect national demographics in casting Latinas, the types of roles offered some change. Latinas still contended with non-Latinas portraying them, an issue since the beginning of Hollywood films. Nonetheless, Latina and Latino actors began writing parts for themselves. These films presented the group as other than domestics and vamps and included groundbreaking films like *Stand and Deliver* (1988), *Mi familia* (1995), *Lone Star* (1996), *Las luminarias* (1999), and *Girlfight* (2000). Showtime's *Resurrection Blvd.* has also given Latinas the opportunity to demonstrate their intelligence and abilities.

Jennifer López, currently a top Hollywood box-office star, exemplifies an actress who has benefited from the changes. She played a vamp in *U-Turn,* a psychologist in *The Cell,* a wedding coordinator in *The Wedding Planner,* a police officer in *The Money Train, Out of Sight,* and *Angel Eyes,* and a Tejana singer in *Selena*. These roles do not always identify her as a Latina. The New York–born Puerto Rican has also engaged in a high-profile singing career. Rosana de Soto, Constance Marie, Lupe Ontiveros, Liz Torres, Jaime Sigler, and Evelina Fernández are Latina actresses who can be seen in big-budget films as well as small independent films and television.

Salma Hayek has become a major star in recent years. A veteran of theatre and *telenovelas* in Mexico, she moved to California in the early 1990s and received her first break in *Mi vida loca* (1993). *Desperado* (1993), with Antonio Banderas, made her a celebrity. Hayek played the lead and coproduced the film *Frida* (2002) for which she was nominated for an Academy Award as best actress.

A 2000 report conducted by the Tomás Rivera Policy

Institute for the Screen Actors Guild found that casting directors retain stereotypical images and misconceptions regarding Latinos. Until casting directors and studio executives understand Latino/a ethnoracial and social diversity, Latinas will remain marginal in the industry.

See also Media Stereotypes; Movie Stars

SOURCES: Fregoso, Rosa Linda. 1993. *The Bronze Screen: Chicana and Chicano Film Culture.* Minneapolis: University of Minnesota Press; Garcia Berumen, Frank Javier. 1995. *The Chicano/Hispanic Image in American Film.* New York: Vantage Press; Noriega, Chon, ed. 1992. *Chicanos and Film: Essays on Chicano Representation and Resistance.* New York: Garland Publishing; ———. 2000. *Shot in America: Television, the State, and the Rise of Chicano Cinema.* Minneapolis: University of Minnesota Press; Rodríguez, Clara E., ed. 1997. *Latin Looks: Images of Latinas and Latinos in the U.S. Media.* Boulder, CO: Westview Press.

Alicia I. Rodríquez-Estrada

CÍRCULO CULTURAL ISABEL LA CATÓLICA

Originally known as Círculo Social Femenino Mexicano, the Círculo Cultural Isabel la Católica was a civic, social, religious, and philanthropic organization in San Antonio, Texas, during the Great Depression. Founded in 1938, this association, composed of middle-class members, sought to uplift the Mexican American community and elevate the status of women of Mexican descent through morality and charity. The civic club helped needy families and promoted Mexican nationalist civic activities. Unlike the League of United Latin American Citizens (LULAC), which emphasized Americanization and assimilation, this civic group merged Mexican nationalism with ideas of uplift.

Concerned with art and aesthetics, the group organized an exhibit of popular Mexican art at the Witte Museum in 1939, in an era when many U.S. museums ignored Mexican art. It also donated curtains and plants to the Biblioteca Mexicana, a Spanish-language library, where the group held its meetings. Members sponsored fiestas, distributed food and toys, and donated funds to the patriotic celebrations organized by the Mexican consul.

Carolina Malpica Munguía, a prominent middle-class activist and the grandmother of the future mayor of San Antonio, Henry Cisneros, served as the first president of Círculo Cultural Isabel la Católica, and legendary activist María L. de Hernández served as the first board member. Women members were married, usually Mexican citizens between the ages of twenty-one and forty-six. This organization operated like a *mutualista* or mutual-aid society in that in addition to charitable and civic activities, it attended to sickness and death of members and their families. Some San Antonio members of LULAC also belonged to this important local organization. In 1938 and 1939 the club sent delegates to the convention held by the Cruz Azul Mexicana, a women's mutual-aid society. The group also helped raise funds for the Clínica de la Beneficencia Mexicana, a health clinic for the poor on the West Side of the city. Members of Círculo Cultural Isabel la Católica met bimonthly on Sundays, but the organization disappeared during the early 1940s. The club represented civic activism by Mexican immigrant women and their enduring Mexican nationalist sentiment in an era in which Mexican Americanization, as exemplified by LULAC, was in full swing.

SOURCES: Garcia, Richard A. 1991. *Rise of the Mexican American Middle Class, San Antonio, 1919–1941.* College Station: Texas A&M University Press; Orozco, Cynthia E. 1996. "Círculo Cultural Isabel la Católica." In *New Handbook of Texas,* 4:680–682. Austin: Texas State Historical Association.

Cynthia E. Orozco

CISNEROS, SANDRA (1954–)

"I'm a bell without a clapper. A woman with one foot in this world and one foot in that. A woman straddling both," explains Chayo in Sandra Cisneros's story "Little Miracles, Kept Promises." Like her character, Cisneros's own experiences reflect a similar sense of fluidity. Transported back and forth between Chicago, where her mother was raised, and Mexico City, where her father's family still lived, Cisneros grew up viewing life from both sides of the U.S.-Mexico border. These travels filled her with rich memories that later shaped her writing, but the family's frequent moves and economic hardships also forced her to deal with feelings of displacement at a young age. For many years Cisneros longed for a permanent home, a dream that was only partially realized in 1966 when her parents succeeded in borrowing enough money for a down payment on a cramped, dilapidated bungalow on Chicago's North Side. There Cisneros encountered a number of colorful individuals and realized the struggles she shared with many through the effects of poverty. In *The House on Mango Street* (1984) Cisneros draws on the characterization of several of these people and explores the particular issues that face young Latinas by telling the story through the eyes of a spunky adolescent named Esperanza. Throughout the book's vignettes Esperanza's coming-of-age tale is paired with the decisions she must make regarding her own aspirations and the culture's expectations for women.

As the only girl among six male siblings, Cisneros was exposed early on to the precarious position of being female within Latino culture. For example, while he did it unintentionally, her father often forgot to include her when he would boast that he had "seven sons." A mistranslation of the fact that he had seven children (*hijos*), her father's linguistic error signaled to Cisneros the need for women to actively seek out their own place. As she comments, within a large family, "You had to be fast and you had to be funny—you had to be a *storyteller*." Cisneros credits the opportunity to hone this interest to her mother's atypical child rearing: "I'm the product of a fierce woman who was brave enough to raise her daughter in a nontraditional way, who fought for my right to be a person of letters. And she did that in a household where she could have certainly trained me to be a housewife, but, instead, she let me go and study during times when perhaps I should have been helping her out." Cisneros also received encouragement from her father, who doted on her; however, she notes that he mostly saw her furthering her education as a means to find a husband. In 1976 Cisneros graduated from Loyola University and entered the prestigious University of Iowa Writers' Workshop, where she received an M.F.A. in 1978. It was during graduate school that Cisneros realized that she had more boundaries to traverse. While as an undergraduate she was influenced by such writers as Donald Justice, James Wright, and Mark Strand, she had difficulty developing her own voice. Initially, she entered the program as a poet and attempted to mimic the writing styles of her teachers and classmates. However, unhappy with the results and inspired by Vladimir Nabokov's memoirs, she began experimenting with traditional writing genres. During this time she also nurtured a friendship with Joy Harjo, a Native American and fellow classmate who wrote largely about her southwestern culture and shared Cisneros's alienation from the workshop's elitist environment. Motivated by Harjo, Cisneros began to write about her experiences as a Latina—a topic she realized was left out of most mainstream American literary discussions. The combination of these various creative forces ultimately led to *The House on Mango Street,* a work now in its sixth reprinting that has won the Before Columbus American Book Award and was performed as a play in Chicago at the Edgewater Theater in 1992.

In *Woman Hollering Creek and Other Stories* (1991) she continued her literary experimentation by writing a series of inner monologues in which characters describe their own borderland experiences. In addition, Cisneros has authored three poetry collections, *Bad Boys* (1980), *My Wicked, Wicked Ways* (1987), and *Loose Woman* (1994), and published a children's book, *Hairs: Pelitos* (1994). Cisneros's work is also widely anthologized, and she has contributed to various periodicals, including *Americas Review, Imagine, Contact II, Glamour,* the *Los Angeles Times,* the *New York Times, Texas Humanist,* and *Village Voice*.

Despite her success, critics remain divided regarding Cisneros's style. Some find that her blend of various genres deviates too far from the standard sensibilities of American fiction. *The House on Mango Street,* in particular, is criticized for its supposedly simplistic use of children's speech and themes. Others have also taken issue with her frequent depiction of male violence toward women, claiming that she paints an excessively negative portrayal of Latino culture. There are even those who believe that she is not sufficiently political, a charge Cisneros strongly disputes. Admitting that she is more likely to have to "tone back" her work, she argues that it is not her writing that is subtly political, but rather its approach, which falls outside of traditional protest literature. The disjuncture between these dissenting perspectives and the vast praise she has also garnered suggests that Cisneros's early split consciousness has followed her into her career. As Cisneros herself comments, "As woman and writer . . . I'm always aware of being on the frontier. Even if I'm writing about Paris or Sarajevo, I'm still writing about it from this border position that I was raised in." A crosser of many types of borders, Cisneros appears to keep readers most intrigued with her ability to straddle several perspectives at once.

See also Literature

SOURCES: *Chicano Writers, Second Series,* ed. Francisco A. Lomeli and Carl R. Shirley, 77–81. Detroit: Gale Group; Cisneros, Sandra. 1997. "Only Daughter." In *Máscaras,* ed. Lucha Corpi, 119–123. Berkeley, CA: Third Woman Press; McCracken, Ellen. 1989. "Sandra Cisneros' *The House on Mango Street*: Community-Oriented Introspection and the Demystification of Patriarchal Violence." In *Breaking Boundaries: Latina Writing and Critical Readings,* ed. Asunción Horno-Delgado, Eliana Ortega, Nina M. Scott, and Nancy Saporta Sternbach, 62–71. Amherst: University of Massachusetts Press.

Maythee Rojas

CLÍNICA DE LA BENEFICENCIA MEXICANA

During the Great Depression Mexican women established a health clinic for the poor, predominantly Mexican community on the West Side of San Antonio, Texas. Alicia and Ignacio Lozano of *La Prensa* newspaper, a statewide Spanish-language newspaper, and the Beneficencia Mexicana, a women's club composed of Mexican immigrant women, joined forces to establish this clinic. Racially segregated and economically marginalized, the Mexican community of San Antonio reportedly had the worst health conditions in the city.

In 1930 Ignacio E. Lozano, *La Prensa*'s editor, raised

more than $27,000 to build this clinic. Numerous Mexican community organizations joined in to make this health clinic a reality. The Finck Cigar Factory Workers, Club Femenino Orquidia, and the Club de Jovenes Católicos donated funds, and grocer Matilde Elizondo purchased medical equipment. Alicia Lozano, Ignacio's wife, headed Beneficencia Mexicana, a group that proved instrumental in launching and maintaining the clinic that bore its name. This motto of this middle-class women's club was "charity, order, and efficiency," and club members' support of this clinic represented moral uplift in action.

Clínica de la Beneficencia Mexicana was located at 623 South Saba in a Spanish colonial stone building. Clients paid 25 cents for a first visit. This public health clinic was run by a male board of trustees, probably doctors, as well as a board of directors made up entirely of women. Alicia Lozano presided over this board until 1938. That year a serious disagreement over the clinic's management emerged that resulted in a court settlement. Women took over the entire management. The clinic moved to 207 San Fernando Street during the 1940s, and by 1949 it became known as a prenatal clinic. Unlike the Freeman Clinic and Newark Maternity Hospital in El Paso, in which services to poor Mexican immigrants were provided by Methodist missionaries and largely European American volunteers, Clínica de la Beneficencia Mexicana represented Latinas organizing for public health in their own community and in an era before government aid was common.

SOURCES: Garcia, Richard A. 1991. *Rise of the Mexican American Middle Class, San Antonio, 1919–1941*. College Station: Texas A&M University Press; Orozco, Cynthia E. 1996. "Clinica de la Beneficencia Mexicana." In *New Handbook of Texas*, 2:162–163. Austin: Texas State Historical Association; Woods, Frances Jerome. 1949. "Mexican Ethnic Leadership in San Antonio, Texas." Ph.D. diss., Catholic University of America. Rpt. as Catholic University of America Studies in Sociology 31. New York: Arno Press, 1976.

Cynthia E. Orozco

COLLAZO, ROSA CORTÉZ (1904–1988)

Puerto Rican patriot Rosa Cortéz Collazo was the daughter of Ramón Cortéz, a one-time merchant marine and native of Ponce, and Juana E. Fernández, a seamstress and sometimes a tobacco worker, a native of Vieques. Rosa was born in Mayagüez, but spent her adolescent years with her father's family in Ponce after her parents divorced. She graduated from high school in Ponce in 1923 and shortly thereafter completed a six-week nurse's aide program. Her career in nursing was cut short when she had to deal with her first corpse, a suicide victim. Without work or job prospects, she moved to New York City in mid-1925, where her father had settled two years earlier.

She found a job in a hat factory earning eight dollars a week. These wages enabled her to take a room in her godmother's cold-water flat at Ninety-eighth Street and Lexington Avenue for two dollars a week and to send another two dollars weekly to her mother in Mayagüez. When jobs disappeared during the depression years, she survived with the help of the Salvation Army, which provided food and inexpensive clothing to the poor of the city.

During this period of economic stress she became politically active for the first time. In 1934 she joined the Club Caborrojeño, a Puerto Rican organization in the city that organized protests against landlords and employers who discriminated against Puerto Ricans. Two years later she joined the Club Obrero Español, a militant workers' group that was attempting to unionize the employees where she worked at the Majestic Specialties Company. Participation in the struggles supported by these two clubs, coupled with news of the 1937 Ponce massacre in which 19 Nationalists were killed and more than 100 were wounded, shaped her political vision and led her to join the Nationalist Party cell in New York and to become active in the Nationalist movement to free Puerto Rico from the United States. During the 1930s she married Justo Mercado, with whom she had two daughters, Iris and Lydia. The marriage to Mercado, however, ended in divorce a few years later, and she brought her mother to New York City to help care for the children.

In 1940 she married Oscar Collazo, one of the two Nationalists who on November 1, 1950, attacked Blair House in an attempt to kill President Harry Truman. The attack resulted in the deaths of Oscar's compatriot Griselio Torresola and of White House guard Leslie Coffelt. Oscar, captured while wounded, was tried and sentenced to death. Following Oscar's capture, Rosa was arrested on charges of collaboration to depose the government of the United States by violent means. When she could not make bail of $50,000, she was sent to the Women's House of Detention on Greenwich Street in Lower Manhattan. On December 24 her lawyer, Abraham Unger, had her released after the charges against her were dropped for lack of evidence.

Once released, she joined a campaign organized by friends of Oscar to demand that his death sentence be commuted to life in prison. Within months the campaign produced 50,000 signatures and hundreds of letters, many of them from top world figures, asking President Truman to spare Oscar Collazo's life. In July 1952 President Truman commuted Oscar's death sentence to life in prison.

Rosa remained active with the Nationalist party and in 1954 was again arrested when four Nationalists

Puerto Rican nationalists Rosa and Iris Collazo seated in the center. Courtesy of the Ruth M. Reynolds Papers. Centro Archives, Centro de Estudios Puertorriqueños, Hunter College, CUNY.

from New York launched an attack against the House of Representatives, wounding five congressmen. She was again taken to the Women's House of Detention on Greenwich Street in Lower Manhattan and charged with conspiring with the attackers to overthrow the government of the United States by force. This time she was convicted and sentenced to serve six years in the Federal Correctional Institution for Women in Alderson, West Virginia. She was joined there by Dolores (Lolita) Lebrón, one of four Nationalists convicted of the attack against the U.S. Congress. Except for the general complaint that life in prison was hard, and that she and Lolita found solace in the prison's chapel, she offered very little information about her time in prison.

Released from prison in 1960, she visited her mother in Puerto Rico and Oscar in Leavenworth, Kansas, before returning to her apartment in the Bronx and to the Nationalist Party. Her prison term and her connection to Oscar Collazo made her a minor celebrity among some Latin American revolutionaries. She was quite proud of the fact that she had met Ernesto (Ché) Guevara when he visited the United Nations in the 1960s.

In 1968, after more than forty years in New York City, she decided that it was time to return to Puerto Rico. In poor health and tired of the declining quality of life in the Bronx, where she was assaulted at knifepoint by two young drug addicts, she took her grandson Carlos Turner (Lydia's son) and moved to her mother's house in Mayagüez until Lydia arrived a year later. Together they purchased a house in Levittown, a suburb of San Juan. Lydia found a job as an art teacher, and Rosa divided her time between caring for her grandson and collaborating with the independence movement in Puerto Rico.

In 1977 Rosa became involved in a campaign that originated in Puerto Rico to free the Nationalists being held in U.S. prisons. Two years later, in September, President Jimmy Carter pardoned them, and Rosa flew to Kansas City to greet Oscar, separated from her for twenty-nine years. She accompanied him through many days of celebration in Chicago and New York. She looked forward to a life with Oscar in Puerto Rico, but the long separation and the pressures placed on Oscar by his newfound status as a hero of the independence movement dissolved the ties between the couple. She remained by Lydia's side until her death in May 1988. Oscar survived her by another six years.

See also Puerto Rican Women Political Prisoners

SOURCES: Collazo, Rosa. 1993. *Memorias de Rosa Collazo.* Compiled by Lydia Collazo Cortéz. San Juan: Gráfico; *New York Times.* 1950. "Assassin's Kin and Friends Are Rounded Up in Bronx." November 2, 1, 18; ———. 1950. "Assassin's Boasts Trapped Suspects." November 10, 24; ———. 1954. "91 Puerto Ricans Rounded Up Here." March 9, 1, 7, 21; ———. 1954. "Anti-U.S. Plot Is Laid to 17 Puerto Ricans." May 27, 1, 14; ———. 1954. "Puerto Ricans in Court." June 2, 26; ———. 1954. "13 Puerto Ricans Get 6-Year Terms." October 27, 12.

Olga Jiménez de Wagenheim

COLÓN, MIRIAM (1936–)

Actress Miriam Colón is without a doubt one of the best-known Puerto Rican actresses in America. In an industry known for its quick turnover of talent, her enviably long and distinguished career has earned her the unofficial title of "la Gran Dama" of the theater.

Colón was born on August 20, 1936, in Ponce, Puerto Rico. Her parents, Josefa Quiles and Teodoro Colón, divorced when she was very young, eventually remarried, and started new families. Throughout her early life Colón shuffled between her parents and an array of five half siblings.

Her dramatic career began while she was attending junior high school in Old San Juan. She was cast in the lead role in a school production of *La azotea* (The Roof), a play by Alvarez Quintero, directed by Marcus Colón. This first experience ignited her love for the theater. Impressed by her performance and potential, Marcus introduced Miriam to Leopoldo Santiago, head of the Department of Drama at the University of Puerto Rico (UPR). Santiago allowed Miriam to observe and participate in theatrical training classes at UPR even though she was not a student at the school or affiliated with the department in any way. For years, while she was attending high school, she sat in on evening classes at the university. Although she did not gain academic credit for her involvement, the practice she received helped her develop the commitment and presence necessary to succeed on the stage. She was eventually placed in the university's traveling theater, an experience that proved pivotal in later years. This early exposure to high-level training left an indelible mark on young Colón that set her on a course for eventual stardom.

After completing high school she officially entered the theater program at UPR to continue her theatrical studies and hone her talents. Hers was a unique situation. She had already had years of theatrical training and experience at the university and could not be expected to register in basic acting classes. In recognition of her level of achievement and talent, a special scholarship was established for Colón that allowed her to come to the United States and continue her training in New York. She studied for two years at the Dramatic Workshop and Technical Institute on Broadway under the direction of Erwin Piscator. Afterward she auditioned for and was accepted into the Actors' Studio, where she studied for several more years. A role in the Broadway production of *Summer House* was the first of several in which she was recognized for her talent.

In 1956 she moved to Hollywood to reprise her Off-Broadway role in *Me, Candido.* During her time in California she had the opportunity to act in major shows and films, including two with Marlon Brando, *One-Eyed Jacks* and *The Appaloosa.* After seven years on the West Coast she returned to New York City, where she met her first husband, George P. Edgar, a securities analyst, whom she married in 1966.

Since the early 1950s Colón has performed countless roles in films, television, and theater that have garnered her national and international acclaim. Among

Actor Miriam Colón, 1958. Courtesy of the Justo A. Martí Photograph Collection. Centro Archives, Centro de Estudios Puertorriqueños, Hunter College, CUNY.

these are *Almost a Woman* (2002), *All the Pretty Horses* (2000), *The Blue Diner* (2000), *Lone Star* (1996), *A Life of Sin* (1992), *The Lightning Incident* (1991), *The Possession of Joel Delaney* (1972), *The Outsider* (1961), and *One-Eyed Jacks* (1961). She has received honorary doctorates from Montclair State College, St. Peter's College, Marymount Manhattan College, and Rutgers University and the Presidential Medal from Brooklyn College, New York.

Of all the accomplishments for which Colón can take credit, the one that she is most proud of is founding the Puerto Rican Traveling Theater (PRTT), formally incorporated in 1967 as a nonprofit organization. Its original intention was to take the theater to the streets and bring it to poor neighborhoods. It has grown to include acting classes in both English and Spanish, signing body movement, improvisations, and a playwrights' unit. Her inspiration for PRTT was the early training she received in the University of Puerto Rico's Traveling Theater. Not only has PRTT played an important part in Colón's professional life, it has also played an equally important role in her personal life. It was at an audition for a PRTT production of *The Oxcart* that she met Dr. Fred Valle, a plastic surgeon who was auditioning for a part in the play. They eventually married and have made a home in New York. Today Colón is still at the helm of PRTT as its creative director and driving force, providing a protected and nurturing environment for the development of future Latino artists.

See also Theater

SOURCES: *Latina*. 1998. "La Gran Dama del Teatro." June. http://www.latina.com/new/magazine/books/98/story2.html (accessed July 26, 2002); Newlon, Clarke. 1975. *Famous Puerto Ricans*. New York: Dodd, Mead; TVTome.com. n.d. "Miriam Colón Biographical Information." http://www.tvtome.com/tvtome/servlet/PersonDetail/personid-8710 (accessed November 2, 2003).

Georgina García

COLÓN, RUFA CONCEPCIÓN FERNÁNDEZ "CONCHA" (1903–1958)

Rufa Concepción Fernández, known to her family and friends as Concha, was born in 1903 in San Juan, Puerto Rico. Her parents were José Fernández and Guadalupe Bernat. According to her steamship cabin ticket, Concha arrived in New York City on January 29, 1925. On December 31 of that year she wed her fiancé, Jesús Colón. Concha Colón lived in Brooklyn with her husband for thirty-two years and died on June 25, 1958, of "natural causes." Much of what is known about Concha Colón is found in the Jesús Colón Collection housed in the archives of the Center for Puerto Rican Studies at Hunter College in New York City.

The early letters written between Concha and Jesús Colón reflect the struggles of migration and acculturation and the difficulties in maintaining a long-distance relationship. They illustrate Concha Colón's preparedness for the vicissitudes of daily life in the city. In these letters her fiancé encouraged her to complete her education. In and of itself, a diploma meant little to him; her kindness and character were what he valued. However, he told her that education determined the quality of employment in the city and, therefore, the quality of her life. Concha completed her high school education in Puerto Rico and later listed her occupation as "clerk." She became politically active alongside her husband. As his secretary, Concha assisted in the founding of various community and grassroots organizations in the fledgling New York Puerto Rican barrio. Through her letters and activism Concha Colón became a link between the home culture of Puerto Rico and the host culture of New York, especially Brooklyn. For Jésus Colón, Concha was a conduit of information, the anchor for his cultural values, family news, and local home events. She eased the struggles of those seeking jobs and a better life in the city during the early decades. Later her kindness and generosity were documented and eulogized by a community that saw Jesús and Concha Colón as community leaders and looked to them for direction and guidance.

Jesús Colón wrote an essay titled "My Wife Doesn't Work" (translated from "Mi mujer no trabaja") for a workers' newsletter titled *Oye, Boricua,* but it was not published until 1993 in *The Way It Was and Other Writings*. In this satirical essay Jesús Colón wrote that when men boast, "My wife doesn't work," what they really mean is "I don't want my wife to work outside the home because other women at the office or the factory can spoil her. (These men always emphasize the term *mi mujer* as if she was a possession.)." Colón wrote that when men get home from work, a few sweet terms of endearment get them their dinner, a can of cold beer, and even their slippers, while women's work was unending, tireless, and unpaid. He added that someday women would earn their own daily allowance and be part of the working class. By all known accounts, Jesús Colón made sure that his wife, Concha, was his equal partner, and together they helped to raise political consciousness on this and many other issues concerning El Barrio.

The world of the Puerto Rican migrant from the 1920s through the 1950s was, in general, characterized by meager wages, inadequate health care, substandard housing conditions, marginal education, and poor sanitation conditions. Yet, at the same time, it was a period of increasing growth in the population of Puerto Ricans seeking better jobs and opportunities. Concha Colón stood alongside her husband and helped develop community leadership through their many organizations and campaigns for unionization. She became the secretary of la Liga Puertorriqueña e Hispana, which fostered mutual aid in the collective struggle and solidarity with all Hispanics in New York City. Much like her husband, she

Community organizer Rufa Concepción Fernández "Concha" Colón, 1925. Courtesy of the Jesús Colón Papers. Centro Archives, Centro de Estudios Puertorriqueños, Hunter College, CUNY.

believed in the "people's capacity to achieve revolutionary change."

Concha Colón left no wills or archival papers, but the letters, pictures, poems, and articles she felt important enough to preserve reflect her politics, her concern for her community, and her position as partner and confidante of Jesús Colón. Her daily life and routine tasks were in part contributions to the growth and acculturation of the New York Puerto Rican community.

SOURCES: Colón, Jesús. 1993. *The Way It Was and Other Writings*. Edited by Edna Acosta-Belén and Virginia Sánchez Korrol. Houston: Arte Público Press; ———. Jesús Colón Collection, Center for Puerto Rican Studies Library and Archives, Hunter College, CUNY; Matos Rodríguez, Félix, and Linda C. Delgado, eds. 1998. "Rufa Concepción Fernández: The Role of Gender in the Migration Process." In *Puerto Rican Women's History: New Perspectives*. Armonk, NY: M. E. Sharpe.

Linda C. Delgado

COMISIÓN FEMENIL MEXICANA NACIONAL (CFMN) (1970–)

In 1970 women at the Mexican American National Issues Conference in Sacramento, California, convened a workshop. Under the leadership of Francisca Flores and Simmie Romero, both longtime activists in the Mexican American community of Los Angeles, and in response to the male domination of Chicano politics and the noninclusion and racism in the feminist movement, approximately forty women at the workshop founded one of the first Chicana feminist organizations in the nation, the Comisión Femenil Mexicana Nacional (National Mexican Women's Commission). They identified their mission as leadership, dissemination of information, problem solving for Chicanas/Mexicanas, and networking with other women's organizations and movements.

The Comisión provided Chicanas with opportunities for leadership and mentoring. Since Comisión members varied in age from their early twenties through their late sixties, a de facto mentorship program emerged as the older women, many of whom had engaged in political activism during the 1940s and before, guided the younger women in the realms of political strategy and leadership.

In 1972 the Comisión Femenil established the Chicana Service Action Center (CSAC), which still operates today. As part of the Comisión Femenil's vision of economic empowerment for Mexican American women, the Chicana Service Action Center, with start-up funds from the U.S. Department of Labor, began to provide job training for women with low incomes and lack of skills. Through strong networking by the founders of the Chicana Service Action Center, the program pulled together resources for training women that included the Los Angeles County Department of Social Services, Southern California Edison, and the White House.

During the 1970s the Comisión Femenil also opened a battered women's shelter and two bilingual and bicultural child-care centers (centros de niños), organized a national Chicana conference in Goleta, California, attended the United Nations–sponsored International Women's Year Tribune in Mexico City in 1975, helped formulate both the Hispanic women's plank and the minority women's plank for the National Women's Conference in Houston in 1977, participated in the 1975 lawsuit *Madrigal v. Quilligan* (a struggle waged to end forced sterilization of Latinas at the University of Southern California–Los Angeles County Medical Center), and established more than twenty chapters nationwide. In 1978 members of the Comisión Femenil attended the National Equal Rights Amendment March in Washington, D.C., and in 1980 several members were present at the United Nations Mid-Decade Conference on Women in Copenhagen, Denmark. In 1982, continuing its community programs, the Comisión Femenil established Casa Victoria, a treatment center for adolescent girls.

The Comisión steered a course of engagement with the Chicana community that ventured beyond political rhetoric and produced tangible representations of its vision for Chicanas. Because of its explicit Chicana orientation, its successful community programs, and its establishment of a viable Chicana leadership, the Comisión stands as one of the most important Chicana organizations of the twentieth century. Within the contexts of Chicana/o and women's history, the Comisión Femenil Mexicana Nacional provides an alternative framework for understanding women's activism because it reveals a link to pre–Chicano movement politics. Through its physical, emotional, and political community building, the Comisión Femenil went beyond consciousness-raising to provide concrete solutions to the problems many Chicanas faced in labor and political leadership.

The Comisión did not arise out of a vacuum. Without the experiences of its founders in political organizing for more than three decades, which entailed originating organizations, networking, building alliances, running electoral campaigns, registering voters, and providing the so-called organizational backbone, the Comisión Femenil itself would never have been founded. Although the political vision, goals, strategies, and structure of the Comisión Femenil resonate with past associations, the organization of the group and its immediate predecessor, the League of Mexican American Women, stands within the context of the social movements of the 1960s and 1970s. The previous generation, dubbed the "Mexican-American Generation" by historian Mario T. García, was unified under the shared experiences of living through the Great Depression, World War II, and the cold war, a political ideology based on a profound and sometimes patriotic belief in democracy, and a hope for social reform. The Comisión is a prime example of what historian Vicki L. Ruiz has identified as one of the foundations of Chicana feminisms: leadership that empowers others. The Comisión Femenil's founders took to heart ideas about inclusion and self-determination and focused on Mexican American women. By building on the activism of women in the previous generation and effectively negotiating state, local, and national politics to build concrete and lasting institutions serving Latinas, the Comisión Femenil became a viable and powerful organization.

See also Chicano Movement; Feminism

SOURCES: Chávez, Marisela R. 2004. "Despierten Hermanas y Hermanos: Women, the Chicano Movement, and Chicana Feminisms in California, 1966–1978." Ph.D. diss., Stanford University; García, Alma M. 1989. "The Development of Chicana Feminist Discourse, 1970–1980." *Gender and Society* 3:217–238; García, Mario T. 1989. *Mexican Americans: Leadership, Ideology, and Identity, 1930–1960*. New Haven: Yale University Press; "History of the Comisión Femenil Mexicana, Nacional, Inc." Comisión Femenil Mexicana National Archives, California Ethnic and Multicultural Archives, University of California, Santa Barbara. http://cemaweb.library.ucsb.edu/cfmn_history.html (accessed February 17, 2004); Ruiz, Vicki L. 1998. *From out of the Shadows: Mexican Women in Twentieth-Century America*. New York: Oxford University Press.

Marisela R. Chávez

COMMUNIST PARTY

The complex relations of Latinas and the Communist Party of the United States (CPUSA) are obscured in historical accounts by red-baiting, blacklisting, fear, and historical amnesia. Yet Juan Gómez Quiñones estimates that "perhaps over five hundred" Mexicans belonged to the Communist Party. Many more worked with and supported Communist and progressive organizing that, as many said, "helped the working people." Latinos were attracted to the CPUSA, founded in 1919, because the group organized the unemployed, supported strikers, and fought for the civil rights of people of color. In short, the CPUSA addressed issues that concerned most working-class Latinos. Abysmal working conditions, racism, political disenfranchisement, discrimination, violence, and segregation also contributed to making Latinos as a group open to working with the CPUSA.

Mexicans involved in labor and other struggles in Mexico and across the Southwest had been exposed to left-wing ideology and harbored little of the staunch anti-Communism of the United States. Some Mexicans had participated in or were affected by the binational and multiracial alliance of the anarcho-syndicalist Partido Liberal Mexicano (PLM) and the Industrial Workers of the World (IWW). The IWW and PLM, which organized together across Mexico and the Southwest, provided a model for later cooperation between Mexicans and Euro-American on the left. Mexicans had also been affected by the Mexican Revolution of 1910–1920.

The CPUSA hierarchy, the Comintern, and the Mexican Communist Party, however, did not envision Mexicans in the United States as part of their collective or individual strategies. The CPUSA as a whole ignored Mexicans as a group. The CPUSA seemed oblivious to Mexican organizing, sent non-Spanish-speaking organizers to Mexican areas, at times refused to aid Mexican leftists facing legal action, and shut down its Spanish-language newspaper in 1938. Yet a number of CPUSA organizers, such as Dorothy Ray Healey, Stanley Hancock, and Pat Chambers, worked closely with Mexican leftists in struggles across the United States.

Mexican leftists joined the CPUSA and formed Spanish-speaking CP cells and branches of the Young Communist League (YCL). They organized in their own communities and worked with various unions and movements. Communists in the border regions had frequent contact with their counterparts in northern Mexico. Although Mexican Communists are usually obscured in historical accounts, they were critical to the CPUSA's successes in strikes and organizing, especially in the Southwest. Mexican leftists sought out support from CP allies and sympathizers in strikes, and they formulated strategy and acted as conduits between Euro-American organizers and workers.

Texas-born Emma Tenayuca became one of the best-known Latinas in the CPUSA. As a teenager, she supported striking cigar and garment workers in San Antonio, took on the city's political machine, and in 1935 became secretary of the West Side Unemployed Council. She joined the Workers' Alliance in 1936 and was appointed to the organization's National Executive Committee the same year. In 1937 she became a member of the Communist Party. Tenayuca is best known for her leading role in the 1938 strike by 10,000 pecan shellers in San Antonio. She and Homer Brooks, her husband and secretary of the Communist Party in Texas, coauthored the only CP tract on the Nationalist question as it concerned Mexicans. Although she left the Communist Party after the Hitler-Stalin pact, she remained a socialist. She said, "I don't think that women or any of the minorities will ever be completely and totally free until you have socialism." Other women, such as Manuel Solis-Sager of San Antonio, also worked closely with the CPUSA.

Guatemalan-born Luisa Moreno worked as an organizer with the United Cannery, Agricultural, Packing, and Allied Workers of America (UCAPAWA) and was principal organizer of el Congreso de Pueblos de Hablan Española (Congress of Spanish-Speaking Peoples). A year before the organization was established in 1939, she traveled around the country, contacting labor unions and local *mutualistas* and forming pro-Congreso clubs, which became the base of el Congreso. At the founding convention Mexicans, who represented three-fourths of those present, were joined by Puerto Ricans, Cubans, Spaniards, and other Latin Americans from around the country. The Congreso stressed the unity of all Spanish speakers in the United States, supported labor organizing, defended immigrant workers, and backed Republican Spain. The Congreso also supported progressive New Deal politics against mounting criticism and advocated an end to discrimination in education, employment, and housing.

Latinas were a crucial part of the progressive Congreso. Josefina Fierro de Bright helped Moreno organize the Congreso's meeting and became its first executive secretary. Fierro de Bright was the daughter of an anarchist mother, Josefina Arancibia, who had belonged to the Partido Liberal Mexicano. Fiarro had learned organizing while traveling around to labor camps with her mother as they cooked food for campesinos and explained to them their rights as workers. Women were a priority for the Congreso, which formed a women's committee and stipulated that women were required to be represented on the executive committee. Approximately 30 percent of the Congreso's membership was women. The degree to which the Communist Party was involved in el Congreso remains debated among historians. Juan Gómez-Quiñones and Mario García squarely set the organization within the popular-front strategy of the CP, while George Sánchez downplays the party's influence in this first civil rights assembly among Latinos, but certainly two of its principal organizers, Fierro de Bright and Moreno, had been party members.

Latinas were also an integral part of the Asociación Nacional México-Americana (ANMA), founded in 1949. ANMA was formed by Mexican members of progressive unions, in particular the Mine, Mill, and Smelter Workers Union. ANMA, recognizing the value of women, focused on organizing around families. Women were also prominent within the organization. Ramón Welch, a former local leader in el Congreso and member of the CPUSA, was ANMA's publicity director. Isabel Gonzáles served as the vice president, Virginia X. Ruiz was the first secretary general, and Florencia Luna was the first secretary-treasurer. Other women were also active, such as Grace Montañez, Mary Jasso, Amelia Camacho, Virginia Montoya, Carmen Contreras, and Dolores Heredia. ANMA faced an uphill battle as a fledgling civil rights organization with CP members in the cold war era. Again, historians have debated the extent of the direct influence of the Communist Party in ANMA. The relationship between Latinas and the CPUSA remains obscure, but further research will eventually demonstrate the importance of those who supported progressive community and labor organizing and worked in sympathy with the Communist Party.

SOURCES: García, Mario T. 1989. *Mexican Americans: Leadership, Ideology, and Identity, 1930–1960*. New Haven, CT: Yale University Press; Gómez-Quiñones, Juan. 1994. *Mexican American Labor, 1790–1990*. Albuquerque: University of New Mexico Press; Ruiz, Vicki L. 1998. *From out of the Shadows: Mexican Women in Twentieth-Century America*. New York: Oxford University Press; Tenayuca, Emma. 1987. Oral history interview by Jerry Poyo, February 21. http://www.texancultures.utsa.edu/memories/htms/Tenayuca_transcript (accessed August 10, 2003); Vargas, Zaragosa. 1997. "Tejana Radical: Emma Tenayuca and the San Antonio Labor Movement during the Great Depression." *Pacific Historical Review* 66 no. 4: 553–580.

Devra A. Weber

COMMUNITIES ORGANIZED FOR PUBLIC SERVICE (COPS) (1974–)

For more than thirty years Communities Organized for Public Service (COPS), a grassroots organization in San Antonio, Texas, has fundamentally altered the political and physical landscape of the tenth-largest city in the United States. Based on the principles of legendary organizer Saul Alinsky, COPS reflects not only the hopes and dreams of Latinos and African Americans who live in West Side and South Side neighborhoods but also represents their substantial political empowerment. In 1973, with the support of local Roman Catholic parishes, especially parish women, Ernie Cortés Jr. began to organize neighbor by neighbor in San Antonio's West Side. This grassroots approach drives the infrastructure of COPS, with leadership emerging from these local networks. As in Mothers of East Los Angeles (MELA), women's voluntary parish work now became channeled to civic improvement, and indeed, Tejanas have often been elected president of the organization.

In 1974 COPS called a public meeting with a city manager at the local high school to address issues of drainage problems and dirt roads in West Side neighborhoods. According to the former mayor of San Antonio and Clinton cabinet member Henry Cisneros, the area was so poor that the Peace Corps trained new recruits there. More than 500 people attended the meeting, and the city manager seemed at a loss in the face of both the numbers of concerned citizens and the thorough research conducted by COPS members. Through the use of demonstrations, political mobilization, research, and negotiation, COPS has significantly improved the material conditions of West Side and South Side neighborhoods. Focusing on municipal issues and boards, members of the twenty-six chapters of COPS ensure that developers, planners, school administrators, city officials, and North Side politicians do not ride roughshod over their communities. They have also been active in local utility and environmental issues and opposed the funneling of more than $1 million of federal urban renewal funds into a suburban country club. COPS also engages in voter registration drives, and while it is committed to nonpartisanship, its members closely monitor the positions taken by local politicians.

Tejanas have played key roles during the organization's three decades. According to former COPS president Beatrice Cortez, "Women have community ties. We knew that to make things happen in the community, you have to talk to people. It was a matter of tapping our networks." While one political scientist considered COPS's reliance on "housewives" as an inherent weakness of the organization, other scholars have contextualized women's leadership in COPS as part of a long history of women's community organizing in the United States and more particularly as representing a strong tradition of Latina grassroots political action. For its local accomplishments, COPS was recognized in 1995 by a United Nations panel as one of the fifty winners of the We the Peoples: Community Awards, one of nine U.S.-based organizations so honored. On the COPS page linked to the award's website, its mission is stated frankly and clearly: "COPS is committed to neighbourhood and family values, democratic participation, leadership development, and public accountability of local and state officials."

Unlike other community-based organizations in which leverage seems to rise and ebb, COPS continues to be a respected grassroots confederation with considerable municipal power. As a model for community empowerment, COPS has brought more than $750 million for affordable housing, public works improvements, recreation, and education. Members study the issues, attend city council meetings, write grants, and organize voters around municipal issues. In 2002 the city council considered the development of PGA Village, an almost 3,000-acre project with significant environmental impact and with the creation of a special taxing district where the developers would "collect and retain all of the property, sales, and hotel-motel taxes for the next fifteen years." Although council member Julián Castro (the son of Chicano movement activist Rosie Castro) had led an impassioned dissent against the project, the city council approved the development project with only two objections. COPS swung into action, collecting more than 68,000 signatures to put the approval of PGA Village to the voters as a citywide referendum. According to journalist Cecilia Ballí, the developers withdrew the project "and have entered negotiations on a compromise."

In addition to urban renewal, land-use, and environmental issues, COPS is also fundamentally committed to educational initiatives. Members were largely responsible for the passage of a major bond issue for the funding of libraries and literacy centers and lobbied successfully for a community college on San Antonio's West Side. In partnership with a local business confederation, the Metro Alliance, COPS has initiated a program to provide jobs or college scholarships to high-school students who both maintain good grades and have an almost perfect attendance record. The organization is also concerned with affordable health care and community policing initiatives. Local Catholic parishes continue to be the backbone of the organization, and priests and nuns, such as Sister Consuelo Tovar, have participated fully in the organization.

While it is an overstatement to assert that slums no longer exist in San Antonio, COPS has dramatically reconfigured West Side and South Side neighborhoods. As political scientist Joseph Sekul stated, "COPS has taken giant steps toward raising the quality of life in older neighborhoods, some of which may now become places where people can stay if they choose, rather than leave because they must." Ernie Cortés Jr., the founding organizer, perhaps best summed up its impact on the political education of San Antonio's Tejano and African American population: "COPS is like a university where people come to learn about public policy, public discourse, and public life."

SOURCES: Ballí, Cecilia. 2002. "Twin Peaks." *Texas Monthly,* October 1989; Communities Organized for Public Service, USA. http://www.iisd.org/50comm/commdb/desc/d19.htm (accessed October 6, 2004); Evans, Sara. *Born for Liberty: History of Women in America.* New York: Free Press; Ruiz, Vicki L. 1998. *From out of the Shadows: Mexican Women in Twentieth-Century America.* New York: Oxford University Press.

Vicki L. Ruiz

COMMUNITY SERVICE ORGANIZATION (CSO) (1947–1995)

Documentation has begun to reveal the involvement of Latinas in various types of labor and political movements. Biographies of women such as Emma Tenayuca, Luisa Moreno, Lucia González Parsons, and Dolores Huerta now exist. However, a place where the Latina presence is often less well documented is in grassroots civic and mutual-aid societies.

Mutual-aid societies took root in the history of Mexicans in the Southwest from the earliest settlements of the 1600s. They evolved for a variety of reasons. Most important was the building of community, group protection, and self-benefit. In these societies the role of women is often unrecorded. In the Community Service Organization (CSO) in Los Angeles, numerous men were associated with the leadership of the group, but the role of women was also important. Throughout the life of the organization various women emerged in leadership positions as directors of programs, administrators, and program developers.

Research on the founding of the Community Service Organization in 1947 has yielded valuable information. Of the thirty individuals listed as founding members, thirteen were women. Life-history interviews document the lives and motivating factors of ten of the women, and one interview focused on the daughter of an original female founder.

The CSO earned its place in Los Angeles Mexican American history because it helped elect Edward Roybal, who won the city council seat for the Ninth District in 1949. He was the first Mexican American to hold such a position in seventy-five years. The CSO undertook an unprecedented voter registration and citizenship drive. The voter registration drive proved to be one of the CSO's most successful projects. In the first three months of the drive the number of registered Mexican Americans in the Ninth Council District increased by 15,000, and seventeen new precincts were created in the Belvedere area alone.

It was primarily in membership and voter registration drives that CSO women took the lead. They organized citizenship classes and produced bilingual materials. Opening their homes for meetings (the CSO did not have an office in its beginning days), Lupe Morales, Lucy Rios, Lucille Roybal, María Durán, and other women invited family and neighbors and introduced them to CSO concepts and goals. Meetings were held all over Boyle Heights, in East Los Angeles, and in county areas like Watts, El Monte, Lincoln Heights, and the San Fernando Valley. In two years the CSO developed from a thirty-member core group into a 3,000-member civic action group dedicated to "helping people help themselves." The CSO women were in the vanguard of this movement.

Interviews with Marian Graff, Ursula Gutiérrez, Estelle Guzmán, Carmen Méndez, Margarita Durán Méndez, Lupe Morales, Lucy Rios, Lucille Roybal, Mary Sparkhul, and Henrietta Vellaescusa shed light on who these women of the early (1947 to 1953) CSO movement were. While the Mexican women of this era were often described as poorly educated, unskilled recent immigrants, the founding women of the CSO did not generally fit this image. With the exception of Durán Méndez and Villaescusa, CSO women did not call themselves Chicanas. Most identified as Mexican Americans. In fact, Carmen Méndez joined the CSO as a way to validate her ethnic identity, something she felt that the schools had tried to denigrate. Essentially, CSO women formed part of the generation that first called itself "Mexican American." They were the antecedents of the Chicana/o baby-boom generation.

Of the eleven women who were founding members of the CSO, only two had been born in Mexico. The rest had been born in the United States. Estelle Guzmán specifically stated that her family had been in New Mexico "since day one," meaning since the days of the first Spanish settlements. Lucille Roybal, the candidate's wife, called herself a Californio, stating that her mother's family had been in California when it was still Mexico. Henrietta Villaescusa recalled that she and her father were born in the same house in Tucson, Arizona. Many came of age during the Great Depression or World War II and witnessed the deportation of Mexicans in the 1930s and 1950s, the zoot-suit riots, and the Sleepy Lagoon murder case in Los Angeles.

In education CSO women also did not follow the path of most Mexican women. Only one did not graduate from high school: Estelle Guzmán received an A.A. degree. Henrietta Villaescusa and Mary Sparkhul became registered nurses, and Villaescusa received a B.A. and an M.A. in public health. Margarita Durán Méndez was one of the first Chicanas to receive a B.A. in political science from UCLA in 1946. In 1950 she earned an M.S.W. from the University of Southern California. Durán Méndez retired in the late 1980s as chief of the Northeast Mental Health District of Los Angeles County. She is credited statewide with developing innovative programs to serve mental health patients, specifically Latinas/os. When the CSO was founded, three of the women were students, only two were housewives, and five were employed full-time in occupations ranging from factory workers to secretaries and salesclerks.

As volunteers, the women shaped leadership in various ways. Lucille Roybal recalls, "We learned as we went along." As members of the organizing committees, the women were guaranteed full rights as members, including voting rights. "I didn't join the League of United Latin American Citizens [LULAC] because women were brought in only as an auxiliary group.

CSO granted us full membership with full voting rights. Also in LULAC you could only speak English. In the CSO Spanish was allowed. In fact, most meetings were bilingual," said Lucy Rios. The CSO was supported by Saul Alinsky's Industrial Areas Foundation, which produced funds for a community organizer, Fred Ross, a secretary, Carmen Méndez, and an office. However, most of the internal fund-raising was handled by Durán Méndez.

Margarita Durán Méndez was an important player in the early days of the CSO and a staunch supporter of labor, civil, and women's rights. Independent and outspoken, Durán Méndez brought financial and in-kind support from the United Steel Workers' Union, the International Ladies Garment Workers' Union, the NAACP, and the Jewish community. As a member of the executive committee of the CSO, she ensured that women's rights and visibility would be protected. CSO women looked to Durán Méndez as a role model and leader.

The spirit of organizing and the dramatic leadership by the women of the CSO continued to enhance this important and representative organization. In time the CSO had nineteen chapters throughout California and Arizona. In the 1950s César Chávez and Dolores Huerta joined the CSO through individual chapters in San Jose and Stockton. In the CSO they learned skills in organizing and advocacy that later brought them international recognition as leaders of the United Farm Workers.

In Los Angeles in the ensuing years the CSO came to be the representative group for Latinos and Latinas in East Los Angeles. In 1964, under the direction of Flavia Vásquez, the CSO opened a credit union. Margot Benavides started a second CSO credit union in 1968. Ursula Gutiérrez organized community members to act as an advisory group; she served as president of the CSO during the 1960s. In 1971 Margaret Gutiérrez developed and directed the PADRES Program. PADRES (Parents Activated for the Development of Relevant Education) provided after-school programs for first and second graders and their parents. In the 1980s, under the leadership of Rosario Vásquez, the CSO in Los Angeles County became a clearinghouse for the 1986 Immigration Reform and Control Act. Simultaneously the CSO assisted families with homes in foreclosure through a Department of Housing and Urban Development program. The Los Angeles CSO remained open and functioning under the leadership of Rosario Vásquez until October 1995.

SOURCES: Apodaca, M. Linda. 1994. "They Kept the Home Fires Burning: Mexican American Women and Social Change." Ph.D. diss., University of California, Irvine; ———. 1999. "Mexican American Women and Social Change: The Founding of the CSO in L.A., an Overall History." Working Paper Series, University of Arizona, no. 27, January; Gutiérrez, David G. 1998. *Walls and Mirrors.* Berkeley: University of California Press.

Linda Apodaca

CONGRESO DEL PUEBLO (1956–)

As Puerto Ricans consolidated a significant presence in New York City during the early decades of the twentieth century, hometown clubs emerged as one of this community's most important forms of organization. Hometown clubs were primarily cultural and social organizations established by Puerto Rican working-class migrants in New York City on the basis of their towns of origin on the island. The earliest, such as the associations for Arecibo, Yauco, Rincón, San Germán, and Cabo Rojo, were founded in the 1930s. In the post–World War II period, as the size of the Puerto Rican population in the city mushroomed from 61,463 in 1940 to 612,574 in 1960, community leaders established additional hometown clubs. For example, in 1958 migrants from the town of Barceloneta organized the Hijos de Barceloneta, while those from the city of Mayagüez founded the Círculo Cívico y Cultural de Mayagüez in 1959. Migrants from the town of Aguada formed the Club Social Aguadeño in 1962.

In 1956, under the guidance of the respected community leader Gilberto Gerena Valentín, a pioneer who had lived in El Barrio since 1936 and a human rights commissioner, many hometown clubs banded together to form the Congreso del Pueblo, a self-supported, voluntary organization that functioned as a conference of hometown clubs. According to Gerena Valentín, who became president of the Congreso, in addition to their role as cultural and social organizations, hometown clubs operated as mutual-aid societies and played an important role in the settlement of Puerto Rican migrants in the city. They helped newcomers with English and those in need with clothing, food, job referrals, and medical assistance. Moreover, existing clubs aided and encouraged the formation of new clubs so as to ensure that all new settlers form Puerto Rico would find an organization representing their town of origin that would welcome and be of help to them.

Hometown clubs also played an important role in the political life of the Puerto Rican community in New York. Some became important political centers. The Congreso del Pueblo considered cultural traditions an important force in the political struggle for Puerto Rican civil rights and sought the proliferation and amalgamation of hometown clubs as a vehicle for addressing political and economic issues, as well as the

Puerto Rican Day Parade, New York City. Courtesy of the Offices of the Government of Puerto Rico in the United States. Centro Archives, Centro de Estudios Puertorriqueños, Hunter College, CUNY.

social and cultural problems confronting recent Puerto Rican migrants in cities across the nation.

At its height in the 1960s the Congreso del Pueblo comprised some eighty hometown clubs throughout New York City and helped lead campaigns for improved housing and educational and employment opportunities, as well as mass protests against discrimination, racism, and police brutality. The Congreso was also instrumental in the organization of the Puerto Rican Day Parade, which was first held in 1959 as a highly visible demonstration of ethnic pride and political unity.

SOURCES: Ribes Tovar, Federico. 1970. *The Puerto Rican Heritage Encyclopedia: The Puerto Rican in New York*. New York: Plus Ultra Educational Publishers; Valentín, Gilberto Gerena. 2002. Interview by Carlos Sanabria, October.

Carlos Sanabria

CÓRDOVA, LINA (1921–)

Lina Córdova was born in Peña Blanca, New Mexico, a small town about an hour's drive from Albuquerque, in 1921. She was the eighth of fifteen children, but one of only five who lived past the age of four. Lina Córdova's father, Jacóbo Martínez, was a sheepherder and worked as a coal miner during the Great Depression. He also farmed wheat, which he took to grind at a mill north of the town. "I used to love seeing the big piles of wheat," Córdova recalls. "I used to say, 'It looks like gold.' "

Life was tough in the Southwest in those days. Before World War I her father was tending sheep in the Magdalena Mountains. One night bandidos came and blindfolded him before making off with all of his lambs. They took him to Magdalena, twenty miles away, and dropped him off. That meant that he had to walk to his home in Socorro thirty miles away. While he was going there, his feet suffered frostbite. He then had to walk to Albuquerque (another seventy-five miles) to get medical care. "They had to amputate the toes from both feet, and for that reason he did not go to service in World War I," Córdova recalls.

When her father died in 1936, her mother, Fulgenica Martínez, had to support their family. She worked in a sewing factory, which they used to call "the Sewing Project." To help the family, one of her brothers taught school during the winter and attended a local university during the summer. Córdova attended a public school and was taught by Catholic nuns because there was a shortage of teachers. "I didn't know a word of English when I went to school," she said. "With the sisters, you had to learn or else. They were very strict."

In the summer of 1938, when Córdova was fifteen years old, she met her husband. Alfredo Córdova was very popular because he was the only young person with a car. One summer day, as she was walking with her cousin, they heard a car coming up the road. "Just as we got to a big cottonwood tree by the road, the car pulled up," Lina Córdova said. She met Alfredo that day but did not see him again until fall, when school resumed. They did not date until she was sixteen, and they were married in May 1940, toward the end of her senior year.

Alfredo and Lina Córdova moved to Albuquerque to live with Alfredo's parents while he searched for a job. He found a position working at a restaurant, serving ice cream and milkshakes for fifteen cents an hour. "It was hard days for us," she said. "It was the end of the Depression, but it was still hard." Her first child was stillborn, but in 1941 she gave birth to a baby girl, Naida. In 1942, she had a son, Alfredo Jr. Instead of going to a doctor for the deliveries, she went to a midwife, who charged $25 for a male and $20 for a female. She laughed when recalling that midwives charged more for a male than a female, saying that she did not know why there was a price difference.

In 1943 the Córdovas went to San Diego, California, because Alfredo had heard that there were jobs there. He was successful in finding work, and they bought two acres of land, on which they planned to build a house. But just as their new life began, Alfredo was drafted into the army. The family decided to move back to Albuquerque before he reported for duty. Alfredo Córdova paid $150 for a Plymouth, and the same day they began a three-day journey back to Albuquerque.

Lina Córdova. Courtesy of the U.S. Latino and Latina World War II Oral History Project. University of Texas, Austin.

After Alfredo Córdova left for the war—he fought in combat infantry in France, Germany, and Austria—Lina Córdova and her two children lived with his parents. Her in-laws insisted on taking the tires off the car because they did not believe that women should be driving. Lina Córdova said that that was the way women were treated then, but she has seen the roles of women change drastically. "When I was young, every decision was made by my husband," she said. Today, she has an equal voice. "I guess he figured sometimes my ideas were better than his," she said. "So we'd work it out."

Lina Córdova prayed each night for her husband's safe return from the European battlefields of World War II. "I used to pray every night. Every night I would pray, 'Please God, bring him home,' " Córdova said. "I didn't care how he (came) home,—without an arm or without a leg—as long as he came home to me and the kids."

While Alfredo Córdova was away, Lina Córdova wrote him two or three times a week. When he wrote back, the letters were sometimes censored, with some passages blacked out. She sent him packages with cans of Vienna sausages and cookies. To make the cookies, she cut back on the rationed sugar used in other things and saved up for her baking. Other items she recalls being rationed included gasoline and nylon stockings. The nylon stockings were seventy-five cents per pair, and each woman was allowed only two pairs if they were available.

While her husband was away, Lina Córdova recalled sitting on the front porch writing letters to him. She sometimes saw the faint glow of tiny bicycle headlights approaching. She knew that bicycles delivered telegrams with bad news about wounded or dead soldiers, and she prayed that this bicycle would not be for her, bringing her bad news about Alfredo. "One night they gave me a scare. (The messenger) was looking for an address. My heart sank. Luckily, it was not for me," she said.

Lina Córdova scoured local papers, which ran the names of men returning from the war. One day, she found Alfredo Córdova's name on such a list, two years after he had left. After his return, the Córdovas had a third child, a daughter they named Dorothy. Recalling her past experiences, Lina Córdova concluded, "God was good to me."

See also World War II

SOURCES: Córdova, Lina. 2002. Interview by Maggie Rivas-Rodríguez, Albuquerque Vet Center, November 2; Sayre, Katherine. 2003. "Wife Remembers Sending Cookies, Letters to Her Soldier." *Narratives: Stories of U.S. Latinos and Latinas and World War II* (U.S. Latino and Latina WWII Oral History Project. University of Texas at Austin) 4, no. 1 (Spring).

Katherine Sayre

CORRIDOS

One of the oldest forms used to record historical data is oral tradition. The Mexican *corrido* (ballad) is included in this tradition. *Corridos* or folk songs operate as literary texts by telling a story and providing entertainment. More important, they emerge as social documents that detail the daily life and vast experiences of Mexicans and Mexican Americans on both sides of the U.S.-Mexico border throughout the nineteenth and twentieth centuries. The diverse issues and emotions explored in *corridos* (immigration, honor and vengeance, banditry, revolution and hard times, racial tension, gender roles, love, death, and many more) also provide a window into self-perception, personal identity, and class status. The ballad became the main medium of communication and enabled all Mexicans, rich and poor, to actively participate in recording their own history and producing a lasting legacy.

The origins of the *corrido* date back to the romance ballads brought from Spain during the conquest of the New World. Chronicler Bernal Díaz del Castillo cites several romances in his *Historia de la conquista de la Nueva Espana* (History of the Conquest of New Spain) (1632). By the mid-nineteenth century the production of *corridos* shifted to a variety of geographic centers. Increasingly, *corridos* were produced by the Mexican American population residing in the Lower Rio Grande Valley of southern Texas soon after the Mexican-American War (1846–1848) and depicted cultural conflict with the encroaching Anglo population. The exploits of Mexican American folk heroes and outlaws, such as the Texan Gregorio Cortéz and the Californian Joaquín Murietta, became its ultimate manifestation.

Within Mexico proper the production of *corridos* entered their most creative phase during the Mexican Revolution (1910–1920), in what has become known as the golden age of the *corrido*. Prominent individuals, such as revolutionaries Pancho Villa and Emiliano Zapata, the *soldaderas* or Adelitas who fought or followed their men into battle, and battlefield exploits became common themes. Another outpouring of *corrido* production occurred during the Cristero Civil War (1927–1929), a peasant revolt defending the Catholic Church against liberal reforms initiated by the Mexican government.

It was not until the efforts of César Chávez and the valiant struggles of the United Farm Workers in the 1960s to organize migrant farmworkers in California and throughout the American Southwest that a new explosion of *corridos* began to deal with protest and socioeconomic exploitation. In the 1970s and 1980s a prominent theme in *corridos* on both sides of the U.S.-Mexico border highlighted the experiences of undocumented workers.

Despite the geographic origin of any specific *corrido,* the highly migratory nature of Mexicans within Mexico and northward into the United States in the pursuit of economic security ensured the broadest audience possible because *corridos* either accompanied Mexicans in their travels or inspired them to write new ballads. In particular, these migrations typify the peasant classes of Mexican society from which the *corrido* has primarily evolved. Mexican peasants remain at the forefront in composing, buying, listening to, and singing *corridos*. Thus the *corrido* has developed a strong connection to the *tierra* (land), agriculture, and hard work and recognizes the labor of tillers of the soil and dedicated wage earners.

The formal structure of the *corrido* is based on a very flexible rhyme scheme that follows a narrative structure that tells a story in the first or third person. This differs from *canciones* (songs), which tend to follow a more lyrical and sentimental pattern that primarily deals with topics of love, nostalgia, and loss of love. The most popular rhyme schemes are *abac, abcb, abba,* and *abbc,* and there are usually four lines to each stanza, but this can also vary. As noted by María Herrera-Sobek in her study of *corridos,* they have historically yielded six primary formulas and eight secondary ones, not all of which appear in every ballad. The primary formulas are the following:

1. Initial call from the *corridista* (singer) to his or her public
2. Place, date, and name of the protagonist
3. Formula preceding the protagonist's arguments
4. Message
5. Protagonist's farewell
6. *Corridista*'s farewell

The singing of the *corrido* can be done by males, females, or mixed-gender duets. Women such as Linda Ronstadt from Arizona, Lydia Mendoza from Texas, and Lola Beltrán and Irma Serrano from Mexico have become world-famous *corridistas.* The protagonist at the center of the ballad may also be male or female, but the patriarchal nature of Mexican society, centered on machismo, an exaggerated notion of masculine authority, has promoted the *corrido* as a male-dominated genre in both production and perspective. This patriarchal system has produced stereotypical representations of women. The five most common are (1) the Good Mother, who is of utmost importance in the maintenance of the Mexican family, and who readily transforms into the weeping mother when confronted with tragic events such as the death of the male hero; (2) the Terrible Mother, who is depicted as harmful, destructive, and evil and is often the source of the hero's death; (3) the Mother Goddess, a benevolent, passive, religious figure personified by the overglorification and sincere worship of the Virgen de Guadalupe (Virgin of Guadalupe), the patron saint of Mexico, who reportedly appeared before the Indian peasant Juan Diego in 1531; (4) the Lover, who is simultaneously chaste and obedient, yet erotic and traitorous, as depicted by the legend of La Malinche, the native mistress and interpreter of Hernán Cortés, the conqueror of the Aztec Empire (1519–1521); and (5) the Soldier, operating in various capacities as spies, cooks, nurses, fundraisers, camp followers, and *soldaderas* (soldiers), yet repeatedly marginalized as love objects and anonymous *mujeres* (women) and *galletas* ("cookies"). Each of these models can be labeled an archetype, an unconscious idea or pattern of thought inherited from the ancestors of any regional group and universally found in individual psyches. As women become more involved in writing and producing *corridos,* the themes will increasingly reflect a more diverse Latina experience.

SOURCES: Hernández, Guillermo. 1978. *Canciones de La Raza: Songs of the Chicano Experience.* Berkeley, CA: El Fuego de Aztlán; Herrera-Sobek, María. 1990. *The Mexican Corrido: A Feminist Analysis.* Bloomington: Indiana University Press; ———. 1993. *Northward Bound: The Mexican Immigrant Experience in Ballad and Song.* Bloomington: Indiana University Press; Paredes, Americo. 1976. *A Texas-Mexican "Cancionero": Folksongs of the Lower Border.* Urbana: University of Illinois Press.

Steven Rosales

COSSIO Y CISNEROS, EVANGELINA (1879– ?)

The face that in all probability shifted American sympathy toward the Cuban cause in that country's struggle for independence from Spain (1895) was that of eighteen-year-old Evangelina Cossio y Cisneros. Accused of conspiracy in 1896 for attempting to lure a Spanish military officer into an ambush on the Isle of Pines, Cossio y Cisneros was imprisoned in Havana's Casa de Recogidas. Her story, emblazoned across the pages of William Randolph Hearst's *New York Journal,* magnificently exemplified the genre of yellow journalism and swayed public opinion. Americans, including prominent women like Julia Ward Howe, joined the *Journal* in mounting a petition for Cossio y Cisneros's release. While Americans were not eager to enter into armed confrontation over Cuba, support for the Cuban cause was greatly enhanced.

Unable to secure her release, Hearst assigned a reporter, Karl Decker, to engineer a spectacular jailbreak to free the young beauty with exclusive coverage by the *Journal.* Feted triumphantly by her supporters, Cossio y Cisneros arrived safely in the United States in October 1897. Throngs awaited her arrival in New York City, and a few days later President William McKinley welcomed her to the White House. Seldom mentioned in the literature, Cuban exile communities in New York, Key West, and Tampa particularly rejoiced, celebrating the Cossio y Cisneros affair with dances, music, and parades. More than 2,000 people, among them the leading Cuban citizens of Tampa, marked the event with floats and pageantry that interpreted the experience as a Cuban triumph over Spanish tyranny. A women's club in support of the insurrection was named after Cossio y Cisneros. That Cossio y Cisneros's freedom was obtained at the hands of an American bore disturbing implications for others who anticipated broader intervention in Cuba in the coming years. After the Cuban-Spanish-American War in 1898, Cossio y Cisneros', footprints appear to fade into history, and little else is known about her.

Almost immediately after the incident newspapers launched accusations of fraud and deception against the *Journal,* and journalists left no stone unturned in digging out the truth. Was Cossio y Cisneros's rescue aided by the Spanish military? Was this a hoax, merely a ploy to increase Hearst's newspaper sales? For more than a century Cossio y Cisneros's story has read more like a romantic novel than a factual incident and until now has remained unchanged. However, new information supports the validity of the saga. More complicated than previously suspected, the case involved numerous individuals. Cossio y Cisneros's rescue rested on the collaboration of the senior U.S. diplomat in Havana, Consul General Fitzhugh Lee, who took a personal interest in the case, and a Cuban American banker, a graduate of Rensselaer Polytechnic Institute, Carlos Carbonell, who married Cossio y Cisneros in the United States eight months after the incident. Along with Decker, Donnell Rockwell, a clerk on the consulate staff in Havana, and the U.S. consul in Sagua la Grande in central Cuba, Walter Barker, were also involved.

Representing the consulate, Rockwell met Cossio y Cisneros on several occasions when he visited American women held at the prison and mentioned her to Karl Decker, who in turned informed Hearst of her plight. Hearst encouraged Decker to attempt a rescue. Decker knew, and probably confided in, Fitzhugh Lee, the highest-ranking American on the island, who also supported the mission. The abominable conditions of the prison were well noted by Lee, whose wife and daughter had visited with Cossio y Cisneros, and at his suggestion she had been removed to slightly better quarters. The rescue plot required all collaborators to enact active roles and was so fraught with danger that it could not have been known to the Spaniards.

According to Lee's unpublished manuscript, a saw that proved useless and pastries laced with opium to induce sleep among her cellmates were smuggled to Cossio y Cisneros. The jailbreak took place on October 7, 1897. She was hidden for two days in the Havana home of Carlos Carbonell. According to Lee, this was a highly distressing period for Cossio y Cisneros, who vowed that she would kill herself rather than surrender. Cossio y Cisneros's flight from prison was discovered by the authorities, who mounted a search for her throughout the city. Cossio y Cisneros was disguised as a boy smoking an unlit cigar and with the help of ship's captain Frank Stevens was smuggled on board the *Seneca,* bound for New York City. She remained hidden in a stateroom until they were well at sea. It appeared that she had friends on board, because the diplomat, Walter Barker, had also booked passage on the *Seneca.* His presence on board was crucial to the plot in the event that the ship's voyage was halted by the Spaniards.

On June 10, 1898, less than a year after her arrival, Cossio y Cisneros married Carlos Carbonell in Baltimore, Maryland. She settled in the United States for several years after her daring flight to freedom. When the United States entered the war on the side of Cuba in 1898, Fitzhugh Lee was commissioned to lead the U.S. Seventh Army Corps. Carbonell served under him with the rank of lieutenant. Like many other Americans, Lee was interested in investing in the country once the conflict ended. Carbonell was instrumental in exploring financial options for Lee. Evangelina Cossio y Cisneros entered the pages of history as a symbol of courage, bravery, and Cubanidad.

Evangelina Cossio y Cisneros on board the *Seneca* bound for New York after a spectacular jailbreak from prison in Cuba, 1897. Photograph from *Under Three Flags in Cuba* by George Musgrave. Courtesy of General Research Division, The New York Public Library, Astor, Lenox and Tilden Foundations.

See also Cuban-Spanish-American War

SOURCES: Campbell, W. Joseph. 2004. "Not a Hoax: New Evidence in the *New York Journal*'s Rescue of Evangelina Cisneros." Online paper, June 29. www.academic2.american.edu/%7Ewjc/wjc2/wjc2.html (accessed June 24, 2005); Hewitt, Nancy A. 2001. *Southern Discomfort: Women's Activism in Tampa, Florida, 1880s–1920s.* Urbana: University of Illinois Press.

Virginia Sánchez Korrol

COTERA, MARTHA (1938–)

Martha (Valdez Martínez) Cotera was born into a middle class family in Nuevo Casas Grandes, Chihuahua, Mexico. Cotera spent a great deal of time with her grandparents, Don Miguel Valdez Martínez and Doña Romanita Martínez de Valdez Martínez. Her grandfather taught her to read the Bible when she was just four years old. Five years later Cotera immigrated to El Paso, Texas, with her mother, Santagracia (Catano) Valdez Martínez, her stepfather, and her older sister and enrolled in the first grade. Within a year, however, her stepfather died, and Cotera's middle-class lifestyle vanished because her mother had to find work in the garment industry.

Despite her family's change in social status, Cotera remained in school and maintained a proud record of perfect attendance through elementary school and to seventh grade. These early experiences influenced her decision to become an advocate for education. Throughout her childhood she acted as her mother's interpreter, a role that served as the foundation of her activism for the rights of Chicanos, Chicanas, and the poor. In an interview she recalled a situation in junior high school where she learned how to negotiate the politics of the educational system. Her best friend, who was Irish Catholic, taught her "how to use the PTA [Parent-Teacher Association]; how to have a good relation with the principal; how to speak up; how to defend myself; how to defend others; and if everything else failed, how to be downright nasty." After that she discovered that she could help other Mexicanos who were having difficulties in school.

Cotera graduated from the University of Texas at El Paso in 1962 with a degree in English and later earned her master's degree in education from the Antioch Graduate School of Education, where she and her husband worked as volunteer faculty. In 1959 she met Juan Cotera, and they married in 1963. They moved to Austin, Texas, where she translated manuscripts for the Memorial Museum at the University of Texas at Austin Archives and worked as a department head at the Texas State University in San Marcos. In 1964 Cotera began her career as a political activist for the Political Association of Spanish-Speaking Organizations and had her first child, María. Her political career continued with activism supporting the farmworkers movement and the upholsterers' union and protesting issues surrounding police brutality. In 1964 she helped found Texans for Educational Advancement of Mexican Americans (TEAMS), whose members were primarily teachers and which in December 1969 sent members to Crystal City to help tutor students who had participated in the walkouts there. At that time Crystal City students were demanding bilingual education, participation in federal programs, such as a lunch program, better physical plant conditions, Chicano counselors, scholarships, the right to bring whatever literature they wanted into the schools, and an end to racist practices in the selection of cheerleaders.

In the late 1960s Cotera became an active member of Texas's first Chicano political party, La Raza Unida, as a strong advocate of Chicana rights. She was a leader in the Chicana conferences. In 1972 she ran for office in the Twenty-third Congressional District on the La Raza Unida ticket and garnered 23 percent of the vote. During this time she had her second child, Juan Javier. Seven years later Cotera summarized the philosophy that drove her political activity on behalf of Chicanas: "It is important that the cultural evolution resulting from the Civil Rights Movement, our participation in the Women's Movement, and the emergence of women as heads of families shall be incorporated into the ideological fabric of our intellectual expression."

Cotera's groundbreaking works include *Diosa y hembra: The History and Heritage of Chicanas in the U.S.*, *The Chicana Feminist,* and *Multicultural Women's Sourcebook: Materials Guide for Use in Women Studies and Bilingual/Multicultural Programs.* Throughout her life she has played a pivotal role in the community, forming community organizations across race, class, and gender lines.

Martha Cotera has been described as a Chicana feminist pioneer and a mentor to women of all ages, as is evident in her community work and in her publishing. In a follow-up report after the 1977 International Women's Year, "Chicanas Change Course of Texas IWY," an unidentified participant wrote, "Through all this, Mexico City to present, remember the name Martha Cotera; the energy, anger, stamina. If anyone deserves an award for the one who put it together, kept it together, encouraged the disillusioned—give it to her." She has never ceased organizing Chicanas and in the 1980s started the Mexican American Professional Business Women's Association. In 1998 the Indigenous Women's Network selected Cotera as the recipient of the Rebozo Award for Development of Cultural and Traditional Arts, and she was awarded the 1999 Women of Significance Award given by the Lone Star Girl Scout Council.

See also Feminism; La Raza Unida Party

SOURCES: Cotera, Martha. 1964. Papers. Benson Latin American Collection, University of Texas at Austin; ———. 1973. "La Mujer Mejicana: Mexicano Feminism." *Magazin* 1, no. 9; ———. 1976. *Diosa y hembra: The History and Heritage of Chicanas in the U.S.* Austin, TX: Information Systems Development; ———. 1977. *The Chicana Feminist.* Austin, TX: Information Systems Development; ———. 1995. Interview by Mary Ann Villarreal, June.

Mary Ann Villarreal

CRAWFORD, MERCEDES MARGARITA MARTÍNEZ (1940–)

Known as "Ms. Marci" to her students, Mercedes Margarita Martínez Crawford taught adult basic education in the Nebraska state prisons for twenty-seven years. An instructor for the Corrections Division at Southeast Community College (SCC) in Lincoln and Metropolitan Community College in Omaha, she helped hundreds of incarcerated men earn their high-school diplomas and associate's degrees. With a matter-of-fact attitude she ardently promoted the reformative goals of prison schools and described her job as a mission "working for changes in men so we don't have to support them forever in an institution."

While her students ranged in age from teenagers to senior citizens, came from varying backgrounds, and possessed different skill levels, Crawford rarely found a student unable to learn and strove to find new ways to encourage their personal and educational development. She taught core subjects, including reading, math, science, grammar, Spanish, English as a second language (ESL), and General Educational Development (GED). In 1990 Crawford won the SCC Burlington Northern Faculty Achievement Award for excellence in teaching. With funding from the Nebraska Department of Education she designed and implemented the first elective science course offered in a Nebraska correctional institution. She copublished the results of the course, which became part of SCC's adult basic studies curriculum, in the *Journal of Correctional Education.*

Crawford described her passion for teaching, compassion for humanity, and willingness to embrace hard work as qualities she learned from her mother, Mercedes Rodríguez Martínez, and from her hometown community in Laredo, Texas. When Crawford was six,

Nebraska educator Mercedes Margarita Martínez Crawford. Courtesy of Natasha Crawford.

her father, a master carpenter, died in a bicycle accident. Her mother subsequently converted their custom home into a neighborhood grocery store called El Tendajito. Crawford, along with her older siblings María Beatriz and Uvaldo Jr., began working in the family enterprise, which they operated for the next decade. At fifteen she joined the high-school Distributive Education Clubs of America (DECA) and clerked for Richter's, Laredo's largest department store. When she graduated from Martin High School in 1958, the family moved to San Antonio.

Crawford attended San Antonio Community College, Laredo Junior College, and the University of Nebraska, Lincoln. Although she received a scholarship to attend Our Lady of the Lake University, she declined the offer to support her mother and her brother, who was attending Texas A&I University in Kingsville. She worked briefly for the Atomic Energy Commission in San Antonio until its offices closed in the early 1960s. Returning to Laredo, she resumed her job at Richter's and devoted her spare time to neighborhood activities at Our Lady of Guadalupe Catholic Church, where she met her husband Weston Crawford, a Volunteers in Service to America (VISTA) volunteer from Nebraska. Together they established a bilingual newspaper and a recreational youth program. In 1969 they relocated to Lincoln and served as houseparents for the Nebraska Center for Children and Youth.

Among the few Mexican Americans living in Lincoln in the early 1970s, Crawford found a rare opportunity teaching migrant youth in the federally funded High School Equivalency Program (HEP) administered by the University of Nebraska and the Nebraska Human Resources Research Foundation. Local philanthropists associated with HEP lauded Crawford's bilingual teaching abilities and encouraged her to create programs for Lincoln's Mexican immigrant population. In 1974, with support from the Lincoln Foundation, she directed Lincoln's first prekindergarten for Spanish-speaking youth, called Learning Enhancement for Mexican American Children (LEMAC). LEMAC acclimated children to school through Spanish-language retention. In 1975 the Nebraska Department of Corrections hired Crawford to assess the possibility of creating educational programs for Spanish-speaking inmates and subsequently hired her to teach bilingual GED courses at the Nebraska State Penitentiary. During this time Crawford also taught evening GED classes for SCC. When SCC contracted with the state to operate its prison education programs in 1976, she joined the faculty of the new SCC Corrections Division. She taught at the penitentiary and the minimum-security Lincoln Correctional Center until she retired in 2002.

Throughout her career she served on the boards of director for the Lincoln Foundation, Women in Community Services, and the Nebraska Office of Community Development. She held memberships in the GI Forum and the Legion of Mary. She continues to teach Spanish privately and works part-time as data collector for the University of Nebraska Medical Center. She has a son, Thomas, and a daughter, Natasha.

SOURCES: Crawford, Mercedes Margarita Martínez. 2001. Interview by Laura K. Muñoz, January 1; Dirkx, John M., and Mercedes Crawford. 1993. "Teaching Reading through Teaching Science: Development and Evaluation of an Experimental Curriculum for Correctional ABE Programs." *Journal of Correctional Education* 44, no. 4 (December): 172–176; Marlette, Marj. 1981. "Education of Inmates Is Teacher's Reward." *Lincoln Star* (Nebraska), November 1.

Natasha Mercedes Crawford

CRUZ, CELIA (1924–2003)

Cuban singer Celia Cruz is one of the most legendary figures in the history of Afro-Cuban music, salsa music, and Latin music internationally. Epithets such as the Queen of Salsa, la Guarachera de Oriente, and la Reina Rumba reflect the central role that she played as a representative and icon of Cuban music for more than half a century. Her legendary status is based not only on her fame as a vocalist and *sonera* (improviser), but also on the longevity of her career, which spanned fifty years or more. While Celia Cruz never identified the year of her birth, historians and music critics have traced the beginnings of her singing career to the 1930s, when she entered amateur singing contests common in radio stations at the time. Born in the working-class neighborhood of Santos Suárez in Havana, Cuba, during a decade of economic need that also affected the island, Cruz won prizes such as food baskets and other edibles that helped feed her family. She was later hired as a singer by radio stations and theaters. She joined a group of dancers called Las Mulatas de Fuego, in which she performed as their lead singer. They toured the Caribbean and Mexico in 1948.

Her most important role as the embodiment and voice of Afro-Cuban music was cemented when she was hired by the orchestra la Sonora Matancera in 1950. Highly popular in the entertainment venues of Havana, Cruz and la Sonora also toured throughout Latin America, where Cruz had the opportunity to share the stage with other great figures in the entertainment world, such as Matilde Díaz and Toña la Negra. After touring Mexico for a year and a half, Cruz and some members of la Sonora arrived in the United States as exiles. In 1962 she married Pedro Knight in New York, where she began a very important career within the Latin music industry. A seasoned performer with Tito Puente and later with Johnny Pacheco under the Fania label, Celia Cruz put her own Cuban stamp on the diverse and multiple musical forms that salsa music constituted. It has been said that she brought the Sonora Matancera style into the U.S. Latin music scene.

For Celia Cruz, the term *salsa* was a commercial term used to market Cuban music internationally. She did not differentiate between Cuban music and New York or Nuyorican salsa, partly because she herself imbued the New York scene with her own "Cuban accent," as she said. Cruz likewise interpreted many Latin American folkloric songs in her performances, thus revitalizing old musical traditions and catering to a larger, Latin American audience that could relate to those canonical and folkloric melodies.

Salsa sensation Celia Cruz (center) in New York, 1957. Courtesy of the Justo A. Martí Photograph Collection. Centro Archives, Centro de Estudios Puertorriqueños, Hunter College, CUNY.

Indeed, Celia Cruz's vast and diverse repertoires, the ease with which she could perform numerous pieces without rehearsing, and her "musical genius" also led to her immense popularity. Because of these talents, Celia Cruz truly performed for and related to her audiences. She maintained the flexibility, after decades in the entertainment business, to gratify local audiences and to offer them a repertoire with which they could identify. In the 1980s Celia Cruz extended her fame as she traveled internationally and made incursions into Hollywood and the U.S. entertainment industry. She created a truly global market where she performed not only for communities of Cubans and Caribbean and Latin Americans, but also for African Americans in the United States. Her appearances in Europe, in Japan, and at New York City's Carnegie Hall, for instance, reflected the versatility of her music and the very diverse audiences that found pleasure in her voice and interpretations. She spanned national boundaries, as well as generational ones.

One of the most unusual aspects of Celia Cruz is that from the beginning of her singing career she maintained significant control over her repertoire, her dress, and her artistic identity. Because of this high degree of autonomy, Cruz was able to perform songs that have had a tremendous impact on the history of salsa music and of Latin music in general. Some of her most popular hits, such as "Quimbara," "Toro Mata," "Que le den candela," "Burundanga," and "Usted abusó," were personally selected by her for production. Her dresses and unique shoes were selected by her in order to construct a serious and respectful professional aura on stage while simultaneously embodying a Caribbean-style brilliance and flashiness. According to critic Raúl Fernández, Celia Cruz represented "art and autonomy."

Under the management of RMM Records and Ralph Mercado during the 1990s, Celia Cruz extended her artistic work to include acting in soap operas and guest-star appearances in Hollywood films. She also produced musical videos, including the obviously feminist song "Que le den candela," an alert to men against domestic violence and infidelity. Celia stated that she would love to record unpublished *boleros,* a musical genre that she did not incorporate as part of her repertoire.

Celia Cruz donated a traditional Cuban rumba dress, a blonde wig, and a pair of her stage shoes to the National Museum of American History at the Smithsonian. Her contributions to Latin music are now an official part of U.S. history. She died of a brain tumor at her New Jersey home on July 16, 2003. She served as a role model for women salsa singers, such as La India and Albita, both of whom have publicly honored Cruz for her contributions and musical talent. She was not only a female pioneer in a male-dominated musical industry, but also a legend by virtue of her powerful voice, her improvisatory talent, her vitality, and her charisma.

See also Salsa

SOURCES: Aparicio, Frances R. 1999. "The Blackness of Sugar: Celia Cruz and the Performance of (Trans)Nationalism." *Cultural Studies*. 13:2:223–236; Arce, Rose. 2003. "Latin Music icon Celia Cruz dies." July 17. CNN.com. www.cnn.com/2003/SHOWBIZ/Music/07/16/cruz.obit/index.html (accessed June 25, 2005); Fernández, Raúl. 1997. "La mulata de fuego: arte y autonoomía de Celia Cruz." In *Mujer* 4 (August–September): 36–41; Sabournin, Tony. 1986. "Celia Cruz." In *The New Grove Dictionary of American Music Vol 1,* eds. H. Wiley Hitchcock and Stanley Sadie. London: Macmillan.

Frances R. Aparicio

CUBAN AND PUERTO RICAN REVOLUTIONARY PARTY (1892–1898)

Considered the "Apostle of Cuban Independence," José Martí founded the Cuban Revolutionary Party (Partido Revolucionario Cubano, PRC) in New York City in April 1892 and presided over it until his death in 1895. Sections of the PRC simultaneously appeared in Cuba and Puerto Rico and in cities with significant concentrations of Cuban exiles, including New Orleans, Louisiana, and Ybor City, Jacksonville, and Tampa, Florida. Intent on seizing the independence of Cuba from Spanish colonial control, the PRC also had a secondary agenda, to liberate Puerto Rico. The New York section of the PRC included a Puerto Rican branch of the organization. Among the leaders of the Puerto Rican PRC section were expatriates living in the city at that time, Arturo Alfonso Schomburg, Dr. José Julio Henna, Sotero Figueroa, and Robert H. Todd.

The official order for the Cuban uprising under the command of Martí, Antonio Maceo, and Máximo Gómez was signed in New York City on January 29, 1895. Until then mobilization toward war was the PRC's primary objective. During the conflict, however, the PRC intensified its efforts. This required engendering broad support in the United States and throughout the Caribbean for the Cuban cause—Cuba Libre! The supporters of Antillean independence, among whom women played a major role, organized hundreds of clubs with the express purpose of raising funds, buying arms and weapons, securing medical supplies, maintaining morale, sewing uniforms, and recruiting Anglo allies. Sympathizers with the Cuban cause in Haiti and the Dominican Republic aided the insurgents, and Martí personally visited Cuban communities throughout the United States on numerous occasions, speaking at mass rallies, in cigar factories, and in meeting halls to stimulate patriotism and commitment.

Las Obreras de la Independencia was organized in Tampa in 1892 in response to the PRC's call to arms. Under the leadership of women like schoolteacher Adelaide de Rivero and club president Dorotea Ruiz, members included many of the wives, widows, relatives, and daughters of veterans of the Ten Years' War (1868–1878). They performed a variety of patriotic deeds for the revolution, contributed money to the PRC, and supported its newspaper, *Patria.* They hosted meetings, bazaars, dinners, festivals, concerts, and dances. The PRC recognized the work of women organizers, inviting them to speak at mass rallies and extolling their actions in the pages of *Patria.* Women's organizations soon served a dual function as the sacrifices and heroics of insurgent women during actual warfare raised consciousness about the role of women overall. Powerful images evoked by patriots like businesswoman Paulina Pedroso, the early independence supporter Carolina Rodríguez, the founder of a Spanish-language school, Adelaide de Rivero, and Ana Merchan, also identified with the Ten Years' War, went well beyond the limitations of helpmate and supporter envisioned by the PRC.

Historian Nancy A. Hewitt identified at least forty-six clubs, of which fifteen women's, six mixed-sex, and four youth organizations were affiliated with the PRC. Once war was declared, clubs proliferated, among them las Patriotas, las Discípulas de Martí, Gonzalo de Quesada, and 24 de Febrero. Cigar workers donated two to five dollars from their weekly salary, and women sold their jewelry, silverware, and furniture for the war effort. Like their white counterparts, Afro-Cubans were heavily involved in revolutionary activities. Paulina Pedroso operated a boardinghouse for cigar workers in Ybor City and made her home Martí's base in the city. A natural organizer, Pedroso and her husband, Ruperto, who headed a group of pro-independence Afro-Cubanos, donated their wages to the cause, cementing one of Martí's principles that the war was to be equally waged by blacks and whites.

In New York City la Liga Antillana exemplified a racially integrated women's group composed predominantly of women who worked in, or were connected to, the cigar industry. Its mission was to support the liberation efforts through diverse fund-raising activities. Other political and social organizations that appeared in support of Cuba Libre! were las Hijas de Cuba, headed by Angela R. de Quesada and Carmen Matillas; Mercedes de Varona, under the leadership of Inocencia M. de Figueroa and Emma Betancourt; and las Hijas de la Libertad, led by Natividad R. de Gallo and Gertrudis Casano. As was the case in Florida, many of the women involved in organizational activity were related to men active in the revolution.

In February 1898 the United States entered the war against Spain. In less than a year the United States occupied Cuba, Puerto Rico, Guam, and parts of the Philippine Islands. The PRC ceased to exist after that.

See also Cuban-Spanish-American War; Ten Years' War

SOURCES: Hewitt, Nancy A. 2001. *Southern Discomfort: Women's Activism in Tampa, Florida, 1880s–1920s.* Urbana: University of Illinois Press; Pérez, Louis A. 1999. *On Becoming Cuban: Identity, Nationality, and Culture.* Chapel Hill: University of North Carolina Press; Sánchez Korrol, Virginia. 1994. *From Colonia to Community: The History of Puerto Ricans in New York City.* 2nd ed. Berkeley: University of California Press.

Virginia Sánchez Korrol

CUBAN INDEPENDENCE WOMEN'S CLUBS

In the aftermath of the Pact of Zanjón of 1878 that ended the Ten Years' War with the defeat of the Cuban insurgents and the emigration of many of them to the United States, the president of the Cuban Revolutionary Committee, Calixto García, signed a document that formally invited Cuban women to participate in Cuba Libre. An ardent separatist who himself had taken the path of exile to New York City, García gave credit to the direct participation of many women in the insurrection. Praising their capacity to adjust from the life of plantation mistresses to the nomadic life of the insurgents, he addressed women with glowing praise for their sacrifices for *la patria.*

García called on the women to help "clean our *patria* from the Spaniard epidemics." Making New York the center for a new insurrection in the name of freedom and sacrifice for the *patria,* the newly founded Cuban Revolutionary Committee (CRC) was honored to invite Cuban and sympathetic foreign women to contribute to the cause of Cuba Libre by founding secret patriotic organizations, such as Hijas de la Libertad. These women were to raise funds for the coming uprising, devise new forms of propaganda, and attract sympathizers to the cause. All these clubs, together with those already founded in other American cities and abroad, were dependent on the central organization of the CRC. Only the CRC knew the real activities of these secret clubs, whose members had to accept very strict bylaws. In the following decade Cuban exiles in New York and other American cities founded several hundred men's and women's clubs that became the basis of the Partido Revolucionario Cubano (PRC), the most advanced form of political organization devised by José Martí.

Some clubs of Cuban women in New York dated as far back as 1869, when Emilia Casanova de Villaverde founded the Liga de las Hijas de Cuba. But women's clubs flourished after 1892, the year of the founding of the PRC, and numbered eighty by 1898. These organizations, like their male counterparts, belonged within the democratic process of party building. When the PRC was founded in 1892, the Mercedes de Varona was the only woman's club in New York. However, the number of clubs swelled after Martí's death. Most club leaders, both in New York and in Florida, were the wives, widows, sisters, mothers, or daughters of male leaders of the PRC. The names of women's clubs showed this relationship: Hijas de . . . , Hermanas de . . . , and so on. In other words, in the public arena, as in the private, the status of Cuban women was secondary to that of men. Naming a club after a revolutionary female figure was not the rule, although an exception was made for Mercedes de Varona, the young heroine of the Ten Years' War. In general, women's clubs were named after a male public figure: a martyr, a hero, or someone who was still living, like José Martí, whose devotion among Cuban women certainly preceded his death.

Martí wrote in *Patria* that the primary role of women's organizations was the promotion of civic awareness among Cuban and Puerto Rican women, yet no woman served on the editorial board of *Patria* or held an important office in the party. Until 1895 women's club activities were largely for purposes of PRC propaganda and raising funds for the insurrection in the islands. After 1895 most women's clubs provided services for widows, orphans, and war prisoners and developed autonomous and creative forms of fund-raising, including picnics and staging theatrical events.

Because women's clubs held lesser importance than men's, and their public involvement was limited due to existing social conventions and family duties, even the leadership of a woman's club was under the supervision of a male figure. In fact, a woman's club would elect the husband, the father, or the brother of one of the leading ladies as its representative to the PRC. During the late nineteenth century, despite such constraints on their visible political leadership, women, both in Cuba and in the United States, had their left domestic circles to enter public life for the cause of independence.

See also Cuban and Puerto Rican Revolutionary Party; Ten Years' War

SOURCE: Hewitt, Nancy A. 2001. *Southern Discomfort: Women's Activism in Tampa, Florida, 1880s–1920s.* Urbana: University of Illinois Press.

Alessandra Lorini

CUBAN WOMEN'S CLUB (1968–)

On October 10, 1968, a group of Miami Cuban women, inspired by the success of the Lyceum Lawn Tennis Club of Havana, Cuba, in offering a vast program of social assistance and cultural and educational activities geared to women, founded the Cuban Women's Club. This club was meant to become a vehicle to orient exiled Cuban women, and women in general, to adjust to the new society in the United States. Another equally important objective was to denounce the oppression, terror, and lack of civil liberties in Castro's Cuba. The charter officers were Dr. Lilia Vieta, Dr. Elvira Dopico, Carmelina Guanche, Julieta O'Farrill, Migñon Pérez, Inés Segura Bustamante, Ofelia Tabares, Elena de Arcos, and Dr. Marta de Castro.

The goals that the founders set for themselves and other club members were thoroughly achieved. Throughout its existence the Cuban Women's Club has greatly contributed to the welfare and cultural enhancement of women in southern Florida by sponsoring workshops, lecture series, and all types of educational and social activities geared to meet the needs of women in that area. It has also funded numerous scholarships for deserving women according to the club's criteria.

In 1976, on the initiative of one of the founding members of the Club, Mercy Díaz Miranda, the Floridana Award was instituted. Each year this award is granted to women who have demonstrated leadership in their profession or in community service. The Floridana became a coveted and prestigious award in the Miami-Dade community. The roster of prestigious recipients reflects the great achievements of Hispanic women in southern Florida and, in the process, the history of Latinas in general. In 1978 Lourdes Aguila, the founder of Liga contra el Cancer in southern Florida, received the award. The new Liga contra el Cancer collected millions of dollars for the treatment of cancer as the original Liga had done in the former Cuban republic. Dr. Elvira Dopico, a highly respected educator and community leader, also received the award that same year. In 1979 Sonia Díaz and Marta del Pino, founders of Ballet Concerto, a prestigious ballet school and company, were the joint recipients. Olimpia Rosado, an accomplished linguist, was honored in 1980. Five years later Pili de la Rosa, accomplished artist and founder of the Compañía Grateli, which promotes and produces ballet, musicals, and theatrical performances, received the award. The following year the award honored the educator Dr. Mercedes García Tuduri. Lydia Cabrera, the great Cuban ethnographer, and Pautita Grau Aguero, one of the initiators of the program that brought thousands of unaccompanied minors fleeing from Communism to the United States, were the honorees of 1990. The Cuban *guarachera* Celia Cruz and the renowned bolero singer Olga Guillot received the Floridana in 1991, along with Dr. Moravia Capo, a civic activist in the Cuban municipalities in exile. The following year the honoree was Leticia Callava, who for many years was the news anchor of Telemundo and later Univision. Clara María del Valle received this award in 1993.

Del Valle is a good example of the type of woman who has earned the Floridana Award. She has dedicated most of her life as a volunteer assisting in social services programs and charitable causes. First in Colombia and then in Panama she worked closely with Catholic Charities in establishing vocational schools for at-risk youths and a home for the aged. In the 1980s del Valle assisted Cuban refugees in Panama through the Cuban American National Foundation's (CANF) Exodus program. Later she supervised that program in several other countries where Cubans sought refuge. Exodus successfully reunited more than 10,000 Cubans with their loved ones in the United States through a privately funded program. Del Valle joined the CANF Board of Directors in 1988. The CANF is an indepen-

Cuban Women's Round Table at Koubek Center, Miami. From left to right: Rosita Abella, Josefina Inclán, Minita Cantero, Marta de Castro, and Josefina Kouri. Courtesy of the Cuban Heritage Collection, Otto G. Richter Library, University of Miami.

dent not-for-profit organization founded in 1981 by exiled Cubans for the purpose of gathering and disseminating data concerning the economic, political, and social welfare of the Cuban people, both on the island and in diaspora. The foundation supports programs to promote respect for human freedom, democratic values, and the pursuit of prosperity with dignity and justice for all. Del Valle directs a CANF human rights project, the Foundation for Human Rights in Cuba.

Other women who have similarly served their communities have earned the coveted Floridana. These include Annie Betancourt, a civic leader elected to the Florida legislature; Zenaida Bacardi Argamasilla, a leader in the municipality of Santiago de Cuba; Elena Díaz Versón, philanthropist and activist; and Sylvia Oriondo, founder of Madres y Mujeres Anti-Represión (Mothers and Wives Against Repression) (MAR), a nonprofit organization whose goals are to promote democratic values and to waken the international community to the reality of the Cuban people under a totalitarian system. For more than ten years, Sylvia Oriondo was a director of the United Way and the Salvation Army and served as the chair of the board for the Little Havana Activity Center, which provides social services and meals to the elderly. Through the Cuban Women's Club and other organizations, women seek to make difference in their communities, both in the United States and in Cuba.

SOURCES: Rodríguez, Luis David. 2001. "Extraordinario jubileo de plata de los Premios Floridana." *Diario de las Americas,* October 14; Rovirosa, Dolores F. 1988. *Cuban Women's Club Directorio.* Miami.

Mercedes Cros Sandoval

CUBAN-SPANISH-AMERICAN WAR (1898)

The conflict that eventually erupted between the United States and Spain in the spring of 1898 originated in the economics and politics of the early nineteenth century. In the years before the U.S. Civil War the slave-owning plantation interests of the Southern states and their political representatives in the U.S. Congress had articulated an interest in purchasing Cuba and Puerto Rico from Spain and incorporating these islands into the Union as "slave states." However, even after the defeat of the Southern Confederacy in 1865, interest in Spain's Caribbean possessions continued, and even increased, because of a growing fear that the United States would become a second- or third-rate power in the competitive global environment of the late-nineteenth-century European-dominated imperialism. Corporate investors in the United States were already heavily involved in the Cuban sugar and tobacco sectors. At the same time other corporate interests wanted to establish trading networks with Latin America, the Caribbean, and eastern Asia, especially China. Alfred Thayer Mahan, an admiral in the U.S. Navy, called for strengthening the armed forces and the establishment of strategically located naval bases to protect the new trade routes in the Caribbean and the Pacific. There was talk of building a canal across Panama or Nicaragua to facilitate the trade with eastern Asia.

By the mid-1890s rebellions in Cuba and the Philippines were providing an excuse for possible U.S. military intervention on the side of advocates for independence from Spain. The war in Cuba, initiated by José Martí and his followers in New York, was a follow-up to the earlier conflicts that had taken place on that island between 1868 and 1880. As would be expected, Cuban women played an active role in the conflict, along with their counterparts in the movement for independence in Puerto Rico. In the years before the war of the 1890s, Cuban and Puerto Rican women, such as Emilia Casanova de Villaverde and Lola Rodríguez de Tió, created or participated in organizations that raised money and generated support for the independence movements. These organizations included la Liga Antillana, Las dos Antillanas, Hijas de Cuba, and Hijas de la Libertad, among others. Cuban and Puerto Rican women also functioned as nurses, combat soldiers, spies, couriers, and informal diplomats during the war itself. Antolina Agripino, Casimira Aquilino, Fermina Candelario, and Fabiana Buenaventura were some of the many Cuban women who served as combat soldiers in the Cuban war for independence.

Cuban women were also used in a manipulative way by the propagandists for U.S. intervention in the Cuban conflict. Evangelina Cossio y Cisneros, an attractive young Cuban woman imprisoned by the Spaniards on the Isle of Pines, was used by newspaper publisher William Randolph Hearst as a sensationalized symbol of the "atrocities" committed by the Spaniards in Cuba. But it was the explosion on the battleship *Maine* in Havana's harbor in February 1898, which killed hundreds of U.S. sailors, that served as the catalyst for intervention and the war against Spain.

As it turned out, the Spaniards were woefully unprepared to fight a war against both the United States and the rebels in Cuba and the Philippines. Elements of the U.S. Army quickly joined Cuban rebels to defeat the Spanish military forces in eastern Cuba in late June and early July 1898. The United States also landed another force in the southwestern part of Puerto Rico and easily defeated elements of the Spanish army on that is-

Scene from the rooftops of Havana during the flight of the exiles. Courtesy of the Cuban Heritage Collection, Otto G. Richter Library, University of Miami.

land in late July and early August. However, the fate of the Spanish military forces in both the Caribbean and the Pacific was sealed by the destruction of the Spanish naval forces at Manila Bay on May 1, 1898, and later off the coast of southeastern Cuba near Santiago on July 3, 1898.

With their land forces cut off from reinforcements and supplies in Europe, the Spaniards sued for peace. At a truce that was signed on August 12, 1898, the Spaniards agreed to cede both Cuba and Puerto Rico to the United States and to surrender their military forces on both those islands for eventual repatriation to Spain. They also agreed to negotiations that were to take place in Paris later that year to settle the conflict in a formal manner. These negotiations resulted in a peace treaty between the two governments and the surrender of the Philippines and the Pacific island of Guam to the United States in December 1898.

See also Cuban Independence Women's Clubs; Ten Years' War; Treaty of Paris

SOURCES: "Focus/En foco 1898–1998, Part I." 1998. *CENTRO: Journal of Centro de Estudios Puertorriqueños* (Hunter College, CUNY) 10:1–2; Jones, Jacqueline, Peter Wood, Thomas Borstelmann, Elaine Tyler May, and Vicki L. Ruiz. 2003. *Created Equal: A Social and Political History of the United States.* New York: Longman; Library of Congress. "The Spanish American War." http://www.loc.gov/rr/hispanic/1898 (accessed June 25, 2005); Williams, William Appleman. 1962. *The Tragedy of American Diplomacy*. New York: Dell.

Gabriel Haslip-Viera

CUERO, DELFINA (C. 1900–1972)

Although not a Latina in a literal sense, Delfina Cuero represents a Native American foremother to contemporary Mexican American women and her life brings into sharp relief the lives of native peoples whose lands and cultures straddle both sides of the political border separating Mexico and the United States. Delfina Cuero was a Kumeyaay Native woman. The Kumeyaay territory covers much of today's San Diego County in California and extends into northern Baja California in Mexico. The traditional lands of the Kumeyaay straddle the current international border of the United States and Mexico. The Kumeyaay people are also known by the Spanish term Diegueño. This word refers to the mission at San Diego established in 1769. In the unratified Treaty of Santa Ysabel (1852) the United States continued to use the term Diegueño. Some anthropologists also use the terms Tipai and Ipai to refer to the Kumeyaay. In the 1950s Florence Shipek interviewed many elders who confirmed that the term "Kumeyaay" remained more preferred as the general term the tribe favors.

Delfina Cuero was born around 1900 to parents Vincente Cuero and Cidilda Quaha in Xamca (Jamacha) in southern California. Her family faced many challenges. When she was a young girl, rapid change caused upheaval in the Kumeyaay homeland because of the increasing numbers of nonnatives entering the San Diego region. Extended growth of farms, houses, businesses, and other developments pressured many of

Cuero's people to move out of the San Diego–Mission Valley. Although the Kumeyaay people traditionally moved with the seasons for food gathering, white expansion depleted many native food resources and forced them to move into other areas.

Delfina Cuero chronicled the displacement of herself and her people through a collaborative book with Florence Connolly Shipek titled *Delfina Cuero: Her Autobiography, an Account of Her Last Years, and Her Ethnobotanic Contributions.* According to this account, Cuero's father worked for ranchers around the El Cajón and Jamul areas who gave him food and at times old clothes for his labor. The family did not live in a house but rather camped near her father's work. Forced farther south by people invading Kumeyaay lands, as well as seeking new places to live and work, her family was initially unaware of the political border between the United States and Mexico. Her grandparents crossed the border first, and later Cuero and her parents joined them. In the late 1800s, according to the book, the federal government established reservations in the San Diego area. However, Cuero explained that while they were aware of the reservations, it was traditional to remain with one's family group, even if this meant living off-reservation.

Delfina Cuero spent much of her life gathering food and materials in her native homelands. She traveled to the ocean and fished, in addition to gathering shellfish, abalone, and other items along the shoreline. She also went into the mountains to collect staple foods of many native peoples, acorns and pine nuts. Cuero grew up native, hearing traditional stories of her people, speaking the Kumeyaay language, and playing with other children, her relatives. She learned much about ethnobotany, as well as traditional crafts such as basket making. After a while Cuero's parents separated. Her father left and never returned. Cuero's mother urged her to marry so that there would be a man to hunt for them. As was common in Kumeyaay tradition, a man asked her family for her hand in marriage. Sebastian Osun was respected in the village, and Cuero's family suggested that she accept his offer of marriage. After marriage they had children. Osun died when her oldest child was about eleven years of age. After his death, as was customary, they burned everything, including their grass house. The family prayed and spiritually cleansed themselves. Cuero and her children went through many difficult times and were often hungry even though they worked diligently.

Delfina Cuero remains an important example of life experiences of a Kumeyaay woman during her time period. Her story is told from her perspective. She faced border issues while attempting to return to the land of her birth. Many records had been destroyed in fires, and the political border between the two larger nations divided her people. Her autobiography illuminates some of the historical and cultural reasons for the displacement. In addition, Delfina Cuero offers a wealth of information on ethnobotany in her homelands. She presents an in-depth knowledge of plants, foods, and lifeways of the Kumeyaay people.

SOURCES: Cuero, Delfina, and Florence Connelly Shipek. 1991. *Delfina Cuero: Her Autobiography, an Account of Her Last Years, and Her Ethnobotanic Contributions.* Menlo Park, CA: Ballena Press; Shipek, Florence Connelly. 1987. *Pushed into the Rocks: Southern California Indian Land Tenure, 1769–1986.* Lincoln: University of Nebraska Press.

Annette L. Reed

D

DAVIS, GRACE MONTAÑEZ (1926–)

Born on November 24, 1926, in Los Angeles, Grace Montañez grew up in Lincoln Heights and attended Albion Street School, Sacred Heart High School, Immaculate Heart College, and the University of California, Los Angeles. Before entering college she worked in a soap factory and for a time became the factory's manager. In 1952 she married Raymond C. Davis and three years later graduated from UCLA with a master of science degree in microbiology.

Her early life mirrors many themes in Mexican American history. Although she recalls the hardships of the Great Depression, she has many happy memories of family trips to the Los Angeles River and to the outlying orange groves and sheep ranches in then rural southern California. Remembering the deportation and repatriation campaigns of the 1930s, she tells stories of waking up to find neighbors gone, because immigration authorities had picked them up the previous night. The family had other fears as well. One of her two brothers had tuberculosis and lived away from the family for four years. He eventually recovered and as a young man wore a zoot suit. During World War II he served as a paratrooper and fought at Normandy, but like many other Latino veterans, when he came home, he had trouble finding a job.

Her mother introduced her to community activism and took the young Grace with her to help their neighbors. Davis witnessed police brutality and remembers going with mothers of the neighborhood to interpret for them in the courts. "Our community was experiencing a lot of discrimination from the police and from immigration, we had no recourse. . . . I remember going to the coroner's office to identify bodies with the mothers." The bodies she saw had "all these bruises." "It looked," she said, "as if they'd been choked . . . hung." Her mother was actively involved in the Sleepy Lagoon Defense Committee that worked tirelessly to free a group of young men unjustly tried and convicted of murder.

Davis graduated from Immaculate Heart College and entered UCLA in 1949. There she became politically active. The university opened new perspectives for her as McCarthyism and cold war hysteria surrounded her. "This was an awakening for me." During this time she met Paul Robeson and W.E.B. DuBois. In the early 1950s she became involved with the Community Service Organization (CSO), a community self-help and civil rights organization.

As a member of the CSO from 1954 to 1960, she taught citizen and voter registration classes that reached thousands of residents. She was actively involved in Edward Roybal's campaigns for political office from his first race for the Los Angeles City Council to his successful election and reelections to the U.S. Congress. "CSO was able to get 50,000 to 60,000 people registered when the organization had a registration campaign." "Then of course, we followed up by getting out the vote. The unions provided transportation, provided food. We walked all over the place and had car caravans and everything else." "It was a very positive influence on the whole community. CSO was a family oriented organization. The women always came. They were housewives . . . you didn't have school teachers and stuff like that then." She planned community canvassing in her living room with her three children playing at her feet. "Women played an active role in the organization from its very beginning. We licked stamps, ran . . . headquarters and answered phones during political campaigns. We made the food and sold it."

One of the original founding members of the Mexican American Political Association, Davis served on the Democratic Party Minority Committee of Los Angeles. In 1965 Congressman George E. Brown asked her to work as one of his field representatives. In this post she was part of a team that helped implement in Los Angeles the antipoverty or Great Society programs of President Lyndon Johnson.

Davis also helped plan Julian Nava's campaign for the Los Angeles Board of Education. She was also a member of the Federal Executive Board, an organization that consisted of the heads of every federal agency in southern California. An active member of the Los Angeles County Democratic Committee, she worked with Senator Alan Cranston in the Democratic Party's Californians for Liberal Representation, belonged to the statewide Democratic Committee, and supported Thomas Bradley in his first unsuccessful mayoral campaign in 1969.

Bradley, successful in his second campaign in 1973, became the first and to date only African American mayor of Los Angeles. He appointed Grace Davis as the director of the city's Human Resources Department, a position especially created to address public resources to the city's social needs. At that time no Latinos or Chicanos held seats on either the city council or the board of supervisors. The Mexican community of the city of Los Angeles was effectively without any governmental representation. In 1975 Bradley selected Grace Montañez Davis as his deputy mayor. She was well aware of her position as the highest-ranking Latina in city government. "I was their representative." "That was very obvious to me. I took that very seriously. I thought of it as a great responsibility."

In this post Davis developed the city's Department of Aging and established a Department of Justice, an Office of Volunteers, and an Office for Youth. Her responsibilities included meetings with the mayor and the twenty-six heads of the city departments; she wrote the agendas and acted as chair for these meetings. She oversaw the Department of Community Development and represented the mayor on the Grants Committee. She worked for and closely with the homeless and with the Salvation Army and the Red Cross helped in the creation of Los Angeles' first Homeless Camp.

Davis was a constant defender of immigrant rights and served as an advocate of several organizations, like One Stop Immigration. She was also a founding mother of the important Los Angeles–based Chicana feminist organization Comisión Femenil Mexicana and campaigned for her Comisión compañera Gloria Molina in her first state assembly campaign. She retired in 1990; Mayor Bradley remained in office until 1993. Today Grace M. Davis lives in the Highland Park area of Los Angeles. She has three children and two grandchildren.

Grace Montañez Davis was appointed Deputy Mayor of Los Angeles in 1975. Courtesy of Grace Montañez Davis.

See also Community Service Organization; Politics, Party

SOURCES: Acuña, Rodolfo F. 1998. *Anything but Mexican: Chicanos in Contemporary Los Angeles.* New York: Verso; Davis, Grace Montañez. 1994. Oral history interview by Philip Castruita; Soneshein, Raphael J. 1993. *Politics in Black and White: Race and Power in Los Angeles.* Princeton, NJ: Princeton University Press.

Philip C. Castruita

DE ACOSTA, AIDA (1884–1962)

Even before Wilbur and Orville Wright's epochal flight in December 1903, Aida de Acosta became, possibly, the first woman to pilot a motorized airship. In the early days of aviation humankind conquered the skies in balloons, dirigibles, and gliders. The first dirigibles—consisting of little more than a gas-filled bladder, a gondola or basket in which the passenger(s) rode, a motor, and a propeller—allowed people to go aloft in controlled flight at the end of the nineteenth century. Brazilian Alberto Santos-Dumont, who developed both dirigibles and aircraft, gained international fame for his flying exhibitions in France.

Born in Elberton, New Jersey, on July 28, 1884, Aida de Acosta grew up in New York City, the daughter of a prominent immigrant family. Her Cuban-born father was reared in Spain and then subsequently returned to Cuba to help drive out the Spanish during the Spanish-American War of 1898. A daughter of privilege, Acosta became fascinated with Santos-Dumont's airship while traveling in Paris in the summer of 1903. After striking up a friendship with the Brazilian airman, she convinced Santos-Dumont to allow her to pilot his dirigible "IX." Because the basket was so small, she would have to fly solo. After three lessons, on June 29, 1903, Acosta become the first woman to pilot a powered aircraft, nearly six months before the Wright brothers' flights at Kitty Hawk. Santos-Dumont's "handy little runabout" traveled at about fifteen miles per hour, and he tracked the dirigible while riding a bicycle. The flight lasted "considerably over a half mile."

Unfortunately, Acosta's parents made Santos-Dumont promise never to reveal the identity of their daughter as the pilot of the dirigible because they were mortified by the publicity surrounding the flight. They believed that a woman's name should appear in newspapers only at the time of her birth, upon her marriage, and at her death. Furthermore, Santos-Dumont did not name Acosta in his book *My Airships*. The story of Acosta's flight surfaced some thirty years later at a dinner party in New York City when a young U.S. Navy officer explained to his hostess why he wanted to fly dirigibles. Acosta, the hostess, explained that she too had flown a dirigible and understood his interest. At the time she was married to Colonel Henry Breckinridge. Her two marriages, the first to Oren Root and the second to Colonel Breckinridge, both ended in divorce. Oren Root was the nephew of Elihu Root, who had been secretary of war for President William McKinley and secretary of state for President Theodore Roosevelt. Colonel Breckinridge had been an assistant War Department secretary, a battalion commander during World War I, a friend of Charles Lindbergh, and an Olympic fencer.

During World War I de Acosta sold $2 million worth of liberty bonds. After the war she traveled to Europe to work for the American Committee for Devastated France. She was also interested in the arts. A story from a book about filmmaker Robert J. Flaherty, most famous for his *Nanook of the North*, credited "Mrs. Ada de Costa Root [sic] and Colonel Henry Breckenridge" as being moving forces behind Flaherty's 1927 documentary about Manhattan, *Twenty-Four-Dollar Island*. In 1935 New York mayor Fiorello La Guardia named Acosta chair of a newly formed art committee to "stimulate the artistic life and expression of the city." Afflicted with glaucoma, Acosta helped countless others with sight problems. She led a multimillion-dollar campaign to help establish the Wilmer Ophthalmological Institute at Johns Hopkins University. In her sixties she served as the first director of the Eye Bank for Sight Restoration, a position she held from 1945 until she retired in 1955. Aida de Acosta, socialite, philanthropist, and first woman pilot, died in Bedford, New York, on May 26, 1962.

SOURCES: De Acosta, Mercedes. 1960. *Here Lies the Heart*. New York: Reynal; Donovan, Frank. 1962. *The Early Eagles*. New York: Dodd, Mead; *New York Times*. 1962. "Mrs. Aida Breckinridge Dies; Former Director of Eye Bank." May 29; Santos-Dumont, Alberto. 1973. *My Airships*. Reprint ed. New York: Dover Publications.

Bruce Ashcroft

DE ACOSTA, MERCEDES (1893–1968)

Mercedes de Acosta was born in New York City on March 1, 1893. The youngest of eight children, she became a substitute for her mother's desire for a son and grew up believing herself to be a boy. Even after the age of seven, when she learned the "truth" about her sex, she insisted on living between genders.

The child of an aristocratic Cuban family transplanted to Fifth Avenue in New York City, Acosta saw herself as the unique product of three separate worlds, Spanish, Cuban, and American. Her father fought for independence from Spain and narrowly escaped execution in Cuba by immigrating to New York. Her mother, orphaned at an early age, arrived in New York, at least in Acosta's memory, as an independent and fearless woman. Acosta, a second-generation immigrant aware of her Spanish bloodlines, believed that they limited her social adaptability. She reinvented herself as an independent Latina lesbian in ways that seemed to fall through the cracks of turn-of-the-century U.S. society.

An important figure in the café society of the late 1930s, Acosta influenced a generation of public figures who challenged sexual politics, refused conformity with sexual norms, and saw themselves as their own unique invention. She was a poet, novelist, playwright, scriptwriter, and set and costume designer, which made her well known within New York theater circles, European literary circles, and the Hollywood movie colony. These circles also included luminaries like Auguste Rodin, Edith Wharton, Igor Stravinsky, Sarah Bernhardt, Eleonora Duse, Pablo Picasso, Cecil Beaton, Sri Ramana Maharshi, and Krishnamurti. Nonetheless, Acosta is perhaps most commonly remembered for the affairs she is believed to have had with several noted celebrities, including Isadora Duncan, Eva Le Gallienne, Greta Garbo, and Marlene Dietrich. As a lesbian icon, Acosta wore her difference "on her sleeve." She wore pants, cloaks, pointed shoes with a gold buckle, and an old-fashioned tricorner hat. Her black hair was usually slicked straight back. She dressed in all black or all white and owned several versions of the same item. Acosta "looked Spanish," and her "ordinary butchness" set long-standing trends in lesbian iconography. Her offstage "cross-dressing" also influenced female actresses like Pola Negri, Greta Garbo, and Marlene Dietrich to wear pants on (and off) stage.

If Acosta's role in American cultural history was transformative, her professional contributions have often been overlooked. Only two of her plays were ever produced, *Jehanne d'Arc* (1922), which starred Eva Le Gallienne, and *Jacob Slovak* (1923). In 1934 she adapted *Jehanne d'Arc* for Garbo and the Hollywood screen, but it was never filmed. Acosta was known for her convictions, which included not only devotion to vegetarianism and the guidance of gurus, but also professional integrity. In 1932, for example, she was fired for refusing to write a historically inaccurate scene for the film *Rasputin and the Empress*.

After Acosta published her memoir in 1960, *Here Lies the Heart,* she found herself increasingly isolated in her small Manhattan apartment, located at 315 East Sixty-eighth Street. Many of her former lovers resented the book's exposure, particularly after the repressive period experienced in Hollywood during the McCarthy era. During this time Acosta sold off her jewelry to pay medical bills. She died in 1968. Her life and work were portrayed in the theater, in Odalys Nanin's *Garbo's Cuban Lover* (2001), MACHA Theatre Company of Los Angeles, and in the film *Here Lies the Heart* (2001).

See also Literature

SOURCES: Cooper, Ilene. 1994. "Loving Garbo." *Booklist* 90 (May 1): 1562; De Acosta, Mercedes. 1960. *Here Lies the Heart.* New York: Reynal; Kaye, Lori. 2001. "Garbo's Girlfriend." *Advocate* 64 (October 23): 64; Vickers, Hugo. 1994. *Loving Garbo: The Story of Greta Garbo, Cecil Beaton, and Mercedes de Acosta.* New York: Random House; White, Patricia. 2001. "Black and White: Mercedes de Acosta's Glorious Enthusiasms." *Camera Obscura* 45:226–265.

Nicole Trujillo-Pagán

DE ARAGÓN, UVA (1944–)

As a Cuban American writer, educator, and cultural leader, Uva de Aragón is committed to making a difference in the Hispanic and wider American community. She has dedicated her life to writing and emphasizes that "writing is a vocation for me and I always dreamed of becoming a writer."

Born in Cuba in 1944, the same year as the Afro-Cuban poet Nancy Morejón, she wrote her first story at the age of nine when her father died. This preliminary novel was a *guajira* version of the Cinderella fairy tale and marked the beginning of her exploration of feminist theory in her work. She was able to accomplish this at this early age because of the literary background in which she had been raised. Her grandfather, father, and stepfather had all been prominent literary figures in Cuba, and they all played a role in the formative years of the young writer.

In 1959, at the age of fifteen, Uva de Aragón emigrated with her family to the United States. She adapted to the new environment, language, and culture and for the next five years experimented with writing in English. Finally she returned to writing in Spanish and in 1972 wrote *Eternidad,* her first book in her adopted homeland. Since that time she has produced a number of literary works in a variety of genres: poetry, short stories, essays, theater, and the novel. Her books include *Memoria del silencio* (2002), *El caimán ante el espejo: Un ensayo de interpretación de lo cubano* (1994), and *Alfonso Hernández Cáta: Un escritor cubano, salamantino, y universal* (1996). One of her plays and several of her short stories have been translated into English and appear in anthologies such as *Cuba: A Traveler's Literary Companion* (2002) and *The Voice of the Turtle: An Anthology of Cuban American Stories* (1997).

The recurrent themes of displacement, nostalgia and longing for the homeland, the immigrant experience, and a sincere concern for the fate of Cubans in Cuba appear in all of Aragón's works. Her literary production reflects the experience of life in exile and the realities of the Cuban diaspora in the United States. The feminist ideology is also expressed in her works, and she believes that it is a "marvellous, well deserved and important achievement" that more women writers have been recognized and included in the Latin American canon.

Among the writers who have influenced Aragón's work are José Martí, Rubén Darío, Juan Ramón Jiménez, the writers of the Latin American Boom, and Edgar Allan Poe. Over the years her literary work has evolved from that of spontaneous expression to the expression of a more confident literary aesthetic. She has received many awards and honors for her achievement and contribution in the fields of education and literature in the United States, Latin America, and Europe.

Uva de Aragón identifies herself "as a voice of my time, a Cuban American, Hispanic American, and Latina." Through her dedication to the creation of literary works she serves and contributes to the community and future generations. She expresses her pro-

Author Uva de Aragón, 2003. Courtesy of Uva de Aragón.

found commitment to literary expression with the conclusion that "my greatest anguish is to not have all the time needed to create all the books that I still have within."

Uva de Aragón is associate director of the Cuban Research Institute and associate editor of *Cuban Studies*. She holds a Ph.D. in Latin American literature from the University of Miami.

SOURCES: De Aragón, Uva. 2003. Interview by Wendy McBurney-Coombs, October 24; Uva de Aragón online. http://www.uvadearagon.com (accessed October 6, 2004).

Wendy McBurney-Coombs

DE ARTEAGA, GENOVEVA (1898–1991)

Puerto Rico is widely recognized as the birthplace of great popular musicians and important popular music traditions. Classical music has also played a role in the island's cultural history, and Puerto Rico has had and continues to have its share of world-renowned classical artists. Genoveva de Arteaga was one of these artists.

An Argentine newspaper article dated October 22, 1944, and titled "The Work of Genoveva de Arteaga" describes her as "sensational!" and goes on to say, "For years we have known and admired Dalmau, but we had only heard Genoveva de Arteaga accompany admirably. We had no idea what a great pianist she is! Last night she gave an impeccable virtuoso performance. . . . the audience gave her a resounding ovation and she had to play an encore for which she received long applause." These comments are significant because for much of her musical career Genoveva de Arteaga was best known as the talented piano accompanist of her famous violinist husband, Andrés S. Dalmau. Yet from all the evidence in her papers and in the biographical book *Latinoamerica en dos mil conciertos* by Hernándo Merchand it is obvious that she was a gifted musician who deserved star billing.

Although Arteaga's artistic career began and ended in New York City, she was born in Ponce, Puerto Rico, the youngest of five children and the only daughter of prominent musicians Julio C. de Arteaga and Nicolasa Torruella. Between 1909 and 1913 she attended the Colegio Universidad del Sagrado Corazón in Santurce. In 1907 she began musical studies in the Academia de Arteaga, a music school founded by her father, who was an acclaimed pianist and composer. She trained there until 1920 and in 1921 received a scholarship from the New York College of Music and moved to New York.

Arteaga graduated from the New York College of Music in 1922 and stayed on as an instructor for four years. In the meantime she performed publicly at Carnegie Hall and other New York venues. In 1923 she married Eduardo Fort, with whom she had her only child, Rodolfo. By 1927 she was back in Puerto Rico, where, in addition to performing, she taught at Santurce High School. In 1929 she founded the Chopin Music Academy, which gradually was transformed into the prestigious San Juan Conservatory of Music. She served as its president until 1937.

The 1930s were specially active and creative years for Arteaga, who was engaged in organizing and producing numerous musical events, as well as giving concerts. She performed, for example, with the Puerto Rico Symphony Orchestra as a soloist, produced concerts at the San Juan Conservatory, and produced and directed Puccini's opera *La Bohème* and Pietro Mascagni's *Cavalleria Rusticana* at the San Juan Municipal Theater. During those years she was also gaining prominence as an important interpreter of the works of Bach.

Music was not her only interest. Arteaga was also active in cultural and political organizations such as the First Assembly of Puerto Rican Women of the Red Cross and was a supporter of nationalist causes. A woman of strong opinions, she wrote articles for such publications as *Ambito*, *Poliedro*, *El Mundo*, *La Correspondencia de Puerto Rico*, and *Curso de música*, among others.

The arrival of the Argentine violinist Andrés S. Dalmau in Puerto Rico changed Arteaga's life dramatically. She became his accompanist, and after giving several concerts together in Puerto Rico and New York, they left in 1936 for a prolonged tour throughout Latin America and parts of Europe. Theirs was both a professional and romantic partnership. They were married in Venezuela in 1948. Arteaga's son was left behind with relatives in Puerto Rico and later continued to live apart from her in New York.

In 1950 Arteaga and Dalmau returned to Puerto Rico after fifteen years of travels. Once again she gave solo performances, including an acclaimed organ concert in the Cathedral of San Juan. Dalmau died in 1955, and Arteaga took up residence close to her family in New York, where she remained until her death in 1991. In New York she dedicated herself mainly to teaching young people and preparing them for musical careers. Her papers bear testimony to her great love of teaching. In 1956 she was named faculty member, judge, and adjudicator of the National Guild of Piano Teachers. She was also a member of the American Guild of Organists and the Choral Conductors' Guild. An active member of the New York community, she frequently offered free concerts in schools and churches and worked with organizations such as the New York Folkloric Festival, the Baroque Music Society, the Liga cívica y cultural de Mujeres Puertorriqueñas, and la

Genoveva de Arteaga playing the organ. Courtesy of the Genoveva de Arteaga Papers. Centro Archives. Centro de Estudios Puertorriqueños, Hunter College, CUNY.

Asociación de Cultura Hispánica Puertorriqueña. She contributed columns to such newspapers as *El Tiempo* and *El Diario* and founded two magazines: *Euterpe*, dedicated to music, and *Voz Femenina*, dedicated to women.

In 1970 she performed in Carnegie Hall at a concert celebrating fifty years as a music artist. Genoveva de Arteaga was a highly accomplished pianist, organist, and composer. She was also a daring woman who took a nontraditional path, deciding that her fulfillment as an artist and her dedication to her musical career came above all else. As Merchand states, "she lived not by, but for music."

SOURCES: De Arteaga, Genoveva. 1913–1991. Papers. Centro Archives, Centro de Estudios Puertorriqueños, Hunter College, CUNY; *La gran encyclopedia de Puerto Rico*. 1976. Vol. 7, *Música*. San Juan, Puerto Rico: Puerto Rico en la Mano y La Gran Enciclopedia de Puerto Rico, Inc.; Merchand, Hernándo. 1974. *Latinoamerica en dos mil conciertos*. New York: Unida Printing.

Nelida Pérez

DE AVILA, DOLORES C. (1946–)

Dolores De Avila was the innovative principal of Ysleta Elementary School, in El Paso, Texas, nationally known for its extensive parental engagement efforts. De Avila is committed to lifelong education and to sharing her expertise on education with students, teachers, and parents. She does this within the Alliance School structure, an organized grassroots approach to empowering parental leaders to join with teachers to strengthen students' education and improve educational policies.

De Avila describes her own parents as her "key teachers in terms of who I am today." Although their educational levels were modest by today's standards, their intelligence and love of learning made them role models for their daughter Dolores. Her mother, for example, read a great deal and worked the crossword puzzles daily. Her father helped raise her awareness about social justice issues. They visited orphanages and supported church collections for the poor. Both parents were actively involved in their church. At the community level her parents struggled along with their neighbors to include residential income diversity within their neighborhood. Her parents, De Avila recalled, taught her the importance of sharing and giving. De Avila earned a B.S. in education from the University of Texas at El Paso and an M.Ed. from Stephen F. Austin University.

De Avila shares much in terms of power, voice, and leadership opportunities with parents and other community residents. In the early 1980s, just after the El Paso Inter-religious Sponsoring Organization (EPISO) was established, De Avila became involved in community affairs through her church. EPISO is affiliated with the Texas Industrial Areas Foundation (IAF), a Saul Alinsky type of community organization that unites the unorganized to use power and engage with local and state decision makers to press government to become accountable to all the people.

In El Paso EPISO's faith-based organizing draws on the strengths of its 50,000-person base, largely from Catholic churches, to address the following issues. Initially, in the 1980s, EPISO focused attention on water and sewer problems in *colonias*, unplanned settlements outside the city boundaries. In the 1990s EPISO prioritized both workforce training for living wages and changing campus cultures to induce parent-teacher collaboration to prepare and place students on pathways toward higher education, better job opportunities, and decent wages. During the 1990s EPISO worked with approximately 10 percent (or ten to twenty campuses, depending on the year) of El Paso's schools, most of them near the historically neglected U.S.-Mexico border, with more than 95 percent Latino/Latina student populations.

Ysleta Elementary School has been a strong Alliance School since EPISO's strategy began. De Avila, a forceful and self-reflective leader, opened the school to parent leaders. Together with parents, campus leaders improved the school and its surroundings. In the first of several victories, parents who were concerned about traffic safety used their collective power to get traffic lights installed, a seemingly simple, but challenging feat in impoverished communities with relatively unresponsive local governments. Parents organized with parents and residents of other neighborhoods to press for Ysleta Elementary School remodeling and later for laptops for student and parental use. The school is now an attractive and hospitable site for students and parental involvement. Many parents participate in school activities, from volunteering to attending classes and expressing themselves in school decision-making processes. Some of the parents, mostly mothers, rethink their own situations and make life-changing decisions to acquire GEDs or attend higher educational institutions.

Ysleta Elementary School has become famous as a result of its successes as an Alliance School under De Avila's leadership. Education researcher and former Rice University professor Dennis Shirley featured the story of Ysleta Elementary School as one of four Texas success cases in his 1997 book *Community Organizing and Urban School Reform*. Also in 1997 the Washington, D.C., Center for Law and Education highlighted Ysleta Elementary School in its *Urgent Message: Families Crucial to Educational Reform*. Ysleta Elementary School is also in partnership with the University of Texas at El Paso in its teacher-training programs. De Avila has attended leadership institutes at the Seattle-based Institute for Educational Inquiry and at the University of Texas at El Paso.

De Avila, married and the mother of two grown sons, pursues her leadership with parents to share the importance of educational achievement, accountability systems, and parental advocacy and also to strengthen education both with their own children and at various levels of government. Her early introduction to community advocacy within the church successfully bridges both charity and justice. Dolores De Avila retired from the Yselta Independent School District in 2003, but not from issues of educational equity as she and her husband remain active members of EPISO.

See also Education

SOURCES: Lewis, Anne Chambers. 1997. *Urgent Message: Families Crucial to School Reform*. Washington, DC: Center for Law and Education; Shirley, Dennis. 1997. *Community Organizing for Urban School Reform*. Austin: University of Texas Press.

Kathleen Staudt

DE BURGOS, JULIA (1914–1953)

Known for her feminist, revolutionary, and sensual poetry, Julia de Burgos has become a cultural icon for Puerto Rican women's and political liberation struggles. Julia Constanza Burgos García was born in the rural community of Carolina, Puerto Rico. The oldest child in a family of thirteen siblings, Julia was light skinned since her mother was of mulatto origin and her father was a white Puerto Rican of German descent. During her formative years the family experienced the poverty shared by many other large rural families on the island, and Burgos witnessed the loss of six siblings. From her early years of schooling she was a dedicated student, and after she graduated from high school, her academic abilities garnered a scholarship for her to enroll at the University of Puerto Rico in 1931. After receiving a normal degree she became an elementary-school teacher.

The 1930s were a decade of political turmoil and social destitution in Puerto Rico. Just before the island began to experience the effects of the Great Depression, it was hit by a devastating hurricane. Poverty, malnutrition, and desolation dominated the Puerto Rican landscape. These conditions, along with the

Julia de Burgos poster advertising a poetry reading at the Longwood Casino, New York, 1940. Courtesy of the Pura Belpré Papers. Centro Archives, Centro de Estudios Puertorriqueños, Hunter College, CUNY.

failed policies created during three decades of U.S. occupation in Puerto Rico, became the target of a revitalized nationalist movement. All of these circumstances contributed to shaping Burgos's social and political consciousness. She joined the Nationalist Party in 1936 and shortly thereafter gave the passionate speech "La mujer ante el dolor de la patria" (Women Facing the Pain of the Nation), trying to rally women to the independence struggle. She also joined a committee to free nationalist political prisoners. At the time she was a scriptwriter for a children's radio program sponsored by the island's Department of Education and was fired as a result of her political activities. During these years of political activism Burgos also began to publish her poems in newspapers and literary journals. It did not take long before her first three collections of poetry, *Poemas exactos a mi misma* (Exact Poems to Myself) (1937), *Poema en veinte surcos* (Poem in Twenty Furrows) (1938), and *Canción de la verdad sencilla* (Song of the Simple Truth) (1939), appeared under the pen name Julia de Burgos.

The poet's personal life was quite unconventional for a Puerto Rican woman living during those years. She had married in 1934, but the marriage ended in divorce three years later. After this experience she was known for her behavior as a free spirit. Her involvement in Puerto Rico's literary and nationalist political circles produced many friendships and a rumored love affair with Luis Lloréns Torres, one of the island's most prominent writers. A few years later she began a relationship with a Dominican doctor and moved with him to Havana, Cuba. After the relationship ended in 1942, she left Cuba and moved to New York City, where she had lived for a few months in early 1940.

In New York Julia de Burgos wrote a weekly column for the newspaper *Pueblos hispanos* (Hispanic Peoples) (1943–1944), founded by Puerto Rican nationalist poet and former political prisoner Juan Antonio Corretjer. She left New York for Washington, D.C., in 1944 when she married musician Armando Marín. They returned to New York two years later, and the marriage dissolved shortly thereafter.

Until 1953, the year of her death, the poet's life of turbulent and short-lived love affairs was complicated by acute health and alcohol problems that sent her to the hospital on several occasions. The last time she was hospitalized, she wrote her famous poem "Farewell from Welfare Island," written in English. This poem foreshadows her approaching death. Soon thereafter she collapsed on a Harlem street, and her unidentified body was buried in a common plot at New York's Potter's Field for several weeks until her friends and relatives located her remains and sent them to Puerto Rico. Before she was buried in her hometown's cemetery, her casket was displayed at the Ateneo Puertorriqueño (Puerto Rican Athenaeum), where she was honored by many prominent writers and public figures. Another collection of her poems, *El mar y tú* (The Sea and You) (1954) was published posthumously and includes many of the poems she wrote during the years she lived in New York.

Almost half a century after her death, Julia de Burgos's poetry remains a powerful source of inspiration to readers and writers alike. Her poems speak to the poor and dispossessed, to people of color, to those who fight for Puerto Rican independence, and to women who love passionately, defy stifling social conventions, and forge their own lives. The soul of this feminist free poetic spirit is best captured in the verses of her composition *Yo misma fui mi ruta* (I Forged My Own Path):

> I wanted to be like men wanted me to be:
> an attempt at life;
> a game of hide and seek with my being.
> But I was made of nows.

See also Literature

SOURCES: Agüeros, Jack, ed. 1997. *Song of the Simple Truth: The Complete Poems of Julia de Burgos*. Willimantic, CT: Curbstone Press; Solá, María, ed. 1986. *Julia de Burgos: Yo misma fui mi ruta*. San Juan: Ediciones Huracán.

Edna Acosta-Belén

DE LA CRUZ, JESSIE LÓPEZ (1919–)

"It doesn't take courage. All it takes is standing up for what you believe in." This outlook has served as the guiding principle for Jessie López de la Cruz in her lifelong quest to improve the conditions of Mexican and Mexican American farmworkers. Born in Anaheim, California, in 1919, de la Cruz was abandoned by her father when she was nine and lost her mother to cancer a few years later. She resided with her grandparents and was reared by her grandmother after her grandfather's death in 1930. "As far back as I can remember as a child," she recalled, "I've done farm work." Her extended family joined the stream of migrant workers who traveled up and down the state hoeing beets, picking prunes, apricots, and grapes, harvesting vegetables, and chopping cotton during the Great Depression in California. Moving from job to job, Jessie de la Cruz was in and out of school and only received a sixth-grade education. The family settled in Parlier, a small town not far from Fresno in the San Joaquin Valley.

She married her farmworker husband, Arnold de la Cruz, in 1938 at the age of nineteen. Very soon in their relationship she challenged the traditional expectation that wives defer to husbands. "I'd been trained as a child that the woman just walked behind the husband and kept quiet, no matter what the husband does. But in work I've been equal to men since I was a child, working alongside men, doing the same hard work and earning the same wages." At her insistence the couple developed a more equal division of labor based on mutual respect and sharing. The de la Cruzes had six children born between 1939 and 1947. When Jessie's sister died, the family adopted her daughter, Susan. The family struggled to make a living, endured poor living conditions in migrant labor camps, and faced illness and injury. She lost a baby daughter to malnutrition, lack of adequate sanitation, and inferior health care.

In her early forties, she found her life dramatically changed when farm labor organizers visited her home. One was a man named César Chávez. Having struggled all her life, she was immediately receptive to their objectives to obtain higher wages, adequate housing, improved working conditions, educational opportunities, and ethnic dignity. A beneficiary of the spirit of reform and social justice unleashed by the civil rights movement, she joined the National Farm Workers Association (the precursor to the United Farm Workers union) in 1965. Two years later she became a union organizer. She experienced a great sense of pride as the first woman field representative in the Fresno area, but her job was not always easy. "It was very hard being a woman organizer," she remembered. "Many of our people my age and older were raised with the old customs in Mexico." Holding fast to her beliefs and always outspoken, she persisted in hosting meetings at her home and in visiting and speaking at workers' houses. By providing services to union members, such as translating, writing letters, filling out forms, and advocating for their rights before various government agencies, she wore down initial resistance and earned the loyalty of workers.

Because of her seemingly boundless energy, enthusiasm, and organizing skills, Jessie de la Cruz was tapped to participate in collective bargaining talks with the Christian Brothers Winery. "I want you to learn this," union cofounder Dolores Huerta told her, "because eventually you might have to take over the negotiating of the contracts." This experience proved valuable when she served on the ranch committee (equivalent to a union local) and helped enforce contracts and pursued worker grievances against the company.

Workers took to the picket lines to enhance their bargaining power at their own ranches, as well as to further the union's leverage with the industry at large. De la Cruz was always at the forefront of these efforts to encourage coworkers, and women in particular, to ignore growers' intimidation and to become active in pressuring agribusiness to improve conditions in the fields and to recognize the union as the bargaining agent. When the union turned its strategy to the boycott, she again urged them to take part. Union members, led by de la Cruz, visited supermarkets in the area to plead with consumers not to purchase grapes, wines, lettuce, and other crops.

As the union became more established in the area, she assumed the responsibility for running the local union hiring hall. This innovation eliminated the abuses of labor contractors who often took advantage of workers, charging them exorbitant prices for transportation to jobs, as well as for housing, work tools, food, and clothing. The hiring hall also operated on the basis of seniority. Those who had worked with the union the longest received the first call when jobs became available.

The union served as a significant catalyst for her involvement in the affairs of the community. Her visibility, eloquence, and confidence made her a valuable community advocate and resource. She was appointed to a variety of boards and organizations, including the Fresno County Economic Opportunity Commission, the Central California Action Associates (a community education project in which she taught English to farmworkers), and the state's Commission on the Status of Women. She became active in school board and city council meetings and pushed for bilingual education. Her political activism reached a special highlight for her when she served as a delegate to the Democratic Party National Convention in 1972.

Always industrious, Jessie de la Cruz achieved a family dream in 1977 when the de la Cruzes, together with other farmworker families, purchased farmland outside of Fresno and established a cooperative. The venture was a success, and she went on speaking tours to talk about family farming, cooperative landownership, and the struggle of farm laborers. That same year she returned to school.

Currently, de la Cruz lives in a retirement community in Fresno. Although her husband died in 1990, she continues to derive joy from her children and grandchildren. She also volunteers for the UFW and participated in its convention in 2000. She is the recipient of many awards, including recognition from the League of Mexican American Women. Her life has been an inspiration for union and community members alike. Since 1980 she has served as a symbol of the grassroots origins of the UFW and provided a lesson in individual courage and determination for a generation of college students who have read her noteworthy oral history. Her life has demonstrated how one individual overcame abject poverty and limited education to make a difference. "[N]o matter who I talk to I always talk about the union because that's the best thing that ever happened to farm workers." Her remarks serve as a testament to the transformative power of the UFW to accomplish social and individual change. "It gives me great pride to know that I had something to do with it—that I was involved, that I was organizing people."

See also Labor Unions; United Farm Workers of America (UFW)

SOURCES: Cantarow, Ellen, ed. 1980. "Jessie de la Cruz: The Battle for Farmworkers' Rights." In *Moving the Mountain: Women Working for Social Change.* Old Westbury, NY: Feminist Press; O'Farrell, Brigid, and Joyce Kornbluh, eds. 1996. *Rocking the Boat: Union Women's Voices.* New Brunswick, NJ: Rutgers University Press; Rose, Margaret Eleanor. 1988. "Women in the United Farm Workers: A Study of Chicana and Mexicana Participation in a Labor Union, 1950 to 1980." Ph.D. diss., University of California, Los Angeles; Soto, Gary. 2002. *Jessie de la Cruz: A Profile of a United Farm Worker.* New York: Persea Books.

Margaret Eleanor Rose

DE LA CRUZ, SOR JUANA INÉS (1648–1695)

The most famous writer of colonial Latin America, known in her own times as the Tenth Muse, was Sor Juana Inés de la Cruz. She was born in San Miguel de Nepantla, near Amecameca, Puebla, Mexico, as the out-of-wedlock daughter of Isabel Ramírez y Vargas and Pedro Manuel de Asuaje. Isabel, who remained illiterate throughout her life, had three daughters with Asuaje and three other children—two daughters and one son—with Diego Ruiz Lozano. She did not marry either of them. Therefore, her children were considered "natural children" (*hijos naturales*) born of two single parents, as opposed to illegitimate, those born from adulterous relationships of a married parent. Juana was baptized as a "daughter of the Church." This humble and unorthodox birth was not uncommon in colonial Mexico, even among people of Spanish descent, as Sor Juana was. Her family had some social status as medium-size landowners. Her birth took place either in 1648 or in 1651; the date remains unclear due to the disappearance of the parochial birth record book. Historians are currently accepting 1648 as her birth date.

Two major sources provide almost all the surviving biographical information about Sor Juana: a letter addressed to the bishop of Puebla, Manuel Fernández Santa Cruz (*La respuesta*), and a biography inserted in the 1700 edition of her works by Diego Calleja, S.J. Sor Juana described herself as a child with a precocious desire for learning. She pressured her mother to allow her to join her older sister's lessons with the local teacher for girls and, having learned to read and write at an early age, continued to teach herself a variety of subjects in the library of her maternal grandfather. Her dream to attend the university—which was closed to women—dressed as a man was never fulfilled, but her mother sent her to the home of a well-married maternal aunt in Mexico City. Her uncommon erudition allowed her to be introduced to the viceregal court. There she remained for several years as a protégée of Vicereine Leonor Carreto, the marchioness of Mancera, whose husband was viceroy between 1664 and 1673. During the short period of time she stayed at the court, she established her name as a poet of wondrous knowledge, which was once tested in a baroque examination by forty scholars. Despite her apparent success in court, in 1667 she took the decision to enter a convent. Her first choice was the Convent of Santa Teresa, of the spartan Carmelite order.

Her choice to become a nun has been much debated. In the seventeenth century a beautiful and wise woman of obscure birth had few other choices. Her own explanation points to her lack of desire for a marriage that would deprive her of her unbounded desire for freedom and for studying. Nonetheless, she could not adjust to the Carmelite discipline and left after three months on grounds of ill health. Her decision to take the veil was firm, however, and in February 1669 she professed in the Convent of San Jerónimo, of the Hieronimite order, adopting the name Sor Juana Inés de la Cruz. She lived there for the next twenty-six years.

As a nun, she was orthodox in her faith but unusual in her dedication to writing and maintaining good relations with erudite men and members of the viceregal court. She wrote little for her first twelve years in the convent, probably as a result of the influence of her confessor, Antonio Núñez, S.J. The arrival of Viceroy Marquis of Laguna in 1680 and his wife María Luisa Manrique, countess of Paredes, marked the beginning of a special relationship between Sor Juana and the viceregal couple. During the six years of their stay in Mexico Sor Juana wrote copiously and was read widely, although she was never published. The countess nurtured a special friendship with Sor Juana, and before her departure for Spain she collected all of her writings and succeeded in publishing them in 1689 under the title *Inundación Castálida.* A second revised edition was issued in 1690. This work earned Sor Juana universal acclamation in the Iberian Peninsula and some parts of the New World.

Her writing received both praise and criticism from male members of the church. Her mentor, the Jesuit Antonio Núñez de Miranda, a much-admired preacher and religious writer, felt betrayed by Sor Juana's inclination to mundane writing. Their relationship was abruptly cut short. In a recently found letter that most critics accept as authentic, Sor Juana bitterly denounced his intransigence, asserting her own freedom to write.

Her intellectual exchanges with men of letters included one with the bishop of Puebla, Father Manuel Fernández de Santa Cruz, at whose request she wrote a critique of the theological statements of a well-known Portuguese Jesuit, Father Antonio Vieira. Some historians argue that the object of her critique was Núñez de Miranda and his theological outlook. This work was published by the bishop without Sor Juana's permission under the title *Carta Atenagórica*. While Fernández de Santa Cruz was behind the publication, he did not support Sor Juana's ideas or stance. He answered the nun's points with his own critique of her writings and lifestyle under the female pseudonym of Sor Filotea de la Cruz. The bishop urged Sor Juana to abandon her mundane interests and return to the higher objectives of her religion with her pen and her faith.

As a response to the bishop's critique, Sor Juana wrote a lengthy autobiographical letter that has become known as *La respuesta* (The Response) to Sor Filotea. It was a fiery defense of her faith and a defense of the right of women to think and write, invoking biblical examples and female saints who had authority within the church and a voice of their own. This letter—not published until 1700—circulated at the time in manuscript form and caused a stormy controversy among ecclesiastics and laypersons. Unfortunately for Sor Juana, this exchange took place after 1691, under the episcopacy of the strict and reputedly misogynist archbishop of Mexico, Father Francisco de Aguiar y Seijas. Under pressure from the latter and a potential confrontation with the Inquisition due to the nature of the arguments she had expounded in her *Carta Atenagórica*, Sor Juana made a public renunciation of her writing in 1694, sold her books, and reconsecrated herself as a nun, signing the pledge with her own blood. In 1695, during an epidemic in San Jerónimo, she contracted the plague and died on April 15, 1695.

For centuries it was believed that she had not written a single word between 1693 and 1695, especially after her official renunciation. A recently discovered inventory of her possessions at her death describes more than 200 books and several bundles of writings, unfortunately now lost. Sor Juana continued to write in the shelter of her cell but kept her work away from worldly publicity. During the eighteenth century the memory of her writings and fame began to fade, and it was not until the early twentieth century that philologists and literary critics began to recover and extol her work. Today she is a national icon, and her image is printed on the Mexican ten-peso bill. Her works have been extensively analyzed and given universal acclamation. Her copious production includes two lay plays and several religious plays (*autos sacramentales*), numerous religious poems, religious songs for religious feasts (*villancicos*), lay and love poetry, and a long philosophical analysis of the nature of knowledge in verse, titled *Primero sueño*. She felt intensely and personally her identity as a woman of the New World, a separate entity from Spain. In regard to the evangelization of the indigenous peoples, she appreciated their history but as a Catholic nun praised the blessings of Christianity. Her poetic writings are baroque, complex, and densely worded, with numerous allegories and metaphors, but the subtlety and finesse of her writing is without rival in Latin American literature.

See also Feminism; Nuns, Colonial

SOURCES: Arenal, Electa, and Amanda Powell. 1994. *The Answer/La respuesta*. New York: Feminist Press; Bénassy-Berling, Marie-Cécile. 1982. *Humanisme et religion chez Sor Juana Inés de la Cruz: La femme et la culture au XVIII siécle*. Paris: Sorbonne; De la Cruz, Sor Juana Inés. 1982. *A Woman of Genius. The Intellectual Autobiography of Sor Juana Inés de la Cruz*. Trans. Margaret Sayers Peden. Salisbury, CT: Lime Rock Press; ———. 1985. *Sor Juana Inés de la Cruz. Poemas*. Trans. Margaret Sayers Peden. Tempe, AZ: Bilingual Press; ———. 1988. *Sor Juana Anthology*. Trans. Alan Trueblood. Cambridge, MA: Harvard University Press; Paz, Octavio. 1988. *Sor Juana; or, The Traps of Faith*. Cambridge, MA: Harvard University Press; Sabat de Rivers, Georgina. 1998. *En busca de Sor Juana*. Mexico: UNAM.

Asunción Lavrin

DE LA GARZA, BEATRÍZ (1943–)

A writer, scholar, attorney, former elected official, and a Renaissance woman from the Texas-Mexico border, Beatríz de la Garza was born in Ciudad Guerrero, Tamaulipas, Mexico, also known as Old Revilla. She uses Old Revilla as the setting for several of her works, including the novel *Pillars of Gold and Silver* and the short story of the same name in *The Candy Vendor's Boy and Other Stories.* As a result of the flooding and destruction of her hometown by the Falcon International Reservoir in the early 1950s, Beatríz moved with her family to Laredo, Texas, where she grew up. Enrolled in school in Laredo without knowing English, she began writing short tales and poetry in Spanish. When she learned English, she also began to write in this language. In high school she entered the short-story contest and twice won honorable mention awards for her writing in consecutive years from the teen magazine *Seventeen*.

She received a scholarship from the *Caller-Times* of Corpus Christi, Texas, to attend the University of Texas at Austin, where she studied journalism and creative writing. At the University of Texas she won the undergraduate short-story contest in her senior year and had

Writer and attorney Beatríz de la Garza. Courtesy of Beatríz de la Garza.

her short stories published in the student magazine, *Corral.* Her first collection of short stories, *The Candy Vendor's Boy and Other Stories*, received a star review from *Publisher's Weekly* that commented that "[t]he author shows a remarkably polished craft for a first time writer, imbuing her characters with rare emotional resonance." *The Candy Vendor's Boy and Other Stories* was selected by the New York Public Library for its list "1996 Books for the Teen Age."

Pillars of Gold and Silver, a novel for young adults, was published in the fall of 1997. *Booklist* said of *Pillars of Gold and Silver*, "De la Garza weaves a story of sunlight and moonlight, memory and affection, and the crossing of two cultures."

Her latest book, *A Law for the Lion: A Tale of Crime and Injustice in the Borderlands*, the true story of a double killing that took place in southern Texas in 1912, was published in the fall of 2003. *A Law for the Lion* exemplifies regional history at its best and represents a signal contribution to the field of Chicano history.

Beatríz de la Garza received four degrees from the University of Texas beginning with a bachelor's with honors. She earned a master's degree and then a doctorate in Spanish literature. Not yet finished with her formal education, she went on to earn a J.D. from the University of Texas' School of Law. She writes and practices law in Austin, Texas, where she has lived for more than twenty-five years. Her love of letters has led to visiting professorships at various colleges and universities in the Austin area. She has taught courses in Spanish language and literature and Basic Legal Principles for Legal Assistants at her alma mater, the University of Texas, Austin, Austin Community College, and Texas State University (formerly Southwest Texas State University) in San Marcos, Texas. De la Garza has been active in civic affairs and in 1988 was elected to her first term on the Austin Independent School District (AISD) Board. She served on the AISD School Board from 1988 to 1994, a total of three terms. During her final term (1992–1994) she served as board president, which made her the first Mexican American woman (and Latina) ever to hold this elected position in the history of the state capital's public school district.

SOURCES: de la Garza, Beatríz. 1994. *The Candy Vendor's Boy and Other Stories*. Houston: Arte Público Press; ———. 1997. *Pillars of Gold and Silver*. Houston: Piñata Books. ———. 2003. *A Law for the Lion: A Tale of Crime and Injustice in the Borderlands*. Austin: University of Texas Press; ———. 2004. Personal Communication with Roberto Calderón. September 13.

Roberto R. Calderón

DE LEÓN, PATRICIA DE LA GARZA (C. 177?–1850)

Patricia de la Garza was born in Soto la Marina, Tamaulipas, Mexico, the daughter of ranching parents, and married thirty-year-old Martín de León, a muleteer and militia captain, in 1795. The couple is known for their establishment of the settlement of Victoria, Texas. Following their marriage, they settled in Burgos, Nuevo Santander, where Martín completed his enlistment, and where their first two children were born, Fernando in 1798 and María Candelaria in 1800.

The following year the young couple applied for Martín's captain's grant of land and used Patricia's sizable dowry of almost 10,000 pesos to establish the Santa Margarita Ranch on the Nueces River in southern Texas, known today as San Patricio. Through revolts, revolution, and invasions, Patricia gave birth to eight more children in Texas: José Silvestre in 1802, María Guadalupe in 1804, Felix in 1806, Agapito in 1808, María de Jesús in 1810, Refugia in 1812, Agustina in 1814, and the last child, Francisca, in 1816. Patricia wanted her children to be well educated, and, according to the 1811 census, she and Martín hired a tutor to teach their growing family to read and write. She also asked her children not to carry guns, a difficult request in frontier Texas, since "only bandits and reprobates were armed." They created close ties to neighbors who became godparents and in-laws. The family established a second ranch on the Aransas River in 1818, next door to their new in-laws, the Aldrete family.

After Mexican independence in 1821, Martín de León applied to the Provincial Deputation of San Antonio de Béxar for permission to grant lands to colonists, much as Stephen F. Austin was doing. In 1824 Martín and Patricia were given approval to settle forty-one families on the banks of the Guadalupe River and to found the town of Nuestra Señora de Guadalupe Victoria, subsequently shortened to Victoria. Their own sons and daughters were first among the families to be granted the large ranches of 4,545 acres. Within the first five years of the Victoria colony Doña Patricia married off six of her ten children to fellow colonists or to settlers in San Antonio or nearby Goliad.

Martín de León died of cholera in 1834, leaving Patricia as the matriarch of the family. Among the new immigrants were Placido Benavides, teacher and militia captain for Victoria, and José María Jesús Carbajal, educated in the United States and surveyor for the colony. The two young men became Patricia's sons-in-law and influential members of the colony's government. They also created a split in the family by siding with the Anglo rebels in the Texas Revolution. Fernando, her eldest son, joined Carbajal and Benavides against his brothers, who remained on their ranches out of the fight. Patricia did her best to care for and protect her son when he was jailed, first by Mexican troops and then by the Anglos.

In June 1836, fearing for the safety of her family in the new Republic of Texas, Patricia gathered her relatives and moved to New Orleans. She sold the family ranch and invested the money in mortgages in land in Opelousas, Louisiana. Fernando, who had acquired land titles from many of the families who had left Texas, lost close to 50,000 acres through the unscrupulous actions of his enemies. Patricia, however, under the protection of John Linn, later senator from Victoria, retained possession of her property in town, although most of the household possessions were lost. The family remained in Louisiana with Benavides relatives and then moved to Soto la Marina in Mexico. When Texas at last gained statehood in 1845, Patricia returned to Victoria. She encouraged her sons and daughters to fight, and win, court cases to regain the family ranch lands.

As matriarch of the de León family, Patricia de León lived comfortably from mortgages on land in Victoria and Louisiana. She loaned money to her sons and daughters and cared for her grandchildren, several of whom had been left orphaned. She also financed José María Jesús Carbajal in his attempt to found the Republic of the Rio Grande. When she died in 1850, Patricia had divided her land and cattle among her three widowed daughters and deeded her property on the town square to the Catholic Church for the construction of St. Mary's Cathedral in Victoria, Texas. Her greatest legacy, however, has been the thousands of de León descendants who live in southern Texas today.

See also Spanish Borderlands

SOURCES: Barrera, Manuel. 1992. *Then the Gringos Came: The Story of Martín de León and the Texas Revolution.* Laredo, TX: Barrera Publications; Castillo Crimm, A. C. 2004. *De León: A Tejano Family History.* Austin: University of Texas Press; Hammett, A.B.J. 1971. *The Empresario: Don Martín de León, the Richest Man in Texas.* Kerrville, TX: Braswell Printing Co.

Carolina Castillo Crimm

DEL CASTILLO, ADELAIDA REBECCA (1950–)

Born in Los Angeles of Mexican parents, Adelaida R. Del Castillo grew up in the Maravilla Housing Project of East Los Angeles. By the time she was seventeen, she had joined a local theater group, El Teatro Chicano, trained with Luis Valdez's Teatro Campesino, and become politically active in the Chicano movement. While she was a student at the University of California, Los Angeles, she was arrested during a protest against then Governor Ronald Reagan's proposed cuts to bilingual education. As an active member of the United Mexican American Students (UMAS) and then el Movimiento Estudiantil Chicano de Aztlán (MEChA), she joined Ana Nieto Gómez and other early Chicana feminists in the publication of the short-lived journal *Encuentro Femenil.*

Her seminal article on La Malinche ("Malintzin Tenepal: A Preliminary Look into a New Perspective") was first published in *Encuentro Femenil* and then reprinted in 1977 as part of the first anthology of Chicana writings, *Essays on la Mujer,* edited by Rosaura Sánchez and Rosa Martínez Cruz. Historian Vicki L. Ruiz, in assessing the importance of this article to Chicana feminism, notes that given the symbolism of La Malinche as a race traitor, "one of the first tasks Chicana feminists faced was that of revising the image of La Malinche." Ruiz praises Del Castillo's "path-breaking article" for providing "a new perspective by considering Malinche's captivity, her age, and most important her conversion to Christianity." "What emerges from Del Castillo's account," Ruiz further adds, "is a gifted young linguist who lived on the margins and made decisions within the borders of her world."

In 1975 Del Castillo participated actively in CASA (el Centro de Acción Autónoma–Hermandad General de Trabajadores) and served as part of the collective that published the newspaper *Sin Fronteras.* Like other members of CASA, Del Castillo articulated a passionate belief in the ideal of working-class solidarity between Mexicanos and Chicanos—"Somos un pueblo sin fronteras" (We are one people without borders). As she notes in her introduction to her groundbreaking anthology *Between Borders,* "the relation between the history of women in Mexico to that of Mexican women in the United States is one between a people who share a similar historical, cultural, linguistic, demographic, and at one time, a similar geographic experience."

In addition to her work with CASA and the cogent articles she wrote on Chicana feminism, Del Castillo earned a B.A. in linguistics at UCLA in 1977. She then entered the graduate program at UCLA in social anthropology, where she received her M.A. in 1981 and her Ph.D. in 1991.

In 1980, while still a graduate student, she coedited with Magdalena Mora the benchmark anthology *Mexican Women in the United States: Struggles Past and Present*, a collection of articles that documents and appraises "Mexican women's participation in the struggle against national oppression, class exploitation, and sexism." Delineating the interconnected and concurrent nature of gender and class struggles, her essay "Mexican Women in Organization" evaluates the earlier efforts and difficulties faced by Chicana feminists in organizing as women during the Chicano movement, as well as the sexist practices that they encountered within one particular Chicano/Mexicano leftist group in Los Angeles. Del Castillo's essay "Sterilization: An Overview" is also one of the earliest Chicana commentaries on state violence against Latina women's bodies as manifested in forced sterilization practices.

An associate professor in the Department of Chicana and Chicano Studies at San Diego State University, Del Castillo has taught there since 1990. Always the transnational scholar, in her more recent scholarship she has focused on Mexican gender spaces, and in *Displacing Gender Identity: The Negotiation of Gendered Behavior in Mexico City's Domestic Space* (forthcoming) she examines the economic survival strategies of women in Mexico City who work as *ficheras* (dance hall girls) in the entertainment sex industry, and who, through financial empowerment, are able to renegotiate their domestic arrangements and relations with male partners. At the forefront of feminist issues during the Chicana/Chicano movement, Adelaida R. Del Castillo is a distinguished teacher, a pioneering researcher, an international lecturer, and a writer.

See also Chicano Movement

SOURCES: Del Castillo, Adelaida R. 1977. "Malintzin Tenepal: A Preliminary Look into a New Perspective." In *Essays on La Mujer*, ed. Rosaura Sánchez and Rosa Martínez Cruz. Los Angeles: UCLA Chicano Studies Center Publications; ———. 1990. *Between Borders: Essays on Mexiana/Chicana History*. Encino, CA: Floricanto Press; ———. 2002. E-mail correspondence with Rosaura Sánchez, July 29; Ruiz, Vicki L. 1998. *From out of the Shadows: Mexican Women in Twentieth-Century America*. New York: Oxford University Press.

Rosaura Sánchez

DEL PRADO, PURA (1931–1996)

Pura Del Prado, a talented Cuban American writer, was born in Santiago de Cuba in 1931. She began her literary career at the age of nine with the publication of her first short story in the children's section of a Cuban national magazine. As an adult in Cuba, she was a teacher and a writer. She graduated from the Escuela Normal of Santiago de Cuba and also studied journalism at the University of Havana.

Del Prado held a number of leadership positions in both literary and educational associations in Cuba. In 1951 she was president of the literary club La Avellaneda and was assistant director and writer for the magazine *Hosanna* in Santiago de Cuba. Throughout that time in her life she developed a firm commitment to her literary vocation, but left Cuba in 1958 before the Castro regime was established. She traveled widely in the United States and Europe and settled in the United States for a number of years until her death in 1996.

Having published her early works, *De codos en el arcoiris, Canto a Martí, Los sábados y Juan*, and *El río con sed*, in Cuba, she continued her literary production in the United States with a number of publications in Spanish. These included *Color de oricha, Otoño enamorado,* and *En la otra orilla*. Her literary talent was most apparent in the area of poetry. As colleague Rosanna Hull stated in the *Miami Herald,* 1996, "Su talento natural para la poesia era simplemente deslumbrante y digo 'natural' porque aparecía de la forma más generosa y espontanea no solo en sus versos, sino en cualquier apunte, en cualquier dedicatoria que estampara en sus libros." ("Her natural talents in poetry were simply brilliant and I say 'natural' because her poetry

Pura Del Prado and Uva de Aragón in Maryland, 1974. Courtesy of Uva de Aragón.

was appealing and spontaneous, not only in her verses but everywhere, in whatever dedication she printed in her books.")

Pura Del Prado is considered a Cuban poet because her poetry expressed a great exaltation of the homeland. In her poetry she was able to articulate the feelings and the spirit of the Cuban community in exile. Her verses make use of rich Cuban idioms and imagery that therefore express a strong connection with the Cuban homeland and traditions. In turn, the verses of Del Prado also reflect on the present experiences and life conditions of Cubans in their adopted homeland. They seem to protest against the loss of the freedom to inhabit the land of their birth, and also against the separation of the Cuban people. In the poem *Por qué se van*? one can see many examples of these characteristics. Another poem written by Del Prado became very popular in exile and was made into a song by the Cuban *trovador* Pedro Tamayo. The verses of this song can frequently be heard on radio stations in Miami: "Aquí no, que va. . . . , El día que yo me muera, se va a morir Cuba un poco, porque mi espiritu loco, tiene zumo de palmera." ("The day I die, Cuba will also die a little because my crazy spirit bears the essence of the palm trees.") These poems became very popular in exile because they captured the spirit of the Cuban community in the United States in a lyrical and meaningful way. They have contributed to the preservation of the Cuban past and to the history and the heritage of Cuban Americans.

SOURCES: Correa, Armando. 1996. "Pura Del Prado, poeta y escritora cubana a los 64 Años." *El Nuevo Herald*, October 18, 4A; Laurencio, Angel Apracio, ed. 1970. *Cinco Poetisas Cubanas, 1935–1969*. Miami: Ediciones Universal.

Wendy McBurney-Coombs

DEL RÍO, DOLORES (1905–1983)

Dolores Del Río was born Lolita Dolores Asúnsolo Martínez y López Negrete in Durango, Mexico. Her family fled her home to Mexico City in 1910. Raised in an upper-class Mexican family, at the age of fifteen she married Jaime Martínez Del Río, the son of a wealthy Mexican family. They spent their honeymoon in Europe, traveling for two years, before settling in Mexico City. In 1925, while on his honeymoon, the director Edwin Carewe met the Del Ríos. Taken in by her beauty, Carewe inquired if Dolores would be interested in making movies. With Jaime's consent, the couple traveled to Hollywood.

The film *What Price Glory?* (1926) made Del Río a star. Under Carewe's guidance Del Río made *Resurrection* (1927), *The Loves of Carmen* (1927), and *Evangeline* (1929). In these roles she mainly portrayed European peasant women.

After divorcing Jaime Del Río in 1928, Del Río married Cedric Gibbons, head art director for MGM studios in the 1930s. No longer under Carewe's tutelage, Del Río made the transition to more exotic and sophisticated roles. *The Girl from the Rio* (1932), *Bird of Paradise* (1932), and *Flying down to Rio* (1933) are her most memorable films from this period. At the same time she and Gibbons stood out as one of the best-known couples in Hollywood. Unfortunately, by the late 1930s Del Río's career and her marriage were on the decline. She divorced Cedric Gibbons in 1941.

Already in a relationship with Orson Welles, Del Río hoped that the film *Journey into Fear* (1943) would help revive her career. It did not, and her relationship with Welles fell apart. Leaving Hollywood, Del Río returned to Mexico. She explained her reasons to a *Variety* reporter: "I didn't want to be a star anymore, I wanted to be an actress and with all those gowns they put on me, all of those millions of feathers, I couldn't be. I chose instead the chance to be a pioneer in the movie industry of my country, an exciting new challenge."

Choosing her own directors, scripts, and camera crews, she entered into a new generation of filmmaking in Mexico. Her films during this period included *Flor Silvestre* (1943), *María Candelaria* (1944), *La malquerida* (1949), and *La cucaracha* (1960). In her debut film in Mexico, Del Río worked with director Emilio Fernández, cameraman Gabriel Figueroa, and leading man Pedro Armenadáriz. Their film, *Flor Silvestre*, landed Del Río an Ariel Award (equivalent to an Oscar). She won three more Ariels for the films *Las abadonadas* (1944), *Doña Perfecta* (1950), and *El niño and la niebla* (1953).

Years later Hollywood invited Del Río to appear in another film, but she continued to work in Mexico, as well as Spain and Argentina. Del Río and Henry Fonda starred in director John Ford's *The Fugitive*, filmed in Mexico in 1947. In 1954, the same year that *Salt of the Earth* was blacklisted, Del Río attempted to return to Hollywood to make the film *Broken Lance* with Spencer Tracy, but was denied a visa. Katy Jurado took the role and won an Oscar nomination for her performance. It was not until 1960 that Del Río returned to Hollywood to film *Flaming Star* with Elvis Presley. She starred in *Cheyenne Autumn* (1964) as "Spanish Woman" with Ricardo Montalban, Gilbert Roland, and Richard Widmark.

Del Río married producer Lewis A. Riley in 1959. Her later years were spent on the stage and doing charity work. Del Río appeared with Anthony Quinn and Katy Jurado in her last film, *The Children of Sánchez*, in 1977. She died in 1983 in Santa Monica, California.

Dolores Del Río's transformation from poor waif roles to sophisticated ingénues demonstrated her acting capabilities. Unfortunately, Hollywood did not permit her to be anything but the "other." Whether Del Río represented "nationness," as Ana M. López argues, or selected images that best suited her at the appropriate times, she instinctively chose roles that merged her thespian abilities and physical attributes.

See also Movie Stars

SOURCES: De Witt, Bodeen. 1967. "Dolores Del Río Was the First Mexican of Family to Act in Hollywood." *Film in Review* 18 (March): 266–283; Hershfield, Joanne. 2000. *The Invention of Dolores Del Río*. Minneapolis: University of Minnesota Press; López, Ana M. 1991. "Are All Latins from Manhattan? Hollywood, Ethnography, and Cultural Colonialism." In *Unspeakable Images: Ethnicity and American Cinema*. ed. Lester D. Friedman. Urbana: University of Illinois Press; Rodríquez-Estrada, Alicia I. 1997. "Dolores Del Río and Lupe Vélez: Images on and off the Screen, 1925–1944." In *Writing the Range: Race, Class, and Culture in the Women's West*, ed. Elizabeth Jameson and Susan Armitage, 475–492. Norman: University of Oklahoma Press.

Alicia I. Rodríquez-Estrada

The Hispanic Women's League in Buffalo, New York. Standing from left to right: Juanita Negrón, Lillian Orsini, Susan González, and Blanca Rodríguez. Sitting from left to right: Margarita Santiago, Carmen Del Valle, and Rosa Avilés. Courtesy of Blanca Rodríguez.

DEL VALLE, CARMEN (1949–1995)

Family therapist and activist Carmen del Valle, originally from the town of Aguas Buenas, Puerto Rico, came to live in the area of Lackawanna, New York, in 1952 at the age of five with her mother and thirteen brothers and sisters. Like many other Puerto Rican families who migrated to the northeastern corridor of the United States, they were casualties of the commonwealth government's economic strategy for industrialization called Operation Bootstrap. Doña María del Valle, Carmen's mother, worked in the garment industry and by herself raised her thirteen children in the town of Lackawanna. Carmen's life is a testimony to the success of her mother's struggles.

Del Valle had a sense of pride in her cultural heritage as well as a strong belief in women's ability to contribute to the betterment of the Hispanic community in Buffalo. She believed in the role of education and women's solidarity as instrumental elements to transform the social conditions facing Hispanic women and their families in the United States. She was a passionate advocate in Buffalo's West Side, the heart of the Puerto Rican community, on issues of education, women's health, and violence against women and in the promotion of programs strengthening Puerto Rican identity and cultural pride. It was her strong leadership that led her to be a cofounder of the Hispanic Women's League/la Liga de Mujeres Hispanas and the Hispanic Network of Health and Human Services. To this day these groups remain active and well recognized by the community of western New York.

Del Valle, like many other Hispanic women, had to manage her academic career while working and raising two daughters. In 1975 she received a bachelor of science degree with a concentration in social work, and four years later she earned a master's degree in social work from the State University of New York at Buffalo. She was a recipient of the Outstanding Student Award from the School of Social Work. She then joined the Child and Family Services of Buffalo, where she had completed her fieldwork as a graduate student. She became the first Hispanic woman in Buffalo to obtain certification as a social worker. She worked for this agency for twelve years and during that time became the first Hispanic woman to be the director of the West Side Services Office. In 1994 del Valle and her staff received an award from the American Association of Marriage and Family Therapy in New York State for their work toward cultural diversity in family therapy.

In 1979, the year she earned her master's degree, Del Valle founded the Hispanic Professional Women's League with the help of a small group of Hispanic women, María Rosa-Rey, Sara Norat, Lillian Orsini, and Carmen Faccio. Reminiscing about the origins of the league's work in her speech as outgoing president in 1989, she recalled: "In 1979, a group of Hispanic women, mainly educators and social workers, responded to an editorial opposing bilingual education. The need for an organization to address issues in the Hispanic community from a women's perspective became apparent and the Hispanic Professional Women's League was born. That year a group of Hispanic women (who) were educators and social workers banded together to oppose an attack on bilingual education. We recognized that the needs of the Hispanic Community went beyond that one event, so we decided to build an ongoing organization which could address issues in our community from a women's perspective."

In 1983 the group changed its name to the Hispanic Women's League, recognizing the excluding connotations and class difference established by the word "Professional." Del Valle also helped develop and establish the league's scholarship program to help Hispanic women pursue higher education.

In 1990 Del Valle assumed the position of trainer for the Center for Human Services in charge of educating future social workers at the State University of New York College at Buffalo. She became one of the first Hispanic women leaders in the Buffalo area, and her legacy is still alive among Hispanic women, community advocates, and health professionals of western New York. Recognizing her legacy of service, on January 19, 1996, the Children's Hospital of Buffalo named its Women's and Children's West Side Health Center in her memory.

In 1998 Carmen Del Valle became one of the two Hispanic women included in the Western New York Women's Hall of Fame, an entity created in order to recognize women who worked to enrich their communities either in the public spotlight or in private. In March 2001 her name became part of the Bricks for Buffalo Women's Walkway to be located in the Niagara Frontier Transit Authority's Terminal across the HSBC Arena.

In community politics Del Valle was also one of the first women to confront Hispanic male leaders' limited views on women's roles and political participation. "She confronted our Hispanic men with their Machismo," recounts her mother. Her commitment to Puerto Ricans in the island also led her to organize a community-wide campaign for victims of the 1986 mudslide. A plaque in the West Side community clinic honors her legacy with these words:

> Her actions were those of peace making and bridge building. Her leadership expressed itself in constant joyous discovery of others' strengths.
>
> Her skills as a therapist brought families closer to each other and to the community networks which she recognized to be the source of her own strength.
>
> She was our sister, her spirit will be felt here when we support each other's small efforts and when we take united action. Particularly, then she will be with us smiling.

Carmen Del Valle passed away in 1995 from malignant cancer. Her memory still is a source of strength for women of the Hispanic Women's League. Her life struggles and actions are part of the history of the Puerto Rican and Hispanic women in Buffalo, New York.

SOURCES: Buffalo General Hospital. 2004. "Kaleida Health Dedicates Del Valle Health Center." June 18. http://bgh.kaleidahealth.org/news/news_display.asp?artID=39 (accessed June 27, 2005); Del Valle, María. 2001. Oral history interview by Janine Santiago, August 19; "Health Center Honors Late Hispanic Leader." 1996. *Buffalo News*, January 19; Rodríguez, Blanca. 2001. Oral history interview by Janine Santiago, August 25; Text on plaque honoring her memory at the Carmen Del Valle West Side Health Center. "Women's Hall of Fame to Honor Inductees." 1998. *Buffalo News*, September 28.

Janine Santiago

DELGADO, JANE L. (1953–)

Jane L. Delgado was born in Havana on June 17, 1953. Two years later she immigrated to Brooklyn, New York, with her mother and sister. She attended local public schools while her mother worked in several factories. Because she spoke little English, her teachers placed her among slow learners in English classes, but recognized her academic strengths and advanced her to the top of her grade in math classes. By third grade Delgado was at the top of her grade in all subjects. In fifth grade, sensing Delgado's innate ability to listen to and help her classmates, her teacher suggested that she become a psychologist.

Delgado skipped eighth grade, took honor classes in high school, increased her course load, graduated from high school in the eleventh grade, and when she was sixteen enrolled in college at the State University of New York, New Paltz. She entered her first professional job in 1973 as an assistant to the editor of the Children's Television Workshop. There, handing out payroll checks one Friday afternoon, she let colleagues know about her interest in child development and inquired if she could be considered for another position. By Monday Delgado was interviewed for the position of children's talent coordinator for *Sesame Street*.

In 1975 Delgado left *Sesame Street* to attend graduate school on a full-time basis. She received a master's in psychology from New York University that same year and in 1979 began a cross-national longitudinal study on child language development. She also accepted a position with the Immediate Office of the Secretary of the U.S. Department of Health and Human Services (DHHS). Believing that social problems require both personal and institutional change, she completed a second master's degree in urban and policy sciences at the W. Averell Harriman School of Urban and Policy Sciences and a Ph.D. in clinical psychology at the State University of New York at Stony Brook in 1981. By the time she left DHHS in 1985, she had become a key researcher on the "Report of the Secretary's Task Force on Black and Minority Health."

Delgado's family support and her personal and educational experiences taught her that "health," particularly among Latinos, requires the integration of body, mind, and spirit. She maintains this philosophy as a practicing psychologist and president and chief executive officer of the National Alliance for Hispanic Health (the Alliance). Formerly known as the National Coalition of Hispanic Health and Human Service Organizations (COSSMHO), the Alliance remains the largest and oldest organization of Latino community-based health providers.

Delgado has directed the Alliance's growth. She made environmental health a major program effort by 1988 and initiated the first technology program for community-based organizations in 1991. She has also published *¡Salud! A Latina's Guide to Total Health* (1997). This first health book for Latinas is now in its second printing. Delgado writes a column for the Los Angeles Times Syndicate. She serves as chairperson of the National Health Council and is on the board of directors for the Patient Safety Institute, the Health Care Quality Alliance, and Hispanics and Philanthropy. She is on the honorary board of the Alaska Native Heritage Center and is a trustee for the Foundation for Child Development, the Kresge Foundation and the SUNY New Paltz Foundation and a member of the Carter Center's Task Force Foundation for Child Development, the National Advisory Council for Mrs. Rosalyn Carter's Task Force on Mental Health, and the EPA's Clean Air Act Advisory Committee. She is an advisor to the American Academy of Family Physicians and the March of Dimes.

Delgado's work helps everyone. *Ladies Home Journal* named her one of seven "Women to Watch . . . unsung heroines who are forging ahead to improve our health," and *Hispanic Business* listed her as one of the 100 "Most Influential Hispanics" in 1988. She was awarded the Community Leadership Award in 1996 from the Puerto Rican Family Insitute, the Dr. Harvey Wiley Award in 1995, the Carter-Bumpers Award in 1995, and Las Primeras Award in 1994 from the Mexican American Women's National Association (MANA). While Delgado works well over sixty-five hours per week, she has a healthy family life. Her husband, Mark, and her daughter, Elizabeth, not only support her, but also see Delgado's work as their own. Together they try to move "humanness forward" and promote cooperation among people and cultures.

SOURCES: AuthorTracker. "Jane L. Delgado." http://www.authortracker.com/author.asp?a=authorid&b=2428 (accessed July 22, 2004); Delgado, Jane L. 2004. Interview by Nicole Trujillo-Pagán, April 27; LDI (the Leonard Davis Institute of Health Economics). "Jane L. Delgado." http://www.upenn.edu/ldi/delgado.html (accessed July 22, 2004).

Nicole Trujillo-Pagán

DEMOGRAPHY

Demographers often use data from the U.S. Census Bureau to identify changes in the population of the United States, including Latinos and Latinas. The first official counting of the U.S. population, which took place in 1790, fulfilled the constitutional mandate to apportion political representation and to collect taxes. However, there was no explicit manner of collecting information about any Latino ethnicity in the decennial census until 1930, when Mexican was included as an option in the question about race. Since 1930 there have been dramatic changes in the collection of federal data about the Latino population, including using linguistic criteria and Spanish surname to identify Latinos. Current federal standards call for self-identification by Hispanic descent, national origin, and race. The federal government defines a Hispanic as a "person of Cuban, Mexican, Puerto Rican, South or Central American, or other Spanish culture regardless of race." The U.S. Census Bureau commonly refers to this group as Hispanic, but others prefer to use the term Latino to signify Hispanic men and women and Latina to refer to Hispanic women only.

According to the 2000 census, Latinos are concentrated in particular areas of the United States. The largest concentrations of Latino men and women are in the West and South, with 43.5 percent and 32.8 percent of all Latinos, respectively, living in those regions. Much lower proportions of the total Latino population live in the American Northeast and Midwest: 15.9 percent and 8.9 percent, respectively. Latinas have similar geographic patterns: 43.5 percent in the West, 32.6 percent in the South, 15.4 percent in the Northeast, and 8.5 percent in the Midwest (see table 1). They are most likely to live in California (31.2 percent), Texas (19.1 percent), New York (8.5 percent), and Florida (7.8 percent).

Like Latinas, Asian women, Native Hawaiian and other Pacific Islander (NHPI) women, and American Indian or Alaskan Native (AIAN) women also prefer the West (49.4 percent, 76.6 percent, and 48.2 percent, respectively). However, the regional distribution of Latinas is quite different from those of Caucasian and African American women. Indeed, non-Hispanic white women are more equally distributed across regions of

Table 1
Regional Distribution of Women by Race and Hispanic Origin, 2000

	Hispanic Origin (of any race)	Non-Hispanic White	African American	Asian	Native Hawaiian and other Pacific Islander	American Indian or Alaskan Native
Midwest	8.5%	26.9%	18.8%	11.5%	5.6%	16.1%
Northeast	15.4%	20.5%	17.9%	20.3%	5.3%	6.5%
South	32.6%	33.9%	55.0%	18.8%	12.5%	29.2%
West	43.5%	18.7%	8.4%	49.4%	76.6%	48.2%

Source: U.S. Bureau of the Census, Census 2000 SF1, Tables P12 b, c, d, e, h, i.

the United States, but tend to prefer the South (33.9 percent). African American women are also concentrated in the South (55.0 percent), though significant proportions live in the Midwest and Northeast.

As was true for the total Latino population in the United States in 2000, the majority of Latinas are of Mexican origin. Indeed, the March 2000 Current Population Survey (CPS), another census data source, indicates that approximately 64.6 percent of Latinas are Mexican. Significant proportions of Latinas are Puerto Rican (9.1 percent), Cuban (4.1 percent), Central and South American (15.4 percent), and of other Hispanic origins (6.7 percent). Census 2000 data about the total Latino population suggest that the largest Central and South American groups in the United States are Colombians, Dominicans, Guatemalans, and Salvadorans.

The age, marital status, and household composition of Latinas are also noteworthy. Latinas are a young population: the median age of Latinas is 26.3 years. The majority of Latinas over fifteen years old in 2000, 54.3 percent, are married. Far fewer are never married (31.4 percent), widowed (5.6 percent), or divorced (8.7 percent). Further, Latinas living in family households in 2000 tend to be members of married-couple households with at least one child (67.4 percent). Female-headed households are the next most prominent type of Latino family households (32.4 percent).

Latinas have higher fertility than women of other racial and ethnic groups. A 2002 National Vital Statistics Report documents that in 2000 the fertility rate of Latinas was 105.9, compared to 58.5 for non-Hispanic white women and 73.7 for non-Hispanic black women. There is significant variation in the fertility rate of Latinas. For example, Cuban women have fertility rates that are even lower than those of non-Hispanic white women, 57.3, while Mexican women have the highest fertility rates of all Latinas, 115.1. Table 2 presents the number of children ever born for Latinas, non-Hispanic white women, African American women, and Asian and Pacific Islander women. At every age Latinas have significantly more children, with the exception of African American women fifteen to twenty-four years old.

The educational attainment of Latinas and other women is also important, given the relationship between education, occupation, income, health, and other factors. In general, Latinas have the lowest levels of education of all women (see table 3). For example, 27.2 percent of Latinas have less than a ninth-grade education, compared with 4.6 percent of non-Hispanic white women, 7.7 percent of African American

Table 2
Children Born per 1,000 Women by Age, Race, and Hispanic Origin, June 2000

	Hispanic Origin (of any race)	Non-Hispanic White	African American	Asian and Pacific Islander
Women 15 to 24 years old	535	270	529	214
Women 25 to 34 years old	1,724	1,183	1,589	868
Women 35 to 44 years old	2,351	1,798	1,937	1,684

Source: Bachu and Martin O'Connell (2001), Table 3.

Table 3
Educational Attainment for the Female Population 25 Years Old and Over by Race, 2000

	Hispanic Origin (of any race)	Non-Hispanic White	African American	Asian	Native Hawaiian and other Pacific Islander	American Indian or Alaskan Native
Less than 9th grade	27.2%	4.6%	7.7%	12.9%	7.7%	10.8%
9th to 12th grade, no diploma	18.7%	10.0%	19.0%	9.3%	13.9%	17.5%
High-school graduate (includes equivalency)	22.4%	31.4%	28.4%	17.1%	34.6%	28.3%
Some college, no degree	16.2%	22.2%	23.4%	13.4%	23.5%	24.7%
Associate's degree	4.7%	7.1%	6.3%	7.0%	7.3%	7.2%
Bachelor's degree	7.0%	16.3%	10.0%	27.2%	9.3%	7.8%
Graduate or professional degree	3.7%	8.5%	5.2%	13.2%	3.8%	3.8%

Source: U.S. Bureau of the Census, Census 2000 SF3, Tables P148 b, c, d, e, h, i.

women, 12.9 percent of Asian women, 7.7 percent of NHPI women, and 10.8 percent of AIAN women. Moreover, Latinas are significantly less likely to have bachelor's degrees (7.0 percent) than women of non-Hispanic white (16.3 percent), African American (10.0 percent), Asian (27.2 percent) or NHPI (9.3 percent) origins. In sum, with only a few exceptions, Latinas are significantly less educated than non-Latinas.

Latinas vary with respect to education level by national origin. As shown in table 4 and verified by analyses of sampling variability, Mexican-origin women have significantly lower levels of educational attainment than other Latinas. For example, approximately 32.2 percent of Mexican women have less than a ninth-grade education, compared with 16.9 percent of Puerto Rican women, 20.0 percent of Cuban women, 23.5 percent of Central and South American women, and 16.4 percent of other Hispanic women. This variation between Mexican women and other Latinas is also present and statistically significant at the highest levels of education. However, other analyses document that there are no statistically significant differences between the educational attainment of Puerto Rican women and women of other Hispanic origins and between Cuban women and their Central and South American counterparts. Therefore, variation by national origin in educational attainment among Latinas is primarily present between Mexican women and non-Mexican Latinas.

Census 2000 data (not shown) indicate that Latinas have lower labor-force participation than women of other racial and ethnic groups. For example, 47.2 per-

Table 4
Educational Attainment by Hispanic Origin, Female Population 25 Years Old and Over, 2000

	Hispanic Origin (of any race)	Mexican	Puerto Rican	Cuban	Central and South American	Other Hispanic Women
Less than 9th grade	27.4%	32.2%	16.9%	20.0%	23.5%	16.4%
9th to 12th grade, no diploma	15.1%	16.0%	17.7%	9.2%	13.0%	14.0%
High-school graduate (includes equivalency)	27.6%	25.7%	29.3%	33.6%	28.8%	32.5%
Some college or associate's degree	19.4%	18.9%	23.8%	15.5%	17.4%	25.2%
Bachelor's degree	7.3%	5.3%	7.8%	12.3%	11.8%	8.0%
Advanced degree	3.3%	1.8%	4.5%	9.5%	5.4%	4.0%

Source: U.S. Bureau of the Census, March 2000 Current Population Survey, Table 7.3.

Note: Percentages are rounded to the nearest tenth of a percent; therefore, the percentages in a distribution do not always add to exactly 100 percent.

Table 5
Major Occupation Groups of the Employed Civilian Female Population 16 Years and Over, March 2000

	Hispanic Origin (of any race)	Non-Hispanic White	African American	Asian and Pacific Islander
Managerial and professional	17.8%	34.6%	25.2%	38.7%
Technical, sales, and administrative support	38.0%	41.3%	38.0%	32.4%
Service occupations	25.9%	15.4%	25.8%	17.7%
Precision production, craft, and repair	3.3%	2.1%	2.0%	2.7%
Operators, fabricators, and laborers	13.1%	5.4%	9.0%	8.1%
Farming, forestry, and fishing	1.9%	1.3%	0.1%	0.4%

Source: U.S. Bureau of the Census, March 2000 CPS, Table 10.3, Table 11.

cent of Latinas were employed in the civilian labor force in 2000, significantly lower than their non-Hispanic white (55.3 percent), African American (52.8 percent), Asian (53.3 percent), NHPI (53.8 percent), and AIAN (50.0 percent) peers. In addition, there is significant variation in the labor-force participation of Latinas by national origin. Approximately 50.3 percent of Mexican women, 55.5 percent of Puerto Rican women, 47.2 percent of Cuban women, 57.4 percent of Central and South American women, and 57.9 percent of other Hispanic women were employed in the civilian workforce in 2000. Statistical analyses confirm that Latinas differ in their labor-force participation rates. For example, Central and South American women are significantly more likely to be employed than their Cuban and Puerto Rican counterparts.

The types of occupations in which Latinas are employed are important, because there can be significant differences in income, job stability, and employee benefits by occupation. In general, Latinas in the civilian labor force tend to be concentrated in three primary occupational groups: managerial and professional occupations (17.8 percent), technical, sales, and administrative support occupations (38.0 percent), and service occupations (25.9 percent) (see table 5). However, Latinas are less likely to be employed in managerial and professional occupations but more likely to work in precision production, as operators, and in agricultural occupations than non-Hispanic white, African American, and Asian and Pacific Islander (API) women. Approximately 38 percent of Latinas and African American women are employed in technical, sales, and administrative support, and these groups have similar rates of employment in service occupations (25.9 percent and 25.8 percent, respectively). Non-Hispanic white women and API women are far less likely to hold such positions (15.4 percent and 17.7 percent, respectively).

Latinas differ in occupation by national origin (see table 6). For example, Puerto Rican women are significantly more likely to be employed in professional specialty (11.2 percent) or administrative support (29.9 percent) occupations than Central and South American women (8.0 percent and 18.6 percent). Further, some Latinas are more likely to be associated with particular occupations than their other Latina peers. For instance, significantly higher percentages of Mexican women work in farming (2.8 percent) than non-Mexican Latinas. Similarly, Central and South American women are more likely to be working as service workers in private households (9.4 percent) than their other Latina counterparts. Thus there is significant heterogeneity in the occupations in which Latinas are employed.

According to 2000 census data, the median earnings of Latinas in 1999 who worked full-time, year-round were $21,634. Latinas earn the lowest annual incomes of nearly all racial and ethnic groups (see table 7). For instance, approximately 43.8 percent of all Latinas earned less than $19,999 in 1999, a significantly higher percentage than women of non-Hispanic white (25.1 percent), African American (32.0 percent), Asian (32.4 percent), or NHPI (30.3 percent) origins. The differences in earnings between Latinas and AIAN women are not statistically significant.

As is true with education and occupation, the annual incomes of Latinas vary by national origin. For example, 55.8 percent of Mexican women working full-time and year-round earned less than $19,999 in 1999 (see table 8). Analyses of sampling variability, not shown here, indicate that significantly higher proportions of Mexican women earn less than $19,999 compared with their Puerto Rican (40.9 percent) and other Hispanic (42.5 percent) counterparts. Variation also exists for Latinas at the highest incomes. For example, Central and South American women (8.6 percent) are

Table 6
Detailed Occupation of the Employed Civilian Latina Population 16 Years and Over by Hispanic Origin, March 2000

	Hispanic Origin (of any race)	Mexican	Puerto Rican	Cuban	Central and South American	Other Hispanic
Executive, administrators, and managerial	9.0%	9.0%	8.7%	12.1%	8.0%	9.8%
Professional specialty	8.9%	7.7%	11.2%	13.7%	9.4%	13.8%
Technical and related support	3.0%	3.1%	3.4%	2.6%	2.4%	3.1%
Sales	11.6%	11.2%	13.2%	15.1%	10.8%	12.3%
Administrative support, including clerical	23.4%	23.3%	29.9%	27.5%	18.6%	25.3%
Precision production, craft, and repair	3.3%	4.0%	2.6%	1.3%	2.9%	1.6%
Machine operators, assemblers, and inspectors	9.6%	10.2%	7.8%	8.4%	10.0%	7.2%
Transportation and material moving	0.7%	0.7%	0.0%	0.0%	0.9%	1.1%
Handlers, equipment cleaners, helpers, and laborers	2.8%	2.8%	2.6%	2.6%	3.1%	2.2%
Service workers, private household	4.1%	3.3%	0.9%	2.9%	9.4%	2.0%
Service workers, except private household	21.9%	22.4%	19.6%	13.9%	23.6%	21.3%
Farming, forestry, and fishing	1.9%	2.8%	0.1%	0.0%	0.8%	0.6%

Source: U.S. Bureau of the Census, March 2000 CPS, Table 10.6.

more likely to earn more than $50,000 compared with Mexican women (4.1 percent), a difference that is statistically significant. Variation in income by national origin for Latinas may reflect heterogeneity in educational attainment and other characteristics not explored here, such as nativity.

In conclusion, the 2000 demographic data for Latina and other women presented here point to at least two important findings. First, statistical analyses of 2000 census and 2000 CPS data document that for many demographic characteristics, Latinas vary significantly from other women in the United States. Unfortunately, the results indicate that Latinas fare worse than other women on a variety of dimensions. For example, Latinas tend to have the lowest educational attainments and incomes of all women. These trends indicate that improving the economic mobility of Latinas is critical. Second, the analyses confirm that there is significant heterogeneity in the demography of Latinas, which underscores the value of disaggregating Latinas by national origin. Further, substantial research has documented variation among Latinas by nativity. Thus it would also be important to compare these demographic characteristics for U.S.- and foreign-born Latinas. In sum, these findings highlight the need for further study of how women in the United States, especially Latinas, differ by race and national origin.

Table 7
Earnings for Females 16 Years and Over Who Worked Full-Time, Year-Round in 1999

	Hispanic Origin (of any race)	Non-Hispanic White	African American	Asian	Native Hawaiian and other Pacific Islander	American Indian or Alaskan Native
Under $19,999	43.8%	25.1%	32.0%	32.4%	30.3%	38.9%
$20,000 to $29,999	27.4%	28.6%	30.4%	23.6%	32.4%	30.6%
$30,000 to $39,999	14.6%	19.8%	18.1%	18.0%	18.9%	15.6%
$40,000 to $49,999	6.5%	10.9%	8.9%	11.8%	8.4%	7.0%
Over $50,000	7.8%	15.6%	10.6%	23.2%	10.0%	7.9%

Source: U.S. Bureau of the Census, Census 2000 SF3, Tables PCT73 b, c, d, e, h, i.

Table 8
Earnings of Full-Time Year-Round Female Workers 15 Years and Over by Hispanic Origin, 1999

	Hispanic Origin (of any race)	Mexican	Puerto Rican	Cuban	Central and South American	Other Hispanic
Under $19,999	51.7%	55.8%	40.9%	40.3%	51.5%	42.5%
$20,000 to $24,999	14.1%	13.6%	15.0%	11.8%	14.2%	18.4%
$25,000 to $34,999	16.7%	15.7%	22.7%	20.2%	14.1%	20.0%
$35,000 to $49,999	11.5%	10.7%	13.7%	16.3%	11.6%	11.2%
Over $50,000	5.9%	4.1%	7.6%	11.4%	8.6%	8.0%

SOURCES: Bachu, Amara, and Martin O'Connell. 2001. *Fertility of American Women: June 2000.* Current Population Reports, P20-543RV. Washington, DC: U.S. Bureau of the Census. http://www.census.gov/prod/2001pubs/p20-543rv.pdf (accessed February 19, 2003); Guzmán, Betsy. 2001. *The Hispanic Population: Census 2000 Brief.* U.S. Bureau of the Census. May. http://www.census.gov/prod/2001pubs/c2kbr01-3.pdf (accessed February 19, 2003); Therrien, Melissa, and Roberto R. Ramirez. 2000. *The Hispanic Population in the United States: March 2000.* Current Population Reports, P20-535. Washington, DC: U.S. Bureau of the Census. June 2003. *The Hispanic Population in the United States: March 2002.* Washington DC: Government Printing Office. ———. (2001). *2000 Census of Population and Housing.* Summary File 1 (SF1), 100-Percent Data and Summary File 3 (SF3), 5-Percent Data. http://fact finder.census.gov/ (accessed February 19, 2003).

Eileen Diaz McConnell

DEPORTATIONS DURING THE GREAT DEPRESSION

On Thanksgiving Day, November 27, 2003, the *News Hour with Jim Lehrer* became the first national television news program to present a dark and tragic chapter of American history—the unconstitutional deportation and repatriation of Mexicans and Mexican Americans—to the American public. A survivor of this horrific experience was María Ofelia Acosta, who testified to the viewers how her parents, legal residents of the United States, and their American-born children were rounded up for deportation to Mexico. "I could have gone to school . . . my sisters and brothers. I could have had a better life," she lamented. Still, Acosta is convinced that recent legal action on behalf of the survivors for reparations will never remedy the injustice. "No money can pay for that." She wants only that the American public recognize this wrong. Along with Acosta, thousands of other women experienced unconstitutional deportation and coerced emigration wherein federal, state, and local authorities captured between 1 and 2 million persons for forced expulsion to Mexico.

Even before the deportation campaigns Mexican and Mexican American women were battling the economic crisis of the Great Depression at home and in the workplace. In many Mexican families women were responsible for handling family finances. Vera Gody remembered that her mother "took care of the money, largely because her father had no time to make decisions. . . . He was either working or looking for work." Jesusita Solis recalled, "We were accustomed to my handling the household budget." Many women also worked outside the home in agriculture, canneries, and garment factories.

As unemployment spread and more families confronted the pressures of deportation and repatriation, Mexican and Mexican American women were often in charge of preparing for the trip to Mexico. They organized and packed household items. As Emilia Castañeda observed, "A man, well he . . . just packs up his sleeping bag and throws it over his back and that's good enough for him. Now a woman, she'll think about whether she wants her sewing machine, her bed, and her dishes." Women bravely traveled alone without spouses. Adela S. Delgado and her three young daughters drove an old, jam-packed Dodge automobile from Pueblo, Colorado, to Santa Eulalia, Chihuahua. Delgado's experience was not an isolated case. The San Diego Consulate reported in 1932 that 27 out of 100 repatriation cases consisted of women traveling alone to Mexico.

Expulsion from the United States formed only part of the tragic experience of repatriation for Mexican and Mexican American women; adjusting to life in Mexico was another traumatic episode. Many Mexican nationals were returning after a ten-, twenty-, or thirty-year residence in the United States. They encountered a new and different Mexico. U.S.-born women and girls

The repatriation of Mexican men, women, and children from Los Angeles, March 9, 1932. Courtesy of the Security Pacific Historical Collection. Los Angeles Public Library.

found themselves in a foreign country with a different culture and language. It was not their home. At best, Mexico was only an ancestral home.

For women repatriates, living in Mexico was regarded as a struggle against poverty and despair, according to survivors Emilia Castañeda and María Ofelia Acosta. It was not the "Mexico, lindo y querido" (Beautiful and Beloved Mexico) celebrated in song and folklore. One reason for adjustment difficulties was that Mexico itself was undergoing the Great Depression. Employment opportunities for the Mexican working class were limited. It therefore was not surprising that Mexican workers disdained repatriates as unfair competition. Some upper- and middle-class Mexican families, however, welcomed young repatriate women who could be hired inexpensively as English-language tutors for their children.

With few jobs available, most repatriates resorted to living with relatives, who often despised them as additional and unwanted burdens. Living conditions were deplorable and crowded, especially for women and girls, who were regarded as responsible for maintaining the home. One woman remembered that as a young girl, "We just had a bedroom for all of us [the entire family]." Another survivor recalled that "We used to have to sleep outdoors. . . . If it rained we couldn't go into the house." Further conflict occurred because many women repatriates were used to American household appliances and conveniences, such as washing machines, sewing machines, and gas stoves. This created tension between repatriate women and their Mexican and other relatives who favored the traditional ways of doing housework.

Outside the home women encountered little freedom of movement and expression. Many women had either grown accustomed to the more liberal ways of American society or had difficulty conforming to a more conservative Mexican lifestyle. They were frequently criticized for their American dress and appearance, including bobbed hair, nail polish, lipstick, and other cosmetics. "The people didn't like the way I dressed. . . . They didn't like for us to wear lipstick, rouge, or anything," Teresa Martínez recalled. Mexican modesty required that mothers and daughters not appear to be loose women.

Language emerged as a particularly sensitive issue because children frequently lacked Spanish fluency and had difficulties communicating. Carmen Martínez recalled that she "spoke very little Spanish in the United States and learned to read and write in Spanish in Mexico." Moreover, schools in the United States frequently disciplined children who spoke Spanish. "The school teachers used to tell us that we shouldn't be speaking Spanish. We used to get scolded and told that we shouldn't speak Spanish but that we had to speak English," Emilia Castañeda said of her school experience in Los Angeles. Some repatriate women and girls therefore endured name-calling that criticized them as *pochas, tejanas,* or even *gringas*.

Many women repatriates maintained their American identity and dreamed of returning to the country of their birth. Teresa Martínez recalled: "I would always say, oh what if I could go back to my country again. . . . I always had intentions of going back home." At the beginning of World War II the need for workers encouraged some repatriation survivors to return to the United States. Emilia Castañeda, for example, remembered her trip on a "crowded train coming back to the United States. . . . There was no place to sit down since servicemen came first." The servicemen regarded Castañeda as a "novelty" and were "surprised" that she could speak English. Yet she never forgot "the fact that I was an American citizen."

Some seventy years after the repatriation drives, women survivors are still defending their American citizenship and identity by lobbying local, state, and federal authorities for recognition of the deportation injustice. With the support of the Mexican American Legal Defense and Educational Fund they also have played key roles in filing the lawsuit *Emilia Castañeda v. the State of California, County of Los Angeles, and Los Angeles Chamber of Commerce.* Though filed on July 15, 2003, the suit has since been withdrawn to avoid an unfavorable ruling given that previous legislation that would have extended the statute of limitations failed. Two years later, a similar bill was passed by members of the California Senate and is being considered in the California Assembly. If this bill is approved and signed into law by Governor Arnold Schwarzenegger, MALDEF intends to re-file the law suit. Whatever the legislative and legal outcome, the courage and strength of women repatriation survivors remain unquestioned.

SOURCES: Balderrama, Francisco E., and Raymond Rodríguez. 1995. *Decade of Betrayal: Mexican Repatriation in the 1930s.* Albuquerque: University of New Mexico Press; Carreras de Velasco, Mercedes. 1974. *Los Mexicanos que devolvió la crisis, 1929–1932.* México, D.F.: Secretaría de Relaciones Exteriores; Guerin-Gonzales, Camille. 1994. *Mexican Workers and the American Dream: Immigration, Repatriation, and California Farm Labor, 1900–1939.* New Brunswick, NJ: Rutgers University Press; Hoffman, Abraham. 1974. *Unwanted Mexican Americans in the Great Depression: Repatriation Pressures, 1929–1939.* Tucson: University of Arizona Press; Sánchez, George. 1993. *Becoming Mexican American: Ethnicity, Culture, and Identity in Chicano Los Angeles, 1900–1945.* New York: Oxford University Press.

Francisco Balderrama

DIMARTINO, RITA (1937–)

Rita DiMartino, a prominent Latina in business and politics, was born in Williamsburg, Brooklyn, on March 7, 1937, and was raised there. Her parents, Juan Dendariarena and Frances Cruz Dendariarena, migrated to New York City from Puerto Rico in the early years of the Great Depression. Like many others who migrated in that era, they arrived with the aspiration of economic stability. Juan worked for the Fisher Company in New York as a machinist in 1927. Frances arrived in New York City in 1932 on the ship *Coamo* and worked for some time at the Emerson Company in New Jersey. After marriage Frances became a homemaker for her family. When her husband passed away, she was left to raise six girls on her own. Serving as a role model to her daughters, she spent her time teaching Bible school to children, played the piano at church, and was the church organist. Frances made it a priority to ensure that her daughters were instilled with strong work ethics, the value of education, and respect for the church. This influence has followed DiMartino throughout her life and has contributed to her successes, ambition, and prominence today.

Rita DiMartino graduated from Eastern District High School in Brooklyn, New York. Shortly thereafter, in 1957, she married and started a family. While she was raising her three children, Vickie Ann, Anthony, and Celeste, she continued to work and became politically active. While she was employed as a legal secretary and assistant to the party chairman of the Republican Party, her interest in politics grew. DiMartino's responsibilities included administrative duties, inspecting the voting polls during campaigns, and serving as a translator. Her involvement encouraged her to begin her own Spanish American Republican Club. Early in her life she recognized that the best way to help people in all areas was by becoming involved in politics.

A good role model for her children, as her mother had been for her, DiMartino returned to school to further her education. Although this meant sacrificing time spent with her family, DiMartino still managed to create a balance that enabled her to be the positive role model her children needed. Despite many obstacles, in 1974 DiMartino earned an associate's degree at Richmond College. Currently she holds a bachelor of arts from the College of Staten Island, a master's in political administration from Long Island University (C. W. Post), and an honorary doctorate of civil law from Dowling College. In addition, she completed courses at the Harvard Business School and at the University of California at Berkeley in leadership and executive management programs.

When DiMartino graduated from college, her involvement in politics made it easier for her to find a job that took her out of the secretarial slot. She was placed into a senior business consultantship position at the New York State Department of Commerce's Office of Minority Business Enterprise. She worked there for some time before taking time off to work with Perry Duryea on a gubernatorial campaign in 1978 despite the risk to her job; if her candidate lost, she too would need to look for a new job. Perry Duryea was not successful and lost the election; DiMartino was faced with seeking new employment.

In 1979 DiMartino was hired at AT&T in public relations, where she worked for the next twenty-five years. Once again drawing upon persistence and dedication, she climbed the ranks at AT&T and was promoted to the Government Affairs division and eventually to vice president of congressional relations. In this role DiMartino developed fruitful relations with the administration, the U.S. Congress, and state governments. She consistently met with members of Congress and advocated for AT&T's interests. Maintaining an interest in Hispanic affairs, she served as a resource for the company, providing leadership and counseling.

In 1982 she was appointed by President Ronald Reagan as an ambassador to the UNICEF Executive Board. As the U.S. representative, DiMartino helped increase financial support and the program's agenda in areas of child health, nutrition, water supply, sanitation, and education. Presently DiMartino serves on numerous boards and councils representing the voice of Latinos worldwide, including the Board of Trustees of the City University of New York (CUNY), the Hispanic Council on Foreign Relations, the Cuban American National Council, the Congressional Hispanic Caucus, the Ana G. Méndez University System, the William J. Fulbright Scholarship, and the National Association of Latino Elected Officials. She is also a delegate to the

Prominent Latina businesswoman and politician Rita DiMartino, 2004. Photograph by and courtesy of Jorivette Quintand.

Inter-American Commission of Children and the Inter-American Commission of Women. An active participant on these boards, DiMartino is serving her Latino/a community and setting an example.

Rita DiMartino's accomplishments continue to mold the history of Latinas all over the world. Continuously setting new goals for herself, she has made an impact, and future achievements may include lobbying for an ambassadorship in Latin America or becoming the Treasurer of the United States. She advises anyone looking to follow in her footsteps to never get discouraged, to set goals, and always to remember to lend a helping hand to others. These are the qualities that enabled her to succeed and are the true qualities of a leader.

See also Entrepreneurs

SOURCES: College of Station Island (CSI) News and Media. 2003. "Island Republican to join CUNY Board of Trustees." June 8. http://www.csinews.net/IntheNews/061803dimartino.html (accessed August 30, 2004); DiMartino, Rita. 2003. Oral history interview by Jorivette Quintana. December 15; DiMartino, Rita. 2003. Résumé, biography, and political profile; Organization of American States, 2002. "United States Appoints New Chief Delegate to OAS Women's Commission." February 21. http://www.oas.org/OASpage/press_releases/press_release.asp?sCodigo=E-035/02 (accessed August 30, 2004).

Jorivette Quintana

DIMAS, BEATRICE ESCADERO (1923–)

Raised under a strict father on border farms on the outskirts of El Paso and Clint, Texas, young Beatrice Escadero hardly had time for social events. But as fate would have it, on February 14, 1942, her father allowed her to attend a fiesta at the small San Antonio Church in El Paso. Most of her friends, as well as soldiers from nearby Fort Bliss, were in attendance.

She must have looked stunning to catch the attention of a soldier whose country was in the middle of the greatest war the world had ever seen, World War II. Although he did not exactly ask the girl in the fitted pink dress to be his Valentine, Alfred Dimas did have plans for the two of them. "He said, 'See that girl in the pink dress and the beautiful legs? I'm going to marry her,' " recalled Escadero Dimas about her husband. "And he did." Beatrice and her friends agreed that young Alfred looked handsome in his uniform, but she does not remember what caught her eye. "But I know that I liked him," she said. After a few months of dating, closely monitored by her father, the two were wed on July 22, 1942, although her mother did not want her to marry. "My mother said it wasn't going to work out because he was in the service," Escadero Dimas said. "But here I am, married 61 years to the man!"

Alfred and Beatrice Dimas, circa 1940s. Courtesy of the U.S. Latino and Latina World War II Oral History Project, University of Texas, Austin.

Alfred Dimas had enlisted in the cavalry at Fort Bliss, but shortly after the marriage he was sent to Fort Benning, Georgia. There he became a paratrooper and later was transferred to Fort Meade, Maryland. After arriving at Fort Meade, he sent for his wife, who had been living with her in-laws. The young girl from El Paso traveled across the country by herself to be with the man she loved. While the experience was traumatic, she said, it was necessary. "You don't say this is bad, this is wrong," Escadero Dimas said. "You just don't." It was in Maryland that the young couple found out they were going to have a child. After giving birth to a baby boy in Phoenix, Arizona, surrounded by Alfred Dimas's family, Escadero Dimas returned to Fort Meade.

For a small woman like Escadero Dimas, traveling across the country with a baby by railroad was a difficult task. Soon she began to travel with other women and mothers to and from the fort. Together they made the experience easier for one another to handle. But greater hardships lay ahead. While he was jumping out of an airplane, Alfred Dimas's parachute malfunctioned, and the harsh landing left him permanently disabled. Because of the injury, he never went overseas to fight against the Axis powers.

After the accident Alfred Dimas was confined to a resort that had been turned into a military hospital in White Sulphur Springs, West Virginia. He was released from the army on October 31, 1945, and had the choice to go to Florida or Arizona. He picked the latter in order to be with his family. Times were difficult after the war for the Dimas family. "We didn't have a home to live," Escadero Dimas said. "It was bad for us—the veterans and the wives. There are a lot of agencies nowadays, but we didn't have that. We called the City of Phoenix, and three months after that they called back and said they still didn't have anything for us."

They were thankful, she said, that her in-laws were building a home and allowed them to live in it, though it was not complete. "Luckily for us, (my husband) was highly intelligent and got a job," Escadero Dimas recalls. "But it was very sad for us."

Her husband was able to acquire a loan from the Veterans Administration in 1950, and the couple built a house of their own in Phoenix. Escadero Dimas had been through hard times before. During the depression her family had to sell their land and livestock to survive. She and her eight brothers and sisters were forced to quit school and help out in the cotton fields of Clint. Through the tiny radio her parents owned, she learned about the stifling effects of the Great Depression. "I could hear the news. Everybody was perishing; everybody had to move."

From that point on, Beatrice Dimas was determined to go back to school. After she and her husband settled in Arizona, Alfred Dimas attended school on the GI Bill and learned the art of leather crafting. Beatrice Dimas, like many women of the time, stayed home to take care of the house and children. However, in the 1970s her determination won out, and she decided to finish her education. After receiving her GED in 1973, she enrolled in Glendale Community College. In 1985 she received her associate's degree with a major in Spanish and a minor in psychology. For her, graduation was very fulfilling. "I was going to go back and finish my studies and my education," said Beatrice Dimas, "because I loved school."

Today, she says, she loves her husband even more, and they still learn many things from each other. "I have never fallen out of love with that fellow," Beatrice Dimas remarks. Alfred Dimas has been a hardworking person who has provided their family with a beautiful life. Recently the couple was honored at their granddaughter's wedding. The day marked their sixtieth anniversary. Beatrice Dimas attributes their long life together to overcoming each other's differences and remaining in love.

See also World War II

SOURCES: Alexander, Jonathan. 2003. "Love Helped Wife Endure Hardships." *Narratives: Stories of U.S. Latinos and Lati-*

nas and World War II (U.S. Latino and Latina WWII Oral History Project, University of Texas at Austin) 4, no. 1 (Spring); Dimas, Beatrice. 2003. Interview by Maggie Rivas-Rodríguez, Vets Center, Phoenix, Arizona, January 4.

Jonathan Alexander

DOMESTIC VIOLENCE

Intimate partner violence (IPV) has reached epidemic proportions in the United States. It is estimated that 30 to 40 percent of non-Hispanic American women have suffered violence in their intimate relationships. Among Latinas of diverse national origins, estimates range from 50 to 60 percent. These figures refer to heterosexual relationships. Accurate data on the extent of IPV among Anglo gays and lesbians are scarce and for Latina lesbians nonexistent.

The legal definition of IPV includes the use of physical violence, sexual violence or coercion, and emotional or psychological abuse against a partner or spouse. In addition, when violence is present in intimate associations, a number of relational dynamics occur that are considered abusive as well. Among these are control of finances, thus limiting women's access to money; restriction of freedom and isolation such that women are not allowed to have friends, visits, or family contact; and threats and intimidation intended to control women's behavior through fear. At the core of IPV is one partner's use of power tactics in order to control the other.

IPV is a cycle that occurs when pent-up frustration and stress are not managed or released in appropriate ways and explode in an act of violence toward an intimate partner. Generally, after the first few incidents the aggressor asks forgiveness and expresses shame and remorse. This may be followed by a honeymoon phase during which the couple believes that it will never happen again. However, violence is likely to recur. The cycle is repetitive and episodic. The victims of violence come to live in fear, experience hypervigilance, and try to anticipate the aggressor's mood and predict when the next assault will come. Over time the cycle is likely to escalate, with a commensurate increase in fear, distancing, and psychological distress among the family members. Being a victim of IPV engenders feelings of shame, guilt, and culpability. Secrecy may surround the situation, further increasing the isolation of those who suffer it and rendering them more vulnerable to continuing assaults. Unless outside intervention occurs, the cycle is not likely to end on its own.

A number of etiological explanations can be found in the literature for the occurrence of IPV among heterosexual couples. Psychological theories grounded in psychodynamic notions posit that at the root of male violence against women is fear of women and dependency needs that are masked through tactics to attain power and control. These theories also suggest that women do not leave abusive relationships because of their own psychological dependency needs, low self-esteem, and the "secondary gains" (positive sequelae of being a victim) obtained in abusive relationships.

Feminists counter that such theories designate women's behavior as pathological and excuse male violence. Furthermore, feminist writers argue that males commit violence against women because they can. Until the 1990s IPV was not a crime. In fact, patriarchal notions of male superiority entitled men to rule over their households and "discipline" women and children. Feminists argue that the patriarchal system has legitimized violence against women. British common law, which is the basis of American jurisprudence, included the "rule of thumb." This meant that a man could hit his wife and children with a stick as long as it was no thicker than his thumb. Feminists argue that violence against women will not cease until the patriarchal system is replaced by one in which gender equity and respect toward women and children are the norm.

Other psychologists, informed by learning and behavioral theories, argue that all violence is learned; thus men learn to be violent toward women through social conditioning that allows violence and promotes it through media and from models of violent behaviors by important men in their life. Individuals who have grown up in families where violent or aggressive tactics were used to resolve conflict learn to emulate those behaviors. Since violence is learned, it can be unlearned. In fact, these theories provide the foundation for most treatment programs for men who batter.

Family systems theorists propose that IPV can be explained in terms of relationship dynamics, family rules and roles, and learned intergenerational patterns. Families with rigid sex roles, strict adherence to traditional values, hierarchical patterns of communication, and aggressive family members run the risk of members behaving violently toward one another. Moreover, system theories view intimate partner violence as dyadic; that is, it must be understood not just as men behaving violently, but also as a series of transactions between intimates in a relationship that culminate in violence. The danger in this analysis is ultimately blaming women for the violence that they suffer. Family theorists argue, however, that intimate partner violence is a very complex situation that must be understood in terms of the individual psychology of the partners, the family environment, organization, and structure, and the larger social context within which families form and function.

Intergenerational family theorists expand the lens of analysis to look at how issues in the birth family precipitate violence in subsequent generations. Likewise, family disruptions, traumas, or significant losses can influence dysfunctional patterns of relating in subsequent generations. More recently, other theories have challenged both individual and family theorists to consider the influence of injustice, racism, classism, and the impact of migration on the development of IPV.

Flores-Ortiz, among others, suggests that in the case of Latinos and other people of color, the violence of men must be understood in terms of the men's own experience of exploitation and the psychological sequelae of their victimization. Furthermore, specific cultural and family dynamics are viewed as characteristic of Latino families with a problem of violence.

Latino cultures emphasize interdependence, respect, loyalty, and sacrifice as a way to maintain harmony in family relationships. Families with a violence problem are families out of balance; the adults, particularly the men, transform these idealized cultural values into dictas: women should be passive and self-sacrificing, children must obey unquestioningly. If the man feels that he has been disrespected, he feels entitled to use violence "to correct" and discipline the woman or child. Within a larger context of racial oppression men of color often aggress against their loved ones as a way to vent their pent-up rage and frustration, sometimes not realizing that they are replicating the violence they suffer at work and in society in their homes. In these families communication suffers; the men are feared and avoided, the women may become depressed or anxious, and the children will learn violent ways of behaving and may use alcohol or other drugs to cope.

In Latino families with problems of violence alcohol abuse often is a contributing factor. A number of studies have found that in at least 50 percent of the cases of IPV among Latinas, the men had been drinking prior to or during the assault. Alcohol disinhibits aggression, and the men subsequently may feel remorse but blame the alcohol for their loss of control rather than be accountable for their violence. Women also may blame the substance and not hold the man accountable for his actions.

Latina feminists argue that certain Latino cultural factors, in particular, ideals of loyalty, sacrifice for the family, and the gendered expectation that women take care of the emotional needs of men, make it difficult for Latinas to leave abusive relationships. However, few studies have examined how Latinas explain or understand IPV or how violence affects their intimate relationships.

Several studies have recently examined how Mexican-origin women on both sides of the border understand IPV and their perceptions of the severity, as well as the prevalence, of IPV in their lives. Peek, McArthur, and Castro (2002) did not find differences between Mexican and Anglo women in terms of which events were considered severe; however, Mexican women rated most events as less severe than Anglos. In both countries physical violence was perceived as the most severe type of violence, followed by sexual and then emotional violence.

Flores-Ortiz, Valdez Curiel, and Andrade Palos's (2002) study of women from Mexico City and rural Jalisco found that the women did not focus on type of abuse but rather severity of abuse. Specifically, the women did not consider one form of abuse more serious than another but rather categorized it in terms of severity. The most severe forms of abuse included losing consciousness after being struck, partner seeking medical attention after a fight, destroying partner's property, striking partner with an object that could cause harm, insults that attack self-esteem, sexual coercion utilizing physical force, using weapon (gun, knife) against partner, and pushing or shoving the partner against a wall.

Moreover, women who experienced violence in their intimate relationships feared their partners, yet wanted to remain connected to them, perhaps hoping that in time the men would cease their violence. Likewise, women who experienced violence held very traditional cultural views that privileged men over women. These studies underscore the importance of exploring the role of cultural values in the etiology of IPV.

Latinas who suffer violence in their intimate relationships rarely leave their partners. Several factors may account for this. Often they lack the economic resources to move out on their own, particularly if they have children. Latinas have less education than other women in the United States and consequently are overrepresented in unskilled jobs. For immigrant Latinas, those who have limited English proficiency, or those who are undocumented, fear of detection and deportation and limited Spanish-language services may impede leaving the batterer.

Latinas, like most women, underreport instances of IPV. There are many reasons for this. Cultural values may inhibit reporting, because the woman may feel disloyal to the family. Many Latinas understand the discrimination and racism Latino men experience on a daily basis, feel compassion for them, and may not want to subject them to a legal system that likely will punish the men more severely because of their ethnicity. Thus Latinas may feel that they must protect the men even at the expense of their own safety.

In addition, reporting violence often leads to an escalation of the abuse. Most homicides related to IPV occur after the woman has left the batterer. The shame, isolation, and fear that women in violent relationships experience also serve as potent barriers to reporting. Moreover, many women do not disclose the abuse because no one asks, even when the abuse results in physical injuries. Recent efforts at training medical staff to inquire about, assess, and report IPV are promising, since battered Latinas have reported that few medical staff inquired about the cause of their injuries when they sought medical attention.

Heterosexual Latinas experience IPV at high rates, yet few seek social services or leave their batterers. There are complex reasons that impede women from leaving abusive relationships, including gender and cultural scripts that promote loyalty and dependence on men and the family. Moreover, barriers to seeking help and reporting must be reduced in order to assist women who live in fear, isolation, and despair. Ultimately IPV must be understood contextually if it is to be treated successfully and eradicated.

See also Marianismo and *Machismo*

SOURCES: Carillo, Ricardo, and Jerry Tello. 1998. *Family Violence and Men of Color: Healing the Wounded Male Spirit.* New York: Springer Publishing; Flores-Ortiz, Yvette. 1993. "La mujer y la violencia: A Culturally Based Model for the Understanding and Treatment of Domestic Violence." In *Chicana Critical Issues*, ed. Norma Alarcón, Rafaela Castro, Emma Pérez, Beatríz Pesquera, Adaljiza Sosa Riddell, and Patricia Zavella. Berkeley: Third Woman Press; ———.1997. "Fostering Accountability: A Reconstructive Dialogue with a Couple with a Problem of Violence." In *101 More Interventions in Family Therapy*, ed. Thorana Strever Nelson and Terry S. Trepper. New York: Haworth Press; Flores-Ortiz, Yvette, E. Valdez Curiel, and Patricia Andrade Palos. 2002. "Conflict Resolution among Mexicans in Jalisco and Mexico City." Research report to UCMEXUS_CONACYT, University of California; Straus, Murray A. and Richard Gelles. 1989. *Physical Violence in American Families: Risk Factors and Adaptations to Violence in 8,145 Families.* New Brunswick, NJ: Transaction Publishers; Walker, Lenore E. 1979. *The Battered Woman.* New York: Harper and Row.

Yvette G. Flores-Ortiz

DOMESTIC WORKERS

Domestic work operates as an unregulated field structured by loose, verbal agreements, where rules, rates of pay, pay stubs, and time off are rarely addressed. Since agreements between employers and domestic workers are largely based on oral, unwritten contracts, and domestic work is frequently perceived as an extension of female duties, many employers do not identify themselves as such and fail to draft contracts delineating explicit rules. Thus the boundaries between work and free time often remain blurred, and this places *domésticas* in precarious, abusive situations in which they experience discrimination, isolation, exploitation, and limited power.

Working to meet standards of cleanliness while attending to child-care duties, domestic workers routinely perform multiple jobs for the price of one. In exchange for around $250 a week, live-in *domésticas* confess to toiling for as long as twelve hours a day, seven days a week, and even during holidays. Sleeping in small beds in storage rooms or in cold garages, some *domésticas* rise before 7:00 A.M. on Saturdays to begin outdoor work.

Domestic workers' duties involve varied and diverse tasks such as changing household linens, emptying and washing refrigerators, dredging and emptying beach sand from bathtubs and showers, knocking down spiderwebs, washing and vacuuming cars, fishing leaves from swimming pools, scouring fishponds, polishing outdoor metal lamps, and using trash bags to collect gutter debris. Some domestic workers are expected to help employers prepare materials for work, such as cutting and laminating shapes for kindergarten classes, and to take children on outings, often spending their own salary on snacks and treats. Domestic workers clean hamster cages, look after family pets, and clean houses, yards, and family cars.

Another common complaint is the demand to work during national holidays. Some *domésticas* labor during national holidays such as Thanksgiving by cleaning up leftovers, tidying up after their employers' guests, helping cook and prepare the big feast, and even being loaned off to nearby neighbors' kitchens, where they are also expected to baby-sit while the guests eat. In extreme abusive cases *domésticas* complain about performing outrageous duties, such as grooming an employer's toenails and even giving massages.

Domésticas conduct tiring and mind-dulling chores, as well as help raise multiple children. The combination of various duties leads to exhaustion and depression by the end of the week. Complaining of sore backs, weak knees, dry hands, and shortness of breath, *domésticas* stress a different type of aching related to the humiliation of daily food prohibitions; they clean and restock refrigerators and cupboards while always keeping in mind that refrigerated items and gourmet goods are for family consumption only. *Domésticas* complain of living an invisible existence, excluded from family meals, cleaning without disturbing, blending into the background, and then stepping out into a world where officially they do not exist.

Driven north mostly from Central and Latin America by war, poverty, or simply the hope for a better future, they pay high prices to be smuggled into the country by coyotes, or they make the dangerous trip up north as *solas*. In the United States *domésticas* often work in gated communities, where they feel sequestered in beautiful but constricting homes, and where they raise other people's children while neighbors and extended family look after their own.

Because of their vulnerable immigrant status, some live-in *domésticas* find themselves working under quasi-slave conditions. This setup seems to be more prevalent among those *domésticas* who are recruited abroad and agree to work for wealthy couples in the United States for an extended period of time. Questioned about their motivation for leaving their countries, many confess that they are influenced by salaries quoted in dollar amounts, representing earnings impossible to match at home.

Another motivating factor stems from the sense of safety domestics feel when they are protected by the prospective employers' ethnic, racial, or religious milieu. Unfortunately, many *domésticas* courted and recruited abroad have found themselves toiling in sweatshops where they are treated as indentured servants, are forced to labor without wages, and have their passports locked up and their mail screened and withheld. By the time they realize that they have accepted a contractless agreement, and that they lack the financial means to return home, overwhelming feelings of isolation and boredom emerge. Immigrant women lured into domestic positions are easily misled about what their work will entail, how they will be treated, and how much they will get paid. In most abusive cases few *domésticas* knew where to seek help, and many believe that they have no rights to contest unfair and cruel treatment.

In some cases *domésticas* experience the freedom to leave the workplace and attend classes at local community colleges. The classroom setup has proven extremely helpful and encouraging not only in improving English skills, but, most important, in providing a forum to congregate, forge social ties, and develop supportive communities. The classroom setup offers a space to build friendships and to discuss and compare working environments and pay. For *domésticas*, to gather at centers is a crucial step toward improving their working conditions, negotiating wages, and learning about workers' rights.

Not all *domésticas* experience abuse and isolation. Despite the multiple challenges and duties of domestic workers, many make time and find spaces to foster community ties and create social spheres for conversation, laughter, and the promotion of solidarity. For the *domésticas* who take bus line 576, "the nanny express," to Beverly Hills, Bel Air, and Pacific Palisades, the trip represents much more than a ride. This particular bus line, created in 1968 to cut across Los Angeles to get domestic workers to their jobs in the quickest time possible, has developed camaraderie and friendship among longtime riders. The daily bus ride presents an opportunity to smile, laugh, and celebrate each other's lives. What keep them stepping on board, sometimes for thirty years, are the dreams that they are creating better lives for their children and grandchildren. This mostly female world offers a place to gossip, pool resources for needy friends, and celebrate birthdays aboard the bus. When the "nanny express" strikes, *domésticas* experience financial difficulties, since they are forced to stay at their employers' homes overnight, often without extra pay.

Informing *domésticas* at bus stops and parks about workers' rights, an organization known as the Coalition for Humane Immigrant Rights in Los Angeles (CHIRLA) advises on negotiating raises and asserting workers' needs. Organized immigrant networks such as CHIRLA offer an invaluable array of resources that include English-language classes, legal awareness, and community empowerment. The value of having a place where immigrants can congregate and discuss their particular situations has proven extremely crucial. Whether attending local community college classes or gathering at bus stops, on board bus 576, at a park, or at CHIRLA meetings, *domésticas* are talking and learning how to keep their jobs while also asserting their rights as workers.

SOURCES: Baxter, Kevin. 1997. "The Sunday Profile: Domestic Policy: She Scrubs Floors, Cleans Bathrooms, and Cares for Three Young Girls, All for $200 A Week." *Los Angeles Times*, August 31; Gold, Matea. 1997. "Labor Center Seeks to Offer More Than Jobs." *Los Angeles Times*, December 15; Healy, Melissa. 1999. "Caring for Our Children: Giving Mary Poppins a Run for Her Money." *Los Angeles Times*, July 25; Hondagneu-Sotelo, Pierrette. 2001. *Doméstica: Immigrant Workers Cleaning and Caring in the Shadows of Affluence*. Berkeley: University of California Press; Morrison, Patt. 1995. "Perimeters: A Sweatshop of a Different Sort." *Los Angeles Times*, August 30; O'Connor, Anne-Marie. 2000. "A Tough Balancing Act Made More Precarious: For the Nannies Who Care for the Children of LA's Privileged, the Loss of Bus Service Can Be a Disaster." *Los Angeles Times*, September 28; ———. 2001. "Study Offers Complex Portrait of Domestic Workers." *Los Angeles Times*, April 11.

Soledad Vidal

DOMINICAN AMERICAN NATIONAL ROUNDTABLE (DANR)

The Dominican American National Roundtable (DANR) is an advocacy organization created to serve the interests of the Dominican community living in the United States and Puerto Rico. As the first and only national lobbying organization for Dominican Americans, it addresses specific issues on behalf of Dominican Americans in areas concerning immigration, education, civil rights, health and aging, economic development, housing, race, ethnicity, gender, and sexuality. The organization seeks to empower the Dominican community by offering programs of voter registration drives, leadership institutes, internships, and policy forums.

The DANR emerged in 1997 during a meeting in Miami of about 200 Dominican American leaders from different parts of the United States to discuss numerous issues related to Dominicans in the United States and Puerto Rico. This initial meeting was organized and hosted by a few concerned entities, including the Dominican American National Foundation of South Florida, then under the leadership of Margarita Cepeda-Leonardo. In 1998, at a subsequent meeting held in New York City, Dominican community leaders formed a national interim steering committee charged with developing the structure and agenda of what was to become the Dominican American National Roundtable. A year later the steering committee elected the first board of directors, its officers, and the first president.

Since its founding the organization has been active in sponsoring a number of educational programs and advocacy activities. In 2000 DANR was incorporated and set up in Washington, D.C., giving Dominicans a means to provide input on national issues and a way to undo negative stereotypes. The headquarters was opened with the appointment of José Bello, the first and current executive director. In 2002 DANR established the Dominican American Voter Registration Project and has been successful ever since in registering thousands of voters. The Dominican Internship Program, centered in Washington, coordinates summer internship positions for Dominican students seeking professional opportunities. Students are placed in congressional offices, federal agencies, and national or international organizations. The Dominican Leadership Institute serves as a development center that prepares current and upcoming Dominican leaders, especially women, to acquire the necessary organizational skills. In January 2003 Congressman Lincoln Diaz-Balart of Florida recognized DANR on its fifth anniversary for its contributions to the Dominican American community. DANR also organizes business conferences; the most recent was held as the Dominican American Business Legislative Meeting (2003), where Dominican business leaders met with elected officials to discuss certain policy issues. In the same year DANR organized the first U.S. congressional delegation visit of ten members to the Dominican Republic to meet with the president and other elected officials. As of 2005, DANR has held eight national conferences in such cities as Miami, Providence, New York, and Washington. At the 2003 national conference, held in Atlantic City, the membership discussed important timely issues: education of youths and underfunded schools, struggles of small businesses, and personal economic struggles and financial independence.

In 2004 the national conference held in New York City turned to international issues. Addressing both the merits and drawbacks of free trade, this DANR conference focused on the importance of including the Dominican Republic as a negotiating partner in the proposed Central American Free Trade Agreement (CAFTA). As noted on its website, the Dominican American National Roundtable is a non-partisan organization dedicated to including "the different voices of all people of Dominican origin in the United States" and to safeguard "for U.S. Dominicans the full exercise of the rights and freedoms guaranteed in the Constitution of the United States of America."

SOURCES: Dominican American National Roundtable (DANR). http://www.danr.org (accessed June 29, 2005); McCoy, Kevin. 1998. "Dominicans Organizing to Raise Their Voice, Flex Political Muscle." *New York Daily News*, July 15, 22.

José A. Díaz

DUETO CARMEN Y LAURA

Carmen y Laura was one of the most popular and successful female Tejana duets in the years after World War II. The two Hernández sisters were born in Kingsville and grew up singing together for their own enjoyment. Carmen was born on October 16, 1921, and Laura was born in 1926. Among the four other children in the family, their brother Lupe was the only one who also displayed musical talent, and he later played the saxophone in some of Carmen y Laura's recordings.

Carmen Hernández married Armando Marroquin of Alice, Texas, in 1936. The shortage of shellac during World War II limited the production of phonograph records. This hurt Armando Marroquin's business when he had trouble filling the nickelodeons with the Tejano music that was popular with his clientele. He decided to buy recording equipment, and Carmen became his first recording artist. In their kitchen she recorded the new company's first song, accompanied by Reynaldo Barrera, a blind guitarist. The records were pressed without a label. When Carmen's sister Laura returned from school in Mexico, Armando Marroquin began to have their records pressed by 4-Star Records in Los Angeles. Although it was expensive, Carmen believes that "it paid off, because we would send the recording and they would send us back 100 or 200 [records] and we would sell them for more and we started making a profit from that." Soon her husband and Paco Betancourt, a distributor for RCA and Columbia Records of San Benito, formed a partnership and started Ideal Records. Ideal's first recordings were of

Carmen y Laura, accompanied by Narciso Martínez, in the kitchen. They did not stay in the kitchen for long since Carmen could no longer take the mess or all the people who were curious about what was going on at her house. She told her husband, "Take everything outside . . . go to the garage." She recalled, "It was a novelty. Everyone wanted to see what we were doing in the kitchen. If it would rain . . . my house was a mess. They would see music and cars and all of that . . . they wanted to see what was going on." After their first big hit, "Se me fui mi amor," they continued making records with all types of accompaniments, including the *conjunto* accordion of Narciso Martínez and the *orquesta* of Beto Villa. Some of their other songs include "No tengo la culpa yo," "Sos palomas al bolar," and "Solo pero contento."

The sisters continued to be the most popular act on the Ideal label and toured extensively, often performing with dance bands signed to Ideal, such as those of Beto Villa and Pedro Bugarín. To promote Ideal records, they toured throughout the 1950s to cities in California such as Fresno, Los Angeles, and Oakland and also made appearances in Salt Lake City, Phoenix, and Kansas City. Carmen y Laura also made personal appearances at record shops to autograph records, but at no time did they see it as their show. Rather, they promoted the Ideal label, which recorded other artists besides themselves. Today both women live in Alice, Texas. Unfortunately Laura's health prevents her from participating in extensive activities outside of her home. Carmen, on the other hand, appeared at the summer festivities when she and her sister were inducted into the Tejano Hall of Fame. But she is busiest with La Villita, a popular southern Texas dance hall, which she has owned since the 1950s.

SOURCES: Marroquin, Carmen. 1988. Interview by Clay Shorkey, March 19; ———. 2000. Interview by Mary Ann Villarreal and Deborah Vargas, July 7; Vargas, Deborah Rose Ramos. 2003. "Las tracaleras: Texas-Mexican Women, Music, and Place." Ph.D. diss., University of California, Santa Cruz; Villarreal, Mary Ann. 2003. "*Cantantes y Cantineras*: Mexican American Communities and the Mapping of Public Space." Ph.D. diss., Arizona State University.

Mary Ann Villarreal

DURAZO, MARÍA ELENA (1953–)

María Elena Durazo is the president of Local 11 of the Hotel Employees and Restaurant Employees Union in Los Angeles. This union local, whose members are predominantly low-wage Latina and Latino immigrant workers, represents the cutting edge of the new social movement unionism, and Durazo has emerged as a key leader in this revived labor movement.

Born in 1953 in Madera, California, Durazo was the seventh of eleven children. Her father came to the United States as a bracero, and the entire family picked crops from California to Oregon. Although she generally considers her childhood to have been a happy one, the death of a younger brother remains a searing memory. He died because of a lack of accessible health care, and this profound lesson in inequality contributed greatly to her commitment to social justice.

When she was a teenager, one of her older brothers began attending college at California State University, Fresno. This would have a significant impact on Durazo in two ways: first, her brother became involved in the Chicano student movement, which exposed Durazo to the beliefs and goals of movement organizing, and second, he helped prepare her for college and guided her through the application process. As a result, she received a scholarship to St. Mary's College in Moraga, California. At St. Mary's she helped create a Chicano studies program and became involved with el Centro de Acción Social Autónomo (CASA), an organization that focused on immigrant and workers' rights. In her words: "The thing that clicked for me from the very beginning, my parents being immigrants, was the class analysis. All they did was cross the border, they were still workers, and they were really getting screwed. [Although] they're Mexican and I'm Mexican, there was the bottom line of class."

Shortly after graduating from college Durazo married and had her first child, Mario. The marriage eventually disintegrated, and she moved to Los Angeles, where she worked at various odd jobs and continued her affiliation with CASA. She later remarried and had another son Michael. In 1977 she took a pivotal trip to Mexico City with a group of organizers from the International Ladies Garment Workers' Union (ILGWU). Impressed with the ILGWU's focus on immigrant workers, she joined the union as an organizer shortly thereafter. She worked for the union until 1981, when she left to attend the People's College of Law while working part-time at Levy and Goldman, a labor-law firm. At that time, Levy and Goldman represented Local 11, and she began to do legal work for the union. Eventually she was asked to assist with a strike, and this subsequently led to a permanent position as an organizer with Local 11. During the mid-1980s, however, Local 11 suffered huge membership losses. As Durazo explained, "It became obvious that this union had far more potential than what it was doing. There was a lot of racism. No respect for the members. No inclusion of the members as far as negotiations, no inclusion of the members to build leadership. The union would refuse to translate the meetings into Spanish. Even as a business union it wasn't responding to the members. It was like a love-hate relationship."

Durazo decided to run for president. The election, held in March 1987, was plagued by numerous irregularities that caused the International to place the local in trusteeship for eighteen months. In 1989, after having worked closely with the International, Durazo ran for president and won. Durazo's victory and subsequent efforts to transform the local have proven significant for both the union and the larger labor movement. Local 11's emphasis on Latina/o organizing and promoting worker leadership and community alliances reflects a radical departure from traditional union culture, as well as a new direction on the part of the AFL-CIO. Because service unions are composed increasingly of women, immigrants, and people of color, who have often been excluded from mainstream labor organizations, they have become the driving force in the push to create a new labor movement, and Local 11, under the leadership of Durazo, has been at the forefront of this effort.

As historian Vicki L. Ruiz succinctly stated, "With drive and conviction, Durazo leads a union that cannot be ignored." Workers seek a living wage and social justice, and although they have been hard hit by the tragedy of September 11 (layoffs have become commonplace because tourism has dramatically declined in southern California), the union continues to be a national model for Latino grassroots empowerment. The revitalized labor movement in southern California, however, has been shaken by the sudden loss of Miguel Contreras, the charismatic leader of the politically powerful Los County Federation of Labor. On May 6, 2005, Contreras, María Elena Durazo's husband of eleven years, died of a heart attack at the age of fifty-two. At his funeral, his widow, her union colleagues, and thousands of workers vowed to honor his legacy. In a 1992 interview, María Elena Durazo eloquently stated, "I hope people will see unions as a tool for change and I hope we in the unions can respond to the challenge."

See also Labor Unions

SOURCES: Durazo, María Elena. 2000. Interview by Laura Pulido, Los Angeles, CA, February 24; Milkman, Ruth, and Kent Wong, eds. 2000. *Voices from the Frontlines: Organizing Immigrant Workers in Los Angeles.* Los Angeles: UCLA Center for Labor Research and Education; Morin, Monte, and Carla Hall. 2005. "Laborers, Leaders Mourn 'the Real Miguel Contreras.'" *Los Angeles Times*, May 13, B1; Ruiz, Vicki L. 1998. *From out of the Shadows: Mexican Women in Twentieth-Century America.* New York: Oxford University Press; Sipchen, Bob. 1997. "Labor of Love." *Los Angeles Times,* March 9, E1, E8.

Laura Pulido

E

ECHAVESTE, MARÍA (1954–)

In 1992, when presidential candidate Bill Clinton named a political unknown to head his Latino outreach effort, Hispanic political veterans were skeptical. Who was María Echaveste, this Stanford-educated, Mexican American Jewish woman from New York, and how would she connect to the increasingly powerful Hispanic political community? By all accounts she was smart, organized, methodical, and inclusive, and, as she has acknowledged, she had the good sense to pick a winning candidate. By the end of the Clinton presidency in 2001, María Echaveste was well known in political circles. She had helped lead the Latino community in a second Clinton presidential election and had risen to the highest White House position of any Hispanic woman in history.

Refugio and María Echaveste, María's parents, came to the United States from Mexico with their seven children. They worked as migrant farmworkers in Texas during María's early years and then moved to California, where they earned a living in the central and coastal valleys picking cotton, strawberries, grapes, tomatoes, and carrots.

Echaveste was a bright student who loved to read. She worked hard and earned a scholarship to Stanford University, where she majored in anthropology. After a brief stint in the nation's capital, she earned a law degree from the University of California at Berkeley. From there she went to New York City, became a corporate attorney, and married Stanley Schlein, a Jewish attorney from the Bronx. She also served for several years on the New York City Board of Elections. Although she was raised Catholic, Echaveste had fallen away from the religion. She converted to Judaism, which she says she found more "life-affirming." The marriage to Schlein ended during her White House tenure.

After Clinton's election in 1992 Echaveste went to work on the presidential transition. Her first appointment (1993–1997) in the new administration was as wage and hour administrator at the U.S. Department of Labor. Echaveste was a strong defender of workers' rights and took on critical responsibilities that included overseeing minimum-wage laws, child labor laws, and the Family and Medical Leave Act. In 1996 her anti-sweatshop campaign titled "No Sweat" received an Innovations in Government Award from Harvard University's John F. Kennedy School of Government and the Ford Foundation.

In 1997, at the start of President Clinton's second term, Echaveste moved to the White House and became assistant to the president and director of public liaison. In this high-profile and very public position Echaveste assumed charge of conducting outreach to politically significant constituency groups, including women, minorities, and issue groups. As one of her many projects, she led the presidential initiative on race relations.

In 1998 Echaveste was promoted to assistant to the president and deputy chief of staff, becoming what some have called the most influential Latina in the administration. She was a strong, practical, and serious deputy chief of staff. In this new position she had, and used, the opportunity to influence much of the president's agenda. She chaired the White House Interagency Immigration Working Group, tackling an issue about which she felt strongly. At a March 2000 conference on migration she noted, "Whether it's the flow of legal or illegal migrants, or the issue of the treatment of migrants once they've arrived, or the importance of the remittances that are sent from migrants to their home countries, these are issues that are no longer relegated to the lower levels of government . . . they are at the very top of the list." Continuing, she said, "The thing that most excites me about the issue . . . is that in so many ways it represents the best of the human spirit—that desire to try to do better, to go someplace else, to provide a better future."

Echaveste, the daughter of migrants, eldest of seven, was provided a better future. She earned a B.A. from Stanford University in 1976 and a J.D. from the University of California at Berkeley in 1980. An attorney, she has worked for law firms in Los Angeles and New York. She is married to Christopher Edley, the dean of the School of Law (Boalt Hall) at the University of California, Berkeley, and they have one son. Since leaving the Clinton administration, Echaveste is the co-founder of a consulting firm in Washington, D.C. called Nueva Vista and appears with regularity on the PBS show "To The Contrary." She is a member of the Executive Committee of the Democratic National Committee.

See also Politics, Electoral

SOURCES: Dart, Bob. 1999. "From Migrant Worker, She Rose to Key White House Role." Cox News Service, Washington, DC. www.coxnews.com (accessed December 12, 2001); Millbank, Dana. 1998. "White House Watch: The Deputy." *New Republic*, July 20. www.thenewrepublic.com (accessed December 11, 2001); Nueva Vista Group. "Personnel Profiles: María Echaveste." www.nuevavistagroup.com/bio_echaveste.html (accessed June 29, 2005); Ross, Alex. 2000. "Maria Echaveste: A View from the Top." *Horizon* (magazine of the Enterprise Foundation). http://horizonmag.com/6/maria-eschaveste.asap (accessed December 8, 2001).

Bettie Baca

EDUCATION

"We always tell our children they are Americans," affirmed Felicitas Méndez in what is perhaps the most important school segregation case in Mexican American and Latino history. *Méndez v. Westminster* (1946), a lawsuit against four school districts in Orange County, California, was brought by a group of parents, Gonzalo Méndez, William Guzmán, Frank Palomino, Thomas Estrada, and Lorenzo Ramírez assisted by the League of United Latin American Citizens. Méndez had attempted to enroll his children into the Main Street School, which he had attended as a child, but due to residential boundary redistricting, the children were sent instead to the Mexican elementary school. The parents essentially protested de facto segregation, the separation of their children, based on ethnicity and limited English proficiencies, into separate "Mexican schools," often substandard and understaffed. Judge Paul McCormick ruled in favor of the parents. He contended that the segregation of the Mexican youngsters was a clear denial of the equal protection clause of the Fourteenth Amendment. On appeal, the U.S. Ninth Circuit Court upheld Judge McCormick's ruling, and the Orange County school districts moved toward desegregation.

The case set precedent for judicial decisions in Texas and Arizona and garnered support from various civil rights organizations, including the NAACP, with Thurgood Marshall coauthoring the NAACP's amicus curiae brief. *Méndez* has several concrete connections with *Brown v. Board of Education*, such as the use of social science research. Furthermore, the case signals the high value placed on education by Latinos in the United States. Latinos have always prized education but have not always had access or opportunity. They have participated as involved parents, teachers, and reformers, fought for access, confronted discrimination, and contributed to the creation of new fields of knowledge.

Educational opportunities increased for Latinas during the late nineteenth century in concert with social and economic transformations of the period. The Tempe Normal School in Arizona, exemplary of southwestern teaching institutions, graduated more than sixty Mexican American teachers between 1885 and 1936. Most came from middle-class families who supported women's education, but some, like María Urquides, enrolled against the wishes of their parents. Many taught an Americanization curriculum in segregated Mexican schools, and a handful became teachers of Spanish at the secondary level.

Cuban middle-class families customarily sent their daughters to the United States for an education. Aurelia Castillo de González observed that "as in 'every civilized country' North American women are 'formed by physical and intellectual education that creates possibilities for an infinite number of lucrative occupations.' " Impressed with the freedom and intellectual alternatives available to women in the United States, Castillo de González advocated for the education of women in her native country. Julia Martínez completed secondary school in Baltimore and received a doctorate in pedagogy in Havana.

During the late nineteenth and early twentieth centuries, teaching opened the way for Latinas to work outside of the home in a respectable setting that did not threaten traditional gender roles. For many women, teaching offered a broadening of the private sphere. Most of the earliest feminists, journalists, writers, politicians, and community organizers came from the ranks of teachers. Before she became a noted newspaperwoman and feminist, Jovita Idar was a teacher. Her friend and colleague Leonor Villegas de Magñón opened a school in her home when she found herself stranded on the U.S. side of the border. Labor organizer and feminist poet Sara Estela Ramírez received a graduate degree from the Ateneo Fuentes in Mexico and taught Spanish in Laredo, Texas. In New Mexico former suffragist Adelina Otero Warren created a school curriculum that incorporated Hispano customs and traditions.

The Puerto Rican Pilar Barbosa de Rosario became the first woman to teach at the University of Puerto Rico. She received a master's degree and a doctorate from Clark University in the early 1920s. Amelia Agostini de del Río moved to New York in 1918 after working as a teacher in Puerto Rican schools. She worked her way through Vassar College, received a master's degree from Columbia University, and was appointed

Luisa Flin, at her Arizona school graduation, August 1905. Courtesy of the Arizona Historical Society Library, Tucson, Arizona.

to the faculty of Barnard College in her field of Spanish. Camila Henríquez Ureña, the only daughter of the revered poet Salomé Ureña (who had founded the first schools for girls in the Dominican Republic), earned a master's degree from the University of Minnesota in 1918. She became a professor of literature, with prestigious appointments at Vassar and Middlebury Colleges.

The majority of Latina educators were not professors, but elementary educators who taught in remote, rural one-room schoolhouses in the U.S. Southwest and Puerto Rico. Many never married because they made their students the center of their lives. Often relegated to schools with limited resources and administrative neglect, they became the innovative problem solvers who took responsibility for the minutest details of their positions. Amelia Margarita Maldonado, a pioneer in bilingual education, began to teach in 1919 in Arizona. Aware that her students did not get enough to eat during the depression, Maldonado "used the school kitchen to bake corn muffins, boil a pot of beans, and prepare hot chocolate" for her hungry pupils. Before Maldonado retired after forty years in the classroom, countless others replicated her experiences, and some penned memoirs about their experiences in country schools. The Puerto Rican community activist Antonia Pantoja recalled leaving the mountain school where she taught in the early 1940s to return home on the weekend "with my arms full of gardenias, pineapples, and oranges. . . . *'Maestra, regresará el domingo?'* " She would respond, *"Si, volveré!"* Born and raised in poverty, Pantoja hungered for an education and went on to create the venues and institutions to instruct the children of the barrios.

For the most part, Latina and Euro-American teachers served Mexican American communities in the Southwest that were overwhelmingly poor. Between 1910 and 1930 more than 1 million Mexicans crossed the border to escape the ravages of the revolution. Lured also by the promise of jobs in agriculture and industry, Mexican immigrants determined to make a better life for themselves, created new barrios in *el norte,* or settled into existing communities throughout the Southwest and Midwest. Within twenty years Mexican Americans were outnumbered by Mexican immigrants at least two to one, and their *colonias* or communities became immigrant enclaves. In urban areas like Los Angeles, residential and educational segregation based on restrictive real-estate covenants and segregated schools increased dramatically between 1920 and 1950.

Teacher expectations were frequently low with regard to the education of Mexican children. Assumed to bring diseases such as lice infestations, impetigo, and tuberculosis into the classroom, students were also thought to lack the ambition to move ahead in life or the requisite intelligence to be successful. The curriculum prioritized vocational learning because teachers and school administrators believed that Mexican students had few aspirations and fewer abilities beyond farm and domestic work.

In addition to civics, the primary component of Americanization was English-language instruction, and children were forbidden to speak Spanish. Educator Sonia Nieto remembers, "We spoke Spanish at home, even though teachers pleaded with my parents to stop doing so." In an eagerness to replace Spanish with English, schools delivered the message that the Spanish language was worthless, even shameful, and was to be discarded as soon as possible. To compound the situation, children of migrant families who moved according to the seasons attended school sporadically because they were needed to work with the family in the fields. Some school districts denied admission to migrant children; others placed migrant children in segregated classrooms because of their limited English capabilities or poor attendance.

Primary-school graduation, 1958. Courtesy of the Justo A. Martí Photograph Collection. Centro Archives, Centro de Estudios Puertorriqueños, Hunter College, CUNY.

Concurrently, Puerto Ricans in the Northeast, particularly New York, faced a similar situation. Puerto Rican students, like their Mexican American counterparts, were expected to navigate a sink-or-swim system when it came to English-language instruction. By the 1950s and 1960s the enormous increase in the city's Puerto Rican population alarmed school officials, who resuscitated old methods for teaching non-English speakers. These incoming students were placed one or two years behind their age-appropriate grade or in classes for "slow or retarded learners." Some educators preferred to pair the new student with a proficient English speaker in a buddy system. Nonetheless, countless Mexican American and Puerto Rican children could not understand the language of instruction. Many parents, teachers, and community leaders understood the long-range implications of inadequate instruction and called for dramatic school reform. By the mid-twentieth century some Latinos advocated for bilingual education, which they believed was the most viable tool for achieving equal education and opportunity.

In regions with large concentrations of Latinos, such as California and New York, steps toward some form of bilingual instruction were already under way. As early as 1948 María Urquides initiated the first bilingual program in Arizona. In the same year Ana Marcial Peñaranda began to work as a bilingual teacher in Public School 25 in the South Bronx. Coteries of Latina teachers, often bilingual and experienced professionals, were well positioned to pioneer the new field. For twenty years bilingual teachers mobilized for recognition of the field, organized professional groups, developed materials and methodology, and lobbied for federal protection of language-minority students. With passage of the 1968 Bilingual Education Act, the education of language-minority students began to improve. However, it took the Supreme Court decision in *Lau v. Nichols* (1974) to guarantee equal opportunity and safeguard the civil rights of non-English-speaking children in American schools. *Lau v. Nichols*, a case brought to the Supreme Court on behalf of Asian American students in San Francisco, argued that unequal educational opportunities violated the Fourteenth Amendment. The case became the major precedent on the educational rights of language-minority students.

The ASPIRA Consent Decree was an agreement between ASPIRA and the New York City Board of Education to provide equal educational opportunity and transitional bilingual programs for Spanish-speaking students in city schools. The consent decree established the model for numerous states, including Massachusetts and Connecticut, to negotiate consent decrees. The ASPIRA Consent Decree was not limited to Spanish speakers, but provided for the education of all language-minority students, including Haitians, Russians, Italians, and Chinese speakers, who resided in the city.

During the 1960s and 1970s, as part of global student movements, Mexican American, Puerto Rican, and other Latino youths mobilized against continuing problems of discrimination, especially in educational representation. For example, in March 1968 more than 10,000 Mexican American youngsters (calling themselves "Chicanos") in East Los Angeles staged the

United Bronx Parents, Inc., circa 1970s. Courtesy of the Records of the United Bronx Parents, Inc. Centro Archives, Centro de Estudios Puertorriqueños, Hunter College, CUNY.

largest student walkout in the history of the United States. They demanded a revised curriculum that according to one participant, Vickie Castro, covered a listing of demands "from better food all the way to . . . we want to go to college." Castro helped organize the East Los Angeles "blowouts," which she called a "massive display of discontent with the education system."

In calling for educational excellence and greater access, high-school and college students demanded curricular reforms in the public schools and universities, urging the creation of history and culture courses that related to their own experiences—Chicano studies in the Southwest and Puerto Rican studies in the Northeast. They also demanded the hiring of Latino teachers and school administrators. Furthermore, students protested substandard education in poorly equipped schools and the tracking system that funneled them into domestic work, clerical jobs, or industrial employment. Students mobilized to create militant campus organizations connected to their barrio communities.

Latino students and teachers figured prominently in fighting for the establishment of Puerto Rican, Mexican American, Chicano/a, Hispanic American, and Cuban studies departments and programs. These proliferated in the Southwest, the Midwest, the Northeast, and the Southeast. Committed to social and political transformations based on a philosophical framework that prioritized the union of learning and practice, departments and programs pledged accountability to their communities and became the venues for increasing student enrollment and faculty representation in academic institutions. Their mission further emphasized the use of innovative methodology and research designed to promote solutions to community problems.

Community service and a relevant curriculum remain common themes in ethnic studies. Returning to one's community with an education served as the informal credo for student activists of color in the late 1960s and early 1970s and still resonates today. Experiential education became an essential component of an ethnic studies curriculum, and internships with community-based organizations allowed young people to serve as links between themselves, the academy, and the community.

Latinas have made their mark throughout the academy, and some have assumed positions of university leadership. For example, Isaura Santiago Santiago and Dolores Fernández have served as presidents of Hostos College. Marta Casals Istomin is president of the prestigious Manhattan School of Music, Elsa Gómez is president of Kean College in New Jersey, and Millie García is president of Berkeley College in New York City. Juliet V. García is president of the University of Texas at Brownsville, Blandina Cárdenas is president of the University of Texas, Pan American, and France Córdova is chancellor of the University of California, Riverside, the first Latina University of California chancellor. For the majority of Latinos in the United States, however, educational equity remains an unrealized promise and a critical political and social issue.

SOURCES: Hewitt, Nancy A. 2001. *Southern Discomfort: Women's Activism in Tampa, Florida, 1880s–1920s.* Urbana: University of Illinois Press; Navarro, Marysa, and Virginia Sánchez Korrol. 1999. *Women in Latin America and the Caribbean.* Bloomington: Indiana University Press; Pérez,

Louis A. *On Becoming Cuban: Identity, Nationality, and Culture.* Chapel Hill: University of North Carolina Press, 1999; Ruiz, Vicki L. 1998. *From out of the Shadows: Mexican Women in Twentieth-Century America.* New York: Oxford University Press.

Vicki L. Ruiz and Virginia Sánchez Korrol

EL CONGRESO DE PUEBLOS DE HABLAN ESPAÑOLA (1939)

Held in Los Angeles on April 28–30, 1939, el Congreso de Pueblos de Hablan Española (the Spanish-Speaking Peoples' Congress) was the first national civil rights assembly for Latinos in the United States. From 1,000 to 1,500 delegates representing more than 100 organizations attended this historic meeting. Although the majority of these men and women hailed from California and the Southwest, some had traveled from as far away as Montana, Illinois, New York, and Florida. They gathered to address issues of jobs, housing, education, health, and immigrant rights. Over the course of three days they drafted a comprehensive platform.

Bridging differences in generation and ethnic background, they called for an end to segregation in public facilities, housing, education, and employment and endorsed the rights of immigrants to live and work in the United States without fear of deportation. Advocating for the rights of immigrants was a courageous course, given that a few short years earlier, an estimated one-third of the Mexican population in the United States had been deported or repatriated even though the majority (an estimated 60 percent) were native-born American citizens. Equally important, the delegates encouraged immigrants to become U.S. citizens and to preserve their cultural traditions. In a gesture that foreshadowed the nationalist student movements of the 1960s, they called upon universities to create departments in Latino studies.

Veteran labor leader Luisa Moreno spearheaded the national conference. At first she attempted to organize a planning meeting in Albuquerque, New Mexico, but received little support. In Los Angeles she met a coterie of civil rights activists who shared her vision of a national conference rooted in community networks. Working in tandem with Josefina Fierro, Eduardo Quevedo, and Bert Corona, Moreno drew upon her contacts with Latino labor unions, mutual-aid societies, and other grassroots groups in order to ensure a truly national assembly.

Even before the April meeting occurred, the Los Angeles team, led by Josefina Fierro, had organized a local chapter. In February 1939 Congreso members had lobbied local government officials for affordable housing. Indeed, public housing remained an important agenda item for southern California branches. Despite the promise of the national conference, local chapters failed to develop outside of southern California, but these local California branches continued for several years to take on significant community issues. Members also were attuned to the circumstances of working-class Latinas. Historian Mario García brought to light the following resolution passed by the second California convention in December 1939:

> Whereas: The Mexican woman, who for centuries had suffered oppression, has the responsibility for raising her children and for caring for the home, and even that of earning a livelihood for herself and her family . . . suffers a double discrimination as a woman and as a Mexican.
>
> Be It Resolved: That the Congress carry out a program of . . . education of the Mexican woman . . . that it [a Women's Committee] support and work for women's equality, so that she may receive equal wages, enjoy the same rights as men in social, economic, and civil liberties, and use her vote for the defense of the Mexican and Spanish American people, and of American democracy.

These California chapters did not survive the cold war era. Almost from the beginning conservative politicians branded the organization "subversive" and claimed that it was controlled by the Communist Party. As a civil rights group that prided itself on inclusion, Congreso members welcomed individuals from various leftist and liberal political persuasions, from Communists to New Deal liberals. Many of the causes associated with el Congreso later resonated in the voices of Latino student activists of the 1960s—educational equity, affordable housing, immigrant rights, women's rights, and Latino studies.

SOURCES: García, Mario T. 1989. *Mexican Americans: Leadership, Ideology, and Identity, 1930–1960.* New Haven, CT: Yale University Press; Gutiérrez, David G. 1995. *Walls and Mirrors: Mexican Americans, Mexican Immigrants, and the Politics of Ethnicity in the Southwest, 1910–1986.* Berkeley: University of California Press; Molina, Natalia. 2001. "Contested Bodies and Cultures: The Politics of Public Health and Race within Mexican, Japanese, and Chinese Communities in Los Angeles, 1879–1939." Ph.D. diss., University of Michigan; Sánchez, George J. 1993. *Becoming Mexican American: Ethnicity, Culture, and Identity in Chicano Los Angeles, 1900–1945.* New York: Oxford University Press.

Vicki L. Ruiz

EL MONTE BERRY STRIKE

On June 1, 1933, 1,500 Mexican berry pickers went out on strike in the fields surrounding El Monte, California. Organized initially by the Cannery and Agricultural Workers Industrial Union (CAWIU), the workers demanded a pay increase because some earned as little as nine cents per hour. Jesusita Torres remembered that she picked berries for less than one penny per basket. Her employers were not European American farmers, but Japanese leaseholders. Within the social structure of El Monte, both groups were minorities and were subject to segregation.

Less than a thirty-minute drive from downtown Los Angeles, El Monte was a small town with a population of fewer than 10,000 residents. European Americans made up 75 percent of the locals, Mexicans 20 percent, and the Japanese 5 percent. Despite its rural hometown feel, it was demarcated by race in neighborhoods, schools, and commercialized leisure. The children of Japanese farmers and Mexican farmworkers attended the same segregated grammar school, and at the local cinema Japanese and Mexicans were relegated to the same side of the aisle, away from European American patrons. While they shared these same segregated spaces, the worker-employer relationship significantly influenced the nature of their interactions. In Torres's words, "They [the Japanese farmers] would work in the field, but you knew they were the *boss*."

Early in the strike Mexican workers were caught between two rival unions—the CAWIU and la Confederación de Uniones de Campesinos y Obreros del Estado de California (CUCOM), a union supported by the Mexican consul. While the strikers received hefty donations from politicians in Mexico, the Japanese consul tried to broker a settlement in order to avoid negative publicity for the farmers. This international intervention in a U.S. labor action seemed unprecedented. Furthermore, the strikers themselves appealed to the U.S. federal government to step in to mediate the dispute.

Both farmers and strikers relied on their community networks. The residents of El Monte's Hick's Camp barrio rallied around the strikers. For example, Sadie Castro "used to cook rice and beans and take it to the people who were striking." Barrio merchants also donated food. Perhaps in a dilemma because of rising rents charged by European American landowners and the demands for higher wages among their workers, Japanese farmers relied on family and friends throughout Los Angeles to pitch in and pick the highly perishable berries. Furthermore, in an attempt to garner local support, they opened their fields to the general public, charging people a penny per box for "pick-your-own" berries.

A month into the strike a settlement was reached that resulted in significant wage increases. The U.S. and California Departments of Labor, the Mexican and Japanese consuls, and the Los Angeles Chamber of Commerce all had a hand in brokering this agreement. After Pearl Harbor the El Monte Japanese growers and their families were forced to abandon their homes and their land when they were ordered into internment camps. The berry fields would never be the same. As Jesusita Torres remembered, "After they were taken to the concentration camps, the fields were not good." The El Monte berry strike reveals that the struggle for a living wage in California fields extends beyond a one-dimensional notion of poor workers against rich growers and can reflect a more complicated picture of California agriculture.

SOURCES: Acuña, Rodolfo. 1981. *Occupied America: A History of Chicanos*. 2nd ed. New York: Harper and Row; López, Ronald L. 1970. "The El Monte Berry Strike of 1933." *Aztlán* 1 (Spring): 101–114; Ruiz, Vicki L. 1998. *From out of the Shadows: Mexican Women in Twentieth-Century America*. New York: Oxford University Press.

Vicki L. Ruiz

EL MOVIMIENTO ESTUDIANTIL CHICANO DE AZTLÁN (MEChA) (1969–)

The 1960s, a period of tremendous turmoil and activism within the Mexican communities of the United States, ushered in the Chicano movement. The movement itself was not a homogeneous endeavor, but rather a collection of simultaneous crusades that included the United Farm Workers struggles led by César Chávez, a highly vocal anti-Vietnam War movement, and rising student expectations at the high-school and university levels. Student activism probed poor educational attainment and opportunities, the tracking system, de facto segregation, and limited Latino representation among the faculty and curricula of institutions of higher learning. In March 1968, over 10,000 dissatisfied students at five area high schools in East Los Angeles walked out of their classrooms. Known as the "East Los Angeles blow-outs," these protests galvanized Mexican American students throughout California, the Southwest, and even the Midwest. The "blowouts" signified the tumultuous collective environment that led to the foundation of El Movimiento Estudantil Chicano de Aztlán (MEChA).

In April 1969 MEChA was established at a three-day conference at the University of California, Santa Barbara, sponsored by the Chicano Coordinating Committee on Higher Education. Attended by approximately 100 delegates consisting of students, instructors, administrators, and community activists, this convention drafted the *Plan de Santa Barbara*, an educational reform program that called for the establishment of Chicano studies programs in high schools and universities and a student organization, MEChA, intended to unite all other student groups under the banner of cultural nationalism and political and community activism. It drew inspiration from the Chicano Youth Liberation Conference held in Denver, Colorado, where 1,500 participants unveiled the *El Plan Espiritual de Aztlán*, a call for an autonomous Chicano homeland comprising the territories ceded to the United States by Mexico following the Mexican-American War (1846–1848).

"Mechistas" sought to promote cultural awareness and *hermandad*—brotherhood and spiritual unity for the entire community. By distancing themselves from mainstream American values and Spanish antecedents, this group favored *indigenismo*, or indigenous ancestry, the glorification of the motherland (Mexico), and Aztlán, the mythical origins of their heritage. Mechistas further attempted to connect university campuses to inner-city barrios to establish a mutually beneficial relationship that promoted advancement for the entire Chicano community. Issues such as police brutality, discrimination in hiring and renting practices, and teaching the fundamentals of La Causa (the Cause) to high-school and junior-high-school students were also some of their objectives.

Almost immediately MEChA suffered from serious internal divisions that led to a diminished status by 1973. Many original leaders left college, while the nationalist emphasis compelled socialist-influenced students who favored the commonality of class interests to leave the organization. Chicanas, generally relegated to stereotypical clerical and administrative jobs in the organization and frustrated by a reluctance to deal with feminist issues, also left. Today MEChA remains a loose federation of chapters scattered throughout various campuses in the American Southwest. It is primarily concerned with the recruitment and retention of Chicano college students.

See also Chicano Movement

SOURCES: Gonzáles, Manuel G. 1999. *Mexicanos: A History of Mexicans in the United States*. Bloomington: Indiana University Press; Muñoz, Carlos, Jr. 1989. *Youth, Identity, Power: The Chicano Movement*. New York: Verso; Vargas, Zaragosa, ed. 1999. *Major Problems in Mexican American History*. Boston: Houghton Mifflin.

Steven Rosales

EL PASO LAUNDRY STRIKE

In the first decades of the twentieth century ethnic Mexican women constituted a significant portion of the labor pool in the border city of El Paso, Texas. The 1920 U.S. census revealed that more than half of El Paso's female working population was of Mexican origin, and the majority of those women labored as domestics or as laundresses in private homes or in one of the city's various laundries. Historian Mario T. García notes that Mexicanas—both residents of El Paso and women who crossed the border daily from Ciudad Juárez—easily constituted anywhere from 60 to 80 percent of the workforces at local laundries. However, Mexican laundresses found that despite experience or longevity, they earned only about half what their Euro-American co-workers earned. Racial assumptions about Mexicans' ability to subsist on less pay, the perceived inexperience of Mexican workers, and the nearly constant supply of workers from across the border functioned to keep wages low. While Mexicanas earned between $4 and $6 per week in the laundries, Euro-American workers in the same plants were paid more than double that amount. Moreover, Mexicana laundresses in El Paso made less than half what laundry workers in other major Texas cities earned at the time for the same work.

In October 1919 hundreds of ethnic Mexican women who toiled as laundresses in El Paso walked off their jobs, demanding an end to a dual wage system, as well as union recognition. With the assistance of local and state organizers from the American Federation of Labor (AFL), several El Paso Mexicana laundresses formed the Laundry Workers' Union at the Acme Laundry, one of the city's largest firms. After the company refused to recognize the union and fired two of its organizers, nearly 200 Mexicana laundresses went on strike against the company. Bolstered by financial and moral support from workers at other area laundries, the Central Labor Union and other AFL locals, the International Union of Mine, Mill, and Smelter Workers, and Mexican and Mexican American mutual-aid organizations, nearly 600 workers and sympathy strikers went on strike against the city's laundries. Women played a vital role in the strike, even going so far as to block the international bridges to prevent strikebreakers from Mexico from crossing into El Paso. However, male leaders, including C. N. Idar, brother of Tejana activist and journalist Jovita Idar, directed the strike and represented the laundresses in all negotiations with laundry owners.

Despite the wide range of support garnered by the laundry workers, the union's efforts were ultimately hampered by its exclusion of Mexican nationals. The AFL maintained a strong anti-immigrant policy (membership in its unions was restricted to U.S. citizens) that created a cleavage between Mexican American and Mexican workers and proved to be a fatal flaw for the Laundry Workers' Union. In a border setting employers easily replaced striking workers not only with American workers, but also with a vast supply of Mexican workers from Ciudad Juárez who were willing to work despite the poor conditions and low pay, and were thus able to keep their laundries running. Although ultimately thwarted by the very nature of the border economy it hoped to alter, the 1919 El Paso laundry workers' strike became what García calls "one of the earliest displays of ethnic solidarity among Mexican female workers in the United States."

The strike continued through the end of 1919, but the strikers were never able to attain their demands, and many of the women lost their jobs permanently. Yet despite the ultimate loss, the 1919 laundry strike stands as a symbol of the determination of Mexicanas to improve their lives and working conditions. The example set forth by these women served as a galvanizing force for future union efforts in El Paso and the U.S. Southwest.

SOURCES: Acosta, Teresa Palomo, and Ruthe Winegarten. 2003. *Las Tejanas: 300 Years of History.* Austin: University of Texas Press; García, Mario T. 1980. "The Chicana in American History: The Mexican Women of El Paso, 1880–1920—A Case Study." *Pacific Historical Review* 49, no. 2 (May): 315–337; ———. 1981. *Desert Immigrants: The Mexicans of El Paso, 1880–1920.* New Haven, CT: Yale University Press; Leyva, Yolanda. Chávez 1995. " 'Faithful hard-working Mexican hands': Mexicana Workers during the Great Depression." *Perspectives in Mexican American Studies* 5:63–77.

Monica Perales

EL RESCATE (1981–)

El Rescate was founded in 1981 by Santana Chirino Amaya Refugee Committee members, along with the Southern California Ecumenical Council. From 1980 to 1987 between 1 and 1.5 million people in El Salvador were driven from their homeland as a result of the civil war and the persecution of military death squads. An estimated one-tenth of El Salvador's population fled. In response to the high influx of immigrants fleeing political persecution, El Rescate was the first U.S. agency to provide legal and social services to these refugees. The Los Angeles-based organization opened Clínica Monseñor Romero, which offered free health and medical attention. In 1987 El Refugio, a transitional housing shelter for refugees, was opened. El Rescate incorporated legal services in addition to social services. In 1984 El Rescate launched the Children's Advocacy Project and assisted in the prevention of family disunification and the separation of children that often occurred when families were detained by immigration officials.

El Rescate also assisted people affected by the 1986 earthquake in El Salvador. The organization raised $55,000 for the purchase of food, medical supplies, and construction materials to help the thousands left homeless and injured by the earthquake. Through the 1980s El Rescate aided war-torn communities in El Salvador, in addition to serving refugees in the United States. In 1989 the organization led the Caravan of Material Aid—a campaign that brought $3 million of necessary supplies to more than ten war-torn communities.

Among its many accomplishments, El Rescate has been instrumental in reversing discriminatory immigration policies and advocating passage of just legislation. In 1991, to secure political refugee status for Salvadoreños, the agency initiated its Temporary Protected Status Campaign and registered more than 60,000 individuals for permanent residency. El Rescate also played a key role in gaining residency for immigrants after the settlement of the *American Baptist Churches v. Thornburg* case. American churches—mostly Baptist—began the sanctuary movement during the 1980s. This movement garnered support from Washington to Texas and began in light of the restrictive and discriminatory immigration policies that denied asylum to political refugees from El Salvador and Guatemala. Religious leaders in the Southwest responded to this situation by offering immigrants sanctuary in churches. U.S. government officials targeted these churches for breaking federal laws and harboring undocumented immigrants. The American Baptist Churches fought the indictments. El Rescate submitted more than 7,000 applications. In response to continued political turmoil in Central America, El Rescate adamantly advocated for the passage of the Nicaraguan Adjustment and Central American Relief Act (NACARA), which allowed for the consideration of refugee cases under less restrictive rules. When NACARA underwent changes in 2003, El Rescate was instrumental in getting clauses included that made it easier for some Salvadoreños and Guatemaltecos to become legal residents.

El Rescate continues to serve Central American communities. It provides legal representation and advice in political asylum cases. Policy analysis and recommendations are central to El Rescate's efforts in maintaining fair immigration and naturalization legislation. It also provides community outreach orientation to individuals and families new to the United States and Los Angeles.

SOURCES: Crittenden, Ann. 1988. *Sanctuary: A Story of American Conscience and Law in Collision.* New York: Weidenfeld & Nicholson; El Rescate Website. www.elrescate.org (accessed June 29, 2005); Golden, Renny, and Michael McConnel. 1986. *Sanctuary: The New Underground Railroad.* New York: Orbis Books; Menjívar, Cecilia. 2000. *Fragmented Ties: Salvadoran Immigrant Networks in America.* Berkeley: University of California Press.

Margie Brown-Coronel

ENTREPRENEURS

The development of increased business ownership among Latinas is significant, given their past history of limited socioeconomic opportunities. A brief demographic profile of the Latino population will provide a better understanding of the recent increase of Latina entrepreneurs.

With the general exception of the Cuban American population, Latino communities continue to experience socioeconomic barriers within U.S. society. For example, in 2000 only 55 percent of the total Hispanic population had completed four years of high school, in comparison with 88 percent of the total Euro-American population. Similarly, only 11 percent of the total Hispanic population had completed four years of college or more, in comparison with 28 percent of the total Euro-American population. Interestingly, there is only a 1 percent difference between Latino males and females for each of these two educational statistics. Historically, they have always had higher rates of unemployment and poverty in comparison with the total population. The median family income for Hispanics is 58 percent of that of the total Euro-American population. A comparison of occupational distributions indicates that although a limited trend in upward mobility can be seen among Latinos, especially among Cuban Americans, Latinos are concentrated in the lower middle and lower rungs of the occupational ladder, while Latinas are concentrated largely in the lower clerical and service categories.

Cary de León, president of the Latin Business and Professional Women's Club, 1988. Courtesy of the Cuban Heritage Collection, Otto G. Richter Library, University of Miami.

An understanding of trends among Latina business owners requires an understanding of the impact of ethnicity and gender on rates of entrepreneurship. Between 1987 and 1992 business ownership among Latinas increased by 114.2 percent. Despite this dramatic growth, Latina-owned businesses accounted for only a small percentage of the total number of minority-owned businesses in 1987 (9.5 percent) and 1992 (12.5 percent). The 1997 Economic Survey also shows that sales/receipts taken in by Latina businesses increased by 297 percent. In 1987 Latina businesses took in about $4 million in sales, but by 1992 the amount of sales/receipts had increased to $17 million.

The 1997 Economic Census Survey of Minority-Owned Businesses Enterprises reports that these firms grew four times faster than the national average between 1992 and 1997. Rapidly expanding Latino-owned businesses totaled about 1.2 million firms in 1997 and employed more than 1 million people. Mexican Americans own about four out of ten of these firms. Latino businesses are concentrated geographically; about 73 percent of all Latino businesses are located in California, Texas, Florida, and New York. These businesses are also concentrated by ethnic group. The majority of Mexican American businesses are located in California and Texas. About 70 percent of Cuban American firms are in Florida, and more than half of Puerto Rican–owned businesses are in New York, Florida, and New Jersey. The 1997 Economic Census Survey also shows that Latino and Latina businesses are concentrated within five metropolitan areas: (1) Los Angeles–Long Beach, (2) Miami, (3) New York, (4) Houston, and (5) San Antonio. Wholesale businesses account for the largest number of firms run by Latinos, followed by manufacturers and retailers.

Women-owned businesses, like minority- and Hispanic-owned businesses, have also been growing at significant rates since 1992. The number of women-owned businesses increased 16 percent from 1992 to 1997, compared with only a 6 percent growth rate for all U.S. firms. Women-owned firms are geographically concentrated in four states: California, New York, Texas, and Florida. These four states account for 33 percent of all women-owned firms. California has the largest percentage of businesses owned by women. The Census Survey of Women-Owned Business Enterprises (1997, 1) points out that "a short drive on Interstate 5 in southern California will take you through three of the 10 counties with the largest number of firms owned by women—Los Angeles, Orange and San Diego." More than seven of every ten women-owned firms were in services or retail trade industries such as bookstores and jewelry stores.

California restaurateur María Elena Avila and her mother, Margarita Avila. Courtesy of María Elena Avila.

The usual categories found in most census reports and economic surveys make it difficult to study Latina entrepreneurs. The data provided by the 1997 Economic Census Survey of Minority-Owned Businesses and Women-Owned Businesses represent the most valuable source for the study of business ownership, but data on ethnicity and gender are not always included. The U.S. Census Bureau's Economic Census is currently revising its data collection to fill this gap in the study of business ownership by women of color such as Latina entrepreneurs. The 1997 Economic Census Survey of Minority-Owned Businesses provides its usual summary table that compares business ownership by minority groups. The data reveal that Latinos have the largest percentage (39.5) of all minority-owned firms. Asian/Pacific Islanders own 30 percent; blacks, 27.1 percent. American Indian and Alaska Natives have the smallest percentage of the total with 6.5 percent. This report now contains data for minority-owned firms by gender and includes information on black, Hispanic, American Indian/Alaska Native, and Asian/Pacific Islander men and women entrepreneurs.

These data show that Latina-owned firms account for a little more than a quarter (28.1 percent) of the total number of Hispanic-owned firms. In comparison, black women own 38 percent of all black-owned firms, the group with the largest percentage of women-owned businesses. According to a report issued in 2001 by the U.S. Census Bureau, Latina entrepreneurs represent the fastest-growing sector of new business owners.

Social science research on Latina entrepreneurs has added a human dimension to the quantitative demographic profiles provided by census reports. Social scientists and journalists have focused on the reasons women start their own businesses and the problems they encounter once they establish their firms. Interviews with Latina entrepreneurs reveal common reasons for their decision to set themselves up as business owners. Latinas, like other women business owners, express strong feelings about being "their own boss," but more important, they see business ownership as a means to increase the family income. Latina entrepreneurs express their goal as one of providing a better life for their children, usually by providing the financial means to a good education. Although they realize that they will be working longer hours once they start their own businesses, Latina entrepreneurs, most of whom had worked in the paid labor force for many years, stress that they work for their children. As Socorro Ramírez, a beauty-shop owner, said, "I work for my daughter's future." She wanted to own her own beauty shop because this would bring in more money for her family and for her children.

> I wanted to be successful for the sake of my children. I wanted them to have a better life. I wanted my daughters to get an education. I thought to myself, if I'm successful with such a limited education then my daughters will achieve more since they are getting a good education. They will better themselves by getting some career or profession. I see my business as a way to provide my children with more opportunities. I wanted to earn more money so they could go to private school. This is what kept me going during hard times.

The sentiments expressed by this Latina beauty-shop owner are not atypical. Other Latina entrepreneurs identified business ownership as a step toward upward mobility for their children as a result of their ability to use their business profits to pay for better schooling. A key theme among Latina entrepreneurs, in contrast to Euro-American women entrepreneurs, is that they do not want their children to become business owners. Latina entrepreneurs with businesses in the services sector are most likely to want their children to become some kind of professional rather than follow their examples as business owners. Interviews in such magazines as *Hispanic Business* and *Latina,* however, are reporting a reversal in this trend. Latina entrepreneurs who own businesses outside the traditional service sector state that they encourage their children, particularly their daughters, to start their own businesses. As Latina entrepreneurs continue to establish businesses outside the service sector, the practice of supporting an entrepreneurial tradition among their children promises to increase.

Latina entrepreneurs continue to face many obstacles shaped by the impact of ethnicity, gender, and social class. Start-up money for business ownership is one of the most basic problems for any entrepreneur, but this issue is particularly difficult for Latinas. Many turn first to their families for loans and then attempt to secure bank loans. With the slow but steady growth of a Latino middle class, it is estimated that the children of the middle class will have access to more financial resources that can be used for business ventures. A growing trend seen among Latina business owners involves partnerships with Latinos or men from other ethnic backgrounds. The Census Bureau has only recently included a category of "equally male/female owned" in its reports on minority businesses. In 1997 these "equally owned" business firms constituted 16 percent of all Latino businesses.

Since 1997, studies of Hispanic businesses have focused on Hispanic women-owned businesses. More than one-third (35 percent of all Hispanic-owned firms are owned by women. Hispanic women-owned companies employ 18.5 percent of the workers in all Hispanic-owned firms and generate $44.4 billion in nationwide sales. Hispanic women control 39 percent of the 1.4 million companies owned by minority women in the United States, generating nearly $147 billion in sales. Hispanic women own four in ten minority women-owned firms. Between 1987 and 1996, the number of Hispanic women-owned businesses grew by 206 percent, compared with 47 percent of all businesses. Between 1997 and 2004, the number of Hispanic women-owned businesses grew by 206 percent, compared with 47 percent of all businesses. During this same seven-year period, the number of firms owned by Hispanic women increased by about 64 percent to 553,618 and their combined revenue climbed to more than 62 percent or $44.4 billion. The five states with the largest number of Hispanic women-owned firms were California (17 percent), Texas (18 percent), Florida (16 percent), New York (14 percent) and Arizona (13 percent).

Latina entrepreneurs also face the problem of gender and ethnic discrimination in the workplace. Discrimination against Latina entrepreneurs can occur at different levels, ranging from business ownership in service industries to high-tech companies. As one Latina entrepreneur who owned her own public relations firm stated, "I have had friends of mine—men—who have their own agencies tell me that they have referred prospective clients to me but then they tell them they don't want a woman handling their accounts." Latina entrepreneurs in the service sector related similar stories of clients who make disparaging remarks. In sum, they are not immune to the everyday occurrences of prejudice that Latinos and Latinas continue to confront in other occupations.

Latina entrepreneurs represent a growing sector of Latino business owners, women business owners, and minority business owners. Their firms are getting larger, hiring more employees, bringing in larger revenues, and concentrating outside the service sector. They have begun to draw national attention, but more studies, interviews, and oral histories are needed in order to document this important group of Latinas whose strength and contribution to U.S. society will increase in the years to come.

SOURCES: García, Alma M. 1995. "I Work for My Daughter's Future: Mexican American Women and the Development of Entrepreneurship." *California History,* October, 262–279; Limón, Anthony. 2005. "Raising the Bar: Hispanics benefit as law firms bid to reflect diversified clientele." *Hispanic Business,* June, 104–106; U.S. Bureau of the Census, 2001. *Survey of Minority-Owned Business Enterprises: Hispanic-Owned Businesses, 1997.* Washington, DC: Government Printing Office; ———. 1997. *Economic Census: Survey of Minority-Owned Business Enterprises.* Washington, DC: Government Printing Office; ———. 1997. *Economic Census Survey of Women-Owned Business Enterprises.* Washington, DC: Government Printing Office.

Alma M. García

ENVIRONMENT AND THE BORDER

The U.S./Mexican border has emerged as one of the most significant sites in the ever-evolving geography of the United States and Mexico. In many ways *la frontera* represents a microcosm of the larger processes and shifts that are transforming both countries. As the border region becomes increasingly integrated through industrialization, urbanization, and flows of capital, labor, and commodities (both legal and extralegal), environmental degradation has become an increasingly severe problem. While the challenges are immense, there is also a growing movement to protect the border environment and its communities that features significant participation and leadership on the part of Chicanas and Mexicanas, especially at the grassroots level.

Transecting 2,000 miles of semiarid and desert environment, the U.S./Mexican border is one of the few that joins a third- and a first-world country. This economic inequality shapes and informs many aspects of the border, including its environmental problems. *La frontera* was established in 1848 under the Treaty of Guadalupe Hidalgo, which brought to a close the Mexican-American War and resulted in Mexico surrendering about one-third of its northern territory to the United States. In 1853 the Gadsden Purchase, encompassing what is now southeastern Arizona, completed the contemporary border configuration. The border skirts four states in the southwestern United States,

Texas, New Mexico, Arizona, and California, and six along the Mexican side, Baja California, Sonora, Chihuahua, Coahuila, Nuevo León, and Tamaulipas. When the border was initially drawn, the border region was sparsely populated by indigenous nations with deep roots in the region, such as the Yaqui and Tohono O'odham, both of which had adapted to the extreme aridity of the border environment by practicing such strategies as seasonal migration and flood irrigation. Although the border is punctuated by two major north/south mountain ranges, the Sierra Madre Oriental and Occidental, both of which are sites of great ecological diversity, the majority of the border is characterized by minimal precipitation, which renders much of the region a desert. The significance of aridity cannot be overstated. Not only does water availability set the upper limit of human activities, but attempts to overcome those limits require massive water transfers and exploitation of groundwater reserves, both of which have major ecological consequences. In addition, aridity causes the border to be a fragile environment. Essentially, the scarcity of water intensifies ecological damage, because plants, soils, and animals cannot readily restore themselves. As a result, the environmental challenges facing the border are of great concern.

The urban and industrial development of the border did not begin in earnest until the early twentieth century with the Mexican Revolution. Although a number of border skirmishes occurred, the major impact on the border was the large numbers of northbound immigrants who sought to escape the war. The refugees and immigrants of this period transformed the region because many settled along the northern edge of the Mexican border and helped create a whole series of urban settlements, known as border towns. In addition, at roughly the same time the southwestern United States experienced its own metamorphosis as corporations and entrepreneurs sought to develop railroads, agriculture, and mining, all heavily reliant upon Mexican labor.

Despite this early growth, the border remained home to relatively few people, and its urban development was limited to a series of twin border towns, until the 1960s. In 1964 the Bracero Program (a formal guest-worker scheme) was terminated, and the Mexican and U.S. governments created the Border Industrialization Program (BIP). The purpose of the BIP, whose factories were known as *maquilas,* was to help ameliorate the unemployment associated with the cessation of the Bracero Program, to facilitate Mexican industrialization, and to provide low-wage labor to U.S. corporations. The United States offered tax incentives to manufacturers who relocated their assembly activities along Mexico's northern border. Not surprisingly, millions of Mexicans were drawn to the border's new opportunities, and this population growth, in turn, provided the basis for widespread urbanization and development. More recently the North American Free Trade Agreement (NAFTA) has continued this growth trajectory. The current population of the U.S./Mexican border is approximately 12 million and is expected to double by 2020. As a result, the border has not only become the fastest-growing region in Mexico, but also has some of the most severe urban and environmental problems. In addition to phenomenal population growth, these problems have been exacerbated by limited infrastructure capacity, weak environmental regulations, and the economic logic of global inequality.

The environmental problems of the U.S./Mexican border are almost legendary and have incited great concern along both sides. One observer has described the situation in the following way: "Lack of adequate housing, exposure of workers to dangerous toxic substances, and contamination of drinking water with industrial pollutants have turned the Mexican side of the border into an environmental wasteland and industrial slum." The fact that the Mexican side of the border is more ecologically devastated than the U.S. side does not imply that the latter is a better ecological steward, but rather reflects the geography of uneven economic and political power so that the majority of ecological devastation is concentrated on the less powerful side. Despite this very real difference, however, it must be recalled that the border is composed of two political units that share a single ecological home.

The environmental problems associated with the industrialization of the border (both manufacturing and agriculture) are extremely severe. Both sides of the region are plagued by industrial emissions and agricultural runoff, which affect the air, water, plant and animal life, and, of course, humans. The use of hazardous substances directly affects workers, adjacent neighborhoods, and communities that share contaminated air and water resources, sometimes with tragic consequences. For instance, in just over a one-year period in the 1990s, fifteen cases of anencephaly (babies born without a brain) were documented in the Brownsville-Matamoras area. Although many attribute these birth defects to pollution, local leaders claimed that they were due to either malnutrition or a genetic predisposition among Mexicans. Another example of border contamination is the New River, which runs through Mexicali and Calexico, labeled as "the most hazardous waterway in all of North America." While estimates of the cost to clean up the border range from $5.5 billion to $18 billion, in 1993 the U.S. Congress allocated only $240 million, while Mexico budgeted $460 million over a three-year period—clearly an insufficient level of resources in both cases.

Environment and the Border

Although pollution is severe on both sides of the border, it is worse in Mexico because of less stringent regulation, weaker enforcement, and greater industrial and urban growth. Once again, this problem must be seen in light of the geographic proximity and economic inequality between the United States and Mexico. As a poor country, Mexico has historically argued that it can ill afford to impose strict environmental regulations on industries, which provide much-needed jobs. At the same time the weaker regulatory environment has provided a haven to some U.S. polluters who consider U.S. regulations to be too burdensome. For example, a large percentage of southern California's furniture industry relocated to Mexico in the wake of the imposition of new air-quality regulations. In Mexico manufacturers can take advantage of both low-wage labor and less expensive production techniques. During the BIP program the La Paz Agreement required that all hazardous materials imported by the *maquilas* be returned to the country of origin. A 1989 study conducted by the Environmental Protection Agency, however, found that approximately 1 percent of *maquilas* were in strict compliance.

In addition to these regulated forms of pollution, there exists a serious problem with illegal pollution. As hazardous materials and toxic waste have become more tightly regulated in the United States, more than a few firms and handlers have sought to dispose of waste in Mexico, essentially using an impoverished area as a dumping ground. Investigators have found barrels and containers of hazardous waste stored in the backyards of unsuspecting Mexicans and in warehouses, industrial districts, and rural areas. Neither U.S. nor Mexican officials have a grasp of the full dimensions of the problem, nor do they have the resources to stop it.

Another source of environmental concern involves the intensification of large-scale commercial agriculture along the border. Although the border has long supported agricultural activity, most of it was sustainable insofar as it did not deplete local water supplies or rely upon the importation of resources. During the last few decades, particularly after NAFTA, agriculture along the border has undergone significant intensification, with great environmental consequences. The most noteworthy problem is water consumption. The development of major irrigation projects on both sides of the border, including water transfers and greater utilization of groundwater reserves, has not only allowed more intensive production, but has opened up millions of new acres for cultivation. For example, along the Rio Grande/Rio Bravo, 95 percent of the native habitat has been transformed by agricultural development. In addition, border agriculture is extremely energy dependent. Mechanization, fertilizers, and pesticides are all fossil fuel based, which has implications for both the global consumption of these resources and the quality of life for local residents.

In 1994 the North American Free Trade Agreement was passed in an effort to integrate the economies of the United States, Mexico, and Canada. Many environmentalists were opposed to NAFTA because of the potentially adverse environmental impacts, while advocates argued that the economic development of Mexico was the only way to enable it to have the resources to protect its environment. There is little doubt as to the growth—the region now has an economic output of $150 billion, and trade between the United States and Mexico increased from $80 billion to $200 billion between 1994 and 2003. However, it remains less certain how this economic juggernaut will affect the border environment and the millions of people who rely upon it.

In addition to the hazards of industrial and agricultural pollution, the rapid urbanization of the border has led to a different set of environmental challenges. Both Mexican and U.S. towns were ill prepared to accommodate the large number of new residents that came to the region, beginning in the 1970s. As a result, thousands of *colonias* have sprung up along both sides of the border. The U.S. General Accounting Office has defined a *colonia* as "an unincorporated subdivision along the U.S./Mexican border in which one or more of the following conditions exist: substandard housing, inadequate roads and drainage, and substandard or no water and sewer facilities." In some cases large numbers of people build homes for themselves as squatters, while at other times they buy land from a developer. In addition, while some municipalities offer utility services to *colonias*, many others do not, forcing residents to devise alternative strategies. The end result is a settlement pattern that exists at the margins of regulated urban development. Although *colonias* do provide housing and community to those in need, they are also associated with some very serious health and environmental problems, in particular, a lack of potable water. One study found, for example, that only 64 percent of residents of Nogales, Sonora, had access to potable water. Access to clean water is considered a cornerstone of both human and environmental health, and without it, people, particularly children, suffer from numerous health problems, especially intestinal disorders. It is the lack of such basic resources as potable water that produces the high infant mortality rates associated with the border region.

In addition to problems related to environmental health, there are numerous other environmental concerns. For instance, rapid population growth has contributed to deforestation as people collect wood for fuel and building materials; it has intensified the depletion of groundwater sources; and a severe air-pollution problem has developed due to auto emissions and open fires. Although environmental degradation is overwhelming, it should also be pointed out that the poverty of many border dwellers also encourages the complete use of goods and materials. The United States, as the largest producer of trash in the world, provides a whole variety of items that resourceful Mexicans and Mexican Americans recycle into such things as homes, household goods, transportation, and toys.

In discussing the U.S./Mexican border it is important to keep in mind one of the purposes of an international border: to regulate the flow of people and commodities. The United States and Mexico are becoming increasingly integrated in their economies, culture, and demographics. For instance, almost 300,000 Mexican workers legally cross the border on a daily or weekly basis to work in the United States. In 1999 there were more than 4.2 million truck crossings. The contradictory nature of the border has led to a situation whereby policy makers acknowledge that it is impossible to stop the flow of border crossers, yet spectacular efforts have been made not only to channel the flow of immigrants, but also to create the illusion of efficacy. As a result of substantial public sentiment against Latino immigrants, the United States has embarked on a tremendous buildup of military infrastructure along the border. This can be seen in a dramatic increase in expenditures: Between 1993 and 1997 the budget for INS enforcement along the U.S./Mexican border doubled from $400 to $800 million. The INS has invested in the installation of massive walls, sometimes consisting of multiple layers; the placement of extraordinarily bright lights to "keep them out"; frequent flights by aircraft; and nearly a tripling of personnel. While the public supports "protecting our borders," such initiatives have had negative consequences for local flora and fauna. It should be obvious that the U.S./Mexican border is a human-made political line, not one that plants and animals comprehend, but one that they are affected by in a multitude of ways. For instance, many species rely on local migrations in order to reproduce, but are blocked by doing so because of the international border, as well as roads. In addition, the bright lights of the border have been linked to stress on particular species, which are then unable to reproduce, while in other cases the lights have made some snakes more vulnerable to predators. For human beings, the implementation of Operation Gatekeeper, a policy initiative centered on the buildup of the border, has pushed immigrants into more isolated, remote, and inhospitable areas. As a result, almost 2,000 persons have died trying to cross the border. As can be seen, there are many ways in which the human, animal, and plant ecology of the border has been dramatically transformed.

During the last two decades, fortunately, there has been growing attention to the border environment from constituencies on both sides. NAFTA, in particular, focused attention on the region because many became concerned with the possibility of the further deterioration of the environment. With the adoption of NAFTA, the La Paz Agreement was essentially replaced by the Border XXI Program, which establishes nine technical working groups centered on key issues: natural resources, water, air, hazardous and solid waste, contingency planning and emergency response, environmental information resources, pollution prevention, environmental health, and cooperative enforcement and compliance. In addition, three new institutions were chartered: the Border Environment Cooperation Commission, the North American Development Bank, and the Commission for Environmental Cooperation. While these organizations have begun important work along the border, it is still too early to assess their efficacy, but their bi-national nature and emphasis on sustainability are promising. The Border XXI Program has been replaced by the Border 2012 Program, which emphasized bottom-up strategies and regional approaches. In addition, growing activism has emerged among border residents, particularly on the U.S. side, where government policy encourages the growth of nongovernmental organizations. Examples include Arizona's Border Ecology Project, New Mexico's Interhemispheric Resource Center, and the Texas Center for Policy Studies. Finally, there has been an increase in more grassroots initiatives, many of which, building on an environmental justice model, seek to connect environmental and economic justice concerns. Such organizations include the California Environmental Health Coalition, which succeeded in banning the pesticide methyl bromide in poor Latino neighborhoods in San Diego, the Southwest Network for Economic and Environmental Justice (SNEEJ), and La Red Fronteriza de Salud y Ambiente. These latter groups garner their strength from their bilateral nature and refusal to allow the state or polluters to pit Mexican and U.S. communities against each other in their struggle for social and environmental justice.

SOURCES: Lewis, Sanford, Marco Kaltofen, and Gregory Ormsby. 1991. *Border Trouble: Rivers in Peril.* Boston: National Toxics Campaign; Liverman, Diana, Robert Varady, Octavio Chávez, and Roberto Sánchez. 2000. "Environmental Issues along the United States–Mexico Border: Drivers of Change and the Response of Citizens and Institutions." *Annual Review of Energy Environments* 24: 607–643; Nabhan, Gary. 1996. "Cryptic Cacti on the Borderline." In *The Late Great Mexican Border*, ed. Bobby Byrd and Susannah M. Byrd, 122–138. El Paso, TX: Cinco Puntos Press; Peña, Devon. 1997. *The Terror of the Machine*. Austin: University of Texas; Pulido, Laura. 1994. "Restructuring and the Contraction and Expansion of Environmental Rights in the United States." *Environment and Planning A* 26:915–936.

Laura Pulido

ESCAJEDA, JOSEFINA (1893–1981)

Josefina Escajeda was one of the first Mexican American woman folklorists in the twentieth century. Like Tejanas Jovita González Mireles and Fermina Guerra, she published Mexican American folklore during the 1930s and collaborated with prominent European American folklorists. She belonged to a longtime Tejano family in El Paso County and herself was a pioneer of Fabens, Texas. As a young woman, she taught school in nearby Clint, Texas, but as was expected for women of her day, when she married, she left the schoolhouse. Her husband was J. M. "Joe" Escajeda, a local farmer who had a daughter from a previous marriage whom Josefina raised.

During the Great Depression she developed a reputation as a talented folklorist of West Texas as she published a number of essays. In 1935 she wrote the following stories: "The Witch of Cenecu," "Doña Carolina Learns a Lesson," "La casa de la labor," "Agapito Brings a Treat," and "A Hanged Man Sends Rain." All of these were included in *Puro Mexicano*, a collection of folktales edited by the legendary University of Texas professor J. Frank Dobie. Two years later Charles L. Sonnichsen, another well-known folklorist, used her stories in his "Mexican Spooks from El Paso," published in *Straight Texas*, a collection edited by J. Frank Dobie and Mody C. Boatright.

Escajeda lived all her life in El Paso County and was well known in the small Lower Valley communities of Fabens, Clint, and San Elizario. She lived a fairly quiet life whose activities revolved around her church, where she played the organ. Escajeda organized fundraisers in order to preserve Our Lady at Mount Carmel Catholic Church, one of the old missions in the El Paso area. It remains a mystery why she stopped collecting and writing folktales. She died in 1981. Josefina Escajeda was a pioneering Tejana folklorist who has yet to receive more scholarly study.

SOURCES: Dobie, J. Frank, ed. 1935. *Puro Mexicano*. Austin: Texas Folklore Society; *El Paso Times*. 1981. March 11; Orozco, Cynthia E. 1996. "Josefina Escajeda." In *New Handbook of Texas*, 2: 887. Austin: Texas State Historical Association.

Cynthia E. Orozco

ESCALONA, BEATRÍZ ("LA CHATA NOLOESCA") (1903–1979)

"La Chata Noloesca" was the most renowned comic actress in Spanish-language vaudeville in the United States; her comic persona of *la peladita* reigned supreme for more than four decades. Born in San Antonio, Texas, on August 20, 1903, Beatríz Escalona was raised by her widowed mother, the proprietor of a boardinghouse facing the Union Pacific Railroad station, where the young Beatríz sold food and coffee to train passengers. At age thirteen she began working in the box office of the Teatro Zaragosa and at seventeen as an usherette in San Antonio's premier theater, the Teatro Nacional. Here she met her future husband, José Areu, and joined up with his family's troupe, in which she was trained as an actress, song and dance girl, and comedienne. Escalona made her stage debut at the Teatro Colón in El Paso in 1920.

The Areus, of Spanish-Cuban roots, were one of the most important theatrical families on the Spanish-language vaudeville and zarzuela (Spanish operetta) circuits in the Southwest. During the entire 1920s the Areus, including Beatríz "Noloesca" (her stage name), toured Mexico and the Southwest, especially spending a great deal of time in Los Angeles. By 1930 Beatríz, now known as "La Chata Noloesca," the name of the comic underdog character (*peladita*) she had developed, had separated from her husband and formed her own vaudeville company, Atracciones Noloesca. Escalona, who had started out as a beautiful song and dance girl, had originally gotten into comedy after becoming too overweight to make it as a chorine. Her *peladita* was destined to become the most famous and beloved comic character on Hispanic stages from Los Angeles to New York. Escalona's *peladita* "La Chata" was a streetwise fast talker in the tradition of Mexican comediennes such as Emilia Trujillo, Lupe Rivas Cacho, and Delia Magaña. Dressed in a costume that, at times, was that of a housemaid and, at other times, was made to look like that of a naughty child, she developed a picaresque style that allowed her character to survive and ironically get the upper hand at all times. Her comedy was topical, often relating to current events and locales, and incorporated working-class language and humor, including Spanish-English code switching.

In 1936, at the height of the depression, Escalona formed a new vaudeville company made up predominantly of women, most of whom had been raised in San Antonio. In 1938, in order to survive, the troupe, now called the Compañía Mexicana, hit the road for points east and north, where other Hispanic populations were still growing and in possession of enough resources to support live theater. Escalona's novel idea was to bring to Cubans, Puerto Ricans, and others dis-

Beatríz Escalona as "La Chata Noloesca" in a comic sketch. Courtesy of Arte Público Press.

tinctively Mexican variety acts. There was one problem that at times led to embarrassment: the women had been raised in San Antonio, and some of them did not speak Spanish very well. Escalona was always trying to teach them Spanish or transform their Tex-Mex dialect into standard Spanish. They were really Americans attempting to represent Mexico in their art. By the 1940s not only was language becoming hybridization, but also hybrid characters, such as the *pachuco*, who represented the emergence of Mexican American culture began to appear in Escalona's sketches and song and dance routines.

In 1938 Escalona's company began a long string of successes in Tampa, Miami, and Cuba. In 1941 the company took Chicago Latino communities by storm and eventually made its way to New York City, where it stayed for nine years. "La Chata Noloesca" and her Compañía Mexicana played the Teatro Hispano, Teatro Puerto Rico, Teatro Triboro, the Fifty-third Street Theater, and radio and television. Escalona, besides being an important company manager, was able to introduce other San Antonio and Texas talent to New York. In the 1950s, once again residing in San Antonio, Escalona worked with a radio-drama group, acting in half-hour segments of *Espuelas de Plata* (Silver Spurs), and later pioneered Spanish-language variety on television in San Antonio with her *Las Tandas de la Chata* (La Chata's Shows).

On her seventy-second birthday in 1975, Escalona was honored with a gala theatrical tribute, and Mexico's National Association of Actors awarded her the diploma of honor; she thus became one of the few non-Mexico-born actors to receive such an honor. Beatríz Escalona died on April 4, 1979.

See also Theater

SOURCES: Arrizón, Alicia. 1999. *Latina Performance: Traversing the Stage*. Bloomington: Indiana University Press; ———, and Lillian Manzor, eds. 2000. *Latinas on State*. Berkeley: Third Woman Press; Kanellos, Nicolás, ed. 1984. *Hispanic Theater in the United States*. Houston: Arte Público Press; ———. 1989. *Mexican American Theatre: Then and Now*. Houston: Arte Público Press; ———. 1990. *Hispanic Theatre in the United States: Origins to 1940*. Austin: University of Texas Press; Ybarra-Frausto, Tomás. 1989. "La Chata Noloesca: Figura del Donaire." in *Mexican American Theatre: Then and Now*, ed. Nicolás Kanellos. Houston: Arte Público Press.

Nicolás Kanellos

ESCOBAR, CARMEN BERNAL (1911–)

Carmen Bernal Escobar's life is emblematic of twentieth-century Mexican immigrant women's experiences in the United States. She combined traditional Mexican and Catholic values with American working-class progressivism to fashion a life that included marriage, motherhood, and labor activism.

Carmen Bernal was born in the city of Durango in north central Mexico on either January 22 or 24, 1911. Her family had been part of Durango's middle class, but her father's death, shortly before her birth, and the ravages of the Mexican Revolution left the family impoverished. Conditions in Mexico meant that Bernal never received more than a fourth-grade education. The family barely survived on her mother's occasional work as a governess and through the scavenging and odd jobs of her older brother and sister.

The desperate economic situation in Mexico forced first her brother and sister and later, in 1925, Bernal and her mother to immigrate to Los Angeles. At the age of fourteen she began to work as a live-in domestic and subsequently in various light industries. In her late teens she did seasonal work in canneries, the industry in which she would later make her mark as a union activist.

Throughout her teenage and young adult years Bernal attempted to integrate herself into American society. While she gave her earnings from her various jobs to her mother to support the family, even in the dark years of the Great Depression she earned enough to buy makeup and the latest fashions. She strove to learn to speak, read, and write English and to engage in those aspects of American life that did not conflict with her obligations as the youngest daughter of a Catholic Mexican family.

In 1935 Carmen Bernal married Steve Escobar, a furniture worker who had been born and raised in the Segundo Barrio of El Paso, Texas. In 1923 he fled racist and restricted opportunities in western Texas in hopes of a better life in Los Angeles. There he became a highly skilled craftsman in furniture finishing, a trade in which he worked for the rest of his life.

By the time they married, Steve and Carmen had steady employment, Steve with a high-end furniture factory, and Carmen with the California Sanitary Canning Company (Cal San). Carmen took time off to give birth to her first child, Alfred, in 1937. When she returned to work, she became involved in union activity.

Carmen prospered at Cal San and was in a position to bring several members of her immediate and extended family into cannery employment. Nevertheless, she chafed under the cannery's paternalistic, racist, and generally exploitative conditions. These same conditions forged a sense of solidarity among the Mexicans, as well as the Russian Jewish women operatives. In the meantime Steve became a leader in organizational efforts of the Congress of Industrial Organizations (CIO) United Furniture Workers of America and brought home his experiences in the labor militancy of that and other leftist unions. The combination of pro-union sentiment in the home, the exploitative nature of the workplace, and the solidarity among the women workers soon disposed Carmen to join Dorothy Healy, the future leader of the Communist Party in the United States and an organizer for the United Cannery, Agricultural, Packing, and Allied Workers of America (UCAPAWA), in organizing efforts at Cal San. Within weeks an overwhelming majority of the women joined the union, and when Cal San's owners refused to negotiate, the workers walked out on strike on August 31, 1939.

Taking opportune advantage of the leftist union's democratic ideology, Carmen Escobar and other Mexican workers quickly assumed leadership positions in the strike. Escobar, for example, became chair of the secondary boycott committee that pressured retailers and consumers to avoid Cal San products. She also organized the union's float in the annual Los Angeles Labor Day parade. Finally, she was among the strikers who took their children to picket the homes of Cal San's owners in the hope of embarrassing them into settling the strike. Faced with the solidarity of the workers and the pressures of the secondary boycott, Cal San finally agreed to a settlement that included union recognition, a closed shop, and improved pay and working conditions.

Winning the strike thrust Escobar into a leadership position within her local. She became head shop steward for women, a member of the union's negotiating team in subsequent contract talks, and the CIO representative to the state of California's Wage and Hour Board. She remained active with Cal San until it relocated to northern California after the end of World War II.

The union experience was a transformative one for Carmen and Steve Escobar. The leadership positions engendered skills, confidence, and a sense of optimism that they carried with them the rest of their lives. They passed those traits on to their children, all of whom became successful professionals. While at the time she did not recognize the Communist influence embedded in the union, in later years Carmen Escobar spoke excitedly about her days with UCAPAWA and the significance of her activities for herself and her family.

After Cal San left Los Angeles, Escobar stopped working to have another son, Edward, in 1946 and a daughter, Rebecca, in 1952. When Rebecca started school in the late 1950s, Escobar returned to work, this time in the retail industry. In 1960, inspired by the presidential campaign of fellow Catholic John Kennedy, Escobar studied for citizenship and became a naturalized U.S. citizen. At the age of sixty-five she left retail and for several years worked as a teacher's aide in the emerging bilingual education programs in local elementary schools. Retiring in her early seventies, she became a voracious reader, primarily of historical biographies. Her husband died in 1984, but Carmen Escobar continues to live in southern California.

See also California Sanitary Canning Company Strike; United Cannery, Agricultural, Packing, and Allied Workers of America (UCAPAWA/FTA)

SOURCES: Ruiz, Vicki L. 1987. *Cannery Women, Cannery Lives: Mexican Women, Unionization, and the California Food Processing Industry, 1930–1950.* Albuquerque: University of New Mexico Press; ———. 1998. *From out of the Shadows: Mexican Women in the Twentieth-Century America.* New York: Oxford University Press.

Edward J. Escobar

ESPAILLAT, RHINA P. (1932–)

Dominican writer, Rhina P. Espaillat moved to the United States with her family in 1939 at the age of seven. She lived in New York in her early adult life, where she taught public school for several years. A resident of Newburyport, Massachusetts, Espaillat began to write poetry in her mature years. However, as David Robert indicates, "Espaillat has emerged, late in her life, as a poet of sublime formal skill and an increasingly wide readership."

Espaillat writes poetry in both Spanish and English,

although primarily in English. Her poetry has been published widely in literary magazines, including *Poetry* and *Sparrow.* It has also been included in a number of important anthologies, such as *A Formal Feeling Comes* and *The Muse Strikes Back.*

She is a kind and gentle presence, and her demeanor and old-world courtesy define the persona of a poet whose collections of poetry have received significant acclaim. She has four poetry collections in print: *Lapsing to Grace* (1992), *Where Horizons Go* (1998), winner of the T. S. Eliot Prize, *Rehearsing Absence* (2001), winner of the Richard Wilbur Prize, and *The Shadow I Dress*, the 2003 Stanzas Prize winner. She has also published a bilingual chapbook, *Mundo y palabra/The World and the Word* (2001). She has received the Howard Nemerov Award, the Sparrow Sonnet Prize, and recognitions from the Poetry Society of America.

See also Literature

SOURCES: Cocco De Filippis, Daisy. 2000. *Para que no se olviden: The Lives of Women in Dominican History.* New York: Alcance; David Robert Books. "Winner of the 2003 Stanzas Prize." www.davidrobertbooks.com/espaillat.html (accessed October 7, 2004).

Daisy Cocco De Filippis

ESPINOSA-MORA, DEBORAH (1951–)

Deborah Espinosa has journeyed from a childhood of racial exclusion to work as a Chicana activist and now as a major community historian and cultural preservationist. Espinosa grew up in the small towns of western Colorado. Her father, Gilbert Mora-Durán, who had attended school until about the ninth grade, worked as a section foreman on the D&RGW Railroad in Colorado for thirty-three years. He died from cancer shortly after Deborah turned twelve. Although her mother, Calletana Mora-Adargo, had never received more than a third-grade education, she worked at various jobs to support her family—as a housekeeper and cook in private homes and hotels and as a lunchroom manager. Because they had obtained only a limited education, her parents highly valued education for all of their children. The three boys and four girls of the Mora family all received their high-school diplomas. All of the boys and Espinosa also attained a college degree.

Living in small-town Colorado as working-class Chicanos, Espinosa's family experienced much discrimination. "We were always aware of our class distinction," notes Espinosa. Speaking Spanish also marked the Espinosas as different and, to Anglos, as inferior. Her parents "were that first generation who felt the pressure to learn English" and who were stigmatized for speaking Spanish. A priest once refused to hear her grandmother's confessions in Spanish. Espinosa admits feeling ashamed of speaking Spanish when she was a child. "At a very young age, I don't know why, but I would cringe when my mother spoke Spanish on the street." She adds, "There was that subtle awareness of, 'oh, we're different.' "

Other Mexican families suffered other types of discrimination as well. Espinosa's in-laws, also from Colorado, remembered that Mexicans were required to sit in the back of theaters. Espinosa vividly recalls, "I remember shopping with a girlfriend . . . and we were accused of shoplifting. The woman took us into the dressing room and literally felt underneath our clothes, checked our bodies, and then another woman came in and said, 'Oh, there's been a mistake. We found the blouses.' . . . We just left because we were scared and terribly embarrassed, even though we knew we were treated very poorly."

In her parochial elementary school Espinosa often felt isolated because she was one of only two Mexican children. Once she started attending public school, she found support among other Chicano students. However, expectations were low. "There was this underlying feeling of 'you don't really fit, and we don't really care.' " Espinosa started college at Mesa College in Grand Junction in 1969, but dropped out. There was a "wall of exclusion that a lot of Chicanos feel."

Soon Espinosa was unwilling to look past such exclusion. At age nineteen she met Juan Espinosa, a newly radicalized Vietnam veteran on his way back to college in Grand Junction. In 1971 they married and headed for Boulder, where both eventually attended the University of Colorado and became major participants in the emerging Chicano student movement. Juan Espinosa started *El Diario*, a Chicano student newspaper, and became one of the cochairs of United Mexican American Students (UMAS). Together Juan and Deborah Espinosa became involved in many of the major events of the Chicano movement that they covered for *El Diario*—César Chávez and the United Farm Workers, the organizing of La Raza Unida Party in Texas, and Corky Gonzáles's Crusade for Justice in nearby Denver. As Deborah Espinosa observes, "We weren't just students at C.U. Boulder, but we were experiencing, and tasting, and seeing a lot."

On campus Deborah Espinosa and other Chicano activists challenged the lack of coverage of Chicano subjects in the university's curriculum and protested overt discrimination. UMAS, now 300 to 400 strong, occupied campus buildings. Unfortunately, violence engulfed the Chicano student movement in Colorado. During the three-week takeover of an administrative building six Chicano student activists died in two car bombings. Although the police accused the victims of setting the bombs themselves, many activists continue to believe that the police were implicated in the deaths. The cases have never been solved.

After Juan Espinosa graduated from the University of Colorado, the Espinosas went to Mexico to study for six months. When they returned to their home state, they chose to settle in Pueblo, a small industrial city with a large Chicano population, and there they have reared their four daughters. Juan initiated another alternative newspaper, and Deborah returned to college at the University of Southern Colorado. After Deborah graduated in 1975 with degrees in history and Chicano studies, she became a volunteer with Hope Alive, a neighborhood organization, and with El Pueblo Museum.

In 1988 Espinosa became the director of El Pueblo Museum for the Colorado Historical Society. When she first started, the museum operated out of an old airplane hangar. Through her guidance and passion El Pueblo moved downtown to a more visible and historic location. She became involved in city planning and the renovation of Pueblo's historic downtown, including the construction of a new museum and an archaeological excavation of El Pueblo Fort. The museum has sponsored exhibits on the Texas-Mexican system of ranching, Jewish, Italian, and Mormon communities, and other major aspects of southern Colorado history. Cognizant of the many myths regarding indigenous people and Latinos, she plans to continue to promote Native American and Latino history.

SOURCES: Mora-Espinosa, Deborah. 1998. "Teresita Sandoval: Woman in Between." In *La Gente: Hispano History and Life in Colorado*, ed. Vincent C. Baca, 3–20. Denver: Colorado Historical Society; ———. 2001. Interview by Margaret D. Jacobs, April 23; Muñoz, Carlos, Jr. 1989. *Youth, Identity, Power: The Chicano Movement*. New York: Verso; Rosales, F. Arturo. 1996. *Chicano! The History of the Mexican American Civil Rights Movement*. Houston: Arte Público Press; Vigil, Ernesto. 1998. "Rodolfo Gonzáles and the Advent of the Crusade for Justice." In *La Gente: Hispano History and Life in Colorado*, ed. Vincent C. Baca, 155–202. Denver: Colorado Historical Society.

Margaret D. Jacobs

ESQUIVEL, GREGORIA (1931–)

As a child, Gregoria Esquivel understood the importance of a good education. After her mother died and her father moved away to work, Esquivel was raised by her grandparents in Lockhart, Texas, about twenty-five miles southeast of Austin. "My grandfather used to say if you're going to get anywhere, you need to go to school and you need to get your education. I know it was hard. A lot of people did finally continue, but some of their parents just didn't have the necessary things to get them to school, and a lot of the time they had to go to work. They had to quit school to go to work."

Although many at the time were unable to continue their education because of financial problems, Gregoria Esquivel attended school while her family lived off food ration stamps. Her family learned to adapt to changes that World War II brought. Esquivel's education proved helpful because she met new people, began learning English, and could act as a translator for her grandparents. "My grandparents only spoke Spanish, but when I was maybe 6, 7, an African-American family lived next door to us and that's how I started picking up some English. When you went to school, you were not allowed to speak Spanish. What I learned from my neighbors helped in a year or two."

Esquivel's family regularly listened to the radio to obtain news about the war overseas. Often the broadcast was in English, and Esquivel translated the war news for her grandparents. Esquivel felt sorry for her grandmother, who saw three of her four sons drafted during World War II. Her grandmother lived in constant fear of getting bad news from the front lines. She remembers that the draft impacted nearly every family with a son in her community. Like her family, some families had more than one person taken into the military.

During the war Gregoria Esquivel and other Mexican Americans experienced segregation in public places such as schools and even in movie theaters. But she also felt that the war helped make her feel that she was on an equal footing with her Anglo neighbors. "At the time, (segregation) didn't bother me," she said. "I felt like that's the way it was supposed to be. But then I started seeing that maybe we can go (where only whites were allowed). I came to Austin; that's when I saw that everything here was not (segregated). Here in Austin you could do things. It felt good." After moving to Austin, Gregoria Esquivel completed high school and took care of children for a local family while still helping her grandparents. Later she took courses at Austin Community College, aspiring to be a social worker.

Esquivel believed that the war brought about positive changes for Latinos. "I did notice that when the soldiers came back from World War II, there was a lot of education in the families, like they were inspired while they were in the military when they came back. They talked about their GI Bills, and they were all into education and into a better living environment."

On March 29, 1952, Gregoria married Harry Esquivel, and they had five children. Because of her family commitments, Gregoria Esquivel could not continue college classes, but she enjoyed the challenges that college provided. "(School was) just a lot of studying and a lot of hard work and writing papers," Esquivel said. "But I enjoy that and I like that. I like to sit in class." With the knowledge that she gained from her classes, Esquivel worked hard, graduated from Brackenridge Hospital School of Vocational Nursing in 1955, and became a licensed vocational nurse. In March 1986 the nursing department honored Esquivel as the Best of Brackenridge. She demonstrated useful skills of bedside nursing for new nurses and was recognized for exemplary care of her patients.

Esquivel advises that today's generation should set goals and educate themselves to do what they love to do. "Go to school and just work hard at that; then I feel that you can be anybody you can be," she said. "If you have an education, people will respect you. That has a lot to do with it. Go to school as much as you can and educate yourself."

See also World War II

SOURCES: Esquivel, Gregoria. 2002. Interview by Laura Herrera, at Austin, TX, November 11; Slaughenhoupt, Lori. 2003. "Wounded Soldiers Inspired Girl to Become Nurse." In *Narratives: Stories of U.S. Latinos and Latinas and World War II* (U.S. Latino and Latina WWII Oral History Project, University of Texas at Austin) 4, no. 1 (Spring).

Lori Slaughenhoupt

ESQUIVEL, YOLANDA ALMARAZ (1951–)

Born in Donna, Texas, on April 10, 1951, Yolanda Almaraz was raised by a single mother and grandmother. She experienced constant migration and instability early in her life as they looked for agricultural jobs throughout the Southwest. She witnessed corporal punishment and discrimination in school and remembers, "This little boy, just because he turned [away], [the teacher] just hit him so hard across the face. It shocked me and scared him so much. After that, I couldn't read and it seemed like I couldn't write." Although she recovered her abilities in another school in Edinburg, Texas, her new teacher's attitudes lowered Yolanda's confidence: "I was really happy in a different school because I had another teacher. I [gave] her my [math] paper. . . . she took it, tore it up, and said, 'you couldn't have been in my daughter's [class] room.' I was hurt . . . and I felt like there was no hope."

At age fourteen Esquivel and her family moved to Coachella Valley, California, for work in the fields. She graduated from Coachella High School in 1969 and was accepted to California State University, San Bernardino (CSUSB). Emma Lundquist, a local high-school counselor, advocated for financial assistance for Esquivel and her friends Socorro Gómez and Amalia Hernández under the new federal affirmative action program. Although Esquivel and Gómez pursued ambitions to become teachers, the two chose different paths in college. While Gómez became active in the Chicano student group Movimiento Estudiantil Chicano de Aztlán (MEChA), Esquivel worked at a Sears department store, maintaining interest, but distance from the movement.

In 1973 both women earned B.A. degrees and teaching credentials from CSUSB and returned to the Coachella Valley to teach: Gómez at Mecca Elementary School in Mecca, California, and Esquivel at Dateland Middle School in Coachella. "That was my goal," Esquivel remembered. "I had always wanted to be a teacher since I was in the first grade." "But," she added, "then reality set in." In Coachella Esquivel witnessed a veteran teacher, Jane Coffey, physically assault a Mexican boy and girl on two separate occasions. When Esquivel confronted Coffey, Coffey struck her in the chest, asking, "Who do you think you are?" Although the incident occurred in the presence of students, the school principal denied that the assault happened and refused Esquivel her right to file a complaint. Additionally, the school district angered parents by suppressing two charges of molestation against another teacher, Don Cochran.

In response, Esquivel, Gómez, two sympathetic Dateland Middle School teachers, Roman Koenig and Charles Márquez, and Gómez's sister Dora organized with parents to address problems in the district. They formed the group Community Committee for Alternatives in Education (CCAE) to defend Mexican children against abuse in the school and to advocate for bilingual education. Parent George Esquivel went on Spanish-language radio to encourage parents to boycott the school in protest of the district's cover-up of Coffey's and Cochran's misconduct. The following day, April 8, 1976, students from Dateland Middle School

Educator and reformer Yolanda Esquivel with then California governor Jerry Brown. Courtesy of Matt García.

and Coachella Valley High School walked out of class and marched several miles through the valley, evoking the strategies of Chicano students at Garfield, Roosevelt, and Lincoln High Schools in East Los Angeles in 1968. As the children spontaneously left the buildings, Esquivel, Koenig, and Márquez joined the march.

The Coachella Valley Unified School District reassigned Esquivel, Gómez, Roman Koenig, Charles Márquez, and Don Cochran to nonteaching duties while district and union officials sorted out responsibility for the walkouts. Although Coffey was initially absolved of any wrongdoing, upon investigation, the district encouraged her to retire rather than face certification revocation. Superintendent Eugene Tucker also resigned. "When he resigned," Gómez remembers, "he called us all in, all four of us . . . and he said, 'up until now, I have afforded the four of you due process, but I'm leaving and you're gonna be left to the rednecks. God help you.' " According to Gómez, "He was right."

The district pursued revocation of their teaching certification, including Cochran's, and the local chapter of the American Federation of Teachers (AFT) refused them financial or legal support. Eventually the state AFT reversed the local's decision and hired accomplished labor lawyer Abraham Levi to defend them. The American Civil Liberties Union (ACLU) contributed attorney Juan Rodríguez's assistance, and Governor Jerry Brown visited with Esquivel, Gómez, and Coachella Valley Mexican American leaders and publicly campaigned on their behalf. In the end, all retained their credentials, but the events took their toll. Márquez went to East Los Angeles, never to return, while Koenig engaged in binge drug use and went into deep depression. On February 1, 1980, he committed suicide after murdering his wife, daughter, and family dog. Reassigned to a different school in Coachella, Gómez was never allowed to return to Thermal, Oasis, or Mecca schools.

Esquivel moved away from the Coachella Valley after months of public persecution by the local newspaper and school officials. She married local radio station manager and personality Gilberto Esquivel, and together they moved to Indio, California, where they began a family. Although circumstances forced Esquivel to leave Coachella, she believes that their movement improved life for Mexican people in the valley. Soon after the walkouts the Coachella Valley Unified School District begrudgingly implemented bilingual education in response to parent demand and the Supreme Court case *Lau v. Nichols* in 1974.

Today Esquivel is the mother of three children and program supervisor for mostly Latino students learning English in Riverside, California. She does not regret her actions. "It changed my life," she remarked. "I never saw myself before as being involved in a movement, though I believed in César Chávez and I supported him. But before that, I had never seen myself that way. So, it changed me, because I became aware that our people have suffered. . . . I am [no longer] the one who stood there watching [child abuse]. . . . I am not helpless anymore."

See also Bilingual Education

SOURCES: Esquivel, Yolanda. 2004. Oral history interview by Matt García, April 2; John Nicholas Brown Center and The Center for the Study of Race and Ethnicity in America, Brown University. "Educating Change: Latina Activism and the Struggle for Educational Equity." www.brown.edu/Research/Coachella/index.html (accessed July 7, 2005).

Matt García

ESTEFAN, GLORIA (1957–)

Gloria Estefan is widely credited with helping infuse Latin American music into the U.S. mainstream. In addition to her international popularity as a singer and performer, she is regarded as the most successful crossover performer in Latin music history. She was born Gloria Fajardo in Havana, Cuba, on September 1, 1957. Estefan's father, José Manuel Fajardo, was a security officer for Cuban president Fulgencio Batista. After Batista's overthrow by Fidel Castro, the family immigrated to Miami, Florida, when Gloria was not yet two years old.

In the United States her mother, Gloria Fajardo, worked and advanced her education. The young Gloria cared for her ailing father, who had developed multiple sclerosis following exposure to Agent Orange in Vietnam, where he had served in the U.S. Army. A quiet, shy girl, Gloria found solace and escape by retreating to her room, teaching herself to play guitar, writing songs, and singing along to Top 40 tunes. Estefan remembers that "music was the one bright spot in my life."

A serious student, she attended Our Lady of Lourdes Catholic School in Miami and graduated with honors in 1975. When Emilio Estefan's band, the Miami Latin Boys, played at a wedding reception attended by Gloria, she was asked to sing with the band. After receiving a standing ovation, she was invited by Estefan to join the band. The band was renamed the Miami Sound Machine, and Gloria made her official debut in the fall of 1975. She sang with the band on evenings and weekends while attending the University of Miami. Estefan and Fajardo began dating in 1976. Two years later she graduated with a B.A. in psychology. After college she joined the Miami Sound Machine full-time and married Emilio Estefan.

In the late 1970s and early 1980s the band released a few bilingual albums with both North American and

Latin American pop tunes. The band, with Estefan as lead singer, won widespread popularity and acclaim throughout Latin America but remained relatively unknown in the United States. Its idea to record "crossover" music was rejected by its recording company, CBS Records. However, with the release of "Dr. Beat" in English the band received exposure not only in its local community, but also via pop stations throughout the country and, later, Europe. Its subsequent tune, "Conga," was rejected by CBS executives who said that it was "too Latin for the Americans and too American for the Latins." In November 1985 "Conga" was the first song in recording history to be on four different *Billboard* charts simultaneously: dance, pop, Latin, and African American.

As the group's popularity increased, Estefan received more attention and the group's record company opted to focus on its lead vocalist. In 1987 the group's name was officially changed to Gloria Estefan and the Miami Sound Machine. The next album released, *Let It Loose,* which included songs written by Estefan, remained on the charts for more than two years and sold 4 million copies worldwide.

In 1988 Estefan earned the American Music Award for best songwriter, and the band won the Best Pop/Rock Group of the Year. In 1989 Estefan launched a solo career with *Cuts Both Ways.* CBS Records presented Estefan the Crystal Globe Award in 1990 for selling more than 5 million copies outside the United States. That same year she earned the Crossover Artist of the Year at the Lo Nuestro Latin Music Awards.

While she was on tour in 1990, tragedy struck when she was involved in a bus accident en route to Syracuse, New York. Estefan suffered a broken vertebra. After successful surgery and therapy she returned to her musical career in 1991 with the symbolically titled *Into the Light.* Her single from that album, "Coming out of the Dark," marked her emergence from months of therapy and was an international hit.

On a humanitarian level Estefan was instrumental in organizing relief centers and raising funds for the victims of Hurricane Andrew and in antidrug education, AIDS research, and water safety, among other causes. She also has provided support for cancer and spinal-cord patients, the homeless, and educational scholarships for disadvantaged students. For her compassion and educational and charitable efforts she has been awarded the Humanitarian of the Year award by the B'nai B'rith Society, the Ellis Island Medal of Honor, and the Hispanic Heritage Award. She garnered recognition from the Alexis de Tocqueville Society and an honorary doctorate from her alma mater. In 1992 President George H. Bush appointed Estefan as a member of the U.S. delegation to the Forty-seventh General Assembly of the United Nations. In 1993 she was honored for her contributions to Latinos at the Casita Maria Settlement House in New York.

In addition to her international fame, Estefan is a bilingual songwriter whose range includes soulful ballads as well as upbeat dance tunes. Her albums *Mi tierra* (1993), *Abriendo puertas* (1995), and *Alma caribeña* (2000) are noteworthy for their Spanish lyrics and traditional Latin American melodies. She received two Grammy Awards for *Mi tierra* and *Abriendo puertas.* In 1999 she made her acting debut in *Music of the Heart* with Meryl Streep, a story about a kindhearted Harlem music teacher. In 2000 Estefan was voted the Hispanic Woman of the Century by *Vista* magazine readers.

SOURCES: DeStefano, Anthony M. 1997. *Gloria Estefan: The Pop Superstar from Tragedy to Triumph.* New York: Signet Books; Gale Group Online. 2000. "Celebrating Hispanic Heritage: Gloria Estefan." www.gale.com/free_resources/chh/bio/estefan_g.htm (accessed July 6, 2005); Gonzáles, Doreen. 1998. *Gloria Estefan: Singer and Entertainer.* Springfield, NJ: Enslow Publishers; Novas, Himilce. 1995. *The Hispanic 100.* New York: Carol Publishing Group.

Bárbara C. Cruz

ESTEVES, SANDRA MARÍA (1948–)

The exceptional female voice among the Nuyorican poets of the 1970s, Sandra María Esteves was born in the Bronx, New York, of a Dominican mother and a Puerto Rican father who separated before she was born. Raised by an overprotective, single, working-class mother, Esteves was sent at age five to a Catholic boarding school in New York's Lower East Side. There she spent her weekdays in a secluded, disciplined, English-speaking environment that contrasted sharply with the gregarious, Spanish-speaking weekend world she shared with her mother and paternal aunt and cousins in the Bronx. To add to what she has referred to as the "triple life" of her youth, Esteves spent her summers with her godmother, a maid on a Connecticut farm estate, where she experienced the life of a "nature child." After high school Esteves sporadically attended Pratt Institute in Brooklyn and received a B.F.A. in 1978 with a major in fine arts, creative writing, and communications.

In the 1960s and 1970s Esteves began to identify with the ethnic- and racial-consciousness movements taking place around her; in the Puerto Rican barrios the members of the Young Lords, like the African American Black Panthers, were organizing efforts for social and political change. Nuyoricans were also discovering their poetic voices, distinct from those of the island-educated poets who had come before and continued to arrive in those years. Sandra María Esteves began to read her poems in public along with other Nuyorican writers. Her first collection, *Yerba Buena,* was published in 1980, followed by *Tropical Rains: A Bilingual Downpour* (1980) and *Bluestown Mockingbird Mambo* (1990). Her ethnic awareness expanded in later years to encompass the struggles of Native Americans, African Americans, and Chicanos, and her approach also became more woman centered.

A general theme of Esteves's poetry is the search for harmony and for reconciliation of her Afro-Caribbean roots with her experiences in the United States. Her poetry is strongly oral, best appreciated when heard, particularly since Esteves's performance of her art is a vital element of its appeal: body movement, rhythm, and voice modulation combine to expand the aesthetic and intellectual impact of her words.

Esteves's creativity also extends to the visual arts. In the 1970s she was in contact with the Taller Boricua collective, Puerto Rican visual artists born and raised in New York. Esteves has worked as a literary artist with the Cultural Council Foundation of the CETA Artistic Project (1978–1980) and the New York Shakespeare Festival (1985) and served as executive artistic director of the African Caribbean Poetry Theater from 1983 to 1988, a company that staged plays, poetry readings, and similar literary events: "The company was predominantly Latino and African American, but there were also Anglo Americans and Asian Americans. It was called the African Caribbean Poetry Theater because I felt that name was an affirmation of who we are, and after years of growing up in denial of ourselves and in low self-esteem, we wanted to turn the tide around."

Esteves has claimed that the catalysts that produced her the transition from visual to literary artist were, in the first place, a gift of an electric typewriter, followed by a course with a Japanese sculptor and teacher at Pratt Institute who taught students how to create visual art that could exist in the mind of an individual reading a description from the written page, thus helping her understand that words are accompanied by numerous associations of color, texture, sound, and feeling that in combination produce a graphic: "A visual poem became a live process of storytelling with a series of simple images leading to a focused statement." Finally, a community poetry reading in Harlem where all types of persons read their creations—nontraditional, free-form verses—that spoke to the issues close to their lives moved her to attempt the process for herself. "Later that night, my first eight poems were born, and I embarked on a new journey in my creativity."

See also Literature

SOURCES: Esteves, Sandra María. 1989. "Open Letter to Eliana (Testimonio)." In *Breaking Boundaries: Latina Writing and Critical Reading*, ed. Asunción Horno-Delgado, Eliana Ortega, Nina M. Scott, and Nancy Saporta. Sternbach; Amherst: University of Massachusetts Press; Hernández, Carmen Dolores. 1997. *Puerto Rican Voices in English: Interviews with Writers.* Westport, CT: Praeger; Kanellos, Nicolás, ed. 1989. *Biographical Directory of Hispanic Literature in the United States.* Westport, CT: Greenwood Press.

Margarite Fernández Olmos

F

FAMILY

Discussions of Latinas in the family need to reflect upon a special set of social and cultural circumstances. First, Latinas entered into social science discourse well after the discussion of men had been established. Second, in an analysis of Latinas and the family one must take into account subgroups with different historical experiences. Latinas include Mexican Americans (clearly the largest group), Cubans, Puerto Ricans, and, more recently, Dominicans and Central and South Americans. Third, the study of women in the family reveals important class differences, as well as significant differences between rural and urban Latinas. Fourth, recent immigrants to the United States often differ in their familial arrangements from Latinas who have lived in the country for a long period of time.

When interpreting women in the familial setting, one should also be aware that early studies of Mexican American communities still influence the way in which social scientists write about the relationships between men and women. Taking the Anglo culture as a standard for evaluating patterns regarding women as wives and mothers, William Madsen and Arthur Rubel, in their studies of two small communities in southern Texas, defined Mexican American women as passive, and they generally neglected the activities in which women were most active. Social scientists are still being called on to critically evaluate the early stereotypes that have come be accepted as fact as a result of these influential research studies. Not only did Madsen and Rubel focus on small communities at a time when Mexican Americans were increasingly becoming urbanized, but their research efforts were carried out prior to the second feminist movement. The study of Latinas and other women in a variety of cultural settings has shown that women as wives have been considerably more proactive and creative, especially in the private or domestic sphere, than earlier research reports have suggested.

Historical research has filled in significant gaps in knowledge of the place of Latinas in the family. Richard Griswold del Castillo, in his book *La Familia,* has taken the lead in this type of scholarship, though he gives only limited attention to the roles played by women. Vicki L. Ruiz has, more than any other historical researcher, done the most to correct the historical record with respect to the role of Latinas within the community.

Maxine Baca Zinn was a pioneer in the realm of research on contemporary family practices, for she presented data that refute the assumption that Latinas have played a passive role in the family. Her writings on Latinas in the family were followed by the field research of Patricia Zavella, who studied the impact of working wives on familial arrangements and emphasized the role of employment and social networks in changing family relationships (an issue considered later).

The research carried out by Norma Williams has clarified the understanding of Latinas in the familial setting in at least two respects. She is one of the few social scientists who have studied the role of life-cycle rituals among Mexican Americans and how these have changed over time. Through interviews with elderly Mexican Americans in Texas she was able to reconstruct traditional patterns regarding rituals associated with birth, marriage, and death. These life-cycle rituals functioned to bring together members of the extended family. Through participation in these rituals common understandings began to emerge. The older Mexican Americans who were interviewed emphasized that women were the leaders in activities associated with rituals involving, for example, mutual grieving at funerals and sharing of happiness at marriage rites, which helped forge deep emotional bonds among extended kin.

Today, women in both the working class and the professional and business class still take the lead in organizing life-cycle rituals. However, these have declined significantly as a basis for integrating members of the extended family. The only rituals that continue to be of some importance are those involving funerals, though the funeral patterns themselves have undergone significant changes. For instance, they have lost much of their traditional religious significance. In the

Wedding photo of Marcario and Guadalupe Hernández, Santa Paula, California, 1928. Courtesy of Esteban and Elia Hernández.

funerals that Williams attended there has been a good deal of visiting among kin who rarely see one another. It is also important to observe that younger women, as well as men, have little knowledge or understanding of the traditional practices associated with birth, marriage, and death. This loss of social memory is indicative of the rapidity of social and cultural change in recent decades in one aspect of family life among Mexican Americans.

Helen and Willie Guzmán on a Bronx rooftop, circa 1930. Courtesy of Virginia Sánchez Korrol.

Williams also examined decision-making patterns within the working class in Austin and Corpus Christi, Texas, with additional data being collected from the Kingsville region as well. The main objective of Williams's research was to describe and analyze changing patterns with respect to decision-making and role-making patterns within the family by husbands and wives. In the process she compared role-making patterns among married couples in the business and professional class with those in the working class. Women in both groups, far from being passive, have been highly active in making decisions regarding family matters, though women in the professional/business class have had considerably more input than working-class wives.

Williams also documents how married women are seeking to remake their roles. In the face of obstacles posed by traditional male dominance in the family and traditional social expectations within the community, wives in both the professional/business group and the working class are aware of their efforts to modify their relationships with their husbands. In the professional and business class there are four main types of role making on the part of the wives. A few women are reluctantly dependent upon their husbands, and a few are quite independent, but most of the women engage in role-making patterns that lie between these two extremes. In most cases either the wives are semi-independent but family oriented, or they are semi-independent and career oriented.

Role making by working-class wives differs from that in the professional and business class. The role making of the former mainly involves establishing a personal identity apart from that of their husbands. This is an identity that wives in the professional and business class typically take for granted. Yet this social identity seems to be a necessary step if wives are to achieve greater equality with their husbands. Professional and business women have been able to develop this personal identity because of their greater education and their extensive social networks. At the same time one must not underestimate the role-making activities among working-class women. The significance of these is effectively documented by Denise Segura and Beatríz Pesquera in their quite detailed and informative case studies of working-class women. These case studies also reveal the many complex facets of modern life (including divorce) that some Latinas experience. Moreover, along with other scholars, Segura and Pesquera take note of how discrimination in the larger community is an important factor in shaping the lives of Latina wives and mothers.

It is possible to elaborate more fully on the role of family among Latinas by looking closely at the research that has been carried out, especially on working-class women, regarding the impact on the family of their employment outside the home. Patricia Zavella has emphasized the centrality of social networks in the lives of the cannery women she studied in the Santa Clara Valley of California. The social networks that these women developed are a crucial source of social and cultural capital that has enabled them to reshape their relationships with their husbands.

Zavella's original research effort loomed large in informing the research she carried out with Louise Lamphere and others in Albuquerque, New Mexico. These authors acknowledge the complexities that arise in comparing Mexican American and Anglo women once the matter of family is introduced. One of their major findings is that the similarities and differences with respect to familial arrangements are best accounted for not by ethnicity or cultural background but by the relative importance of the woman as a provider in the family setting. Women who play secondary roles as providers in a family tend to be semitraditional: they are more traditional than women who are providers. At the same time these researchers emphasize the contradictions or tensions between family and work, a common theme in the sociological literature on the family. In this situation they found that husbands typically are more willing to take over child care than to assume household tasks—the result being that wives have to work a second shift. It should be emphasized, however, that Lamphere and her coauthors Patricia Zavella and Felipe Gonzáles (with Peter Evans) do not regard class and ethnicity as irrelevant. Rather, they contend that Mexican American and Anglo women have converged because both groups have responded in similar ways to changes in their industrial-urban environment.

The family can be viewed from still another perspective. Vicki Ruiz's widely read work *From out of the Shadows* has taken the lead in emphasizing that Latinas have been active in the public sphere beyond the arena of work. Historically, it would appear that women were most active in the church. In more recent decades, Latinas as mothers have been assuming leadership roles in community activities. According to Segura and Pesquera, a number of working-class women

Garment workers and their families during a vacation trip sponsored by the International Ladies Garment Workers' Union, 1957. Courtesy of the Justo A. Martí Photograph Collection. Centro Archives, Centro de Estudios Puertorriqueños, Hunter College, CUNY.

have developed a rather high degree of political consciousness. In addition, Latinas who are wives and mothers are assuming leadership roles in a variety of grassroots organizations, and they are becoming increasingly active in the more formal political arena as well. These women also experience tensions and contradictions between their role as mothers and their activities in the political sphere, with its multilayered demands on its participants.

Systematic in-depth research that focuses on Latinas as mothers seems to be lacking, but one can piece together data from a wide range of scholars who have discussed motherhood as a by-product of other research. As might be expected, mothers rather than fathers play a central role in socializing their children in areas from language learning to making one's way in the larger society. Mothers also appear to be more involved than fathers in the governance of the schools attended by their children. This pattern conforms to Williams's own rather extensive observations. However, less educated mothers lack the specialized social knowledge about the organizational structure of the schools that the more educated Latinas have often taken for granted. Because of the latter's social knowledge they can exert greater influence on members of the school system.

A discussion of wives as mothers should also briefly consider Latina grandmothers. Elisa Facio, in her *Understanding Older Chicanas,* provides some useful guidelines for future investigations. She studied women in what she terms the Chicano-Mexican community who had limited education and were poor. They were financially dependent on Supplemental Social Security income and Medicaid. Facio reports that the grandmothers she studied were in the process of redefining grandmotherhood. Some were developing networks with other elderly women quite apart from their family connections, and their roles in the family were undergoing change with respect to such matters as caregiving. Her data strongly suggest that the grandmothers were reshaping their roles as a result of major changes in the larger society.

The research on the poor elderly brings up another important matter. Many of the in-depth studies of Latinas in the family have focused on working-class and professional groups, but many Latinas drop out of school and are characterized by a high birth rate (relative to women in the United States as a whole). Elva Trevino Hart has written a moving autobiographical account of a poor Mexican American family whose members at one time were migrant workers. The author grew up in Pearsall, Texas, a small community between San Antonio and Laredo. As a young girl, she traveled with her family to work in the beet fields of Minnesota. Now she is a nationally acclaimed writer. Her stories about her life as a poor Mexican American are not only riveting but also revealing. For her (and for most Latinos and Mexican Americans), education has been the ticket out of the barrio. She attended the University of Texas at Austin and later received her M.A. degree in computer science at Stanford, after which she worked for a number of years as an executive at IBM. But her autobiography is about more than herself. Her stories provide a vivid glimpse into the daily life of her parents and her five siblings. She is able to describe her family's struggles with poverty without making them seem to be victims. The author documents the patriarchal nature of family life among the poor in contrast to the working class and the professional/business group. However, her family is rather atypical among the poor in that her father, not her mother, was the one who insisted that the children acquire a high-school education. She tells how members of her family created a life for themselves despite the

The Gómez family in Kansas City, Missouri.
Courtesy of Lara Medina.

discrimination they experienced from Anglos that limited their opportunities at work, in school, and in the community. Family ties were maintained despite their struggles for basic necessities such as food, clothing, and shelter. Because of the efforts of her parents and older siblings she was able to acquire the social capital (networks) and cultural capital (social knowledge) that permitted her to leave Pearsall in order to attend universities. Both of her parents worked extremely hard, and the children were expected to contribute to the family's livelihood. The life of poor Latinas is a very difficult one.

One should not assume that changing patterns among Latinas in families have resulted from assimilation. Social scientists still tend to assume that Latinas are changing because they are seeking to emulate Anglo women. But the data indicate that the patterns of family life among Latinas and among Anglos are becoming more similar because both groups are responding to the processes of industrialization and urbanization. Latinas in families are not emulating Anglos but are adjusting, often by creating new roles for themselves, to social and cultural changes in the broader society.

See also Aging

SOURCES: Facio, Elisa. 1996. *Understanding Older Chicanas.* Thousand Oaks, CA: Sage Publications; Griswold del Castillo, Richard. 1984. *La Familia: Chicano Families in the Urban Southwest, 1848 to the Present.* Notre Dame: University of Notre Dame Press; Lamphere, Louise, Patricia Zavella, and Felipe Gonzáles, with Peter Evans. 1993. *Sunbelt Working Mothers: Reconciling Family and Factory.* Ithaca, NY: Cornell University Press; Madsen, William. 1964. *Mexican Americans of South Texas.* New York: Holt, Rinehart, and Winston; Rubel, Arthur. 1966. *Across the Tracks: Mexican-Americans in a Texas City.* Austin: University of Texas Press; Ruiz, Vicki L. 1998. *From out of the Shadows: Mexican Women in Twentieth-Century America.* New York: Oxford University Press; Segura, Denise A., and Beatríz Pesquera. 1999. "Chicana Political Consciousness: Renegotiating Culture, Class, and Gender with Oppositional Practices." *Aztlán* 24:9–32; Treviño Hart, Elva. 1999. *Barefoot Heart.* Tempe, AZ: Bilingual Press; Williams, Norma. 1990. *The Mexican American Family: Tradition and Change.* Dix Hills, NY: General Hall; Zavella, Patricia. 1987. *Women's Work and Chicano Families: Cannery Workers of the Santa Clara Valley.* Ithaca, NY: Cornell University Press.

Norma Williams

FARAH STRIKE (1972–1974)

From May 1972 until March 1974, 4,000 employees of Farah Manufacturing at plants located in El Paso, San Antonio, Victoria, Texas, and Las Cruces, New Mexico, walked off their jobs over wages, pension benefits, unrealistic production quotas, and union recognition. Eighty-five percent of the strikers were women, the overwhelming majority of whom were Mexican American. As an example of their grievances, some workers had a daily quota of sewing 3,000 belts onto pairs of slacks. This meant sewing six belts per minute.

The 1972 walkout was not the culmination of an overnight organizing drive by the Amalgamated Clothing Workers (ACW), but the result of a campaign that started in 1969. Farah Manufacturing was the largest private employer in El Paso, a city that had a reputation as an antiunion, minimum-wage town. When picketing began outside the plants, security guards intimidated the strikers with unmuzzled police dogs, and the local police arrested approximately 900 people for breaking an 1880 antipicketing ordinance. The ordinance was declared unconstitutional, and Willie Farah was admonished to "call off" the dogs. The National Labor Relations Board charged Farah with unfair practices with regard to intimidation and harassment.

To many in El Paso, Willie Farah and his families were local heroes. From the newspapers to people on the street, the strikers found few supporters, and when El Paso's Catholic bishop proved sympathetic to the workers' cause, he was publicly castigated. As one activist reflected, "We thought when we went out on strike that our only enemy was Farah . . . but we found out it was also the press, the police, the businessmen. . . . This strike was not just for union recognition." Indeed, the author of one letter to the editor proclaimed, "The Farah family has worked hard for what they have and no-one has the moral right to harm them." Perhaps in response, a union member wrote her own letter, "I say Farah should be grateful to us, the Mexican-American, who from our sweat have [*sic*] worked hard to make the pants that have built his empire."

Recognizing the hostile local climate, the ACW called for a national boycott of Farah suits and slacks. Supported by unions, college students, celebrities, and liberal politicians, Citizens Committees for Justice for Farah Workers emerged across the country. Like the allies of the United Farm Workers, these committees raised money for the strikers and took turns picketing local department stores that carried Farah products. During "Don't Buy Farah Day" on December 11, 1972, an estimated 175,000 people held rallies and parades across the country. The workers themselves were visited by such notables as UFW president César Chávez and the Democratic vice-presidential candidate of 1972, Sargent Shriver. The national boycott began to have its effect as sales of Farah pants dipped by more than $20 million.

The strike divided friends and families because a little less than half the original workforce had walked out. Elsa Chávez remembered, "But you wouldn't believe the number of divorces caused by the strike. A lot of couples broke up; either the wife was inside and the husband was outside or the other way around." Financially the strike was a disaster for union members. One woman explained, "A lot of people lost their homes, cars—you name it, they lost it."

Critical of the ACW, one group of women formed their own committee within the union. According to historians Laurie Coyle, Gail Hershatter, and Emily Honig, they pushed the union to be more accountable to the strikers, founded the Farah Distress Fund, and designed their own leaflets. Moreover, women brought their children to the line in front of the plants and at local department stores. These boys and girls passed out leaflets outside of stores, because adults were less likely to make abusive comments when they were handed a flyer. Indeed, Julia Aguilar recounted a question asked by her children, "Are we going to the picket line today, mommy?" Children on the line are a common occurrence in the annals of Chicano labor history.

The settlement of the Farah strike in March 1974, for many women, came at great personal cost. Few activists enjoyed the benefits because many were fired after a few months, ostensibly for failing to meet inflated production quotas, and union representatives refused to initiate any grievance procedures. Mexican women have not fared well in their affiliation with mainstream labor unions even though they have contributed much of the people power, perseverance, and activism. Yet the Farah strikers had created community with one another and developed confidence in their abilities as they made their claims for social justice. As Coyle, Hershatter, and Honig note, "The Chicanas who comprise the majority of the strikers learned that they could speak and act on their own behalf as women and as workers, lessons they will not forget." Elsa Chávez is one of these women. She came to realize that she wanted—and could achieve—a college education. I first met Chávez when she was a student in my Chicano history class at the University of Texas, El Paso. Two former strikers had enrolled in the class, a fact I discovered as I lectured on the Farah strike and noticed the two reentry women, both bilingual education majors, sitting in the front row giggling. "Oh, we're sorry, Dr. Ruiz, but we were *there.*" I turned the class over to them.

SOURCES: Coyle, Laurie, Gail Hershatter, and Emily Honig. 1980. "Women at Farah: An Unfinished Story." In *Mexican Women in the United States: Struggles Past and Present*, ed. Magdalena Mora and Adelaida Del Castillo, 117–143. Los Angeles: UCLA Chicano Studies Research Center Publications; Farah Strike Newsclipping Collection. Institute of Oral History, University of Texas, El Paso; Ruiz, Vicki L. 1998. *From out of the Shadows: Mexican Women in Twentieth-Century America.* New York: Oxford University Press.

Vicki L. Ruiz

FARMWORKERS

Agriculture is a major industrial and economic sector of the United States and relies heavily on migrant and seasonal farm labor, particularly in California, where agricultural workers grow many of the nation's labor-intensive crops. Migrant and seasonal farmworkers rank among the most underserved and understudied occupational populations in the United States. Like workers in the construction and mining industries, agricultural workers labor in one of the most hazardous occupations in the country.

As many as 5 million migrant and seasonal agricultural workers live and work in the United States. They are composed primarily of laborers from Mexico, Puerto Rico, Haiti, Jamaica, and Central America, as well as Native Americans and African Americans. Three major north-south migrant flows exist in the continental United States. Migrants based in southern California frequently move north to northern California, Oregon, and Washington. Others, working in Texas and Arizona, migrate up the Mississippi Valley to Ohio, Michigan, Indiana, and Illinois. The East Coast stretch finds workers moving from southern Florida through Georgia, the Carolinas, Maryland, Delaware, New Jersey, New York, and New England.

California, the largest agricultural producer of vegetables and fruits in the United States, relies heavily on migrant and seasonal farmhands to work the labor-intensive crops. Estimated to number between 600,000 and 1.1 million, including dependents, California's migrant workers constitute a substantial portion of all farm laborers. Many migrant farmworkers and their families live in established migrant communities with strong ties to Mexico. The gross annual household income averages $15,203; however, households consist of an average of 6.8 members living well below officially defined poverty levels. Counties like Fresno and Tulare house the poorest farmworker communities in California, especially during peak harvest times, when workers crowd into substandard and temporary, makeshift homes. Migrant families typically find housing in labor camps provided by their employers. Housing and sanitation conditions are often substandard, lacking water and bathroom facilities. In addition, drinking water and toilet facilities are often not readily available in the fields.

Occasionally nonprofit developers obtain start-up funds to build homes for the workers. Monetary contributions are placed into a fund to cover start-up costs charged by private developers. Donations sometimes spur other businesses to make contributions to help solve the housing crisis. While many agree that homeless workers should receive shelter, residents from various neighborhoods reject the possibility of having

Migrant farmworker children, Colorado, circa 1968. Courtesy of the Denver Public Library, Western History Department.

farmworker shelters placed within their residential areas. As winter makeshift camps are torn down, farmworkers are left with few options for shelter, and rural communities, shelter supporters, farmworker advocates, and nonprofit developers struggle to find suitable places to build adequate homes.

The socioeconomic status of this population contributes to serious health effects that result from the living conditions and occupational hazards of farmwork. Because of the transient nature of the population, language barriers, the seasonal nature of the work, large distances between fields, and lack of legislative protection to ensure decent and fair working conditions, accurate health data on the agricultural labor force remain an area in critical need of study.

Occupational health problems include accidents, pesticide-related illnesses, musculoskeletal and soft-tissue problems, dermatitis, noninfectious respiratory conditions, reproductive health problems, children's health problems, climate-related illnesses, communicable diseases, urinary tract infections, kidney disorders, and eye and ear problems. In general, health problems such as malnutrition, poor dental health, obesity, cardiovascular disease, diabetes, anemia, and mental disorders further complicate the risk of occupation-related diseases among farmworkers and their families.

Occupational accidents in agriculture include fractures and sprains due to falls from ladders or farm equipment, sprains or strains from prolonged stooping, heavy lifting, and carrying, amputations, lacerations, crushed bones and joints from tractors, trucks, or other machinery, pesticide poisoning from direct spraying or mixing, electrical accidents, carbon monoxide poisoning from running equipment in enclosed areas, and drowning in irrigation ditches. Such injuries are commonly underreported because of workers' fear that missing a workday or reporting an injury could cost them their job. When health complications are reported, they most frequently seem to develop from work injuries and accidents associated with farm equipment.

Heavy physical labor contributes to a variety of musculoskeletal problems, including traumatic injuries, soft-tissue disorders, and degenerative joint disease of the hands, knees, and hips. Farmworkers are exposed to many of the risk factors associated with musculoskeletal injury. Occupational factors that contribute to back strain include previous back injury, heavy lifting and carrying, difficult work positions, an excessively rapid work pace, whole-body vibration, and working in cold or hot climates and in the rain. Workers carry heavy bushels and buckets of produce, often lifting them above their heads to empty into trucks. Orchard workers wear canvas bags held with straps over their shoulders that they fill with as much as thirty to thirty-five kilograms of fruit as they climb up and down ladders. Farmworkers also spend long hours bent over low-lying crops such as cucumbers, beans, strawberries, and squash.

Agriculture has consistently been identified as the major industrial sector with the highest risk of work-related skin disease outbreaks. Grape pickers, more than citrus or tomato workers, suffer from contact dermatitis and widespread rashes. Agricultural operations can also lead to restrictive lung disease and bronchitis that result from continually inhaling dust and from daily exposure to a multitude of respiratory toxins, fumigants, pesticides, insecticides, and defoliants.

Pesticide-related illnesses have been linked to cancer, as well as to reproductive health problems leading to low sperm count and sterility in male workers and inconsistent menstrual cycles, premature births, and involuntary abortions among females. Labor-intensive crops, such as fruits and vegetables, are treated extensively with pesticides, which are absorbed into the body through the skin, by inhalation, and by ingestion. Exposure to pesticides can result in abdominal pain, nausea, dizziness, vomiting, rashes, and chronic health problems leading to fatigue, headaches, sleep disturbances, memory loss, birth defects, sterility, blood disorders, and abnormal liver and kidney functions.

Strenuous working conditions, pesticide-related illnesses, and reproductive health concerns have a detrimental effect on farmworkers' mental health and lead to high levels of anxiety and depression. Feelings of helplessness are compounded by an ineffective social support system, physical isolation, limited access to medical care, discrimination, marginalization, and the sense that there are limited opportunities for change. Expressing feelings of loneliness, workers feel unwelcome in the larger community and confess to living the existence of a "stray vagrant," unable to forge lasting friendships. "Working like burros," they experience an existence of "just passing."

Fortunately, farmworker organizations such as the United Farm Workers (UFW) are doing what they can to improve conditions for agricultural laborers and are currently attempting to track down former farmworkers to provide them with retirement pay. According to the UFW, thousands of aging farmworkers are owed millions of dollars in pension funds under the retirement program established in 1975 by union founder César Chávez. The pension fund is valued at nearly $100 million. The UFW estimates that currently more than 700 retired workers are eligible for benefits but do not know about them.

The question of what to do with the migrant farmworkers has become a major contested issue in presidential elections and has stimulated various discussions on the role of legislation, immigration, human rights, and working ethics. In discussions about immigrant labor and the issue of citizenship, presidential candidates reveal that immigrant farmworkers have become an essential, inextricable part of the U.S. labor force. Most presidential candidates claim that there is a pressing need to intervene, oversee, and force employers who hire immigrant and migrant workers to abide by labor laws.

While advocates support protective laws and workplace improvements for farmworkers, those against granting citizenship to immigrant laborers argue that migrant workers compete for low-end jobs that displace native-born workers. However, most farmworkers earn less than $6,000 a year. This places them among the most economically deprived groups in the United States. Farm labor has the highest incidence of workplace fatalities in the United States and often employs child labor as part of a system that, on average, keeps farmworkers from furthering their educational levels beyond the sixth grade. Undocumented immigrants are tightly woven into the fabric of the U.S. workforce.

Yet legislation alone cannot force those who hire agricultural workers to abide by fair working standards. Conditions for farmworkers will not change until the employers who abuse agricultural workers are prosecuted and fined. Larger efforts need to take place to ensure that farmworkers can become full participants in American society. These include granting the right to gain citizenship, respecting workers' rights, extending access to health care, and protecting their right to organize.

Pesticide-related concerns must be promptly addressed. Greater regulatory oversight is critical, and an in-depth study of farmworker health remains a critical need. Efforts must be made to reduce the risk of chemical exposure and to eliminate dangerous pesticides. Current practices continue to put farmworkers and their families at grave risk of toxic exposure. No government agency at this time is responsible for examining these impacts. California and Washington are the only states with mandatory reporting of pesticide-related illnesses, but underreporting consistently occurs because many of the migrant and seasonal farmworkers never see a physician. Migrant farmworkers deserve adequate housing, clean water, restroom facilities, fair pay, health coverage, educational opportunities, respect, support, legislative protection, workplace protection, and the right to gain citizenship.

See also Environment and the Border

SOURCES: Alvarez, Fred. 2003. "$76,891 Check Crops Up; A Retired Farmworker, 92, Receives a UFW Pension." *Los Angeles Times*, December 5, California Metro, pt. 2, p. 1; Gaona, Elena. 2003. "Carlsbad Finds Site for a Temporary Farm Worker Shelter." *San Diego Union-Tribune*, December 10, Local, p. B-2; ———. 2003. "Carlsbad Ponders Homeless Shelter: New Facility Would Serve Farm Workers." *San Diego Union Tribune*, December 3, Zone, p. NC-1, NI-3; Hovey, Joseph D., and Cristina G. Magaña, 2002. "Exploring the Mental Health of Mexican Migrant Farm Workers in the Midwest: Psychosocial Predictors of Psychological Distress." *Journal of Psychology*. 136 (September): 493–513; Jones, Gregg. 2003. "UFW Seeks Improved Health Care." *Los Angeles Times*, April 21, B1; Martin, Philip. 2002. "Mexican Workers and U.S. Agriculture: The Revolving Door." *International Migration Review* 36, no. 4 (Winter): 1124–1142; Maxwell, Bill. 2003. "Farmworkers Get Another Raw Deal." *St. Petersburg Times* (Florida), November 16, Perspective, p. 7D; Saillant, Catherine. 2003. "The Region: Farm Labor Housing Gets Seed Money." *Los Angeles Times*, November 18th, California Metro, pt. 2, p. 3.

Soledad Vidal

FEMINISM

Strands of feminist ideology or incipient feminist ideology can be located at various junctures in the history of Latinas in the United States. Ardent feminists from the dynamic Puerto Rican labor organizer Luisa Capetillo to Adelina Otero Warren, a Hispana from New Mexico who campaigned for women's suffrage, form integral links in the Latina feminist narrative. Several organizations similarly represent feminism in action, such as New Economics for Women. Do struggles for gender and social justice equal feminist consciousness? As contemporary Latinas know all too well, it depends on whose feminism and whose context. As one women involved in the Farah strike (1972–1974) bluntly stated, "I don't believe in burning your bra, but I do believe in having our rights."

The quest for civil rights has been a signifying theme running throughout Latino history. A century ago women's educational and voting rights were openly discussed within Latino communities, and for a short period two sisters, Andrea and Teresa Villarreal published *La Mujer Moderna* (The Modern Woman), the first feminist newspaper in Texas. A prominent labor leader in Puerto Rico and Florida, Luisa Capetillo penned *Mi opinión sobre las libertades, derechos y deberes de la mujer, como compañera, madre y ser independiente* (My Opinion on the Liberties, Rights, and Duties of Woman, as Companion, Mother, and Independent Being). In this 1911 feminist manifesto Capetillo railed against the exploitation of women within the household, the church, and the workplace. Adopting a republican motherhood argument popular among elite and middle-class Euro-American women since the American Revolution, she argued that more literate, articulate women would make better mothers. Capetillo, however, added a radical twist—educated women would be better mothers for future leaders of a workers' revolt. More than thirty years later community activist María Hernández of Texas defined her own version of Republican motherhood, more in step with traditional interpretations, that "the domestic sphere was maintained to be the foundation of society and mothers the authority figures who molded nations."

Women were not silent partners in early civil rights organizations, including the League of United Latin American Citizens. Furthermore, Josefina Fierro and Luisa Moreno were the driving forces behind the first national Latino civil rights assembly, el Congreso de Pueblos de Hablañ Española, held in Los Angeles in 1939. While specific women's issues were not addressed at this historic meeting, during a follow-up local convention that occurred six months later, delegates passed a prescient resolution that the Mexican woman "suffers a double discrimination as a woman and as a Mexican." Latina trade union activists, while perhaps not political feminists, were certainly attuned to sex discrimination at work. Women members of the United Cannery, Agricultural, Packing, and Allied Workers of America (UCAPAWA/FTA), in general, developed a job-oriented feminism; that is, they sought equality with men regarding pay and seniority, and they sought benefits that specifically addressed women's needs, such as maternity leave and day care. Similarly, the wives of miners profiled in the landmark film *Salt of the Earth* grew in consciousness as they expressed their own demands for a more egalitarian division of labor within their own homes as the result of their participation on the picket line. The emphasis on working women's leadership was not limited to Latinos in the Southwest. In New York City Antonia Pantoja, an energetic community organizer from Puerto Rico, began a legacy of building neighborhood political and educational institutions that spanned more than four decades. During the 1950s a Vassar professor, Camila Henríquez Ureña, a Dominican immigrant from a distinguished literary and political family, crafted eloquent feminist motifs in her poems and essays.

The bulk of scholarship on Latina feminism has focused on the participation of women in the Chicano student movement, where they demonstrated creative leadership in a myriad of activities, including welfare rights, immigrant services and advocacy, sterilization suits, community organizations, La Raza Unida Party, antiwar protests, campus activism, and literary production. Whether a Brown Beret in Los Angeles or a Young Lord in Philadelphia, Latinas were not always satisfied with the attitudes and behavior of their *compañeros,* but those who called for a discussion of women's issues or an end to gender-specific tasks (e.g., typing or cooking) were labeled "women's libbers" or worse. At the 1969 National Chicano Youth Liberation Conference the facilitator of the women's workshop reported to the general assembly, "It was the consensus of the group that the Chicana woman does not want to be liberated." Feminist activist Francisca Flores had little tolerance for such self-abnegating statements. "Women must learn to say what they think and feel without apologizing or prefacing every statement to reassure men that they are not competing with them." Many Latinas felt caught between two seemingly polar movements—the patriarchy of male-centered, cultural nationalist student groups and the maternalism and condescension of mainstream Euro-American feminist organizations.

Most Latinas kept their distance from Euro-American feminists, preferring instead to organize with their *compañeros* and to address issues of crucial concern to women, such as sterilization abuse. They also organized a number of conferences, such as la Conferencia de Mujeres por La Raza in 1971. This first national Chicana gathering adopted a fairly radical platform for the time, calling for grassroots health care, with Chicanas in charge of providing accessible abortion and birth control. They also pushed for greater educational opportunities, condemned the Catholic Church, and called for companionate marriage and for child care at movement functions. Perhaps as many as half the 600 delegates disagreed with the platform and walked out.

Latinas such as the brilliant student activist Magdalena Mora could be found in all aspects of political organizing from La Raza Unida, the Chicano third party, to the leftist Centro de Acción Social Autónomo (CASA). Women also formed their own organizations, such as Comisión Femenil Mexicana Nacíonal (CFMN), a Chicana professional group whose community service, legal advocacy, and urban planning initiatives have had a great impact on the lives of Latinas in Los Angeles. Latinas with different political perspectives from CASA to CFM participated in a campaign to end sterilization abuse at a local hospital, one that culminated in a lawsuit, *Madrigal v. Quilligan.*

Latinas also built coalitions with other women of color. Salsa Soul Sisters emerged in New York City as a grassroots organization for Latina and African American lesbians. Cherríe Moraga and Gloria Anzaldúa edited the pathbreaking anthology *This Bridge Called My Back: Writings By Radical Women of Color,* the first collective literary work written entirely by women of color. Latina lesbians led the way in building interracial, transnational networks for social change. They articulated a vision that claimed and fused public and private spaces. Though Latino gays and lesbians face considerable homophobia and harassment, they have refused to be silenced, and their work as activists and artists continues to make a difference in Latino communities throughout the United States.

In 1982 Chicana undergraduates, graduate students, and professors gathered at the University of California, Davis, to form Mujeres Activas en Letras y Cambio Social (MALCS). Called together by Adaljiza Sosa Riddell, this small group of women joined together to form a feminist organization with a collective vision and responsibility to Latinas in higher education and in the community. Today MALCS is the largest, most influential Latina academic organization.

Latina feminists continue to make their innovative mark in literature and the visual arts. The Cuban American performance artist Ana Mendieta, for example, combined drama, experimentation, earthworks, and photography in exploring themes like women's relationship to the body, nature, and heritage. Integrating sexual and cultural identities in her work, Mendieta displayed a clear political consciousness that incorporated pre-Hispanic civilizations and fertility icons with Afro-Cuban beliefs.

Grassroots activism, especially with regard to accessible health care and women's reproductive rights, remains an important, though relatively unacknowledged, feminist endeavor. In 1989 Dominican and Puerto Rican women created the Latina Roundtable on Health and Reproductive Rights, which has facilitated collaboration among community health projects and has sought to influence public policy. Self-help workshops, local clinics, community education programs, and public health access are just a few components of wide-ranging activities by Latina health advocates.

What makes Latina feminism distinct is that at its root Latina feminism is about collective politics, not personal politics. Regarding leadership, perhaps Tejana activist Rosie Castro expressed it best: "We have practiced a different kind of leadership, a leadership that empowers *others,* not a hierarchical kind of leadership." Indeed, in the preface to *Making Face, Making Soul,* Gloria Anzaldúa held out a message of hope: "We are continuing in the direction of honoring others' ways, of sharing knowledge and personal power through writing (art) and activism, of injecting into our cultures new ways, feminist ways, mestiza ways."

SOURCES: Anzaldúa, Gloria, ed. 1990. *Making Face, Making Soul: Haciendo Caras.* San Francisco: Aunt Lute Foundation; García, Alma M., ed. 1997. *Chicana Feminist Thought: The Basic Historical Writings.* New York: Routledge; Moraga, Cherríe, and Gloria Anzaldúa, eds. 1981. *This Bridge Called My Back: Writings by Radical Women of Color.* Watertown, MA: Persephone Press; Ruiz, Vicki L. 1998. *From out of the Shadows: Mexican Women in Twentieth-Century America.* New York:

Oxford University Press; Ruiz, Vicki L., and Virginia Sánchez Korrol, eds., 2005. *Latina Legacies: Identity, Biography, and Community.* New York: Oxford University Press.

Vicki L. Ruiz

FERNÁNDEZ, BEATRICE "GIGI" (1966–)

Beatrice Fernández, known professionally as Gigi Fernández, is considered among the best doubles tennis players in the world. She was born in San Juan, Puerto Rico, in 1966 and grew up to become the first female athlete in the country. Fernández's athletic abilities emerged very early in her life when she began to play tennis as a child. Although most serious players are attracted to the sport during their teen years, Fernández managed to graduate from high school in Puerto Rico and attended Clemson University in the United States for a while. At the age of seventeen Fernández turned professional and left college to tour the pro circuit.

At the age of eighteen Fernández represented Puerto Rico in the 1984 Olympics in Los Angeles, California. But in the 1992 Olympics in Barcelona, Spain, Fernández decided to play for the United States. This was not an easy choice to make, but Puerto Rico did not have a doubles tennis category. With Mary Joe Fernández, an equally gifted young tennis player who was born in the Dominican Republic, Gigi Fernández won an Olympic gold medal. In one of her many press interviews she remarked, "And although the Puerto Rican flag didn't go up at the medal ceremony, I felt very proud to be Puerto Rican."

Throughout the 1980s Fernández's career flourished. She continued to rank in the World Tennis Association (WTA) among the best tennis players for most of her career. A meeting with Martina Navratilova led to a doubles players' partnership that proved to be highly successful. For three consecutive years, 1992 to 1994, Fernández and Navratilova won the doubles championship at Wimbledon. In preparation for the Olympics, Fernández moved to Colorado to increase her stamina by training in the high altitude. In 1996 she again brought home the gold, winning the Olympic medal in the doubles competition for the United States. An overview of Fernández's accomplishments in addition to her two Olympic gold medals includes the following victories. She won the Wimbledon doubles title in 1992, 1993, 1994, and 1997; the French Open doubles title in 1991, 1992, 1993, 1994, 1995, and 1997; the U.S. Open doubles title in 1988, 1990, 1992, 1995, and 1996; and the Australian Open doubles title in 1993 and 1994.

In 1997, at the age of thirty-three, Fernández retired from the WTA tour, leaving an impressive athletic legacy in tennis. She enrolled at the University of South Florida, intending to complete the college education she had put on hold in 1983. In an online interview with College Sports, Fernández told of an incident that changed her immediate academic plans. "I was going to school incognito, minding my own business. No one knew that Gigi Fernández was at the university, which was fine with me. I was taking a geography class and a student recognized me." The student worked with the athletic department and, recognizing Fernández, invited her to donate a tennis racket for a fund-raiser. She did more than that. Fernández made contact with the department, and when the coach decided to retire in 2002, the university asked Fernández to take the position. Delighted about the opportunity to coach an NCAA Division 1 women's tennis program, Fernández accepted the appointment. Committed to completing the baccalaureate degree with a major in psychology, Fernández was also committed to developing the best team she possibly could. "I still plan to get a degree. It's just going to take a little longer." Fernández also understood the pressures on students such as meeting deadlines, exams, and research papers.

Fernández established and manages the Gigi Fernández Charitable Foundation, which has contributed more than $500,000 to various Latino and Puerto Rican organizations, the United States Tennis Association (USTA) collegiate committee, and the USTA Sports Science committee. She supports the National Hispanic Scholarship Fund, the Yo Sí Puedo (a say-no-to-drugs program), the Puerto Rico Tennis Association, and the Gigi Fernández Invitational Cup, which also benefits Puerto Rican charities. Fernández coached the Puerto Rico Olympic Team for the 2004 games in Greece. In June 2005 Gigi Fernández resigned from her coaching job at the University of South Florida. However, she left with fond memories of the university where she graduated cum laude with a degree in psychology.

SOURCES: CollegeSports.com. Gagliano, Anthony. "There's no disguising newest South Florida women's tennis coach." www.colegesports.com/sports/m-tennis/iwire/071102aaa.html (accessed May 27, 2003); The Oracle (University of South Florida student newspaper) online. 2005. "Fernandez resigns as tennis coach. June 9. www.usforacle.com/vnews/display.v/ART/2005/06/13/42ad896769ed1 (accessed July 7, 2005); University of South Florida. "Head Coach Gigi Fernandez." http://gobulls.usf.edu/Sports/womenstennis/staff/gigi_fernandez.htm (accessed July 7, 2005).

Virginia Sánchez Korrol

FERNÁNDEZ, MARY JOE (1971–)

Mary Joe Fernández, a two-time Olympic tennis gold medal winner, was born María José Fernández in the Dominican Republic on August 19, 1971. From the age of three she demonstrated an interest and ability in tennis when she accompanied her father and her sister to practice sessions. Two years later, at age five, her father signed her up for professional tennis lessons.

Her father, José Fernández of Spain, met her mother, Silvia Pino, while visiting relatives in Cuba. The couple left Cuba during the Cuban Revolution and settled in the Dominican Republic for a few months, where both Mary Joe and her sister Mimi were born. When Mary Joe was a few months old, the family relocated permanently to Miami.

Fernández's first significant victory occurred in 1981 when at age ten she won the United States Tennis Association (USTA) Nationals title for players twelve and under. At age thirteen she played her first professional tournament and became the youngest player to win a match at the U.S. Open. By the age of fourteen she had won four singles USTA championships, becoming the first girl in tennis history to win that many consecutive titles.

At the start of a promising career, Fernández decided to make her education a priority. Even though she became a professional tennis player, she made it her goal to complete her education, unlike many players who drop out of school to dedicate themselves full-time to the sport. It was after she completed her high-school education that she turned full-time professional and went on to win her first major championship at the Tokyo Indoors (1990).

The major triumph in Fernández's athletic career came in 1992 when she competed at the Olympic Games in Barcelona. She won a gold medal in the women's tennis doubles competition with her Puerto Rican partner, Gigi Fernández (no relation), and a bronze medal in the singles competition. In 1996, at the Olympic Games in Atlanta, she won the gold medal in the women's tennis doubles competition with Gigi Fernández. Throughout her career Mary Joe Fernández has won seven singles titles and eight doubles titles. As an athlete she has excelled in her ground strokes, precise timing, intense concentration, and remarkable footwork and balance.

With her fame, Fernández has become a good role model. She uses her celebrity to support worthy causes and is involved in numerous charities. For example, in 1992, when Hurricane Andrew devastated parts of Florida, she was involved in organizing a charity tournament to aid the victims. When she was diagnosed with endometriosis in 1993, she used her own health problem to reach out and help educate other women on the disease.

In 2000 Fernández married Tony Godsick, vice president of IMG, a sports management agency. From 1999 to 2002 she became interested in television broadcast work and writing for *Tennis Magazine*. Currently she works as a sports analyst on women's tennis events for ESPN.

SOURCES: "Mary Joe Fernández." 1999. *Macmillan Profiles: Latino Americans*. New York: Macmillan Library Reference; Tardiff, Joseph C., and L. Mpho Mabunda, eds. 1996. *Dictionary of Hispanic Biography*. New York: Gale Research; Telgen, Diane, and James Kamp, eds. 1993. *Notable Hispanic American Women*. Detroit: Gale Research.

José A. Díaz

FERNÁNDEZ, ROSITA (1919–)

Born in 1919 to Petra and César Fernández in Monterrey, Mexico, Rosita Fernández was part of a family of sixteen children and was educated in Laredo, Texas. When she was nine, Rosita Fernández and her family moved to San Antonio. Soon thereafter she started singing with her mother's brothers, Sotero, Santiago, and Fernando San Miguel, the Trio San Miguel. They traveled to Robstown and other small towns, performing in carpas, tent theaters with brick walls and a canvas top. Her career advanced rapidly, from singing live to radio and film. At seventeen years of age she was working at KONO radio station in San Antonio for $2.50 a week. In 1936 the Entertainment Committee of the Texas Centennial Exposition chose the Rhumba Kings as its official orchestra, and Fernández was named the featured singer, performing with her sister Bertha. Fernández's career continued to advance following her marriage to Raul Almaguer on March 21, 1938, and the birth of their two children, Raul Javier and Diana Rosa Orellana. Fernández did not step out of the spotlight. She attributes her success to her husband's support: "I married him 61 years ago. He's been my *cómo se dice esa canción?* (how does that song say it?) the wind behind [beneath] my wings. He's been my memory; he's been everything to me."

Fernández's radio presence increased when she won a contest to be the corporate commercial representative of companies like Fritos and Gephardt Chili. In one contest Gephardt said that it would have to change her name to "Rosita," because that was the corporate name of its ad celebrity. She responded, "My name is Rosita!" and was happy that she did not have to change her name. Her career eventually led her, in October 1949, to a spot on San Antonio's first television program, *Curtain Time,* on WOAI-TV (now Channel 4, KMOL-TV). She took roles in several films, such as *The Alamo* (1960) with John Wayne, Walt Disney's *Santiago, the Homing Steer* (1965), and Jesús Treviño's *Sequin* (1980), and NBC-TV's *300 Miles for Stephanie* (1981).

She became an institutional icon when she partnered with the Alamo Kiwanis Club in 1957 to create the first Fiesta Noche del Rio production at the Arneson

The Rosita Bridge dedicated to singer Rosita Fernández. Photograph by Marisol Garza. Courtesy of Mary Ann Villarreal and Marisol Garza.

River Theatre. The money raised went to needy children in the San Antonio area. Fernández retired from performing at the Fiesta Noche del Rio in 1982 but continued to raise money for organizations that benefited children and the Catholic Church. Fernández also played an active role in raising funds for the renovation of Municipal Auditorium and Arneson River Theatre.

Fernández has received international recognition and continues to be honored by Latino and music organizations throughout San Antonio. She has performed for the pope, Queen Elizabeth II, and numerous presidents. For her many performances at the home of President Lyndon B. Johnson, Lady Bird Johnson in 1968 gave Fernández the title San Antonio's First Lady of Song, which was reported in the newspaper and was associated with her over the years. The bridge that spans the San Antonio River at the Arneson River Theatre was named the Rosita Bridge in her honor in 1982. This bridge tells more than the story of the Arneson Theatre or the Fiesta Noche Del Rio. Fernández tells another story of her bridge and its relevance to her past. "My father used to work for the WPA [Works Project Administration] and he would come and let us know about so many things. He thought they were beautiful, all the bridges and the theater . . . so maybe he just happened to put a little rock in my little bridge."

SOURCES: Fernández, Rosita. 2001. Oral history interview by Mary Ann Villarreal, March; Rosita Fernández Collection, The University of Texas, Institute of Texan Cultures at San Antonio; Vargas, Deborah R. 2003. "Rosita Fernández: La Rosa de San Antonio." *Frontiers: A Journal of Women's Studies* 86:2–3: 168–185; Villarreal, Mary Ann. 2003. "*Cantantes y Cantineras*: Mexican American Communities and the Mapping of Public Space." Ph.D. diss., Arizona State University.

Mary Ann Villarreal

FERRÉ AGUAYO, SOR ISOLINA (1914–2000)

María Isolina Ferré Aguayo, "el Angel de la Playa de Ponce," was born in Ponce, Puerto Rico, on September 5, 1914. She was the daughter of Antonio Ferré Bacallao, a Cuban emigrant who amassed a sizable fortune in Puerto Rico in the iron and cement industries, and Mary Aguayo y Casals, daughter of a family of modest means. The couple had six children, among them María Isolina and Luis, who later became the second popularly elected governor of the island of Puerto Rico.

At the age of fifteen, on a trip to Cuba, Ferré Aguayo made a decision to forsake her comfortable life in order to work among the poor as a consecrated religious sister. That decision was not revealed to her family until her twenty-first birthday. That same year she entered the Congregation of the Missionary Servants of the Most Blessed Trinity, whose motherhouse at that time was in Philadelphia, Pennsylvania. The Congregation of the Missionary Servants of the Most Blessed Trinity, or Trinitarians, was established when Father Thomas Augustine Judge, a member of the Vincentian Fathers of Boston, Massachusetts, and a group of lay catechists founded the congregation to return lapsed Catholics to the fold of the Catholic Church. The Trinitarians' apostolate included formal education, home visitation, catechism of youths and adults, and other types of social and religious ministry. Puerto Rico was an early mission field for the Trinitarians, who were dedicated to work in the United States but not in foreign lands.

María Isolina Ferré Aguayo professed in 1937 and received as her religious name Sister Thomas Marie, honoring both the founder of the congregation, Father Judge, and her mother, Mary, who died when Ferré Aguayo was a young girl. The young sister first worked among the Appalachian poor in Norton, Virginia, later with Portuguese immigrants in Cape Cod, and then in the Trinitarian mission in Cabo Rojo, Puerto Rico. Sent back to the United States in 1957, she completed a baccalaureate degree at St. Joseph's College for Women, Brooklyn, New York. While attending college, she worked among Puerto Ricans and African Americans in that part of the city. From 1959 to 1962 she joined the faculty of Blessed Trinity College in Philadel-

Sor Isolina Ferré Aguayo. Photo by Tony Zayas. Courtesy of Centros Sor Isolina Ferré.

phia and collaborated with the Instituto de Relaciones Interculturales of the Catholic University in Ponce, Puerto Rico, the Puerto Rican Forum, and ASPIRA of America in New York. During these years of teaching and studying she earned a master's degree in criminology from Fordham University. From 1963 to 1968 she directed the Dr. White Community Center in Brooklyn and was a member of an advisory committee created by Mayor John V. Lindsay to implement the federal War on Poverty.

The Second Vatican Council altered church roles and the sisters' work within the institution. The new theology stressed engagement in the world. Many sisters returned to using their baptismal names, and Sister Thomas Marie went back to Isolina with the religious title Sor preceding it. Her experiences in Brooklyn with troubled youths and the criminal justice system taught her the importance of social work and the need to identify resources within and outside the community. In 1969, together with other religious sisters and a group of lay volunteers, she founded Juventud y Comunidad Alerta, a multiservice project in La Playa de Ponce, one of the poorest and most neglected neighborhoods of the island. The Centro de Orientación y Servicios, which later became Centros Sor Isolina Ferré, was modeled on these successes. Through the center the Trinitarians offered a program of alternative education, gathering supporters to help in the schooling of young people and work with their families. Workshops on photography, silk screening, ceramics, cosmetology, upholstering, industrial sewing, and gardening became part of the center's mission. The center targeted the needy, handicapped children, runaways, pregnant young women, and the aged. By 1985 these federally funded programs were extended to other towns of the island.

Sor Isolina believed that "God's glory is in the total fulfillment of God's people, men and women." In the eighty-five years of her life Sor Isolina accomplished much on behalf of the poor in Puerto Rico. Most of all, she was able to inspire and help people help themselves by developing their potential and self-esteem. The Taller Tabaiba, Ruta Artesanal de Puerto Rico, for example, trained many artisans and offered them opportunities to be self-sufficient by helping them promote their art through the Internet, catalogs, local exhibitions and artisans' fairs, sponsorships (*intercesores*), and educational opportunities related to promotion and sale of their products.

By the end of her life Sor Isolina had received numerous awards and seventeen doctorates honoris causa from the Pontificia Universidad Católica de Puerto Rico (1974), Marymount College, New York (1975), Universidad Interamericana de Puerto Rico, San Germán (1979), Saint Francis College, Brooklyn (1981), Fairleigh Dickinson University, Rutherford, New Jersey (1982), the Catholic University of America, Washington, D.C. (1984), Universidad Sagrado Corazón, Santurce, Puerto Rico (1984), Bank Street College, New York (1984), Ciencias Médicas de la Universidad de Puerto Rico (1985), Centro Caribeño de Estudios Postgraduados, Santurce, Puerto Rico (1986), Queens College of the City University of New York (1990), Universidad Central del Caribe, Bayamón, Puerto Rico (1991), Yale University, New Haven, Connecticut (1992), College of the Holy Family, Philadelphia, Pennsylvania (1992), Saint Joseph's College, Brooklyn (1994), Escuela de Medicina de Ponce (1994), and Loyola University, New Orleans, Louisiana (1997). Among her awards are the Life Achievement Award of the Puerto Rican National Coalition, Washington, D.C. (1987), the Cruz Alonso Manso from the Pontificia Universidad Católica de Puerto Rico (1987), the Alexis de Tocqueville Award of the United Fund, California (1989), the Humanitarian Award Albert Schweitzer from Johns Hopkins University, Baltimore, Maryland (1989), the Roberto Clemente Humanitarian Award from Boricua College, New York (1990), the International Peace Award from the Milton S. Eisenhower Foundation, and the Andrus Award from the American Association of Retired Persons, San Antonio, Texas (1992). In 1998 she received the Medalla de la Legislatura de Puerto Rico (Puerto Rican Legislative Medal). The following year President Clinton presented Sor Isolina with the Presidential Medal of Freedom, the highest honor that a civilian can receive from the president of the United States.

Sor Isolina's greatest accomplishment was to work with the poor, especially the poor of her homeland, to help them help themselves to achieve a potential that seemed hidden but that for Sor Isolina was nothing less than "God's glory." She died in her native city in the Hospital Santo Asilo de Damas at the age of eighty-five.

See also Nuns, Contemporary; Religion

SOURCES: "Una luminosa autobiografia dialogada." 1990. *El Nuevo Día*, October 21; MedalofFreedom.com. 1999. "Presidential Medal of Freedom Recipient Sister Isolina Ferré, www.medaloffreedom.com/SisterIsolinaFerre.htm (accessed July 7, 2005); *Puerto Rico Herald*. 2000. "Puerto Rico Profile: Sr. Isolina Ferre." January 14. www.puertorico-herald.org/issues/vol4n02/ProfileFerre-en.shtml (accessed July 7, 2005); "Sor Isolina: Concluye una vida dedicada a los demás." 2000. *El Nuevo Dia*. August 3.

Ana María Díaz-Stevens

FIERRO, JOSEFINA (1914–1998)

Born in the border town of Mexicali, Baja California, during the tumultuous years of the Mexican Revolution, Josefina Fierro was raised in a familial heritage of revolutionary activism. Her father was an officer in General Francisco "Pancho" Villa's northern revolutionary army, a fact that made him largely absent from her life. She was raised by her mother, who separated from her husband and immigrated to the United States when Josefina was a baby. The language of revolution and social justice was a constant in her young life. Her mother's family members were followers of Ricardo Flores Magón, a Mexican anarchist banished from Mexico for promoting radical reforms as part of his Partido Liberal Mexicano, a movement he continued while in exile on the U.S. side of the border. As a "Magonista," Josefina's mother taught her daughter to stand up for the underdog, to speak out against injustice, and to treat others with dignity and respect. It was no surprise that Josefina eventually used these qualities as a basis for assuming leadership within the Mexican American community in California when she came of age.

After periods of migration that took Fierro, her mother, and her younger brother through southern Arizona and southern California, the three settled in the sleepy San Joaquin Valley agricultural town of Madera. After graduating from the local public high school—an accomplishment attained by few Mexican students of her generation—Fierro moved from Madera to live with an aunt in Los Angeles. Through her relatives, many of whom were entertainers, Fierro was exposed to Hollywood's night life. There she met, fell in love with, and soon married screenwriter John Bright, later a member of the famous Hollywood Ten, a group of motion-picture writers and producers blacklisted from the industry because of their alleged Communist Party leanings. Influenced by, and with support from, her husband and other Hollywood notables, Fierro began a campaign in Los Angeles during the mid-1930s to defend the rights of Mexican immigrants and Mexican Americans against the widespread discrimination and racism on the rise in southern California during the Great Depression. She helped organize, together with the local Mexican consulate office, the Mexican Defense Committee, an organization that staged boycotts against industries that refused to hire Mexicans, confronted the Los Angeles Police Department over cases of brutality, and led protests to the steps of the state capitol against proposed anti-Mexican legislation.

Fierro's successful organizing efforts and her emergence as a key leader in the Los Angeles Mexican community attracted the attention of Latino leaders, especially Luisa Moreno, who were preparing to launch the first-ever national Latino civil rights organization, el Congreso de Pueblos de Hablan Española. El Congreso was founded in Los Angeles in 1939, and young Fierro was elected national executive secretary, the second-highest-ranking position in the organization. For the next several years she and her colleagues led a broad-based civil rights movement for Mexican Americans and other Latinos in California and in the Southwest. A fiery orator who could captivate an audience, Fierro

A night on the town for civil rights leader Josefina Fierro and her Hollywood screenwriter husband, John Bright. Courtesy of Mytyl Glomboske.

traveled throughout California to participate in various demonstrations and activities aimed at bringing down the walls of discrimination against Mexicans in housing, employment, education, and other public places. She played an instrumental role, in addition, on the defense committee of the infamous Sleepy Lagoon case in wartime Los Angeles, a murder trial involving several Mexican American youths accused and sentenced to prison for a crime they did not commit. The Sleepy Lagoon Defense Committee eventually won the release of the defendants from state prison two years after the original convictions. A year later, in June 1943, Fierro almost single-handedly brought an end to the days of rage and physical assault on Mexican Americans in the downtown and in East Los Angeles during the so-called zoot-suit riots. Because the Los Angeles Police Department was unwilling to stop the brutality in the streets against Mexican American youths, Fierro flew to Washington, D.C., with a Mexican consulate official to prevail upon the vice president of the United States, Henry Wallace, to help bring an end to the violence unleashed against her community. Convinced by her graphic, firsthand stories about the beatings of Mexican Americans by servicemen, buttressed by an armful of newspapers she carried with sensational headlines about the riots, Wallace secured a military order that restricted all service personnel to their respective bases until order was restored.

As Fierro's efforts to advocate for Mexican Americans attracted more notice, she was labeled as a "Communist subversive" by the California Committee on Un-American Activities. After her divorce from John Bright she returned to Madera, where she organized on behalf of Henry Wallace's Independent Progressive Party. In 1948, after being hounded by the FBI and fearing arrest and deportation, she decided to leave the United States and head to Guaymas, the Mexican port city where she lived the rest of her life.

Josefina Fierro was one of the most important Mexican American leaders of her generation during the 1930s and 1940s. In an era when organizing on behalf of the rights of Mexicans in the United States was a sacrifice made at enormous personal and professional costs, Josefina Fierro's work building organizations and advocating for the welfare of Latinos everywhere places her in the company of a select group of pioneering Latina leaders.

See also El Congreso de Pueblos de Hablan Española

SOURCES: Camarillo, Albert. 1984. *Chicanos in California: A History of Mexican Americans.* San Francisco: Boyd and Fraser; García, Mario T. 1989. *Mexican Americans: Leadership, Ideology, and Identity, 1930–1960.* New Haven, CT: Yale University Press; Ruiz, Vicki L. 1998. *From out of the Shadows: Mexican Women in Twentieth-Century America.* New York: Oxford University Press; Sánchez, George. 1993. *Becoming Mexican American: Ethnicity, Culture, and Identity in Chicano Los Angeles, 1900–1945.* New York: Oxford University Press.

Albert M. Camarillo

FIGUEROA, BELÉN (1918–1960)

Religious activist Belén Figueroa was born in San Juan, Puerto Rico, the daughter of Guillermo Figueroa and Alejandrina Giraldi. Her life was never one filled with praise for any childhood or preadolescent accomplishment. Her training as a competent homemaker far outweighed any other accomplishments she might achieve.

"At the tender age of twelve I became a surrogate mother to my two sisters who were merely three years younger than myself. My mother, Alejandrina Giraldi, had already taught me to cook and housekeep by the time I was eight years old. Following my mother's death I comforted my sisters by using the stories my mother had told me between house chores and bedtime. . . . I believe that the greatest inheritance I can leave my children is to cherish their childhood by repeating their real life stores and [to] show others how to cope with younger siblings who faced a bleak future without my [a] mother."

Once Figueroa succeeded in carrying out her duties as the eldest sister, she married Antonio Pagán, a horse jockey. In the 1940s she became part of a wave of unsung "heroes" who migrated to the United States. Unlike many of her countrymen, she traveled alone by boarding a freight ship with her two children, Antonio

Religious reformer Belén Figueroa. Portrait by Isidro Aybar. Courtesy of Fundación Belén Figueroa, Inc.

Jr. and Ariel. Figueroa was also pregnant with a third child, and nine months later her husband followed her to New York's Spanish Harlem as a stowaway in another freight ship.

In 1950 Figueroa faced the most important challenge in her life. With her husband's support she requested permission to enroll in a three-year Bible Institute Program at the Arca Evangélica Bible Institute on West 100th Street. However, the price for completing the missionary program, attending nightly conferences three times a week, was expulsion from a quasi-Pentecostal church in her community, a religious organization to which she and her husband belonged. The organization believed that "woman were supposed to stay home and care for the children." By that time Belén and Antonio had two sons and three daughters.

In 1953 Antonio followed her lead and became a religious worker by day while working the night shift in a steel mill to support the family. Together they opened the first storefront church for Hispanics in Niagara Falls, New York. Their efforts met with opposition from the mostly Italian American neighborhood. While peace never meant the absence of strife, the couple nurtured their family and community and discovered that peace from God meant providing the strength and fortitude to weather storms of rejection and opposition.

As a nondenominational couple in pastoral work, the Figueroas strove to meet the many needs in that Latino community. It was not unusual for their three daughters to wake up and find family and friends sleeping in their two-bedroom apartment simply because there was need for temporary shelter. The Pagán-Figueroa family braved harsh winters, and with very limited resources they began anew. The Vencedores en Cristo Church was another storefront mission founded by the Figueroas. It became a second home to the Spanish-speaking population in the military who longed for the warmth of traditional Hispanic settings, as well as spiritual leadership, at a time when a handful of families constituted the total Puerto Rican and Latino community of western New York. The Figueroas worked diligently in their ministry and encouraged the parents who attended church meetings to teach their children to maintain their Puerto Rican heritage even while reaching out to embrace all nationalities.

In 1957 the family moved to the west side of Buffalo, New York, where they founded the next church in the basement of the family's first-owned wooden home. By this time Figueroa had saved enough money in her Quaker Oats cereal box for a round-trip ticket to Puerto Rico. She visited her beloved island, which was always referred to as "mi casa," a homecoming that seemed to be an earthly prelude to her spiritual home. Belén Figueroa de Pagán believed and preached that there is "no such thing as an untimely death. Every life has a special time and mission to complete." Her accidental death came about from a faulty indoor heating system on an icy cold day in November 1960, when other families were preparing to celebrate Thanksgiving. With barely enough money to cover the expense of a sealed casket that held the unrecognizable remains of the woman who was called "the facilitator of dreams," no wake was held. Funds were unavailable for the simplest of grave markers. Yet her fruitful life did not go unnoticed by grateful friends, community, and the God she served. In celebration of her life's work, the Belén Figueroa Foundation was incorporated in Puerto Rico in 1986. Graphic artist Reyes Meléndez-Rosa donated the artwork and logo used by the organization to honor her memory.

More often than not, it takes just one ordinary person with a mission and a vision to inspire and motivate others to excel beyond their expectations. Today, Figueroa's philosophy of life is kept vibrantly alive through the careers of service that her daughters have chosen. Ahilud, a social worker, serves her community on several boards of trustees and intercedes on behalf of children and youths as a bilingual specialist in a counseling division. Ruth, a registered nurse, is a bilingual health professional for non-English adult patients, and Alicia, a Ph.D., organizes and manages the Belén Figueroa Foundation, provides seminars in education and health.

SOURCES: Figueroa, Belén. Papers. Foundation Belén Figueroa, Orlando, Florida; Pagan-Figueroa, Alicia. 2002. Interview by Hector Carrasquillo, June; ———. 2004. *El Regreso*. Orlando: Foundation Belén Figueroa.

Hector Carrasquillo

FIGUEROA MERCADO, LOIDA (1917–1996)

Noted historian Loida Figueroa Mercado was a dedicated leader in the Puerto Rican independence movement, a member of the island's Socialist Party, and the party's candidate for the mayoralty of the city of Mayagüez. The first woman to become a member of Gran Logia Masónica Gran Oriente de Puerto Rico, Figueroa Mercado was also the recipient of the Cuban Ministry of Culture's National Medal of Culture.

Loida Figueroa Mercado was born on October 6, 1917, in Yauco, Puerto Rico, to Agustín Figueroa, a sugarcane cutter, and Emetria Mercado, a housewife. She was married three times and had four daughters, Eunice, María Antonia, Rebeca, and Avaris. In 1941 she earned the baccalaureate degree and graduated magna cum laude from the Polytechnic Institute, today known as the Universidad Interamericana, in San German, Puerto Rico. In 1952 she had obtained her M.A. from Columbia University, and in 1963 she completed her Ph.D. at the Universidad Central de Madrid, Spain. She was a Yale University Fellow (1975) and visiting professor of history in the Department of Puerto Rican Studies at Brooklyn College, City University of New York (1974–1977). There she became involved in the student movement of the 1970s. At Brooklyn College, in particular, she walked with the faculty and students as they picketed the administration over the issue of departmental autonomy in choosing a chairperson.

Before she became a renowned historian, she was an elementary-school teacher. She taught at Guánica High School in the town of Guánica, Puerto Rico, from 1942 to 1957. Figueroa Mercado was acting principal in 1947 and again in 1955. From 1957 to 1974 she was a professor of history specializing in the history of

Dona Loida para Alcalde, poster for Figueroa Mercado's campaign for mayor of Mayagüez, Puerto Rico. Courtesy of the Department of Puerto Rican and Latino Studies at Brooklyn College, CUNY.

Puerto Rico at the University of Puerto Rico, Mayagüez. A quote from her first publication, *Frente al espejo* (Before the Mirror) (1945) gives some insight into her developing personality:

> Te prohíbo en adelante que te rindas
> O que escondas de las gentes tus valores [*sic*]
> Adelante, extermina ese complejo
> Que tu tienes tú puesto en este mundo!
> (From here on in, I forbid you to give up
> Or to hide your values from people
> Onward, extinguish that complex
> You have your place in this world!)

Her first literary publications were *Acridulces* (poems, 1947) and *Arenales*, a novel published in 1961 (second edition, 1985). She explained that she started her foray into writing the history of Puerto Rico when she was asked to teach a course on the subject and found that there were no textbooks to assign to the students. She began to put together what she thought would be a short history of Puerto Rico. Over time her brief history of Puerto Rico became two volumes, which are now considered classics because of the literary style and the meticulous research she brought to the interpretation of historical data. Part 1 was translated into English in 1971 as *History of Puerto Rico from the Beginning to 1892,* making her as famous in the United States, especially on the East Coast, as she already was on the island.

Although she was a historian, her publications reflect broad interests. Her publications include *Acridulces* (poems, 1947), the novel *Arenales* (1961; 2nd edition, 1985), *Breve Historia de Puerto Rico* (volume 1, 1968; volume 2, 1969), *History of Puerto Rico from the Beginning to 1892* (1971), *Tres puntos claves: Lares, idioma, soberania* (1972), *La historiografía de Puerto Rico* (1975), *El caso de Puerto Rico a nivel internacional* (1980), *Hostos ensayos inéditos* (edited by Emilio Godinez Sosa, 1987), and *Biografías de hombres y mujeres ilustres de Puerto Rico* (with Vicente Reynal, 1988).

Figueroa Mercado was an active member of the Asociación Histórica Puertorriqueña, the Association of Caribbean Historians, the Asociación de Historiadores Latinoamericanos y del Caribe, the Sociedad de Autores Puertorriqueños, the Club de Puerto Rico, the National Audubon Society, Phi Alpha Theta, and PEN. She died in San Juan in 1996 and was buried in Bayamón, Puerto Rico, but on November 12, 2003, her remains were removed to Yauco, in keeping with her last wishes. Her birthplace was renamed Sector Loida Figueroa Mercado in her honor.

See also Education

SOURCES: Baéz Fumero, José Juan. 2004. E-mail correspondence with Andrés Pérez y Mena, July 13; Fernández, Ronald, Serafín Méndez, and Gail Cueto, eds. 1998. *Puerto*

Rico: Past and Present. Westport, CT: Greenwood Publishing; Rayan, Bryan, ed. 1991. *Hispanic Writers: A Selection of Sketches from Contemporary Authors*. Detroit: Gale Research.

Andrés Pérez y Mena

FLORES, DIANA (1951–)

Politician Diana Flores was born and raised in Palacios, Texas, a small Gulf coastal town. The fourth of five children in her family, she is today the mother of five children and grandmother of twelve. While raising her children and working full-time, Flores returned to college to finish her degree. She attended El Centro and Mountain View Colleges in Dallas until she had enough credits to transfer to Dallas Baptist University (DBU). She graduated with a 4.0 grade point average and received the baccalaureate degree from Dallas Baptist University in May 1994.

Flores has lived in the Oak Cliff area of Dallas since the summer of 1979. While her children were young, she was an active member of the Parent-Teacher Associations in their schools, a Girl Scout volunteer, a Sunday-school teacher, and a youth leader in her church. She has always been active in civic organizations, but her primary emphasis has been, and continues to be, education. Because of this she dedicates herself to efforts that enable greater participation of low-income students and families in educational attainment (high-school and college graduation). She firmly believes that education is the pathway to "become your dream" and therefore helps many young people in their dream-making journey by valuing and using education as the commencement of that passageway.

Since 1985 she has been involved in higher-education issues. This led to a position with the Dallas County Community College District (DCCCD). There she distinguished herself and was recognized for her contributions and leadership by being selected in 1992 as the DCCCD Employee of the Year from among 2,500 employees. Flores left her employment with DCCCD in 1995 and in 1996 became the first Chicana (and Latina) elected to the Dallas County Community College District (DCCCD) to represent District 6. Since then she has been reelected and continues to serve in this capacity. Only one other Chicano (Latino) had ever been elected to the DCCCD before Diana Flores; that other person is current Dallas city councilman Steve Salazar. Thus Flores was the second Latina/o elected to this important community college board, and to date, no other Latina/o has been elected to this public body.

While Flores was at the DCCCD, she became involved with the Texas Association of Chicanos in Higher Education (TACHE). TACHE's primary goal is to improve the participation of Chicanos/Latinos in

Politician Diana Flores. Courtesy of Diana Flores.

higher education. The "Closing the Gap" project, envisioned by Flores and others on the board to address these issues, seeks to build college enrollments and increase diversity in higher education by 2015. While serving on the board of this organization, she met with college and university administrators, business leaders, and legislators throughout the state to lobby for greater access to a college education for all students.

Flores is very proud of several accomplishments since her tenure on the board. First, more students enrolled in the district's various college campuses between 1996 and 2004. Second, many of these new students have been undocumented individuals whose enrollment has been approved by the state legislature since 1996. Third, more students were receiving full tuition and book scholarships in 2004 than in 1996. Fourth, during this eight-year period the diversity of DCCCD faculty, staff, and students increased. Fifth, these recent achievements notwithstanding, the DCCCD still enjoys one of the lowest tax rates for a community college district in Texas. In short, Flores notes that the number of Latina/o students increased between the spring of 1996 and the spring of 2004 from 6,144 to 12,188 (an increase of 98 percent), and the number of degrees/certificates awarded to Latina/o students during a similar period (1995 to 2003) grew from 258 to 657, an increase of 155 percent. In both instances Latina/o students posted the greatest such increases among students from the various ethnic groups served by and attending the DCCCD. For her efforts on behalf of Latino/a students, Flores received the Mexican American Democrats' Adelita Leadership Award in 1994, and was listed in *Who's Who in American Junior College Students, 1991–92.*

See also Education

SOURCES: Dallas County Community College District. "Trustee Diana Flores." www.dcccd.edu/trustees/flores.htm (accessed October 6, 2004); Flores, Diana. 2004. Personal communication with Roberto R. Calderón, February.

Roberto R. Calderón

FLORES, FRANCISCA (1913–1996)

Born on December 1913 in San Diego, California, Francisca Flores was a revolutionary, a community organizer and activist, a journalist, an advocate for women's rights, and a forerunner of Chicana feminism. Diagnosed with tuberculosis at the age of fifteen, Flores spent more than a decade isolated in a sanitarium from which she was released at the age of twenty-six. Although she lost a lung, she managed to live a long and productive life. The same year she was admitted into the sanitarium, her older brother died of tuberculosis, a condition common among Mexicans and Mexican Americans during the early part of the twentieth century. The severe and oppressive conditions Mexicans and Mexican Americans like Flores experienced in the Old Town barrio of San Diego left a mark on her and greatly influenced her social and political development.

The Mexican Revolution and massive emigration from Mexico to the United States influenced Flores's youth. She met veterans of the Mexican Revolution at the sanitarium who imparted their political and ideological fervor. Profoundly affected by these interactions, Flores helped form a women's organization, Hermanas de la Revolución Mexicana. The organization offered women the space to discuss politics and encourage social activism. This was a totally new experience for Flores that helped shape her feminist views. Bill Flores, Flores's nephew, relates her conversations about Hermanas: "I knew that the men didn't take us seriously. They only wanted us to make tortillas. They couldn't accept that we had our own ideas." Thus began Flores's long campaign for women's rights.

By the time she was released from the sanitarium, World War II had erupted, and Flores had gained political organizing experience. According to Bill Flores, she was inspired by the Spanish civil war and resistance to Hitler, whom she saw as a terrible enemy of freedom. However, she loved the art of resistance and the artistic revolution of Diego Rivera, José Clemente Orozco, David Alfaro Siqueiros, and Pablo Picasso. Her ideological solidarity with Mexico's independence from the economic and cultural influence of the United States underlined her belief that Mexican Americans needed to fight on two fronts: one in the United States for equality and another in support of liberty in Mexico. Her love for Mexican history and culture nourished her sense of pride, and she used every project to instill cultural pride in others.

Francisca Flores moved to Los Angeles, honed her organizational skills, and engaged in numerous social and political activities. In 1943 she joined the Sleepy Lagoon Defense Committee, a group of progressive California activists that worked toward the release of twelve Mexican American young men wrongly convicted of murder. A year later the 2nd District Court overturned their convictions. During the 1940s she emerged at the forefront of community organizing in Los Angeles and served as a leader of the Asociación Mexico-Americana (ANMA), a left of center civil rights group.

Under the scrutinizing glare of the postwar "red scare" era, Flores's activities in progressive organizations made her a target of McCarthyism. During this period she openly criticized the House Committee on Un-American Activities (HUAC) and its persecution of labor activists. She arranged for underground screenings of the controversial movie *Salt of the Earth* about Mexican women's role in a 1950 miners' strike in Silver City, New Mexico.

Flores also became active in the Democratic Party and eventually helped cofound the Mexican American Political Association (MAPA) in 1960. MAPA remains an active organization to this day. As an activist with important information to disseminate, Flores succeeded in reaching a wider audience through her work as a writer and journalist. She served as a writer for both *La Luz Magazine* and *Mas Gráfica* and helped edit *Carta Editorial* and other political periodicals that focused on Latino issues. Of major significance was her role as editor of *Regeneración,* a magazine modeled after the Flores Magón brothers' newspaper during the Mexican Revolution. However, throughout the 1970s Flores's focus on the rights and conditions of women became the centerpiece of *Regeneración.*

Flores continued her unique brand of activism into the civil rights era. In the 1960s she embraced Chicanismo as an identity, but challenged the more sexist aspects of its guiding ideology, cultural nationalism. A lightning rod for her times, she attracted and garnered the support of a critical mass of Chicanas who collectively triggered a social and political campaign for the rights of Chicana and Mexican women. Flores became the founding president of a major organization that reflected her views, the Comisión Feminil Mexicana Nacional. In a 1971 article published in *Regeneracion* she described the important role of the Comisión, stating that "more Chicanas are fighting for their own identity, and they do not care who does not like it. Women must learn to say what they think and feel and [be] free to state it without apologizing or prefacing every statement to reassure men that they are not competing with them."

Founded by resolution on October 10, 1970, at a National Issues Conference in Sacramento, Comisión Feminil recognized that "the effort and work of Chicana/Mexican women in the Chicano movement is generally obscured because women are not accepted as community leaders, either by the Chicano movement or by the Anglo establishment." Flores's most ardent dreams for women were fulfilled in the purpose and scope of the organization, which sought to "direct its efforts to organizing women to assume leadership positions within the Chicano movement and in community life, and: [to] concern itself in promoting programs which specifically lend themselves to help, assist and promote solutions to female type problems and problems confronting the Mexican family." The following year the organization developed the Chicana Service Action Center, and Flores became its director in 1972. The Chicana Service Action Center was established to provide low-income, unskilled women with job training. The center continues to grow, provides shelter assistance to battered women, and links other Chicana-related resources together. Both the Comisión Feminil Mexicana Nacional and the Chicana Service Action Center have served and represented Chicanas and Mexican women for more than thirty years.

Flores continued her activism with Comisión Nacional and the Chicana Service Action Center. She participated in the National Equal Rights Amendment March to Washington, D.C., in 1978 and lobbied for the extension of equal rights to women and for strengthening protections and institutions for Chicanas. She also attended the United Nations Mid-Decade Conference on Women in Copenhagen, Denmark, in 1980, becoming in the process an instrumental force for ushering in the age of Chicana feminism that defied the rigid cultural roles of women as passive and subordinate. She aligned herself with other Chicanas who sought to end sexism, exercise their autonomy, and engage as independent and collective agents of social change in their communities.

By the 1990s Flores's health began to fail, and she passed away on April 27, 1996, at the age of eighty-two. She left an incredible, powerful legacy of a true revolutionary spirit. Bill Flores recalls, "Francisca once told me that she felt that Chicanos could be the bridge for America, the link that closes two critical gaps—the chasm between white and black and the hemispheric rift between North and South America." He quotes her as stating, "We are the hope for this country. We are also the hope for America, not just the country, but the hemisphere." Flores proved to be fearless in the face of injustice and a beacon of light for many women and men who continue to work for social change. In emphasizing the dynamic roles Chicanas and Chicanos have played in this society and the contributions they have made, the memory of Francisca Flores embodies what is best about Chicana/o and Mexican culture.

See also Chicano Movement

SOURCES: Comisión Femenil Mexicana Nacional. 1967–1997. Archives. CEMA California Ethnic and Multicultural Archives, Special Collections, Donald Davidson Library, University of California, Santa Barbara; Flores, William. 1996. "Francisca Flores." May 2. 1996. http://www.clnet.sscnet.ucla.edu/research/francisca.html (accessed October 4, 2003); García, Alma, ed. 1997. *Chicana Feminist Thought: The Basic Historical Writings.* New York: Routledge; ______. 2000. "Chicana Civil Rights Organizations." *Reader's Companion to U.S. Women's History.* Houghton Mifflin. http://www.college.hmco.com/history/readerscomp/women/html/wh_005100_chicanacivil.htm (accessed October 7, 2004).

Naomi H. Quiñonez

FLOREZ, ENCARNACIÓN VILLARREAL ESCOBEDO (1898–1968)

Curandera Encarnación Villarreal Escobedo Florez, also known as Chona, was born in Yucatan, Mexico, to Ramón Villareal and Carnuta Escobedo. The family consisted of five sisters and one brother. After Chona's birth her parents moved to Fresnillo, where Ramón operated a cattle ranch. In many ways the first eight years of her life were idyllic; she often rode horses with her father and enjoyed watching him work with the family's animals. No one in the family is certain when or how, but it was during these years that she was introduced to the art of *curanderismo* (healing). The desire to heal and help others through the use of herbs and prayer became a central aspect of Chona's life and eventually earned her the epithet *"la santa entre los santos"* (Mormons).

Circumstances changed dramatically for the clan in 1906 when Chona witnessed the murder of her father at the hands of Porfirio Díaz's troops. The soldiers knocked Ramón off his horse and dragged him to his death. Carnuta saved her children by hiding them under straw and manure. After burying Ramón, the siblings helped Carnuta sustain the family by taking in laundry and selling tortillas. Conditions worsened by the early part of the next decade when the family faced the dangers and uncertainties produced by the Mexican Revolution.

In 1911, the time she turned fifteen, Chona met and married Reyes Florez. In the midst of this national upheaval the couple found solace in their love and began having children. Unfortunately, economic conditions were abysmal, and Reyes faced great difficulties in providing for his family. Within eight years, Chona gave birth to nine children, including two sets of twins. These unfortunate offspring faced a grim reality of want and disease. Although Chona plied her *curandera* skills to provide succor for her children, seven of them succumbed to a variety of maladies before the family left Mexico in 1920.

With heavy hearts and an immigrant's hope for economic improvement, the couple took their two remaining children and abandoned their troubled homeland. Like thousands of other Mexicanos, they eventually found their way to El Paso, where Reyes and Chona looked for work among the many *enganchistas* (labor contractors) that carried on their trade in the city. They found work as *betabeleros* (beet pickers) and onion pickers in southern Idaho. Chona often recalled the trip north in language common to many Mexicanos who made the trek to *el norte*: "They put us in a box car with nothing more than a bag of *pinole*, a piece of baloney and bread." Ultimately the Florez family migrated to the west side of Salt Lake City when Reyes was hired as a *traquero* (track worker) with the Denver and Rio Grande Railroad. Other family members supplemented his salary by working in nearby beet fields during the spring and autumn.

By the early 1930s Chona had given birth to three more children and confronted the deaths of the last two offspring born in Mexico. The family lived in a boxcar, subdivided into a kitchen and living quarters, provided by the company and located a mere twenty feet from the tracks. Chona fought a never-ending battle to keep the quarters clear of dirt and dust. Although they were very poor, she worked diligently to raise her remaining children with a deep sense of pride in their Mexican heritage, teaching them about Aztec history, culture, and art. In addition to domestic duties, she also rendered a valuable service to west side residents by practicing her healing arts. Apparently Chona's skills must have been considerable, for her son John recalls that "patients" came from as far away as Texas and Arizona seeking cures and spiritual intercession. A 1973 article from the *Utah Historical Quarterly* provides a brief overview of Chona's work. "She combined prayer, ritual, and medicine, denying her power to cure and stating that God merely used her as an instrument of his will. She accepted no money for her services, only an occasional gift to help defray expenses, and she consulted with anyone who needed her services."

Encarnación Florez died on May 2, 1968. During her years in Utah she touched the lives of many sick and troubled individuals. In addition, she worked diligently to instill pride and awareness of Mexico's history and culture into her children. The story of Chona and others like her demonstrates that Latinas, using a variety of skills, rituals, and beliefs, worked to benefit the spiritual and social lives of their families and communities in locales throughout the United States.

SOURCES: Benavides, E. Ferol. 1973. "The Saint among the Saints: A Study of Curanderismo in Utah." *Utah Historical Quarterly* 41 (Autumn): 373–392; Iber, Jorge. 2000. *Hispanics in the Mormon Zion, 1912–1999*. College Station: Texas A&M University Press; Ulibarri, Richard O. 1989. "Utah's Unassimilated Minorities." In *Utah's History*, ed. Richard D. Poll, 629–650. Logan: Utah State University Press; Wright, Lili. 1994. "Latinos: Rich Heritage of Church, Family Nurtures Activist." *Salt Lake Tribune*, April 3, A13–A14.

Jorge Iber

FOLK HEALING TRADITIONS

In Latino and Latina forms of folk medicine it is difficult to divorce these systems from religious or spiritual practices. Two such practices, Santería and Espiritismo, are primarily of Caribbean origin, but are now popularly found in major cities in the United States. They have often been identified within the rubric of folk medical treatments by mental and public health officials. For example, Espiritismo is included in contemporary cultural competency programs that are interested in understanding non-Western healing systems. This entry first provides a historical account of these traditions and then compares them with other Western nonbiomedical forms of healing.

Santería as a religion emerged from Cuba as a direct result of the slave trade and is more authentically referred to as la Regla Lucumí or la Regla Ocha. It is commonly described as a syncretic religious practice that developed because Catholic slave masters would not allow slaves to overtly practice their Yoruba-based religion. The worship of the African deities called *orichas* was considered sacrilegious. In response, slaves drew relations between their *orichas* and Catholic saints, and Santería as a religious practice was conceived.

Those initiated in the religion recognize that the similarities drawn between Catholic saints and *orichas* served as a means to practice an African-based religion. In recognizing similarities, the priests and priestesses of this religion, who are called *santeros* and *santeras*, believe that *orichas* and saints are not interchangeable. Instead, they simply share particular characteristics. For example, Saint Barbara became associated with Shango (or Chango) because of the principle of force and thunder. Scholar Andrés I. Pérez y Mena does not think that Santería is a product of syncretism. Instead, certain characteristics of a particular *oricha* became associated with different saints, and the saints merely represent aspects of the *orichas*. Thus the

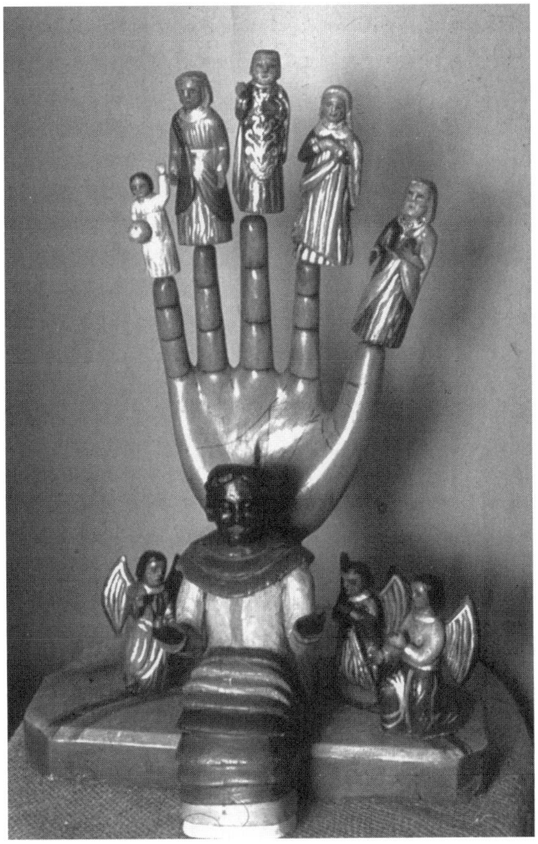

Artistic representation of popular Catholicism. Photograph by and courtesy of Carlos A. Cruz.

Symbolizing Catholicism and Santería. Photograph by and courtesy of Carlos A. Cruz.

Catholic saints are not exact representations of the *orichas*. This idea demonstrates that African slaves did not simplify their religion to mirror Catholicism, but instead understood both practices as two different religious ideologies that happened to share similar characteristics. As a survival mechanism, then, slaves were able to maintain the complexity of their religion by masking their belief system under that of Catholicism.

Because of this legacy of persecution, Santería holds a tradition of secrecy whereby knowledge is conveyed through tightly knit kinship relations between godchildren (*aijados* and *aijadas*) and initiated priests and priestesses who act as godfathers and godmothers (*padrinos* and *madrinas*). A basic distinction between Santería and Palo Mayombe, also referred to as Palo Monte, is that the former is a Yoruba-derived religion, while the latter traces its origins to the Congo. Practically speaking, la Regla Lucumí or la Regla Ocha deals with a pantheon of deities, the *orichas,* while the latter primarily deals with spirits of the dead.

Kinship is at the forefront of Santería in that the familial ties that develop as a result of initiation transcend the physical world while also providing the means for social organization within the material world. The primary relationship between godfather and/or godmother and godchild that develops is based on reciprocity in which the godparent directs the spiritual development of the godchild and the godchild, in turn, provides support in the form of labor or resources. Basically, the knowledge system of the religion is developed through social activity, which can only be maintained through strong social ties.

Anthropologist George Brandon believes that Santería developed in Cuba as a full-fledged religion in the late nineteenth and early twentieth centuries. Its presence in the United States can be traced to the Cuban Revolution when Cubans sought refuge from Castro's government. Brandon focuses on the years from 1959 to 1962 as a historically important time period. In the United States the areas where this religion first emerged are predominantly located in the East, especially in New York, New Jersey, and Florida. In essence, this practice provided immigrants to the United States with a social and metaphysical support system that is similar to what it provided the slaves who created it. That like the rationale of Voudou, the ideas and practices of Santería are flexible in that this religious system provides a tangible means of addressing social circumstances, including those associated with health and well-being, especially when facing unanswerable problems in life.

If a potential practitioner decides to join the religion, he or she must go through a complex initiation process that begins with a *misa espiritual* (séance) and culminates in *asiento*, also referred to as making *ocha*. The *misa espiritual* is held to determine the initiate's destined and corresponding *oricha*. Once the initiate "receives" the *oricha*, he or she is bound in service to this deity for life. The *asiento* is the actual ceremony in which the initiate receives his or her *oricha*. The process is long, arduous, and complicated and requires a myriad of preparations. Also, the initiation ceremony is costly, with an average price ranging from $5,000 to $15,000 for the weeklong preparations.

Divination is an important method by which problems are uncovered or resolved in this religion. As in other non-Western religions, divination reveals causes for misfortune, including illness and death. In this sense divination becomes a form of social analysis that provides salient prescriptions for tangible maladies, including health problems. Because of this, *santeros* and *santeras* are highly valorized in the community as agents in diagnosing and resolving problems. Of specific interest in this practice is the gendered aspect present, as exemplified by the roles ascribed to men and women. In particular, women are provided with opportunities for leadership not readily available in other European-derived Christian institutions. The possession experience in which the female body becomes a vehicle for communication with divine entities is one form in which these opportunities are manifested. However, while women may participate in this manner, it is the men who seem to be the leaders of the community. In fact, only men can become high priests, or *babalawos*. In some instances women are allowed to become *babalawos,* but only after they have stopped menstruating.

Santería has received unwanted attention in the United States because of the controversial practice of animal sacrifice. The case commonly cited as bringing this issue to the forefront of U.S. popular knowledge occurred in Hialeah, Florida. In 1987 the Hialeah City Council in Florida banned animal sacrifice. The case went to the Supreme Court in 1992, and in June 1993 the ruling was in favor of the *santeros* in that they were allowed to perform animal sacrifice as part of their religious practice.

Espiritismo (roughly translated as Spiritism) and Spiritualism are belief systems that have had different historical developments from that of Santería. Spiritism is traced to the teachings of Leon Denizarth Hippolyte Rivail, better known by his pseudonym Allan Kardec. Kardec is the one who opposed the term Spiritualism and introduced the term Spiritism, explaining that it was a general term that could be applied to anyone "who believes that there is in him something more than matter." Spiritualists formally distinguish themselves from Spiritists by stating that their set of beliefs constitutes a religion, while Spiritism deals with the occult. The Argentinian adherents of Joaquín Trincado agree that Kardec laid the groundwork for Spiritism. However, they believe that Trincado's approach was more "scientific" and "rational." Trincado adherents are usually of a higher socioeconomic status in their communities than Kardecists.

Elements of Spiritualism. Photograph by and courtesy of Carlos A. Cruz.

The major points of Kardec's doctrine are based on traditional Christian doctrine. The doctrine also reflects such ideals of the nineteenth century as the primacy of the spiritual over the material. This is based on an evolutionary model of progress derived from the Enlightenment where spirits climb through hierarchical ranks, and progress through these ranks is based on individual merit. Thus human effort becomes rewarded in the spiritual realm and consequently is demonstrated through class-based distinctions. This belief system spread and became widely adopted in Latin America. In Brazil Spiritism is socially divided according to class, with the mediums coming from a predominantly upper Anglo and middle class, while the clients tend to be ethnically diverse and poor.

Spiritualism, on the other hand, developed in the United States in the mid-nineteenth century. The doctrines of Spiritualism were popular because of the promise that they would provide a "new moral world" in which social and individual needs could be met. The genesis of this movement is most often traced to the three Fox sisters, who in 1848 heard rapping that was eventually identified as coming from the spirit of a dead peddler. While this is the most common explanation given for the inception of Spiritualism in the United States, other accounts credit André Jackson Davis for having been in communication with spirits in

1843. The goal of nineteenth-century Spiritualism was toward public edification, not toward personal growth.

The medicinal value of herbs in association with a type of religious practice also influenced the development of Spiritualism as an alternative religious doctrine. Robert C. Fuller discusses how this developed in the United States and Europe in the nineteenth century with the advent of such practices as Thomsonianism (medicinal value of herbs), homeopathy (small herbal dosages of what is causing the ailment are given with the understanding that "like cures like"), hydropathy (water cure), Grahamism (the stomach is the physiological agent for delivering "vital power" in order to overcome disease), Mesmerism ("animal magnetism" as an invisible fluid that permeates the universe must be kept in balance for good health) and Swedenborgianism (a positive bodily health status is the product of harmony among the spiritual, mental, and physical levels). Mesmerism and Swedenborgianism were important influences in the later development of Spiritualism. These examples demonstrate the strong association between notions of health and religiosity in Western folk medical models.

Mexican Spiritualism is defined by anthropologist Kaja Finkler as having a relatively separate development from Kardecian Spiritism and from the Spiritualism attributed to the Fox sisters. Finkler defines Mexican Spiritualism as a "dissident religious movement vehemently anti-Catholic, and a nonbiomedical health-care delivery system" and traces it to Roque Rojas in 1861. Finkler acknowledges that most other Latin American countries trace their practice to Allan Kardec, but this was not evident in her research. As with the divinities associated with Santería, those who are associated with Spiritualist practices in Mexico are perceived more as "forces" or "powers" than as personalities. Spiritualist healers in Mexico believe that there are four powers, divinities that are identified as the Father God, the Father Jesus, the Father Elijah, and the Holy Mother. This is in contrast to the larger pantheon of *orichas* in Santería. There are also spirits who are contacted, both good and bad, and are primarily of deceased humans but can also be such creatures as dwarfs and aliens. The crossing over of entities is most visible in Puerto Rican Spiritualism, where Andrés I. Pérez y Mena posits that religious objects and ideology are drawn from Cuban-based Santería with aspects of French Kardecian Spiritism added. George Brandon refers to the melding of Puerto Rican Spiritualism and Santería as Santerismo.

As with Santería, most of the people who practice Spiritism and Latino forms of Spiritualism are women. Women primarily seek assistance because of what is described as failing health. For the most part, they seek this form of treatment because their maladies have not been alleviated by other means, that is, biomedicine. There is participation by both men and women, but women are usually the mediums because they are supposedly more apt to "receive" a spirit. One possibility for the predominance of male spirits inhabiting female bodies during séances is that this is a form in which women are able to overcome their social condition of powerlessness. In June Macklin's study, female spirits outnumbered male spirits four to three. This contrasts with other studies where the predominant presence accounted for is that of male spirits.

June Macklin believes that the major difference between Kardec's Spiritism, where the spirit follows a series of incarnations in the pursuit of reaching a topmost rung of the spiritually oriented hierarchical ladder, and American-English Spiritualism, where the soul only has the opportunity of being incarnated once, is this idea of multiple incarnations. Macklin further explains that Kardec's system was most likely not accepted by the English and by Americans because "the English and Americans did not need the romantic, idealistically based, nationalistic ideology which Kardec synthesized" because both were pursuing material interests. One main difference between the value system of Spiritualism and that of Spiritism is the emphasis that Spiritualism places on individual agency, as opposed to Spiritism's emphasis on communal well-being. This divide is attributed by Macklin to the divergent religious traditions each draws from. Spiritualism, with its Protestant roots, emphasizes the achievement of individual physical well-being, whereas Spiritism, with its predominantly Catholic roots, emphasizes the healing relationship that develops between the medium and the client in the form of public diagnosis.

One predominant feature of these religions is how the body is perceived. The body is understood as multifaceted. Thus the physical body that experiences pain as a result of illness is deeply connected to its spiritual counterpart. Also, as the brief account of the historical development of these traditions demonstrates, social circumstances shape the manner in which life is experienced. Health cannot be addressed outside of this context. *Santeros, santeras,* and *espiritistas* realize that in order for health to be experienced in terms of the absence of pain, an entire lifestyle must be devoted toward this endeavor. While positive health may be one aspect of a person's life, it is most definitely a substantial one because an unhealthy life assures personal discord. As a result, Santería and Espiritismo are two Latino forms of identified folk medicine that provide holistic perceptions of life, health, and (bodily) well-being. It is also worth noting that one of the primary reasons cited for why members join these practices is that maladies, including physical ones, have not been successfully addressed through other systems, including the biomedical one.

SOURCES: Brandon, George. 1997 [1993]. *Santeria from Africa to the New World: The Dead Sell Memories*. Bloomington: Indiana University Press; Finkler, Kaja. 1985. *Spiritualist Healers in Mexico*. South Hadley, MA: Bergen and Garvey; Fuller, Robert C. 1989. *Alternative Medicine and American Religious Life*. Oxford: Oxford University Press; Macklin, June. 1974. "Belief, Ritual, and Healing: New England Spiritualism and Mexican-American Spiritism Compared." In *Religious Movements in Contemporary America*. Ed. Irvine Zaretsky, and Mark P. Leone, 383–417. Princeton, NJ: Princeton University Press; Pérez y Mena, Andrés I. 1991. *Speaking with the Dead: Development of Afro-Latin Religion among Puerto Ricans in the United States*. New York: AMS Press.

Karen V. Holliday

FONTAÑEZ, JOVITA (1942–)

Boston community activist Jovita Fontañez was born in New York City in 1942, the daughter of a Bermudan mother and a Puerto Rican father. Her family lived in Spanish Harlem, where Fontañez grew up, tagging after one of her paternal aunts, who engaged in political activities in El Barrio. At the age of ten Fontañez moved to Boston, where she has continued to live all her life. Fontañez grew up in the South End and attended the Jeremiah E. Burke High School for girls. Afterward she received a bachelor's degree from the University of Massachusetts at Boston. Fontañez was married and is the mother of two children, Herminio Nicolas (1962–) and Melina Tamar (1963–).

Throughout her life Fontañez has been active in numerous community and social service organizations that have served Boston's and Massachusetts's broader Latino community. Her community roots and bilingual skills opened the doors for her participation in numerous antipoverty programs developed in Boston in the 1960s. A longtime resident of the South End—Boston's historical Puerto Rican enclave—she was a member of the Association Pro-Constitutional Rights of the Spanish Speaking (APCROSS) in the 1970s. Her interest in racial issues led her to join PoroAfro, an organization created by young Latinos, mostly Puerto Ricans, in the late 1960s to promote Latino and African American coalition building around political and social issues. Its emphasis on racial issues and immediate action placed the group at odds with more senior Puerto Rican community leaders. Fontañez was one of the first Latinos, along with longtime activists Tony Molina and Tony Ortiz, to work for the South End Neighborhood Action Program (SNAP), at the time a predominantly African American organization. At SNAP Fontañez worked as a social worker in a family service clinic. Fontañez was also involved in the creation and development of Inquilinos Boricuas en Acción (IBA), a community-owned and operated nonprofit organization that managed the Villa Victoria housing complex. IBA was created by the Puerto Rican community to stop gentrification efforts and urban renewal in the South End. During the 1990s Fontañez was the director of Latinas y Niños, a social service organization that helped develop a more comprehensive agency called Casa Esperanza. Latinas y Niños was the first residential treatment center for Latinas recovering from substance abuse in Boston.

Fontañez has also been a longtime player in Boston Democratic Party politics. That, combined with her ethnicity and sex, has led Fontañez to compile a long list of "first" accomplishments. She was the first Latino/a and the first woman to be selected as chair of the Election Commission for the city of Boston in 1991. Previously Fontañez had been the first Latina selected as fair housing commissioner and also the second one selected Democratic state committeewoman. In her political career Fontañez had also been the second Latina appointed as Metropolitan District Commission associate commissioner, following Conchita Rodríguez. In all her public appointments Fontañez has protected the interests and concerns of Latinos.

Fontañez continues her activism on behalf of the Latino community in Boston. She completed a master's degree in public policy at Northeastern University in 2003.

SOURCE: *Boston Globe*. 1991. "Hispanic to Head Election Division." May 28, 67.

Félix V. Matos Rodríguez

FORNÉS, MARÍA IRENE (1930–)

The winner of eight Obie Awards for her Off-Broadway dramas, the prolific writer María Irene Fornés ranks among the most productive playwrights and directors on the American stage. One of six daughters, Fornés was born on May 14, 1930, in Havana, Cuba, to Carlos Luis Fornés, a government worker, and Carmen Hismenia Collado. In an educated family Carlos Luis nurtured the intellectual development of his daughters enabling María Irene to receive a good academic foundation even though she attended public school for only the third to the sixth grade. In 1945 Carmen Hismenia, now a young widow, brought her daughters to live in New York City. María Irene, who was just fifteen years of age and spoke only Spanish, decided against returning to school and found employment on a local factory assembly line. A series of jobs that included doll making, translating, waiting tables, and clerical work supported Fornés and permitted her to study painting at night. She studied with Hans Hoffman at the Provincetown School and left New York for Europe to further her painting career in 1954. She soon discovered that while she lacked the discipline required to paint, the structure of producing art led her to another art form, the composition of plays.

It is said that Fornés discovered her true calling by helping her roommate, writer-philosopher Susan Sontag, overcome writer's block. The result was her first published play, *La viuda*. In an interview with Rachel Koenig and Kathleen Betsko, Fornés explains, "I started writing late; I was around thirty. I had never thought I would write; as I said, I was an aspiring painter. But once I started writing it was so pleasurable that I couldn't stop." In 1961 Fornés received a John Hay Whitney Foundation fellowship, followed by a second fellowship from the Centro Mexicano de Escritores in 1962. Within a year Fornés had written a two-character play, *Tango Palace,* hailed as a critical success. A second hit about prisoners who willingly return to confinement after exposure to a chaotic world, *Promenade,* was dubbed by critics as "a protest musical for people too sophisticated to protest." It, too, was a success. Both *Promenade* and *The Successful Life of 3,* her fourth play, garnered Fornés a prestigious Obie Award.

Fornés's theatrical achievements attracted attention. She received a Yale University fellowship in 1967 and a University-Tanglewood fellowship in 1968 and produced two more plays, *A Vietnamese Wedding* (1967) and *Dr. Kheal* (1968). The latter was produced both in the United States and abroad. Fornés's work flourished, and soon her productions were seen in numerous venues, including La MaMa, the Judson Poets' Theatre, the Open Theatre, the New Dramatists, the Actors' Workshop in San Francisco, and the Firehouse Theatre in Minneapolis. In a *Village Voice* interview Fornés commented on her work: "Writing is like your fingerprints. You have no idea what they look like, but wherever you go, you are leaving your mark."

From 1973 to 1979 Fornés was managing director of the New York Theatre Strategy, an experimental theatrical group that she founded with other playwrights. In 1981 she became director of the International Arts Relations (INTAR) Hispanic Playwrights-in-Residence Laboratory. This program provided a resourceful theatrical outlet for Latino playwrights that nurtured their creative talents through workshops and productions. During this period Fornés also found time to work with the board of education in a program titled Theatre for the New City in New York City.

Throughout the 1980s and 1990s, Fornés continued to write and produce plays. She has received a number of prestigious grants from the Rockefeller Foundation, the American Academy and Institute of Arts and Letters in Literature, and the Lilia Wallace-Readers' Digest Fund. She was also awarded a Guggenheim Fellowship. Her awards include the Distinguished Artists Award from the National Endowment for the Arts and the New York State Governor's Award. She was also a finalist for the Pulitzer Prize. Among the forty-one plays written by Fornés, eight have received Obies and she received an Obie for Sustained Achievement in Theater. Her Obie-winning productions include *Promenade* (1965), *Successful Life of Three* (1965), *Fefu and Her Friends* (1977), *The Danube* (1982), *Mud* (1983), *Sarita* (1984), *The Conduct of Life* (1985), *Abingdon Square* (1988), and *Letters From Cuba* (2000). An extraordinary role model, Fornés teaches students at the Padua Hills Festival in southern California, at INTAR, and at Manhattanville College in New York.

See also Theater

SOURCES: Besko, Kathleen, and Rachel Koenig. 1987. *Interviews with Contemporary Women Playwrights.* New York: Beech Tree Books. 1981. MacNicholas, John ed. *Dictionary of Literary Biography. Vol. 7: Twentieth-Century American Dramatists.* Detroit: Gale Research.

Virginia Sánchez Korrol

FRIENDLY HOUSE, PHOENIX (1920–)

At a meeting of the Phoenix Americanization Committee (PAC) on April 11, 1920, Grace Court, principal of Adams School in Phoenix, proposed that the committee secure a permanent space as a "community house" for its Americanization projects in South Phoenix instead of relying on space borrowed from schools and churches to hold its English and citizenship classes. Court was the project's primary advocate, lining up financial support for the effort not only from the Kiwanis and Rotary clubs but also from the Alianza Hispano Americana, the state's largest *mutualista* or self-help organization.

By 1922 the Phoenix Americanization Committee had rented a small house, quickly named Friendly House, where Carrie Green, a former public school teacher fluent in Spanish, taught classes. She served as the director of Friendly House from 1922 through 1931, and her work was framed by her belief that "immigrants should be loyal to the United States but should be encouraged to take pride in their native culture as well." In 1928 the PAC spent $5,250 to purchase a permanent home for the work on South First Street. In 1931 Green resigned for health reasons and was replaced by Plácida García Smith, a career educator who had relocated from Colorado in 1928.

From the 1920s through the 1950s Friendly House served as a social service agency linking the Mexican American community to the rest of Phoenix. A product of both the Americanization and settlement-house movements, it made a long-term commitment to the employment and education of Mexican American women. During this era, while the project was funded by Euro-American residents of Phoenix and civic organizations, an increasing number of Mexican American men and women held seats on the board and were members of the staff.

During the depression a great demand arose for the services of this settlement house, particularly since no social welfare organizations served the Mexican American population of South Phoenix. Friendly House participated in depression relief efforts, particularly in the distribution of food. Between 1929 and 1934 more than 500,000 Mexicans, an estimated one-third of the population, were deported or repatriated to Mexico, even though the majority of those affected were U.S.-born children. In a controversial move García Smith and Friendly House supported the repatriation effort and facilitated the relocation of hundreds of Mexican residents of Phoenix. Decades later García Smith revealed in an interview that although she participated in the program, she was anti-repatriation because it was disrespectful and relocated people who had gainful employment.

In 1933 Friendly House obtained federal New Deal monies to fund classes in English and citizenship, two classes in high demand within its community since citizenship was necessary to benefit from relief programs. It also obtained funds under the Federal Emergency Relief Act (FERA) to support an *orquesta* employing local musicians and to partially fund a day-care program. Under García Smith's leadership and influence Friendly House became an integral part of Phoenix's social service community.

Friendly House emphasized Americanization through classes in civics, English, and homemaking. It also operated a job placement service that provided both temporary and permanent positions to applicants. Most of the clients were Mexican American women and girls who found low-wage employment as domestic workers in Phoenix's middle- and upper-income homes. Imbued with a maternalism typical of the times among settlement-house workers, Friendly House leaders envisioned these positions as an opportunity for their clients to gain an introduction to American culture while also meeting employment demands and economic needs. Men who sought employment through Friendly House were placed in other low-wage positions in such fields as construction and groundskeeping. These types of jobs, however, offered little in the way of economic mobility. By the end of the 1930s Friendly House was known for its formal roles in job placement and education, as well as for its more informal role as a community center hosting meetings for many different clubs and *mutualistas*.

Throughout the 1940s and 1950s the programs offered by Friendly House expanded according to the interests and concerns of Placida García Smith and other leaders. García Smith became a spokesperson for the Mexican American community in Phoenix. In 1963 another former teacher, Mari Marín, replaced García Smith as director of Friendly House, although García Smith remained involved with the project as an educator. Like other settlement houses that have continued to the present, Friendly House shed the Progressive-era pronouncements and became a community center.

Friendly House continues to serve the Spanish-speaking population of Phoenix by offering services in six general areas: adult education and job development, youth services, parenting, immigration, home care, and family counseling. Friendly House also operates the Adam Díaz Early Childhood Development Center, named for Arizona's first Mexican American city council member, and the Joseph I. Flores Academia del Pueblo, a charter school teaching grades K–3 and 7–8. Funding for some programs derives from the state government and the United Way, but most monies are raised through private donations and such activities as the annual Tamale Dinner, now in its sixty-eighth year.

Friendly House has established itself as a lasting place in the community. Salvador Pastraña, director of Youth Services, attributes the success and longevity of Friendly House to its "long history in the community, so people know they can trust us."

See also Americanization Programs

SOURCES: *Arizona Republic.* 2001. "Day Care Tough to Find in Central Phoenix, Many Centers Stretched to Limit." May 11; Friendly House. http://www.friendlyhouse.org (accessed review October 7, 2004); Titcomb, Mary Ruth. 1984. "Americanization and Mexicans in the Southwest: A History of Phoenix's Friendly House, 1920–1983." M.A. thesis, University of Santa Barbara.

Eve Carr

FUERZA UNIDA (1990–)

On January 17, 1990, 1,115 predominantly Latina workers at the South Zarzamora Street Levi Strauss and Company plant in San Antonio, Texas, were informed that the plant was shutting down. With less than twenty-four hours notice, the workers had lost their jobs. The women, some of whom had been with the company for as long as forty years, were shocked by the news that came despite their record as one of the highest-producing Levi's factories and the company's record-earning profits of $272.3 million the year before. Workers at the South Zarzamora plant learned that their plant was the twenty-sixth Levi's plant closure since 1985 and part of a trend among multinational corporations to transplant production abroad in search of lower labor costs. Levi's relocated its plants to Costa Rica, where it could pay workers less than $3.80 a day, about half the average wage of San Antonio workers. For the South Zarzamora workers, job stability had remained the saving grace of a job that paid mediocre wages, reneged on promises of bonuses, routinely led to carpal tunnel syndrome and other injuries, and offered only limited retirement benefits.

Fomenting the first-ever protest against a plant shutdown by Levi's, the San Antonio workers met on February 12, 1990. They formed an independent workers organization called Fuerza Unida to demand severance pay and to pressure the Levi's corporation to improve its policy regarding plant closures. In 1997 Levi Strauss and Company announced eleven more plant closures across the United States, amounting to 6,395 worker layoffs. This time, according to a Levi Strauss spokesman, "because of some of the lessons learned in San Antonio," the company offered these workers eight months' notice, three weeks' pay for each year of service, and eighteen months of health benefits. Empowered by the evidence of its activism, Fuerza Unida continued to demand similar compensation for the San Antonio workers. With the motto "La mujer luchando, el mundo transformando," roughly translated as "Women in struggle transform the world," Fuerza Unida broadened its protest to demand attention to sweatshop labor conditions. It waged numerous protests in cities across the Southwest, in Seattle, Portland, Chicago, Albany, and New York City, and into Mexico and France. Among its actions were a nationwide boycott against Levi Strauss clothing and the building of alliances with other women's and worker organizations. Throughout the 1990s its struggle remained tied to the movement against the North American Free Trade Agreement (NAFTA) and was committed to raising awareness about the negative consequences of economic globalization on labor. "We don't want free trade," its members chanted. "We want fair trade."

Fuerza Unida is remarkable for its significant contributions to the growing international consciousness of economic globalization and, in particular, of the deplorable sweatshop conditions rampant within the garment industry. The actions of Fuerza Unida, as well as other social justice movements, catapulted a new anti-sweatshop movement across college campuses and demanded public awareness to government-business collaboration on trade policy. In addition, Fuerza Unida presents an alternative vision to mainstream labor unions through its linkage of community and labor economic concerns. It contends that the Levi's plant closure contributed to community decay and asserts that corporate-run plants have a responsibility to the communities in which they function. Key to its vision of community-based labor activism is the training of former garment worker employees as Fuerza Unida organizers. With limited access to economic resources and without formal education, the women of Fuerza Unida have nonetheless managed to sustain their actions through various innovative practices, ranging from the maintenance of a volunteer sewing cooperative to the operation of a food bank to support some of its members. In these ways Fuerza Unida continues to work toward the empowerment of the working-class women of San Antonio.

See also Labor Unions

SOURCES: American Friends Service Committee (AFSC), Texas, Arkansas, Oklahoma (TAO). "The Birth of Fuerza Unida." http://www.afsc.org/tao/112k03.htm (accessed October 7, 2004); Hollens, Mary. 1993. "Catfish and Commuity: People of Color Organize in and around Unions." *Third Force*, June 30, 13; Martínez, Elizabeth. 1998. "Levi's, Button Your Fly—Your Greed Is Showing!" In *De Colores Means All of Us: Latina Views for a Multi-colored Century*, 82–90. Cambridge, MA: South End Press; Ruiz, Vicki L. 1998. *From out of the Shadows: Mexican Women in Twentieth-Century America*. New York: Oxford University Press.

Julie Cohen

G

GALLEGOS, CARMEN CORNEJO (1926–)

"El que quiere puede" (Those who want to can achieve). These words propelled softball champion and community activist Carmen Gallegos through life. They are her mother's words. Born to Mexican immigrants from Tepic, Nayarit, Carmen Gallegos was the fourth of five children and the first to be born in the United States. She grew up in Orange, California, keenly aware of discrimination against Mexican Americans in a predominantly Anglo community.

"I was sent to a segregated school, far from home with no school buses available. We weren't allowed in certain theaters, the public swimming pool, and local stores." Despite the climate of adversity, Gallegos flourished. Home was a happy and secure place with a high value placed on education. With her mother's words in mind, Gallegos was an honor student, sang in the choir, had a part-time job, and played sports. "Baseball was the popular sport and we women wanted a team of our own." The Orange Tomboys, composed entirely of Mexican American women, won their league's championship in 1947.

Carmen married Tony E. Gallegos in 1948; the couple had two children. Michael is an economist, and Lori is a lawyer. Tony Gallegos is a former chairman of the Equal Employment Opportunity Commission in Washington, D.C. Carmen Gallegos received a California teaching certificate and taught English as a second language (ESL) and Spanish for eleven years, from 1971 to 1981, in elementary school and in an adult education program.

A supporter of César Chávez, founder of the United Farm Workers union, and his cause, Gallegos was an active participant in the civil rights movement, joining the American GI Forum in 1963, an organization dedicated to the promotion of education and civil rights for Mexican Americans. In addition, she was PTA president, a member of the El Rancho Unified School District's advisory board, a member of the Sister City Committee of Pico Rivera, a member of the Women's Democratic Party, and a volunteer at the White House for the Public Liaison for Hispanic Affairs. In 1974 the Mexican-American Opportunity Foundation honored her as the Hispanic Woman of the Year for community service. Through her untiring commitment to civil rights and community service, Carmen Gallegos serves as an inspiration for other women. Consistent with her Hispanic heritage, she considers her children to be her most important achievement.

SOURCES: Griswold del Castillo, Richard, and Richard A. Garcia. 1995. *César Chávez: A Triumph of Spirit.* Norman: University of Oklahoma Press; Johnson, Connie Peterson, and Margie Wright. 1984. *The Woman's Softball Book.* New York: Leisure Press; Ramos, Henry A. J. 1998. *The American GI Forum: In Pursuit of the Dream, 1948–1983.* Houston: Arte Público Press.

Lori Gallegos-Hupka

GANADOS DEL VALLE (1983–)

Ganados del Valle is a community-based economic development organization located in Rio Arriba County, New Mexico. Ganados represents highly innovative efforts to provide alternative forms of economic development that are environmentally sustainable, offer meaningful opportunities to local residents, and build upon the Hispanic culture of the region.

Northern New Mexico is one of the oldest and poorest rural communities in the United States. During the 1960s the region gained visibility when Reies López Tijerina and la Alianza de Mercedes Federales attempted to reclaim communal grant lands lost through Euro-American conquest and subsequent capitalist penetration. While la Alianza never achieved its goals, it resonated with locals and tapped into a deep frustration. As a result, many were encouraged to consider alternative forms of landownership and economic arrangements. Although many Hispanos were wedded to a pastoral lifestyle, the growing tourist economy and rising land prices made it prohibitively expensive to acquire the necessary land and/or capital to initiate a successful economic venture. Consequently, the region has suffered from severe out-migration as growing numbers of Euro-Americans have been drawn to the region. While tourism has brought much-needed money into the area, it has also created a series of low-wage, seasonal jobs that not only are environmentally pernicious, but also do not build upon or cultivate the talents and leadership potential of the local population.

Ganados began in 1983 when three local residents, Antonio Manzanares, Gumercindo Salazar, and María Varela, began to discuss the obstacles to building a viable livestock operation. Ranchers Manzanares and Salazar, along with Varela, a community development specialist, soon realized that in addition to limited access to land, the small size of most operations proved a key impediment. Accordingly, the three sought to achieve economies of scale by encouraging local livestock owners to cooperate. In addition to promoting cooperation, Ganados has built a series of integrated businesses that allow money to stay in the community, rather than be spent elsewhere. Ganados describes its mission in the following manner:

> To demonstrate how . . . land-based rural cultures can secure, use, and protect their ancestral land and water by developing sustainable economies and environments that strengthen the culture. It does this by helping residents form cooperative enterprises that both create jobs and preserve the region's cultural identity. Ganados' definition of sustainability is that pastoral cultures and environments depend on each other; one cannot survive without the other.

Ganados del Valle has created a complex of businesses and social and economic programs that serve the community. The heart of the organization, however, remains the livestock, because most of the businesses and related programs center on sheep products. Ganados actively seeks to build and develop local flocks through a variety of initiatives, including assisting its members as they strive to increase their individual flocks, promoting the breeding of the almost extinct Churro, and training members on the most up-to-date livestock management techniques. In addition to actual livestock, additional businesses include Pastores Feed and General Store, Pastores Lamb (marketing high-quality, organically grown meat), Pastores Collection (offering linen and home decorations), and Otra Vuelta (which recycles tires into mats).

Perhaps the most successful venture, Tierra Wools produces high-quality woven products. Tierra Wools has recently spun off from Ganados to form an independent worker-owned weaving cooperative. In addition to businesses, Ganados has also developed a series of social and education programs that include establishing a scholarship fund and offering community college courses. Currently more than 150 individuals actively participate in Ganados, and it has become one of the largest employers in the county.

In addition to foundation grants, Ganados has received recognition and awards for its members' weavings, including an exhibition at the Smithsonian. Central to the success of Ganados has been the development of the rural community. Many locals, especially Hispanas, have been transformed by Ganados. Not only have they learned tangible skills, but the organization has also provided an alternative to outmigration and poverty. According to María Varela, one of "the most heartening success[es] of Ganados was the flowering of the women. Many were shy and passive when they began. I learned not to push, to wait till they were ready. One woman could hardly take her eyes off the floor when we started. Now she's making speeches. Another said all she could do was crochet, and she became the store manager."

One of the biggest challenges facing Ganados is a lack of summer grazing land. This is an ongoing problem that Ganados must confront every year. In the summer of 1989 Ganados faced its usual crisis, and in order to dramatize their plight, members, along with 2,000 sheep, trespassed onto a wildlife management area (WMA). This act of civil disobedience helped generate alternatives. For instance, Ganados members discovered that a $100,000 donation had been made to the Sierra Club Foundation in 1970 for the express purpose of buying land for a Hispano co-op in the area. An inquiry revealed that the money had never been spent on its intended purpose. The benefactor and the New Mexico attorney general's office sued the Sierra Club Foundation, and ultimately the foundation chose to settle out of court. In the settlement, Ganados received $900,000—roughly the value of the land if it had been purchased as intended in 1970.

Ganados del Valle has become a model for low-income rural communities across the globe that are struggling to build a viable economic base, preserve their homeland, and develop the skills and talents of the local population. Referring to the customers of Tierra Wools, Tina Ulibarri explained, "You can tell when people come in here they are really impressed with what we do. It is not something from Wal-Mart. It is carefully made here and they will cherish it for the rest of their life."

SOURCES: Jackson, Donald Dale. 1991. "Around Los Ojos, Sheep and Land Are Fighting Words." *Smithsonian* 22:37–47; Pulido, Laura. 1996. *Environmentalism and Economic Justice: Two Chicano Struggles in the Southwest.* Tucson: University of Arizona Press; Tierra Wools. www.handweavers.com/abouttw.htm (accessed July 9, 2005); Tierra Wools Newsletter. 2005. "News and Inspirations." Spring and Summer. www.handweavers.com/newltr%20pub%20file%201_files/newltr%20pub%20file%201.htm (accessed July 9, 2005).

Laura Pulido

GANGS

Juvenile delinquency, especially in the form of gang participation, has been a growing concern in the last several decades. Annual arrest rates for youths have increased between 20 and 40 percent during the 1990s. Within this national increase in delinquency, an unexpected trend of female youth offenders has emerged. Evidence indicates that juvenile arrests of females rose dramatically, between 30 and 80 percent, depending on the offense, from 1984 to 1993. The notable increase in female delinquent behavior has provoked an interest in the participation of women in gangs, a realm of antisocial behavior formerly defined as solely masculine.

There is evidence of female participation in gangs as early as the mid-nineteenth century. Anthropologists and sociologists in the 1930s and 1940s made specific reference to Latina, especially Puerto Rican and Mexican American, gang membership in urban areas of the West and East Coasts. These early studies, however, often dismissed female participation in the gang structure, labeling the women as "auxiliaries" to the male gangs or simply reducing the women's behavioral participation to "sexual delinquency." These stereotypes about Latinas in gangs have only recently been challenged. Generally, these women have been ignored by the scientific community and have served more as journalistic curiosities than as real social phenomena. In the last decade social scientists have helped flesh out the true nature of the Latina gangsters (la Chola, the homegirl), who currently constitute between 5 to 10 percent of all gang members in the United States. It is believed that approximately 600,000 gang members are found in the continental United States, and about 15 percent are female. Moreover, gangs are no longer urban or coastal phenomena. There are identifiable gangs throughout the Midwest and some rural areas of the United States.

Latina gang members tend to have certain attributes in common. First, they tend to be young. The average age of these young women is approximately fifteen years, but the predominant period of active participation ranges from twelve to seventeen years of age. Contrary to popular stereotypes, Latina gangsters tend to hold many traditional values. They hold motherhood as a prominent role in their development, expressing that a child should not be exposed to the "street life" and that a child is a primary motivator to distance oneself from severe risk-taking behavior. Latina homegirls also show a regard for serial monogamy, often ostracizing young women in their groups who may be more promiscuous. As among other oppressed groups, Latina gang membership is often a function of poverty, protection, and lack of education.

Research indicates that one of the most robust factors contributing to gang membership for Latinas is peer relationships. There is a recurring theme in the literature illustrating how young women who have friends, siblings, or other family affiliated with the gang lifestyle adopt similar attributes and behaviors. Additionally, for many young Latinas, especially those who have recently immigrated or are without an integrated social network, the gang provides a venue for meeting friends and creating peer relationships. Furthermore, given the tenets of adolescent development, the gang gives a young Latina a chance for heterosexual contacts.

Yet peer pressure is not the only reason for joining gangs. Proximity is also an influential factor in becoming a homegirl. Simply put, these women live in areas that are gang infested. Becoming a gang member is part of joining the larger social network of their ecological reality. For many Latinas, gangs have been part of their lives since birth or early childhood. Therefore, becoming an active participant during, or in some cases before, adolescence is natural to the environment in which they must survive.

Unfortunately, many of the young Latinas who are part of gangs come from dysfunctional families. The research indicates that these young women are disproportionately victims of neglect and abuse in their homes. Often the less fortunate and more psychologically distressed homegirls tend to join gangs for survival, seeking a substitute for their own lacking family dynamics. Despite efforts at reparenting themselves through the gang, these homegirls, victims in their own homes, tend to be at higher risk for drug addiction, violence, and other harm.

The literature also reveals that many Latinas join the gang structure in order to gain status in their neighborhoods. Joining and belonging to a feared, cohesive group bring some benefits to the individual's ego. For example, gang membership carries with it some semblance of pride and respect. Others fear the young Latina who dons the cloak of a known gang. She becomes the object of reverence, if not respect or fear. People think twice about giving her a hard time on the street or at school. Such reactions may inspire feelings of importance, personal satisfaction, and self-confidence in young Latinas who otherwise have very little in their lives to support positive feelings about themselves.

Economic needs and opportunities, or lack thereof, are also cited in the literature as contributing factors to Latina gang membership. However, the role of economics is quite complex. In the case of all-female gangs that are autonomous from any male counterpart, the economic gains of drug sales may play a central role in maintaining gang membership. However, the gang generally serves to perpetuate economic survival, not enhancement, for most of its Latina members. That is, gang membership provides for a collective of persons to help in the economic maintenance of the individual. For example, when a homegirl needs somewhere to sleep or something to eat, she can count on her gang affiliates to help. Furthermore, many women in gangs often "double up" or gather in groups in order to help each other raise their children when the fathers are absent. It should be noted that not all homegirls are helped economically. Generally, those who become addicted to drugs and show themselves untrustworthy lose economic assistance over time.

The factor of protection is tied to the ideas of proximity, family dysfunction, and economics. Growing up and being overrepresented in poverty-stricken, urban neighborhoods, Latina gang members often cite protection as a major reason for their decision to join a gang. Ethnographic data suggest that for a large proportion of Latina youths, there is perceived danger in their environment. This danger is perpetual and can come at the hands of peers, often from neighboring communities, or from illicit activity in the neighborhood of residence such as drug trafficking, or even from within the family system. When interviewed about their choice to join a gang, Latina youths specify that they needed support to avoid victimization or harm. This protective support is called "backup" and represents one of the fundamental features of gang structure—the idea that a member can rely on the loyalty of other members for protection from external harm. Ironically, it is this very protection provided by gang allegiance that can lead to one's becoming a greater target, as in the case of attacks by rival gangs.

There are several methods of gang initiation. Almost all methods involve some form of pain or humiliation. It should be noted that some gangs, usually in very old and established neighborhoods, do not require initiation, but rather function by invitation only. These gangs, however, have little documentation because of the exclusivity of the membership and tend to be male only. For Latina gangsters, initiation usually consists of "walking the line," "pulling a train," or participation in a criminal act. "Walking the line" is a classic method of initiation. It is often also referred to as "getting jumped in." The premise is that the young Latina must prove that she is tough, can hold her own, and is not easily beaten down. Therefore, she must go through a double line (*doblefila*) of homegirls and homeboys who beat her with their fists as she goes through. An alternative is for her to be "jumped" and have to fight three to five other gang members for a designated length of time. While involved in this initiation rite, the Latina youth cannot cower and must fight back in order to gain acceptance. She must show that she has the physical prowess and willingness to fight for her gang.

The other forms of initiation are less popular among Latina gangsters but exist nonetheless. To "pull a train" or be "sexed in" is the least respectable method for a young Latina to gain gang membership. This initiation rite requires her to have sex with several of the male gang members on a single occasion. The problem with this choice of initiation is that the young Latina subsequently continues to be treated as sexual property by the males in the gang. Furthermore, she is not respected by the other females in the gang, who see her as promiscuous and as a "lesser" member. Once a young Latina is initiated in this manner, it is difficult to acquire a higher status in the gang. The homegirl who was "sexed in" must prove herself to be even tougher or crazier than the other women in order to change her reputation and gain respect among her peers in the gang. Research indicates that the young women who are initiated in this manner tend to show more chronic and severe psychological distress and are more likely to become drug addicted and marginalized from the core gang membership.

The third form of initiation involves committing a criminal act with other gang members. Usually the crimes involve participation in a robbery or assault, such as a drive-by shooting. These activities prove to the core gang members that the young Latina is willing to take risks and is unafraid to "back up" her fellow members in their activities. Although these more serious offenses may be necessary to pass the initiation rite, Latina gangsters predominantly commit theft and misdemeanor crimes during the actual tenure of their affiliation with the gang. More serious felonies, such as armed robbery and aggravated assault, are less prevalent in the group, often because the male members do not approve of the women's involvement in such activities.

A recurring question regarding female gang members is whether they are autonomous or are affiliated with a corresponding male gang (coed gang). There is evidence of independent all-female gang enterprises. All-female gangs that have existed, or do exist, tend to have territorial and economic foundations. The women claim a specific area or neighborhood that they protect, usually in order to defend their economic interests. However, rarely have Latina gangs been successful at maintaining complete autonomy from the male counterparts in their area. This interdependence may be rooted in traditional Latino values, such as the importance of the family and machismo, wherein the female naturally takes a less prominent role in the social structure and places herself as secondary to the male.

When the focus of evaluation shifts from the larger

social level to a more intimate level of individual attitudes and beliefs, one notices a distinct difference in how Latino male gang members perceive the role of females within the gang, as opposed to how the women in the gang perceive their own gender roles. Latino male gang members often exhibit an attitude of territoriality toward the women in the gang. The male gang members tend to think of the women as having a lower status in the gang structure and as available sex objects, although this belief may be a form of posturing. Research indicates that the males relegate the women to a second-class status in the gang, believing them to be potential liabilities in giving information to rival gangs, as well as not valuing the women's adeptness in providing "backup" during organized gang activity. Ethnographic interviews also show that gang males tend to view female gang members as sex objects who are readily available for companionship, generally without commitment. A popular belief among male gangsters is that they have the privilege to be "players," or to have more than one concurrent relationship with the homegirls. However, this same behavior is viewed as detrimental and unfavorable if it is exhibited by a homegirl.

Interestingly, Latina gangsters tend to have a different perspective of their own roles in the gangs. Although the research indicates that Latina homegirls will concede their lesser status in the gang, the women often attribute the lower status to the males wanting to protect them by not allowing them to participate in the higher-risk, violent activities. Otherwise, these young women tend to view themselves as quite independent and as major forces within the gang. Specifically, they view themselves as fearless, strong, and autonomous from external or male control. Latina gangsters often describe themselves as vanguards in breaking archaic gender roles that have been perpetuated within their communities and families. Thus they would not tolerate being in an abusive relationship, nor would they allow themselves to become dependent on a male in the raising of their children. Furthermore, the women view themselves as having central roles in making the higher-risk behaviors possible by carrying weapons or delivering drugs for their male counterparts. Latina gangsters also tend to believe that their status can be elevated by increasing their fighting prowess, even though excessive violence in the women is not highly valued by their male peers in the gang.

There are several methods by which a Latina gang member can leave a gang. The most absolute option is death. The second option is for the young woman to request to leave the gang and to be "jumped out." Jumping out involves being beaten by several of the active gang members, usually for a longer period of time than was required to be initiated. Often the person requesting to be "jumped out" will be seen as a traitor by some of the active members, and this person will continue to be targeted and challenged to fight even after leaving the gang.

The most common manner of leaving the gang involves "fading out" or simply distancing oneself from the gang over time. This process consists of the Latina gangster "hanging out" less with the homeboys and homegirls and then eventually not participating at all in gang-oriented activities. The advantage of "fading out" is that the young Latina is able to maintain a friendly but distant relationship with the other members of the gang and is not viewed as a traitor. Fading out is often a function of maturity and life circumstances. As the Latina gangster grows older, she matures and may begin to value different experiences in her life, leading to a shift in priorities from the gang to self-improvement. For many Latina homegirls, the primary factor that incites their maturity is motherhood. As noted previously, motherhood is a highly valued role among Latina gang members. Thus part of being a good mother involves lessened gang participation and a renewed desire to live for and be available to the child. Under such circumstances the process of fading out allows the young Latina mother to exit the gang in a relatively safe and quiet manner.

SOURCES: Campbell, Anne. 1991. *The Girls in the Gang*. 2nd ed. Cambridge: Basil Blackwell; Huff, C. Ronald, ed. 1996. *Gangs in America*. 2nd ed. Thousand Oaks, CA: Sage Publications; Miller, Jody. 2001. *One of the Guys: Girls, Gangs, and Gender*. New York: Oxford University Press; Vigil, James Diego. 2002. *A Rainbow of Gangs: Street Cultures in the Mega City*. University of Texas Press; Walker-Barnes, Chanequa J., and Craig A. Mason. 2001. "Perceptions of Risk Factors for Female Gang Involvement among African American and Hispanic Women." *Youth and Society* 32, no. 3:303–336.

Guadalupe Gutiérrez

GARCÍA, CRISTINA (1958–)

Highly acclaimed novelist Cristina García was born in Havana, Cuba, on July 4, 1958, just six months before the revolution that would shape her life and fiction. Her parents, seeking political asylum, immigrated to Queens, New York, with two-year-old Cristina and her younger sister in 1960.

García admits to having kept to herself when she was a girl: "I was so shy . . . that I refused to answer the telephone until I was 10 years old." As a teenager during the early 1970s, García was sheltered by her mother, who was suspicious and disapproving of the liberal social changes sweeping America. As a result, her parents sent García and her sister to study French in Europe during the summer. "We were packed off in late June," recalls García, "to the safety of a quaint

Swiss town on the banks of Lake Geneva far from the dangerous hippies."

After high school García earned an undergraduate degree in political science from Barnard College, as well as a master's degree in international studies from Johns Hopkins University. Deciding against becoming a diplomat, García became instead a correspondent for *Time* magazine. A successful journalist, she was promoted to bureau chief in Miami, where she covered Latin American assignments.

In 1984 García and her sister traveled to Cuba. Here she "rediscovered half of [her] family": the relatives on her mother's side who had remained since the 1959 revolution. Upon her return to the United States following a two-week visit to the island, García suffered an overwhelming sense of loss due to her separation from her Cuban family, particularly her maternal grandmother, with whom García had been very close as a child.

In 1988 García took a leave of absence from *Time* to try writing fiction. At UCLA she enrolled in a women writers' course and began working on what would become *Dreaming in Cuban* (1992). Inspired by her experiences in Cuba, García began to cull her imagination, basing several of her novel's characters on the family members she had left behind. According to the author, *Dreaming in Cuban* functions as "an exploration of the very different ways you can be Cuban." The core of the narrative focuses on three generations of the del Pino family: Celia, the family's matriarch and loyal supporter of El Líder (Castro); her two daughters, Lourdes, the staunch American patriot and owner of two Yankee Doodle Bakeries, and Felicia, the politically ambivalent and psychologically unstable rebel; and Pilar, Lourdes's daughter, the novel's protagonist and García's alter ego. Fiercely independent and suspicious of her parents' diatribes against Cuba and her relatives there, Pilar is initially elated at her reunion with her beloved grandmother, Celia, only to realize that she ultimately belongs in the United States.

Upon its release *Dreaming* earned high accolades. *The New York Times* hailed the book as a "dazzling first novel . . . [announcing] the debut of a writer, blessed with a poet's ear for language, a historian's fascination with the past and a musician's intuitive understanding of the ebb and flow of emotion." The novel was nominated for the National Book Award in 1992, and García was awarded a Guggenheim Fellowship and a Whiting Writers' Prize.

Continuing to explore historical, national events and the construction of truth, García released her second novel, *The Agüero Sisters* in 1997. "I was curious about the stories people told themselves to get by," reports García, "about what happens when memory and nostalgia and loss get all wrapped up together." The

Popular author Cristina García. Photograph by and courtesy of Norma E. Quintana.

protagonists and title characters, Constancia and Reina Agüero, have been separated for thirty years. Reunited in Miami, the sisters seek the truth behind their mother's suspicious death and their father's suicide. Paralleling the mystery, the natural history of Cuba is revealed through the journal entries of the sisters' father, Ignacio Agüero, an ornithologist.

Like her first work, García's second novel was highly praised. Julia Alvarez called it "a rich and complex novel about the entanglements of family and the possibility of redemption that comes with knowing the story of the past." The *New York Times* referred to the novel as "haunting," noting García's "blending of hallucinatory imagery of Gabriel García Márquez with a homespun American idiom."

García has recently completed her third novel, *Traveling through the Flesh*, which features a middle-aged Chinese-Cuban-American man, Domingo Chen, as the book's protagonist. The writer is working on an idea for her fourth book, and when she is not traveling to writers' conferences and the lecture circuit, she lives in California with her daughter, Pilar.

See also Literature

SOURCES: García, Cristina. 1999. "Star-Spangled." *Washington Post*, July 18, W21; Kirkwood, Cynthia Adina. 1992. "A Cuban Odyssey." *Los Angeles Times*, August 30, E7; *LiteraryEn-*

cyclopedia (online). "Garcia [Garcia], Cristina." www.litencyc.com/php/speople.php?rec-true&UID=5910 (accessed July 9, 2005); Viera, Joseph M. 1998. "Exile among Exiles: Cristina García." *Poets and Writers Magazine*, September/October, 40–45.

Joseph M. Viera

GARCÍA, EVA CARRILLO DE (1883–1979)

María de los Angeles Guadalupe Eva Carrillo y Gallardo was born in 1883 in Los Angeles, California. After her mother's death when she was only five, Eva became a ward of the Methodist Church. She was raised in Mexico under the care of Methodist missionary Dr. Levi Salmans. She attended the Colegio Juárez in Guanajuato, Mexico, and graduated from a nursing school in Kansas. A devout Methodist, she graduated from the Chicago Training School for City, Home, and Foreign Missions, a branch of Northwestern University. She worked as a nurse in the Battle Creek Sanitarium in Michigan, the famous Kellogg health facility of the Seventh-Day Adventist Church.

Eva met her husband Alberto García in Battle Creek. They married in New Orleans in 1911, and the couple had eight children. She worked at the George O. Robinson Orphanage in San Juan, Puerto Rico, and lived in Central America and Mexico with her husband before they moved to Austin, Texas, in 1915.

During the early decades of the twentieth century Mexicans in Austin were segregated by neighborhood and schools and in lower-tier economic opportunities. In 1920 she joined her husband Alberto in publishing the first Spanish-language newspaper in the city, *La Vanguardia*. As a trained nurse, she also sought to educate others about tuberculosis through health education drives. She also worked with youths and city officials to combat juvenile delinquency. In addition to her family and community work, Eva Carrillo García taught Spanish at the Austin Military Academy.

A community activist particularly with regard to public health and child welfare, García joined the League of Women Voters of Texas and during the late 1930s became a founding member of the Ladies League of United Latin American Citizens (LULAC) council in Austin. As a member of LULAC, she fought to desegregate Austin's movie theaters, swimming pools, and schools during the 1940s and 1950s. She and her husband encouraged Mexican Americans to buy property, pay the poll tax, defend their rights, vote, and claim their share of the American dream.

Eva Carrillo García served as an elder at University Methodist Church and participated in a number of Methodist women's groups. She also helped found the second Mexican Methodist church in Austin. She and her husband believed in the importance of education and sent six children to the University of Texas at Austin at a time when few Mexican Americans graduated from high school. She died at the age of ninety-six in 1979 and was honored during National Women's History Month in 1989 by the Austin Commission for Women.

SOURCES: "Eva García." Vertical Files, Austin History Center, Austin, Texas; Orozco, Cynthia E. 1996. "García, Eva de Carillo." In *New Handbook of Texas*, 3:82–83. Austin: Texas State Historical Association.

Cynthia E. Orozco

GARCÍA, PROVIDENCIA "PROVI" (1908–1995)

Provi García was the most successful executive in Latin American music publishing during the epoch when much of the standard repertoire was being created by the most famous and lasting composers from throughout Latin America. In that golden age, spanning the late 1940s through the 1960s, García was the central figure in recruiting and retaining such never-eclipsed composers as the Puerto Ricans Rafael Hernández and Pedro Flores, the Mexicans Agustín Lara, Dámaso Pérez Prado, and Lorenzo Barcelata, the Brazilian Ari Barroso, Cuban Miguel Matamoros, and numerous other Dominican and South American greats for Peer–Southern Music, which became the largest publisher and rights holder for Latin American music in the world.

Born into a large family in Arroyo, situated in the southern sugar belt of Puerto Rico, García became attuned to the Afro-Caribbean music that emanated from the majority black and mulatto population of the southern towns. The strong-willed, daring, and flamboyant redhead defied her parents after graduating from high school and eloped into a disastrous marriage to a womanizer. To escape her husband and the shame of the failed marriage (her divorce became final in 1939), García moved to New York in the early 1930s. In 1936 García began work as a secretary for Southern Music, which later became Peer International, and soon became the director of the Latin American section. Through the force of her charm, exuberance, and honesty, as well as her infallible ear for music and her knowledge of the Hispanic community in New York and later abroad, García became a safe bridge for Latin American composers, band directors, and musicians to the commercial music industry. For this particular market, Provi García was the ultimate word because she represented the owner of the company, Ralph Peer, himself—and after his death, his wife Monique, and still later Ralph Peer II.

In the early days, when composer-performers were living hand-to-mouth by playing in cabarets in New York, San Juan, and Havana, Provi García's infallible taste led her to sign up compositions and even the entire repertoire of such untapped talent as Rafael Hernández, Pedro Flores, Osvaldo Barrés, Consuelo Velásquez, Manuel Espelón, and many others. Her thorough understanding of commercial viability also resulted in her signing for the Peer–Southern Music Company the standards that today are still the heart of the Peer–Southern Music catalog and are considered all-time classics of Latin American music: *Bésame mucho, Frenesí, Brazil, Cuando calienta el sol, Me lo dijo Adela, María Elena, Aquellos ojos verdes, Bahia, Inolvidable primavera*, and *Alma llanera*, among many others.

García was also instrumental in facilitating the "crossover" of Latin American music into mainstream American pop, especially during the years of the mambo and cha-cha-cha crazes in the 1950s and 1960s, when, among others, the Pérez Prado recordings of *Patricia* and *Cherry Pink and Apple Blossom White*, Nat King Cole's *Aquellos ojos verdes*, and Alan Dale's *Sweet and Gentle* shot to number one in the United States and abroad. Provi García's magic extended to the next generation when she became an important link in the success of Spanish crooner Julio Iglesias.

Over the years Provi García built up and became the director of a network of offices that stretched from New York to the major cities of Latin America to Australia and even Japan. She served as the chief administrator over the regional directors, who were all Hispanic men. As the only woman of stature in the field, she faced indignities and insults with a smile and a great capacity for diplomacy. In fact, she was known for her great sense of humor and ribald joking, and on many occasions she easily turned adversity into outrageously funny stories for her close-knit family. At one point, when corruption became rampant in some South American offices and she had to clean house, she was spat upon by a male regional director, but this never dampened her spirits nor her resolve to continue developing the music of Latin culture for the world. In New York's *El Diario/La Prensa* on November 26, 1971, Alberto Alonso published the following sketch of García:

> Seated behind a broad tabletop desk covered with contracts, newspaper clippings, photos of performers, and documents along the lines of records and composers, an elegant and jovial Provi García maintains a frenetic schedule in her large office-salon on Broadway. Each day she receives composers with dreams of making the International Hit Parade with one of their pieces, authors anxious for advantageous advances for their works and recording executives hoping to register a million in sales for their singers, now idols of mass audiences.
>
> Provi García receives them all equally, treating each one individually with proverbial Puerto Rican hospitality and courtesy, which she has elevated to a personality trait.

Although Provi García was sought after romantically by the wealthy and famous, in whose circles she traveled, she decided early in her career that she would never marry again nor ever have to be accountable to a male other than the president of the company. Never interested in her career for financial gain and using her salary as a stopgap and security for her large, extended family, Provi García never became wealthy herself, even while making millions for Peer and for her composers. Always working behind the scenes on the business end of the music industry, in humility Provi García never pursued the publicity and fame of the composers and performers she promoted, and to this day her name and accomplishments are known only to insiders in Latin music. She died of heart disease while in semiretirement in Río Piedras, Puerto Rico, in 1995. Years earlier she had had a massive heart attack that remanded her back to Puerto Rico during New York's frigid winters. Provi García's legacy remains, not only in the continued flourishing Latin music in the United States, but also in the work of her nephew, Nicolás Kanellos, who has tried to emulate her example in the world of Latino literary publishing.

Provi García with Mexican singer Pedro Flores. Courtesy of Arte Público Press.

See also Entrepreneurs

SOURCE: "Providencia García." Dr. Nicolás Kanellos Collection. Recovering the U.S. Hispanic Literary Heritage Archives, University of Houston.

Nicolás Kanellos

GARCÍA CORTESE, AIMEE (1929–)

Reverend Aimee García Cortese is a fully bilingual (English- and Spanish-speaking) Puerto Rican woman born and raised in the South Bronx, New York City. She was nurtured in the Christian faith in a Pentecostal church where she was told by the elders in her church that if she was indeed being called by God to serve as a minister, one of the tests would be to survive street preaching over a period of time. Therefore, her career in public speaking began on the gang-ridden and impoverished streets of New York City, where she engaged in street evangelism by handing out evangelistic tracts, preaching, and giving her testimony "al aire libre" (open air), which was the popular style of Pentecostal Christians, particularly the recently converted and those interested in the ordained ministry. She obtained the credential of license to preach in 1951 and became a missionary evangelist in Latin America (Puerto Rico, Cuba, and Mexico) for the Spanish Assemblies of God denomination. She engaged in pastoral work beginning in 1957 when she served as associate minister to her father, Reverend Rafael García, in the South Bronx congregation of Thessalonica Christian Church, where she had earlier served as educational director. Although she had the theological education required of those seeking to enter the ordained ministry in the denomination, the opportunities for women were nonexistent at the time. Her journey led her to join the Wesleyan Methodist Church in Puerto Rico, where she was ordained in 1962 to become one of the pioneers among Latina women in the ordained Christian ministry. Alongside her husband, Joseph Cortese, she worked as part of the Billy Graham Evangelistic Team in Latin America (Puerto Rico, Venezuela, Colombia, and Guatemala) and served as a delegate to the First Congress on Evangelism in West Berlin, Germany, in 1966, sponsored by the Billy Graham Association.

In her commitment to serve, Reverend García Cortese did not limit herself to the spiritual well-being of people but also sought to gain training as a mental health counselor and psychotherapist. From 1969 to 1972 she served in the political arena as a legislative aide to her brother, New York state senator Robert García, where she worked on the issues of housing, welfare, and drug rehabilitation in the South Bronx. This prompted her to combine community social justice efforts with her ministerial work in 1973, which resulted in her becoming the first female chaplain for the New York State Department of Corrections. She worked with female and male inmates in various facilities such as Bedford Hills, Ossining (Sing-Sing), Taconic, and Bayview until 1983. She continued to be active in civic affairs as a clergy leader of the city of New York and as part of New York City mayor Ed Koch's Commission on Hispanic Affairs and Commission on Bias Affairs.

Although a decade earlier the ordination of women had been a moot issue, García Cortese was ordained in New York State by the Spanish (Eastern District of the) Assemblies of God Pentecostal denomination in 1974. She continued to work interdenominationally as a preacher, counselor, and speaker, as well as fulfill the role of wife and mother to three daughters and a son. While she was volunteering as a counselor at Brooklyn Gospel Tabernacle (currently Brooklyn Tabernacle) in Brooklyn, New York City, during the late 1970s and 1980s, her daughters came to be known as the Cortese Trio, with Dámaris (now Cortese Carbaugh) as the lead singer. They sang with vocal cords that impressed not only the congregants attending the megachurch but also record companies and commercial media. The Cortese Trio became a key component of more than 100-member Brooklyn Tabernacle Choir, with Dámaris as one of the soloists, which later won several Grammy Awards. In 1983 García Cortese founded a church known as Crossroads Tabernacle in the Bronx, associated with the English-speaking Assemblies of God, where she continues her full-time pastorate and spearheads efforts to provide vital services that meet the spiritual and physical needs of her congregants and the surrounding community. Her ministerial life can be summarized by using her own words: "I want to be where the people are; that's where Jesus was."

As a dynamic orator very well grounded in scripture and a wealth of experiences in diverse areas of ministry, she is consistently invited to serve as a keynote speaker, workshop facilitator, and retreat leader in churches, community-based organizations, college campuses, and conferences throughout the United States and in Puerto Rico. Those who have benefited from her talks have credited her effective public speaking and charisma to her good sense of humor and gentle, down-to-earth wisdom.

See also Pentecostal Church; Religion

SOURCES: Pérez y González, María Elizabeth. 2000. *Puerto Ricans in the United States.* Westport, CT: Greenwood Press; Sánchez Korrol, Virginia. 1988. "In Search of Unconventional Women: Histories of Puerto Rican Women in Religious Vocations before Mid-century." *Oral History Review* 16, no. 2 (Fall): 47–63.

María Pérez y González

GARCÍA-AGUILERA, CAROLINA (1949–)

Award-winning Latina author Carolina García-Aguilera was born in Havana, Cuba, to a family with deep roots in the island's history. One of her ancestors, Francisco Vicente Aguilera, was honored for his service in Cuba's war for independence against Spain by having his profile imprinted on the Cuban 100 peso's Cubanos bill. Soon after the 1959 Cuban Revolution García-Aguilera moved to New York City with her family before settling in Miami Beach.

García-Aguilera attended Miss Porter's School in Farmington, Connecticut. She received her B.A. at Rollins College in Florida, from which she graduated with a double degree in history and political science. After Rollins she studied for a master's degree in language and linguistics at Georgetown University in Washington, D.C. In 1973 she moved to Asia and lived first in Hong Kong, then in Tokyo, and later in Beijing. In 1981 she returned to the United States and began studies at the University of South Florida in Tampa, where in 1983 she earned an M.B.A. with a concentration in finance.

After marriage and motherhood García-Aguilera became inspired by the idea of writing mystery fiction with a Cuban American woman as the protagonist. In 1986 she became a private investigator. "I wanted to be a private eye so I could utilize my experience and write about it," explains the author. For ten years she worked in the rough-and-tumble environment of Miami as a private eye, always gathering experience she would eventually incorporate into her novels. Raising three daughters and maintaining a long-distance marriage, she was able to grow a successful business even when it required her to work at all hours, often under hazardous conditions. The experience of handling complex and dangerous cases gave her a solid understanding of the profession that would serve her well as a mystery writer.

Cuban American mystery writer Carolina García-Aguilera. Photograph by Ali, 1999. Courtesy of HarperCollins Publishers.

With the experience gained from having worked as a private investigator, García-Aguilera took a sabbatical and began working on her first novel in the Lupe Solano mystery series. In 1996 her first book, *Bloody Waters*, was published. Her mysteries feature a savvy, sexy, and sophisticated private investigator, Lupe Solano, as the protagonist who works and lives in the vibrant city of Miami. Like the author who breathed life into her, Lupe is a strong-willed, yet family-oriented, Catholic and *muy cubana.* Smart and witty, Lupe Solano drives a Mercedes and hates to shoot people because "it messes up her nails." Combining a compelling story with subplots drawing upon Cuban politics and history, García-Aguilera developed a critically acclaimed six-book mystery series.

More than just a mystery writer, García-Aguilera draws upon her life experiences to write novels that educate as well as entertain. Each book in the Lupe Solano series develops subplots around history, Hispanic culture, and global politics. The series quickly won an international audience, and Lupe's adventures are read in eight languages, distributed in ten countries, and acclaimed for their intriguing historical plotlines and cultural insights. García-Aguilera has been identified with a new wave of Hispanic crime/mystery writers, including Rodolfo Anaya and Lucha Corpi, whose works dispel age-old stereotypes about Hispanics.

García-Aguilera's understanding of the complexities of investigation, law, and criminal behavior permeate her writing. She continues to hold a private investigator's license in the state of Florida and occasionally takes cases, keeping her investigative instincts sharpened. Not resting on her successes, she has taken her first steps toward writing in other genres, as well as for television and film. Depasse Entertainment has purchased the film and television rights for her first book, *Bloody Waters,* and has a series in development at ABC television.

As a wife and mother raising three children, García-Aguilera is also familiar with the fine line many woman walk, balancing professional achievement with personal happiness. She has achieved professional success, developed real-life coping skills, and created and maintained a thriving investigation business while carving her own niche in the supersaturated market of mystery fiction, where novels by Hispanic women were previously nonexistent.

In 2000 García-Aguilera's fifth book in the series,

Havana Heat, received the Shamus Award for best private eye novel published that year. This award is given by the Writers of America to honor excellent work in the detective/private eye genre. In 1999 her fourth book in the series, *Miracle in Paradise*, won the Flamingo Prize for the best novel set in Florida. Her other recent mysteries include *Bitter Sugar* (2002) and *One Hot Summer* (2003). Cristina García-Aguilera just released her eighth book, *Luck of the Draw*, in 2004.

SOURCES: Brinson, Claudia Smith. 2000. "Gun-Toting Mystery Writer to Be Honored." *State*, December 4, 1; Cogdill, Oline H. 2001. "Exploring Cuban Exiles' Lost Heritage." *Sun-Sentinel*, October 17, C+; Fichtner, Margarita. 2000. "House of Mystery." *Miami Herald*, October 1, K+; Flores, J. C. 2000. "Carolina Garcia-Aguilera: Creates a New Kind of Private Eyes." *LatinHeat*, July, 11, 18; García-Aguilera, Carolina. 2001. Interview by Rebecca Torres-Wilkner, September 15; *People*. 1996. "Talking with Carolina Garcia-Aguilera." April.

Rebecca Torres-Wilkner

GARCÍAZ, MARÍA (1957–)

Born on February 13, 1957, in Salt Lake City, Utah, María Garcíaz is the executive director of Salt Lake City Neighborhood Housing Services (SLNHS), a nonprofit housing agency that combines community development with at-risk youth employment. Her dedication to affordable housing and home ownership stems from her own working-class childhood in Salt Lake City. She grew up in a single-parent household with five brothers and one sister. Her mother would repair their dilapidated living quarters, but the landlords would reward her hard work by raising the rent beyond her means. In 1970, with the pooled wages of every family member, including thirteen-year-old María, the Garcíazes purchased their own home.

"The Chicano Movement saved my life." Facing intense discrimination in school, María Garcíaz began to act out. Chicano students at the University of Utah visited her high school and encouraged her and other Mexican Americans to see a world beyond the stifling atmosphere of indifferent and at times hostile teachers. Garcíaz remembers her mentor's words: "Don't become the loser they want you to be." She turned her life around and attended the University of Utah, where she became a very visible and vocal Chicana activist.

Her own identity as a Chicana did not necessarily influence how her mother and siblings viewed themselves. "My mother is Spanish; one brother is Mexican; my sister Mexican-American; I am Chicana. Three brothers are Hispanic and the youngest is Latino." Her family's divergent cultural locations speak volumes about the heterogeneity within Latino communities, a heterogeneity that cuts across region, gender, religion, sexuality, and even individual families.

After graduating from college María Garcíaz worked as a probation officer but was disturbed by the two-tiered justice system she encountered. A Latino youth with a minor infraction would receive a harsh sentence, while a Euro-American counterpart who had committed a more serious offense would merit only a slap on the wrist. She earned a reputation as a skilled, caring probation officer. She asserts that she still feels "more comfortable with gang bangers than politicians." Desiring to help youths on a larger scale, she began to volunteer with Salt Lake Neighborhood Housing Services in 1982 and eight years later became its executive director. Along the way she received a master's degree in education from Utah State University.

Since 1977 Salt Lake Neighborhood Housing Services has revitalized working-class neighborhoods, such as Fairpark and Guadalupe. With the motto "Rebuilding Neighborhoods . . . one block at a time," SLNS embraces a multifaceted approach: building new homes, rehabilitating older structures, conducting home-ownership classes, and providing low-interest financing. Furthermore, since 1982 more than 1,200 adolescents have participated in YouthWorks, a program for at-risk teenagers, many of whom are referred by the juvenile courts. These young people earn money while learning construction trades as they refurbish neighborhood homes. They also participate in other community projects, such as creating a storefront mural. YouthWorks has an 80 percent success rate, with success defined as completing high school and avoiding further brushes with law enforcement. Many former participants have attended college and pursued careers as professionals and small-business owners. Building homes for people like themselves has given teenagers pride in their own efforts and in their neighborhoods. Journalist Bill Moyers profiled YouthWorks in a television special as "one of the leading programs in the country dealing with youth and youth related issues." In 1990, if one drove around the Westside neighborhood of Guadalupe, one would find about half the houses boarded up and abandoned; today only two such structures remain.

Salt Lake Neighborhood Housing Services has responded proactively to the dramatic demographic change that has occurred during the last three decades. In 1970 only 33,000 Latinos lived in Salt Lake City. Today more than 200,000 Latinos call the city home. Although working-class neighborhoods, like Guadalupe, remain predominantly Latino, newcomers from Sudan, Bosnia, and Iraq have also settled in these areas, communities with a greater sense of hope than despair.

María Garcíaz and her husband, real-estate broker David Galván (María jokes that she met David at a 7–11) made the decision to raise their children in the

Guadalupe neighborhood. They have built a Craftsman-inspired home within a block from her office, and across the street is the proposed site for a new affordable housing complex. In her words: "We talk about building communities, but then we don't live there. We talk about celebrating diversity but then we live in all-white neighborhoods." María Garcíaz and David Galván provide a model for community activists, people who give new meaning to the phrase "the personal is political."

SOURCES: "A Morning Conversation with Community Members." 2004. Workshop held as part of the "Mirando Adelante: Looking Forward Conference," Salt Lake City Library, Salt Lake City, UT, October 2; Garcíaz, María. 2004. Interview by Vicki L. Ruiz, October 2; Salt Lake City Housing Services. www.slnhs.org (accessed July 10, 2005).

Vicki L. Ruiz

GARMENT INDUSTRY

The garment industry has been a major employer of Latinas. As a labor-intensive industry, garment manufacturing has sought low-wage workers, relying on immigrants, migrants, and women. Puerto Rican and Dominican women in New York City, Mexican women in Los Angeles, and Cuban women in Miami have all found themselves concentrated in garment-industry jobs. More recently, Central American immigrant women have been following in their footsteps in all three cities. As the garment industry continues its search for cheap labor through globalization and export-processing zones, Latinas are affected by the garment industry in their countries of origin as well.

Puerto Rican women found jobs in New York City's garment industry after World War I. Classified advertisements called for skilled and unskilled garment workers, and by 1925 more Puerto Rican women, 17 percent, were employed in factory work than in any other occupation. Confronting the need to contribute income to their household economies and care for their children, many turned to the home needlework industry despite its low wages and exploitative conditions. Between 1930 and 1936 the employment service of Puerto Rico's Department of Labor placed about 600 women. An overwhelming majority, about 80 percent, secured jobs as domestics or operatives, many in the garment industry.

As Puerto Rican migration increased after World War II, so did women's concentration in the garment industry, especially in undergarments, dressmaking, skirts, and blouses. New York was still the center of the U.S. garment industry. Through social networks women helped each other migrate and find garment-industry jobs. Encountering a wide range of working conditions, many Puerto Rican women found jobs in

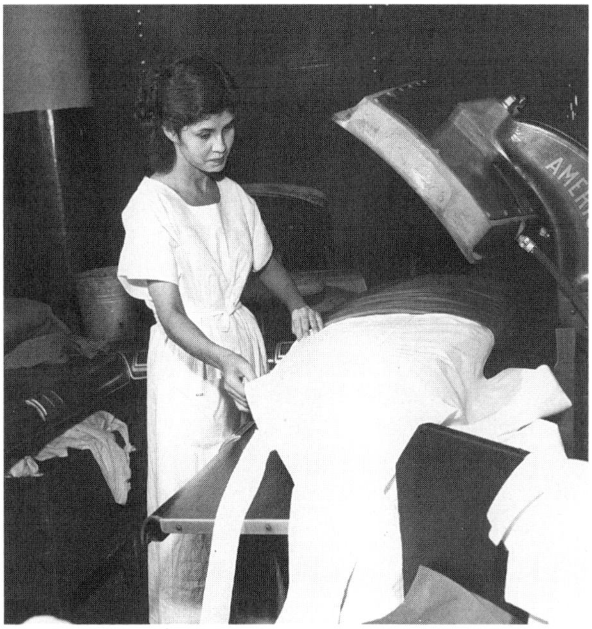

In the 1940s Puerto Rican women migrated to U.S. urban areas and found jobs in low-wage labor industries. Courtesy of the Offices of the Government of Puerto Rico in the United States. Centro Archives, Centro de Estudios Puertorriqueños, Hunter College, CUNY.

union shops and became members of the International Ladies Garment Workers' Union. By 1950, 40 percent of Puerto Rican women were in the workforce, compared with 35 percent of women citywide, and a substantial number of Puerto Rican women, 72 percent, worked in manufacturing. Yet the garment industry was about to change. After a postwar economic boom competition and imports increased, sending the garment industry in search of lower wages. As the garment manufacturers left New York, Puerto Rican women found fewer jobs and deteriorating conditions in the jobs that remained. Section work increased, in which workers sewed only a portion of each garment instead of the entire garment. Contracting and subcontracting increased as manufacturers and retailers sent garments to small shops for assembly. Sweatshops proliferated. Dominican women, whose migration to New York City increased in the late 1960s and 1970s, encountered this two-tiered garment industry, where the remaining decent jobs were engulfed by sweatshops.

The garment industry relocated to lower-wage, nonunion regions of the United States, including Los Angeles, where it grew steadily during the mid-1950s. As early as 1924 Los Angeles had become the fourth-largest garment center in the United States, and by the 1930s the majority of workers were Mexican and Mexican American women. In the post–World War II era the industry grew and shifted from skilled suit and cloak manufacturing to the lesser-skilled sportswear and swimwear trades, as well as lower-cost dresses. Mexican and Mexican American women were concentrated in the lesser-skilled, lower-paid trades. As in New York City, the structure of the industry shifted, with increases in section work and contracting. As Edna Bonacich and Richard P. Appelbaum conclude, there was "a fairly severe ethnic division of labor, with whites at the top, Asians in the middle and to some extent, at the bottom, and Latinos mainly at the bottom." Hence, while a few Mexican Americans became contractors, most were assembly workers in small shops, many of which were underground. Conditions were harsh, with low, piece-rate wages and no benefits, seasonal work and no job security, harsh supervision, long hours, and persisting homework despite its illegality. Undocumented workers were the most vulnerable to exploitation.

Miami's garment industry grew with the arrival of Cuban immigrants and in the context of an economic enclave of immigrant businesses, where employers and employees were of the same nationality. Between the early 1960s and 1973 garment employment increased from fewer than 7,000 to more than 24,000. While most of the manufacturers were Jewish, the overwhelming majority of the contractors, 90 percent, were Cuban men, and the overwhelming majority of the workers, 95 percent, were Cuban women. Like their counterparts in New York and Los Angeles, many worked in unregulated shops or in homework. Scholars debate whether economic enclaves shield workers from exploitation in the broader labor market and benefit the immigrant group as a whole or whether employment in enclaves is just another form of exploitation.

Latinas have also been affected by the garment industry beyond these major garment centers. Puerto Rican women who migrated to Philadelphia after World War II encountered industry changes comparable to those in New York City. Mexican American women in El Paso, Texas, confronted an employer who had left New York in search of cheaper, nonunion labor with a strike lasting from 1972 to 1974 that demanded union recognition and better conditions. Many Cuban women in New Jersey, like their counterparts in Miami, worked in garment-industry jobs. Hence the availability of garment-industry jobs has shaped Latinas' migration patterns. Because Latinas turned to garment-industry jobs as one of the few avenues of employment available to them, their employment in the industry, as well as the wages and conditions in those jobs, has shaped not only their own economic well-being and that of their families, but also the economic well-being of their communities and of the inner cities.

SOURCES: Bonacich, Edna, and Richard P. Appelbaum. 2000. *Behind the Label: Inequality in the Los Angeles Apparel Industry*. Berkeley: University of California Press; Fernández Kelly, M. Patricia, and Ana García. 1989. "Hispanic Women and Homework: Women in the Informal Economy of Miami and Los Angeles." In *Homework: Historical and Contemporary Perspectives on Paid Labor at Home*, ed. Eileen Boris and Cynthia R. Daniels, 165–179. Urbana: University of Illinois Press; Ortiz, Altagracia, ed. 1996. *Puerto Rican Women and Work: Bridges in Transnational Labor*. Philadelphia: Temple University Press; Whalen, Carmen Teresa. 2002. "Sweatshops Here and There: The Garment Industry, Latinas, and Labor Migrations." *International Labor and Working-Class History* 61 (Spring): 45–68.

Carmen Teresa Whalen

GIANT

Based on the novel by Edna Ferber, the epic film *Giant* chronicles twenty-five years in the lives of wealthy rancher and Texan patriot Bick Benedict (Rock Hudson) and his wife Leslie (Elizabeth Taylor). Set amid the backdrop of a dusty Texan wilderness, the film depicts the state's transition from cattle ranching and land wealth to oil-based wealth. The film begins when Bick visits Maryland to purchase a thoroughbred horse from Leslie's father. Despite their different upbringings, the two fall in love, and Leslie returns with Bick to his sprawling 600,000-acre Reata Ranch to embark on their new life. In his final cinema appearance, James Dean portrays Jett Rink, a rough-around-the-edges Reata ranch hand with a grudge against Bick, his employer. Rink's discovery of oil on an inherited patch of land brings initial riches but ultimate ruin.

Throughout the film Leslie and Bick represent the tensions and binaries often perceived between an American East and West, the former civilized yet traditional and unchanging, the latter wild and untamed, but a space of potential and progress. These binaries play out over the issue of Anglo-Mexican relations in Texas. For instance, only a few minutes into the film, and shortly after Leslie has been introduced to her future husband, she asserts, "We really stole Texas, didn't we, Mr. Benedict? I mean, away from Mexico." Bick's face falls and he angrily defends his state, yet his love for Leslie remains unhindered. After marrying, the couple travels to Texas by train, and the screen fills with images of the wild and untamed ranch lands. Once Leslie is settled in Texas, her interest in Reata's Mexican servants leads Bick to instruct, "Don't fuss over those people. You're a Texan now." Despite Bick's warning, Leslie continues to challenge the attitudes of her husband and Anglo-Texan neighbors and sets about trying to improve the living conditions of her Mexican servants. These scenes set Leslie's sophistication and civilized manners apart from her husband. Yet as the film moves forward, Leslie's Maryland home and family remain static and unchanging, while Texas moves rapidly into the future with the discovery of oil.

A central theme of the film addresses the issue of Anglo-Mexican intermarriage. Once married and settled on Reata, Leslie and Bick begin a family. They raise three children and, as the years pass, witness an oil boom and a world war. All grown up, the couple's only son, Jordie (Dennis Hopper), marries Juana, a Mexican woman. A disappointed Bick is forced to rethink his own racist attitudes. His major confrontation with his own and the region's anti-Mexican sentiment serves as the film's climax. The scene begins with Bick, accompanied by Leslie, one of his daughters, his daughter-in-law, Juana, and his mestizo grandson, little Jordie, entering a road-stop diner called Sarge's Place. Sarge and an Anglo waitress eye the family suspiciously, clearly displeased with the mixed company of Anglos and Mexicans. When little Jordie asks for ice cream, Sarge viciously responds, "Ice cream? I thought he'd want a *tamale*." Only begrudgingly does he allow the family to stay. Moments later an elderly Mexican couple and their daughter sit down at a table. "You're in the wrong place, amigo. . . . Your money is no good here," Sarge tells the man as he attempts to usher them out. Bick stands up to defend this family's right to be served, reminding Sarge of the Benedict name. Sarge asks, "And that little papoose back there," referring to little Jordie, "Is he a Benedict too?" This is a pivotal moment in which Bick seems to acknowledge his grandson for the first time. "Yeah. Come to think of it, it *is*." Dramatic fisticuffs ensue to the soundtrack of "The Yellow Rose of Texas." Bick loses the fight, but wins his honor, as well as the renewed respect of Leslie.

Although *Giant* takes a progressive stance on intermarriage, the film's Mexican Texan characters, and Mexican women in particular, are rarely given a voice. Despite the centrality of the taboo love and intermarriage theme to the second half of the film, Juana has few lines and stands by silently while her Anglo counterparts come to terms with their own prejudice. For instance, when Juana is refused service at a beauty salon in Jett Rink's new resort hotel, she silently takes the abuse and calls her husband, Jordie. Smashing lobby furniture and ushering Juana out of salon by the elbow, it is Jordie who arrives to protect and stand up for his wife. In the culminating scene at Sarge's Place, Juana, little Jordie, and the Mexican patrons denied service stand mute while Bick speaks, and fights, for them. Thus the film strips its Mexican characters of their agency. In *Giant* justice is delivered at the initiative, and as the prerogative of, its Anglo characters.

Further, the film depicts Mexican Texans as a racialized "other" whose presence is clearly noted, but only in separate and distinctly marked Mexican spaces. The film ends with a camera focus on Bick's two grandchildren sharing a crib in the Benedict home. Little Jordie stands next to Bick's other blond grandchild while Bick remarks to Leslie, "My own grandson don't even look like one of us. I swear, honey, he looks like a little wetback." Thus even after Bick has seemingly overcome his prejudice following the events in Sarge's Place, he reaffirms the racial otherness of little Jordie. Bick's comments suggest that although he accepts his grandson, he remains unable to question notions of racial difference.

Well received by critics and viewers alike, *Giant* was nominated for ten Academy Awards, and George Stevens won the Oscar for best director. Quickly immortalized as a classic, the film inspired numerous other artistic works, such as Billy Lee Brammer's political novel *The Gay Place* and Tino Villanueva's collection of poems titled *Scenes from the Movie Giant*. Villanueva's poems reveal the enormous impact of the film's theme on his youth while simultaneously capturing the frustration of the Mexicans' silent portrayal in the film. Rehashing the scene in Sarge's Place, he writes: "Two men have organized / Their violence to include me, as I am on the side / Of Rock Hudson, but carry nothing to the fight."

While the film fails to challenge notions of racial difference or grant agency to its Mexican Texan characters, *Giant* remains significant for its portrayal of the postwar nation's increasing attention to issues of equal treatment and inclusion. Released just after *Brown v. Board of Education* and at the dawn of the civil rights movement, *Giant* reveals the growing urgency to overcome racism, segregation, and intolerance. In addition, it brought the reality of Mexican oppression in Texas to the big screen and tackled the highly controversial issue of intermarriage with a progressive position in a decade often remembered for its conservatism.

See also Media Stereotypes

SOURCES: Ferber, Edna. 1952. *Giant.* Garden City, NY: Doubleday; Griffith, Albert J. 1991. "The Scion, the Señorita, and the Texas Ranch Epic: Hispanic Images in Film." *Bilingual Review* 16, no. 1:15–22; Heide, Markus. 1999. " 'When Borders Migrate': The Frontier, Chicano Performance Art, and the Postcolonial in the Americas." *Zeitschrift für Anglistik und Amerikanistik* 47, no. 4:361–377; Pérez-Torres, Rafael. 1998. "Chicano Ethnicity, Cultural Hybridity, and the Mestizo Voice." *American Literature* 70, no. 1 (March): 153–176; Ramírez-Berg, Charles. 1992. "*Bordertown*, the Assimilation Narrative, and the Chicano Social Problem Film." In *Chicanos and Film: Essays on Chicano Representation and Resistance*, ed. Chon A. Noriega, 33–52. New York: Garland Publishing; Stevens, George, director. 1956. *Giant.* From a novel by Edna Ferber. Warner Bros., 201 min. Two-DVD special edition release, 2003; Villanueva, Tino. 1993. *Scenes from the Movie Giant*. Willimantic, CT: Curbstone Press.

Julie Cohen

GÓMEZ CARBONELL, MARÍA (1903–1988)

Vital public servant and stateswoman María Gómez Carbonell was born in Havana on June 29, 1903, the daughter of José Fernando Gómez Santoyo and Candelaria Carbonell Rivero. On her mother's side she came from a long line of political activists involved in Cuba's independence movement. Her maternal grandfather was Néstor Leonelo Carbonell Figueroa, regarded as a hero of the Ten Years' War (1868–1878), who later helped organize José Martí's Cuban Revolutionary Party while he was in exile in Tampa. Three of her maternal uncles, José Manuel, Néstor, and Miguel Angel Carbonell, also had distinguished careers in Cuba's political and civic life. Her own mother's political activism in the Cuban independence efforts earned her praise from Martí himself, who wrote a poem in her honor.

María Gómez Carbonell also dedicated her life to public service, first in Cuba and later in the United States. After graduating from the University of Havana with a doctorate in philosophy and letters, she directed and taught at a primary and secondary school named for her maternal grandfather. She helped found the Alianza Nacional Femenista, which worked for suffrage and women's rights. Gómez Carbonell was the first woman elected to the Cuban Congress. In 1936 she was elected to a four-year term in Cuba's House of Representatives, and she served in the Senate from 1940 to 1944. In Congress she became known for her eloquence, giving more than 160 speeches. As a congressional representative, she focused on issues relating to women's rights, as well as prison reform, juvenile courts, and social welfare legislation. She served in the presidential cabinet in 1941, 1952, and 1958. During World War II she served as the secretary general of the Women's Civil Defense Corps. In addition, she served as president of the National Corporation for Public Assistance, where she focused on issues relating to mental health and homelessness. She was the Cuban delegate to many international conferences in the United States, Europe, and Latin America.

In 1959 she chose political exile in the United States after the overthrow of Cuban president Fulgencio Batista by Fidel Castro. Along with Mercedes García Tudurí and Vicente Cauce, she founded the Cruzada Educativa Cubana (Cuban Educational Crusade, CEC) on August 2, 1962, with the twofold purpose of preserving Cuban culture in the United States and fostering the civic ideals that were necessary to create a democracy once a return to Cuba became possible. Through the CEC she sponsored the Tertulias Infantiles, weekly children's workshops about Cuban history, geography, music, and poetry, as well as about democratic ideals. The CEC had its own weekly show on Spanish-language talk radio, *La Escuelita Cubana,* on radio station WMIE, which informed its audience about the history and culture of Cuba. Over the years the organization sponsored numerous conferences and patriotic celebrations. It offered three prizes, the Juan J. Remos, José de la Luz y Caballero, and Candelaria Carbonell, to honor Cuban exiles who had distinguished themselves in different intellectual enterprises. A 1984 publication edited by Gómez Carbonell compiled the biographies of all those who had received the award.

Gómez Carbonell was also active in the organizations known as the *municipios.* Before the 1959 Cuban Revolution the nation was divided into 126 *municipios* (townships) in six provinces, and each Cuban citizen belonged to a particular *municipio* simply by residence. In Miami Cuban exiles created mutual-aid organizations that were named after each of the *municipios.* When a Cuban arrived in the United States, he or she could contact his or her respective *municipio*-in-exile for referrals and assistance. Gómez Carbonell played an active role in the Municipio de la Habana and published its periodical, *El Habanero* (1969–1980). She also served on the directorate of the Cuban Municipalities in Exile, the umbrella group that supervised the various *municipios.*

Gómez Carbonell was a sought-after speaker in the Cuban exile community, lecturing to various groups around the city on a variety of cultural and historical topics. She contributed essays to the Miami-based newspaper *Diario Las Americas* and authored or edited

As a community icon in both Cuba and the United States, María Gómez Carbonell lectured on cultural and historical topics. Courtesy of Collection Cruzada Educativa Cubana. The Cuban Heritage Collection, Otto G. Richter Library, University of Miami.

several books, including *Cuba y su derecho a la libertad*. Gómez Carbonell died in Miami on May 24, 1988.

SOURCES: García, María Cristina. 1996. *Havana USA: Cuban Exiles and Cuban Americans in South Florida, 1959–1994*. Berkeley: University of California Press; "María Gómez Carbonell." Vertical Files, Cuban Heritage Collection, University of Miami; Rovirosa, Dolores. 1988. "María Gómez Carbonell y una familia excepcional." Manuscript, Cuban Heritage Collection, University of Miami.

María Cristina García

GÓMEZ-POTTER, SOCORRO (1951–)

Born into extreme poverty in El Municipio del Soyate, in the state of Jalisco, Mexico, on May 14, 1951, Socorro Gómez was the last of six children. Her father, a former bracero, sharecropped, while her mother, born and raised in Illinois until she was deported in 1932, taught reading and writing to the children of Soyate. The grinding poverty of the countryside forced the family to seek better work conditions. Initially they moved to Sinaloa, Mexico, where farming was a little better but not adequate to care for six children. Socorro's mother migrated alone to San Diego, California, to become a live-in maid and nanny, while her father moved the family to Tecate, a Mexican border town, to prepare for immigration to the United States. Her mother's job enabled family support, but separated her from the children for more than three years. The separation took an emotional toll, particularly on five-year-old Socorro. "I was reunited with Mercedes Gómez, but I was never reunited with my mother." In 1959 her mother saved enough money to sponsor all of her children to come to the United States, while her father secured employment at Forbes Citrus Ranch in Oasis, California, in the Coachella Valley. At the age of eight Socorro crossed the border with her mother and siblings.

In the United States Gómez experienced discrimination. Reflecting on her educational experiences, she comments: "I knew that there could be pain involved in school experiences from being poor, but not from being Mexican or from being from a different group, or a different language." She adds, "School [in the United States] was painful in a way that was unfamiliar to me." Gómez spent the first years trying to understand English and having the feeling that "people hated [me] for talking." From grades three through seven she felt that she had "no business" being in school and felt deeply inadequate and insecure. "I lost my voice . . . and never reclaimed it." Fortunately, her math skills enabled her to survive. In high school she received encouragement from friends, especially Yolanda Almaraz (later Yolanda Almaraz Esquivel), her teacher, Mr. Keller, and her father. In 1969 she attended California State University, San Bernardino (CSUSB), where she entered a five year B.A./M.A. program in education.

Gómez became one of only twenty-one ethnic Mexican students on campus and an active member of the Chicano student group, Movimiento Estudantil de Chicano de Aztlán (MEChA). She and her friends Analea Torres and Enedina López refused to accept the prevailing attitudes of Chicano leaders regarding women's participation. Jorge and Sal Rios, two MEChA leaders, believed that "the females could cook at their meetings and the females could do certain things, but they could never aspire to a position of leadership." Gómez, Torres, and López mobilized Chicanas, a slim majority among MEChA members, and held new elections. Gómez proudly remembers, "We took it over." As leaders, they organized a food drive to support the United Farm Workers in the Coachella Valley, held cultural activities, and ran symposia on topics such as the antiwar movement and the Chicano moratorium of East Los Angeles. They worked with local African American leaders and welfare activists Frances Grice and Valerie Pope and Chicano organizer Richard González to assist welfare mothers and high-school dropouts in the Mount Vernon area of San Bernardino. Moreover, they secured federal funding from the War on Poverty program to start Casa Ramona Community Center in San Bernardino.

In September 1973 Gómez began teaching elementary school in Mecca, and Yolanda Almaraz took a position at Dateland Middle School in Coachella. Both became outspoken critics of the school system and embroiled in a conflict with school administrators. In her first year Gómez witnessed the superintendent misappropriating federal classroom funds to build tennis courts next to his house. The following year she helped defeat a school bond issue for constructing a new football stadium at the local high school. In 1976 Gómez joined her sister Dora, Almaraz, her colleague Roman Koenig, and parents to form the Community Committee for Alternatives in Education (CCAE), an advocacy group for educational reform, bilingual education, and defending students against abusive teachers. The group raised community awareness that encouraged walkouts by middle- and high-school students in the Coachella Valley to protest physical abuse and child molestation. School officials accused Gómez, Almaraz, Koenig, and a fourth teacher, Charles Marquez, of "unprofessional conduct," removed them from their classrooms, and initiated proceedings to revoke their teaching credentials. Parents and political leaders, including Governor Jerry Brown, rallied to their defense and overturned the district's actions.

Although Gómez won an equal-opportunity lawsuit in 1976 against the Coachella Valley Unified School District for discrimination, she returned to San Bernardino to take a position at Mount Vernon Ele-

Education advocate Socorro Gómez during her first year as a teacher at the Mecca Elementary School, 1973. Courtesy of Matt García.

mentary School and pursue a master's in educational counseling at CSUSB. In 1980 she gave birth to her first and only child, Nadia. In 1983 she accepted a job in San Bernardino as a school counselor at Curtis Middle School, serving low-income black and Latino gang youths. Although the school was ranked ninth from the bottom among low-achieving middle schools in California, Gómez helped create a college preparatory program, College Capable Cats. The success of the program garnered local, state, and national awards and the praise and envy of her peers.

As keynote speaker at an Achievement Council conference at the University of California, Los Angeles, Gómez met members of a team from Rhode Island, including her second husband, Harry Potter. In 1995 she moved to Providence, where she became principal of Alfred A. Lima Elementary School, the only two-way, Spanish-English immersion school in the Rhode Island public school system. With a strong support base of mostly low-income Latino and black Providence parents, Gómez is recognized as a strong defender of bilingual education in Rhode Island and has struggled against administrative and political pressures to reduce the program at Lima Elementary.

See also Bilingual Education

SOURCES: Gómez-Potter, Socorro. 2004. Oral history interviews by Matt García, February 13, 20, and March 12. John Nicholas Brown Center and The Center for the Study of Race and Ethnicity in America, Brown University. "Educating Change: Latina Activism and the Struggle for Educational Equity." www.brown.edu/Research/Coachella/index.html (accessed July 7, 2005).

Matt García

GONZALES, ELVIRA RODRÍGUEZ DE (1883–?)

Born in Mier, Tamaulipas, Mexico, in 1883, Elvira Rodríguez de Gonzales represented the small group of Mexican teachers who taught in segregated schools. Perhaps recognizing her position in the community (similar to that of African American women teachers in the South during the same period), she promoted Mexican American parental involvement in the education of their children, particularly through Spanish-speaking Parent-Teacher Associations (PTAs). Her parents were Nicolás and Prudencia (Reyes) Rodríguez. It is unclear when she arrived in the United States. She married Rafael M. Gonzales, a justice of the piece in San Diego, Texas, and the couple had two children. In 1903 she obtained a college degree from the Laredo Seminary (later the Holding Institute), an institution sponsored by the Methodist Church. She remained a lifelong Methodist. She also taught in Duval and Webb Counties for many years.

During the 1930s she played an important role in the Spanish-Speaking Parent-Teacher Association, a separate organization for Spanish-dominant parents and teachers. From 1927 to 1936 she served as district chair and wrote the yearbook for the small network of Spanish-speaking PTAs. During the celebration of the Texas centennial (the 100th anniversary of Texas independence) she translated articles about Texas history for Spanish-language newspapers. Gonzales was unusual for her times in that as an immigrant, she obtained a college education, and perhaps because of her own position as an immigrant, she proved an effective organizer of Mexican American parents.

SOURCE: Orozco, Cynthia E. 1996. "Elvira Rodríguez de Gonzales." In *New Handbook of Texas*, 5:657–658. Austin: Texas State Historical Association.

Cynthia E. Orozco

GONZÁLEZ, LAURA (1954–)

Laura González writes that her family hails from Mexico, in the coastal areas of Tamaulipas, Veracruz, and

Guerrero. "I was conceived in Acapulco, born in Mexico City [1954] and raised between Mexico City and Acapulco. I started to be bilingual and bicultural since I was 6 years old, when I started kindergarten and later attended 6 years of elementary school at the 'Two United Nations School.' "

González received her licenciatura in social anthropology from the Universidad Iberoamericana in México, D.F., in 1978. Her thesis was published in 1992 by the Universidad Iberoamericana Press as *Respuesta campesina a la revolución en El Bajío.* She received a master's in anthropology from the University of California, Santa Barbara (UCSB), in 1987. This was followed in 1996 by her doctorate in anthropology at UCSB with a dissertation titled "Political Brokers, Ejidos, and State Resources: The Case of Arturo Quiroz Francia, a Peasant Leader from Guanajuato, Mexico." She revised her doctoral dissertation and had it accepted for publication by the Social Science Research Center at the Universidad de Guanajuato, which published it in 1996 as *Political Brokers, Ejidos, and State Resources in Guanajuato, Mexico.*

Her published work reflects twenty-five years' worth of research in peasant communities in the state of Guanajuato, Mexico, and various transnational Mexican communities in the United States in California, Pennsylvania, and Texas. In 1998, for instance, she coordinated and became the de facto editor for the *Proceedings of the International Colloquium on Mexican Migration to the United States.* This was a joint publication of the Gobierno del Estado de Guanajuato, the Universidad de Guanajuato, and the Consejo Estatal de Población.

González is a dedicated researcher and teacher whose teaching appointments stretch across both the United States and Mexico and encompass both academic settings and less traditional community-based settings, including research field stations. In 1979 she was a substitute instructor at the Escuela Nacional de Antropología e Historia in México, D.F. From 1979 to 1982 she served as an assistant professor in the Department of Anthropology, Universidad Autónoma Metropolitana, Iztapalapa, México, D.F. She was tenured at the UAM in 1980 and named associate professor. She continued to teach at UAM until 1984, when she left Mexico to enroll as a full-time graduate student in anthropology at UCSB. From 1984 to 1987 she was a teaching and research assistant in the Department of Anthropology at UCSB.

Once she completed her doctoral coursework, González continued to conduct her research and write her dissertation from 1988 to 1996. Part of her research and writing entailed a stint in Pennsylvania (1991–1993). She received partial funding for this phase of her work from UCSB, the Wenner Gren Foundation, and the Interamerican Foundation. Needing to find full-time employment, however, she returned to Guanajuato, where from 1994 to 1998 she was associate professor and researcher at the Social Science Research Center, Universidad de Guanajuato. She taught at the School of Economics, Philosophy, and History. Once again, she was tenured in 1994.

Doctorate in hand, González returned to the United States. From 1998 to 1999 she held a visiting professorship appointment at the School of Social Sciences at the University of Texas at Dallas (UTD), located in Richardson, Texas. Since 1999 she has been a research scientist in the School of Social Sciences at UTD. Since 2000 she has been the full-time director of the UTD Angel Palerm Field Station based in the Oak Cliff area of Dallas. She teaches undergraduate and graduate courses both at UTD and Mountain View Community College, a campus of the Dallas County Community College District. Since 1998 she has been the director of the Networks of Guanajuato Migrants Research Project, School of Social Sciences, UTD, a project she directed previously from 1994 to 1998 through the Centro de Investigación en Ciencias Sociales (CICSUG), Universidad de Guanajuato, where it was known by the project name Proyecto Redes de Migrantes Guanajatenses.

González's work on Guanajuatense migration networks in the United States and the Dallas–Fort Worth

Laura González. Photograph by Javier González. Courtesy of Laura González.

area in particular is significant because she is probably the only researcher conducting this work full-time, focused as it is on the study of one group of Mexican immigrants. Her research carries important ramifications for the present and future. Guanajuatenses constitute the single largest segment of the Mexican immigrant community in the Metroplex. Among the more than 1 million Mexican immigrants in the northern Texas metropolitan area in 2000, those hailing from the state of Guanajuato accounted for about 225,000, or nearly one-fourth of the total. González's prodigious original research and publications on the subject will long establish a vital link to the history of this community in the United States and specifically in northern Texas.

In addition, she is highly active in the community, and her work is widely appreciated and acknowledged. She sits on the advisory boards of several nonprofit organizations and government agencies, such as Mexican consulates, Latino community centers, and Casa Guanajuato of Dallas, Texas. In October 2002 she was elected as advisor to the new Council of the Institute for Mexicans Abroad, an organization created by the current president of Mexico, Vicente Fox. In this capacity, together with her colleagues, González consults with the Mexican president and his government on designing and formulating policies directed at Mexican communities in the United States. In January 2004 she became the twenty-ninth recipient of the Distinguished Faculty Award presented by the Texas Association of Chicanos in Higher Education (TACHE).

SOURCE: González, Laura. Personal correspondence with Robert R. Calderón, April 25.

Roberto R. Calderón

GONZÁLEZ, MATIANA (1940–)

Born in Edinburg, Texas, in 1940, Matiana González was something of a miracle to her undocumented parents. Both were more than forty years of age, literally dirt poor, and alone in the United States. Matiana survived a mysterious illness as an infant. Her mother swore that St. Jude and Our Lady of Guadalupe had heard their prayers, because certainly there was no doctor in the picture. Matiana spent the early years of her life in a one-room shack. Her parents labored as migrant farmworkers. When things were especially bleak, her mother worked for other Mexican migrant families. As González remembered, "We were indeed, among the poorest of the poor." She also recalls her parents killing crows for food and the constant, sheer terror they all felt about being discovered by *la migra* (the Immigration and Naturalization Service or INS).

When González was five, INS agents did catch up with her family and deported them to Mexico. For the next twenty years González lived and worked with her parents in Jalisco and Reynosa, Mexico. Her parents permitted her to attend school for a few years. After the sixth grade her father declared that she did not need an education to do the domestic work expected of women. Her mother agreed, and González's education in Mexico ended.

There is much more to González's story. She married at twenty-five and as a U.S. citizen moved to the Rio Grande Valley of Texas with her new husband. She informed him that she wanted to learn English, and he wisely agreed. She learned to drive a car, began wearing pants on occasion, and eventually passed the high-school equivalency test or GED, all of which were firsts for any woman in her family and in her husband's family as well.

Matiana González continued on the path of lifelong learning and for more than twenty years has taught elementary school as a certified bilingual education instructor. She and her husband reared four children, all college graduates, from Princeton, Stanford, the University of Pennsylvania, and St. Mary's College. She also provides assistance and mentoring to other women in her family who desire a formal education. Her work ethic, dedication, faith, and compassion have made a difference in countless lives. Simple yet courageous actions like that of Rosa Parks in the 1950s are part of González's fiber. Matiana González's life story continues to unfold each day—teacher, role model, friend, wife, and mother.

See also Bilingual Education

SOURCE: González, Monica. 2000. E-mail to Vicki L. Ruiz, June 13.

Monica González

GONZÁLEZ MIRELES, JOVITA (1904–1983)

Born into a ranching family in Roma, Texas, in 1904, folklorist and educator Jovita González spent her early childhood absorbing the legends and stories of the "ranch folk" on the border. In 1910 the family moved to San Antonio so that González and her siblings could be educated in English. By her own account, the move was a wrenching experience. Indeed, González never fully separated herself from the ranch folk of her childhood, returning frequently to southern Texas for research work and in later years settling permanently in Corpus Christi, Texas. Despite what she refers to as a few unpleasant incidents during her early education in San Antonio, González excelled academically, finishing high school at the age of eighteen (notwithstanding her late start) and completing the requirements for a teaching certificate two years later.

In 1925 she enrolled at the University of Texas, determined to pursue a baccalaureate degree in Spanish, but financial difficulties soon forced her to leave school. A year later González resumed her studies in San Antonio at Our Lady of the Lake College, where she was offered free room, board, and tuition in exchange for teaching two hours a day. During this period González was able to attend summer school in Austin, taking classes with the venerable professor of Spanish at the University of Texas, Lilia Casis. It was through Casis that González met J. Frank Dobie, the celebrated Texas folklorist and then secretary and editor of the Texas Folklore Society. With Dobie's support and encouragement González rose quickly to prominence in the Texas Folklore Society, ascending to the post of vice president in 1928 and then to president for two terms, from 1930 to 1932, the first Mexican American to be elected to this position.

From 1927 to 1935 González published a number of groundbreaking articles on the folklore and cultural practices of Mexicanos in southern Texas in the *Publications of the Texas Folklore Society* and the *Southwest Review.* In 1928 she was awarded a Lapham Fellowship by the American Association of University Woman (AAUW) to conduct research in the Mexicano community of southern Texas and write "a history of the social life of the Texas border from 1760 to the present." The fellowship enabled González to complete a master's degree in history at the University of Texas, where she wrote her thesis, "Social Life in Cameron, Starr, and Zapata Counties" (1930). This work broke new ground in the study of Mexican American culture in Texas and has been used as source material by many contemporary historians and social scientists.

In 1934 González was awarded a Rockefeller Grant to return to her favorite research topic, the history and social life of southern Texas. This time her research resulted in a book-length manuscript, *Dew on the Thorn*, a compendium of border folklore loosely connected through a semi-autobiographical narrative documenting the lives of a ranchero family at the turn of the century.

In 1935 González married activist Edmundo E. Mireles and moved to Del Rio, Texas, to aid him in his struggles for educational equity. After her marriage to Mireles, González increasingly focused her creative energy on teaching and pedagogical politics, contributing with less frequency to the activities of the Texas Folklore Society. Nevertheless, González continued to pursue her own intellectual projects. In 1936 she put together a special display that focused on the role of Mexicanas in the founding of Texas titled "Catholic Heroines of Texas" for the Texas centennial celebration in Dallas. It was perhaps her research on this subject, as well as the triumphant mood of Anglos during the centennial year, that inspired her most important work of fiction, *Caballero*. Written sometime between 1936 and 1938 in collaboration with an Anglo woman, Margaret Eimer, *Caballero* is a historical novel that tells the story of the Mexican-American War (1848) and its aftermath from the perspective of the Mexican *hacendados* who founded Texas. The novel is unique in its attention to the gendered and class politics that undermined the *hacendados'* struggle against the "invading Anglos." Because of the undeniable feminist undertones expressed in its powerful critique of the patriarchal social order, *Caballero* is an early example of what Chicana scholar Sonia Saldívar-Hull has termed "feminism on the border." Though *Caballero* and *Dew on the Thorn* remained unpublished during González's lifetime, both manuscripts were rediscovered as a result of a recovery project and published in the early 1990s. These works significantly shift our understanding of this foundational Mexican American scholar.

Texas folklorist and novelist Jovita González Mireles, 1930. Courtesy of E. E. Mireles and Jovita González Mireles Papers. Special Collection and Archives. Texas A&M University–Corpus Christi Library.

See also Feminism; League of United Latin American Citizens (LULAC); Literature

SOURCES: Cotera, María Eugenia. 1998. "Jovita González Mireles: A Sense of Homeland and History." In *Latina Legacies: Identity, Biography, and Community*, eds. Vicki L. Ruiz and Virginia Sánchez Korrol. New York: Oxford University Press; González, Jovita. 1997. *Dew on the Thorn.* Ed. José E. Limón. Houston: Arte Público Press; González, Jovita, and Eve Raleigh [pseudonym of Margaret Eimer]. 1996. *Caballero: A Historical Novel.* Ed. José E. Limón and María Cotera. College Station: Texas A&M University Press; Limón, José E. 1994. *Dancing with the Devil: Society and Cultural Poetics in Mexican-American South Texas.* Madison: University of Wisconsin Press; Saldívar-Hull, Sonia. 2000. *Feminism on the Border: Chicana Gender Politics and Literature.* Berkeley: University of California Press.

María Eugenia Cotera

GOVEA, JESSICA (1947–)

Jessica Govea is best known for her lifelong efforts to achieve justice, equality, education, and economic opportunity for Latino workers. The eldest of five siblings and a child of the post–World War II baby boom, she was born in 1947 to Juan and Margarita Govea in Porterville, California, in the San Joaquin Valley. Her father received training at the National Conservatory of Music in Mexico City before immigrating as a bracero to the United States during the labor shortages of World War II. For most of his work life he was employed on the Santa Fe Railroad. Her mother, also a native of Porterville, left school at the age of seven and toiled with her parents in the cotton fields, vineyards, and citrus groves of the San Joaquin Valley. Occasionally working during the harvest season while rearing her own children, Margarita returned to school to earn a nursing credential after her children left home.

Jessica Govea represents the generation of Chicano youths who came of age during the turbulent and idealistic civil rights era of the 1960s. Although she was swept up in the currents of change associated with this decade, her parents' economic circumstances, values, and activism set an important example. As a youngster, Govea rose early to work with her mother in the harvests. However, her father's steady salary, along with his wife's economic contributions, provided enough family income to keep their children in school. With a strong belief in a solid education, her parents took an active interest in their children's schooling. Govea's graduation from high school in 1964 and her subsequent attendance at Bakersfield Community College held the prospect for a more comfortable middle-class lifestyle.

Govea also inherited an interest in community activism from her parents. Influenced by the wave of social consciousness that spread throughout barrios, particularly in the Southwest after World War II, her parents became cofounders of the local chapter of the Community Service Organization (CSO), a self-help, grassroots group that promoted civic engagement among urban Mexican immigrants and Mexican Americans. The organization encouraged family involvement, and the young Jessica Govea was an officer of the junior CSO. The entire family knew César Chávez and Dolores Huerta, two prominent executives within the CSO organization.

Chávez and Huerta disagreed with the CSO when the group rejected their plan to organize farm laborers. They resigned and founded the National Farm Workers Association (the precursor to the United Farm Workers union), and many CSO members, like the Goveas, supported this new direction. A college student at the time, Jessica Govea soon began devoting her spare time to organizing in the 1965 Delano grape strike. Exhilarated at the prospect of achieving meaningful change in the lives of impoverished farmworkers, Govea abandoned the ranks of volunteers and committed herself to the union full-time. "I no longer belong to myself," she revealed in a testament to the transforming power of La Causa, "but to the thousands of people who are struggling to be free . . . farm workers, Native Americans, blacks, Vietnamese. They are proud and they are brave, and I am happy that I am part of them."

Putting her words into action, she joined the international boycott in Canada. With the encouragement of her parents, she moved to Toronto with her companion, Marshall Ganz, the son of a local rabbi in Bakersfield and a veteran of civil rights protests in Mississippi (with whom she remained romantically involved for eighteen years). Toronto was a major grape market for California growers, with a consumer population of more than 2 million. It presented a huge challenge for the untested and inexperienced Govea. She threw herself into organizing, making speeches, and picketing. Because of her ethnic and farmworker background, her gender, and her youth, the twenty-one-year-old Govea provided a captivating subject for local activists and reporters and attracted important publicity for the union's campaign. Her passionate appeals brought trade union members, religious supporters, students, and political reformers to their feet in outbursts of applause and needed donations. The boycott quickly made converts and great strides throughout Toronto and the province of Ontario.

Because of her experience, growing confidence, and accomplishments, the UFW leadership asked Govea to open a new Canadian front, the province of Quebec. Although it meant a temporary separation from her partner Ganz, who remained in Toronto, Govea agreed to become the director of the Montreal boycott in January 1969. Her rapid rise to boycott director signaled her clear emergence as a visible and highly regarded Chicana activist. She assumed complete authority for the Montreal operation, devised local and regional strategy, and undertook new administrative responsibilities, joining only a handful of women boycott directors. Govea stayed in Montreal until the summer of 1970, when the union triumphantly announced the historic contracts with Delano grape growers.

That same year Govea turned her organizing skills to the next challenge: the resistant lettuce growers in California and Arizona. "The most successful organizing I have been involved in or witnessed," she declared in one speech, "is where people take real ownership of their organization by exercising both authority and responsibility." Govea practiced this philosophy in the succession of demanding positions she held within the union. When contract talks broke down with obstinate lettuce and grape growers and Gallo executives, she returned to Canada as the codirector of the Toronto boycott for two more years. The renewed economic pressure in the United States and abroad culminated in the historic passage of California's Agricultural Labor Relations Act in 1975. Govea and other staff members plunged into organizing elections in the fields. Afterward she worked on several projects, including reconstituting the UFW health plan. In recognition of her outstanding contributions to La Causa, Govea was elected to the nine-member national executive board in 1977, the only women besides Dolores Huerta to achieve this status.

During the late 1970s and early 1980s the UFW experienced an internal struggle over its future direction. Opinions divided over whether the union would move toward a more centralized structure typical of a traditional union, a plan favored by Chávez, or would pursue a more decentralized organization, characteristic of its social movement origins. After sixteen years of service to the union, Govea resigned her position in 1981 in opposition to the drift of the union to a more standard and conventional posture.

Since her departure from the UFW Govea has turned her talents to other human rights issues, labor struggles, and educational efforts. In the 1980s she worked closely with Central American activists in refugee communities in the United States and with the national leadership of the coffee-processing workers' union in El Salvador. She also served as the associate director of social services and assistant director of civil rights for the Amalgamated Clothing and Textile Workers, a major garment workers' union, and also became the New Jersey state director for the national AFL-CIO. She ventured into the area of education. From 1991 to 1997 she was on the faculty of the Labor Studies and Employment Relations Department at Rutgers University. She is presently director of Labor In-House Programs for the Division of Extension and Public Service in the School of Industrial and Labor Relations of Cornell University. She is married to Kenneth Thorbourne, a former labor and community organizer and currently a reporter.

Govea has been featured in the four-hour PBS series *Chicano! The Mexican-American Civil Rights Movement.* She also appeared in another two-hour PBS documentary, "The Fight in the Fields," broadcast in 1997. In the same year she was featured in "We Were There!"—an audiovisual program about women leaders in American labor history. Her organizing work was recognized in 1994 when she was included in a mural titled *Maestrapeace* that covers the outside walls of the Women's Building located in the Mission District of San Francisco, California. A breast cancer survivor, she is also pictured in the mural *Who Holds the Mirror? Breast Cancer, Women's Lives and the Environment.* Through almost thirty-five years of organizing Govea has never wavered from her commitment to the empowerment of the dispossessed. "I have found a similar desire for power and voice in men, women, and children of all colors and of all economic levels . . . there are tremendous opportunities all over this country [to organize]."

See also Labor Unions; United Farm Workers of America (UFW)

SOURCES: Cobble, Dorothy Sue, ed. 1993. *Women and Unions: Forging a Partnership.* Ithaca, NY: Cornell University Press; Ferriss, Susan, and Ricardo Sandoval. 1997. *The Fight in the Fields: César Chávez and the Farmworkers Movement.* New York: Harcourt Brace; Rose, Margaret Eleanor. 1988. "Women in the United Farm Workers: A Study of Chicana and Mexicana Participation in a Labor Union, 1950 to 1980." Ph.D. diss., University of California, Los Angeles.

Margaret Eleanor Rose

GRAU, MARÍA LEOPOLDINA "POLA" (1915–2000)

Pola Grau was an indomitable human rights activist who, as the spiritual godmother of Operation Pedro Pan, was responsible for bringing thousands of Cuban children to live in the United States following the revolution. Pola Grau was born María Leopoldina Grau Alsina in Cuba on November 19, 1915, the daughter of Francisco Grau San Martín and Paulina Alsina Fernández. She was the niece of Dr. Ramón Grau San Martín, president of Cuba from 1933 to 1934 and from 1944 to 1948. During her uncle's later presidency Pola Grau served as First Lady. After the death of her father in 1930, when Grau was fifteen years old, she and her brothers, sisters, mother, and grandmother went to live with her uncle, who held a professorship in the University of Havana's School of Medicine. In her uncle's home she witnessed periodic meetings between student members of the radical Directorio Estudiantil Universitario and her uncle, conspiring to oust the president, Gerardo Machado. Before long, as she remarks in her writings, "I began to conspire and work for democracy in Cuba." Her uncle and the student plotters were discovered and incarcerated. Because of her uncle's poor health, he was released on condition that he leave Cuba.

Exiled in 1931 for the first time in Miami, Florida, the family was summoned to return to Havana three years later when the Machado dictatorship fell in a coup d'état. In 1933 Dr. Grau became president of Cuba, but was cast out of office the following year by Fulgencio Batista. Sent into short exile to Mexico and later once again to Miami, the family returned to Cuba in 1934, and in September of that year Pola Grau married fellow conspirator Roberto Lago Pereda, leader of the student movement. By August 1935 the couple was in Miami, where Lago Pereda died at Jackson Memorial Hospital following an attack of appendicitis. Four years later Pola Grau married José Agüero, with whom she had a son and a daughter.

Dr. Grau was elected president in 1944, and his ascendancy into public office conferred the title of First Lady on his niece and encouraged her to become more politically active in Cuba. But in 1952 Fulgencio Batista led a coup against Prio Socarrás, Dr. Grau's successor, and Pola Grau immersed herself in antigovernment politics, sheltering dissidents and working with underground forces to oust Batista. Forced into exile in Miami, Pola Grau remained in the United States until Fidel Castro assumed control of the nation. She returned to Cuba in 1959.

At the beginning Pola Grau supported the Castro revolution, but when the government began to nationalize industries, she turned against it. A participant in a series of counterrevolutionary activities, Grau was involved in a coordinated women's resistance movement. She helped secure weapons, hid conspirators, and worked with the U.S. Central Intelligence Agency. Following the aborted Bay of Pigs invasion of 1961, Pola and her brother Ramón were recruited by Miami's Monsignor Bryan Walsh to formulate a plan for the evacuation of Cuban children. The Graus secretly distributed formal invitations from their Havana home that permitted 14,000 children to leave Cuba for homes, orphanages, and shelters in the United States. Among them were Pola's own son and daughter, who were sent to live with friends in Miami while Grau remained in Cuba to care for elderly relatives.

In 1965 Pola and Ramón Grau were charged with being CIA agents and heading an espionage ring. Sentenced to thirty years of incarceration, Pola was released in 1978 after serving thirteen years; her brother was not freed until 1986. Her life as a political prisoner was abominable. She describes movements from

Indomitable human rights activist María Leopoldina "Pola" Grau, circa 1948. Courtesy of the Cuban Heritage Collection, Otto G. Richter Library, University of Miami.

prison to prison throughout the island, brutal beatings and rapes, forced labor, and substandard living conditions. Grau recalls in her writings that fourteen years of prison life for many who had not gone through it are insignificant, but she and all those who have gone through the Cuban political prison system count the years, months, days, and hours of suffering and the lost life during those years. Her freedom was secured as part of the dialogues held between Cuba and the United States under President Jimmy Carter. However, it was her son, Monchy, disguised as a dialoguer, who found his mother and brought her into freedom. Exiled for the fourth time in southern Florida, Grau became an American citizen, officially taking the name of Pola Grau.

For twenty-two years, until the end of her life, Grau worked to increase awareness of and assistance for political prisoners. Afflicted with congestive heart disease, she never forgot the suffering she endured in prison. On March 21, 2000, Grau died at the age of eighty-four. Bernardo Benes, who was involved in dialogue negotiations in 1978, recalled Grau as "a very brave woman. She wasn't afraid of anything. She felt very Cuban."

SOURCES: Cuban Heritage Collection Digital (University of Miami). "Polita Grau de Aguero Collection." http://digital.library.miami.edu/chcdigital/chc0356/chc0356_main.shtml (accessed July 10, 2005); Levine, Robert M. 2001. *Secret Missions to Cuba.* New York: Palgrave; Rosenberg, Carol. 2000.

"Pola Grau, 85, dies; was first lady of Cuba." *Miami Herald*. March 23.

Virginia Sánchez Korrol

GREAT DEPRESSION AND MEXICAN AMERICAN WOMEN

The Great Depression of the 1930s was a period of tremendous economic and social upheaval for Latinos, especially Mexican Americans, who made up the overwhelming majority of Latinos in the United States. Increasing anti-Mexican and anti-immigrant sentiments, rising unemployment and discrimination in the workplace, and a lack of social welfare programs proved formidable obstacles for Mexican Americans during the nation's greatest economic crisis. Despite these barriers, Mexican American women rose to the occasion, playing critical roles in the survival of their families and communities. Women acted individually and in groups to address economic and social issues. It was a time when both middle-class and working-class women assumed leadership positions in a variety of organizations. As historian Cynthia Orozco has argued, Mexican American women have a long history of community organizing and volunteerism. The Depression proved no exception.

"Black Tuesday," October 29, 1929, signaled the beginning of a crisis that engulfed the nation. Across the country unemployment, homelessness, and suffering rose, profoundly affecting communities of color. The Mexican American population, estimated at 1.4 million in 1930, was in a particularly vulnerable position as the depression deepened. Viewed as foreigners whether they were U.S. citizens or not, Mexican Americans were the targets of xenophobic attacks. Mobs attacked Mexican American barrios, government policies excluded them from relief programs, and employers exploited them to new heights.

At the depths of the Great Depression one-quarter of the workers in the United States were unemployed. Unemployment led to increased demands on the already underfunded local and state relief programs, which soon found themselves overburdened by requests. Media and government statements implied that Mexicans and Mexican Americans were chiefly responsible for this situation, although in reality they made up less than 10 percent of those on relief. As cities, counties, and states came under increasing pressure to provide relief, social welfare programs excluded Mexican nationals in order to give assistance to those considered more "worthy." Cities passed laws denying relief work to immigrants. Other local governments denied Mexicans relief in order to force them to work for low wages, particularly in agriculture and domestic work. In El Paso, after a series of cotton pickers' strikes in the early 1930s and a domestic workers' strike in 1933, relief agencies began to refuse any assistance to Mexicans and Mexican Americans unless they accepted low-paying work provided through these agencies. Mexican American women were caught in a double bind. They would be cut off relief if they did not accept extremely low-paying work for which local officials and employers believed they were "naturally suited." If they did accept these jobs, their relief aid would end. Employers hoped to benefit from these policies, believing that Mexican American women would be trapped, unable to improve their wages or working conditions.

Some states, such as Texas and California, made it a requirement that Mexicans either show their naturalization papers or prove that they were in the process of becoming citizens before they could receive relief. This proved to be an alarming obstacle for Mexicans who had come to the United States earlier in the century when crossing the border without documents was commonplace. The federal government also denied New Deal work relief to Mexican Americans who could not prove their citizenship.

Under these conditions Mexican American women found creative ways to feed and care for their families. They took in boarders, sold food, scavenged for scraps, and made their own clothes. Some organized to fight for better conditions, and still others left the United States, either voluntarily or under pressure. Other women organized self-help groups to provide services for their members. For example, middle-class Mexican American women in San Antonio formed la Beneficencia Mexicana, which organized a health clinic to dispense prenatal services to poor women. Other San Antonio women created the Catholic Relief Association to distribute food, clothing, and shelter to the unemployed in San Antonio's Mexican American community.

Between 1931 and 1934 one-third of the U.S. Mexican population faced either deportation or repatriation. Somewhere between 500,000 and 1 million Mexican-origin people left the United States, the majority of whom were children born in the United States. The federal government initiated a deportation campaign in response to popular opinion that blamed Mexicans for the national economic crisis. Government officials carried out highly publicized deportation raids in both urban and rural areas. U.S.-born Mexicans who could not produce proof of citizenship faced immediate deportation. These tactics were intended to scare Mexicans into leaving the United States. Unemployment, fear of violence and deportation, and worsening wages pushed thousands of Mexicans and Mexican

Mexican family stranded with car troubles, California. Courtesy of the Library of Congress, America from the Great Depression to World War II: Photographs from the FSA-OWI, 1935–1945 (Digital ID: fsa 8b38214).

Americans out of the country through a process called repatriation.

Although some counties instituted formal programs, most repatriation was carried out informally. Repatriation proved especially difficult for children born and reared in the United States. Many children did not even speak Spanish. Newspapers reported that children asked "to go home." Fellow Mexicans treated many repatriates badly because repatriates were viewed as too "American" and "foreign." Already in the 1920s popular *corridos* (ballads) had complained that women in the United States had changed for the worse. Their dress, speech, and behavior—all deemed too American—were suspect. Mexican American women experienced culture shock as they tried to accommodate to different gendered expectations. While their opportunities had been limited in the United States, Mexican American women found life in Mexico even more restricting, economically and socially.

On the eve of the Great Depression Mexican American women were concentrated in low-paying occupations such as domestic work, agricultural labor, fruit and vegetable packing, and the garment industry. Wages and working conditions worsened with the depression. In 1935, for example, the Texas State Department of Vocational Education called the wages of domestic workers "starvation pay." A 1933 survey of Los Angeles manufacturers showed that more than 40 percent of the women working in the garment industry earned less than $5 per week for a sixty-hour week. The recommended minimum wage at the time was $15 weekly. The same year a Texas physician filed a complaint with the State Department of Labor accusing El Paso garment manufacturers of paying Mexican American women as little as ten cents per week, forcing women to work on a piece-rate basis. As agricultural prices declined, wages fell disproportionately low; moreover, competition from Dust Bowl refugees and other hungry unemployed Americans drove wages down even further. Dismal wages and working conditions inspired Mexican American women to organize in the workplace.

The 1930s were a time of heightened labor organizing within the Mexican American community. Women performed a variety of essential roles during this period. As historian Vicki Ruiz has stated, they "distributed food, formed picket lines, taunted scabs, and when attacked by police, fought back." Labor activism brought Mexican American women into contact with women from other communities, strengthened their leadership abilities, and gave them more confidence.

Mexican American women founded and participated in a number of labor organizations across the Southwest. In 1933, for example, domestic workers in

El Paso created the Asociación de Trabajadoras Domésticas (Domestic Workers Association), demanding an increase in wages to $6 per week. The same year the International Ladies Garment Workers' Union (ILGWU) led a strike among garment workers in Los Angeles, and Mexican American women were the most active on the picket lines. The passage of the New Deal's National Industrial Recovery Act in 1933 helped encourage the domestic workers' union and the ILGWU, as well as other labor organizations. The act bolstered workers' confidence in the federal government because it gave workers the right to organize and bargain collectively, free from employer interference. Mexican American domestic workers in El Paso, for example, threatened to report employers to the National Recovery Administration (NRA) if they did not increase wages. Although the NRA was inconsistent in its economic benefits to Mexican American workers (in the case of the ILGWU, the NRA worked with employers to fire employees for union activities), it gave Mexican American women a sense of confidence and possibilities. The NRA helped Mexican Americans feel that the federal government stood behind them, protecting their rights as citizens and workers.

Latinas emerged as influential labor organizers. For example, Manuela Solis Sager organized garment and agricultural workers in Laredo, Texas, acting as the first organizer for the South Texas Agricultural Workers' Union. She also worked with the pecan shellers' union in San Antonio. Throughout her life she continued to work for other progressive causes, including immigrant rights and the Chicano movement. Emma Tenayuca, a Tejana teenager, began organizing Mexican American cigar workers in San Antonio early in the depression, but she is best known for her work in the pecan shellers' strike of 1938. In 1934 wages in the pecan-shelling industry had fallen to less than $2 per week. Although employers had mechanized pecan shelling by the end of the 1920s, they found it more profitable to return to hand shelling once wages dropped in the 1930s. Employers justified the low wages by saying that shellers could eat as many pecans as they wanted. Low wages and dismal working conditions created an unbearable environment for the mostly Mexican American, mostly female workforce. In addition to starvation wages, pecan shellers worked in cramped spaces with little ventilation. The dust from the pecan shells filled the air as they worked. In 1938 organizers called a strike, and an estimated 6,000 to 10,000 workers walked off their jobs for six weeks, fighting for higher wages and better working conditions. Strikers faced police brutality, and many, including strike leader Tenayuca, were jailed. The United Cannery, Agricultural, Packing, and Allied Workers of America (UCAPAWA) sent Guatemalan-born organizer Luisa Moreno to San Antonio, where she organized pecan shellers into a viable union. UCAPAWA won recognition, and the piece rate was increased to meet the recommended minimum wage of twenty-five cents per hour. The victory was short lived, however, because employers soon began replacing workers with machines once again.

In the mid-1930s UCAPAWA was a rapidly growing union. A 1939 strike at the California Sanitary Canning Company brought 400 workers, mostly Mexican American and Russian Jewish women, out to the streets, successfully demanding higher wages and improved working conditions. As in other locales, UCAPAWA encouraged women's leadership, particularly among the rank and file. The best-known agricultural strikes of the era, including the El Monte berry strike and the San Joaquin Valley cotton strike, included Mexican American women. Involvement in labor organizations empowered Mexican American women to claim public space at a time when their communities were under siege.

During the Great Depression Mexican and Mexican American women participated in politics, ranging from the Democratic Party to the Communist Party. During the New Deal President Franklin D. Roosevelt's Democratic Party reached out to Mexican American voters, initiating a relationship that lasted for the remainder of the twentieth century. In Tucson, Arizona, Mexican Americans organized the Spanish American Democratic Club, which registered voters and campaigned for Democratic candidates. The leadership of the organization was composed largely of U.S.-born Mexicans who believed that their civil rights could be gained through participation in the electoral process. María Urquides, who later gained national attention as "the mother of bilingual education," was a young woman in her twenties when she became involved with the Spanish American Democratic Club.

Founded in 1929 in Corpus Christi, Texas, by middle-class Tejanos, the League of United Latin American Citizens (LULAC) provided another venue for Mexican American organizing. LULAC was founded in response to the profound discrimination and disfranchisement experienced by Mexican Texans. LULAC's leadership believed that Mexican Americans could achieve civil rights by integrating themselves fully into U.S. society. Early on LULAC restricted its membership to U.S. citizens and focused on the electoral process and the legal system to gain equality. When working-class Mexican American pecan shellers went on strike in 1938, LULAC condemned them.

Mexican American women participated in LULAC from its founding conference, although initially its chapters were segregated by sex. During the Great Depression LULAC provided Mexican American women, such as Ester Nieto Machuca and Alice Dickerson Montemayor, leadership opportunities around issues of education, child welfare, and women's equality. Mexican American women organized local and regional fund-raisers, established women's councils, and served as national leaders.

Although historians argue over the extent to which the Communist Party influenced Mexican American politics during the 1930s, numerous leaders identified with the party, of whom Emma Tenayuca was the most visible. Both UCAPAWA and el Congreso de Pueblos de Hablan Española (the Spanish-Speaking Peoples Congress) were red-baited as Communist-dominated organizations. Founded in 1939, el Congreso took strong stands on such issues as housing, employment, education, and immigrant rights. Its leaders included Luisa Moreno and Mexican-born Josefina Fierro, a dynamic Los Angeles organizer. The Great Depression was a turning point for Mexican women in the United States. Confronting terrible social and economic obstacles, women across the political spectrum responded by organizing for their families, their communities, and themselves.

SOURCES: Balderrama, Francisco E., and Raymond Rodríguez. 1995. *Decade of Betrayal: Mexican Repatriation in the 1930s*. Albuquerque: University of New Mexico Press; Guerin-Gonzáles, Camille. 1996. *Mexican Workers and American Dreams: Immigration, Repatriation, and California Farm Labor, 1900–1939*. New Brunswick, NJ: Rutgers University Press; Leyva, Yolanda Chávez. 1995. " 'Faithful hard-working Mexican hands': Mexicana Workers during the Great Depression." *Perspectives in Mexican American Studies* 5: 63–77; Monroy, Douglas. 1999. *Rebirth: Mexican Los Angeles from the Great Migration to the Great Depression*. Berkeley: University of California Press; Orozco, Cynthia E. 1992–1993. "Beyond Machismo, la Familia, and Ladies Auxiliaries: A Historiography of Mexican-Origin Women's Participation in Voluntary Associations and Politics in the United States, 1870–1990." In *Renato Rosaldo Lecture Series Monograph* 10. Tucson: University of Arizona Mexican American Studies and Research Center; Ruiz, Vicki L. 1998. *From out of the Shadows: Mexican Women in Twentieth-Century America*. New York: Oxford University Press.

Yolanda Chávez Leyva

GUERRA, FERMINA (1893–1988)

Fermina Guerra was born on her family's Buena Vista Ranch, a 3,000-acre ranch fifty miles northeast of Laredo, Texas. In 1860 her grandfather Justo Guerra had settled the area to raise goats and sheep. As a member of a long-standing Texas family, she attended the Ursuline Academy in Laredo and received both her undergraduate and master's degrees at the University of Texas at Austin. The Guerra family valued education. Near the ranch house they built a one-room adobe school named Buena Vista Elementary and Las Blancas Junior High. As an adolescent, Fermina Guerra served as a tutor and taught her mother to read.

Guerra is best known for her work in Texas folklore. Her master's thesis, "Mexican and Spanish Folklore and Incidents in Southwest Texas," which she completed in 1941, documented border folktales. Following in the footsteps of prominent folklorist Jovita González, Guerra studied with J. Frank Dobie, the Texas professor who dominated the field of southwestern folklore. Her thesis addressed the region's history, families, ranch work, and folk songs. On the basis of interviews with men and women, including her own mother, she addressed women's domestic labor, an area often ignored by male folklorists. In 1941 she also published "Rancho Buena Vista: Its Ways of Life and Tradition" in *Texian Stomping Grounds,* an important publication of the Texas Folklore Society edited by her mentor J. Frank Dobie. This study covered a variety of subjects: Spanish missionaries, the Texas Rangers, folk remedies, water use, and sheepshearers. She also included a story about Indian captive Antonia Hinojosa. According to the legendary Tejano folklorist Américo Paredes, "She situated the history of her people and the development of the Mexican ranching industry within the historical events in the United States." Two years later she published "Mexican Animal Tales" about ranch and brush-country animals in *Backwards to Border*, another Texas Folklore Society book.

For more than fifty years Guerra was a fixture in education in Webb County. At Texas A&I University in Kingsville she taught English and Spanish and also served as an assistant principal at Central Elementary School in Laredo. During the 1950s and 1960s she tutored border patrol and other law enforcement agents in Spanish. After she retired, she continued to tutor in Spanish, often volunteering her services. She was reportedly an avid newspaper reader, an independent voter, and an active member of St. Augustine Church. One of the first Tejana folklorists, she died in 1988 at the age of ninety-five.

SOURCES: Garza-Falcon, Leticia M. 1998. *Gente decente: A Borderlands Response to the Rhetoric of Dominance*. Austin: University of Texas Press; Guerra, Fermina. 1941. "Mexican and Spanish Folklore and Incidents in Southwest Texas." M.A. thesis, University of Texas at Austin; ———. 1941. "Rancho Buena Vista: Its Ways of Life and Traditions." In *Texian Stomping Grounds,* ed. J. Frank Dobie. Austin: Texas Folklore Society; Orozco, Cynthia E. 1996. "Fermina Guerra." In *New Handbook of Texas*, 3: 368. Austin: Texas State Historical Association.

Cynthia E. Orozco

GUERRERO, ROSA (1934–)

Born in El Paso, Texas, on November 14, 1934, Rosa Ramírez de Guerrero is an internationally known choreographer of Ballet Folklorico and a pioneer in multicultural education. Her life mirrors the important gains achieved by Mexicans in this border city during the past fifty years. As a child, she was punished for speaking Spanish in class, but now an elementary school in El Paso bears her name. Through dance, music, and multicultural, bilingual curricula, Rosa Guerrero has participated in the transformation of a border public school system from one where the Spanish language and Mexican culture were shunned to one where diversity and bilingualism are now embraced.

Both literally and figuratively, Rosa Guerrero is a *mestiza*. Her father identified as *español* and her mother as *india*. Guerrero remembered her father as a "beautiful, Socratic man." "We would sit and conjugate verbs in Spanish just for the love of it." Her mother was a party person (*fiestera*) who lived life to the fullest. Recalling her childhood as the youngest of six siblings, she noted, "We were so poor though; we had that one bathroom. I remember we had to share it with about thirty people and everybody was constipated." Her father took charge of the children while his wife worked as a maid and as a "fortune teller." Decades later, still stung by a friend's accusation that her mother was a witch, Guerrero recited the conversation verbatim. "No, my mother is not a witch; and if she's a witch, she's a good witch. She's a beautiful lady and she's my mother." She then elaborated, "She has a different gift from God—to psychoanalyze people, to question them, and through her cards, and her way she helps them." Guerrero herself began to work outside the home around the age of ten or eleven as a maid, earning fifty cents per day.

Throughout her schooling in El Paso she was punished for speaking Spanish. Teachers would routinely remark, "Don't speak that ugly language, you are an American now, you Mexican child." "They degraded us horribly." As an adult, remembering these experiences steeled Guerrero's commitment to bilingual and multicultural education. A chronic overachiever, Guerrero became one of the first Mexican American students to integrate Austin High School in the early 1950s and quickly emerged as a student leader. "I was president of PE leaders, of the National Rifle Association, of the Courtesy Club, the Pan American Club. My own kids call me the social climber of the fifties." She received a dance scholarship at Texas Tech College for Women in Denton, but after a miserable year in which she witnessed and endured considerable discrimination, she returned home to El Paso. "You have to learn that . . . you are not going to be born for people to like you." She continued, "I can change my name to Rose Guerry . . . and dye my hair, but . . . I'm just kidding myself and I'm cheating myself." She married her high-school sweetheart Sergio Guerrero and graduated

Internationally renown choreographer of Ballet Folklorico Rosa Guerrero. Courtesy of Rosa Guerrero.

from Texas Western (now the University of Texas, El Paso) with a degree in physical education. In 1977 she earned a master's degree in education.

A talented dancer and choreographer, she founded the Rosa Guerrero International Ballet Folklorico in 1974. From 1974 to 1997 the group was one of the most respected dance troupes of its kind, and in 1991 it performed to a sold-out crowd at the Kennedy Center in Washington, D.C. She was a high-school teacher for more than twenty years and during the 1970s developed the first curricula in multicultural education implemented in El Paso's public schools. Her 1974 dance film *Tapestry* is a moving affirmation of Chicano border culture widely used in classrooms throughout the Southwest. In 1995 she produced an updated film, *Tapestry II*. In building cultural awareness and appreciation, Rosa Guerrero notes the importance of history and homeland for Mexican Americans. "Many of us didn't cross the border, the border crossed us." The mother of three children and the grandmother of five, she credits the support of her husband and family for her achievements.

Her awards have been many, including being the first Latina in El Paso to have a public school named after her. In addition, a college scholarship designated for local students is named in her honor. In 1993 she was inducted into the Texas Women's Hall of Fame, and in 1999 the National Education Association bestowed on her the George I. Sánchez Memorial Award for her contributions to multicultural education. The Valley Forge Freedoms Foundation and the National Women's Political Caucus have also recognized her work as an artist and educator. Though retired from choreography and musical direction, Rosa Guerrero is currently artist-in-residence in the Chicano Studies Research Program at the University of Texas, El Paso. "I have so many dreams. I have so many goals. . . . And every day is a new horizon and every day a new dream."

See also Bilingual Education; Education

SOURCES: Ruiz, Vicki L. 1987. "Oral History and la Mujer: The Rosa Guerrero Story." In *Women on the U.S.-Mexico Border*, ed. Vicki L. Ruiz and Susan Tiano, 219–231. Boston: Allen and Unwin; Texas Women's University. "Texas Women's Hall of Fame: Rosa Guerrero." www.twu.edu/twhf/tw-guerrero.htm (accessed October 7, 2004); The University of Texas Institute of Texan Cultures at San Antonio. "The Mind has to be opened like a parachute. Guerrero, Rosa Ramírez. 1995. Oral interview by Sarah Massey, July 26. www.texancultures.utsa.edu/memories/htms/guerrero_transcript.htm (accessed October 7, 2004.

Vicki L. Ruiz

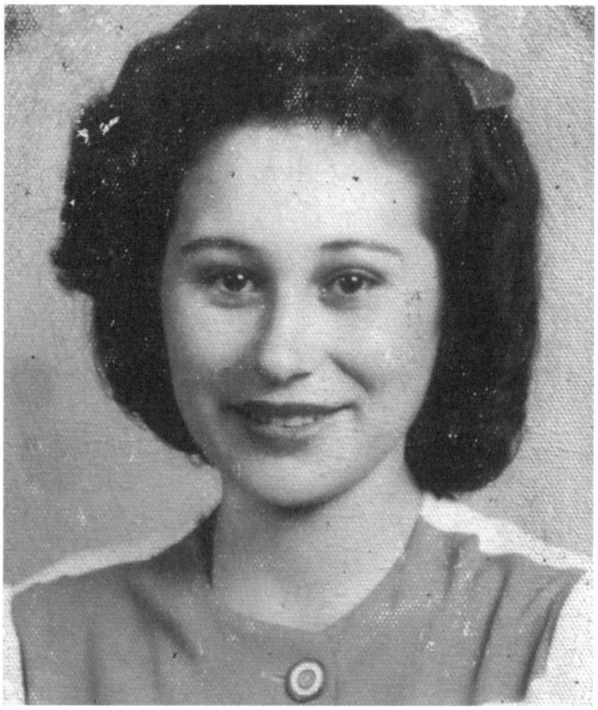

Victoria Partida Guerrero during World War II. Courtesy of the U.S. Latino and Latina World War II Oral History Project, University of Texas, Austin.

GUERRERO, VICTORIA PARTIDA (1925–)

Victoria Partida Guerrero was born in 1925 and grew up in the southern Texas Rio Grande Valley, where she remembers everyone being friendly and knowing everyone else. Her father died when she was three, and her mother remarried a few years later. The family worked in the fields to harvest spinach, potatoes, carrots, and cotton.

"It was hard working out in the hot sun," Guerrero said. "It was hard, but we were happy. We were poor but very happy because we shared each other." For entertainment her mother would sing while a neighbor played the guitar. Guerrero also enjoyed listening to her grandmother tell stories, especially Spanish versions of "Snow White" and "Cinderella."

At nine Guerrero entered first grade at Fort Sam Houston but was then skipped to the third grade. "I don't know whether we were smart, or they just wanted to get rid of us," she said. The shy girl found it hard at first. "Some of the white girls were nice; others were not very nice. After a while we mingled and got along." Her teacher worked to get the Hispanic and white children to relate to one another. By her late teens Guerrero felt comfortable associating with white students.

Guerrero met her husband in 1941. She was sixteen and traveling by train with her family, headed for the sugar-beet fields of Michigan. The train stopped in San Antonio, Texas, so migrant workers could be screened for tuberculosis. While the train was in San Antonio, Luis Guerrero pulled his cousin aside, pointed to Victoria Partida, and said, "See that girl? That's the girl I'm going to marry!" After moving to Saginaw, Luis Guerrero asked Victoria's father for permission to court her, and the two began dating regularly, always chaperoned by her younger brother, Pedro.

The couple worked hard to save money to start a life together, but World War II postponed their plans. Luis Guerrero enlisted in the marines in 1943. The oldest child in his family of fifteen, he was trained as a cannoneer. He was sent to Guam in 1944 as a member of the Third Marine Division, which took part in Operation Forager, the invasion of Saipan, Tinian, and Guam. Later, Luis Guerrero spent time in Tiensing, China. "We wrote back and forth all the time," Victoria Guerrero said. "The fear (that he could be wounded or killed) was within you constantly."

She and her mother, aunts, and cousins hoped and prayed that their loved ones would return home safely. "We prayed for peace; we prayed night and day," Guerrero said. Her family listened to the radio for reports of those killed or wounded. Two of her cousins were killed, one as a gunner in an Air Corps warplane and the other when his tank exploded. "That's when you pray the hardest," she said. "It was very hard for our families." She attended the funeral of one cousin in Brownsville, Texas, with her family in 1945. The remains had been shipped back in a casket, with orders that the casket was not to be opened. She remembered that two sentries took turns standing by the casket, even in the family's home. "My aunt said, 'Maybe it's just a casket,' " Guerrero recalled.

The war years were hard for the family. Clothing, shoes, sugar, coffee, and meat were all rationed. Only a certain amount of gasoline was allotted per month for their Model A car, limiting travel. The family worked hard harvesting crops to feed the nation and the troops overseas. During the family's years in Michigan, German prisoners of war worked in the fields with them. They had "POW" printed on their shirts, and Guerrero remembered some of them as "great, big, husky fellas." She remembers being a bit afraid of the POWs escaping, but there were no problems while she was there.

Victoria Guerrero remembers the telephone call as though it were yesterday. A man rushed into the office where she was working in May 1946, yelling to her that she had a phone call across the street. She dashed to the phone and heard the voice of the man she had been waiting to hear from for two long years. It was her fiancé, Luis Guerrero, who had been at war in the South Pacific. He said the words she had long wanted to hear. "You'd better get ready, because I'm coming down," he said. He had been discharged from the marines a few weeks earlier, on May 30, 1946. After years of being separated by war, they were married on June 23, 1946, in La Feria, Texas. It was not a big wedding, because they did not have the financial means. She bought a simple white wedding dress; he wore his marine uniform.

Victoria Guerrero described her husband as a quiet, intelligent man, serious about everything, and a perfectionist. He seldom talked about his war experiences, but he loved to take pictures and brought some home that he had taken in Guam and China. He was aboard the USS *Missouri* in Tokyo Bay on September 2, 1945, when Gen. Douglas MacArthur signed the formal surrender documents of Japan, and had a picture of the historic moment.

The couple settled in Raymondville, Texas, for a year, where Luis Guerrero hauled pipe for oil pipelines on eighteen-wheelers. After their daughter, Ester, was born on April 7, 1947, the couple moved back to Michigan and moved in with his family in Saginaw. "They welcomed me as another child into the family," Victoria Guerrero said. They lived with his family until they could afford their own home. They had a second child, Diane, in Michigan. Two other daughters, Patricia Ann and Catherine Gloria, followed.

Luis Guerrero worked in a steel mill that had produced machine guns and cannon parts during the war and then produced automobile parts. Eventually he quit that job and returned to his first love, trucks, working for Bender and Louden Motor Freight Company. For Victoria Guerrero and her husband, hard work had always been a way of life. World War II had an effect on them both as young people and for the rest of their lives. "He always said, 'I can go anywhere I want to go. I'll go in, and they'll let me in.' He was like that, and it made a difference," Victoria Guerrero said. "In those years you matured quite early." On December 19, 1989, Luis Guerrero died.

See also World War II

SOURCES: Desimone, Christa. 2003. "War Delayed Marriage for Daughter of Migrants." *Narratives: Stories of U.S. Latinos and Latinas and World War II* (U.S. Latino and Latina WWII Oral History Project, University of Texas at Austin) 4, no. 1 (Spring); Guerrero, Victoria Partida. 2002. Interview by Elizabeth Aguirre, Mexican American Cultural Center, Saginaw, MI, October 19.

Christa Desimone

GUILLEN HERRERA, ROSALINDA (1951–)

Rosalinda Guillen Herrera, farmworker and union organizer, was born to Jesús Guillen and María de Jesús Herrera on December 28, 1951, in Haskell, Texas. The oldest of eight children, Rosalinda spent the first years of her life in Coahuila, Mexico, with her family, eventually settling in the northwestern part of Washington State in La Conner when she was about nine years old. Situated about an hour south of the Canadian border along the coast, La Conner was a small town of predominantly Scandinavian immigrants who had settled into logging, farming, and fishing. In the 1960s the town also became an artist colony and home to a variety of bohemian artists and intellectuals, providing the unusual backdrop to Guillen's early life. Throughout her childhood her family was one of three Latino farmworker families in town. Guillen remembers discussing politics with her parents and their eclectic group of friends. She was introduced to progressive thought and theorists, as was characteristic of the late 1960s.

Brought up in a family of avid readers, she was encouraged to argue and discuss her ideas with her parents and their friends. Therefore, it was not a surprise when at the age of fifteen, Guillen announced that she was going to spend her life working to liberate the poor and contribute to social change. Her parents were not as enthusiastic over this revelation. Deciding to take her life into her own hands, she ran away with her farmworker boyfriend to work toward liberating the downtrodden.

Marrying her boyfriend, Guillen worked as a migrant laborer for several years before eventually leaving that grueling work to raise her two sons in a more settled life. She found work with Skagit State Bank in Skagit County, Washington, as a bookkeeper, eventually became an operations officer, and remained employed there for about fifteen years. During this time she remained active in community work and in the late 1980s became involved with the Rainbow Coalition and worked to elect Jesse Jackson as the Democratic Party presidential nominee.

In the early 1990s the workers at Chateau Ste. Michelle Winery in central Washington sought the support of the Rainbow Coalition in a boycott against the winery. Eventually the workers asked Guillen to assist them to lead the four-year-old boycott, and at the age of forty, in an act that was reminiscent of an earlier calling, she quit her job with the bank to work with the United Farm Workers (UFW) union in Sunnyside, Washington. Although her family and parents were anxious about her decision (by then she had three sons, the youngest of whom was thirteen), she began immediately to organize the workers of Ste. Michelle Winery, "a tightly knit workforce from Michoacán, Mexico." She explains that their strength of character

Union organizer Rosalinda Guillen Herrera. Photograph by Jay Donnelly. Courtesy of Rosalinda Guillen.

motivated her to work long days and nights together learning how to organize a boycott against one of the largest wineries in the state.

Although the workers were predominantly men, women constituted about 30 to 40 percent of the winery workforce. Not accustomed to union work, women did not attend the initial organizing meetings in 1993, although she asked them to participate. By the close of the boycott in late 1994 women and children were a regular part of the union meetings. It had become their issue as well. As she explains: "The workers had transcended gender—they did not see each other—or me—as men or women; rather they saw themselves as workers, organizers, a community with common goals. . . . I didn't go in with an agenda of forcing the men to work with the women or of forcing the women to stay for the initial planning meetings. Their 'critical consciousness' sort of emerged organically." In this way traditional Mexican men found themselves supporting women, their wives, and their friends' wives to pursue "men's jobs," such as working the machinery or in other technical areas. Guillen continues: "When the possibility of actually winning a good labor contract began to be realized, the men could see for themselves the women being courageous and taking on responsibilities through union organizing which resulted in changes in all of their lives . . . changes in the way they would work . . . changes in the way they worked at home."

The seven-year-long boycott was a success, resulting in the first UFW labor contract won outside of California since 1972. It was a favorable contract, lauded by both workers and winery officials. Guillen attributes the success of the boycott to the workers' vision and strength of character, to assistance and guidance throughout the boycott years from key Rainbow Coalition activists, to union organizers, and to the spirit of César Chávez. Guillen, now an elected national vice president of the United Farm Workers of America and headquartered in Sacramento, California, states that the "ultimate goal of organizing is to empower people to change their lives. . . . it is like a little seed that grows. . . . It is the best thing I have ever done."

See also United Farm Workers of America (UFW)

SOURCES: Bobo, Kim, Jackie Kendall, and Steve Max. 1996. *Organizing for Social Change: A Manual for Activists in the 1990s.* 2nd ed. Santa Ana, CA: Seven Locks Press; Freire, Paolo. 1990. *Pedagogy of the Oppressed.* New York: Continuum Press; Gonzáles, Sylvia. 1980. "Toward a Feminist Pedagogy for Chicana Self-Actualization." *Frontiers: A Journal of Women Studies* 5, no. 2: 48–51; Guillen Herrera, Rosalinda. 2001. Interview by María D. Cuevas, Sacramento, CA, October 8; Pardo, Mary. 1998. *Mexican American Women Activists: Identity and Resistance in Two Los Angeles Communities.* Philadelphia: Temple University Press; Sivanandan, Ambalavaner. 1990. *Com-*

munities of Resistance: Writings on Black Struggles for Socialism. London: Verso Books.

María D. Cuevas

GUTIÉRREZ, LUZ BAZÁN (1945–)

Luz María Bazán Gutiérrez was born on August 4, 1945, in Falfurrias, a small southern Texas town, to well-established fourth-generation Texas Mexicans. As she states to the hapless person who raises the "problem of immigration" to her, "My family never crossed any border—the border crossed them!" She, her two brothers, and her sister enjoyed a wonderful childhood in which they were raised by hardworking and loving parents. Gutiérrez recalls fond memories of her mother and father taking her and her sister to political rallies in town, where streets were blocked off so candidates could appear to a captive audience, lured by plenty of Mexican food, drinks, and music.

Memories of the determined women in her family contributed to her passion and love for politics and social activism. Her "Tia Chinda" had been one of the first Chicana elementary-school principals hired in southern Texas to preside over a predominantly Mexicano/Chicano student population, but had been fired for insubordination when she refused to accept used and old school furnishings while other schools received new furnishings and equipment. Closer to home, she remembers her parents' divorce during high school, when divorce was taboo and divorced women were known behind whispers as *dejadas* (someone who abandoned her family). The divorce forced her mother into the labor force with no skills other than her determination to keep her family intact.

Upon graduation from high school in 1963 Gutiérrez headed off to college at Texas A&M in Kingsville, Texas, where the organizations of choice for Chicanos at the time were the Spanish Club and the Young Democrats. It was at this time that she met her soul mate, Jose Angel Gutiérrez.

Luz married José Angel after graduating from college in 1967 and settled in San Antonio, where she taught school as one of the first bilingual teachers; he attended graduate school. Buzzing with activity, laughter, and music, their home was always the site for strategic planning sessions, reminiscent of Luz Gutiérrez's childhood. The establishment of the Mexican American Youth Organization (MAYO) by José Angel Gutiérrez and four of his college friends served as a catalyst for the beginnings of La Raza Unida Party.

Moving to Crystal City, they worked hand in hand to organize the Chicano community. The idea for a third political party that would more adequately address the needs of the Chicano community had inspired them. During that time Ciudadanos Unidos, an all-men group organized toward this goal, met regularly on Sunday afternoon. Women were excluded from participating in the meetings but were expected to cook tamales and hold fund-raisers to support the group. Luz Gutiérrez and some of the women in the group decided that they had had enough, and an ultimatum was given to the men: "We are treated equally as voting members or we will no longer cooperate in any way." They forced the membership to vote. The women won, but the result caused some of the men to walk out in protest. Nevertheless, the organization was successful in electing a slate of Chicanos to the school board and city council, and in 1970 Luz Gutiérrez was elected to serve as the first Raza Unida Party county chair for the state of Texas.

Since then, Gutiérrez has served the Chicano and Latino communities in the fields of health care and economic development for more than twenty years. In the early 1980s she settled in the Northwest. She wasted no time establishing a Latino presence in the predominantly white communities of northern Oregon and central Washington. Not settling for the status quo, she leaves behind structures to address the growing Latino population in the Northwest. She established various clinics, programs, commissions, and small businesses serving the Latino community.

Despite her success in addressing the needs of minority communities, she was terminated from a top-level position with the Department of Health and Human Resources in Yakima, Washington, for "ruffling the feathers" of the old guard, which was not used to being challenged. Gutiérrez then obtained her real-estate license and assisted immigrants to buy their first homes. She organized and solely financed the Washington Association of Minority Entrepreneurs (WAME), which was based on a model of economic development she initiated in Oregon. She has served as the president and CEO for thirteen years. WAME provides business assistance for new and emerging businesses, and since its inception the demand for services has established the organization as the only Latino group to create wealth in the Latino community in the state of Washington. WAME has financed more than 120 Latino-owned businesses and loaned more than $2 million.

Luz Bazán Gutiérrez has overcome enormous obstacles to establish a better quality of life for the Chicana/o communities she has resided and worked in. Known for her "strong" personality, she shows no signs of slowing down. Her current goal is to prepare and train Chicanas and Chicanos for political office and leadership positions in the Northwest.

SOURCES: Acosta, Teresa, and Ruthe Winegarten. 2003. *Las Tejanas: 300 Years of History.* Austin: University of Texas

Press, 2003; Rosales, F. Arturo. 1996. *Chicano! The History of the Mexican American Civil Rights Movement*. Houston: Arte Público Press.

María D. Cuevas

GUZMÁN, MADRE MARÍA DOMINGA (1897–1993)

María Dominga Guzmán was born in Río Piedras, Puerto Rico, on September 3, 1897, one of nine children of José Guzmán Cancel and Belén Florit Oliveras. She lost her father at the age of eight and her mother when she was eleven. Because of financial circumstances she spent one year in the Colegio Para Niñas Huérfanas, an orphanage in Santurce. A scholarship made it possible for her to study in the United States. Those who knew her as a child described her as somewhat shy and serious, but of good disposition and affable smile.

On August 26, 1913, she entered the religious congregation of the Dominican Sisters of the Holy Cross, otherwise known as the Amityville Dominicans, in Brooklyn, New York, but shortly thereafter became ill and was sent home to recuperate. She returned to the convent in 1914 and in less than three years formally made her first vows to the religious life as a professed sister of the Amityville Dominicans. The life of Sister María Dominga, as she was known in the Amityville Dominicans, was punctuated by periods of ill health that inconvenienced but did not deter her from her ministry, first as a parish schoolteacher and later as a founder and first mother general of the second Puerto Rican congregation of women religious to be founded on the island.

Shortly after professing in 1916 she was sent to teach at Colegio Santa Rosa de Lima in Bayamón, Puerto Rico, where she remained until 1921, when she transferred to Colegio Santo Tomás de Aquino in San Juan for a year. It was during this period of the young sister's missionary work that news reached Puerto Rico of the first apparition of the Virgin Mary in Fátima on May 13, 1917. Because of her deep devotion to the Catholic tradition of the Holy Rosary, this news was of great importance. Later she chose this appellation of the Virgin Mary for the congregation of native religious she founded.

Despite frail health and the exigencies of the religious life, at the age of twenty-six Sister María Dominga vowed to remain permanently faithful to a life of poverty, chastity, and obedience. Faced again with poor health in 1924, she was sent for treatment to St. Catherine's Hospital in Brooklyn. She resumed normal conventual obligations, and for the remainder of that year and most of the next she was assigned to St. Agnes School in Rockville Center, New York. On August 25, 1925, she returned to Puerto Rico to teach in Colegio Santísimo Rosario. Henceforth Yauco was her home and Puerto Rico her ministry field.

Madre María Dominga Guzmán. Courtesy of Hermanas Domínicas de Nuestra Señora del Rosario de Fátima.

In 1927 Sister María Dominga was given charge of the boardinghouse for Santísimo Rosario, a post she held for twenty-two years. From 1943 to 1949 she assumed the responsibility of sister superior for the Yauco Amityville Dominicans. When her term as sister superior ended, Sister María Dominga petitioned her congregation for permission to be "on loan" to a new group of Puerto Rican women catechists seeking to form a congregation. Though the bishop of the Diocese of Brooklyn was not in favor, the mother general of the Amityville Sisters acted on her behalf to obtain the necessary permissions for a "leave of absence." Thus on November 3, 1949, Sister María Dominga and four Puerto Rican women founded a congregation of religious women under the auspices of Our Lady of Fátima. The new congregation was housed in an old, dilapidated chapel, Santuario de la Milagrosa, in Yauco. Three months after its foundation Sister María Dominga fell seriously ill and was hospitalized in Ponce. Despite her illness, the scarcity of material resources, and the arduous work that the establishment of a new religious congregation entailed, the incipient congregation grew in strength and numbers. On February 22, 1953, las Hermanas Dominicas de Nuestra Señora del Rosario de Fátima, hereafter known as las Hermanas de Fátima, acquired an old but spacious house in the village of Santa Rita. This house, leased from the Guánica Central, became their motherhouse and novitiate.

The first step in founding a new religious congregation was to petition for its establishment to the local bishop, in this case, James MacManus, C.SS.R., bishop of Ponce. A second step was to petition and to be received by the master general of the Dominican order as a member congregation. Las Hermanas de Fátima was received into the Dominican religious family on the feast of the patron saint of Puerto Rico, St. John the Baptist, June 24, 1954, and on August 4 the sisters wore the Dominican habit for the first time. With the approval of the Dominican master general and the acceptance of the bishop of the Ponce Diocese, the group's status changed from that of pious union to that of diocesan congregation of religious women. In 1965 las Hermanas de Fátima celebrated its first general chapter, and Sister María Dominga was unanimously elected the first mother general. Henceforth she was known to las Hermanas de Fátima and to all others as Madre Dominga. She was reelected six years later for a second term. In 1983 the congregation received its pontifical decree of approval from Rome. For the rest of her natural and religious life, rather than returning to the Amityville Dominicans, Madre Dominga remained with las Hermanas de Fátima at the motherhouse.

Madre Dominga's work on behalf of the Puerto Rican people has been amply recognized and celebrated. In 1967 she received a doctorate *honoris causa* from the Universidad Católica de Puerto Rico. She lived to see the native congregation she helped found grow and extend its work beyond Puerto Rico. Madre Dominga had the pleasure of welcoming to the motherhouse many visitors, including Mother Teresa, whom she admired and respected. Mother Teresa of Calcutta and Madre Dominga met at the Fátima Motherhouse at Santa Rita on July 4, 1986. Two years before, on July 12, 1984, Madre Dominga had received a special blessing and a petition for prayers from John Paul II upon his visit to the island.

During her long and fruitful life three things guided her actions: love of God as expressed in the consecration of her life to religious life and the foundation of a religious congregation of women; love for others as manifested in the motto of the congregation she founded, "llevar a Cristo a la familia y la familia a Cristo" (To take Christ to the family and the family to Christ); and love for the country God chose as her place of birth. A candidate for canonization, Madre María Dominga Guzmán died at the age of ninety-five on January 16, 1993.

See also Nuns, Contemporary; Religion

SOURCES: El Visitante Online (Catholic Periodical of Puerto Rico). Chévere, Sor Ana. 2005. "Madre Dominga Guzmán frente al successor de Pedro." April 10–16. www.elvisitante.biz/vistante-web/evwebed1505/edespecial/o.php (accessed July 11, 2005); Hermanas Dominicas de Nuestra. Señora del Rosario de Fátima. 1985. "Special Publication of las Hermanas Dominicas de Nuestra Señora del Rosario de Fátima marking seventy-five years in religious life of Madre M. Dominga Guzmán, O.P." *Destellos* 6 November 3; ———. 2005. "Madre M. Dominga Guzmán Florit, O.P." http//netdial.caribe.net/~promvoc/madredominga.htm (accessed July 11, 2005); Parroquia San Isidro Labrador, Puerto Rico (parish Web site). "Las Historias Hermanas." http://sanisidropr.com/historiahermanas (accessed July 11, 2005); "Un proyecto de restauración de nuestra herencia historia." Promotional flyer. Dominican Sisters of the Holy Cross General Archives, Amityville, NY.

Ana María Díaz-Stevens